# A HISTORY OF MINNESOTA

## Volume II

# A HISTORY OF MINNESOTA

**BY**

WILLIAM WATTS FOLWELL

**IN FOUR VOLUMES**

VOLUME II

ST. PAUL

THE MINNESOTA HISTORICAL SOCIETY

1961

♾ The paper used in this publication meets the minimum
requirements of the American National Standard for Information
Sciences—Permanence for Printed Library Materials,
ANSI Z39.48-1984.

MINNESOTA HISTORICAL SOCIETY, St. Paul 55101
First edition published 1924
Revised edition copyright 1961

International Standard Book Number: 0-87351-001-1
Library of Congress Catalog Card Number: 21-20894
Manufactured in the United States of America
10 9 8 7 6 5 4 3

*But nothing is too improbable for history,—though, according to Boileau's maxim, it may be for fiction.*—Prescott, Conquest of Mexico, *volume 2, book 4, chapter 6.*

# INTRODUCTION

ALTHOUGH nearly four decades have passed since this book was first published in 1924, it remains unquestionably the best single source on Minnesota's history during its first seven years of statehood from 1858 to 1865. In these pages William Watts Folwell gave the state a classic account of its early years — a trying period of experimentation and growth in which the young commonwealth struggled to lay the foundations of sound government, to finance the railroads that were desperately needed, to quell the tragic Sioux Uprising within its own borders, and to make its heroic contributions to the Civil War effort. This work, the second in Folwell's monumental four-volume history, has been out of print for some years. Its reappearance in a reprint edition seems particularly appropriate on the eve of the centennials of the Civil and Sioux Wars—the two events that dominate its pages.

In a concise "Editor's Introduction" to the original edition, Dr. Solon J. Buck, then superintendent of the Minnesota Historical Society, pointed out that the "formative years of the state of Minnesota coincide with the most critical period in the history of the nation. Scarcely had the process . . . of installing Minnesota in the sisterhood of states been completed when the smoldering fire of antagonism between the North and the South burst into the flames of secession and Civil War." With skill and accuracy, Folwell relates in detail the story of those eventful years. He writes of Alexander Ramsey's offer of the first troops to the Union cause on April 14, 1861; the roles of Ramsey and Stephen Miller as war governors; the state's attempt to build railroads without money; the famous charge of the First Minnesota Regiment at the battle of Gettysburg; the triumphs and defeats of Minnesota troops on such other well-known battlefields as Bull Run, Ball's Bluff, Mill Springs, Shiloh, Fair Oaks, Savage's Station, Antietam, Iuka, Corinth, Fredericksburg, Vicksburg, Chickamauga, Missionary Ridge, Nashville, Murfreesboro, Allatoona, and Guntown, and their participation in the lesser known campaigns in Arkansas and Louisiana.

But only a small portion of the book deals with the Civil War, for in the midst of that conflict, as Dr. Buck put it, "Minnesota found herself confronted with one of the most disastrous Indian uprisings in the long and painful history of the contact between white men and red in the area of the United States. . . . In the history of the nation," Dr. Buck continued, "the Sioux Outbreak is only an incident, while the Civil War is a major event. In the history of Minnesota, however, the relative importance of the two is reversed." The Indian war, which was fought exclusively on Minnesota soil, took the lives of more than five hundred people during the summer of 1862. Others fled, leaving almost the entire southern half of the state depopulated. The effects of the Indian uprising were severe and immediate, and until it was quelled the development of the state could not go forward.

Many participants in the Sioux Outbreak were still living when Folwell began gathering material for this book, and he was able to obtain their stories. Utilizing these and other sources, he presented an objective, well-balanced view of the Indian uprising that brought a temporary halt to settlement in Minnesota, absorbed the energies of troops during the critical years of the Civil War, and served as a prelude to the long Indian wars on the plains in the years that followed.

As a distinguished scholar and long-time resident of Minnesota, Folwell was singularly well equipped to write about the formative period in the state's history. His early association with Minnesota, which began in 1869, brought him into personal contact with virtually all the principal figures in these pages. His experience as a Civil War soldier made it possible for him to understand the heroism, cowardice, horror, and grim humor of the battlefield. His skill as a writer enabled him to tell the story in an engaging fashion, and the candor and genial tone of his personal observations add greatly to the reader's pleasure. His ability and persistence as a historian prodded him to an exhaustive examination of the voluminous materials in the collections of the Minnesota Historical Society — especially the Sibley, Ramsey, and Donnelly papers that are so rich for this period. His zeal carried him into the treasures of the state archives, which gave him added insight into the subjects under consideration.

The author's passionate attention to detail and documentation, his deep interest in clarifying controversial points and elusive events are everywhere apparent in the footnotes and appendixes of this book. These provide a wealth of sources on Minnesota history, some of which have been little exploited since Folwell wrote. Where sources were lacking, Folwell created them by interviewing people who had firsthand knowledge of the men and events discussed. His notebooks and letters, as well as the reports, reminiscences, and maps he gathered, constitute one of the Society's valuable collections.

Folwell's work has stood the test of time. In making this reprint edition available for a new generation of readers, the Minnesota Historical Society did not find it necessary to make major revisions in the author's text. No attempt has been made to bring this work up to date in the light of later research. Minor errors have been corrected; the maps have been simplified; and new illustrations have been added.

It is fitting that this volume should be reissued to take its place beside its companion, volume 1, which the Society reprinted in 1956. Perhaps these two durable books will prove to be the most lasting of the many contributions their wise and learned author made to his adopted state.

RUSSELL W. FRIDLEY

MINNESOTA HISTORICAL SOCIETY
January, 1961

# CONTENTS

# MAPS

# LIST OF ILLUSTRATIONS

# A HISTORY OF MINNESOTA

## VOLUME II

# I. ADMISSION TO THE UNION

THE constitution framed by the ambiguous convention of 1857 provided for an election to be held on the thirteenth of October. On that day the electors were not only to vote on the ratification of the constitution, but also to elect members of the national House of Representatives, a governor and a lieutenant governor, supreme and district judges, members of the legislature, and all other state officers designated in the constitution.[1] As no census had been taken since 1850, the convention bodies were constrained to divide the state into congressional, legislative, and judicial districts according to the best available estimates of the population. Neither body accepted the generous forecasts made by Governor Willis A. Gorman the year before, but they meant to make no mistake in underestimating a population which from its feverish activity and incessant movement gave the appearance of great numbers. Relying in part on late election returns as a guide, they tacitly assumed a total population of 247,500 as a reasonable approximation sufficient for the exigency.[2] In the division of the state into twenty-six senatorial and representative districts and the distribution of thirty-seven senators and eighty representatives, the schedule adopted

---

[1] Minnesota, Constitution, schedule, section 16. The best edition of the constitution, with all the amendments proposed and ratified up to 1921, is in William Anderson (in collaboration with Albert J. Lobb), *History of the Constitution of Minnesota with the First Verified Text*, 207-275 (University of Minnesota, *Studies in the Social Sciences*, no. 15 — Minneapolis, 1921). This volume contains also a full and accurate account of the creation of the constitution. The authors have placed the state under a lasting obligation. See also *ante*, 1:ch. 15, for an account of the constitutional convention. An analysis of the constitution as originally adopted may be found in the Appendix, no. 1, *post*.

[2] Minnesota Territory, *Council Journal*, 1856, appendix, 2; *Daily Pioneer and Democrat* (St. Paul), August 25, 1857. The census required by section 4 of the enabling act was not completed until July, 1858. See the report of the secretary of the interior for 1858 in *Message of the President*, 35 Congress, 2 session, 1:93 (*Senate Executive Documents*, vol. 1; *House Executive Documents*, vol. 2 — serials 974, 997). The total population as returned was 150,092. The imperfections of this census are discussed in the *Congressional Globe*, 35 Congress, 1 session, 1403.

was precisely the same as that of the Democratic draft.[3] As Joseph R. Brown was chairman of the committee which reported that schedule, it may safely be assumed that it was chiefly his handiwork. The schedule added the new requirement that election judges and clerks should forward immediately by mail to the secretary of the territory, not only the usual returns, but also certified copies of the poll books.[4] The final canvass of the votes at large was imposed by the constitution on the governor of the territory, who was to be assisted by Joseph R. Brown and Thomas J. Galbraith.[5] As returns had to come from distant points over common roads in bad condition at that time of year, the canvass was much delayed. The board did not meet until December 3 and its labors were not completed until the seventeenth. The vote for the adoption of the constitution was practically unanimous: for the constitution, 30,055; against the constitution, 571.[6]

The Democrats obtained majorities in both houses of the legislature and elected their candidates for state offices and for the delegacy in Congress and three aspirants for membership in the national House.[7] The forty-five days intervening between the close of the convention and the election were none too many for the opposing parties to strengthen and

[3] Minnesota Constitutional Convention (Democratic), *Debates and Proceedings*, 563, 591-595 (St. Paul, 1857); Constitution, schedule, section 12. Because the report on the schedule was delayed until the compromise committee was about to report, it was laid on the table and not adopted in the Democratic convention. The Republican apportionment as reported from committee provided for twenty districts with twenty-six senators and sixty-six representatives. A member of the committee stated in debate that eight thousand had been made the basis for senators and three thousand for representatives. Those ratios would have assumed a population of about two hundred thousand. The draft was debated at great length, amended in details, and engrossed for passage. Minnesota Constitutional Convention (Republican), *Debates and Proceedings*, 506, 526-537 (St. Paul, 1858).

[4] *Debates and Proceedings* (Democratic), 119; Constitution, schedule, section 20.

[5] Constitution, schedule, section 21.

[6] *Daily Minnesotian* (St. Paul), December 4, 18, 1857; report of the committee on territories on the Minnesota constitution, in 35 Congress, 1 session, *Senate Reports*, no. 21, p. 32 (serial 938). A footnote to Governor Medary's certificate of the votes on the constitution states that 6,451 votes for and 132 votes against the constitution, having been informally returned, were rejected by the canvassers. These figures added to those of the text give the sums 36,506 and 703.

[7] *Pioneer and Democrat*, December 2, 3, 13, 15, 19, 1857; *Minnesotian*, December 18, 19, 1857.

perfect their organizations. The campaign was a busy one for both; neither spared pains or expense to discover and rally all possible supporters. It was no time to be indifferent or illiberal in regard to suffrage, as a section of the schedule had provided that every free white male inhabitant over the age of twenty-one years who had resided within the limits of the state for ten days previous to the day of election might vote upon the adoption of the constitution and for all officers to be elected under it. The reader may form his own opinion of a provision of the schedule which forbade voting on the constitution on ballots separate from those cast for officers. The election machinery was, of course, that of the territory, which had remained unchanged since the adoption of the Code of 1851.[8]

The contest was keenest between the two candidates for the governorship, Alexander Ramsey and Henry H. Sibley. Up to the last moment both parties claimed a victory, and it was not until the official canvass was published on December 19 that the Democrats were assured of a triumph in the election of Sibley by the slender majority of 240 in a total vote of 35,340. And this figure would have been reduced to 42 but for the operation of a rule adopted at the outset by the board that only the canvassed returns from the several counties be adopted as the basis of calculation. Commissioner Brown had proposed that votes returned by the proper canvassing officers together with the returns from extra precincts of the establishment of which the board had been legally informed should be the basis. Governor Medary voted against this proposition on the ground that it would take six months to complete the count. Under the ruling 1,930 votes for Sibley and 2,128 for Ramsey were rejected. Both before and after the canvass allegations of frauds were bandied by the party newspapers. The *Pioneer and Democrat* charged the Republicans, among other things, with the

---

[8] Constitution, schedule, sections 17, 18; *The Revised Statutes of the Territory of Minnesota, Passed at the Second Session of the Legislative Assembly*, 44-53 (St. Paul, 1851). See *ante*, 1:262, for an account of the framing of the Code of 1851.

intimidation of voters in St. Anthony, the importation of voters from Wisconsin in Stillwater, and the entering of 399 votes for Ramsey on forged poll books. The *Minnesotian* was not less liberal in its denunciation of Democratic activities in obtaining Indian votes at Long Prairie, of frauds in many counties, of the forgery of poll books in St. Paul for northwestern precincts, and of the "rascality" of the "scoundrels," Medary and Brown, who rejected a thousand honest votes for Ramsey and counted seven hundred forged and fraudulent votes for Sibley.[9] Ramsey gave notice of his intention to contest but refrained from doing so, and some were ungenerous enough to suggest that he was wise to avoid a controversy which might have revealed irregularities on his side not easily justified.[10] The two candidates remained for over thirty years close personal friends and many a joke passed between them turning on the distinction between governors *de facto* and governors *de jure*. Ramsey could well afford to wait for honors in store. Governor Sibley before his term was closed might have been quite content to see his opponent in his official shoes.

Section 6 of the schedule fixed December 2, 1857, as the time for the first session of the state legislature to assemble. It was the natural expectation that the Democratic Congress meeting within a week of that date would without delay

[9] *Pioneer and Democrat*, November 18, 19, December 19, 1857; *Minnesotian*, December 18, 19, 1857. The *Minnesotian* of November 16, 1857, specifically charged that on the night of October 24 a party of Democratic politicians met in the American House in St. Paul and then and there forged poll books for St. Vincent precinct in Pembina County. This story might well be suppressed but for the elaborate denials of the *Pioneer and Democrat* on November 19 and 20.

[10] In an interview with the author on June 29, 1905, Earle S. Goodrich, who was the editor of the *Pioneer and Democrat* in 1857, said that he went carefully over the election returns in the secretary's office and became satisfied that Sibley was fairly elected. To an inquiry as to how near right one would be in stating that Ramsey did not care to contest for fear of exposure of irregularities on his side, the answer was, "He would be exactly right." In the *Pioneer and Democrat* of June 26, 1858, there is an assertion that Sibley's course afforded a pleasing contrast to that pursued by Ramsey. In the Sibley Papers there is a copy of a letter, dated June 21, 1858, from David Cooper, attorney for Ramsey, to Francis Baasen, secretary of state, asking for a statement of the vote for governor at the last election. "The fees," wrote Cooper, "for such information will be paid whenever the same is furnished, or in advance if desired." Hercules L. Dousman wrote to Sibley on April 12, 1858, that Ramsey said that he had beaten Sibley honestly a thousand votes, but that "he had been *ciphered* out of it." Sibley Papers.

pass an act admitting a new Democratic state sending two senators and three representatives to swell the ranks of the majority. It was believed that, in accordance with the principle of ignoring trifles in legislation as well as in judicial proceedings, the act of admission would "relate back" and legitimate all proceedings of the Minnesota state legislature before the expiration of the territorial government. It was expressly provided in the schedule that all territorial officers should hold their offices until "superseded by the authority of the state."[11]

The houses were not precipitate in proceeding to legislation. A week and more passed while they elected officers, considered and adopted rules, and disposed of resolutions deprecating the extension of slavery. On the ninth of December both houses passed resolutions to notify the "acting Governor" by a joint committee that they were duly organized and ready for any communication he should be pleased to make.[12] Two days later a member of the Senate presented a solemn protest, dated December 8 and signed by seventeen Republican senators, against the recognition by the Senate of the claims of Samuel Medary "to exercise any of the rights, authority, privileges, powers or functions of the Governor of the State of Minnesota," declaring any such exercise to be usurpation.[13] On the same day, December 11, the houses were in joint convention and upon a motion to send a committee to notify "the Governor" that they were so met and ready to receive any communication from him, fifty-nine members voted in the affirmative and forty-seven in the negative. So His Excellency — the title was still in vogue — departing from the custom of appearing in person, sent in his message by a secretary and thereby recognized the bodies as a state legislature. It was a well-composed and judicious document. The executive congratulated the state on the low

[11] Constitution, schedule, section 5.
[12] Minnesota, *House Journal*, 1857-58, p. 27; *Senate Journal*, 19.
[13] *Senate Journal*, 27.

constitutional limit placed on state debts and advised a firm adherence to a gold and silver standard and great caution in the framing of banking laws. "The banker," said he, "becomes the common endorser for all who leave money in his hands. What then must be the consequences, when such business is left to the unrestricted license of the unprincipled and designing." He concluded by promising cheerfully to coöperate in legislation during the remnant of his term.[14]

Still there was hesitation as to the status of the legislature and the right of the governor to exercise a veto power over its acts. Numerous were the notices by members of bills which they would upon leave introduce. A few were introduced, but only one was seriously taken up — that to prescribe the manner of electing United States senators. While it was pending, thirty-two representatives filed their protest against any attempt of the chambers to make laws and against the recognition of any official acts of the territorial governor. The bill passed, however, but by a majority of only four in the lower house. It was approved by the governor on the nineteenth of December.[15] On that day the two houses met in joint convention and consummated the action of the Democratic caucus, which had designated the Honorable Henry M. Rice and General James Shields to be elected senators of the United States.[16] This capital piece of business, for which a state legislature had been elected in a still-existing territory, disposed of, most of the members departed, leaving a corporal's guard to adjourn from day to day during the Christmas holidays.

The election of Rice was a foregone conclusion, and it must be admitted that he had earned the promotion at the hands of his party; furthermore, no Democrat was more acceptable to the opposing party.[17] The second place had been expected

14 *House Journal*, 31, 32-42.
15 *House Journal*, 57, 58, 59-63, 69; *Senate Journal*, 47, 51; *General Laws*, 1858, p. 273.
16 *Pioneer and Democrat*, December 20, 1857; *House Journal*, 69-72.
17 There is a tradition that Rice with some reluctance aided in the nomination and election of Sibley to the governorship to get him out of his daylight. Interview of the author with William Pitt Murray.

by Sibley, Gorman, Brown, Steele, and perhaps others, and if long residence in the territory, familiarity with its interests, and services performed in its behalf had governed the choice, to some one of them it would have fallen. It fell, as if by the turn of a card, to General James Shields, that soldier of fortune who in the previous spring had been commissioned to distribute the Sioux half-breed scrip. Shields was born in County Tyrone, Ireland, and had come to the United States in 1826 at the age of sixteen. He studied and began the practice of law in Illinois. In 1836 he was a member of the Illinois legislature, in 1839 he served as state auditor, and, after four years, judge of the supreme court of that state. In 1845 he was appointed commissioner of the general land office at Washington, and on the outbreak of the Mexican War he was commissioned a brigadier general of volunteers. During the two years of his service in Mexico he fairly justified that extraordinary promotion. After the battle of Cerro Gordo, in which he was wounded, he was brevetted major general. At Chapultepec he displayed much gallantry and was again wounded and severely. Shortly after his muster out of service in July, 1848, he was appointed governor of Oregon Territory, which office he resigned to become United States senator from his state of Illinois. He served the full term, from 1849 to 1855, and after its close came to Minnesota.[18] Shields was a graceful and engaging public speaker, possessed of an unusually rich and sonorous voice, which he used with art. His attractive personality and charming manners made it always easy for him to attract and captivate, in spite of an irascible temper and an ill-concealed arrogance.[19]

Sibley, against the desire and counsel of friends, had accepted the nomination of his party for the governorship.

[18] See *ante*, 1:483; *Appletons' Cyclopædia of American Biography*, 5:509 (New York, 1887–1900); Henry A. Castle, "General James Shields, Soldier, Orator, Statesman," in *Minnesota Historical Collections*, 15:711-730; and Archbishop John Ireland, "Address at the Unveiling of the Statue of General Shields, October 20, 1914," in *Minnesota Historical Collections*, 15:731-740.

[19] Interview of the author with Mrs. D. A. Robertson.

Gorman had alienated the Democrats of St. Paul by leading
the movement to remove the capital. The supporters of
Joseph R. Brown resigned all hope after the first ballot in
caucus. Franklin Steele, the pioneer proprietor of St.
Anthony, widely known and admired, then felt confident
of the nomination; but on the fourth ballot Shields led by
five votes out of sixty-one.[20] He was everybody's second
choice. Steele's friends never forgave Rice for his failure
to give him the support which they alleged he had promised.[21]
It was a bitter draught for these veteran wheel horses of
Minnesota Democracy to be supplanted by this meteoric
stranger. Among the considerations contributing to his
election was the belief, much emphasized, that the experience
and address of General Shields would secure offices for his
supporters and good things for the new state from the
administration. The opposition press lost no opportunity
to rowel the defeated expectants, set aside by "a pauper
politician, sent out by Douglas to the Territory to get the
place."[22]

General Shields was a senator from Minnesota for less
than a year and thereafter maintained but a brief residence
in the state. He served with no little distinction as a brigadier general of volunteers in the Civil War between the
states. Later for a few years after his resignation from army
service in March, 1863, he resided in California, where he
held the office of railroad commissioner. His closing years
were spent in Missouri. In 1874 and 1875 he was a member
of the Missouri legislature and in 1878 he was elected to
serve out an unexpired term in the United States Senate
occasioned by a death. He died in private life in 1879.
This long and varied series of public employments, civil
and military, would be sufficient to make General Shields a
notable personage; but it is not for these alone that his
name will survive on the historian's page. He will be

[20] *Pioneer and Democrat*, December 16, 1857.
[21] Statement of Colonel William E. Steele to the author.
[22] *Pioneer and Democrat*, December 19, 1857; *Minnesotian*, December 17 19, 1857.

known in the distant future as the absurd and irascible Irish politician who challenged Abraham Lincoln to mortal combat in a duel. The latter, to protect a lady, had assumed the authorship of a bit of metrical lampoon. Lincoln, as was his privilege, chose cavalry broadswords for weapons and a point opposite Alton, Illinois, beyond the Mississippi, as the place of combat. The intervention of judicious friends persuaded Shields to withdraw and Lincoln to explain his part in the public ridicule. Lincoln in later life did not encourage inquiry into this episode, in which he took no pride.[23]

The reasonable expectation of the people of Minnesota of a prompt admission to the Union on the assemblage of the Thirty-fifth Congress was not fulfilled. A correct copy of the Democratic version of the Minnesota constitution was delivered to the president by Rice on January 6 but it was not until January 11 that the document reached the Senate. It was as usual referred to the committee on territories, of which Douglas of Illinois was still chairman. On January 26 Douglas submitted a report accompanied by a bill to admit Minnesota. The preamble of the bill stated that the constitution had been framed by "delegates elected for that purpose" — a slight variation from the usual form, "by a convention of delegates." In an effort to secure consideration of the bill on February 1, Douglas was opposed by Senator Gwin of California, who claimed precedence for his Pacific railroad bill.[24]

In the course of a long debate on the question of taking up the Minnesota bill, the reasons for bolting the door to Minnesota and for keeping it shut for months to come came

[23] Castle, in *Minnesota Historical Collections*, 15:719-728; Ward H. Lamon, *The Life of Abraham Lincoln; from His Birth to His Inauguration as President*, 253-269 (Boston, 1872); Abraham Lincoln, *Works*, 1:221-240 (Gettysburg edition, New York, [1905]); William H. Herndon and Jesse W. Weik, *Abraham Lincoln*, 1:217-245 (New York, 1906). The tradition, mentioned by Castle, that General Shields was offered the command of the Army of the Potomac upon the retirement of McClellan is improbable and lacks confirmation.

[24] See *ante*, 1:421; *Pioneer and Democrat*, January 17-21, 1858; 35 Congress, 1 session, *Senate Reports*, no. 21 (serial 938); *Congressional Globe*, 246, 405, 497-505; United States, *Statutes at Large*, 11:285.

to light. It is a matter of common knowledge that from the formation of the Union under the Constitution of 1787 new states had come in alternately slave and free. By southern statesmen this custom had come to be regarded as a part of the unwritten constitution; and it was with alarm and apprehension that under the compromise act of 1850 California was admitted as a free state out of turn.[25] To secure the admission of another slave state and thus restore the "equality of states" and the "equilibrium of the senate" at once became a chief and immediate demand of the proslavery propagandists. By noisy threats of secession the South, to its ultimate undoing, had secured the repeal of the Missouri Compromise so as to open the way for the spread of "the institution" into any territory likely to be the first to ask for admission to the Union.

The romance of "bleeding Kansas" cannot here be retold, but it chanced that on the very day on which this debate ended, February 2, a constitution purporting to have been framed by a convention duly and freely chosen by the people of that territory was laid before the Senate. This was that famous and infamous "Lecompton constitution," framed by a rump convention elected by proslavery votes alone and not submitted to the electors for ratification. Instead of the constitution there was submitted the question of retaining or rejecting the following provisions: (1) "The right of property is before and higher than any constitutional sanction, and the right of the owner of a slave to such slave and its increase is the same, and as inviolable as the right of the owner of any property whatever"; (2) "The legislature shall have no power to pass laws for the emancipation of slaves without the consent of the owners, or without paying the owners previous to their emancipation a full equivalent in money for the slaves so emancipated." Of the 6,226 votes counted for these clauses against 569 in the negative, more than half were from border counties which had not, all told, more than a thousand voters. It was the desire and the intention of the southern senators and representatives that Kansas should be admitted with this constitution before the case of any other applicant should be considered, no matter if it did have the parliamentary right of way. The old game of bluff, which had won in so many previous emergencies, was resorted to successfully. Said Brown of Mississippi: "Do Republican Senators hope to have two more Senators on this floor to aid them in the exclusion of Kansas?" "If you admit Minnesota and exclude Kansas . . . the spirit of our revolutionary fathers is utterly extinct if the Government can last for one short twelvemonth." In vain did Douglas urge that the case of Kansas was not before the Senate and that of Minnesota was. The opposition secured an adjournment, leaving the question of consideration undecided. It was, of course, now understood that Minnesota must stand waiting at the door until after Kansas had been ushered in.[26]

On March 23 the Senate passed the bill for the admission of Kansas with the Lecompton constitution.[27] On the day following friends of the Minnesota bill renewed their efforts for its consideration. After further debate the opposition yielded and the bill was taken up by the Senate as in committee of the whole.[28] That body, however, had no disposition to expedite the measure. The Lecompton constitution had still to run the gantlet of the lower house and might fall

[26] *Congressional Globe*, 497-505, 518, 521. The report of the committee on territories, to which was referred the Lecompton constitution, in *Senate Reports*, no. 82 (serial 938), is accompanied by the acts of the Kansas legislature calling the convention and ordering a census of the population, the census returns, the text of the Lecompton constitution, and the vote thereon (pp. 20-47). Two minority reports follow (pp. 52-88). See also Theodore C. Smith, *Parties and Slavery, 1850-1859*, 209-222 (*The American Nation: A History*, vol. 18 — New York and London, 1906).

[27] *Senate Journal*, 280 (serial 917); *Congressional Globe*, 1264.

[28] *Congressional Globe*, 959, 1258, 1297-1299. On March 4 Senator Green of Missouri introduced as a substitute for the previous bill pending a bill for the admission of Kansas and Minnesota in a single act. It remained before the Senate until March 23, when it was withdrawn.

by the way; at any rate, its fate could not be determined for some days or weeks. That Minnesota ought to be admitted and sooner or later would be admitted was perfectly plain to everybody; but the southern senators were resolved that Kansas should come in first, and that it should come in with the forced assistance of the friends of Minnesota; and they had no difficulty in prolonging debate on the Minnesota bill. The first point of attack was the number of representatives from the expectant state. The enabling act had provided for one representative in Congress and more if the census to be taken should warrant it. That census, though begun before the Minnesota conventions had finished their work, was not completed until many months after.[29]   As already related, the apportionment of state senators and representatives was based on a guess of 247,500 inhabitants. No loyal Minnesotan would reduce that sum by a single unit. The newspapers regarded it as ridiculously inadequate. In the minds of the delegates in convention the idea of one representative in Congress, or even of two, was not to be entertained for a moment; three at least must the populous North Star State demand. Accordingly, section 9 of the schedule modestly provided for that number; and three were elected, all stanch Democrats. Along with the senators elect they had made the long journey to Washington and had been waiting since the opening of the session for the opportunity to employ their talents in legislation and, incidentally, to see their names on the pay roll. One member of the delegation, General Shields, doubtless acting for all, had made a statement of their case in a letter which was read to the Senate on February 25. The position taken in this letter was that the Territory of Minnesota having conformed to the enabling act in framing and adopting a constitution had thereby been instantly

---

[29] 35 Congress, 2 session, *Senate Executive Documents*, no. 1, p. 93 (serial 974); *Congressional Globe*, 35 Congress, 1 session, 1300. The returns were filed on July 23, 1858, and the total population was found to be 150,092. The enabling act may be found in any issue of the Minnesota *Legislative Manual*.

transformed from a territory into a state. He expressed
the hope, therefore, that the Minnesota representatives
would be promptly admitted. This novel proposition
excited enough interest to be referred, after an interesting
debate, to the judiciary committee. Crittenden of Kentucky, who presented the letter, presented also General
Shields's credentials as a senator from Minnesota, supported
the claim, and declared that he could "see no reason why
the gentleman in question had not a just, constitutional,
and lawful privilege to take his seat here." Pugh of Ohio
gave a hearty approval, citing an example from his own state.
Seward announced his intention to vote for the seating of
General Shields and his associate on the ground that swear-
ing in the senators and representatives from Minnesota
would work her admission to the Union. The opposition,
led by Mason of Virginia, rested its argument on the clause
of the Constitution which reads "New States may be
admitted by the Congress into this Union." This Mason
interpreted as requiring an act of admission. On March 4
the judiciary committee submitted a report accompanied by
a curt and unanimous resolution that "Minnesota is not a
State of the Union, under the Constitution and laws."[30]

The debate over the number of representatives to be
accorded to Minnesota occupied the Senate for the greater
part of four days. Northern Democrats, Douglas among
them, were ready to grant the three. Southerners for the
most part were unwilling to concede more than one. Brown
of Mississippi held that there had been no valid election
in Minnesota. She could hold no state election until after
her admission. Her pretended state legislature had no right
to legislate and the election by it of putative senators was
void. Republican senators divided. Some were of the
opinion of Senator Brown; others would admit one representative and would authorize a new census. A new census

[30] See *ante*, p. 1; *Senate Journal*, 215 (serial 917); *Senate Reports*, no. 104 (serial 938);
*Congressional Globe*, 861-867, 957.

was not desired by Democratic senators; the result was uncertain, and here were three orthodox representatives at the door of the House. After voting down various propositions, the Senate at length reconsidered one offered by a Georgia senator that Minnesota be allowed two representatives until the next apportionment among the states. It was adopted by a vote of 29 to 21. The mere number of representatives was not the only point on which the debate was spun out. The question was mooted how, if two representatives should be granted, they should be selected from the three elected and waiting to be sworn in. This was left for the House to decide when it should come up. Another objection which furnished occasion for talk was the fact that Minnesota, by virtue of her constitution, had elected her three members from the state considered as a single district. To this the reply was made that the "mandamus act" of 1842 providing for the election of representatives by districts, although never repealed, in many instances had not been conformed to, and Congress had condoned the disregard. Some senator also made the discovery that the Minnesota constitution did not in definite words limit the terms of state representatives. This part of the debate closed with the last day of March.[31]

On April 2 there was a wrangle over the question of resuming consideration of the Minnesota bill, and it was not resumed on that day. On the fifth it was again postponed, but on the day following it was taken up and the debate was prolonged until late on the seventh. Various minor objections gave opportunity for speeches. One related to the preamble, which, in spite of the departure from the usual form, did not, it was claimed, correspond with the facts. Another was to the excess of delegates in the Minnesota convention over the number provided for in the enabling act, which might possibly invalidate the whole proceeding.

---

[31] *Congressional Globe*, 1300-1302, 1322-1329, 1402-1411, 1417-1423. There are seventy-seven columns of debate on the number of representatives.

The provision permitting unnaturalized aliens to vote received some attention, as did that opening the suffrage to civilized Indians. The whole subject was threshed over until every possible point had been touched. Senator Douglas, who had wisely let the debate run on, replying at times with great ingenuity, made a brief speech, finely adapted to conciliate. After several senators had explained why they would vote for the bill in spite of the objections made by themselves and others, the roll was called on April 7, and but three out of fifty-two votes were recorded in the negative.[32]

The concurrence of the House was asked on the next day, April 8, but that body was not pleased to take up the bill until the fourth of May, the very day on which the Kansas bill became law.[33] There was, of course, no further occasion for dilatory proceedings; it was too well known that the bill would pass. But the minority resisted with a ferocity the more intense, perhaps, because it was hopeless. The old straw of the Senate debate was superfluously beaten over. The alien vote objection, however, became the main topic of discussion. The well-understood distinction between the rights of citizenship and the privilege of voting was ignored and even denied by more than one speaker. One ground of opposition to granting suffrage to foreigners before naturalization held but unavowed by many was blurted out by Anderson of Missouri. Said he: "I warn gentlemen from the South of the consequences. . . . The whole of the Territories of this Union are rapidly filling up

[32] *Congressional Globe,* 1445-1447, 1461, 1487-1492, 1511-1516. The preamble was finally amended by striking out the words "in pursuance of said act of Congress."

[33] *House Journal,* 736 (serial 940); *Congressional Globe,* 1544, 1946. The "Kansas Bill" which was passed was not the Senate bill for admission with the Lecompton constitution but a compromise bill submitted by a conference committee of the two houses and named the "English Bill" from William H. English, who reported it to the House. It was in the form of an enabling act, with certain unusual provisions for securing a "fair and free" election. For the text see *House Journal,* 675-678, or *Statutes at Large,* 11:269. The conditions of the act were not agreed to by the people of Kansas and her admission to the Union was postponed three years. For the documents relating to the Lecompton constitution see *Kansas Constitution* (*House Reports,* no. 377 — serial 966). See also Leverett W. Spring, *Kansas: The Prelude to the War for the Union,* ch. 10 (*American Commonwealths* — Boston, 1885), and James F. Rhodes, *History of the United States,* 2:277-301 (New York, 1893).

with foreigners. The great body of them are opposed to slavery. Mark my word: if you do it, another slave State will never be formed out of the Territories of this Union. They are the enemies of the South and her institutions."

The most spirited attack on the bill came from an unexpected quarter. John Sherman of Ohio, a Republican, afterwards a United States senator and a cabinet officer, offered a substitute for the bill providing for a new convention in Minnesota and a complete novation of proceedings. The proceedings so far, he declared in his speech, had been irregular and were void. The enabling act had been transgressed by the presumed election of 108 instead of 78 delegates. There had been no convention, only "two mobs." The pretended constitution was defective. The election held according to its appointment was illegal and attended with fraud. The putative legislature had been employed in passing invalid acts, had presumed to elect senators, and to aid certain companies of land-jobbers had already framed and submitted to the electors of Minnesota an amendment to the pretended constitution, before its approval by Congress. All these atrocities he attributed to "your Sibleys and Medarys and Gormans who are sent there, and, to gratify their senatorial aspirations, infuse their poison among the people."[34] Granted that Sherman was correct in his general charge, his selection of examples was unhappy, especially in the case of Sibley, who had lived more than half his life in the territory. There is ground for the surmise that Sherman's action was inspired from Republican sources in Minnesota. A new deal might give the Republicans the winning cards and enable them to swing the delegation at Washington to the Republican column. A printed letter from Minnesota circulated among Republican senators

---

[34] *Congressional Globe*, 1946-1956, 1978-1981, 2004-2012, 2057. There are seventy-eight columns of debate. In the *Pioneer and Democrat* of February 9, 1858, there is a letter, dated January 14 and signed by the whole Minnesota delegation, explaining the convention split. See also a letter from General Shields to Richard G. Murphy, president of the state Senate, dated February 8, 1858, in the issue of February 24.

and representatives which raised objections against the admission of the state under the constitution so irregularly framed contains too many points in common with those of Sherman's speech to be explained as mere accident. The St. Paul *Pioneer and Democrat* did not hesitate to insinuate broadly that it was inspired by Ramsey. Lorenzo A. Babcock, secretary of the Republican wing of the convention, presently admitted that he had written the letter, but Ramsey was still credited with using his personal influence while he was in Washington to defeat the Minnesota bill. The House turned down the Sherman substitute by a vote of 141 to 51.[35]

The main debate in the House closed on May 6, but it was not until the eleventh that Alexander H. Stephens as chairman of the committee on territories could make his closing speech and bring the House to vote. The bill was passed as it came from the Senate, the vote standing 157 to 38. Early on the following day the president communicated to the Senate his approval of the bill and Rice and Shields were sworn in and seated. There was a brief opposition on the ground of their election before the admission of the state. This, said Seward, was only a metaphysical, not a practical, objection. In lawyers' phrase, the proceeding was "*de bene esse.*"[36] On the thirteenth the credentials of William W.

[35] *Minnesotian*, May 13, 1858; *Pioneer and Democrat*, May 14, 1858; *Congressional Globe*, 2061. The *Pioneer and Democrat* of May 9, 1858, gives the text of the "Secret Circular." The editor says it betrays "the peculiar genius of Dr. FOSTER," who was understood to be Ramsey's man Friday.

[36] *Senate Journal*, 440-442; *Congressional Globe*, 2057-2061, 2075-2079. The resolution of the Minnesota legislature in joint convention expressing its wish that Henry M. Rice represent the state of Minnesota in the Senate of the United States for the long term was referred to the committee on the judiciary, which on May 14 reported a resolution that "the Senate proceed to ascertain the classes in which the Senators from the State of Minnesota shall be inserted, in conformity with the resolution of the 14th of May, 1789, and as the Constitution requires." This resolution was agreed to by the Senate and, accordingly, on the same day the two Minnesota senators drew lots. In a first drawing Shields got the short term expiring on March 3, 1859. In a second separate drawing Rice had the fortune to draw a term expiring on March 3, 1863. See Minnesota, *House Journal*, 1857-58, p. 73; *Senate Journal*, 450; *Congressional Globe*, 2123; and *Annals of Congress*, 1 Congress, 1 session, 25. For the abortive attempts of the first legislature to elect a successor to Senator Shields for a full term see *House Journal*, 1857-58, pp. 1071-1077, and John P. Owens, "Political History of Minnesota from 1847 to 1862," 497, in the possession of the Minnesota Historical Society.

Phelps and James M. Cavanaugh, claiming to be members elect, were presented to the House. Sherman's motion to refer to the committee on election was carried. The vote on the question to refer indicates the persistence of a hope that the Democratic representatives elect might be rejected and a new election ordered. The yeas were 91, all Democrats; the nays were 84, all Republicans.[37] Just a week later the report of the committee, accompanied by two reports of minorities, was submitted. The committee had no hesitation in recommending that the applicants be seated. As to the objection that the claimants had been elected prior to the admission of Minnesota to the Union, the committee held that the admission of the state related back to and legitimated every act of the territorial authorities exercised in pursuance of the enabling act. To the objection that three representatives had been elected in Minnesota, it replied with a delightful simplicity that no information of such fact had been received; but two certificates of election had been presented. In the course of the debate it had been revealed that the three men elected had cast lots to eliminate the odd man. The result was to throw out George L. Becker, much the best of the lot, and he did not present his credentials. After two days of the rankest filibustering the vote was taken on the question to admit. It stood 127 to 63, and Minnesota was a state in the Union, abundantly represented.[38] The needless palaver over the admission of Minnesota covers nearly three hundred columns of the *Congressional Globe*, averaging almost a thousand words each.

[37] *House Journal*, 792-798; *Congressional Globe*, 2108-2111.
[38] *House Journal*, 883-886, 1136; *Senate Journal*, 592; *Congressional Globe*, 2275-2278, 2292-2296, 2310-2315. The report of the committee is printed in full on page 2310, followed by the two dissenting statements. All abound in ingenious argumentation. See also *Minnesota Election Case* (*House Reports*, no. 408 — serial 966). Both houses refused to allow the Minnesotans compensation for their long period of waiting. Becker sent a resignation to the governor. See Minnesota, *House Journal*, 1857-58, p. 605, and Owens, "Political History of Minnesota," 490-492. For biographical sketches of Becker see J. Fletcher Williams, *History of the City of Saint Paul, and of the County of Ramsey, Minnesota*, 250-252 (*Minnesota Historical Collections*, vol. 4 — St. Paul, 1876), and Thomas M. Newson, *Pen Pictures of St. Paul, Minnesota, and Biographical Sketches of Old Settlers*, 155 (St. Paul, 1886).

A little afterpiece followed the comedy. As a compliment William W. Kingsbury had been elected delegate to Congress from Minnesota Territory at the October election, in place of Henry M. Rice, to serve for the few days at the opening of the session while Congress should be putting the Minnesota bill through the usual stages and to draw a tidy sum for mileage. Of course he held his seat until the passage of the act of admission and participated in the debates. When the state representatives were qualified Kingsbury did not vacate his seat. A few days after the Minnesota representatives had been seated, one of them, Cavanaugh, offered a resolution authorizing the committee on elections to inquire into and report upon the right of Kingsbury to sit as a delegate from that portion of the Territory of Minnesota left outside of the state boundaries. The speaker, Orr of South Carolina, thereupon remarked that, while he felt obliged in deference to precedent to consider Kingsbury as a delegate, he should be pleased to have the House relieve him of the responsibility of deciding whether or not he should be recognized. The resolution to refer was agreed to after an amendment had been added, which read: "And in the meantime no person shall be entitled to occupy a seat as a delegate from said Territory." The committee on elections on May 29 submitted its report, which strongly recommended that Kingsbury be allowed to retain his seat, arguing that the excluded area remained as the Territory of Minnesota and as such was entitled to representation. The Sibley case of 1848–49 was cited and a similar one from Ohio in 1802. The minority in a separate report did not dispute the existence of a rump territory, but held that as Kingsbury was not a resident of it and had received no votes therein he was not entitled to represent it. The debate on the report added little to the enlightenment of the subject, but two unofficial letters, which had not been seen by the committee, were read to show that Kingsbury had received more than two hundred votes in the excluded area. An

impatient member moved that the whole subject be tabled,
pending which motion the House adjourned. On the following morning, June 3, the member who had made the motion
to table bethought himself to inquire of the speaker the
effect of his motion if agreed to. He was informed that the
"meantime" amendment to the resolution of inquiry
became void upon the submission of the report of the committee on elections and that the chair would recognize
Kingsbury as the delegate from Minnesota Territory. The
House, after a brief but heated debate, ordered the main
question. The decisive vote came on an amendment declaring that "the admission of the State of Minnesota . . .
operates as a dissolution of the territorial organization of
Minnesota; and that so much of the late Territory of
Minnesota as lies without the limits of the present State
of Minnesota, is without any distinct, legally-organized
government, and the people thereof are not entitled to a
Delegate in Congress until that right is conferred upon
them by statute," which was agreed to.[39]

There was a bit of harmless byplay, which added to the
interest of the main plot. No sooner had the Cavanaugh
resolution for inquiry into the status of Kingsbury been
agreed to than a memorial of Alpheus G. Fuller was introduced asking that he be recognized as delegate from the Territory of Dakota, identical in area with the excluded portion
of Minnesota Territory, and soon, it was believed, to be
organized by a pending act of Congress. This memorial was
also at once referred to the committee on elections. That
committee, having recognized the Territory of Minnesota
as still existing and having recommended that Kingsbury
be allowed to retain his seat as delegate, refused to admit
the existence of any Territory of Dakota. The minority
in its report had no difficulty in recognizing the existence
of the Minnesota remnant as a territory and as *the* Terri-

---

[39] *Minnesota Territory Election Case* (*House Reports*, no. 435 — serial 967); *House
Journal*, 932; *Congressional Globe*, 2428, 2660-2664, 2677-2679. On the Sibley case, see
*ante*, 1: 241.

tory of Dakota. Upon the strength of a certificate of three county officials of Midway County, Dakota Territory, that they had canvassed the votes of their own and four other counties and had found a majority of all the votes cast in favor of Fuller as delegate, they recommended that he be seated as such. The trivial proposition was not seriously entertained. A final effort to lay the whole subject on the table and thus leave Kingsbury to serve out a full term was negatived by the decisive vote of 128 to 53, and he was obliged to surrender his seat.[40] The story of the entrance of Minnesota into the Union with its irregularities, procrastination, tricks, and blunders teaches the facility with which democracies may overcome such obstacles and reach their reasonable ends.

The ambiguous Minnesota legislature which was elected on October 13, 1857, and began its session on December 2, as related, was dubious at the outset about its right to legislate. In December it enacted but one statute, the one already mentioned providing for the election of United States senators. This was the only act signed by Governor Medary, who not long after departed for Washington and later returned to his home in Columbus, Ohio, where he became postmaster.[41] In the month of January four general and eight special acts were passed, all of minor importance. They were approved by Charles L. Chase, secretary of the territory, as acting governor. During February confidence in legitimacy increased and there was a marked access of legislation. Six general laws and thirty special laws were passed, most of the latter acts to lay out counties, to incorporate cities and villages, and to provide for the opening of roads.[42] Growing more confident that they were senators

[40] *Minnesota Territory Election Case; House Journal*, 1005-1009; *Congressional Globe*, 2429, 2660-2664, 2679.

[41] *Congressional Globe*, 35 Congress, 1 session, 2109, gives the remarks of Representative Sherman on Medary's status. The Minnesota *Legislative Manuals* give the termination of Governor Medary's term as May 24, 1858. Whether he drew salary to that date is not known.

[42] *General Laws*, 1858; *Special Laws*, 1858.

and representatives of a sovereign state and not councilors and assemblymen of a territory, the amphibious statesmen proceeded from law-making to amending the constitution still awaiting the approval of Congress. In the first week of March, 1858, an act was passed by large majorities submitting to the electors an amendment to section 10 of article 9 to authorize the loan of the credit of the state to certain railroad companies, a thing forbidden by the original section. The notorious "Five Million Loan" which resulted will be considered later.[43]

Another legislative diversion proved less mischievous. There was a clause in section 7 of article 5 of the constitution which provided that the terms of the state executive officers should begin after the admission of Minnesota to the Union. Disposed to assert actual statehood and to suggest to Congress that the approval of that body was not needed in state matters, the legislature in the first week in March submitted an amendment to the effect that state officials might qualify and begin their terms on May 1. April 15 was designated for an election to ratify or reject the two proposals. Both were ratified; the first, by a vote of 25,023 to 6,733; the other absurd proposition, by an "imposing majority" in a very small vote. The state officers wisely refrained from taking advantage of it. On March 25 the legislature adjourned until June 2.[44]

Early on the morning of May 13, 1858, a telegram forwarded from Prairie du Chien brought the news of the admission of the state. The leading St. Paul newspaper mentions "a thrill of joy," but there was no tumultuous rejoicing. Some days passed before the official notice of congressional action was received. Meanwhile the state

[43] See *post*, ch. 2.
[44] *General Laws*, 1858, p. 13; *House Journal*, 1857–58, pp. 599, 604; *Pioneer and Democrat*, April 18, 1858; *Minnesotian*, April 29, 1858. The amendment to section 7 of article 5 was to be void if the state should be admitted before the date of the election. In his message to the legislature on June 3, 1858, Governor Sibley, referring to the latter amendment, said: "The people, by an imposing majority, endorsed the recommendation of their representatives, thereby administering a deserved rebuke to all who had been instrumental in delaying the admission of the State."

officers elect, executive and judicial, were assembling at the Capitol. On May 24 they took their oaths of office in the governor's room and the state government in all departments was in operation.[45] On June 2 the legislature met pursuant to adjournment and on the next day went into joint convention to hear the governor's message. Governor Sibley gave expression to his own indignation and that of fellow Minnesotans that the state had been kept out of the Union for many months without "a single valid objection . . . because it subserved the purposes of Congressional politicians to allow her to remain suspended for an indefinite period, like the fabled coffin of the false prophet, between the heavens and the earth." He denounced Representative Sherman's accusation against him (Sibley) as "basely calumnious and without the shadow of foundation." After disclaiming any knowledge of frauds or irregularities in the election, he invited "the strictest judicial investigation into the facts" and declared that if not legally elected governor he would "scorn to fill that station for a single hour." The challenge was not accepted. Proceeding to particular measures which would need legislative action, he advised great caution in regard to banking laws. "Banks are, at best," he said, "but a necessary evil." Referring to railroad legislation of the previous session, he declared that it would be his policy to hold the railroad associations to a strict compliance with law. The common schools and the university should be the peculiar care of the legislature, and the funds to accrue from the lands granted by Congress should be "preserved . . . 'forever inviolate and undiminished.' " The early and complete organization of the militia in view of the proximity of two nations of warlike savages should not be delayed. Without expressing an opinion on the merits or demerits of constitutional amendments recently adopted, Governor Sibley vigorously attacked as one of the most serious defects in the constitution of the state the facility

[45] *Pioneer and Democrat*, May 14, 25, 1858.

afforded for its own amendment. "The 'Magna Charta'
. . . of a sovereign State" ought, he said, to be held sacred
from innovation, and placed beyond the reach of feverish and
temporary excitement.[46]

On the third day after the state officers were inducted,
public attention was turned from that highly interesting
civic act to a scene of battle within an easy day's drive of the
Capitol. Ever since the Dakota had been exiled to their

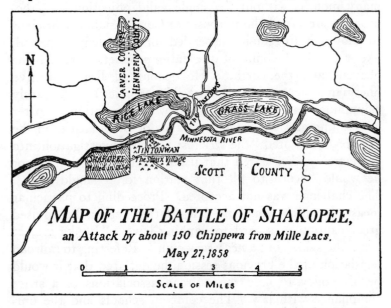

MAP OF THE BATTLE OF SHAKOPEE,
an Attack by about 150 Chippewa from Mille Lacs,
May 27, 1858

SCALE OF MILES

reservations on the upper Minnesota some of the bands were
wont to return in the summer to their ancient homes, where
they were tolerated and even welcomed by the whites. In
May, 1858, some one hundred and fifty of Shakopee's band
were in camp just below the nascent village on the Minnesota which had taken his name. On the early morning of the
twenty-seventh one of the men fishing in the Minnesota
River was shot at from the north bank. The Sioux warriors
recognized the hostile shot, instantly rallied at Murphy's

[46] House Journal, 1857-58, pp. 600, 602-609.

ferry, and were rapidly put across by the women. Had they known that some one hundred and fifty Chippewa warriors who had made a clandestine march from Mille Lacs were in hiding in the timber of the bluff not more than a mile away, they would have been less adventurous. They did not, however, allow themselves to be tolled into a possible ambush, but found cover at a point called "The Narrows," where the road leading to the ferry is closely flanked by two lakelets. The Chippewa attacked repeatedly in detachments, but before the day was far advanced gave up their enterprise and departed with great speed homeward. Four Chippewa bodies were carried back by the Sioux, scalped, beheaded, and fearfully mutilated by the squaws. This was the last battle between the two great Indian nations in Minnesota. The conflicting reports of the affair and its results afford a striking example of the uncertainty of human testimony, even when there is no motive for misstatement.[47]

The first state legislature when it reassembled on June 2 had no fears that it was not in all respects regular and competent. The Senate had its constitutional president in the person of Lieutenant Governor William Holcombe and a state governor had been installed to approve or disapprove legislative acts. A large number of acts were passed, many of them well conceived. Some were new enactments, but more were codifications of territorial statutes. They were concerned with state, county, and town officers; with courts, "high, middle, low"; with roads, railroads, ferries, and bridges; with taxation, banks, and corporations; and with militia, liquor traffic, logs and timber, homestead exemption, and mechanics' liens.[48]

Governor Sibley's first official act was to authorize the use of the territorial seal for the authentication of documents. This action was in response to a letter from Francis Baasen,

[47] *Pioneer and Democrat*, May 28–June 2, 1858; *Minnesotian*, May 28–June 3, 1858; recollections of Myron S. Staring, in the *Minneapolis Journal*, May 14, 1911. An interview with H. E. Staring, an eyewitness, is recorded in the author's notebooks, 4: 2–11.

[48] *General Laws*, 1858.

secretary of state, informing the governor that no seal of the state had been adopted by the legislature and suggesting the continued use of the territorial seal with the omission of the word "territory." In his special message of June 15, 1858, Governor Sibley informed the legislature of his action and gave notice that the territorial seal would continue in use until provision should be made by law for a permanent seal of the state.[49]

In his inaugural message to the legislature on June 3, 1858, Sibley mentioned the Inkpaduta massacre of the previous year and derived the lesson that to hold the warlike savages on her frontiers in order Minnesota must depend upon her own energies "rather than upon the tardy movements of the General Government." In his special message of June 15 he urged the entire revision of the militia laws and in particular the encouragement of volunteer companies always prepared to obey the requisitions of the state authorities.[50] The Code of 1851 contained an elaborate statute relating to the militia. It provided for an enrollment by company commanders of all able-bodied free white male inhabitants between the ages of eighteen and forty-five, within the limits of their respective districts, and an annual rendezvous of each regiment or battalion in September or October. Further provision was made for the organization of "volunteer companies" of thirty or more persons, who should furnish themselves with uniforms and other equipage according to law. Arms were to be furnished by the general government, under existing statute. Adjutant General James M. Boal in a report dated January 20, 1852, stated that the whole militia force as computed from the census was 2,003 and that the secretary of war was ready to supply

[49] *House Journal,* 1857–58, p. 674; *Senate Journal,* 1858, p. 426. A copy of the letter from Secretary Baasen, dated May 25, 1858, may be found in a manuscript report on the seals of Minnesota prepared by Edward K. Milliken for Governor Andrew R. McGill. The report is in the possession of the Minnesota Historical Society. Governor Sibley's answer of May 25 is the first entry in volume A of the Records in the Governor's Archives, now in the custody of the Minnesota State Archives Commission. See the Appendix, no. 2, *post,* for a discussion of the origin of the state seal.

[50] *Senate Journal,* 1858, pp. 377, 423. On the Inkpaduta massacre, see page 223, *post,* and the Appendix, no. 10.

HENRY H. SIBLEY, GOVERNOR, 1858
*Photograph owned by the Sibley House Association,
Minnesota Daughters of the American Revolution*

GREAT SEAL OF MINNESOTA TERRITORY, *Actual Size*

GREAT SEAL OF THE STATE OF MINNESOTA, *Actual Size*

about fifteen rifles or muskets upon requisition of the governor. Two independent companies had been organized and had applied for arms. It was recommended that an enrollment be ordered and a day of general muster be specified. The patriotic adjutant general thus voiced his appreciation of a true militia: "But to arm the whole people, and to make each and every man an efficient soldier, well skilled in the use of fire-arms, and ready, upon emergency, to do his country service upon the battle field, has ever been the aim of our General Government." He recommended a memorial to Congress for the supply of arms for the militia of the territory.[51] No further reports of the adjutant general of Minnesota for the territorial period have been found. The law cited seems to have been a dead letter except that volunteer or independent companies were organized in the larger cities and villages, but no list of them has been found.[52]

In response to Governor Sibley's exhortation the legislature of 1858 made a complete revision of the militia law of 1851. The act established a distinction which has ever since been in effect — that between the body of men capable of bearing arms, called simply "the militia," and the "active militia . . . composed of volunteer companies." The principal part of the act relates to the active militia. A few introductory sections provide for an enrollment of all the able-bodied white male citizens between the ages of eighteen and forty-five, but require no attendance at a general muster. No active military duty is required except in case of actual or threatened riot, insurrection, or invasion.[53]

Governor Sibley lost no time in taking up the duties devolved upon him as commander in chief of the militia. The state was geographically arranged in division, brigade, and regimental districts, and within ninety days after the

[51] *Revised Statutes*, 1851, pp. 581-600; *House Journal*, 1852, p. 217. The figure 2,003 is an evident error — for 20,030?
[52] *Senate Journal*, 1859-60, p. 755.
[53] *General Laws*, 1858, pp. 231-254.

passage of the act the governor had made thirty or more appointments of general officers, members of the commander's staff, and division and brigade staff officers. Before the close of his term, December 31, 1859, large additions had been made to the list of militia officers. The roster of that year shows a complement of field and staff officers. Six of the twenty-eight geographical regiments included thirteen volunteer companies; the remaining twenty-two reported "no returns" for companies. The state auditor on June 4, 1859, reported to the governor the number of white male citizens liable to enrollment in the militia as 23,972.[54]

Before the conclusion of his two-year term of office Governor Sibley was able to quote an example of the usefulness of a military force in support of the civil authority. In the

[54] Report of the adjutant general for 1859, in *Senate Journal*, 1859–60, pp. 755–808. The roster is a curiosity. The major generals appointed in October, 1858, were Lorenzo D. Smith, Willis S. Gorman, Horatio P. Van Cleve, and Joseph R. Brown. John H. Stevens was a brigadier general. E. St. Julien Cox, Samuel E. Adams, John B. Sanborn, and William W. Kingsbury were division inspectors with the rank of lieutenant colonels. George L. Becker was quartermaster-general, Martin McLeod was a division quartermaster, and Sylvanus B. Lowry was commissary general. William Ashley Jones was engineer in chief with the rank of colonel, Charles E. Flandrau was judge-advocate-general with the rank of colonel, and Alfred E. Ames was surgeon-general with the rank of colonel.

Among the colonels commanding the paper regiments were: Samuel McPhail, the First; Alexis Bailly, the Sixth; William H. Dyke, the Eighth; Thomas Cowan, the Tenth; Francis Baasen, the Eleventh; William J. Cullen, the Twelfth; Cyrus Aldrich, the Sixteenth; Richard Chute, the Seventeenth; Daniel A. Robertson, the Twenty-third; and Norman W. Kittson, the Twenty-fourth. Other less-known names on the roster were those of William B. Dodd, Charles L. Emerson, Charles H. Oakes, Mahlon Black, Jacob J. Noah, Henry Poehler, Henry J. Horn, Charles H. Berry, Jacob H. Stewart, John J. Knox, William S. Drew, William B. Gere, William Freeborn, Hans Mattson, A. K. Skaro, John E. Tourtellotte, Charles H. Mix, Ara Barton, John Vander Horck, Eugene M. Wilson, Abram M. Fridley, Stewart B. Garvie, Oscar Taylor, John S. Prince, William H. Forbes, William Crooks, William H. Acker, William H. Mower, Edward W. Durant, and Clement Beaulieu. In the Sibley Papers there is a letter from Joseph R. Brown, dated December 11, 1858, thanking Sibley for his appointment as major general. "I shall I think go east this winter," he wrote, "and will then procure a uniform 'suitable to the occasion' and if I live will make a *splurge* at the musters next summer. Probably my generalship may be necessary to 'repel invasion' of the Yanktonais or old Inkpaduta next spring."

For later militia developments see the report of the adjutant general, in Minnesota, *Executive Documents*, 1860, no. 11. This testifies to the absolute inefficiency of this system and suggests a commutation tax, to be collected as a poll tax, for those not ambitious of military glory. The report of 1861 is accompanied by a draft of a militia bill. See *Executive Documents*, 1861, no. 2, pp. 51–76. For the new military law which made drill compulsory, see *General and Special Laws*, 1862, extra session, 22–44. The report of the adjutant general for 1862 in *Executive Documents*, 1862, pp. 398–401, criticized the law here mentioned, condemned volunteering, and recommended compulsory military service with pay for time devoted.

summer of 1858 a certain citizen of Wright County disappeared and it soon came to be believed that a neighbor named Oscar F. Jackson, who showed notes of a certain bank similar to some known to have belonged to the missing man, had murdered him. Complaint was made and Jackson was arrested and held in custody in the Ramsey County jail or Fort Ripley until the spring of 1859, when he was tried and acquitted. Still the belief persisted that Jackson was guilty and a conspiracy was formed for the purpose of executing justice in an irregular manner. A charge of theft was laid against him and the sheriff of the county proceeded with a posse to Jackson's house to serve the warrant. He found the place surrounded by a party of armed men, made the arrest, and had gone but a short distance with his prisoner when the mob relieved him of his charge. The circumstances indicate that the sheriff was privy to the rescue. On Monday, April 25, Jackson was hung from the gable of the house of the man supposed to have been murdered. On May 2 Governor Sibley offered a reward of five hundred dollars for the apprehension and conviction of participants. Weeks passed without arrests. On July 26 the widow of Jackson made complaint against one Aymer W. Moore of Rockford, a relative of hers having recognized him at Minnehaha Falls. The accused was at once sent to Wright County and placed in custody of a deputy sheriff to await examination. On the following night a party of thirty or more men, armed and disguised, assembled about the deputy's house, overawed him with threats, and took Moore away. Governor Sibley was at once notified by the attorney-general, whom he had sent to prosecute Moore. On August 5 Sibley issued a proclamation declaring the county of Wright in a state of insurrection and, to "assert the majesty of the law and to subdue the spirit of ruffianism," he ordered a body of police and three armed and uniformed companies of volunteers to that county. When the military in their wagons arrived at Monticello they found the village at peace. The insurgents had disappeared and tradition has it that they might have been found in haystacks, cornfields, cellars of cabins, and some upon an island in Lake Beebe. The county officials promised to arrest three suspects, at least, if the troops would be withdrawn; and three men, Moore among them, were arrested, bound over to the October term of court, and released on five hundred dollars bail. The troops returned to their homes after a week's absence, and so ended the "Wright County war," as some opposition newspapers derisively called the excursion. The complaints against the three men released on bail came in due course before the grand jury of Wright County. It probably occasioned no surprise that the body found no reason for indictment. The accused were released by the court on October 4. Governor Sibley discussed the matter in his message of December 8, 1859, as an illustration of the usefulness of a volunteer militia, armed and equipped for the suppression of insurrection, and vindicating the power as well as the will of the state to enforce her laws. His adjutant general concurred in this view.[55]

The financial proceedings of this first state legislature were not all such as to furnish models for those following. The state salary scale was put so high that the next legislature had to cut it down.[56] The culminating fiscal act was one which has had too many analogies in later and present days. Early in the adjourned session it was ascertained that after the expenses of that session were paid there would remain a balance of some ten thousand dollars of the reservation of forty-six thousand dollars made on June 29 for the estimated expenses of the adjourned session of the legislature. Members, mostly in the lower house, easily conceived it to be a worthy and proper thing to relieve the treasury of that

[55] Franklyn Curtiss-Wedge, *History of Wright County, Minnesota*, 1: 194-205 (Chicago, 1915); Return I. Holcombe, in *Minnesota in Three Centuries*, 3:77 (New York, 1908); Williams, *Saint Paul*, 389; *Pioneer and Democrat*, August 4-7, 9, 11, 12, 1859; Daniel R. Farnham, "History of Wright County," in the *Wright County Eagle* (Delano), February 3, 10, 17, 1881. For Sibley's account, see *House Journal*, 1859-60, p. 28.

[56] *General Laws*, 1858, p. 107; 1860, p. 102.

money and divide it in equal shares among the senators and representatives who had borne the burden and heat of so many legislative days for a "per diem" of three dollars. They had earned it many times over and needed the money. The ingenuity displayed in the concoction of schemes to reach this coveted treasure testifies that intellect was not wanting in that legislature. The session was not five days old when a House resolution directed its committee on judiciary to report its opinion on the legal right of members to per diem during the recess of the legislature from March 25 to June 2 — sixty-eight days. That committee, through its chairman, George L. Otis, reported on June 11 that, in its opinion, the right to per diem during the vacation, if not wholly imaginary, was one "dangerous to assert, and magnanimous to surrender." In the Senate the problem in division was attacked by a resolution offered on the twenty-fourth of June to allow to every senator the amount of fifty dollars as compensation for mileage, for which a clear receipt up to June 2 should be rendered. The report of the joint committee to which the resolution was referred is not of record, but the minority, composed of William Sprigg Hall and William H. C. Folsom, declared the disguised claim for per diem during the recess to be entirely devoid of equity, no services having been rendered. But the theory of "per diem during the vacation" was persisted in until the last working day of the session, August 11, when an opinion of Attorney-General Charles H. Berry, who had been appealed to by both chambers, gave it a quietus. He advised them that if they could adjourn and go home for two months and draw pay the while, they might adjourn for any number of months and draw more than double the compensation allowed by the constitution.[57]

In anticipation, probably, of this discouraging ruling the two houses had already adopted another scheme for the

---

[57] *General Laws*, 1858, p. 297; *House Journal*, 1858, pp. 624, 647, 1096; *Senate Journal*, 1858, pp. 461, 618, 717.

distribution of the treasury balance. On the ninth of August the House by a vote of 38 to 25 agreed to a resolution instructing its chief clerk to draw certificates for stationery to the amount of seventy-five dollars in favor of members wishing to take them, each member taking a certificate to sign a receipt in full for all demands for pay during the vacation. On the following day the Senate passed by a vote of 19 to 9 a resolution in similar form for the issue by its secretary of certificates to the amount of seventy-five dollars to each member. This resolution, however, was superseded by one adopted on August 11, authorizing the secretary to issue to officers and members of the Senate certificates for postage to the amount of seventy-five dollars in lieu of mileage, each member to give a release of all claims for per diem during the recess.

The proceedings in the separate houses, however, could have no effect unless the proposed payments were provided for in the general appropriation bill. That measure, which originated in the Senate, came up in the House on August 11, with a paragraph appropriating six thousand dollars for payment of members for "services during the recess." The House amended by striking out this phrase and inserting the word "stationery." This House amendment came up in the Senate in the evening session of August 11. An amendment to appropriate in addition thirty-five hundred dollars "for payment of members and officers of the Senate in full for postage stamps" was put and lost. The House amendment was righteously rejected by a vote of 1 to 29. The House insisting, conferees were appointed. The stubborn representatives refused, on recommendation of their conferees, to recede from their amendment for six thousand dollars for stationery. The Senate thereupon revived and passed its defeated amendment for thirty-five hundred dollars for postage stamps and tacked it on to the House amendment. The House concurred by a vote of 44 to 18 and the bill was ready for approval. On the following morning, August 12, the Senate, having finished its business, waited half an hour for the message of Governor Sibley signifying his approval of the appropriation bill. "There are items embraced in the Bill," said he, ". . . involving great injustice to the State"; but, since the passage of the bill was absolutely necessary for the carrying on of the government, he had given the act his "reluctant approval." Appended to the act as printed in the *Laws* of 1858 may be found the following sentence: "I have signed the above bill, protesting against the items of $6,000 and $3,500, contained in specification number twenty-eight. HENRY H. SIBLEY."[58]

The protest was creditable, but a veto would have been heroic. The legislature was still in session and should have been compelled to choose between passing the bill by a two-thirds vote over a veto and, should better counsel prevail, passing it shorn of the objectionable paragraph.[59] Another extraordinary measure passed by this legislature, by a vote nearly unanimous, provided for the squandering of the state school lands. Sibley's pocket veto of this bill should stand to his credit to the end of time.[60]

The year 1858 witnessed the culmination of Democratic control in Minnesota. A consciousness of waning influence had rendered the leaders of that party sensitive and even irascible. The Republicans, on the other hand, inspired with a hope of victory not far away, gave expression to their elation to a degree bordering on insolence. The state of mind general throughout the state may be inferred from a single incident, which, did it not so well illustrate the situation, might be passed by as a local episode not worthy of recognition in a general history.

On the seventh day of June, 1857, there appeared in St. Cloud, Stearns County, Minnesota, a woman forty-two years

[58] *House Journal*, 1858, pp. 1052, 1086, 1098, 1099; *Senate Journal*, 1858, pp. 691, 723, 726, 730, 735, 736; *General Laws*, 1858, p. 110. The vote in the Senate was: ayes, 19; nays, 10. Senator Van Etten explained that he had voted for the bill that the wheels of government might not stop.

[59] *Minnesotian*, August 13, 1858; *Pioneer and Democrat*, August 13, 15, 1858.

[60] See *post*, volume 4.

of age, physically slight, with kind eyes, a soft voice, and winning manners, Jane Grey Swisshelm by name. She was a native of Pennsylvania, but a residence of four years in Kentucky after her marriage had aroused in her soul a bitter, burning hatred of slavery. She had edited a short-lived antislavery newspaper in Pittsburgh and had been a Washington correspondent of the *New York Tribune*. For raciness and vigor of style she had few equals.[61]

In January, 1858, Mrs. Swisshelm became editor of a weekly newspaper called the *Visiter*, for which she asked the support of her townsmen. The most important of them at the time was the Democratic boss of the northern counties, General Sylvanus B. Lowry, whom she describes as wealthy, splendidly housed, liberally educated, born to command, and conscious of superiority. It was supposed that no paper could survive in St. Cloud unless it was at least approved of by General Lowry. He assured the editor of the *Visiter* that he would give his countenance to that paper if it would support the administration of President Buchanan. She promised so, but when the next issue appeared the support was of a most unexpected variety. An editorial stated that the *Visiter* would in the future support Buchanan's administration, and went on to say that the objects of that administration were "the entire subversion of Freedom and the planting of Slavery in every State and Territory, so that Toombs could realize his boast, and call the roll of his slaves at the foot of Bunker Hill." Such sarcasm was ill-adapted to gain support from the friends of General Lowry. James C. Shepley, a Democratic attorney, in a lecture on woman in which he divided women into classes, characterized the "strong-minded woman" in terms such that Mrs. Swisshelm believed he was using her as a typical example. She replied

[61] William B. Mitchell, "St. Cloud in the Territorial Period," in *Minnesota Historical Collections*, 12:643; *National Cyclopædia of American Biography*, 2:316 (New York, 1892); William B. Mitchell, *History of Stearns County, Minnesota*, 1: 61-66 (Chicago, 1915). See also Lester B. Shippee, "Jane Grey Swisshelm: Agitator," in the *Mississippi Valley Historical Review*, 7:206-227 (December, 1920).

in the *Visiter* that the speaker had neglected to mention one class of women — frontier belles — who sat up all night playing poker with men. A few nights later the printing office of the *Visiter* was entered, the press was damaged, and some of the type was carried out and flung into the river. A note signed "Vigilance" gave warning that a further attempt by Mrs. Swisshelm to publish a paper in St. Cloud would bring down on her treatment similar to that which had been given her office. On April 2, 1858, the *Pioneer and Democrat* of St. Paul published a letter signed by Shepley in which he took upon himself the whole blame, if any there was, of the transaction, accusing Mrs. Swisshelm of "a most infamous attack on his wife." Fearing a repetition worse than the first, he had destroyed the type, always intending to pay the owner on his return.

Citizens of both political parties, forty in number, contributed to the repair of the printing outfit and the St. Cloud Printing Company was organized to continue the publication of the *Visiter*. General Lowry threatened to bring an action for libel, and suit was brought against the company to recover damages to the amount of ten thousand dollars. Mrs. Swisshelm took a bill of sale for the plant, but not until after the complaint had been served. The company was therefore obliged to defend. With her acquiescence a settlement of a novel variety was made. At the dictation of the prosecution it was agreed that the *Visiter* should publish a card acknowledging that the damage to the press and types had been done solely on account of the defamation of a lady and had no political significance; and, further, that the *Visiter* should never again make any reference to the matter. To guarantee this engagement a penal bond in the sum of ten thousand dollars was duly signed and acknowledged. The next issue of the *Visiter* appeared in a half sheet and contained the promised card. That was the last issue. The next day there appeared a new paper, the *St. Cloud Democrat*, with Mrs. Swisshelm as editor and proprietor; in it were reprinted some of the alleged libelous articles. The opposition at this point gave up the contest and Mrs. Swisshelm continued for some years to write and lecture according to her taste and pleasure.[62]

[62] Jane G. Swisshelm, *Half a Century*, 171-173, 178-195 (Chicago, 1880); Daniel S. B. Johnston, "Minnesota Journalism in the Territorial Period," in *Minnesota Historical Collections*, 10:344-347. In a letter published in the *Minnesotian*, September 13, 1859, Mrs. Swisshelm charged Lowry with being present and assisting in the destruction of her press and then invited him to prosecute her for slander. For an interesting biographical sketch of Mrs. Swisshelm, see S. J. Fisher, "Reminiscences of Jane Grey Swisshelm," in *Western Pennsylvania Historical Magazine*, 4:165-174 (July, 1921).

## II. THE FIVE MILLION LOAN[1]

THE granting of public lands by Congress to aid in the construction of railroads began in 1850 but did not become an established policy until 1856. In the congressional session of that year after elaborate debate thirty grants carrying some fifteen millions of acres were made, about equally divided between the South and the West.[2] When Minnesota appeared as an applicant for admission to the Union as a state a year later, the moment was naturally regarded as an appropriate one to renew her request for a railroad grant. The fact that the territory had been deprived of a generous benefaction through no fault of her own but by the mistake or misconduct of those who had tampered with the act of June 29, 1854, aroused a degree of prejudice in favor of the renewed claim. It was true that the Minnesota and Northwestern Railroad Company was still contesting the right of Congress to repeal that grant; but Congress, having passed the act of repeal, could not charge the grant against Minnesota. It required no extraordinary effort, therefore, to secure the passage on March 3, 1857, of a bill carrying a generous land grant for Minnesota railroads. To conciliate a certain opposition an amendment securing a grant to the state of Alabama was tacked on. The bill was peculiar in that it did not make a definite grant to Minnesota to be disposed of freely by the legislature, but designated in a general way the routes of the roads to be built and constituted the territory and future state trustee and agent of the government for its purposes. It provided that the lands,

[1] This chapter is a revision of the first part of an article by the author entitled "The Five Million Loan," in *Minnesota Historical Collections*, 15:189-214.

[2] Thomas Donaldson, *The Public Domain*, 261-273 (47 Congress, 2 session, *House Miscellaneous Documents*, no. 45, part 4—serial 2158); Lewis H. Haney, *A Congressional History of Railways in the United States to 1850*, 363 (University of Wisconsin, *Bulletins*, no. 211 — Madison, 1908). Grants for rights of way had been made frequently before 1850.

being every alternate section for six sections in width on each side of the lines, could be sold only in batches of sections, as building progressed, and that all lands not sold for the purposes of the act within ten years should revert to the United States.[3]

If the reader will trace on the map the routes named in this act he will perceive that taken together they formed a well-devised scheme for a primary system of Minnesota railroads. He will remember that northern Minnesota was to remain for many years a wilderness. The congressional scheme included the following elements: (1) a road crossing the state north of the forty-fifth parallel; (2) a road running diagonally northwest from this road to a navigable point on the Red River; (3) a line running up the valley of the Minnesota from St. Paul and St. Anthony via Minneapolis and continuing southwest to the southern boundary of the territory in the direction of the mouth of the Big Sioux River; (4) a line from Winona by way of St. Peter to a point on the Big Sioux River south of the forty-fifth parallel; (5) a road from La Crescent up the Root River Valley to a point of junction with the last-mentioned route east of range 17; (6) a line leaving the Minnesota Valley line at some point and running south through Faribault to the Iowa line west of range 16.[4] The location of the southern roads was doubt-less made in expectation of connection with Wisconsin roads.

[3] See *ante*, 1:329-350; Matthias N. Orfield, *Federal Land Grants to the States with Special Reference to Minnesota*, 151 (University of Minnesota, *Studies in the Social Sciences*, no. 2 — Minneapolis, 1915); *Statutes at Large*, 11:195-197; 34 Congress, 3 session, *Senate Journal*, 205, 313 (serial 873); *House Journal*, 619-625 (serial 892); *Congressional Globe*, 613, 626, 699, 973, 1068, 1069, 1072. The act provided that when lands within the six-mile limit had been preëmpted, other lands might be selected within fifteen miles of the roads. It provided also that whenever a stretch of twenty miles of railroad should be "completed" one hundred and twenty sections of land might be sold. The grant was extended to ten miles by act of Congress on March 3, 1865. See *Statutes at Large*, 13:526. In the *Pioneer and Democrat* of April 26, 1857, Richard Chute praises Rice's efficiency in securing the passage of the bill. "RICE stood up nobly." The *Minnesotian* of March 20 and 30 gives Chute the chief credit for the land grant. There was no opposition, or but little, to the Minnesota bill on its merits, but two hundred thousand dollars in bonds of the St. Paul and Milwaukee Railroad Company had to be promised to thirty members of the House. After the passage the custodian of the bonds disappeared, and none of them were delivered. Henry T. Welles, *Autobiography and Reminiscences*, 2:53-69 (Minneapolis, 1899).

[4] *Statutes at Large*, 11:195. The map opposite is based in part on a map of Minnesota by William R. Wood, Charles A. F. Morris, and Henning von Minden, 1861.

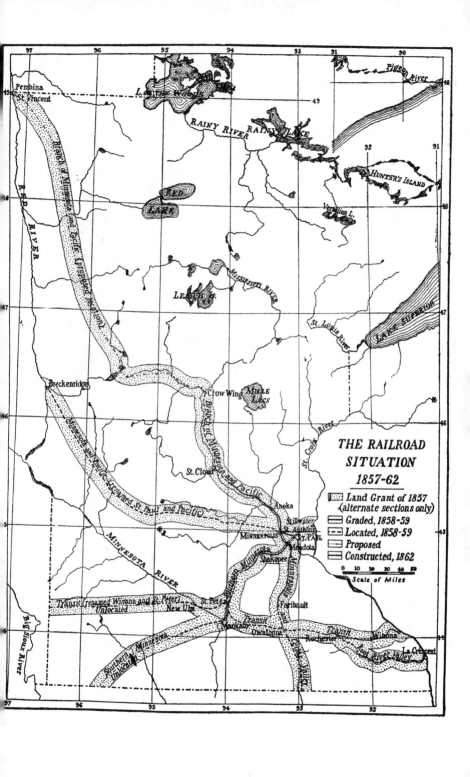

Pembina
St.Vincent

RED RIVER

Breckenridge

Branch of Minnesota and Pacific (Proposed section)

Branch of Minnesota and Pacific

Minnesota and Pacific (renamed St. Paul and Pacific)

MINNESOTA RIVER

Big Sioux River

Southern Minnesota (Unlocated)

Transit (renamed Winona and St. Peter) Unlocated

L. of the Woods

RAINY RIVER    RAINY LAKE

Pigeon River

HUNTER'S ISLAND

RED LAKE

Vermilion L.

Mississippi River

LEECH L.

St. Louis River

LAKE SUPERIOR

Crow Wing    MILLE Lacs

St.Cloud

Anoka

Stillwater

MINNEAPOLIS    St.Anthony    St.PAUL
Minnesota    Mendota
Shakopee

St.Croix River

St.Peter
New Ulm    Faribault

Mankato    Transit
Owatonna    Rochester    Winona

La Crescent

Root River Valley

Minnesota and Pacific

THE RAILROAD
SITUATION
1857-62

▨ Land Grant of 1857
(alternate sections only)
▤ Graded, 1858-59
▦ Located, 1858-59
⋯ Proposed
▥ Constructed, 1862

0  10  20  30  40  50
Scale of Miles

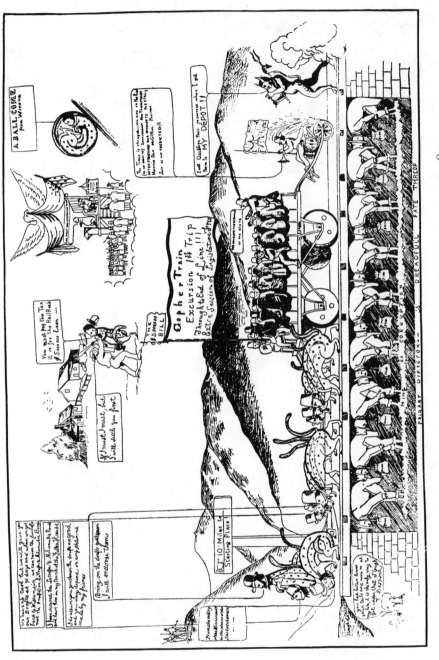

BROADSIDE RIDICULING THE FIVE MILLION LOAN OF 1857

The scheme was an ambitious one, in marked contrast with the more reasonable counsel of Governor Gorman that the first effort be to secure a single road connecting with the outside world. But it was struck out in a period of great elation preceding the panic, which came on in the late summer of the year 1857. It was no time for timidity or even moderation in business ventures. Previous to 1857 Minnesota legislatures had chartered fifteen railroad companies and nearly as many more were incorporated in that year.[5] Had all built their contemplated roads, the state would have been thoroughly gridironed. Probably all the companies had hopes, and some, expectations, of being aided by land grants. That all would receive grants was, of course, impossible. To establish a condition under which the fittest might survive and flourish, the leading spirits of four interests got together and worked out a plan for a railroad system which would reach all the principal centers of business, concentrate the largest possible amount of influence, political as well as commercial, and eliminate much undesirable competition. Of this "combine" of four corporations — three existing and one inchoate — the Honorable Edmund Rice of St. Paul, brother of the Minnesota delegate, was the leader. The incorporators were mostly Minnesota men, among them the head men of both political parties and representatives of the largest towns. The few names of eastern men indicated the expectation that fiscal coöperation would be needed from that quarter. It was the belief of Minnesota people that the system of roads was to be so much under home control that no clique of outside investors could dominate it. The united interests were so influential at Washington that they easily dispersed a slight and disunited opposition and triumphantly carried through the bill, virtually conveying to themselves

[5] *Council Journal,* 1854, p. 29; *Laws,* 1853–56; Rasmus S. Saby, "Railroad Legislation in Minnesota, 1849 to 1875," in *Minnesota Historical Collections,* 15:11. Before the passage of the general act of 1858 "for the Incorporation and Regulation of Railroad Companies," all railroad charters had been made by private or special acts. *General Laws,* 1858, p. 166.

millions of acres of public lands, provided, of course, that
the annexed conditions were fulfilled.[6]

It has already been related that Governor Gorman in the
last days of his service called an extra session of the legislature of 1857 to meet on April 27 and that one of the chief
objects of this session was to pass the measures necessary to
give effect to the enabling act for the formation of a state
government. That duty was tardily discharged just before
adjournment.[7] From the opening hour, however, all interest
centered on three railroad bills, which had been drawn up
by the skillful attorneys of the parties chiefly interested.
Governor Medary had transmitted a copy of the land grant
act of Congress of March 3 with a special message and had
counseled strict conformity to its provisions and careful
protection of the public interest. A separate bill accepting
the trust of the general government was promptly passed.
The conditions of this trust were such that small discretion
was left to the Minnesota legislature. There was some skirmishing in the chambers to secure additional branches and
the location of routes through certain towns, which was quite
ineffective. After sufficient delay to allow opposition to
expend itself in unwelcome amendments, three bills were
passed in a bunch in the third week in May by votes nearly
unanimous.[8] The newspapers of St. Paul abound in allusions
to the presence of crowds of outside speculators, "moneyed
vultures," keen for plunder, but their efforts seem to have

[6] Welles, *Autobiography*, 2:53-69; Newson, *Pen Pictures*, 153. See Anderson, *History of the Constitution*, 46-55, for a discussion of the relation of this legislation to the issues of the division of the territory and the location of the capital and to the local political situation.

[7] See *ante*, 1:394; *Laws*, 1857, extra session, 342; *House Journal*, 5, 19-22, 31, 80, 93; *Council Journal*, 30, 56. On the second day of the extra session Representative Joseph R. Brown moved the appointment of a committee to report its opinion on the legality of such a session. A week later a report was submitted by Brown and two colleagues. They said that the question admitted of argument on both sides, but indicated their belief that the session was legal. The House ordered 250 copies of the report printed; no further action was taken.

[8] *Council Journal*, 5-11, 15, 17, 19, 22-24, 26, 27, 29, 30-32, 36; *House Journal*, 25, 30, 35-37, 39-47, 51-54, 57, 58; *Laws*, 3-26, 70. The bill accepting the grant was approved on May 19; the three railroad bills were approved on May 22. Since the journals of the extra session are without indexes, the reader is advised that the bills were Council File 1, House File 5, and Council File 10. The votes in the Council were 12 to 1, 10 to 3, and 9 to 2; in the House, 32 to 3, 26 to 7, and 26 to 6.

been in behalf of town site interests and railroad connections eastward. Congress had put the division of the lands beyond their power.[9] A proposition for a consolidated bill, submitted to the House early in the session, had been lost by a vote of 18 to 19. No sooner, however, had the separate bills been carried through the third readings than there was a general desire to have them merged into one omnibus bill. The House had passed a bill to encourage the destruction of gophers and blackbirds and had asked the concurrence of the Council. The latter body in committee of the whole made merry with the measure by amending the title to include the Sioux Indians, and Joseph Rolette moved its reference to the military committee. On May 20 the Council went into committee of the whole for the further consideration of this bill and after some time spent therein reported an amendment striking out all after the enacting clause and inserting a consolidation of the three railroad bills transferring the land grant to four corporations. The amendment was agreed to and the title was changed to correspond. The next day the message of the Council announcing its concurrence in the House bill to encourage the destruction of gophers and blackbirds, with an amendment, was received by the House. A ruling by the speaker, Joseph W. Furber, that the amendment was not truly such but was an entire new matter was appealed from effectively by a vote of 28 to 8. There were but three negative votes on concurrence.[10]

The act thus passed and promptly approved forms chapter 1 of the extra session laws of 1857, entitled "*An Act to execute the trust created by an Act of Congress . . . and granting certain Lands to Railroad Companies therein named.*" The division into three subchapters indicates that the act

[9] *Pioneer and Democrat,* May 13, 16, 1857; *Minnesotian,* May 1, 5, 7, 9, 1857. In his *Autobiography,* 2:67, Welles says: "'The charter was finally passed; but not until a large amount of money had been distributed among a set of as corrupt and avaricious men as ever disgraced the halls of legislation in this state. Who furnished the money is well known to myself, and also a good part of those who received it." An interview on this subject with William P. Murray is recorded in the author's notebooks, 2:3.
[10] *House Journal,* 36, 41, 52-55, 56, 59, 73; *Council Journal,* 38, 41-44.

was made up by simple assemblage. The first chapter of
the act incorporated the Minnesota and Pacific Railroad
Company and empowered it to build from Stillwater via
St. Paul, St. Anthony, and Minneapolis to Breckenridge on
the western boundary, with a branch from St. Anthony via
Anoka, St. Cloud, and Crow Wing to St. Vincent near the
mouth of the Pembina River. The second chapter authorized
the existing Transit Railroad Company to build from Winona
via St. Peter to the Big Sioux River south of the forty-
fifth parallel. The last chapter embraced two companies
and three roads. The Root River Valley and Southern
Minnesota Railroad Company was empowered to construct one road from La Crescent up the Root River Valley
to a point of junction at Rochester with the road from
Winona to the Big Sioux, and another line from St. Paul and
St. Anthony via Minneapolis up the valley of the Minnesota
River to Mankato and thence to the southern boundary of
the territory in the direction of the mouth of the Big Sioux
River. The Minneapolis and Cedar Valley Railroad Company was authorized to build from Minneapolis to a junction
point near Mendota and thence via Faribault to the south
line of Minnesota west of range 16.[11]  To each of the companies severally the act assigned all the estate and interest
of Minnesota in the lands granted by Congress in aid of railroad construction for its particular route or routes. As soon
as each of them located twenty miles, it was to receive title
to 120 sections, and thereafter to a like amount whenever
twenty continuous miles had been completed so as to admit
the running of regular trains. All the lands were to be ex-
empt from taxes as long as they remained in the possession
of the companies and in consideration of the grants, privileges, and franchises conferred the companies were required

[11] The Transit Company had been incorporated by an act of March 3, 1855; the Root
River Valley and Southern Minnesota Company, by an act of March 2, 1855; and the
Minneapolis and Cedar Valley Company, by an act of March 1, 1856. *Laws*, 1855, pp. 73,
84; 1856, p. 325.

to pay annually into the state treasury three per cent of their gross earnings in lieu of all taxes and assessments.

When the legislature of 1857 broke up on May 25 the members dispersed to their homes to congratulate their constituents upon the prospect of the immediate beginnings of railroad building and the development of a great system of a thousand miles or more in the course of a few years.[12] A cloud was soon to cover this bright prospect. The panic of 1857 struck the country late in August. Its effect upon Minnesota has already been noted.[13] Not one dollar could these four Minnesota railroad companies raise. Their interests in the lands were only expectant. They must each survey and locate at least twenty miles before title could pass to a first batch of 120 sections. At five dollars an acre these would be worth $384,000. It would require great faith in a capitalist to lend more than half of this sum on wild lands in good times. With millions of acres of railroad lands offered in the market elsewhere, neither large nor rapid sales could be expected. The Transit Company offered all its prospective lands between Winona and the site of Waseca, some five hundred thousand acres, at one dollar an acre, and found no buyers.[14] If the stockholders had been disposed to pay in a large per cent of the face value of their shares, the slump in business would have made it impossible for them to do so. Many of them could not save their private fortunes from wreck. The people of Minnesota felt sorry for themselves and extended their sympathy to the members of the corporations which had planned generously for the public advantage.

[12] Senator Stuart of Michigan informed the United States Senate that the total length of the roads provided for was 925 miles. His further statement that on 527 miles of the proposed roads there were no public lands and that the amount along the remaining 398 miles was 1,528,320 acres is not explainable. Governor Ramsey in his message to the legislature of 1860 gave the aggregate as six million acres. The kindly disposition of the Minnesota legislature may be inferred from the joint resolution passed on the last day of the extra session, May 25, 1857, asking Congress to suspend preëmptions along the lines of the roads till they were definitely located or for four months to enable the companies to press construction. *Congressional Globe*, 34 Congress, 3 session, 699; Minnesota, *House Journal*, 1859–60, p. 178; *Laws*, 1857, extra session, 350.

[13] See *ante*, 1: 363, and Sibley's message in *Senate Journal*, 1859–60, p. 10.

[14] Verbal statement of William Ashley Jones, a stockholder, to the author.

During the fall months of 1857 the people were occupied with the question of ratifying their new constitution, with the election of representatives to Congress, and with the choice of a legislature, which would have among its duties the selection of two national senators. The railroad interests were naturally alert to discover any possible escape from the mire into which they had sunk. They had no money, of course. There was almost none in the territory. The military and Indian disbursements furnished the little in sight. Could each company but survey and locate a twenty-mile section of road it would receive 76,800 acres of land, which might be sold or hypothecated. Could it build and set in operation twenty miles, as many more acres would be acquired and the business begun would yield an income. Population would flow in, cultivation would extend, towns would develop, land values — especially those of railroad lands — would mount. In the course of a few years Minnesota would have a great railroad system, worth millions, which had cost her not a cent. All these companies lacked was a start, just a little sum to locate and build, say, fifty miles apiece. The whole state was interested; why should not the state, following the example of the national government, assist these worthy enterprises, of so much account to her? Other states had rendered such assistance for internal improvements. The proposition was not novel.[15] But there was the state constitution forbidding the legislature to contract a debt in excess of $250,000 and providing that in case any debt should be incurred the legislature should in the act authorizing the debt provide for a tax sufficient to

[15] Report of the select committee on the Five Million Loan Bill, in Minnesota, *Senate Journal*, 1858, pp. 172-179. A reprint of the report also forms the first of a number of pamphlets and newspaper clippings relating to the Five Million Loan which have been bound in a volume with the back title, "Five Million Loan." This volume is in the library of the Minnesota Historical Society. See also pamphlet no. 3 in the same volume, entitled *An Act Proposing a Loan of State Credit to the Land Grant Railroad Companies; with Arguments in Favor of Its Approval by the People*, 8 (St. Paul, 1858). In this pamphlet are reprinted a number of articles which appeared in the *Pioneer and Democrat* of March 11-14, 18, 20, 21, 1858.

cancel it within ten years.[16]  A loan of money by the state
was out of the question.  The framers of the constitution
had borrowed from that of Wisconsin a paragraph reading,
"The credit of the State shall never be given or loaned in aid
of any individual, association or corporation."  This pro-
hibitory provision furnished a clew.  It appeared to suggest
that there was such a thing as lending "credit" without
incurring liability for ultimate payment and thus making a
debt.  The case of an indorser protected by ample collateral
duly assigned was quoted.  Could not the state take some
such part?  A scheme was worked out whereby the state was
to furnish her promissory obligations to the railroad companies, which should obligate themselves to pay principal and
interest and secure the state against possible loss.  The
state was merely to furnish "accommodation paper" to
wealthy corporations in a pinch for ready cash, taking ample
security.[17]

The "Five Million Loan Bill" did not appear in the legislature, at least in its final form, until the twenty-fourth of
February, 1858.  The railroad interests seem to have had
some influence in convincing that body that it was competent
to do all manner of legislative business, which had been so
much doubted until about that time.  So favorable a sentiment had been disseminated that the bill met with no serious
opposition in the Senate.  After moving through the usual
stages, it was passed by that body on March 2 by a vote of
24 to 7.  Three days later the House of Representatives
concurred by a vote of 47 to 24.  Some opposition was made
in the House, but a favorable report from a select committee
of nine secured a concurrence.  Objection was made to such
hasty action, one member declaring that the legislature had
given more time to changing a county seat than to this

[16] Article 9, section 5.
[17] Constitution, article 9, section 10; Franklin B. Hough, *American Constitutions*,
2:513 (Albany, 1872); *St. Paul Advertiser*, February 20, March 27, 1858; *Minnesotian*,
December 1, 1858.  For a glorification of the scheme, see James W. Taylor, *The Railroad
System of the State of Minnesota, with Its Connections* (Five Million Loan Pamphlets, no. 5
— St. Paul, 1859).

important bill. There were then and later insinuations, even
open assertions, that the legislative bodies had been corrupted.[18] The proof thereof is yet to be revealed. It was not
necessary to bribe a body of men so willing to believe in a
plausible scheme for which their constituents were clamoring.

The bill thus passed proposed to add to article 9, section
10, of the constitution, quoted above, in substance the
following: except that to aid the four companies in the construction of their roads special bonds bearing seven per cent
interest, payable semiannually, should be "issued and delivered" to an amount not exceeding five millions of dollars
as a "loan of public credit." These bonds were to be
denominated "Minnesota State Railroad Bonds" and the
faith and credit of the state were pledged "for the payment
of the interest and the redemption of the principal thereof."
The bonds were to be issued in batches as construction progressed. Upon the completion of "any ten miles" of road,
ready for the superstructure, the governor on satisfactory
evidence thereof was to cause to be issued and delivered
bonds to the amount of one hundred thousand dollars; and
when "any ten miles" of road should be actually completed
and cars running thereon, a like amount was to be issued and
delivered; and so on, for further ten-mile sections. The state
was to lend its credit and see the good work go on without
further concern. As assurance that no claim could ever
arise, the companies were bound, if they accepted the
conditions of the act, to make provision for paying the
special state bonds, interest and principal, when due. As
security for faithful performance, they were to execute proper
assignments of their net profits to pay the interest which
should accrue; they were each to execute and deliver to the

[18] *Senate Journal,* 255, 259, 261, 263, 265, 267, 268; *House Journal,* 422, 429, 437,
445-453. The number of the bill was changed from Senate File 113 to Senate File 52.
See also the *Minnesotian,* March 1, 6, 1858. The special committee to which the bill was
referred said in its report that it believed "the principle and policy of a State loaning its
credit to works of internal improvement a bad one." This proposition, however, was "an
exception of the general rule." The previous legislature had not stipulated that failure
to build would forfeit charters. The bill would remedy this defect. See *House Journal,* 445.

governor a conveyance to the state of the first 240 sections — 153,600 acres — of land free from encumbrances; and the proceeds of all sales of these lands were to be applied to the payment of interest if defaulted and to form a sinking fund to meet any future defaults in the payment of interest and principal. Finally, "as further security," each company was required to transfer to the treasurer of the state at the time of the issue of the state bonds an amount of its own first mortgage bonds corresponding to the state bonds issued to it. These corporation bonds the governor was authorized to sell in case of default by the companies and he might also foreclose the mortgages given to secure them. In case of default by any of the companies in payment of interest or principal of the state bonds, no further issues were to be made to the company.[19]

This elaborate amendment to section 10 of article 9 of the constitution was to be submitted to the voters of the territory at an election to be held on April 15, 1858. For the six weeks immediately before the election the loan bill was the uppermost topic of public and private discussion. There was a remnant of conservative men who did not lose their heads, and they pointed out with unerring foresight the weaknesses and vices of the bill, which experience later revealed to the mass of the voters. The members of the legislature had not mistaken the sentiment of their constituents, which had indeed been voiced in numerous public meetings. The greatest effort made by those chiefly interested in ratification was to assure the people that in no conceivably probable event would the state have to come in and pay those bonds. Sixty-seven members of the two houses

---

[19] *General Laws*, 1858, pp. 9-12. Each company was required to construct at least fifty miles of road ready for the superstructure within two years after the acceptance of the act. The essential words of the Minnesota state railroad bonds of 1858 were: "The State of Minnesota acknowledges to owe, and promises to pay to the —————— Railroad Company . . . the sum of One Thousand Dollars, on the first day of December, A.D. One thousand eight hundred and eighty-three, with interest at the rate of seven per centum per annum. . . . Witness the Great Seal of the State of Minnesota and the signatures of the Governor and Treasurer of the State." Five Million Loan Pamphlets, no. 17, p. 3.

united in a published statement pledging themselves
"individually and collectively, to vote against any proposition to levy a tax either for the interest or principal of the
proposed loan of State credit. We claim to have removed
all probable chance of taxation . . . and we shall resist, as
one man, any proposition of the kind." Senator Rice and
thirty-eight Democratic leaders, including Joseph R. Brown
and Franklin Steele, published a letter strongly urging
ratification; but it cannot be said that the measure was
Democratic. Gorman opposed it vigorously and Daniel A.
Robertson contributed to newspapers a series of strong and
clear critical articles. A correspondent wrote to Alexander
Ramsey, "Judge Cooper is raising the De . . l and making every possible exertion to defeat the Loan."[20] Sibley
and Ramsey were both on the directorates of one or more
companies and remained silent. The former certainly
voted in the negative. The *Pioneer and Democrat* refrained
from comment while the bill was pending before the legislature, but before the election it advocated ratification in a
series of editorial articles, which were reprinted in pamphlet
form.[21] The Republican organ at the capital, the *Minnesotian*, edited by Dr. Thomas Foster and George W. Moore,
opposed the loan consistently from the earliest proposal,
but the Republican party did not take issue against it.[22]

The election was held as appointed. Few expected any
such majority of votes for the loan as was shown by the
official canvass published on the sixth of May: yeas, 25,023;

[20] *Pioneer and Democrat*, March 2, 13, 17, 18, 27, 31, April 6, 9, 15, 1858. The issue of
March 27 contains a strong letter from Gorman against the bill. It *"does not secure the
State,"* he says. See also the *Minnesotian*, December 1, 1858, and Benjamin Thompson
to Ramsey, April 3, 1858, in the Ramsey Papers.

[21] *Pioneer and Democrat*, March 4, 10–14, 18, 20, 21, 28, 30, 31, 1858. In the issue of
March 14 the editor represented that Canada, Massachusetts, Maryland, Virginia, South
Carolina, Georgia, Florida, Alabama, Tennessee, and Missouri had all lent their credit to
aid in railroad building and not one of those states had ever paid a dollar. See also the
*Minnesotian* of April 17, 1858, and *An Act Proposing a Loan of State Credit* (Five Million
Loan Pamphlets, no. 3). In a speech before the state House of Representatives on February
8, 1871, Sibley stated that he voted against the loan. *Saint Paul Daily Pioneer*, February 9,
1871.

[22] See the issues of the *Minnesotian* for February, March, and April, 1858.

nays, 6,733. Only in a few rural counties were the nays the more numerous. The cities and towns, large and small, gave large majorities for the loan. In the city of Winona, out of 1,182 votes but one was cast in the negative, that of the Honorable Thomas Wilson, later chief justice of the Minnesota supreme court. All the people wanted railroads, for the best of reasons. These twenty-five thousand who voted for the amendment, misled by public men who ought to have known better, deceived themselves into the belief that a "loan of public credit" pledging the faith and credit of the state did not create a debt, unless in empty form. In any event, if the companies should ever default in payment of the state bonds and their assigned "collateral" should prove insufficient, their confiscable property and franchises would certainly protect the state against ultimate loss.[23]

The four corporations promptly accepted the conditions of the amendment and immediately there was great show of activity. By midsummer contracts were let and construction was begun. On the fourth of August Governor Sibley, who had promised in his inaugural message to hold the railroad companies to a strict and yet reasonable compliance with law, gave them formal notice to that effect, reciting the conditions of the loan of credit substantially as expressed in the constitutional amendment, with one deviation of importance: the first mortgage bonds of the companies to be transferred to the state treasurer in exchange for the special state bonds should have priority of lien over all other bonds which the companies might issue. The talk was that they would be likely to issue some twenty million dollars.[24] Two days later the Senate by resolution called on the judges of the supreme court for their opinion on the state of the law

[23] *Minnesotian*, May 6, 1858; *Pioneer and Democrat*, April 18, 1858, citing the *Winona Republican*. Justice Wilson, in conversation with the author, confirmed the *Republican's* statement. See also the *St. Paul Advertiser*, March 27, April 3, 10, 1858.

[24] Sibley's address to the House, February 8, 1871, in the *Saint Paul Pioneer*, February 9, 1871; *St. Paul Advertiser*, June 12, 1858; *Pioneer and Democrat*, July 8, 1858; *House Journal*, 1859–60, pp. 15-20; *Senate Journal*, 1857–58, p. 376; Governor's Archives, Records, A : 7, 30. See also *Laws*, 1858, p. 179, for elaborate instructions to the governor in case of default by any of the companies.

in this regard. Justice Charles E. Flandrau, for the court, declined to depart from the traditional usage of deciding cases only as they arise in actual litigation.[25] The Minnesota and Pacific Railroad Company, by its attorney, thereupon moved in the supreme court of the state that a mandamus issue commanding Governor Henry H. Sibley to accept its bonds in their usual form without stipulation of priority of lien. Counsel was heard and on November 10 the court, having found in the terms of the amendment no warrant for the demand of the governor, ordered that the mandamus issue. The journals of the legislative bodies show that propositions to secure to the state priority of lien were voted down. The amendment had been purposely and most adroitly drawn so as to exclude any such priority. The state's bonds were "special bonds"; those of the company were not. The company was merely obligated to transfer "an amount of first mortgage bonds," that is, as the court held, a quantity of the whole amount of first mortgage bonds that it might issue in the course of its enterprises.[26]

As advised by the attorney-general, Governor Sibley obeyed the order of the court and presently issued and delivered to the plaintiff company state bonds to the amount then reported as earned. He was severely criticized both for taking the position that he did and for yielding to the court. He was counseled by friends to ignore the action of the court and to assert the right of the executive as a coördinate branch of the government to act according to his own best judgment and discretion. Sibley was capable of

[25] *Senate Journal*, 1858, pp. 669, 718. See page 694 for the failure of a motion to reconsider.

[26] Minnesota and Pacific Railroad Company *v*. H. H. Sibley, governor, 2 *Minnesota Reports*, 13; *Pioneer and Democrat*, November 11, 13, 19, 23, 1858. Justice Flandrau dissented from the decision of the court. An insurmountable objection to Governor Sibley's ruling, in the opinion of the court, was that it would have rendered unnecessary and absurd the provision of the act for the payment of the net profits of the roads and the conveyance of the first 240 sections of land. See also a memorandum in Sibley's handwriting, dated November 12, 1858, in Governor's Archives, Records, A: 63. An amendment to make the bonds a first lien was voted down by a vote of 13 to 18 in the Senate, while a similar amendment was rejected in the House by a vote of 27 to 37. *Senate Journal*, 1858, p. 266; *House Journal*, 1858, p. 447.

such independence but he doubtless decided to conform, not
because the court had commanded, but because he was convinced that it had properly construed the law. Senator
Rice is reported as having declared that the court had
decided against Governor Sibley justly and properly and
that "the idea that the Democratic Governor should be
compelled to do his manifest duty by mandamus from a
court was disgraceful."[27] Sibley got little credit with
political opponents, whose principal organ charged that,
interested as he was in the Minneapolis and Cedar Valley
road, he was at heart desirous to accept the bonds of the
companies as offered and therefore welcomed the mandamus.
It is safe to say that this was but one of a long series of de-
famatory exercises in which that newspaper delighted. The
court, however, in a well-known case decided two years
later, declared that "the governor [*Sibley*] seemed only
desirous of obtaining for his guidance a judicial interpretation of a clause in the constitution." It may be added that
but for the action of the Minnesota and Pacific the other
three companies would have acceded to the executive
demands and would have given the bonds exchanged with
the state a prior lien. In fact some issues had already been
made in exchange for companies' bonds conceding the
state's prior lien, though under protest.[28] Had the companies conformed to Governor Sibley's demand and transferred bonds securing to the state an exclusive prior lien, it
may be questioned whether the outcome would have been
materially changed. The mischief which resulted was not

[27] *Pioneer and Democrat*, December 7, 1858; letters to Sibley from J. J. Noah, November 13, 1858, from William G. Le Duc, November 20, 1858, from Ramsay Crooks, November 22, 1858, from W. W. Phelps, December 10, 1858, Sibley Papers. Phelps regretted that Governor Sibley did not refuse obedience to the mandamus. Crooks says, "The attempt of the Rail R. Companies . . . to coerce you into the Exchange of their bonds for those of the State, *before the Iron is laid* upon their roads, is looked upon here [*New York*], as nothing less than an attempt to defraud & swindle the State." For Sibley's explanation see his message in *Senate Journal*, 1859–60, p. 11.

[28] *Minnesotian*, November 11, 19, December 1, 10, 1858; Selah Chamberlain *v.* Henry H. Sibley, governor, 4 *Minnesota*, 309; memorial of the Transit Company, in *Senate Journal*, 1859–60, p. 197; Sibley to James W. Taylor, secretary of the Minnesota and Pacific Company, November 5, 1858, in Governor's Archives, Records, A: 62.

caused by any depreciation of the companies' bonds; they
were never worth anything and could not be in fact a "further security."

The beginnings of construction made in the late summer
and fall of 1858 were continued in the following season, the
contractors having accepted the state bonds at a figure
agreed upon, doubtless much below par. The decision of the
supreme court had not helped in maintaining their value.
By July 1, 1859, all the companies were in extremities. The
special state bonds, their only effective resource, had sunk
to a figure so low that they were of no further use as collateral.
The contractors, therefore, at the advice of the companies,
ceased work. The next six months were a period of dejection
in Minnesota. The railroad system which in April, 1858, the
people believed they were calling into being by the magic of
their vote had appeared only to sink into chaos. Many
who had performed labor, supplied subsistence, and furnished tools and materials for railroad construction were
unpaid or were possessors of state bonds of uncertain and
declining values. The distress caused by the continued
scarcity of real money was much aggravated by considerable
issues of depreciating circulating notes by state banks,
based on deposits of the special state railroad bonds.[29]

The first state legislature, which did not close its adjourned
session until the middle of August, 1858, provided by law
that there should be no further session until the first Wednesday in December, 1859, unless sooner convened by the
governor. No extra session was called and the second state
legislature convened on the date prescribed, December 7,
1859. Its proceedings were awaited with great interest and
some apprehension. Governor Sibley was still in office and
delivered his message in person to the houses in joint convention. The railroad bonds were, of course, the uppermost
topic. After reciting the issue and delivery of those bonds in

conformity to the constitutional amendment as judicially
interpreted, their failure to acquire a market value, which he
attributed to "the determined and mischievous efforts of a
portion of our own citizens," the suspension of work on the
roads, and the default of the companies to meet the interest
as stipulated, Sibley informed the legislature that the companies had graded in all 239 miles and 2,897 feet, not very
unequally divided, and that there had been delivered to them
special bonds to the amount of $2,275,000. These he
declared to be state obligations, voluntarily assumed. He
hoped that the legislature would "not for a moment tolerate
repudiation. Better, far better that we be visited by pesti-
lence or famine, for these are the instruments of God, for
which we are not responsible." Governor Sibley's simple,
high-minded counsel was that the state should acknowledge
its indebtedness and its willingness to pay as soon as it should
be in condition to do so.[30]

On January 1, 1860, Sibley was succeeded in office by
Alexander Ramsey, who had been elected in the previous
October over George L. Becker.[31] In Governor Ramsey's
message the matter of "transcendent importance" was that
of the state railroad bonds, which, he declared, ought to be
"rightly adjusted and settled satisfactorily to all parties,
upon principles of justice, equity, and honor." Assuming
that the state would acquire by foreclosure the properties
and franchises of the four companies, he proposed that new
charters of liberal character be granted to parties who should
receive from the state "a bonus of ten thousand dollars a
mile, in State Bonds bearing a graduated interest of less than
7 per cent per annum" for every twenty miles of continuous road completed, on condition that an equal amount of

---

[30] *General Laws*, 1858, p. 114; *Senate Journal*, 1859–60, pp. 10-27. In his message Sibley
traces the history of the bond issue to date. The message is otherwise important and very
well composed. See Governor's Archives, Records, A: 115, 120, 121, 125, 126, 204, 212,
228 for references to the defaults in the payment of interest. See also the memorial of the
Transit Company in *Senate Journal*, 1859–60, p. 197.

[31] *House Journal*, 1859–60, pp. 38, 39. The votes for the state officers were opened and
announced by the speaker in the presence of the legislature.

Minnesota state railroad bonds be returned to the treasury for cancellation. In this way the construction of about 250 miles of railroads might be secured within the state. The governor was of the opinion that the greater part of the special bonds were still in the possession or control of the companies or "their immediate representatives, the contractors." His expectation was that their stockholders would immediately and eagerly accept the charters and resume work. The greater proportion of the old bonds would then be provided for. As for the small remainder, his proposition was to retire them by issuing to holders other and general bonds at a rate to be ascertained by the legislature. The constitution should be amended so as to reduce the maximum amount of state debt for railroad purposes from five million dollars to two and one-half million. With characteristic intuition Governor Ramsey proposed this plan not as ideal but as one which could be worked. His chief concern was to secure an immediate settlement; next to that he desired the immediate building of the railroads. He warned the legislature and the people that if this "vexing" question were not settled it would remain to disturb politics, divide the people, and annually occasion discord and possibly corruption in the legislative halls. The end, he declared, would be as in other states: the men who would have obtained possession gradually of all the bonds for a few cents on the dollar would "knock, year after year, at the door of the legislature for their payment in full," would subsidize the press, would raise the cry of repudiation, and, finally, would "pile up almost fabulous fortunes obtaining a recognition of their disputed paper and its payment at par!" He felt that "Now is . . . the very time to settle, arrange, adjust these unfortunate and deplorable Railroad and Loan complications." This man of common sense amounting almost to genius never counseled more wisely.[32]

[32] *Senate Journal*, 1859–60, pp. 123-130; *House Journal*, pp. 173-180. Ramsey stated that "others" argued that the Minnesota state railroad bonds of a "special and restricted character" did not create an ordinary general state obligation and that this was understood

The legislature thus addressed, composed in great part of inexperienced men, was too completely saturated with an existing public sentiment regarding these bonds to give much heed to sound business counsel. The public had been assured, by none more emphatically than by the agents of the four companies, that the state railroad bonds were evidences of company debt, amply covered by company securities. The people took them at their word and held to the faith inculcated. The bonds were "special bonds," known so to be by all who took them, and those who bought them took all risks. The railroad companies were perfectly aware of this understanding on the part of the people, who had given expression to it at the election on April 15, 1858. The Minnesota people of 1859, believing that they had been tricked by the companies into voting for an ambiguous constitutional amendment, could easily suspect that the companies had never intended to build the roads, but had planned only to secure as many bonds as possible in return for grading at the rate of ten thousand dollars a mile. The report was widely spread that the grading done was in detached portions where work was light, that lines were excessively crooked and grades much too steep, and that in places the track level was below high-water mark; in short, that the work was generally skimped and scamped and totally unfit for superstructure. In some places even the right of way had not been legally acquired. It was believed that

by the companies which had received them. How far Governor Ramsey sympathized with these arguments is not known, but he probably had reason to believe that his proposed plan of settlement would be acceptable. In his message of January 9, 1861, he said: "Certainly, equity neither seems to require, nor have we in any event the ability now to assume the burden of paying them at a par value." The legislative committee on railroads in its report recommended a plan similar to that proposed by Governor Ramsey. The suggestion was made that twenty-five cents on the dollar would cancel all claims of bondholders. The plan proposed by the minority of the committee consisted of the following points: the state must finally pay the railroad bonds; each company should be required to complete fifty miles within twelve months; the state should then issue to each company "State bonds at large" to the amount of $425,000, while a like amount of Minnesota state railroad bonds with unpaid coupons should be returned by the company to the governor, and the state should relinquish all securities held by her. See *Senate Journal*, 1861, p. 21; *House Journal*, 1859–60, pp. 391, 396. A plan of adjustment proposed by one company — probably for all — "after long and full consultation with parties East," is given in *Senate Journal*, 1859–60, p. 199.

certain experienced contractors had worked their will with
the incompetent officials of the companies.  Over all was the
bald truth that all the state had to show for two and a
quarter millions in special bonds was 240 miles of discon-
tinuous, ill-executed grading.[33]

Influenced by this sentiment and sharing in it, the legislature raised a joint committee of fourteen to consider and
report on railroads, railroad grants, and Minnesota state
railroad bonds.  This committee was unable to come to
any agreement.  Six reports were submitted, all but one
accompanied by proposed constitutional amendments.
One member, Senator Charles N. Mackubin of St. Paul,
proposed a full payment of principal and interest with an
apparatus for redemption much too complicated to be comprehended by the average man.[34]  If the best heads of the
two houses could come to no agreement, the members at
large were less likely to; and they did not.  Weeks passed in
unprofitable discourses and projects.  There was but one
thing which that legislature could at length agree upon
touching these bonds.  It could, in sea phrase, simply "clap
a stopper" on the whole proceeding and leave successors to
wrestle with the problem which it had vainly essayed to
solve.  This purpose was effected partly by the passage of a
joint resolution submitting to the people two amendments to
the state constitution: one provided that no law making
provision by tax or otherwise for the payment of the bonds
should take effect until adopted by a majority of the electors
voting thereon; the other expunged the entire amendment to
section 10 of article 9 adopted in 1858 lending the credit of
the state to the land grant railroads.  Both these amendments were adopted at the election held on November 6,
1860.[35]

[33] House Journal, 1859–60, pp. 173, 176, 390; Proceedings of the Board of Commissioners
Appointed by the Governor of Minnesota under the Provisions of an Act Approved February
28, 1866, pp. 49-52 (Five Million Loan Pamphlets, no. 13 — St. Paul, 1867).
[34] Senate Journal, 146, 151, 343-358, 370, 380, 382; House Journal, 186, 389-398, 424.
[35] General Laws, 1860, p. 297.  The vote on the amendment requiring a referendum
for the payment of the bonds was: yes, 18,648, no, 743; that on the expunging of the amend-

The legislature of 1858 passed a general banking law for the issue of circulating notes by corporations which should be organized under the act, substantially on the New York plan. Upon the deposit of "public stocks" of the United States or of any state with him, the state auditor was authorized by law to issue circulating notes countersigned and registered in his office to an amount not exceeding the current market value of such securities as determined by the average price on the stock exchange in New York City during the preceding six months. In case of failure, bill holders had a first lien on assets. At the very close of the session an amendatory act was passed providing that public stocks of the United States and of the state of Minnesota should be received by the auditor "at their current value," without designating any particular method of ascertaining that value, while the stocks of other states to be eligible must not have sold at less than par on the stock exchange in New York during the preceding six months.[36]

Within a short time after the first issue of the special state railroad bonds, the auditor was furnished with affidavits of "reputable citizens" to the effect that considerable sales had been made in New York and that therefore the current value of the state railroad bonds was ninety-five cents on the dollar. Upon this information he delivered to twelve or more banking corporations, which had deposited special bonds, circulating notes to the amount of $509,000. In some cases contractors accepted the bonds from the companies in payment, with the purpose of using them to bank on. Before the close of 1860 seven of these banks had failed and their deposited stocks had been sold at public

ment of 1858 was: yes, 19,308, no, 710. The essential words of the expunging amendment were: "nor shall there be any further issue of bonds denominated 'Minnesota State Railroad Bonds,' under what purports to be an amendment to Section ten (10) of Article nine (9) of the Constitution . . . which is hereby expunged from the Constitution." See also the report of the secretary of state, in Minnesota, *Executive Documents*, 1860, no. 4, p. 12, and Governor's Archives, Records, A: 272.

The long and disagreeable sequel to this bond story will be told in volume 3.

[36] *General Laws*, 1858, pp. 68-81. This act replaced and repealed a previous act that the same legislature had adopted.

auction in New York at prices averaging less than thirty cents on the dollar. One batch went at sixteen and a quarter cents. A year later but two survived and those did not completely retire their circulation until the national bank act went into operation in 1863. That act was nowhere more gladly welcomed than in Minnesota. Indeed, the losses through state bank circulation, so trifling when estimated from present circumstances, were felt keenly by the pioneers.[37]

[37] Ramsey's message of January 2, 1860, in *House Journal*, 1859–60, pp. 168, 177; reports of the state auditor, in *Executive Documents*, 1860, no. 2, p. 5; 1861, pp. 553-556; 1862, p. 587; Ramsey's message of January 7, 1863, in *Executive Documents*, 1862, p. 21. For a detailed account of this experiment in state banking, see Sidney A. Patchin, "The Development of Banking in Minnesota," in the *Minnesota History Bulletin*, 2: 143-161 (August, 1917).

## III.  MINNESOTA ON THE EVE OF THE REBELLION

THE territorial status of Minnesota ceased on May 24, 1858, when the state officers elected in the previous autumn were sworn into office.  As already related, the Democratic legislature elected at the same time met in adjourned session on June 2.  Among its acts was one providing for annual state elections on the second Tuesday of October and for annual sessions of the legislature to open on the first Wednesday of December.  Governor Sibley in his special message of June 15, 1858, recommended deferring the session of 1858–59 to July or August.  The legislature preferred to omit that session entirely, unless it should be convened by a proclamation of the governor.[1]  It was the belief of Republican leaders that in case of a Democratic victory in the election of 1858 Governor Sibley would call a special session of the legislature for the election of a United States senator to succeed General James Shields.  The hopes of the Democrats were blasted by a vote which would give the Republicans a majority in joint convention of the two houses should they be assembled.[2]  Surprised by their success in this campaign, heartened by the recollection that it was by only a slender majority that their candidate for governor had been defeated in 1857 — and that majority challenged for trickery — and encouraged by the general advance of their forces in neighboring states, the Republicans of Minnesota looked forward to the election of 1859 with high hopes.  In their state convention held in St. Paul

[1] See *ante*, p. 25.  *General Laws*, 1858, p. 114; *House Journal*, 674.
[2] *Saint Paul Minnesotian*, September 10, 1858; Republican address of Jared Benson, in the *Minnesotian*, October 1, 1858.  Although it was expected that no session of the legislature would be held in the winter of 1859, the annual election of 1858 was held.  The vote was light and in many precincts was virtually neglected.  The returns are published in the *Minnesotian* of October 26, 1858.

on July 20 and 21 they nominated Alexander Ramsey for
governor by acclamation.[3]  They organized in every county,
spread their campaign documents broadcast, and sent their
"spellbinding" orators to every village and crossroads.
As one seat in the United States Senate and two seats in the
House of Representatives were in issue, the national Republican managers thought it important to send able speakers to
Minnesota.  John P. Hale of New Hampshire, Galusha A.
Grow of Pennsylvania, Schuyler Colfax of Indiana, Francis
P. Blair, Jr., of Missouri, and Carl Schurz of Wisconsin
were heard in the principal cities.[4]

Of all the orators who participated in the spirited campaign of 1859, none rendered more effective service than a
late comer to Minnesota, who was to play a conspicuous
rôle in her politics for more than forty years — Ignatius
Donnelly of Nininger.  He had come from Philadelphia to
make his home in the West in the summer of 1857, at the age
of twenty-six.  After receiving a high-school education in
his native city, he had studied law, had practiced at the bar,
had married happily, had published a volume of poems, had
written editorials for a Democratic newspaper, and had
delivered a Fourth of July oration from the steps of Independence Hall.  The panic of 1857 put a quietus on his
ambitious projects to found a city at Nininger, an hour's
walk to the north of Hastings, and to extend a railroad into
the Minnesota Valley.  Donnelly was now ready for new
employments, public and other.  Like many other Democrats, he had found good reasons for going over to Repub-
licanism soon after this commercial disaster.[5]  To obtain

[3] *St. Paul Minnesotian*, July 22, 28, August 4, September 5, 1859; *Pioneer and Democrat*,
July 21, 1859.
[4] Eugene V. Smalley, ed., *History of the Republican Party*, 165 (St. Paul, 1896); Owens,
"Political History of Minnesota," 521.  The *St. Paul Minnesotian*, September 2-26, 1859,
gives the appointments of the visiting speakers.
[5] Everett W. Fish, *Donnelliana: An Appendix to "Cæsar's Column,"* part 1, pp. 13-15,
25 (Chicago, 1892).  See also Donnelly's letter "To the Foreign-Born Citizens of Minnesota," in the *St. Paul Minnesotian*, August 4, 1859; John D. Hicks, "The Political Career of
Ignatius Donnelly," in the *Mississippi Valley Historical Review*, 8:80-83 (June–September,
1921); and the manuscript thesis by Franklin F. Holbrook, "The Early Political Career of
Ignatius Donnelly, 1857–1863," 6 (University of Minnesota, 1916).  Copies of this thesis

recognition in the new party, in the fall of 1857 he accepted, without the least hope of success, a nomination as state senator. In 1858 the same compliment was paid him and a split in the Democratic ranks gave him warrant for an active canvass; but he failed of election by twenty-five votes. In 1859 Donnelly was early in the field for something better than a local or state position. On May 9 he wrote John H. Stevens that he thought of running for Congress.[6] He soon found, however, that Congress was beyond his reach and he then stood ready to accept a nomination to any state office that his party might accord him. The Republican convention made him its candidate for lieutenant governor. A series of letters "To the Foreign-Born Citizens of Minnesota," published in the course of the month preceding the convention, gained him some votes, but it was probably the favor of Alexander Ramsey and the support of his friends, rallied between adjourned sessions, that gave him the lead over four competitors and secured the nomination.[7]

The estimation in which Governor Ramsey held Donnelly at the time may be inferred from the fact that he invited Donnelly to accompany him on a campaign tour. In a private conveyance the two traveled more than two thousand miles and each made over sixty speeches. It is the deliberate judgment of the present writer, after hearing him on a variety of occasions, that Minnesota has possessed no other public speaker the equal of Ignatius Donnelly in captivating and enchaining audiences. To his eloquence, in no small measure, may be attributed the overwhelming victory of the Republican party in 1859. Alexander Ramsey, as his friends claimed, came to his own again and it was just

are in the libraries of the university and the Minnesota Historical Society. It is a well-written account drawn from Fish, *Donnelliana*, contemporary newspapers, and the Donnelly Papers.

[6] *Minnesotian*, November 5, 1857; *Pioneer and Democrat*, October 20, 21, 1858; Donnelly to Stevens, May 9, 1859, Stevens Papers. Fish, in his *Donnelliana*, 29, erroneously states that Donnelly was beaten in the election of 1858 by but six votes.

[7] *Minnesotian*, June 15, July 19, 22, August 4, 1859.

forty years before a second governor was elected by a Democratic majority.[8]

The second state legislature, the first controlled by the Republicans, convened on December 7, 1859, and listened to the final message of Governor Sibley, who vigorously counseled the redemption of the railroad bonds, the reduction of the legislature to eighteen senators and thirty-six representatives, and the husbanding of the school lands to form an inviolate and perpetual endowment. He also counseled the repeal of the act establishing township organization and the revision of the banking, military, and tax laws. Lieutenant Governor William Holcombe continued to preside over the Senate, but the House elected a Republican speaker. The duty of supreme interest to the legislative body was the election of a United States senator. The choice, virtually made in the Republican caucus, was formally voted in joint convention on the fifteenth of December. It fell on Morton S. Wilkinson of St. Paul. Wilkinson had settled in Stillwater in 1847 and was the first attorney to practice at the bar north of Prairie du Chien. He was an ardent free-soiler, had enjoyed the personal acquaintance of William H. Seward and Abraham Lincoln, and had been active in the organization of the Republican party in Minnesota. His success in politics was largely due to his vigorous and engaging eloquence. He was the first of a more or less unbroken line of Republican United States senators elected from Minnesota until 1923.[9]

[8] Fish, *Donnelliana*, 31, 32. Fish's figures are doubtless an exaggeration. For the itinerary of the orators see the *Minnesotian* for August 27 and September 23, 1859. Owens, in his "Political History of Minnesota," 521, says that Ramsey and Windom "put forth the solid arguments, Goodrich told the funny stories . . . and Donnelly did the same, interspersed with those magnetic and eloquent appeals of which he is master." See also Holbrook, "Early Political Career of Donnelly," 43. The election returns for state officers are given in *House Journal*, 1859–60, p. 39. Ramsey's majority over Becker was 3,753; Donnelly's over Lowry, 3,247. The second governor to be elected by a Democratic majority was John Lind, in 1899.

[9] *Senate Journal*, 1859–60, pp. 10-27, 258; *House Journal*, 4, 15-32; Smalley, *Republican Party*, 286. For biographical sketches of Wilkinson see Holcombe, in *Minnesota in Three Centuries*, 3: 86; *Minnesota Historical Collections*, 8: 533; and the *Daily Pioneer Press* (St. Paul), February 5, 1894. The vote in joint convention was: Wilkinson, 79; Shields, 33; and Gorman, 1.

On January 2, 1860, Alexander Ramsey took his oath of office as governor and on the same day Lieutenant Governor Donnelly assumed the presidency of the Senate. In his inaugural message the new executive denounced the waste and extravagance which Sibley had censured and urged a reduction of expenses. The legislature took him at his word, cut down his salary from twenty-five hundred to fifteen hundred dollars, and also trimmed the salaries of other officials. It reduced the number of senators from thirty-seven to twenty-one and that of representatives from eighty to forty-two and submitted to the electors an amendment to the constitution providing that no session of the legislature should exceed the term of sixty days. By these and similar measures the expenses of the state for that year were reduced about thirty-six per cent below those of the preceding year.[10]

The legislature of 1858 had established a system of county government by boards composed of town supervisors on the model of that of New York. The plan, unsuited to a frontier community, had not worked satisfactorily. Sibley advised that it be abandoned and Ramsey, that it be revised. The legislature of 1860 repealed the law and substituted that plan of administration by county commissioners which has been in use ever since. The laws for town government were also revised. Important amendments or revisions were made in the road, tax, corporation, interest, and election laws. These and other measures of this very industrious legislature may justify the eulogium of Owens that it "laid the foundation of our State structure," in spite of its absurd,

---

[10] *House Journal*, 1859–60, pp. 163-183; *Senate Journal*, 113-133, 134; *General Laws*, 1860, pp. 170, 229, 230, 256. In his message Governor Ramsey arraigned the state officials of the previous year for mismanagement and failure to make full and accurate reports. See also Owens, "Political History of Minnesota," 550, 562. Ramsey recommended a reduction of the number of senators to fifteen and of that of representatives to forty-five. He recommended also that the assembling of the legislature "be made more nearly simultaneous with the induction into office of the members of the Executive department." The legislature accordingly provided for the opening of future sessions on the first Tuesday after the first Monday in January. This has remained unchanged. Governor Ramsey gives the expenses for the year 1860 in his message of January 9, 1861, in *Executive Documents*, 1860, no. 1, p. 7.

not to say dishonest, repudiation of the railroad bonds of 1858.[11]

The decennial census of 1860 was a disappointment to citizens generally, but in particular to hopeful investors in lands and city lots. Instead of an expected total population of at least 250,000, the actual number was but 172,023, including 2,369 Indians. St. Paul had 10,401 inhabitants, St. Anthony had 3,258, and three other cities had about 2,500 each. The main body of the people were dwelling in the river counties and in those immediately in the rear. Spread out on the land, they were deriving a plain but abundant subsistence from virgin soil and abounding waters. Of good sustenance for man and beast there was no lack.[12]

In provision for elementary schooling, religion, and social enjoyments the young and ambitious communities of Minnesota had in many cases progressed beyond those from which the people had migrated.[13] Congress had voted liberal sums to the territory for opening roads. Stage lines carried passengers and mails to all important settlements. The

[11] *General Laws*, 1858, pp. 190-227; 1860, pp. 9-51, 79-93, 110-130, 130-141, 146-165, 226, 239; 1861, pp. 46-48; Owens, "Political History of Minnesota," 561. The act of 1858 required the erection of as many towns as there were townships in the county and made the chairman of each town board of supervisors a member of the county board of supervisors. As the counties generally contained twenty or more towns, these boards were excessively large. The notable change in the election law was that providing for the registration of electors. Owens remarks that before this act was passed "the purity of the ballot box . . . had at almost every election been outrageously tampered with." See his "Political History of Minnesota," 558. Ramsey, in his message of January 9, 1861, in *Executive Documents*, 1860, no. 1, p. 5, asserts that the provision for registration "should accomplish . . . that prevention of fraud which is better than any subsequent punishment."

[12] *United States Census*, 1860, *Population*, 255-263. Stillwater had 2,380 inhabitants; Minneapolis, 2,564; and Winona, 2,464. Of the native-born population — 113,295 people — the Middle States had furnished the major part, 30,075; New England, 18,822; and the Middle West and the West, 24,640. The foreign born numbered 58,728. Of these the Germans, who numbered 18,400, and the Irish, of whom there were 12,831, predominated, while Norway had sent 8,425 and Sweden, but 3,178. Of a total of 53,426 engaged in gainful occupations, 27,921 were farmers and 3,921 were fishermen. See Joseph A. Wheelock, *Minnesota: Its Progress and Capabilities*, 108-112 (Minnesota, Bureau of Statistics, *Second Annual Report* — St. Paul, 1862), and Edward V. Robinson, *Early Economic Conditions and the Development of Agriculture in Minnesota*, 46, 47 (University of Minnesota, *Studies in the Social Sciences*, no. 3 — Minneapolis, 1915).

[13] Interview of the author with Mrs. Mary Briggs Aiton, May 28, 1917. Mrs. Aiton joined the Dakota mission in 1852 and in 1855 she was married. Later the family settled on a farm in Nicollet County. She was emphatic in praising the high and sterling character of the immigrants who forced their way into the Minnesota Valley after the treaties of 1851. Their coming was followed by the immediate opening of churches and schools.

river trade by means of commodious steamers, often splendid in equipment and decoration, was rapidly increasing. It was by them that the exportable produce of the state, which in the census year amounted to nearly four millions of dollars, was moved eastward.[14]

The property of the state as valued for taxation in 1860 stood at $36,753,408. Her indebtedness, exclusive of the state railroad bonds, consisted of $250,000 in eight per cent bonds issued in 1858 and floating obligations of $68,637. The municipal debts, of unknown amount, were large, but had there been an efficient taxing system they need not have given concern. The state taxes of the census year as collected were $113,602, and the accumulated delinquent taxes were $216,594. Although confidence in values and securities had been in a good degree reëstablished and business had much revived, enterprise was restrained by the lack of a sound currency and by a continued interest rate of over two per cent a month. Great and general commercial and industrial developments were waiting, and had still years to wait, for railroad construction to unite Minnesota with the outside world all the year round.[15]

Early in the summer of 1860 the St. Paul newspapers announced the rapid construction of the electric telegraph line which was to put the capital of Minnesota in continual association with the great world. In June the public was informed that the poles were nearly all set between Winona and St. Paul and that the workmen had been much annoyed by rattlesnakes.[16] It was not until August 29 that the opening of the St. Paul office was celebrated by the dispatch of a

[14] *Statutes at Large*, 9:439; 10:150, 306; 11:27; message of Governor Ramsey, January 9, 1861, in *Executive Documents*, 1860, no. 1, p. 4. Ramsey estimated the value of the exportable surplus as follows: grain, $2,800,000; potatoes, $10,000; lumber, $629,000; furs $190,000; ginseng, $70,000; hides, $30,000; cranberries, $20,000; other articles, $100,000; total, $3,939,000.

[15] Report of the state auditor, in *Executive Documents*, 1860, no. 2, pp. 4, 7, 12, 14. The estimated value of the real and personal property of the state was $60,205,009. *United States Census*, 1860, *Statistics*, 306.

[16] *Minnesotian*, May 29, 1860; *Pioneer and Democrat*, June 12, 1860. By an act of March 3, 1855, the legislature had authorized the construction of a telegraph line from St. Paul to Traverse des Sioux by way of St. Anthony and Minneapolis. *Laws*, 1855, p. 69.

message of salutation, at 1:45 P.M., from Morton S. Wilkinson and Aaron Goodrich to William H. Seward. Seward's reply was received at 8:30 P.M. The delay in the installation was due not so much to rattlesnakes and foul weather as to the consumption of time in extracting bonuses from the municipalities along the route. Minneapolis was so tardy with her subscription that it was not until November 14 that the first dispatches appeared in her newspapers. St. Anthony, even less prompt with her bonus, did not get her local office until December 4. For many months newspapers were compelled to apologize for the absence of telegraphic news because the wire was down or because there had been a thunderstorm or a sudden thaw, and in one instance because of some mysterious influence of moonbeams on the electric current.[17]

The political campaign of 1860 was far less boisterous than that of the previous year. The Republicans had good reason to expect a triumph over a united Democracy and their confidence expanded when the supporters of Douglas deserted the Charleston convention and assembled in Baltimore to place their favorite in nomination for the presidency. The main body of Democrats, as the election returns showed, led by Sibley, supported Douglas, while a remnant derisively called "Buchaniers" adhered to Breckinridge under Rice's lead.[18] Still the Republicans maintained an active though not a strenuous campaign. The most notable event of the season was an address delivered from the steps of the State Capitol in St. Paul on September 18 by William H. Seward. It was a clear and forceful presentation of the great issue of the time and contained a powerful appeal to Minnesota Republicans to give their support to Abraham Lincoln, who

[17] *Pioneer and Democrat*, August 30, 1860, January 17, February 13, 24, May 25, 1861; *State Atlas* (Minneapolis), September 26, November 14, 1860; *Falls Evening News* (St. Anthony and Minneapolis), November 15, 17, 22, December 4, 1860.

[18] Owens, "Political History of Minnesota," 568; *The Charleston Convention: Statement of a Portion of the Minnesota Delegation to Their Constituents* (Washington, 1860), a copy of which is in the Donnelly Pamphlets, 11: no. 1, in the library of the Minnesota Historical Society; *Pioneer and Democrat*, November 21, 1860; *Daily Times* (St. Paul), August 14, 23, 1860.

at the Chicago convention had won from Seward the nomination which the latter had expected. The Minnesota delegation, voicing the preference of Minnesota Republicans, had stood firmly for Seward as long as any hope remained of his nomination. In his St. Paul address Senator Seward ventured a bit of prophecy at which he was perhaps not so good as at statesmanship. "Here is the central place," said he, "where the agriculture of the richest regions of North America must begin its magnificent supplies to the whole world. . . . I now believe that the last seat of power on the great continent will be found somewhere within a radius not very far from the very spot where I stand, at the head of navigation on the Mississippi river."[19]

The contest between the great political parties generally in 1860 was far less violent than that which followed within the ranks of the Republican party. It had not yet enjoyed the sweets of government patronage and the prospect of capturing a number of desirable appointments was alluring. For the positions of surveyor-general, United States district attorney, collectors and receivers of the land offices, and those of the principal post offices there was a horde of aspirants. The struggle continued till the various places were filled after President Lincoln's accession to office.[20] It was diversified by an effort on the part of the Republican delegation to Congress to dictate the appointments and thus reduce the prestige of Governor Ramsey at Washington and add to their own importance in state politics. To a number of aspiring gentlemen of his party Ramsey was much in the way. A feeble effort to secure for him the position of secretary of the interior had for its object his promotion out of their daylight quite as much as to pay him a compliment or

[19] *Times*, September 19, 22, 1860; *Minnesotian*, September 19, 1860; *Pioneer and Democrat*, September 20, 1860. The Minnesota Historical Society has in its possession typewritten extracts from the diary of Charles Francis Adams, Sr., and from the recollections of Charles Francis Adams, Jr., relating to the reception of Seward and his party in St. Paul. Both men were in Seward's party. See also Owens, "Political History of Minnesota," 570, and Smalley, *Republican Party*, 166.

[20] See numerous letters to Ramsey and Donnelly, 1860–61, in the Ramsey and Donnelly papers, and Owens, "Political History of Minnesota," 591.

to render the country a service. One outcome, however, was the intrenchment of a "land office clique," which later undertook to balk Governor Ramsey's elevation to the Senate, fortunately without success.[21]

In the legislature elected in October, 1860, the defeated Democracy held but few places. The session which opened on January 8, 1861, was marked by but few measures of permanent importance, but there is one measure of transcendent moment to its credit. In response to a fervent appeal by Governor Ramsey for the rescue of the public lands granted by Congress to Minnesota — in particular of the school lands — from premature sale at low prices with a probable dissipation of the proceeds, this legislature adopted a plan agreeable in principle, if not in administrative details, to that commended to them. The subject will be treated in a later volume, but it ought to be said here that Governor Ramsey, following Sibley's example, and the legislature of 1861 by the salvation of the school fund earned the unending gratitude of the people of Minnesota. The railroad legislation of 1861, which proved wholly abortive, and that of the following year, which became effective only after long and vexatious delays, will be better comprehended if it is reserved for a summary on a later page.[22]

It is important that the reader should understand that the Republican triumph of 1860 did not imply a disposition to interfere with African slavery in the southern states. It did mean, however, an unalterable resolution to prevent its extension into the territories. There was still a general and notable tolerance in the north of the continuance of the

[21] *Pioneer and Democrat*, March 17, 1861. See letters to Ramsey from Aldrich, December 23, 1860, from Wilkinson, January 2, 1861, from Colfax (two letters), January 11, 1861, from North, February 24, 1861, from Miller, February 26, 1861; joint letter from Wilkinson, Aldrich, and Windom to President Lincoln, January 28, 1861; and numerous other letters in the Ramsey Papers for 1860–61. The presidential electors, Stephen Miller, Clark Thompson, Charles McClure, and William Pfaender sent a memorial to Lincoln urging the appointment of Ramsey as secretary of the interior.
[22] Message of Governor Ramsey, January 9, 1861, in *Executive Documents*, 1860, no. 1, pp. 14–19; *General Laws*, 1861, pp. 79–94. See *post*, ch. 12, in regard to the railroad legislation of 1861 and 1862.

institution in the southern states. "Abolitionist" was still a term of scorn among Democrats and among Republicans it was one of reproach. The state of mind was illustrated in a case of liberation which took place in St. Anthony in August, 1860. In 1857 there had been opened in that place a large hotel, the Winslow House, in expectation of attracting visitors from the South in summer time. The journey up and down the Mississippi in the splendid steamboats of the time was one of comfort and pleasure. Southern people in considerable numbers came north and, presuming on the comity which had been accorded, brought colored servants with them.[23] Canada was far away and the chances of escape were few; and, doubtless, some masters rightly presumed on the fidelity of the favored servants brought with them.

On the twenty-first of August complaint was made that a colored woman was "restrained of her liberty" by her master, a guest at the Winslow House. A writ was granted and the woman was brought into court. The master was too well advised of the law to plead any claim to her and she was set at liberty. If the Democratic newspapers can be believed, there was general disgust and indignation against the abolitionist fanatics who had tampered with the girl, as they alleged, and persuaded her to run away from a kind and generous master. In the crowd which remained about the courthouse steps a proposition was made to capture her and give her back to her owner. He had the good sense to frown on the suggestion; and so ended "this sickening and disgraceful performance," says the *St. Anthony Express*. On the night of the same day a party of men assembled about the house of the principal complainant to tar and feather him and possibly to recover the negress. A violent rainstorm and the discharge of a pistol in the house — said to have been accidental — caused the gang to disperse. The Democratic newspapers of the three cities denounced the "abduction" of the negress as the work of

[23] *Pioneer and Democrat*, July 18, 19, 1860.

abolition Republican fanatics. The Republican papers took pains to insist that their party had taken no part in the transaction and was not responsible for it, and they contented themselves with saying that if the woman desired her freedom and of her own motion sought means to secure it, she ought to remain free. They denounced all propositions for kidnaping her and deprecated interference with the servants of southern visitors. A correspondent denounced "some strong, active, enthusiastic, intelligent, high minded Republicans" for talking of lynching those who were concerned in procuring the poor woman's freedom. He was more disgusted with these doughfaces than with the slaveholders.[24] The sentiment of hospitality was so notable that in March, 1860, a resolution was presented in the House and a bill was introduced in the Senate to permit slave owners to bring servants with them and hold them to service for a period of five months.[25]

On the second day of December, 1860, Senator Rice wrote from Washington to Governor Ramsey: "I found everything here much worse than I had anticipated. South Carolina, is virtually out of the Union, other states will follow, and unless the North shall at once show a disposition to recognize the rights of the South, every southern state must go. . . . Within thirty days there will not be a dollar in the Treasury & perhaps no government! Those who took the last loan will forfeit the stakes they put up. . . . the end God only can see. In the South the people now lead — the politicians follow." On the eighteenth of the same month, the senator

[24] *Saint Anthony Weekly Express*, August 25, September 1, 1860; *Falls Evening News*, August 23, 25, 28, 1860; *Minnesota State News* (St. Anthony and Minneapolis), August 25, September 1, 1860; *State Atlas*, August 29, 1860, February 20, 1861; *Pioneer and Democrat*, August 22, 23, 24; *Times*, August 23, 24, 1860. The affidavits of Eliza Winston and two of her rescuers may be found in the *Falls Evening News*, August 28, 1860, and the *State Atlas*, August 29, 1860.
[25] *Senate Journal*, 1859–60, pp. 599-601; *House Journal*, 649. Of the seventeen votes cast in favor of the House resolution, all were Democratic except one, that of Speaker Coggswell. Owens, in his "Political History of Minnesota," 565, relates that after adjournment James H. Baker, meeting the speaker in the hall, said in a jocular way, "Good bye, Coggswell; we are sorry to lose you, but good-bye!" Owens adds that thereafter Coggswell sided with the Democrats.

wrote further: "As yet nothing has transpired to change my former opinion — but much to confirm it. I trust you will recommend to the Legislature the calling of a Convention of the States. If this is not done by the northern Legislatures, good-bye to the Union. Nothing else in my opinion can save it — but if dissolution must come — I hope it may be a peaceable one." Two days later the South Carolina convention adopted an ordinance of secession from the federal union of 1787. Still another letter from Senator Rice, dated January 20, 1861, may be quoted as showing the state of mind of the acknowledged leader of the party which had for years controlled Minnesota affairs. "Most truly do I hope that Minnesota will keep herself out of complicity with the fanaticism of the day. If trouble must come upon our Nation where can those who desire peace find it so surely as in our own State? Should war be brought upon us there are thousands of brave men who will never draw the sword. They will look to our State." The *Pioneer and Democrat* of January 18, 1861, referring to a compromise resolution offered by Rice in the Senate on January 16, credits him with an ingenious scheme to enlarge the states of Minnesota, Oregon, California, and Kansas so as to embrace all the existing "territory" of the United States, and thus remove from discussion the "cause of all our woes — the slavery agitation." On January 2, 1861, Senator Wilkinson wrote to Governor Ramsey: "Rice I think is frightened, he told me today that he feared there would be an attack made upon the Capitol." On January 16 Wilkinson wrote: "The clouds are thick enough. . . . It looks to me as though the Government would be dismembered"; and his counsel was that the executive should at once proceed to organize the militia of the state.[26]

[26] The letters to Ramsey from Rice and Wilkinson are in the Ramsey Papers. In the *State Atlas* of January 16, 1861, there is a bitter denunciation of Rice by William S. King, a Republican opponent. See the *Congressional Globe*, 36 Congress, 2 session, 401, for Rice's compromise resolution. At his request the resolution was ordered to be printed and to lie on the table pending the consideration of the Crittenden resolutions.

The situation as seen through the eyes of Representative William Windom will illustrate another phase of the public opinion of those dark hours. On the twenty-fifth of December, 1860, he wrote to Ramsey: "Nearly all the slave states will *vote* themselves out of the Union in less than ninety days. What is to follow? I confess I can see nothing but civil war. We are truly in a pitiable condition. Traitors in Congress in the Cabinet, and a traitor even in the Presidential chair. The Treasury empty, and the pockets of *public thieves* well filled. . . . However I say let us adhere to principal, & *fight* it out if need be." Another letter, dated January 18, 1861, contains his more deliberate judgment: "I see no prospect whatever of a reconciliation. . . . The sword will have to decide. . . . I think a conciliatory course here on the part of Republicans, is the best, for the reason that it will be most likely to produce unity of feeling at the North. When we commence the fight in good earnest we will want the co-operation of the Democracy."[27]

Senator Wilkinson did not share the fears of his colleague in the Senate for the safety of the Capitol or his belief that the people of Minnesota and the Northwest would not consent to a war to preserve the Union. On February 12, 1861, he presented to the Senate the joint resolution of the Minnesota legislature, adopted on January 22, declaring that secession implied revolution and civil war and pledging to the government aid in men and money, to the extent of the state's ability, for checking the work of rebellion and treason. It declared that under no circumstances would the obstruction of the free navigation of the Mississippi River by any power hostile to the federal government be consented to. Two days later Senator Wilkinson presented a memorial addressed to Congress by several citizens of Minnesota, including the Republican members of the legislature. These petitioners, after reciting the seizure of forts and arsenals, the confiscation of arms and other public property to the

[27] Ramsey Papers.

value of several millions of dollars, the maltreatment of loyal citizens, and the defiance of the national government, prayed Congress to furnish the president with all means necessary to enforce the laws of the United States, to recover forts and munitions of war, to bring traitors to trial and punishment, and generally to see to it that the republic take no harm. Upon the reading of this memorial Senator Rice remarked that it was long on language but short on names and presented a counter memorial, to which were affixed a large number of respectable names, deprecating a fanatical policy and recommending that Congress adopt the Crittenden compromise resolutions or the one submitted by Rice himself, a modification of either, or some combination of the two. Rice stated that within a few days evidences would come from his state that a large majority of the people were for the Union and for peace.[28] It may be reasonably conjectured that he spoke in expectation of a peace demonstration to be made at his home in St. Paul. On the evening of February 27 a public meeting was held in St. Paul at which vigorous protest was made against the coercion of rebelling states. The *Pioneer and Democrat* declared that the memorial of certain citizens — that presented to the Senate by Wilkinson — was "untrue, exceedingly ill-timed," and "uncompromising and fanatical" in spirit.

Firm in the conviction that his constituents were so much devoted to peace that they would consent to secession rather than go to war, Senator Rice on two notable occasions solemnly expressed his intention to represent what he believed to be their wish and sentiment. On March 2, in the course of a debate on the Crittenden compromise resolutions, he said: "We will do all that we honorably can do to keep the southern States with us; but if they are determined to leave us, they must go in peace. . . . I do not believe either one of them [*four northwestern states*] will vote a dollar or a man for coercion. . . . We are a family of brothers; and if

[28] *Congressional Globe*, 36 Congress, 2 session, 862, 897.

we cannot live together in peace, in the name of God, let us agree as brothers to separate in peace." On the twenty-seventh of the same month Rice, speaking upon Breckinridge's resolution that the Senate advise the removal of United States troops from the Confederate states, was even more ardent in his advocacy of peace. "I am," said he, "in favor of peace. If the seceded States are determined to remain out, I am in favor of their going in peace. I would go further than this: I would give them the forts and arsenals within their limits. If they ask more, I would divide the Navy with them. If they wanted more than that, I would release them from the public debt. I would even give them more than that — anything for peace."[29] Upon this ground, which was held also by distinguished persons in Republican ranks, Senator Rice stood firmly and consistently until persuaded that he was not, as he had believed, supported by his constituency. Doubtless his faith must have been shaken when his state was the first to offer to the president a full regiment of her sons to revenge the insolent rebel capture, by an act of war, of a national fortification. It was not until after the decimation of that regiment at Bull Run that he voiced his persuasion that Minnesota was willing to go to war for the preservation of the Union.

On July 24, 1861, the Senate had under consideration a bill to promote the efficiency of volunteer troops. Senator Rice closed the debate with a brief impassioned address, part of which ought in justice to be quoted.

Mr. President, it is well known to the Senate that so far as my humble efforts were used heretofore, they were used for the preservation of peace: that I did all in my power to prevent war. . . . War, however, has been brought on us. . . . It is not for us here now, when the enemy are within a few hours' march of the capital, to look back. . . . They [*our constituents*] expect us to act. They have decided upon a war policy, and it is for us to say whether the war shall be properly prosecuted. . . . The President, his Cabinet, and the high officers of the Army. . . . have perfected the details; and if we approve of the general policy, it is for us

[29] *Pioneer and Democrat*, February 28, 1861; *Congressional Globe*, 36 Congress, 2 session, 1373, 1513.

to give them power to carry out the details. . . . I, Democrat as I am, will give my vote and my support to the Administration . . . so far as the necessary war measures are concerned.

In pursuing this course, I am properly representing the spirit of the State in whose name I speak. Minnesota . . . with impulsive loyalty . . . was among the foremost to tender her gallant sons for the service of the country, and gallantly they acquitted themselves on the field of battle. In the expressive language of an emphatic Senator, who witnessed the dreadful carnage, they "fought like devils." Their heroism is the theme of every tongue; and individual cases . . . are described that have no parallel in Greek or Roman story. My course, then, is no equivocal one. I give the aid of whatever support I can command to the Administration, and to the General-in-Chief. . . . In him and in the Administration I am disposed to yield a becoming confidence. . . . This is no time for us to be fiddling; it is no time for us to be swapping jack-knives when the ship is sinking.[30]

From the course thus laid Senator Rice never for a moment wavered, but stood by his state with full devotion. It is noteworthy that this ardent lover of peace should have been able to render exceptionally valuable service in war. In an address before the Minnesota Historical Society, General John B. Sanborn said: "I heard Senator Wilson, of Massachusetts, chairman of the committee of military affairs, say to Mr. Rice, long years after the war, 'I don't know how we could ever have mobilized our armies, if you had not been on the military committee of the United States Senate;' and he went on to state that they got more information and knowledge from Mr. Rice, as to what was required to move a regiment or any organized force of the army, than from all other sources combined."[31] It is an agreeable duty to introduce here a letter written on January 6, 1863, by Senator Wade of Ohio to Henry A. Swift, at that time a member of the state Senate, which bears testimony to the excellent service rendered by Rice to the nation after he resolved to align himself as a war Democrat.

I have just received a line from our mutual friend R. F. Paine, of Cleveland, who states that he has been writing in favor of the re-election

---

[30] *Congressional Globe*, 37 Congress, 1 session, 242.

[31] John B. Sanborn, "Minnesota in the National Congress during These Fifty Years," in *Minnesota Historical Collections*, 9: 625.

of Senator Rice and wished me to state my views of the matter to you,
which I would cheerfully do, could I do it without seeming to be imperti-
nently interfering with that which concerns your noble State alone.    I
will however say this in behalf of Mr. Rice, that I have served in the
Senate with him now nearly six years, that I know of no Senator who has
been more laboriously and energetically alive to the interests of his own
State and people than he has.   Nor do I believe any Senator *understands*
the interests of his own State and people better than Senator Rice.   In the
fore part of his term he was violently proslavery and acted on all occasions
with the worst of the proslavery Democracy.   This however, as they were
in a very large majority gave him power to do more for his own State than
he otherwise could have done, but since the attack upon Fort Sumter,
he has been thoroughly interested in the War, I believe always acting
cordially with the Republican Party, he is one of my best friends and
avows that he shall act and vote with me on all political questions and I
have no doubt of his sincerity, or his loyalty.   The above I have stated
to you in confidence, with no desire to obtrude my opinions upon you,
but I am sure I have done no more than justice to Senator Rice.[32]

During the winter of 1861 the slaveholders' rebellion was
rapidly maturing; a confederacy of eight states was organized
and its agents proceeded to confiscate arsenals, fortifications,
vessels, and other public property of the United States.
They received the surrender of Union troops and seized
large sums of public moneys.   Still the people of the North
looked upon these proceedings as mere demonstrations
intended to extort compliance with further demands of the
South regarding slave property and interests.   From this
dream they were rudely awakened by the cannonade opened
by express order of the Confederate war department on Fort
Sumter in Charleston Harbor, occupied by a small garrison
of United States Infantry, on the early morning of April 12,
1861.[33]   Governor Ramsey was in Washington on Sunday
morning, April 14, when the news of the occupation of
Sumter on the previous afternoon by a Confederate force
spread through the city.   At once he hastened to the office

[32] Swift Papers.
[33] Rhodes, *United States*, 3: chs. 13, 14, 15; Captain J. G. Foster's engineer journal, in
*The War of the Rebellion: A Compilation of the Official Records of the Union and Confederate
Armies,* series 1, vol. 1, pp. 16-21.   This set of 130 serial volumes of text and 3 atlas volumes
was published by the war department between 1880 and 1902.   It will be cited hereafter as
*Official Records.*

ALEXANDER RAMSEY
*Governor of Minnesota, 1859–63*

HENRY M. RICE
*United States Senator, 1858–63*

of the secretary of war — Simon Cameron, his old Pennsylvania colleague — and tendered a thousand men for national defense. This offer he put in writing at the request of the secretary, who was on the point of going to the president. Without doubt Minnesota has the credit of making the first tender of Union troops for the great contest thus suddenly precipitated.[34]

On April 15 the president called forth the militia of the states to the number of seventy-five thousand and the secretary of war notified Governor Ramsey that Minnesota's quota would be one regiment of infantry to serve for three months. On the same day, Governor Ramsey telegraphed to the adjutant general of Minnesota to issue a proclamation in his, Ramsey's, name calling for one regiment of infantry. The proclamation, however, which appeared on the following day in proper form and duly attested by the secretary of state, was signed "Ignatius Donnelly, *Governor ad interim.*" It gave notice that volunteers would be received at St. Paul for the term of three months and that the adjutant general would issue the necessary orders.[35] On the same

[34] Message of Governor Ramsey, January 9, 1862, in Minnesota, *Executive Documents,* 1861, p. 26; William Lochren, "Narrative of the First Regiment," in *Minnesota in the Civil and Indian Wars, 1861–1865,* 1: 2. The first volume of the latter work was published by the state in 1890 and the second, in 1893. A second edition, printed from the same plates but with numerous corrections and additions, was brought out in 1891 and 1899. Volume 1 contains narratives of the various military organizations of the state and their rosters. Volume 2 includes the official reports and correspondence relating to the organization and services of the Minnesota troops. Citations are from the second edition. See also the same work, 2: 1.

[35] James D. Richardson, *A Compilation of the Messages and Papers of the Presidents, 1789–1897,* 6: 13 (53 Congress, 2 session, *House Miscellaneous Documents,* no. 210 — serial 3265); *Minnesota in the Civil and Indian Wars,* 2: 2, 3. Article 5, section 6, of the Minnesota constitution provides that "in case a vacancy should occur, from any cause whatever, in the office of Governor, he [*the lieutenant governor*] shall be Governor during such vacancy." Whether Governor Ramsey's brief absence from the state on state business constituted a vacancy is a question for lawyers, and some have expressed the opinion that it did not. That Donnelly presumed that such an absence did create a vacancy is obvious from the following extract from a letter in the Donnelly Papers which he wrote to his wife on April 17, 1861: "The President made a requisition upon the Gov' of the State for 1 Regiment of 780 men. It was my duty to issue a Proclamation calling for volunteers. Gov. Ramsey then in Washington, totally ignored my existence here, sent two telegraphic despatches, the first to Jennison his secretary, and the last to Adj. Gen¹ Acker instructing him to issue a Proclamation *in his, Ramsey's, name.* I informed M' Jennison that I held my office by as good a title as Gov. Ramsey — that I was acting Governor, and that if M' Ramsey thought he could ignore my existence and ride over me rough-shod he had mistaken his man. . . . Ramsey

date was issued from the adjutant general's office General
Orders no. 1, "in pursuance of the Proclamation of the
Commander-in-Chief of the Militia of the State," offering
to receive the first ten companies ready for service, but giving
a preference for a period of ten days to existing companies
of volunteer militia upon their compliance with the requirements. Three only of those commands were able to avail
themselves of the preference, but there was no lack of new
organizations more than willing to fill the quota. Within
ten days fourteen companies reported themselves as organized and ready for duty. On the twenty-seventh the
adjutant general announced in General Orders no. 3 the
acceptance of the ten companies first organized under his
previous order. They represented nine different militia
regiments. On the same day the adjutant general ordered a
rendezvous at Fort Snelling, having secured from the pro-

may explain his conduct, but to me it looks very much like a hoggish dread that I might gain
a little bit of credit. Gen¹ Acker very promptly said that it was all wrong in R. and that he
would not act under the despatch. I should not wonder if Jennison was at the bottom of it."
The ruffled plumage was apparently soon smoothed down. Donnelly wrote a number of
executive letters, most of which he signed simply "Ignatius Donnelly." In some cases he
signed as "*Governor ad interim,*" in others as "*Acting Governor.*" Governor Ramsey wrote
him instructions as if he were a subordinate. See *Minnesota in the Civil and Indian Wars,*
2: 6-12, 17-19, 46-48, 66. Donnelly later signed executive proclamations as acting governor.
See especially the *Saint Paul Daily Press* of July 11, 1862.
    There was precedent for the assumption of the governorship *ad interim* by Donnelly.
During an absence of Governor Sibley from the state in the summer of 1858 while the legislature was in session, Lieutenant Governor Holcombe approved nineteen acts as "Governor
*ad interim.*" See *General Laws,* 1858, pp. 62, 63, 136, 297; *Special Laws,* pp. 209, 214, 280,
291, 295, 360, 403, 411, 425, 442, 446, 454, 471, 482, 512. In the case of State *ex rel.* Marr v.
Stearns, 72 *Minnesota,* 209-214, it was held that during a temporary "vacancy from whatever cause" the lieutenant governor becomes governor. The question as to whether the
absence of the governor from the state on state business creates a vacancy was not touched.
So far as is known no "temporary vacancy" in the office of governor of Minnesota has occurred since Governor Ramsey's term. Governor Ramsey appears to have thought that
his absence from the state created a vacancy to be supplied by the lieutenant governor.
On April 24, 1860, he wrote Donnelly that "business of public interest" was calling him to
Washington and that he would be much obliged if Lieutenant Governor Donnelly would
come to St. Paul and see to those public affairs that would be devolved upon him. See also
two other letters from Ramsey to Donnelly written on June 16 and September 24, 1861.
Archibald M. Hayes, writing to Donnelly on May 3, 1860, said that Governor Ramsey
had told him that "he had written you [*Donnelly*] to go to St. P. to go up & 'run
the machine'!" See also Jennison to Donnelly, April 8, May 6, 1861, and Leonard to Donnelly, April 19, 1861. Robert M. Fisk, private secretary to Governor Ramsey, writing to
Donnelly on March 16, 1863, mentions the absence of the governor and adds that he is "running the Executive office" himself, since Lieutenant Governor Swift declined to act. All
these letters are in the Donnelly Papers.

prietor, Franklin Steele, without cost to the state, the use of the old post buildings, vacated three years before. On the twenty-ninth and thirtieth the officers and men to the number of 950 were mustered into the service of the United States. On the former date ex-Governor Willis A. Gorman was commissioned colonel of the regiment and at once took command. His first official act was to inform Governor Ramsey that the First Minnesota Infantry was "ready for duty." The governor, less experienced in military affairs, wrote at once to the secretary of war that one regiment of nine hundred men had been detached from the militia of Minnesota and was "ready for active service."[36]

Here were nearly a thousand young men, as fit for peace or war as any who ever stood in shoe leather, men who had been mustered into the volunteer army without a shilling of bounty money, content, even zealous, to leave their work and their homes for the unknown fortunes of war. Colonel Gorman was certainly discreet in reporting his regiment on April 30 as merely "ready for duty." There were arms enough of various patterns in possession of the militia companies or in the state arsenal to supply the command, but there was little or no ammunition. On May 3 Gorman notified "His Excellency, Alexander Ramsey, Governor and Commander-in-Chief," that immediate provision should be made for uniforms. He asked also for camp and garrison equipage, for knapsacks, canteens, cooking utensils, axes, picks, and spades. Neither the state nor the general government was prepared to furnish clothing for the infant

[36] Report of the adjutant general, in *Executive Documents*, 1861, pp. 82, 231, 232, 233; Lochren, in *Minnesota in the Civil and Indian Wars*, 1: 3; 2: 4. Governor Ramsey sent also a telegram to the secretary of war, in which he merely announced that 950 men were organized and mustered into service, and awaited orders. Lochren gives a sketch of General Gorman in *Minnesota in the Civil and Indian Wars*, 1: 27. In a letter to Donnelly, December 27, 1861, in the Donnelly Papers, Ramsey voices his estimate of Gorman's character. For the aspirations of Lieutenant Governor Donnelly to be colonel of the First, see a letter to his wife, dated April 24, 1861, in the Donnelly Papers. The proclamation and correspondence relating to the organization of the First Minnesota may be found copied in the Governor's Archives, Records, A: 324, 329, 331. For interesting details of the recruiting, see John D. Hicks, "The Organization of the Volunteer Army in 1861, with Special Reference to Minnesota," in *Minnesota History Bulletin*, 2: 331-334, 344, 355-363 (February, 1918).

regiment. An amendment to the militia laws in the previous
winter authorized the colonels of militia regiments to prescribe the uniforms of their respective commands.[37] An
enterprising firm of contractors was found which was willing
to furnish the clothing and look to the United States for
payment. Before many days had elapsed the men were
arrayed in red flannel shirts, black trousers, and slouch hats.
This picturesque attire they wore at the battle of Bull Run,
where they felt that it made them too fair a mark for rebel
rifles.[38]

The selection of ex-Governor Gorman as colonel of the
First Regiment was a happy one. He had been major general
of the state militia for two years[39] and his service in the
Mexican War had qualified him for command in the field.
That he had been a Democratic party leader was at that hour
no disqualification. He began on the instant the work of
making a regiment of soldiers out of untrained civilians.
Squad and company drills, schools for officers, guard duty,
and parades and reviews in hourly succession soon convinced
the volunteers that soldiering was no holiday pastime.
The colonel began at once to enforce discipline by military
sanctions in marked contrast with those of civil justice.
It was not many days before this efficient officer was
cordially hated all along the line, but within a few months

[37] Report of the adjutant general, in *Executive Documents*, 1861, p. 235; *Minnesota in the
Civil and Indian Wars*, 2: 5, 7; *General Laws*, 1860, p. 142.
[38] Report of the adjutant general, in *Executive Documents*, 1861, pp. 83, 197. The bill
for clothing was as follows:

*Culver & Farrington — for 1st Regiment Minn. Vol.*

| | | |
|---|---|---|
| June, 1861. | 868 blankets for men, at $3 | $ 2,604 00 |
| " | 13 blankets for hospital, at $3 | 39 00 |
| " | 800 flannel shirts, at $1.50 | 1,200 00 |
| " | 975 pairs wool socks, at 25c | 243 75 |
| " | 868 hats, at $2.25 | 1,953 00 |
| " | 868 pairs pants, at $4.50 | 3,906 00 |
| " | 868 pairs drawers, at 62½c | 542 00 |

Total amount .......$10,488 25

For correspondence regarding the clothing for the First, see *Minnesota in the Civil and
Indian Wars*, 2:31-38. See also Lochren, in the same work, 1: 3, 13. In Fish, *Donnelliana*,
37, there is an amusing discussion of an alleged "'shoddy' contract."
[39] Report of the adjutant general, in *Executive Documents*, 1860, no. 11, p. 14.

his men learned that he had been doing for them the service of a friend.[40]

The camp routine had been running but a few days when an order came from Washington for a detail of three detachments of two companies each to proceed to Forts Ridgely, Ripley, and Abercrombie to relieve garrisons of regular troops therein stationed. The volunteers were by no means pleased with service of that kind. They had not enlisted as home guards to keep whisky-sellers off Indian reservations. Colonel Gorman was so much disappointed that on Sunday morning, May 5, he called a meeting of all his commissioned officers and took the chair himself. A set of resolutions was passed remonstrating against the obnoxious order and naming Governor Ramsey as agent or attorney to procure its reversal. The *Pioneer and Democrat* declared the proceeding to be "a gross military impropriety" and hoped "in God's name, that our Regiment, and with it our State, is not to be disgraced by the impertinent vanity of its commanding officer." Gorman and his officers, after a night's sleep, appreciated the military impropriety of their action. An explanatory statement, signed by eleven commissioned officers, appeared in the *Pioneer and Democrat,* and the colonel commanding requested the *Saint Paul Press* in writing to make no further mention of the event. The *Pioneer and Democrat,* however, returned to the charge with reiterated accusations, apparently dictated by personal hostility. Governor Ramsey ventured no interference with the government's disposition of the regiment and Colonel Gorman lost no time in responding that detachments would be dispatched as soon as they could be equipped.[41]

[40] Judge William Lochren in repeated conversations with the author.

[41] *Minnesota in the Civil and Indian Wars,* 2: 5, 6; *Pioneer and Democrat,* May 7-9, 1861; *Saint Paul Press,* May 8, 9, 1861. In their explanatory statement the officers denied that Gorman called the meeting. They said that all the officers asked was that Ramsey would offer six new companies to relieve the regular soldiers at the forts. The resolutions were addressed not to the general in chief, but to Ramsey. On April 13, 1861, Lieutenant Governor Donnelly, at the time "governor *ad interim,*" wrote to Governor Ramsey in Washington suggesting that it was important that garrisons be put into the forts and that the state troops should be paid by the United States. A copy of this letter is in the Donnelly Papers.

While the whole regiment was still together at Fort Snelling a request came from the war department that the officers and men who had enlisted for three months consent to be mustered in for three years. The commissioned officers without exception at once consented. The willingness of the enlisted men was far from unanimous. Many who had been willing to leave home and business for ninety days were not prepared for a possible absence of years. In spite of fervid appeals in the newspapers to their patriotism and pride in the regiment, 350 of them declined to be mustered for the extended period. There was no lack of young men ready to take their places. Recruiting officers were sent to the towns which had furnished companies and on June 21 Colonel Gorman was able to report that there were 1,023 officers and men in his regiment.[42]

The camp at Fort Snelling was of great interest to the neighboring cities and lines of coaches were established to carry visitors back and forth. On one day some gallants were made glad by the arrival of six stage loads of young ladies from St. Anthony. There were horse, sword, and flag presentations galore. The women of Winona gave the regiment a splendid national banner, which Colonel Gorman sent home after it had been riddled with bullets at Bull Run and which may now be seen in the Capitol. The command

[42] *Minnesota in the Civil and Indian Wars*, 2: 2-6, 18; Lochren, in the same work, 1: 4; *Saint Paul Press*, May 11, 12, 1861; report of the adjutant general, in *Executive Documents*, 1861, p. 83; Gorman to Donnelly, June 21, 1861, Donnelly Papers. In a letter to Donnelly, dated May 17, 1861, in the Donnelly Papers, W. W. McDougall alleges that the officers tendered the regiment for three years without consulting the enlisted men, that beer was liberally dispensed by Colonel Gorman, and that those who would not reënlist were threatened with disgraceful dismissal or with being kept in the service and sent to the Indian forts. Soon after the return of the regiment from Bull Run to Washington, disaffected soldiers raised the question whether the muster-in for three years without previous muster-out of the three months' service was binding. A case was made up and taken before the United States Supreme Court, which, after hearing, ruled that the second muster-in was legal. See *In re* Edward A. Stevens, 24 *Law Reporter*, 205; letters by "Raisins" (Stevens) in the *Stillwater Messenger*, July 6, 8, 16, 23, August 6, 13, 27, September 3, 10, 24, October 22, 29, 1861, and the editorial in the issue of September 3; and letters to Ramsey from Gorman, August 24, 1861, and from Neill, August 29, 1861, in the Ramsey Papers. On May 16, 1861, Ramsey wrote to Donnelly: "What are you about? Is Gorman's Regt. mustered in for three years or not? Answer at once." Ramsey's letter is in the Governor's Archives, Records, A: 345, and Donnelly's reply follows. See also page 346.

was feasted in St. Paul and Minneapolis. Women made havelocks, scraped lint, and collected testaments for the boys of the regiment. Pandemonium reigned in camp on the night of June 14 when it was noised through the company streets that the regiment had been ordered to the East. The detachments sent to the frontier forts were called in and lost no time in returning.[43]

[43] *Minnesota in the Civil and Indian Wars*, 2: 15, 28; Lochren, in the same work, 1: 4, 5; *State Atlas*, May 8, 15, 22, June 5, 1861; *Pioneer and Democrat*, May 2–June 23, 1861; *Saint Paul Press*, May 1–5, 16, 23, 25, 26, 30, June 18, 22, 1861.

# IV. TWO YEARS OF THE CIVIL WAR

A T DAWN on June 22, 1861, the First Regiment of Minnesota Volunteers paraded at Fort Snelling and was addressed by the chaplain, the Reverend Edward Duffield Neill, already known to the reader as the pioneer historian of Minnesota. He said in part: "Your errand is not to overturn, but to uphold the most tolerant and forbearing government on earth. You go to war with misguided brethren, not with wrathful, but with mourning hearts. . . . To fight for a great principle is a noble work. We are all erring and fallible men; but the civilized world feel that you are engaged in a just cause, which God will defend." With outspread hands he solemnly pronounced the Hebrew benediction, "The Lord bless you and keep you . . ." This address concluded, the command immediately marched on board two waiting steamboats. Half an hour later the vessels rounded up at the upper levee of St. Paul. Here the regiment disembarked and marched through streets crowded with citizens to go on board the waiting transports at the lower landing. This march was repeated by later departing regiments but there was a dramatic interest and novelty in this occasion which could not be repeated.[1]

[1] Lochren, in *Minnesota in the Civil and Indian Wars*, 1: 6; *Pioneer and Democrat* (St. Paul), June 23, 1861; *Saint Paul Press*, June 23, 1861; Edward D. Neill, *History of Minnesota: From the Earliest French Explorations to the Present Time*, 650 (fourth edition, Minneapolis, 1882). The Right Reverend Henry Benjamin Whipple was first elected chaplain of the regiment. Bishop Whipple declined, and the Reverend Benjamin F. Crary, president of Hamline University, and the Reverend Edward Duffield Neill were then considered. An arrangement was made to give the chaplaincy to Neill and let Crary take the office of state superintendent of schools to be vacated by Neill. Crary became chaplain of the Third Regiment on May 4, 1862. Neill resigned his chaplaincy on July 13, 1862, and soon after became a secretary to President Lincoln. For a very interesting account of his experiences in that position see his "Reminiscences of the Last Year of President Lincoln's Life," in *Glimpses of the Nation's Struggle*, a series of papers read before the Minnesota Commandery of the Military Order of the Loyal Legion of the United States, first series, 29-53 (St. Paul and Minneapolis, 1887). In regard to the chaplaincies of the Minnesota regiments see also the *Pioneer and Democrat*, May 31, 1861; the rosters of the First and Third regiments, in *Minnesota in the Civil and Indian Wars*, 1: 49, 178; and the Reverend Cyrus Brooks to Governor Ramsey, June 24, 1861, in the Ramsey Papers.

The scope of this work does not permit us to follow in detail the marches and battles of this regiment or of those which later followed it. They may be studied in the two royal octavo volumes published by the state under the title *Minnesota in the Civil and Indian Wars*.[2] The stories of the separate commands, written by members of them, are in general so simply and temperately told as to inspire confidence in the reader. On July 21, less than a month from the day of its departure, the First had its baptism of blood and fire at Bull Run. Its position was on the extreme right of Heintzelman's turning column, which, moving from Centreville by way of Sudley Springs, at length encountered, not the exposed left flank of the enemy, but the left wing of Beauregard's army, which by a change of front to rear, admirably conceived and executed, was ranged nearly parallel with the Warrenton pike. The first onset, which drove the Confederate line across the pike, seemed like a victory to those amateur soldiers; but the retirement was only to the stronger position about the Henry and Robinson houses, where Johnston's reënforcements were arriving and where Jackson's brigade was "standing like a stone wall." The First Minnesota was one of the last regiments to be led forward to sacrifice. In thirty-two minutes forty-two officers and men were killed and one hundred and eight were wounded. Vain was the desultory effort. The regiment held its ground until it was ordered to the rear, and the two wings, though separated, moved off the field in order. In the evening a halt was made at Centreville for food and rest, after which by McDowell's express order the march to the defenses of Washington was taken up. In the course of this march there was some unavoidable disorganization and separation of the companies, but Minnesota had no cause to be ashamed of her maiden regiment.[3]

[2] Concerning this work, see *ante*, p. 77, n. 34.

[3] *Minnesota in the Civil and Indian Wars*, 1: 1-48, gives Judge William Lochren's "Narrative of the First Regiment." For the battle of Bull Run in particular see the quoted account by Captain William Colvill, of Company F, on pages 9-11. The report of the adjutant

The First Minnesota was engaged in the unfortunate affair at Ball's Bluff; it made the whole Peninsular campaign; it shared in the rescue of Pope from his wretched fiasco in Virginia; at Antietam, posted on the extreme right of the Union lines, it was literally decimated; and at Fredericksburg it underwent an ordeal which only troops equal to veterans could have endured. The Second Company of Minnesota Sharpshooters, recruited after November 23, 1861, and mustered on March 20, 1862, was attached to the First Minnesota Infantry at and after the battle of Fair Oaks and for a year and a half shared its fortunes. At Antietam twenty out of the forty-two of its men present for duty were wounded.[4]

general, in *Executive Documents*, 1861, pp. 254-261, is accompanied by the reports of Colonel Gorman and of Colonel Franklin. These reports occur also in *Minnesota in the Civil and Indian Wars*, 2: 21-26. Colonel Heintzelman's report and that of Franklin may be found in *Official Records*, series 1, vol. 2, pp. 402-407. See also Neill, *Minnesota*, 672-681, particularly the extracts from letters from Javan B. Irvine to his wife on pages 672-675 and the extracts from Chaplain Neill's diary on pages 675-681; J. N. Searles, "The First Minnesota Volunteer Infantry," in *Glimpses of the Nation's Struggle*, second series, 84-87; Josias R. King, "The Battle of Bull Run," in *Glimpses of the Nation's Struggle*, sixth series, 497-510; and Return I. Holcombe, *History of the First Regiment Minnesota Volunteer Infantry, 1861-1864*, ch. 5 (Stillwater, 1916). The last work as originally written was much bulkier but it was reduced by the omission of portions thought by the publication committee not to be germane. Although not supported by cited authorities, the statements generally may be accepted. The author was certainly a conscientious seeker for the truth. In regard to casualties see page 55. A letter from Colonel Gorman to Governor Ramsey, dated August 21, 1861, in the Ramsey Papers, is very graphic. For interesting gossip regarding the early career of the First Regiment, see the letters of Private Henry W. Lindergreen to Donnelly, August 13, September 15, November 12, December 20, 1861, January 18, 30, February 13, March 1, April 26, May 20, June 7, July 7, September 6, 1862, in the Donnelly Papers. The series seems to have been written to keep Donnelly minutely informed as to the movements and gossip of the regiment. Other interesting letters were written to Donnelly by Private Julian I. Kendall, August 3, October 17, 1861, February 1, 1862. The daily newspapers of St. Paul and the weeklies of Minneapolis, St. Anthony, Red Wing, Faribault, Hastings, Wabasha, and Winona from July 19 to September, 1862, abound in narratives and communications from members of the regiment. There is much interesting gossip about the First in the letters of "Raisins," in the *Stillwater Messenger*, May 7, 1861-January 13, 1862. For the experiences of a *New York Tribune* correspondent on the battle field and in the retreat, see William A. Croffut to the author, July 31, 1915, in the Folwell Papers.

[4] Lochren, in *Minnesota in the Civil and Indian Wars*, 1: 15-31; Holcombe, *First Regiment*, 74-79. James A. Wright, in his "Story of Company F., First Regiment," 49-72, gives a very graphic account of the march from Alexandria, the battle, the repulse, and the return march to Washington. Wright was one of the orderly sergeants of the regiment. His story, unpublished unless in fragments and covering 875 typewritten pages without paragraphs or chapter divisions, came into the possession of the Minnesota Historical Society in 1921. The style is that of a practiced journalist. The portions relating to personal experiences and observations derived from the author's diary are often very interesting and valuable. The mass of his work, drawn from well-known sources extending

The First Minnesota had not only an extra company but
also an artillery attachment.  In a letter dated February 22,
1862, the Honorable Henry S. Sanford, United States
minister to Belgium, presented to the state of Minnesota a
small battery of three steel rifled cannons of six-pound
caliber, to be intrusted to the First Minnesota in testimony
of his pride in its conspicuous valor at Bull Run and Ball's
Bluff.  Governor Ramsey on April 28 made an eloquent
acknowledgment of the gift and on the same day he notified
the colonel of the First Minnesota and asked him to have
Sanford's letter and his, Ramsey's, reply read at the head of
the regiment.  At the request of Governor Ramsey the secretary of war directed that the guns be stored in the Washington arsenal.  Whether there had been a previous understanding or whether Governor Ramsey acted spontaneously
out of gratitude for so signal a compliment to his premier
regiment and the state remains a matter of conjecture,
but Sanford was appointed a major general in the Minnesota militia.  An extant letter dated Brussels, March 11,
1862, acknowledges the receipt of the commission.[5]  It is
said that Sanford wore his major general's uniform at court
functions in Brussels.

beyond the entitled subject, is good reading but adds little to existing knowledge.  For the
part taken by the regiment in the unfortunate affair at Ball's Bluff, see the statements
of Colonel Dana and of Brigadier General Gorman, in the report of the adjutant general, in
*Executive Documents*, 1861, pp. 261-267.  Neither of these reports has been found in the
*Official Records*; both, together with the report of Brigadier General Charles P. Stone,
are given in *Minnesota in the Civil and Indian Wars*, 2: 48-58.  See also Josiah B. Chaney,
"Narrative of the Second Company of Sharpshooters," in *Minnesota in the Civil and Indian
Wars*, 1: 513-516.

  [5] *Minnesota in the Civil and Indian Wars*, 2: 62-65.  A twelve-page pamphlet in the
library of the Minnesota Historical Society contains the *Correspondence on the Occasion of the
Presentation by Major-General Sanford, United States Minister Resident at the Court of
Brussels, of a Battery of Steel Cannon, to the State of Minnesota, for the Use of the First Minnesota Regiment of Volunteers* (St. Paul, 1862).  The original Sanford letter of February 22,
1862, and a letter from Governor Ramsey dated March 15, 1864, the latter relating to a proposed shipment of the guns to Minnesota, are in the Governor's Archives, files 184, 185.
These files are now in the custody of the Minnesota State Archives.  Sanford's letter
of March 11, 1862, is in the Ramsey Papers.  Soon after the Indian war of 1862 broke out,
Governor Ramsey asked the president to have the battery sent to the state.  See *Minnesota
in the Civil and Indian Wars*, 2:224.  Following an act of the legislature approved on
March 4, 1864, the Sanford battery was brought from New York and deposited in the state
arsenal.  Two hundred and fifty dollars were appropriated for the transportation of the guns.
They disfigured the State Capitol grounds, old and new, until the 1930's.  Report of
the adjutant general, in *Executive Documents*, 1864, p. 261; *General Laws*, 1864, p. 44.

As already related, four companies offered for the First Regiment had to be rejected. Other companies were being organized in many villages. There was an abundance of patriotism and martial zeal. On May 3, 1861, Governor Ramsey tendered another regiment to the president. Daniel A. Robertson of St. Paul, already known to the reader, had been for three years colonel of the Twenty-third Regiment of Minnesota Militia, which the previous year had reported on its roster a total strength of forty officers and enlisted men. Colonel Robertson, an ardent Democrat who had espoused the Union cause, at once offered his services. On the fourth of May he opened a recruiting office in St. Paul to fill his regiment. He did not confine his efforts to Ramsey County, which was his regimental district, but invited companies and individuals from all quarters. Such progress was made that on the thirteenth the adjutant general was able to telegraph Governor Ramsey, then in Washington, that Colonel Robertson's Twenty-third Regiment was full. On the next day the governor replied that he had made application to the war department for its acceptance. On the same day, May 14, the secretary of war acknowledged the tender of Colonel Robertson's regiment and informed the governor that the make-up of the quota of troops from Minnesota would be left to his discretion. The newspapers continued to announce the readiness of Colonel Robertson's regiment.[6]

A month now elapsed during which six companies of the First Regiment were dispatched to the Minnesota frontier forts, leaving at Fort Snelling but four companies, not yet filled up. The First Regiment seemed doomed to inglorious service on the far borders of civilization. Existing records

    [6] *Minnesota in the Civil and Indian Wars*, 2: 4, 9-11; Richardson, *Messages and Papers*, 6: 15; report of the adjutant general, in *Executive Documents*, 1860, no. 11, p. 42; *Pioneer and Democrat*, May 7, 14, 18, 1861; *Saint Paul Press*, May 18, 24, 1861; Ramsey to Donnelly, Washington, May 19, 1861, Donnelly Papers. Ramsey's offer of another regiment was doubtless in response to the president's call for 42,034 volunteers. He apparently took the offer of Colonel Robertson's regiment quite seriously at first. See the telegram from Donnelly to Ramsey, May 16, 1861, in Governor's Archives, Records, A: 345, and Ramsey to Donnelly, May 17, 1861, in the Ramsey Papers.

show that Senator Rice now became interested in the Robertson regiment and exerted himself to have it called for, accepted, and ordered to the front. On June 10 he telegraphed from Washington to Governor Ramsey that the secretary of war would accept a second regiment if it could be ready in ten days. On the next day Governor Ramsey replied to him that the First Regiment was ready for marching orders and that its place could be filled in ten days by a new regiment. On the twelfth Senator Rice again telegraphed that the secretary of war would not order Colonel Gorman's regiment. "Get the new regiment ready as soon as possible and telegraph me," he said. On the same day Colonel Robertson announced, through a card in the newspapers, the names of his companies and directed them to hold themselves in readiness for rendezvous. Still on that same day Governor Ramsey in his characteristic style telegraphed Cameron: "Do you want Minnesota regiment? If so, Colonel Gorman's . . . can be in Washington in ten days." It is probable that a letter explaining the situation went forward. Two days later, June 14, the secretary telegraphed an order to the Minnesota governor to send the First Regiment east. The assemblage of the companies and the departure of the command on June 22 have already been related. Governor Ramsey, after all his pains and activities in raising the First, escaped the humiliation of having a Minnesota regiment arrive in Washington under the auspices of Senator Rice.

The order of the war department of June 14 sending the First Minnesota Regiment to the front was accompanied by a requisition for a second regiment. On that date the adjutant general of the state published his General Orders no. 8 calling for volunteers. Companies willing to enlist were directed to report themselves to his office. Colonel Robertson's regiment, which had been announced as full a month before, was ignored. Seven of the companies which he had considered as belonging to his regiment offered their services direct to the adjutant general. On the twenty-sixth of June the adjutant general conveyed the thanks of the commander in chief to the ten companies by that time tendered and ordered those selected to assemble, five companies at Fort Snelling and two at Fort Ridgely.[7]

In the *Pioneer and Democrat* of the eighteenth there appeared a card from Colonel Robertson in which he expressed bitter resentment of his treatment. He had filled up his regiment with the knowledge and approval of Governor Ramsey and Adjutant General Sanborn. He had begun and had continued the organization of the regiment with their approval and had anticipated no hostility from them until the previous Saturday, June 15, when the governor had refused a renewed tender of the regiment and a request for an allowance of five days to fill all the companies to maximum. Governor Ramsey knew that Robertson had authority from the secretary of war "through a reliable and high official source" to fill the regiment and get it ready for orders, and that he had accordingly notified his companies to hold themselves in readiness for summons. Robertson's influential friends in Washington had induced the president to make a direct request of the secretary of war with a view to the acceptance of the regiment. It may be surmised that it was the knowledge of this which caused Governor Ramsey to forget about Colonel Robertson's Twenty-third Regiment of Minnesota Militia and to adopt a plan for diverting the companies which had been in some manner promised to its patriotic commander. It is altogether probable that Governor Ramsey, though never vindictive, had not forgotten certain activities of Robertson in connection with the Sioux treaties. It was quite unnecessary for Colonel Robertson to announce that he was not, under the circumstances, a candidate for the colonelcy of the Second Minnesota. The following hitherto unpublished telegram may suggest a con-

[7] *Minnesota in the Civil and Indian Wars*, 2: 14-16; *Pioneer and Democrat*, June 12, 1861; *Saint Paul Press*, June 12, 1861; report of the adjutant general, in *Executive Documents*, 1861, pp. 235-237. The companies selected are given on page 237.

sideration which led Governor Ramsey to reconsider his
offer of the Twenty-third Minnesota Militia to the secretary
of war: "Milwaukie May x111th [1861] Gov. Alex. Ramsay.
of Minn. Washn. Saturday telegram received. Regiment
full. Anxious about acceptance. Pray success. Your
friend[s] think Senator Rice the man for brigadier. If
consistent with your views and his official position. D. A.
Robertson."[8]

The command of the Second was given to Colonel Horatio
Phillips Van Cleve, a graduate of the United States Military
Academy who had served for some years with regular troops.
His field officers had been volunteer officers in the Mexican
War. Early in July six companies were sent to the three
forts on the Indian frontier, from which they were recalled
toward the end of September. On October 14 the Second
Regiment departed for Washington, but at Pittsburgh it was
diverted and sent down the Ohio to Louisville, Kentucky.
This regiment shared honorably in the victory of Mill
Springs, participated in Halleck's fruitless "siege" of
Corinth, joined in the repulse of Bragg at Perryville, won
imperishable laurels at Chickamauga and Missionary Ridge,
and participated in Sherman's march to the sea. Its discipline was such that rarely, if ever, was a man missing.
Those not in the ranks after battle were dead on the field
of honor or were on the hospital rolls.[9]

[8] *Pioneer and Democrat,* June 18, 1861. In a conversation with the author on July 22,
1905, Mrs. Daniel A. Robertson said that the effort to organize his regiment cost her husband
a thousand dollars and the failure to have it accepted broke his heart. She blamed Sanborn
more than Ramsey. The loyalty of Colonel Robertson was ardent and genuine. For
Robertson's connection with the Sioux treaties, see *ante,* 1: 465, 469, 469n. The telegram
was seen by the author in Governor's Archives, file 421, but it has since been lost.

[9] J. W. Bishop, "Narrative of the Second Regiment," in *Minnesota in the Civil and
Indian Wars,* 1: 79-122. The gallant behavior of the Second at Mill Springs is described
on pages 82-86. Van Cleve's appointment was dated July 22, 1861. On that date the adjutant general in General Orders no. 14 instructed the citizens of Minnesota to fill up the
Second Regiment immediately, since two more regiments might soon be demanded. See
his report, in *Executive Documents,* 1861, pp. 238, 239. In a letter to Donnelly dated July 17,
1861, Dr. Thomas Foster states that "the 2nd Regt. is getting along d——d slow."
Lieutenant Governor Donnelly was also an aspirant to the colonelcy of the Second Regiment. On June 26, 1861, he wrote to his wife: "I am afraid my Colonelship has gone up.
Ramsey told Blakely of Rochester . . . that he would not think of appointing any one but
a military man. The old 'cuss' fears that anyone might interfere with his plans for the

On September 18, almost a month before the Second Regiment departed southward, Governor Ramsey, in response to a call from the secretary of war, directed by general order the organization of two more regiments for three years or the war, to be designated respectively as the Third and Fourth regiments of Minnesota volunteers. The latter, it was announced, would be retained to guard the forts on the frontier. The recruiting of these regiments was not so rapid and tumultuous as had been that of the first two regiments, which at Bull Run and Mill Springs had learned that war was no holiday. The yellow hospital flag and the dead march had put another tone and color in. The Third Regiment, however, recruited from all parts of the state, was organized on November 15 with a strength of 901. Two days later it departed for Louisville, Kentucky, uniformed but not armed.[10]

The Third Regiment passed the winter guarding railroads in Kentucky and was ordered early in the spring of 1862 to Murfreesboro, Tennessee, to occupy and hold, along with some other troops, that minor, but still important, strategic point. Midsummer of 1862 found it, after certain excursions, still at that point. To delay Buell's expected movement on Chattanooga, Bragg detached Forrest with a cavalry force not exceeding fifteen hundred in number to make a raid into central Tennessee. A rapid march brought him to Murfreesboro unheralded at daybreak of July 13. Although the town was an important railroad station on the Nashville and Chattanooga Railroad as well as a considerable supply depot, no kind of defensive work had been dug or erected,

U. S. Senate in the future. If it turns out that he does not appoint me I will make him regret it." See also Archibald M. Hayes to Donnelly, June 22, 24, 1861. The writer, at one time a partner of Donnelly, reports a bargain between Donnelly and Governor Ramsey: "He is to appoint you Col. upon condition that you do not stand in his way for Gov!" He adds, "Now if you two Pa. [Pennsylvania] Dutchmen will take advantage of & adopt my Yankee suggestion all will be well." Donnelly Papers.

[10] Report of the adjutant general, in *Executive Documents*, 1861, pp. 240-242; Christopher C. Andrews, "Narrative of the Third Regiment," in *Minnesota in the Civil and Indian Wars*, 1: 147. The act of Congress of July 22, 1861, authorized the president to call for five hundred thousand volunteers for a period not to exceed three years; they were to be disbanded at the end of the war. *Statutes at Large*, 12: 268.

nor were the roads and railroads effectively picketed. The troops consisted of some one thousand fit for duty: six companies of a Michigan infantry regiment, two small troops of cavalry, a four-gun battery, and nine companies of the Third Minnesota. The colonel of the Third Regiment had been until the previous day the ranking officer in command. For reasons of questionable sufficiency he had divided his forces by moving his regimental camp and the camp of the artillery to a point on the Nashville pike about a mile and a half northwest of the town, leaving the Michigan regiment and the cavalry about three-fourths of a mile to the east of the place. At daybreak on July 13 an advance Confederate party captured the unready federal picket guard. Forrest in person led a detachment which took possession of the town and made a prisoner of a new brigadier general who had arrived and taken command the day before. An attack in force was then made upon the Michigan regiment of 250 men and upon the cavalry troops. They made a gallant defense until noon, when the commander, finding but 134 men able to fight, surrendered.

At the first sound of firing the Minnesota colonel moved his command half a mile eastward toward the town, where he took up a well-chosen position for defense. There he held his men throughout the forenoon, while a fight was in progress a mile away and the smoke of burning stores was rising from the town. A brief and feeble demonstration only was made upon the front of the Minnesota regiment; but Forrest in person with a considerable force made a detour and fell upon the camp, which was captured only after a third charge had been made upon the little band of about twenty teamsters, convalescents, and cooks commanded by Corporal Charles H. Green, who showed how the men of the Third would have fought if they had had a commander of his mettle. This brave man received a saber cut and two bullet wounds and died two hours later. Early in the afternoon a messenger came with a flag of truce from the Michigan colonel requesting the commander of the Third Minnesota to come into town for a conference. On his return from the conference the Minnesota colonel called his officers in council and asked their judgment on a question of surrender. The majority promptly voted to fight; but their commander reopened the matter after the departure of some of the officers and insisted on a vote by ballot. There were six votes for a surrender and but half that number for battle. One of the three was cast by Captain Christopher C. Andrews, who afterwards became a colonel and, later, a brigadier general. The shameful surrender was made.[11]

The enlisted men were not long after paroled, but the officers were held in southern prisons for some months. On December 1, 1862, the president dismissed dishonorably all the officers who voted for the surrender. The disgrace of that transaction must be laid mainly upon the shoulders of Colonel Henry C. Lester. Lester had been promoted from a captaincy in the First Minnesota, in which he had proved himself an efficient and capable officer and a brave and gallant leader in action. His fine military bearing, his diligence in instruction, and his constant care for the welfare of his command had obtained for him such a degree of regard and confidence that his officers trusted his judgment rather than their own. The failure to march his command of five hundred brave men to the relief of the Michigan command of half that number, which had been fighting all the forenoon,

[11] Andrews, in *Minnesota in the Civil and Indian Wars*, 1:149-157. The same account, with slight modifications and with Confederate accounts embodied, may be found in Andrews, "The Surrender of the Third Regiment," in *Glimpses of the Nation's Struggle*, first series, 347-359. In *Official Records*, series 1, vol. 16, part 1, pp. 792-811, note especially the reports of Brigadier General Thomas T. Crittenden, Colonel William W. Duffield, Lieutenant Colonel John G. Parkhurst, Colonel Henry C. Lester, and Brigadier General Nathan B. Forrest. See also John A. Wyeth, *Life of General Nathan Bedford Forrest*, 83-97 (New York, 1899); the *Saint Paul Press*, July 16, 19, 26, 27, August 1, 1862; extracts from a "valuable paper" giving particulars of the conference at which the surrender was made, in *Minnesota in the Civil and Indian Wars*, 1:177n.; the address of Colonel Chauncey W. Griggs at a reunion of the Third Minnesota at St. Paul in 1886, a typewritten copy of which is in the possession of the Minnesota Historical Society; and General Christopher C. Andrews to the author, December 31, 1906, in the Folwell Papers. Griggs severely arraigns Lester. Interviews with Major W. E. Hale and with General Andrews are recorded in the author's notebooks, 2:98; 8:14.

was hardly less disgraceful than was the surrender of his own regiment.[12]

The muster of the Fourth Minnesota began on October 2, 1861, and presently the first four companies, and later a fifth, were sent to the forts on the frontier. The five remaining companies were held at Fort Snelling and kept under instruction. In the following March the detached companies were called in and on April 20 the regiment departed by steamboat for St. Louis. The command was given to John B. Sanborn, who had served Governor Ramsey as his adjutant general. The regiment was ordered to join Halleck's army in northern Mississippi and it arrived in time to share in the water haul of that commander at Corinth. An epidemic of typhoid and other fevers soon afterwards sent one-third of the men to the hospitals.[13]

On December 5, before the close of the first year of the war, still another regiment was called for. Mustering began on December 19, but recruiting went on during the ensuing winter in nearly all the more populous counties. On March 20 the last company was mustered. To stimulate the

[12] Andrews, in *Minnesota in the Civil and Indian Wars*, 1:149, 157. See pages 178-197 for the roster of the Third Regiment. The list of the dismissed officers is given in the report of the adjutant general, in *Executive Documents*, 1863, p. 179. In the Ramsey Papers are letters written to Governor Ramsey by Colonel Gorman, August 21, 1861, by Chaplain Neill, November 3, 1861, and by Surgeon Daniel W. Hand, November 16, 1861, all eulogistic of Lester. Gorman, who had already been promised promotion to the rank of brigadier general, wrote: "If a vacancy occurs in the field officers of my Regt you should *by all means* appoint Capt. H. C. Lester." James M. Bowler, writing to Donnelly on January 15, 1862, states that Lester "exceeds expectation" and is "praised by all." The letter is in the Donnelly Papers. Charles E. Flandrau, in his *History of Minnesota and Tales of the Frontier*, 133 (St. Paul, 1900), gives this curious and questionable explanation of Lester's conduct: "Cherchez la femme." See the *Winona Daily Republican* of August 30, 1889, for statements of the Honorable William Mitchell, associate justice of the Minnesota supreme court, in an address before the Winona Old Settlers' Association on August 30, 1889. The speaker refrained from comment on Colonel Lester's military conduct but praised him as a valued intimate friend who felt that he had been unjustly censured and wronged by the refusal of the war department to grant a court of inquiry, which he had earnestly sought. See also the *Saint Paul Press*, July 19, 27, 1862, and the statement of Dr. Levi Butler, surgeon of the Third, in the issue of July 26.

[13] Newson, *Pen Pictures*, 439-442; Alonzo L. Brown, "Narrative of the Fourth Regiment," in *Minnesota in the Civil and Indian Wars*, 1:198-203; Alonzo L. Brown, *History of the Fourth Regiment of Minnesota Infantry Volunteers during the Great Rebellion, 1861-1865*, 48-57, 62 (St. Paul, 1892). Chapters 4 and 5 of the last-named work give an account of the way in which the Fourth participated with much credit and small losses in the battles of Iuka and Corinth on September 19 and October 3 and 4, 1862.

activity of those who were raising the companies, Governor
Ramsey had permitted it to be understood that he would
make his appointments to the field and staff according to the
nominations of the line officers. This arrangement resulted
in the appointment of a German nobleman, who had seen
service in the Prussian army, to the colonelcy of the Fifth
Minnesota Infantry. The experience of a few months satisfied his ambition and proved to himself and others that
personal bravery was not the only requisite for command.
Upon his retirement Lieutenant Colonel Lucius F. Hubbard,
afterwards governor of Minnesota, became colonel of the
Fifth and held that rank until he was promoted to be brevet
brigadier general.[14] Immediately upon the completion of the
muster of the regiment Companies B, C, and D were
detached and sent to relieve the five companies of the Fourth
Regiment distributed at the three Indian posts. The story
of the experience of the three companies may be reserved for
a succeeding chapter. Two of them rejoined their regiment
in the South in the following December and the third, not
until February, 1863. On the twenty-fourth of May, 1862,
the seven companies which had not been sent to the Indian
country reported for duty near Corinth, Mississippi, in time
to take an honorable part in the affair at Farmington and
in the fruitless marches which followed the siege of Corinth.
At the battle of Corinth on October 4 it was the good
fortune of the Fifth Minnesota to render a great service with
little loss. Rosecrans reports that at a moment when the
enemy was penetrating a weak point in his lines Colonel
Hubbard, anticipating orders, led his regiment into the gap,
repulsed the enemy's advance, recovered some guns which
had been captured by the enemy, and saved a battery which

---

[14] Lucius F. Hubbard, "Narrative of the Fifth Regiment," in *Minnesota in the Civil and
Indian Wars*, 1:243, and the roster, p. 282; reports of the adjutant general, in *Executive
Documents*, 1861, p. 248; 1862, p. 206. The adjutant general's call of December 5 stated
that the secretary of war had been "pleased to authorize the organization of a fifth regiment" because it had been represented that loyal citizens of Irish birth were desirous to
enlist in the service. The roster of the Fifth does not indicate a preponderance of Irish
names. Was this an idea of Donnelly's?

had taken up an exposed position.  The gallant survivors
have always claimed that the regiment saved the day.[15]

The chaplain of the Fifth Minnesota was a young Roman
Catholic priest who had lately completed his education

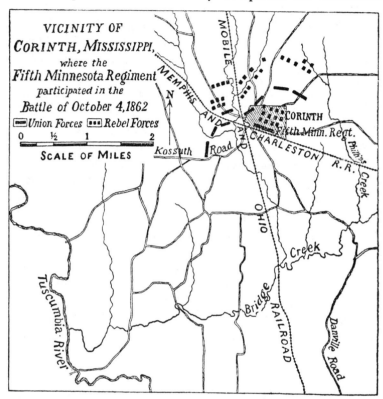

abroad.  During the hardships of a very arduous summer
campaign his tender and kindly ministrations won him the

[15] Hubbard, in *Minnesota in the Civil and Indian Wars*, 1:243, 260-264.  On page 263 is
a letter from General Rosecrans to Archbishop Ireland dated August 26, 1889.  See also
Lucius F. Hubbard, "Minnesota in the Battles of Corinth, May to October, 1862," in
*Minnesota Historical Collections*, 12:531-545, and the remarks of Archbishop Ireland and
General Mark D. Flower which follow on pages 546-551; Hubbard to Ramsey, June 21, in
the *Saint Paul Press*, July 6, 1862; and accounts of the battle of Corinth by a private in the
regiment and by Chaplain Ireland in the *Press* of October 24 and November 1, 1862, reprinted in part in Neill, *Minnesota*, 711-714.  Interviews on this subject with General
Judson W. Bishop and with Archbishop Ireland are recorded in the author's notebooks,
3:1; 4:37.

good will and respect of the whole command.  In the battle of Corinth he not only exercised the offices of his ministry but he also displayed a manly intrepidity on the firing line. After the lapse of half a century and more the survivors of the Fifth still delighted to greet and honor their comrade the Most Reverend John Ireland, archbishop of St. Paul.  He was distinguished in ecclesiastical circles on both sides of the Atlantic and his heart and hand were always in every good cause of his city, state, and nation.  American through and through, he incurred no little censure because of his desire to see and his efforts to establish a distinct American Catholicity in his country.  His commanding yet gracious presence and his powerful and brilliant oratory dignified many an important civic celebration.  As an apostle of temperance he wrought a revolution among his own people and others sufficient to make an epoch in Minnesota history.  No Catholic prelate in America has done more to bridge the chasm between the old church and the descendants of those who in times gone by broke from its fold.[16]

In addition to the infantry sent by Minnesota to the war under the calls of 1861 there were three small commands of other arms.  The First Battery of Minnesota Light Artillery was mustered at Fort Snelling on November 21, 1861, and shortly afterwards, on three different days, the officers and men departed for St. Louis by stage, the river having been closed by ice.  The battery was fitted out with horses and guns and forwarded to Pittsburg Landing, Tennessee, in February, and by the time it was called into action at the battle of Shiloh on April 6, 1862, it had been drilled into a promising state of efficiency.  Its assignment was to Prentiss' division, which was surprised and driven in early in the day. The battery was, of course, forced back, but it maintained its organization and repeatedly checked the rebel pursuit with well-directed fire.  By its splendid stand at the point

---

[16] Warren Upham and Rose B. Dunlap, *Minnesota Biographies, 1655-1912*, 362 (*Minnesota Historical Collections*, vol. 14 — St. Paul, 1912); *St. Paul Dispatch*, May 1, 1909.

called in the tradition of the camp "the Hornets' Nest" it contributed to the delay which made it possible to organize a line near the landing and effectively block the advance of the enemy, thereby saving Buell's shattered army from ruin. Captain Emil Munch was severely wounded and had his horse shot under him.[17]

The Second Battery of Minnesota Light Artillery, which was mustered into service in the midwinter of 1862, left the state on April 21 and a little more than a month later it reached Halleck's army, then investing Corinth, Mississippi. It joined in Buell's race with Bragg for the Ohio River and took an effective part in the action at Perryville. Its commander, Captain William A. Hotchkiss, had served in a regular battery in the Mexican War.[18]

Three companies of cavalry were recruited and mustered in during the autumn months of 1861 and on December 28 were reported at St. Louis. There they were merged with troops from three other states and, because those from Iowa were most numerous, the regiment so formed was designated the "Fifth Iowa Cavalry." It was not until after two years of service that the Minnesota troopers, to their great gratification, were given an independent organization as "Brackett's Battalion of Minnesota Cavalry." In February, 1862, they were sent to Tennessee in time to render arduous and useful, though not dangerous, service, which contributed to the capture of Fort Donelson.[19]

The First Company of Minnesota Sharpshooters, mustered on October 5, 1861, was sent immediately to Washington and placed under the instruction of Colonel Hiram Berdan. In the midwinter following it became Company A of the Second Regiment of United States Sharpshooters.

[17] Henry S. Hurter, "Narrative of the First Battery of Light Artillery," in *Minnesota in the Civil and Indian Wars*, 1:640-649; the same work, 2:91-97; Neill, *Minnesota*, 688; the *Pioneer and Democrat*, December 10, 11, 17, 1861; *Saint Paul Press*, November 28, December 8, 10, 1861.

[18] "Narrative of the Second Battery of Light Artillery," in *Minnesota in the Civil and Indian Wars*, 1:654-665.

[19] Isaac Botsford, "Narrative of Brackett's Battalion of Cavalry," in *Minnesota in the Civil and Indian Wars*, 1:572-584.

This command was not sent to the Peninsula but was kept in northern Virginia and it rendered excellent service in Pope's disastrous campaign. It suffered heavily at the second battle of Bull Run. The Second Company of Minnesota Sharpshooters, although recruited for Berdan's corps of United States Sharpshooters, was but temporarily attached to that corps. As already related, it was transferred to the First Minnesota Infantry and it shared the fortunes of that illustrious command.[20]

Governor Ramsey's first term of office expired with the close of the calendar year 1861. At the election held in November he was reëlected for a second term by a decisive majority of a total vote much reduced on account largely of the absence of so many electors with the Union armies. That an estimable competitor, the Honorable Edward O. Hamblin of St. Cloud, received so considerable a vote is testimony to the power of tradition in politics.[21]

In the year 1861 Minnesota had furnished to the general government all the troops demanded of her. It must have been due to a reliance upon the patriotism and generosity of the state that early in May, 1862, the secretary of war made an urgent call for an additional regiment of infantry. On the twenty-second of that month the adjutant general of the state published the governor's order for the organization of a sixth regiment of Minnesota volunteers. He expressed his confidence that all Minnesotans would "cheerfully and promptly rally in defence of liberty and the country" and, to stimulate the latent enthusiasm of young men, he assured them that the regiment would be moved to the seat of war as soon as it was full. On the last day of the same month another general order was issued appealing to the people of

[20] Francis Peteler, "Narrative of the First Company of Sharpshooters," in *Minnesota in the Civil and Indian Wars*, 1: 507-510; Chaney, in the same work, 1: 513-516. In a letter to Governor Miller, dated April 16, 1864, in the same work, 2: 420, General Winfield S. Hancock says that the Second Company of Minnesota Sharpshooters "is one of the finest and most soldierly body [sic] of men I ever saw." See *ante*, p. 86.

[21] The vote for Ramsey was 16,274; for Hamblin, 10,448. It may be found in any Minnesota *Legislative Manual*. Smalley, in his *Republican Party*, 170, remarks on the persistence of a strong Democratic element.

Minnesota to fill up their old regiments in the field. The response was disappointing. The regiments and battalions already in the field had depleted the number of young men unmarried or with small families and not permanently established in business. New enlistments must embrace men of greater age, with families needing support and business not easily relinquished. It was natural to believe that the six hundred thousand men already in service would presently suppress the rebellion and reëstablish the Union. Recruiting, therefore, was apathetic in the early summer of 1862, not only in Minnesota but throughout the loyal states.[22]

On June 28, the day following the defeat of Porter's corps on the north side of the Chickahominy, Major General McClellan, commanding the Army of the Potomac, dispatched a memorable telegram from Savage's Station to the secretary of war. In it occurred the expressions: "I have lost this battle because my force was too small. . . . You must send me very large reënforcements, and send them at once. . . . If you do not do so now, the game is lost." President Lincoln was so much aroused by the appeal that he instantly resolved upon an immediate increase of the army. For fear of creating a panic if he should issue his call in ordinary form, he secured through Secretary Seward from the governors of the loyal states a request that he should at once call for reënforcements sufficient to crush the rebellion and a promise that they would be promptly furnished. The newspapers of July 6 published the letter of the governors and the president's reply, in which an

[22] Report of the adjutant general, in *Executive Documents*, 1862, pp. 208, 209. By General Orders no. 33 of the war department, issued on April 3, 1862, the recruiting of volunteers was discontinued. General Orders no. 60 revived it. See the final report of the provost marshal general, in Secretary of War, *Reports*, 1865, appendix, part 2, p. 102 (39 Congress, 1 session, *House Executive Documents*, vol. 4, part 2 — serial 1252); the report of the adjutant general, in Minnesota, *Executive Documents*, 1862, p. 408; Charles W. Johnson, "Narrative of the Sixth Regiment," in *Minnesota in the Civil and Indian Wars*, 1: 300; and Secretary of War, *Reports*, 1861, p. 3 (37 Congress, 2 session, *Senate Documents*, vol. 2 — serial 1118). The provost marshal general gives the number of men in the service in the spring of 1862 as 637,126. See his final report, part 1, p. 9 (serial 1251).

immediate call for three hundred thousand volunteers was announced.[23]

On July 11 there appeared an executive proclamation, signed "IGNATIUS DONNELLY Acting Governor," calling for recruits. In impassioned phrases Donnelly implored the young men of Minnesota to rally in defense of their country in an hour of "terrible necessity." The Sixth Regiment would first be filled and the remaining recruits would be assigned to new regiments. The response was not encouraging. The young men were not allured by the prospect of such punishment as had been inflicted upon the old regiments at Bull Run, Mill Springs, Iuka, and Corinth. It may be added also that the shameful retreat of the Army of the Potomac at the end of June was so much overshadowed by the splendid series of rear-guard actions at Savage's Station, Glendale, and Malvern Hill that the people generally did not deeply feel the need of a further increase of the army. McClellan's retreat was continually represented by the press as a mere strategic change of base from which his campaign could be and would be more effectively prosecuted. At the end of July, as shown by the rosters, no recruits had offered for the old regiments and the Sixth had enlisted less than one-fourth of normal strength.[24] It is not known that any of the loyal states were more forward in responding to the call of July 2. Spontaneous volunteering was a failure. Unless this tardiness had been extensive, if not general, the war department would not on August 4, 1862, have given notice by order that if any state should not

---

[23] John G. Nicolay and John Hay, *Abraham Lincoln: A History*, 5:427-429, 441 (New York, 1890); Richardson, *Messages and Papers*, 6:114. See Lincoln, *Works*, 6:344, for a facsimile of Lincoln's letter to Seward, June 28, 1862. See also Frederick W. Seward, *Seward at Washington as Senator and Secretary of State*, 3:100-108 (New York, 1891), and the *Saint Paul Press* and the *Pioneer and Democrat* for July 6, 1862.

[24] *Saint Paul Press* and *Pioneer and Democrat*, July 11, 1862. See also the editorial appeals in the issues of the *Press* for July 9, 10, and 18. The issue of July 25 contains a report of a great war meeting, held on the previous evening, at which speeches were made by Henry H. Sibley, John B. Brisbin, James Smith, William J. Cullen, John M. Gilman, James W. Taylor, Thomas M. Newson, and A. Wolf. Ardent resolutions were adopted. The rosters of the regiments are given in *Minnesota in the Civil and Indian Wars*, 1:49-78, 123-146, 178-197, 221-242, 282-299, 329-346. Up to July 18 only about one hundred men had been enlisted for the Sixth. *Saint Paul Press*, July 18, 1862.

furnish its quota of volunteers by the fifteenth of that month the deficiency would be made up by a special draft from the militia. This powerful medicine had immediate effect. The quota assigned to Minnesota was 5,362 men. The idea of filling up the old regiments, which was the proper thing to do, was discarded and the plan of forming new regiments from companies recruited by men ambitious to obtain commissions was revived. On August 5 Governor Ramsey ordered the organization of a seventh regiment of volunteer infantry. The order contained a paragraph announcing that if this regiment and also the Sixth were not full by the eighteenth day of the same month they would be filled by a special draft from the militia of the state.[25]

On the eighth of August an order was issued for the organization of an eighth regiment, to be composed of citizens of Irish birth, who, it had been represented, "would immediately volunteer en masse" for a separate regiment. On August 13 and 14 additional orders were issued directing the organization of the Ninth, Tenth, and Eleventh Regiments of Minnesota Volunteers. In the last of these orders the time for enlistment in all the new regiments forming was extended from the fifteenth to the twenty-second of the month.[26]

Meantime under direction of the war department arrangements for the threatened draft were expedited. An agent for each county was appointed by the governor to ascertain whether town assessors had made up the lists of men liable

[25] Richardson, *Messages and Papers*, 6: 120. The act of July 17 authorizing a draft of militia is given in *Statutes at Large*, 12: 597. See also the report of the adjutant general, in Minnesota, *Executive Documents*, 1862, p. 215. The Minnesota quota of 5,362 men included one-half that number — 2,681 — to be drafted for nine months under the general call of August 4, 1862. The state furnished the whole required number of three-year volunteers, for which it received credit on later requisitions. See the report of the adjutant general, in *Executive Documents*, 1864, p. 255. For the result of the draft of August, 1862, see the final report of the provost marshal general, in Secretary of War, *Reports*, 1865, appendix, part 1, pp. 11, 28 (serial 1251). The call was for 300,000 men; 292,441 names were drawn, and of these 164,394 were exempted, 52,288 commuted by paying three hundred dollars in cash, and 35,882, less a number who deserted before the men could be sent from their states, were held to service. A small fraction actually joined the army. It would be interesting to know how many held to the service and have been on the pension rolls.

[26] Report of the adjutant general, in *Executive Documents*, 1862, pp. 217, 222, 227, 228.

for militia service and, in cases of failure, to make up or complete the lists themselves. A commissioner was appointed for each county to hear and decide upon applications for exemption and to conduct the draft appointed for September 3. Surgeons were appointed to assist the commissioner in acting on cases of alleged physical or mental disability for service. Detailed instructions were issued for the action of these draft officials. A board of five supervising commissioners was appointed to visit the county draft officials to give them counsel and direction. According to an order issued on August 14, no person was to leave the state without a pass from the attorney-general, or his county without a pass from the sheriff, a novel disability for free American citizens.[27]

Volunteering began immediately upon the promulgation of the draft orders. Because the quota of the state was apportioned among the counties and towns according to the numbers of their enrolled militia all the communities of the state became interested at once in supplying each its contingent. The rural districts felt the appeal for the army as never before and responded to it with admirable promptness; whole companies were made up in neighborhood rallies. To accommodate farmer recruits, furloughs were given to run until the harvest should be gathered. Before the end of the time limited for the acceptance of volunteers nearly enough men had been enlisted to fill five regiments. Because of the Sioux Outbreak of 1862, the draft was postponed until October 3. The full quota was assured by four postponements in all, the last to November 20, 1862.[28]

[27] Report of the adjutant general, in *Executive Documents*, 1862, pp. 217-235; General Orders no. 99 of the war department, issued on August 9, 1862, in Secretary of War, *Reports*, 1865, appendix, part 2, pp. 105-107 (serial 1252).

[28] Report of the adjutant general, in *Executive Documents*, 1862, pp. 238, 250, 255, 260. See page 545 for the table showing the whole number of militia returned (36,296), the whole number of volunteers to November 1 (11,225), the quota in the call of July and August, 1862 (5,362), and the excess or deficiency of each county. Seventeen counties are credited with excesses and forty are indicated as deficient. See also the *Central Republican* (Faribault), August 6, 13, 1862; the *Goodhue Volunteer* (Red Wing), August 6, 13, 20, 1862; the *Winona Republican*, August 20, 1862; and the *Minnesota Conserver* (Hastings), August 14, 21, 28, 1862.

On September 1 about a thousand more men were required to fill the quota. These were raised in an unexpected manner. The experience of Colonel Sibley in his campaign against the Sioux Indians, which will soon challenge the reader's attention, proved the imperious need of cavalry in operations against mounted Indians. Under authority received from the president, Governor Ramsey on September 2 issued a call for about twelve hundred officers and men to form the First Regiment of Minnesota Mounted Rangers to serve for three months. A later order, issued on October 15, announced that the term of enlistment would be one year and that all recruits would be credited to localities on their respective quotas. The twelve companies were therefore rapidly recruited and were full by the day last set for the draft. They were composed in large proportion of citizens who had armed and organized in an irregular manner for the defense of the frontier and had participated in the defense of New Ulm and Fort Ridgely. The personnel was of high quality. Eugene M. Wilson, afterwards a member of Congress, and Horace Austin, a governor of the state, were captains. Minnesota thus furnished all the troops required of her with an excess of 320 and averted the dishonor of a conscription. The Eleventh Regiment of Infantry was not then organized, the recruits for it being transferred to compose the Tenth Regiment.[29]

The selection of field and staff officers for the new regiments, although not reposed in his hands, under the circumstances caused Governor Ramsey much concern and responsibility. The militia law of 1858 authorized the governor as commander in chief to appoint all commissioned officers of regiments, battalions, and companies. Up to September 29, 1862, he exercised that authority, deferring in general, it may be presumed, to the wishes and reasonable

[29] Report of the adjutant general, in *Executive Documents*, 1862, pp. 241, 255, 256; Ramsey's message for 1862 in the same volume, 24; Eugene M. Wilson, "Narrative of the First Regiment of Mounted Rangers," in *Minnesota in the Civil and Indian Wars*, 1: 519-542. Samuel McPhail was the colonel. Joseph Anderson, E. St. Julien Cox, and Jacob Nix, who had been prominent in the suppression of the Sioux Outbreak of 1862, were captains.

expectations of the commands and the public. On the date mentioned the state legislature in extra session, in revising the law of 1858, took this appointing power from the governor and provided that company officers should be elected by the enlisted men, and field officers by the officers of the line. The Democratic organ of St. Paul declared that the object of this legislation was to disenable Governor Ramsey to use his appointing power in a manner to secure votes for his election to the United States Senate. The same newspaper accused him of ignoring this law and of virtually dictating appointments. There is ground for believing that the governor did exert his influence in field and staff elections, but if so it served to secure some admirable selections. Lieutenant Colonel Stephen Miller of the First Minnesota was made colonel of the Seventh, Lieutenant Colonel Alexander Wilkin of the Second became colonel of the Ninth, Lieutenant Colonel Minor T. Thomas of the Fourth was appointed colonel of the Eighth, and Captain James B. Gilfillan of the Seventh later became colonel of the Eleventh.[30]

The political organ mentioned found other pretexts for virulent diatribes against Governor Ramsey. It went to the length of laying the whole blame of the Sioux Outbreak on his shoulders because of his action at the treaties of 1851. It charged him with criminal negligence in failing to provide for the protection of the frontier. It even insinuated that he was content to have the opportunity offered by the Indian war to make appointments of persons who would further his political aspirations. Such absurd ribaldry he knew how to disregard complacently. What gave him more serious concern was a rising opposition in the Republican party to his election to the United States Senate in the place of Henry M. Rice, whose term would expire in March, 1863. On July 22, 1862, Horace Greeley gave him friendly

[30] General Laws, 1858, p. 233; 1862, extra session, 26; Saint Paul Pioneer, November 2, 1862; Ramsey to Donnelly, October 8, 1861, Donnelly Papers. See also the rosters of the various regiments, in Minnesota in the Civil and Indian Wars, 1: 49, 123, 221, 382.

notice of "a secret and determined movement . . . on foot" to defeat his nomination, which he "guessed" would fail. The aspirant favored by this opposition was Cyrus Aldrich of Hennepin County, then in the third year of service as a member of the national House of Representatives, in which position he had made many friends and had acquired more than a local reputation.[31] The intervention of Ignatius Donnelly in the contest is worthy of brief attention because it illustrates that gentleman's cleverness in politics. Donnelly was exceedingly desirous of succeeding Aldrich at Washington. He did not, therefore, discourage him from declining a renomination and entering the race for the senatorship, thus leaving the congressional field open for another. For some months preceding the senatorial election Aldrich was given reason, both directly and indirectly, to depend upon the influence of the lieutenant governor in his favor. After all the favors and courtesies showered on him by Governor Ramsey, Donnelly could not with any propriety oppose his reasonable aspiration to the senatorship; and he was too shrewd an observer of the signs of the times not to perceive that such opposition would not only be futile, but would leave him in the position of an ingrate. He evidently took to heart the counsel of Dr. Thomas Foster, then a staff captain of volunteers, "never to quarrel politically" with "old Alex," who "with all his faults . . . has no salient points of attack before the *people*, and his assailant is always worsted."[32] Friends of Governor Ramsey were therefore allowed to believe that Donnelly was his stanch supporter for the senatorship. As such he was taken

[31] *Pioneer and Democrat*, September 10, 14, October 8, 1862; Greeley to Ramsey, July 22, 1862. See also letters to Ramsey from Stephen Miller, March 25, May 25, 27, June 4, 12, from John Jay Knox, August 21, December 11, from David Heaton, September 1, December 5, from Neill, May 7, 29, December 13, from Gorman, October 26, from Jared Benson, March 14, from Robert F. Fisk, July 21, and from M. J. Severance, June 21, 1862, in the Ramsey Papers.

[32] Aldrich to Donnelly, December 18, 28, 1862, January 2, 21, 1863. In the last letter Aldrich expressed his gratitude for Donnelly's support. See also Donnelly to Aldrich, December 20, 1862, H. G. O. Morrison to Donnelly, June 13, November 25, December 22, 27, 1862, and Foster to Donnelly, June 30, 1862, in the Donnelly Papers; and Holbrook, "Early Political Career of Donnelly," 89, 93, 103.

into their confidence and was kept informed of the progress of the campaign.[33]

The Republican caucus assembled on the evening of January 12, 1863. Upon the last of twenty-four ballots cast Governor Ramsey lacked one vote of the necessary majority. At the adjourned session on the following evening he received twenty-six out of forty-six votes and was thereby virtually elected. At the formal election in joint convention of the legislature on the fourteenth the whole Republican vote was accorded him. The voting in caucus demonstrated that Governor Ramsey's solicitude was not without foundation. There were friends of Ramsey who had believed and openly proclaimed that Senator Rice had been engineering a split in the Republican ranks in the hope of winning over a sufficient number of malcontents to give himself a reëlection or the governorship. If the senator had at any time lent countenance to such a scheme he later washed his hands of it. On December 29, 1862, he wrote Governor Ramsey: "Of the combination you mention I had not heard — yet shall not be disappointed at anything. Some would go for the Devil if they could injure you. I cannot believe that any number of Democrats have thought of making arrangements with such men."[34]

[33] Letters to Donnelly from A. P. Foster, December 29, from D. Heaton, November 28, December 12, 23, 27, from Frederick Driscoll, November 27, and from Joseph A. Wheelock, December 18, 28, 1862, Donnelly Papers.

[34] *Saint Paul Press*, January 13, 14, 15, 1863; Smalley, *Republican Party*, 169; Rice to Ramsey, December 29, 1862, Ramsey Papers. That efforts were made to induce Republican members of the legislature to support Rice is evident from the letter by Senator Wade printed on page 75, *ante*.

# V. THE SIOUX OUTBREAK, 1862[1]

IN THE early morning of August 18, 1862, a large party of Dakota braves, armed and painted for war, surrounded without warning the little village of traders and employees about the lower Sioux agency on the right bank of the Minnesota River some six miles below the mouth of the Redwood. Small parties were detached to surround the traders' stores, the barns, and other principal buildings. At a prearranged signal fire was opened. James W. Lynd, a former state senator but at the time a clerk for the Myricks, was the first to fall dead. Francois La Bathe was killed in his own trading house. At Robert's store Henry Belland, Sr., and two other clerks were shot down. Three white men in charge of the barns were shot by Little Crow's direct order. No women were shot. So keen were the savages to loot the traders' stores of guns, ammunition, and other goods, that they soon suspended their killing. This respite gave the surviving whites, perhaps fifty in number, time to escape to the thickets under the bluff. Many were set over the river by the heroic ferryman, Hubert Millier, who plied his craft until he was barbarously murdered. Those thus and otherwise rescued took their way on foot or by means of casual vehicles toward Fort Ridgely, fourteen miles away by the eastern bluff road. Seven of them were overtaken and murdered, including Dr. Philander P. Humphrey, the

[1] The narrative in this and in the following two chapters has been digested from the many accounts cited in the footnotes and, in addition, from the following: Rudolph Leonhart, *Erinnerungen an Neu Ulm. Erlebnisse aus dem Indianer-Gemetzel in Minnesota, 1862* (Pittsburgh, 1880); Alexander Berghold, *The Indians' Revenge; or, Days of Horror. Some Appalling Events in the History of the Sioux* (San Francisco, 1891), the original of which is in German: *Indianer-Rache, oder die Schreckenstage von Neu-Ulm, im Jahre 1862* (New Ulm, 1876); *Illustrated Album of Biography of Meeker and McLeod Counties, Minnesota* (Chicago, 1888); Charles S. Bryant, "History of the Sioux Massacre of 1862," in Ellis C. Turner and others, eds., *History of Rice County* (Minneapolis, 1882); and an interview with Henry Belland on January 18, 1907, recorded in the author's notebooks, 3:136. These accounts are often discordant in minor particulars and not infrequently in regard to matters of first importance.

agency physician, and Philander Prescott, who had lived in peace with the Sioux for forty years.[2]

At an earlier hour small parties of Indians had been dispatched to raid the adjacent settlements. Some, and the

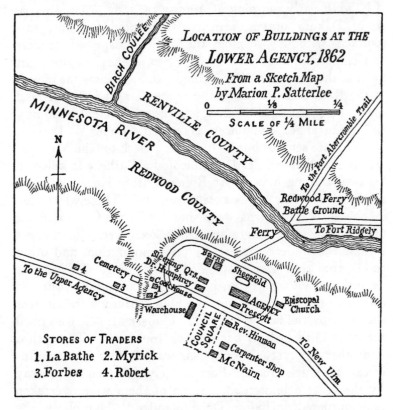

LOCATION OF BUILDINGS AT THE
LOWER AGENCY, 1862
From a Sketch Map
by Marion P. Satterlee

SCALE OF ¼ MILE

STORES OF TRADERS
1. La Bathe   2. Myrick
3. Forbes     4. Robert

greater number, spread themselves up and down the left bank of the Minnesota and made havoc in the nearer townships of Renville County bordering on the river, which were

[2] Isaac V. D. Heard, *History of the Sioux War*, 59–68 (New York, 1864). Heard erroneously calls the ferryman "Mauley." See also Minnesota Valley Historical Society, *Sketches of the Monuments and Tablets Erected by the Minnesota Valley Historical Society in Renville and Redwood Counties*, 6, 23 (Morton, 1902); Marion P. Satterlee, *Authentic List of the Victims of the Indian Massacre and War 1862–1865* (Minneapolis, 1919); and the address of William R. Marshall at the reunion of the Early Settlers of Nicollet County, January 27, 1880, in the *Saint Peter Tribune*, January 28, February 4, 1880. The last is an excellent

# MAP OF THE
# SIOUX OUTBREAK AND WAR
## IN SOUTHWESTERN MINNESOTA
### 1862

Scale of Miles
0    20    40    60

County Boundaries
Reservations with dates
Dakota or Sioux
Ojibway or Chippewa
Winnebago

FORT RIDGELY UNDER ATTACK, AUGUST 22, 1862

*Oil painted in 1890 by Sergeant James McGrew, who participated in the defense of the fort*

occupied largely by German settlers. Although the Dakota
tribes had receded the ten-mile strip on that side of the river
four years before, their hunters had not ceased to wander
over and to camp on it. As they had been peaceable,
friendly relations had been established with many settlers,
who had exchanged pork and flour with them for their
game and fish. Although it was apparent that the Indians
were in a state of excitement, the unsuspecting settlers took
no alarm until after the murders had begun. As the miscreants reached the farms they shot the men, made captives
of the women, and indifferently butchered the children or let
them follow their mothers. After many hours of pillaging
and slaughter they departed on stolen horses for their
rendezvous at the lower agency, the farm wagons loaded
with plunder and the cattle and their prisoners driven before
them. The barns and stacks of hay and grain were commonly burned, but most of the houses were left, probably
for expected occupation later.[3]

sketch of the events of 1862. The lower Sioux agency was in section 8, township 112, range
34 west. George Spencer swore at the trial of Indian no. 21 by Sibley's military commission
of 1862 that he was shot about seven in the morning in Forbes's store. The Proceedings
of the Military Commission, in the Senate files, have been examined by the author. Marion
P. Satterlee, in his *Massacre at the Redwood Indian Agency*, 2, gives the number of people
living there as "some 85." On page 10 he gives the number of people killed as follows:
at the agency, thirteen; in flight, seven; taken captive, about ten; escaped, forty-seven; in
all, about seventy-seven. See Stephen R. Riggs, "Memoir of Hon. Jas. W. Lynd," in
*Minnesota Historical Collections*, 3: 107-114, for some account of this gifted person.

[3] Report of Agent Galbraith, dated January 27, 1863, in the Commissioner of Indian
Affairs, *Annual Reports*, 1863, p. 290; *Statutes at Large*, 12: 1031, 1037; report of Lieutenant
Governor Donnelly to Governor Ramsey, dated August 29, 1862, in Indian Office, *Reports*,
1862, p. 60; Holcombe, in *Minnesota in Three Centuries*, 3: 313. The reports of the commissioner of Indian affairs referred to above will hereafter be cited as Indian Office, *Reports*.
They may also be found in the annual reports of the secretary of the interior, which in turn
are usually included in the serial set among the documents accompanying the president's
message to each regular session of Congress. Thus the report for 1862 is in 37 Congress,
2 session, *House Executive Documents*, vol. 2 (serial 1157) and that for 1863 is in *House
Executive Documents*, vol. 3 (serial 1182). Galbraith's report, which occupies pages 382-416
of the last mentioned volume, may also be found in *Indian Tribes in the Northwest*, 9-40
(37 Congress, 3 session, *House Executive Documents*, no. 68 — serial 1163). See also the
deposition of Stephen R. Riggs, in Sisseton and Wahpeton Bands of Sioux Indians *v.* United
States, *Record, Evidence for Defendant*, 405, 409 (Court of Claims, no. 22,524). For an
account of this case, see the Appendix, no. 12, *post*. A copy of the record — more than a
thousand pages — is in the library of the Minnesota Historical Society. See *post*, p. 426,
n. 46. Extracts from Riggs's deposition are in *Claims for Depredations by Sioux Indians*,
9-12 (38 Congress, 1 session, *House Executive Documents*, no. 58 — serial 1189). This
document includes also extracts from a deposition by Agent Galbraith and the report of
the Sioux claims commission of 1863. See the map on page 112, *post*.

Meantime another tragedy was staged at the agency. By the middle of the forenoon fugitives had reached Fort Ridgely with their appalling tidings. That post was occupied at the moment by a company of the Fifth Minnesota Infantry under the command of Captain John S. Marsh, a brave young officer who, although a citizen of Minnesota, had served in a Wisconsin regiment which took part in the battle of Bull Run. With forty-six enlisted men and his

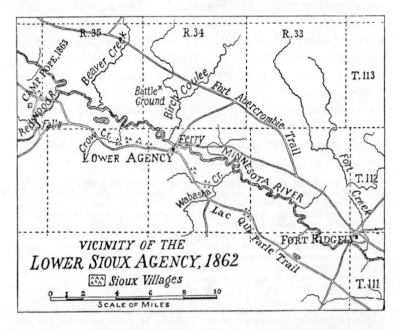

VICINITY OF THE
LOWER SIOUX AGENCY, 1862
ᴧᴧᴧ Sioux Villages
SCALE OF MILES

interpreter, Peter Quinn, he set out promptly for the scene of the massacre. A train of wagons for which he might as well have waited overtook the party three miles away. In them the men rode until an early hour in the afternoon, when they reached a point a mile or more from their destination. On the way many bodies of murdered victims were passed and scores of fugitives were encountered. Their warnings of danger ahead served only to inspire the young commander to quicken his march. Ignorant of Indian warfare, overconfident, and unapprehensive of ambuscade, he moved his men in a body directly to the Redwood Ferry, where he held them in closed ranks. He did not suspect that across the stream behind convenient saw logs and other cover many scores of Indians were lying invisible with cocked guns waiting for a signal.[4]

There was but one Indian in sight on the farther bank and that was White Dog, who had been an overseer of farmer Indians and was regarded as civilized. A parley, which has been variously reported, then took place with him through the interpreter. According to his own statement at his trial, White Dog "told Marsh to come over on the ferry."[5] While the parley was prolonged a number of Indians took advantage of the opportunity to ford the river upstream and take cover in the thicket. One party of them presently got possession of the ferryman's house. It has been reasonably surmised that the Indians' plan had been to reserve their fire until the white soldiers should be crowded on the ferryboat, when the cable should be cut, the boat set adrift, and the slaughter take place. As no movement was made toward crossing, White Dog at length gave the signal for concerted action and a volley of bullets went crashing into

[4] The best account of the "battle of Redwood Ferry" is that by Lieutenant Thomas P. Gere, which is embodied in Hubbard's narrative in *Minnesota in the Civil and Indian Wars*, 1: 248-250. See also Charles S. Bryant and Abel B. Murch, *History of the Great Massacre by the Sioux Indians*, 182-186 (St. Peter, 1872); Heard, *Sioux War*, 71; and Mrs. Nancy M. Huggan to Holcombe, May 24, 27, June 14, 1894, in the Holcombe Papers. Captain Marsh left the fort at 10:30 A.M., according to the letter from Lieutenant Gere to the commanding officer at Fort Snelling, dated August 18, 1862, in Governor's Archives, file 255. An example of discordance in particulars is found in Heard, *Sioux War*, 71. The author states that the Reverend Samuel D. Hinman, who had escaped from the lower agency not later than seven o'clock in the morning, met Marsh's command a mile from the fort at two o'clock in the afternoon. On the following page Heard says that Marsh reached the ferry at sundown, which would be almost exactly seven o'clock at that time of the year. Gere says he reached the ferry "shortly after noon."

[5] Gere, in *Minnesota in the Civil and Indian Wars*, 1: 249; Proceedings of the Military Commission. In his *ante-mortem* statement to Riggs, White Dog said that "At the ferry, he talked with Quinn. First called to them to come over, but when he saw that the Indians were in ambush, he beckoned to Capt. Marsh to stay back. He says that . . . he . . . did not command the Indians to fire. . . . He complains bitterly that he did not have a chance to tell the things as they were. . . . He says that they all . . . think it hard that they did not have a fairer trial." *Saint Paul Pioneer*, December 28, 1862; Return I. Holcombe, "Chief Big Eagle's Story of the Sioux Outbreak of 1862," in *Minnesota Historical Collections*, 6: 391.

the ranks. Perhaps a dozen men, half of the whole number killed, fell dead on the spot. Quinn's body was pierced with many bullets. Captain Marsh was unhurt. Almost at the same moment fire was opened by the Indians in ambush in the right rear. The captain faced his men about, closed ranks, made a short advance movement, and ordered them to fire a volley. All was vain; more of his men were falling and relief was impossible. At his command the survivors broke for the nearest shelter. He and the larger number made their way into the fringe of timber and underbrush which lines prairie rivers. Indians skirted its margin for some distance, but their shots did no harm. At length a point was reached where the cover was too thin. Captain Marsh decided to cross the stream, thus escape the Indians' fire, and make his way toward the fort along the south bank. He would not have so resolved had he known or, if knowing, had he reflected that he would find himself in one of the Sioux villages. Taking the lead, he attempted to wade or swim, got beyond his depth, and was drowned. Because the manly efforts of two soldiers failed to rescue him, it was believed that, overheated as he was, he was seized with a cramp. The Indians now desisted from pursuit and the surviving members of the company straggled into Fort Ridgely. The ambuscade with its resulting slaughter has been called the "battle of Redwood Ferry." It had all the effects of a victory upon the savages. They could kill the white men like sheep.[6]

At eight o'clock in the evening Lieutenant Thomas P. Gere, whom Captain Marsh had left in charge at the fort,

[6] Charles E. Flandrau, "The Indian War of 1862–1864, and Following Campaigns in Minnesota;" in *Minnesota in the Civil and Indian Wars*, 1: 730; Gere, in the same volume, 248-250; Holcombe, in *Minnesota in Three Centuries*, 3: 315-322; Sergeant John F. Bishop's report, in *Minnesota in the Civil and Indian Wars*, 2: 166-170. The last account, with slight variations, may be found also under the erroneous title "The Yellow Medicine Massacre," in *Glimpses of the Nation's Struggle*, third series, 17-25. See also Oscar G. Wall, *Recollections of the Sioux Massacre*, 47-63 (Lake City, 1909). He gives the names of the members of Captain Marsh's party, those of the killed and wounded, and those of the survivors. A footnote on pages 63-76 gives a narrative by one of the survivors. See the report of the adjutant general, in *Executive Documents*, 1862, p. 416, for a variant account. Sergeant Bishop led fourteen of the survivors back to the fort.

wrote the following dispatch and sent Private William J. Sturgis, mounted on the best horse, to carry it: "Hd Qrs Fort Ridgely Minn Aug 18<sup>th</sup> 8 P.M. Comdy officer Ft Snelling Capt Marsh left this post at 10½ this morning to prevent Indian depredations at the Lower Agency. Some of the men have returned—from them I learn that Capt Marsh is killed and only thirteen of his company remaining. The Indians are killing the settlers and plundering the country. Send reinforcements without delay." The following postscript was added: "Please hand this to Gov Ramsey *immediately*."[7]

On the same fateful eighteenth of August in the forenoon a large number of Indians, doubtless from the villages below the agency, made their appearance in the township of Milford, Brown County, some twenty miles from their homes. Before nightfall the fiends had murdered nearly, if not quite, fifty peaceable German settlers engaged in the farm work of the season. The contemporary stories of indescribable mutilation of bodies have not been confirmed.[8] Six persons who had fled from the mouth of the Redwood in a wagon and had made a detour on the prairie to avoid the lower agency were overtaken about eight miles from New Ulm, probably by some of the same Indians. The three men were shot at sight and the three women were taken captive after one of them had been mortally wounded. The alarm spread rapidly throughout the settlements and put the people to precipitate flight. Before morning virtually the whole population of Milford and adjoining towns had congregated in New Ulm. Eight murders were committed the same day, probably by a detachment of the same Indians, in the towns of West Newton and Courtland,

---

[7] Gere, in *Minnesota in the Civil and Indian Wars*, 1: 250. The original dispatch is in Governor's Archives, file 255.

[8] Narrative of John W. Young, in Bryant and Murch, *Great Massacre*, 175-178; recollections of Christopher Spelbrink, in L. A. Fritsche, ed., *History of Brown County*, 1: 189-198 (Indianapolis, 1916); letter of Dr. Thomas S. Williamson, dated September 16, in the *Saint Paul Press*, September 21, 1862; Satterlee, *Victims of the Indian Massacre.*

Nicollet County, on the north side of the Minnesota below Fort Ridgely.[9]

Rumors of the outbreak at the lower agency reached the upper agency on the Yellow Medicine River thirty miles away at an early hour.[10] They seemed so improbable to

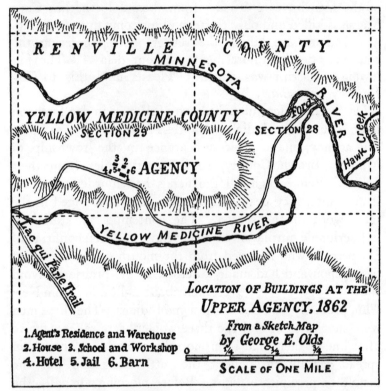

LOCATION OF BUILDINGS AT THE
UPPER AGENCY, 1862

From a Sketch Map
by George E. Olds

1. Agent's Residence and Warehouse
2. House 3. School and Workshop
4. Hotel 5. Jail 6. Barn

SCALE OF ONE MILE

the white people resident there that no serious attention was given to them until they were confirmed by later

[9] Mary Schwandt-Schmidt, "The Story of Mary Schwandt," in *Minnesota Historical Collections*, 6: 461-474. This account was confirmed in an interview recorded in the author's notebooks, 8: 38. See also Satterlee, *Victims of the Indian Massacre.*

[10] The upper Sioux agency was beautifully situated on the north bank of the Yellow Medicine River about two miles from its junction with the Minnesota if measured along its curving bed, but not much, if any, more than one mile in a direct line. It was located in the southwest quarter of section 29, township 115, range 38. See the map in Arthur P. Rose, *History of Yellow Medicine County*, 66 (Marshall, 1914), and the sketch map by George E. Olds, accompanying a letter to the author, August 31, 1917, in the Folwell Papers.

arrivals. The Wahpeton dwelling or encamped thereabouts
and probably some visiting members of other bands assembled in council in the afternoon. There was a long and
heated debate on the question whether common cause should
be made with the lower Indians in killing and plundering.
All that is certain about the result is that the council would
neither resolve to embark in the outbreak nor refuse its

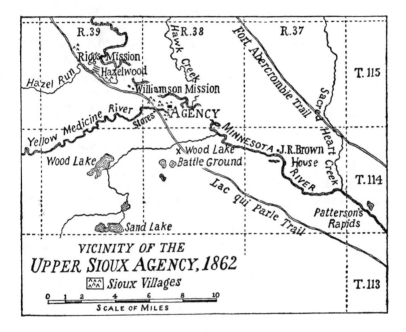

VICINITY OF THE
UPPER SIOUX AGENCY, 1862
Sioux Villages
SCALE OF MILES

sympathy and support to it. Individual members were
uninstructed. The Christian Indians at once perceived the
danger which threatened their white friends and hastened
to reveal it to them. In the early evening John Other Day,
a Christian with a white wife, aided by Joseph Laframboise,
a French half-breed, collected nearly all the whites remaining about the upper agency into the brick warehouse, which
was a good fortification against small arms. In the night of
the eighteenth an attack was made on the four traders'
stores in the Yellow Medicine Valley under the hill. One

employee who had not escaped was killed and another was mortally wounded. At daybreak of the following morning the hostile Indians gathered to plunder the traders' stores. While they were so engaged John Other Day piloted the sixty-two people over whom he and a small group of Wahpeton friends had stood guard during the night safely across the Minnesota and out onto the prairie. Among them were the wife and children of Galbraith, the Sioux agent. There were three wagons and two buggies in which the young children, the feebler women, and the wounded trader were carried. After three days of great anxiety and privation the party, guided solely by the faithful Indian, reached Hutchinson. At that place it disbanded for the river towns.[11]

Three miles above the upper agency on the bank of the Minnesota was the Pajutazee (Yellow Medicine) mission of Dr. Thomas S. Williamson, and three miles farther up was the Hazelwood station of the Reverend Stephen R. Riggs.[12] Near sunset on Monday Antoine Renville, one of Riggs's elders, came in great excitement to tell Riggs that Indians were killing white people. The report seemed to be merely one of a drunken quarrel. Rumors thickened in the afternoon and at dark Riggs's horses were taken. A messenger

[11] See the statement of John Other Day, interpreted by Gideon H. Pond, a letter from Dr. Thomas S. Williamson, dated August 26, and a communication from A. J. Ebell containing information furnished by Frederick Patwell, a refugee from a trader's store, in the *Saint Paul Press*, August 28, 29, 30, 1862; the *Pioneer and Democrat*, August 24, 1862; a letter from Riggs, dated August 24, in the *Missionary Herald*, 58:297-299 (October, 1862); and the testimony of Samuel J. Brown, of Joseph Laframboise, and of the Reverend Charles R. Crawford, in *Sisseton and Wahpeton Claim Case Record, Evidence for Claimant*, 41, 144-147, 159-161. These and others not here cited differ widely in regard to the time of day that the news was received at Yellow Medicine, the time the council was held, the attendance there, and the nature of the deliberations. Other Day gives the time of the first report as eight o'clock in the morning of the eighteenth. Laframboise places it at sundown òn the nineteenth. "About noon" on the eighteenth is the hour fixed by the more reliable. Other Day states that about one hundred Indians were in council at noon — Sisseton, Wahpeton, and about thirty young Yankton. The Sisseton urged the indiscriminate slaughter of all the whites; the Wahpeton advised merely plunder. The only council Laframboise remembered was "a gathering of the people" after dark listening to "three men who had come from the lower agency, and their talk was to get these people to do as they had done." Before his conversion John Other Day was known as "a peculiarly abandoned and fierce savage." *Missionary Herald*, 58:299 (October, 1862).

[12] Dr. Williamson's mission was in the southwest quarter of section 24, township 115, range 39 west; that of Dr. Riggs — Hazelwood — on the south half of section 15, in the same township and range. See the map in Rose, *Yellow Medicine County*, 66.

sent to the upper agency brought word that the stores were
about to be broken in. The young people of the mission,
however, retired and slept, to be awakened after midnight
by Indian friends who told them that instant departure was
necessary. The parents were told that the Indians would
kill them to get possession of their three grown-up daughters.
In a short time twenty-one persons started through woods,
underbrush, and tall grass for the riverside. From there
they were set over onto an island in the Minnesota and left
by their Indian guides. It was believed that the danger
would presently be over and that all could return to their
homes. In the forenoon of Tuesday Riggs went over to the
agency village, to find it deserted and the stores sacked and
to learn of the escape of the white people under the convoy of
Other Day. It became apparent that flight was imperative
and the whole company waded over to the north side of the
river, where they may be left for a moment.[13]

Williamson heard rumors of the outbreak early on Monday, but he refused to credit them. Many Indians came to
him during the day. Some of them said nothing; others
said that the Yankton and the Sisseton were coming down
to kill all the whites and the Indians wearing white man's
clothes and that the lower Indians and the Winnebago
would take the fort and New Ulm. Not until a little after
sunrise on Tuesday did Williamson send off with his son-in-
law, Andrew Hunter, ten of his household in two wagons,
one drawn by horses and the other by oxen. Late in the
day the two missionary companies united and, increased
by some refugees from the government sawmill, bivouacked
on the farther side of Hawk Creek at the old crossing.
The march of Wednesday was tedious, the pace being set by
the ox teams. The bivouac at night was on the prairie, without shelter, under a steady rain, which fell until morning.
The refugees were compelled to devote Thursday afternoon

[13] Stephen R. Riggs, *Mary and I: Forty Years with the Sioux*, 154-156, 171 (Chicago,
1880); letter from Riggs, dated August 24, in the *Missionary Herald*, 58:297 (October,
1862).

to cooking the meat of a butchered cow and baking bread on sticks held over the fire. On Friday morning it was decided to abandon the plan of going to Hutchinson and to take the old Lac qui Parle road, which would lead them to Fort Ridgely. The noon rest was at Birch Coulee, sixteen miles from the fort. At that point the ox wagon in which were traveling Williamson, his wife, and sister, all of whom had remained at Pajutazee until Wednesday morning, overtook the party. While the cavalcade moved slowly on, Hunter with his wife went forward in a buggy on the fort road. When they came near the post they saw the flames of burning buildings. Leaving his wife, Hunter "crawled into" the fort, where he learned of the battle of that day and was advised that the mission people would do better to go on to the settlements. A night's march broken by a brief rest was followed by a long day's journey, which brought the refugees late on Saturday to a place a few miles from Henderson. On Sunday a short Sabbath-day's journey was made, after which the devout fugitives, unwilling to travel on the Sabbath, joined in a service of praise and thanksgiving. On Monday they dispersed to various destinations.[14]

On Tuesday, the nineteenth of August, the sun rose on another day of horrors. The killings in Renville County were renewed. The previous evening thirteen families of the Sacred Heart settlement, so called from the creek of that name, had assembled at the house of Paul Kitzman in Flora Township. After some preparation they began their flight. They had traveled fourteen miles in the general

[14] Letter from Williamson, "On the Prairie," August 26, and from Riggs, Shakopee, August 27, in the *Saint Paul Press*, August 29, 1862; Riggs, *Forty Years with the Sioux*, 156-163; Riggs, in the *Missionary Herald*, 58:298 (October, 1862). See the maps on pages 112 and 117, *ante*. An account by D. W. Moore, a member of the missionary party, is in the *Pioneer and Democrat* of August 28, 1862. See also Jonas Pettijohn, *Autobiography, Family History, and Various Reminiscences of the Life of Jonas Pettijohn among the Sioux or Dakota Indians*, 67-78 (Clay Center, Kansas, 1890). Pettijohn was a teacher at Red Iron's village. He gives interesting details in regard to the escape of his family and those of the mission. Riggs relates that on Thursday afternoon Ebell took a "very good stereoscopic [*sic*] picture of the party." The picture is reproduced in Heard, *Sioux War*, 87. Riggs says that Hunter advanced only to the picket line of the fort, where he was advised by the officer of the day to keep his party out on the prairie.

SIOUX OUTBREAK REFUGEES RESTING ON THE PRAIRIE

*This brief stop by whites fleeing from the Upper Agency area was photographed by Adrian J. Ebell*

THE SECOND BATTLE OF NEW ULM, AUGUST 23, 1862

Scene from a Sioux War panorama painted by Anton Gág, Christian Heller, and Alexander Schwendinger

direction of Fort Ridgely when, sometime after sunrise, they were overtaken by a party of Sioux warriors, who told them that the Chippewa were on the warpath and that safety lay in returning to their homes, where they would be protected. Kitzman, trusting to the Indian spokesman, who used good English and with whom he had hunted, advised compliance. When they were near their homes the Indians opened fire and twenty-five of their number were killed. The women who were not killed were taken captive, with one notable exception.[15] There was a murder the same day on Lac qui Parle, that of Amos W. Huggins, the teacher who had lived among the Wahpeton from childhood.[16]

In Brown County there were new victims on the same day. A party of sixteen men left New Ulm to aid and rescue settlers on the Cottonwood River who might not have made their escape. They were returning in the evening in separate parties when, on nearing New Ulm, they were ambushed and eleven of them were killed. In the afternoon a large marauding party of savages made its appearance at New Ulm and, dismounting, made a formidable demonstration on the town. An account of it will be given on a later page.[17]

For some years Joseph R. Brown had resided in a "fine stone house, elegantly furnished," some seven miles below the upper agency on the opposite side of the Minnesota River. On Monday afternoon two members of his family

[15] Bryant and Murch, *Great Massacre*, 113-116. The exception was Justina Kreiger, who was rescued; her narrative is given on pages 298-312. See also Satterlee, *Victims of the Indian Massacre*, and Upham to the author, March 8, 1922, accompanied by a useful recast of Satterlee's tables, in the Folwell Papers. See the map on page 117, *ante*.

[16] Bryant and Murch, *Great Massacre*, 161; Heard, *Sioux War*, 96; the story of Mrs. Sophia Huggins, in the *Saint Paul Press*, February 3, 4, 5, 1863. Mrs. Huggins' story, with some omissions, is also given in Heard, *Sioux War*, 209-228. See also *Sisseton and Wahpeton Claim Case Record, Evidence for Defendant*, 344-346. According to the witness, the wrong man was hanged for the murder of Huggins. The Proceedings of the Military Commission, however, show that the Indian who was hanged was convicted for participation in the murder. He admitted that he was present. See also the testimony of Julia Laframboise in the Proceedings of the Military Commission.

[17] Bryant and Murch, *Great Massacre*, 178-181; Satterlee, *Victims of the Indian Massacre*. See *post*, p. 133.

were at the agency, where they were told by an old Indian woman to get away as there was going to be trouble. At four o'clock the next morning the Brown family was wakened and advised to escape at once. There was no time to catch the horses grazing somewhere on the prairie. Three yoke of oxen were hastily hitched to as many wagons and in them the family and others who had joined it, in all twenty-six persons, started for the fort, the oxen on a trot. Six miles had been covered when they saw Indians "popping out of the grass on every side," among them "the awful Cut Nose, the terrible *Shakopee* . . . and the impudent and saucy *Do-wan-ne-yay*." With one exception they demanded that the whites be killed on the spot. Major Brown was absent at the time, but his wife was equal to the perilous occasion. She was related to Akepa, a Wahpeton chief of influence. "If you harm any of these friends of mine," said she, "you will have to answer to Scarlet Plume, Ah kee pah, Standing Buffalo, and the whole Sisseton and Wahpeton tribe." After much deliberating in council apart, the demons allowed the men to go but carried the women and children to Little Crow's camp. There they were prudently taken under the protection of that personage, who was just then most ardently desiring the full coöperation of the upper Indians.[18]

[18] Interview with Samuel J. Brown, recorded in the author's notebooks, 6: 72; Brown, "Reminiscences of the Sioux Massacre and War of 1862," 3-26, in the possession of the Minnesota Historical Society. According to a prefatory letter to Charles D. Gilfillan, dated August 18, 1899, this is a revision of Brown's narrative which the *Mankato Review* published in its columns and in pamphlet form under the title, *In Captivity. The Experience, Privations, and Dangers of Sam'l J. Brown, and Others, while Prisoners of the Hostile Sioux, during the Massacre and War of 1862.* It may be found also in 56 Congress, 2 session, *Senate Documents*, no. 23 (serial 4029), and in Brown's testimony in *Sisseton and Wahpeton Claim Case Record, Evidence for Claimant*, 39-74. See Heard, *Sioux War*, 202-208, for the narrative of Samuel J. Brown to Heard. The two Browns who went to the agency were Samuel J. and his sister Ellen, later Mrs. George G. Allanson. Both were living in 1923. In a letter to the author, dated March 13, 1922, George G. Allanson says that the Brown home was on the southeast quarter of the northeast quarter of section 8, township 114, range 37. He writes that "the latch string was always out . . . there were lots of young folks and many gay times in the old house. Mr. Drew, a Scotchman, who, I believe, was Sibley County's first county surveyor . . . gave the old house the name 'Farther-and-gay,'" punning on the well-known Fotheringay Castle in which Mary Stuart was imprisoned and executed. The letter is in the Folwell Papers. The location of the Brown home is shown on the map on page 117, *ante.*

On Wednesday the twentieth the slaughter was extended to remoter points. In the western part of Kandiyohi County about forty miles from the reservation line fourteen murders were committed; thirteen of the victims were members of two families which had been attending a religious meeting.[19] Near Lake Shetek in Murray County, fifty miles to the southwest of the reservation, a raid was made on an advanced settlement of some fifty people, of whom fifteen or more were killed and many were wounded. The settlement was wholly broken up and dispersed.[20] On Thursday there were additional victims in Kandiyohi County. On the same day, at and near the trading post on Big Stone Lake, the Indians killed five government employees and, a short distance away, three men engaged in haymaking. Rumors of Indian disturbances had reached a settlement, mostly of Norwegians, in the town of Belmont, Jackson County, on the upper Des Moines River. A meeting had been called for August 25 to arrange means of defense,

[19] Victor E. Lawson and Martin E. Tew, eds., *History of Kandiyohi County*, 21-23 (St. Paul, 1905), contains a photograph of the monument to the Broberg and Lundborg families in the Lebanon Cemetery, New London. The narrative of Ernestina Broberg is in Bryant and Murch, *Great Massacre,* 401-403. The affidavit of Lena Lundborg at Paynesville, August 21, 1862, is in Governor's Archives, file 255. For the names of the victims see Satterlee, *Victims of the Indian Massacre.* See also the map opposite page 110, *ante.*

[20] Accounts of Mrs. Lavina Eastlick and Mrs. Alomina Hurd, in Bryant and Murch, *Great Massacre,* 343-366, 367-375; Satterlee, *Victims of the Indian Massacre*; Heard, *Sioux War,* 99-110. Heard attributes this atrocity to the bands of Lean Bear, White Lodge, and Sleepy Eyes, sometimes called lower Sisseton. See the map opposite page 110, and that on page 226. The Minnesota Historical Society has in its possession copies of a number of papers written by survivors of the Lake Shetek massacre. They include: a narrative letter of A. Meyers to Neil Currie, Garretson, South Dakota, November 20, 1894; a narrative letter of W. J. Duley, Beeson, Colbert County, Alabama, August 24, 1885, which gives a list of twelve persons buried in one common grave on October 31, 1863, the bodies having been disinterred from hastily made graves; a narrative of Mrs. Hohnmuth of Mankato; questions for Mrs. Hohnmuth, evidently not followed by her in her narrative; a narrative letter of Lillian Keeney, formerly Lillian Everet, to Dr. H. M. Workman, Waseca, Minnesota, August 2, 1894; a narrative of Thomas Ireland, who claims to have shot Lean Bear; and a brief narrative about Charles D. Hatch. See also James Starkey, "Reminiscences of Indian Depredations in Minnesota," in *Glimpses of the Nation's Struggle,* third series, 282. Captain Starkey commanded the military escort of the party which buried the twelve bodies mentioned above. In the order book of Company M, First Regiment, in the possession of the Minnesota Historical Society, are Colonel McPhail's order of October 22, 1863, to Starkey to proceed with thirty men to Lake Shetek, and Starkey's report to McPhail, November 4, 1863. In 1905 the legislature appropriated four hundred dollars for the disinterment and reburial of these bodies, and for the erection of a suitable monument. *General Laws,* 1905, p. 531.

if it should be thought necessary. On Sunday, the day before, a party of Sioux fell upon the settlement and murdered thirteen of its number. Much property was carried off, some of which was soon abandoned. At Breckenridge, more than a hundred miles northwest of the upper agency, three men were murdered on or about August 23.[21]

Whether or not the forays had been deliberately planned for such a purpose, their effect was to strike terror into the hearts of survivors and to put them to instant flight. Practically all the inhabitants of twenty-three counties abandoned their homes and took the roads eastward, many carrying nothing but the clothes worn at the moment of their escape to the sloughs or the timber. The alarm was intensified by rumors that the Winnebago from their reservation ten miles south of Mankato and the Chippewa warriors from the upper Mississippi had made common cause with the Dakota and were closing in on the flanks. This new fear, intensified by sporadic assassinations which lasted for nearly a month, impelled many to continue their flight to the river towns, and thousands of frantic refugees made their way to St. Cloud and Clearwater, to Minneapolis and St. Anthony, to St. Paul and Hastings, and even to Winona. Not a few left the state never to return. In all, a region two hundred miles long and averaging fifty miles wide was devastated or depopulated.[22]

[21] Bryant and Murch, *Great Massacre*, 149-153; Arthur P. Rose, *History of Jackson County*, 101-109 (Jackson, 1910); Orin G. Libby, "Fort Abercrombie, 1857-1877," in *North Dakota Historical Collections*, vol. 2, part 2, p. 12; Satterlee, *Victims of the Indian Massacre*. See also the map opposite page 110, *ante*.

[22] *Claims for Depredations by Sioux Indians*, 8, 16 (serial 1189). The refugee populations of nineteen counties had not returned to their homes up to November, 1863. In remaining counties and parts of counties less than one-half of the people had returned in the winter and summer of 1863. Some of the counties on Galbraith's list have since been subdivided or combined with others. See also Governor Ramsey's messages of September 9, 1862, and January 7, 1863, and the report of the adjutant general, in Minnesota, *Executive Documents*, 1862, pp. 5, 9, 420, 462, 468; Heard, *Sioux War*, 112, 118, 120, 142; Bryant and Murch, *Great Massacre*, 80, 416, 418; Donnelly, in Indian Office, *Reports*, 1862, p. 59; Mrs. Donnelly to her husband, August 24, 1862, Donnelly Papers; *Minnesota in the Civil and Indian Wars*, 2: 195, 199, 200; *Official Records*, series 1, vol. 13, p. 642; *Saint Paul Press*, August 21, 30, 1862; *Pioneer and Democrat*, August 24, 1862; *Minnesota State News*, August 23, 30, September 6, 1862. For an account of the panic in Ramsey County, see a letter from Thomas M. Newson, dated August 25, in the *Saint Paul Press* of August 30, 1862. For the spread of the alarm to Iowa and Kansas and the territories of Nebraska and

From the white man's point of view these operations
amounted simply to a massacre, an atrocious and utterly
unjustifiable butchery of unoffending citizens. The re-
sources of invective were exhausted in the descriptions of
the day. The Indian, however, saw himself engaged in
war, the most honorable of all pursuits, against men who,
as he believed, had robbed him of his country and his freedom, had fooled and cheated him with pretensions of friendship, and who wished to force upon him an alien language
and religion. He was making war on the white man in the
same fashion in which he would have gone against the
Chippewa or the Foxes. There were a few instances of
mutilations of bodies, but they were by no means so numerous as the excited imaginations of refugees made them out.
There were also isolated cases of tenderness and generosity
to captives. The more reputable chiefs would gladly have
restrained their warriors from indiscriminate slaughter,
but that was impossible when there were hundreds of young
braves to whom the eagle feather was the most precious
thing in life; and that could be won by the murder of a baby
as easily as by the killing of a foe in equal combat. In the
absence of records and other testimony it would be unsafe
to assert, as has frequently been done, that the Sioux Outbreak of 1862 was deliberately concocted and that a definite
plan of campaign was agreed upon. But events now to be
described seem to render it probable that the idea of a war
on the whites was by no means novel and that a plausible
scheme of a campaign, which might be put into effect if
ever an opportunity should arise, had been thought about
and kept in mind.[23]

Dakota, see Frederick T. Wilson, "Fort Pierre and Its Neighbors," in *South Dakota Historical Collections*, 1: 298. See also Milo M. Quaife, "The Panic of 1862 in Wisconsin,"
in the *Wisconsin Magazine of History*, 4: 166-195 (December, 1920).

[23] Mrs. Sarah F. Wakefield, *Six Weeks in the Sioux Tepees: A Narrative of Indian
Captivity* (Shakopee, 1864); Bryant and Murch, *Great Massacre*, 199, 340-342; narrative of
Benedict Juni, in Fritsche, *Brown County*, 1: 111-122. Juni, who was kindly cared for by an
Indian woman during his captivity, was known to the author as a student at the University
of Minnesota in the seventies. See also Mrs. J. E. De Camp Sweet, "Narrative of Captivity
in the Sioux Outbreak of 1862," in *Minnesota Historical Collections*, 6: 358-363, and Samuel
W. Pond, "The Dakotas or Sioux in Minnesota as They Were in 1834," in *Minnesota*

Fort Ridgely, some twenty miles above New Ulm and near the head of ordinary navigation of the Minnesota, was the base of operations and supply of the white soldiers of the Great Father. To seize and occupy this stronghold would transfer that advantage to the Sioux nation and, this place captured, it would be easy to sweep down the val-

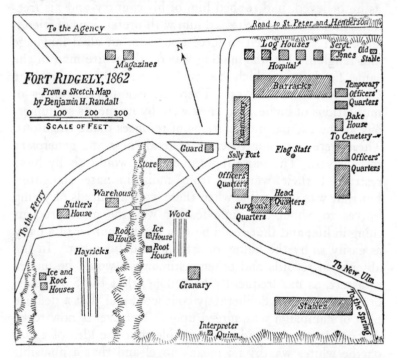

ley and wipe out Mankato, St. Peter, Henderson, Shakopee, and all the settlements down to the defenses of Fort Snelling.

*Historical Collections*, 12: 379. Pond says: "It was the work of a mob, begun by the few and carried on by the many. . . . Some were influenced by . . . clannish feeling. . . . Some were intimidated by the insane violence of those who were drunk with blood. Many joined in the fight because they thought that, if the Dakotas were overcome, little discrimination would be made by the victors between the innocent and the guilty. . . . After all, a great many Indians on the Reserve held themselves aloof from deeds of violence, and did what they could for the preservation of the captives." In a letter to Holcombe, dated June 14, 1894, Mrs. Nancy Huggan says: "I have never been able to find an Indian that did any thing or killed any one at the time of the outbreak. Little Crows brother [*White Spider*] was here not long ago and to hear him talk all Minnesota would of been killed had it not been for him." Holcombe Papers.

Fort Ridgely had been established in 1853 soon after the removal in that year of the Sioux to the reserves set apart under the treaties of 1851. The site was on the north bank, some three-fourths of a mile from the river, a bottom of nearly that width intervening. The plateau is 150 feet above the valley. Ravines of erosion with steep slopes, forming excellent cover, surround the place except to the northwest, where the open prairie extends. The principal buildings were grouped around the sides of a parade about ninety yards square, the two-story stone barracks on the north and a large one-story building adjacent for quartermasters' use being the only structures which were proof against musketry. The officers' quarters were comfortable frame buildings to the right and left of the parade. In the rear of the barracks was a row of log houses in which families of civilian employees were lodged. The commodious house of the commandant stood on the south side of the parade near the western angle. Back of this at some distance was a large log barn or stable, adjacent to which were stacks of hay which made good cover for attack. If Little Crow, the dominating chief of the lower Sioux, could have led his warriors against the fort directly after the slaughter of Marsh's men on Monday or early in the following morning, they might have made an easy capture and worked their will on the remnant of the soldiers and on the settlers who had fled to the shelter of the fort. This, had he so planned, he was unable to do because his young men in considerable numbers were widely dispersed, engaged in carnage and plunder, which to them was glorious work. The delay gave opportunity for reënforcing the garrison.[24]

[24] An anonymous manuscript, entitled "Fort Ridgely, Minnesota," in the possession of the Minnesota Historical Society, contains a full history of Fort Ridgely. The society has also manuscript histories of Fort Snelling and Fort Ripley in the same beautiful hand-writing and accompanied by maps and drawings. These histories were compiled in the war department and sent to the Minnesota Historical Society by order of Alexander Ramsey in 1880 when he was secretary of war. A note accompanying the history of Fort Snelling indicates that a person named Jasper W. Johnson, otherwise unknown, was the compiler or, perhaps, only the copier. The history of Fort Ridgely is composed chiefly of copies of printed documents. There is a tracing showing the lines of the military reservation, the creeks, and the location of the fort, and another showing the location of the buildings from

Before Captain Marsh moved out of Fort Ridgely on Monday forenoon he had the good sense and prescience to dispatch a messenger with an order of recall to overtake First Lieutenant Timothy J. Sheehan, who with a detachment of his Company C of the Fifth Minnesota Infantry had on Sunday marched for Fort Ripley, his proper station, from which he had lately been detached to reënforce the garrison at Fort Ridgely, as will later appear. A rapid night's march of forty miles brought this command, which was overtaken near Glencoe, to the fort before noon on Tuesday.[25] At five o'clock on Tuesday another reënforcement arrived at the fort. The enlistment fever then raging throughout the whole state had seized upon a number of young white men employed on the Indian reservations, whose terms of service were about to expire, and upon some of the mixed-blood idlers. Upon their solicitation Galbraith, the Sioux agent, began enlisting and in the week before the outbreak he had enrolled nearly fifty recruits and had started with them to Fort Snelling. He was in St. Peter with his men on the afternoon of the eighteenth and there "about sundown" he got the news of the massacre. There were in the town some fifty Harpers Ferry muskets with accouterments, which belonged to the state, but there was no ammunition. Galbraith got possession of the muskets, after executing a bond to the exacting custodian.

a survey made in 1874. The fort was on the northeast quarter of section 6, township 111, range 32 west. The *Mankato Daily Free Press* of August 23, 1917, gives an historical sketch of Fort Ridgely by Thomas Hughes, which he derived mainly from this manuscript. See also Wall, *Sioux Massacre*, 73-77, and the map and cuts of the fort on pages 37 and 38; Gere, in *Minnesota in the Civil and Indian Wars*, 1: 251; and an article by Benjamin H. Randall on the defense of Fort Ridgely, in the *Winona Daily Republican* of March 5, 1892. An interview in 1908 with Randall, who was sutler at Fort Ridgely at the time of the outbreak, is recorded in the author's notebooks, 5: 109. See the map on page 126, *ante*, and the sketch accompanying Randall to the author, February 1, 1908, in the Folwell Papers.

    [25] Gere, in *Minnesota in the Civil and Indian Wars*, 1: 245, 248, 251, 731. Marsh in his order to Sheehan said: "Return . . . immediately. . . . The Indians are raising hell at the Lower Agency." Sheehan's testimony is given in *Sisseton and Wahpeton Claim Case Record, Evidence for Defendant*, 271. In an interview with Colonel Timothy J. Sheehan on January 6, 1906, the author was given interesting details of this return march, of the attacks on the fort, of the battle of Birch Coulee, and of Sheehan's night ride to the fort to notify Sibley. This interview is recorded in the author's notebooks, 2: 140. See Holcombe, in *Minnesota in Three Centuries*, 3: 332, for the dispatch sent by Lieutenant Gere to Sheehan after midnight on August 19 to hasten his return. See *post*, p. 229.

Assisted by Lieutenant Norman K. Culver of the Fifth Minnesota Infantry, the agent collected powder, buckshot, and lead and set his men to making cartridges. At four o'clock in the morning of the nineteenth, when they were nearly ready to start to the fort, word was brought of the death of Marsh and the dispersion of his command. Late in the afternoon the garrison at Ridgely welcomed the arrival of Galbraith's "Renville Rangers," a reënforcement so much needed. Meantime the agent had written an account of the situation and dispatched it to Governor Ramsey. By this time two hundred and fifty refugees had come in and about twenty-five of the men at once willingly volunteered to fight, thus increasing Sheehan's force to some one hundred and eighty effectives. The interval allowed by the Indians seems to have been used as well as could be expected of inexperienced troops and commanders in preparing for defense and in picketing the converging roads.[26]

It was not until Wednesday the twentieth that a sufficient number of Sioux warriors could be collected, moved to the vicinity of the fort, and concealed in the surrounding ravines for an attack. At about one o'clock in the afternoon Little Crow appeared on horseback to the west of the post, apparently to obtain a conference, but probably to distract attention from an opposite quarter, from which a galling fire was suddenly opened. By a bold push a party actually drove in the skirmish line and reached the log dwellings in the rear of the barracks. Lieutenant Sheehan, on the alert, was not surprised. An attempt to hold his men in rank

[26] Galbraith, in Indian Office, *Reports*, 1863, p. 275; Gere, in *Minnesota in the Civil and Indian Wars*, 1: 251. For the roster of the Renville Rangers, see the latter work, 1: 780. Bryant and Murch, in their *Great Massacre*, 202, relate that the trader, Louis Robert, gave his bond for a thousand dollars to the custodian of the arms at St. Peter. For the original letters of Galbraith, Culver, and Henry A. Swift, and one signed by four citizens of St. Peter, all written to Governor Ramsey on August 18 and 19, see Governor's Archives, file 255. For conditions at the fort, see Galbraith to Ramsey, with Sheehan's addition, August 20, 1862, in Governor's Archives, file 255. John P. Usher, secretary of the interior, expressed the opinion that the zeal and patriotism of Galbraith which induced him to leave his post at so critical a moment was misdirected. See *Indian Tribes in the Northwest*, 3 (serial 1163). The inscriptions on the state monument erected in September, 1896, on the site of Fort Ridgely show a larger number of effectives by including more citizen defenders. *Minnesota in the Civil and Indian Wars*, 2: 193a.

on the parade he saw at once to be futile; he therefore ordered squads to various quarters of the post, with directions to get under cover and fire at will.

When in the previous year the United States troops were withdrawn from Fort Ridgely, which had been an artillery post, a number of cannon of various patterns and caliber and some ammunition were left behind and Ordnance Sergeant John Jones remained in charge of them. To vary the monotony of infantry drill a number of men of Company B, Fifth Minnesota, had been allowed to practice artillery loading and firing under Sergeant Jones. There were enough to form three gun detachments, and that number of pieces promptly put into position and efficiently served and bravely supported by the infantry soon drove the Indians back to their hiding places. The artillery fire was a surprise to Little Crow and he contented himself with maintaining a desultory distant fire upon the post until nightfall. Sergeant Jones in his report remarks with professional pride that his amateur artillerymen "gave much satisfaction . . . to all who witnessed the action."[27]

[27] Gere, in *Minnesota in the Civil and Indian Wars*, 1: 252; Wall, *Sioux Massacre*, 86; Randall, in the *Winona Republican*, March 5, 1892. In the *Central Republican* (Faribault), September 10, 1862, is a communication from John Whipple, a citizen volunteer and chief of one of Sergeant Jones's gun detachments. He states that upon an alarm given at 2:00 P.M. by a picket west of the fort, Lieutenant Sheehan posted twelve files of men in the grass sixty rods to the west; that after the Indians began firing on the southwest corner of the place, these men, being outflanked, returned inside. The commander endeavored to hold his men in rank near the flagstaff by threatening to cut down any man who should leave his place. After two or three of their number had fallen, the men broke ranks and ran for cover. The successful defense was due chiefly to the coolness and judgment of Sergeant Jones. On this point, see also Bryant and Murch, *Great Massacre*, 197, and a letter from A. B. Murch in the *Saint Paul Press* of September 6, 1862, in which he states that "*Jones saved the post.*" Bishop Whipple, in his *Lights and Shadows*, 130, says, "The Indians were kept at bay by Captain John Whipple and Sergeant Jones." Lieutenant Sheehan's report of August 26, 1862, is given in *Minnesota in the Civil and Indian Wars*, 2: 171. From the brevity of the account of the attack on Wednesday, August 20, it may be inferred that the commander did not consider it one of magnitude. He does state, however, that the large force of Indians was repulsed "in a great measure by the superior fire of the artillery, under . . . Ordnance Sergt. J. Jones." On September 11, 1901, in his testimony in *Sisseton and Wahpeton Claim Case Record, Evidence for Defendant*, 275, Colonel Sheehan is also very brief in his description of the attack on August 20 but he gives it a more serious character. He represents that the Indians "took possession of the outbuildings and drove away all the horses and mules, cattle, etc., and commenced firing on the garrison from every direction. On the north side they charged and got inside of my breastworks, where three of them were killed and one of my men were also killed and two wounded. They had pointed their guns through the window of Sergeant Jones's house on one side and the end door of the building

A heavy rain fell that night and did not cease until the afternoon of the following day, which passed without an attack, as did Thursday night and the forenoon of Friday the twenty-second. Meantime the garrison did what it could to strengthen its defenses. In the absence of intrenching tools, rough epaulements of sacks of oats and cordwood were arranged for the protection of the gunners. Water, which had to be procured from a spring to the south, was brought in at night. The refugees, constantly increasing in number, were put on half rations. Their anxiety and distress may be left to the reader's imagination.[28]

The Sioux leaders were by no means discouraged by the result of the affair of Wednesday and they resolved on a second attempt which should be a "grand affair."[29] To this resolution they were doubtless emboldened by a considerable accession of upper Indians, Wahpeton and Sisseton, to their fighting force. That these Indians joined in the massacres and battles as whole bands has been strenuously, and probably justly, denied. But such denials have ever been accompanied by admissions that many of the younger braves, whom the chiefs could not control, donned war paint, feathers, and breechcloth, mounted their ponies, and rode away on the warpath. The number of warriors collected for the new enterprise has commonly been put at eight hundred, but it may be questioned whether it reached that figure. In the forenoon of Friday the twenty-second the Indian force was quietly disposed in the

and fired several shots at his family." Sheehan in his testimony made no reference to the part played by the artillery. The report of Sergeant Jones, August 26, 1862, is in *Minnesota in the Civil and Indian Wars*, 2: 172. See also Flandrau, in the same work, 1: 733. Flandrau's story of the "spiking" of Sergeant Jones's cannon with old rags by deserters from the Renville Rangers, derived from Heard, *Sioux War*, 83, is farcical.

[28] Gere, in *Minnesota in the Civil and Indian Wars*, 1: 253; Bryant and Murch, *Great Massacre*, 191; Randall, in the *Winona Republican*, March 5, 1892; interview with Major Randall, August 23, 1908, recorded in the author's notebooks, 5: 110. Water had always been obtained from springs distant from the fort. At the time of the dedication of the monument in 1896, a drivewell sunk by R. I. Holcombe to a modest depth near the site of the commissary building furnished an abundant supply. Major Randall attended to hauling the water at the time of the siege.

[29] Big Eagle used this phrase in his story of the massacre, in *Minnesota Historical Collections*, 6: 392.

ravines near the fort and about one o'clock in the afternoon fire was opened from all quarters. The main attack, however, was made from the south and a lodgment was effected in the big log barn which covered a part of that front. Some shell from the artillery, however, soon set this on fire and dispersed the assailants. As the hours passed, firing was maintained from the northeast and other directions, accompanied by "demoniac yells," while preparation was being made for a decisive rush on the southwest angle through the ravine terminating near it. About four o'clock a daring chief led the assaulting party to the attack. As it was about to emerge from the timber a double charge of canister from one of Sergeant Jones's guns so disheartened the warriors that they recoiled and scattered to the rear out of range. The "grand affair" was over. Some discharges from a twenty-four-pounder gun which had been brought into play, sweeping different parts of the field, no doubt added to the panic.[30]

The defense of the place was conducted with so much discretion that but three lives were lost and thirteen persons wounded. The Indian loss was estimated by Lieutenant Gere at not less than one hundred. Four Indian witnesses in a celebrated case tried nearly forty years after could recall the names of only two. It was a well-known custom for Indians after a battle to conceal their dead and to carry off

[30] Accounts of Gere and Flandrau, in *Minnesota in the Civil and Indian Wars*, 1: 253-255, 733; Randall, in the *Winona Republican*, March 5, 1892; Sheehan's report, in *Minnesota in the Civil and Indian Wars*, 2: 171; interview with Dennis O'Shea, one of the artillery men in the defense of the fort, near Fort Ridgely, August 25, 1908, recorded in the author's notebooks, 5: 109. See also Sheehan's testimony in *Sisseton and Wahpeton Claim Case Record, Evidence for Defendant*, 275. One of the best accounts of the two battles is Captain McGrew's address in the *Pioneer Press* of August 24, 1896. The letters of Andrew J. Van Vorhes, dated August 20, 21, 25, in the *Pioneer and Democrat* and the *Saint Paul Press* of August 22, 24, 29, 1862, are clear in statement and free from frantic exaggeration. Van Vorhes was one of the party which brought the gold to Fort Ridgely on August 18. See *post*, p. 238. Holcombe, in *Minnesota in Three Centuries*, 3: 337, states that Chief Mankato was the leader in this assault, Little Crow having been temporarily disabled. For the same reason Little Crow was not present at the second battle of New Ulm on August 23. See also Heard, *Sioux War*, 83-85; Bryant and Murch, *Great Massacre*, 192-195; Holcombe, in *Minnesota in Three Centuries*, 3: 336-338; Big Eagle's story, in *Minnesota Historical Collections*, 6: 392; and a "write up" by Theodore M. Knappen in the *Minneapolis Journal* of March 12, 1898.

the wounded.   The result of the battles of Fort Ridgely was
well described by Chief Big Eagle in an interview with a
Minnesota historian.   "We thought the fort was the door
to the valley as far as to St. Paul, and that if we got through
the door nothing could stop us this side of the Mississippi.
But the defenders of the Fort were very brave and kept the
door shut."[31]

Reference was made on a preceding page to a demonstration made by a raiding party of Dakota braves on the afternoon of Tuesday, August 19, on the village of New Ulm.[32]
This party may have been an aggregate of the smaller groups

[31] Gere, in *Minnesota in the Civil and Indian Wars*, 1: 254; *Sisseton and Wahpeton Claim Case Record, Evidence for Defendant*, 288, 306, 336, 351; Satterlee, *Victims of the Indian Massacre*. The two Indians whose names were recalled by the witnesses were Iron Nest and Striped Wing Feather.  Compare Holcombe's account in *Minnesota in Three Centuries*, 3: 338, with that of Big Eagle, in *Minnesota Historical Collections*, 6: 392.
    The bronze medals presented by the state to the defenders bear in Dakota the motto, "Ti-yo-pa Na-ta-ka-pi," which translated means, "They kept the door shut."  The legislature of 1895 made an appropriation of three thousand dollars for the erection of a monument on the site of Fort Ridgely "to commemorate the attacks" on August 20 and 22, 1862. It was dedicated in an imposing ceremony on the twentieth of August of the following year. The principal address was made by Captain James G. McGrew.  The list of names of the military and of the armed citizens with checks showing the killed and wounded — sixty-one members of Company B, Fifth Infantry, fifty-five of Company C, forty-five of the Renville Rangers, fifty armed citizens, and nineteen women — is inscribed on the monument.  An account of the dedication and woodcuts of the medals presented to the defenders are in the *Pioneer Press* of August 21, 1896.  The issue for August 9, 1896, gives a copy of the inscriptions and a picture and description of the monument.  See *General Laws*, 1895, p. 774. On August 20, 1914, another monument absurdly out of place was unveiled on the site of Fort Ridgely.  It was erected at the expense of the state "to commemorate the loyalty of the Chippewa Indians and the valorous services of chief Mou-zoo-Maun-Nee rendered to the state of Minnesota during the Sioux war of 1862."  Concerning this monument, see *General Laws*, 1913, p. 582, and the Appendix, no. 5, *post*.
    [32] See *ante*, p. 121.  In the spring of 1855 seven houses were built upon a site previously selected by an advance party, members of the Chicago Land Verein.  They were Swabians and they gave the place the name of their home city.  A year later they were joined by members of the Colonization Society of North America, a German organization from Cincinnati. The two were merged into the German Land Association of Minnesota in 1857.  The growth of the village was so rapid that the census of 1860 showed a population of 635 people.  By the time of the outbreak it had probably increased to 900.  In regard to the founding of New Ulm, see Fritsche, *Brown County*, 1:124-140, and R. L. Polk, ed., *The County of Brown, Minnesota*, 56-66, 83 (St. Paul, 1905).  On August 24, 1908, the author had an interview in New Ulm with William Skinner and Richard Pfefferle, residents of that place, both of whom were present in the principal battle of 1862.  Their accounts added personal incidents to what was already known.  On the following morning, under the guidance of Mr. Pfefferle, a study was made of the topography of the place and the sites of the barricades, the ferries, and other principal points were identified.  The results are recorded in the author's notebooks, 5: 119.  In November, 1917, at the request of the author, Mr. Franklin F. Holbrook, at the time field secretary of the Minnesota Historical Society, devoted some days to a careful study of the topography of New Ulm and its vicinity and collected a body of information from survivors.  The author gladly acknowledges his indebtedness to Mr. Holbrook for confirmation of his previous conclusions and much new

which had been doing the murders in the neighboring town of Milford earlier in the day, or it may have been a separate detachment. It was after three o'clock when the Indians dismounted in the rear of the town, advanced to the crest of the terrace next back of the place, and began firing. The reports of refugees and of relief parties sent out from New Ulm the previous day had given good reason for expecting an attack and some preparation had been made for meeting it. The people had been collected into the business part of the town, barricades had been erected about three blocks apart on the principal street and between the buildings fronting thereon, and an organization of some of the able-bodied men present had been made. The few citizens who were armed with rifles replied as effectively as was possible at so long range on enemies of whom little could be seen. The Indians' fire was not hot enough to deter a party of resolute men from advancing to a house well outside of the barricades. Half of the number pushed out to a house still farther away, but they were presently forced to retire. At half past four a dense rain cloud arose from the southwest, with thunder and lightning, followed by a dash of rain. When that had ceased in the course of half an hour, no Indians were to be seen. So ended what has been called the "First Battle of New Ulm." At the first fire a girl of thirteen, who had ventured into the street against warning, was shot dead. There were no other casualties of importance. About the time the Indians were withdrawing, the hearts of the townsmen were cheered by the arrival of sixteen mounted men from St. Peter under the head of L. M. Boardman, the sheriff of Nicollet County.[33]

information. From Mr. Holbrook's survey it appears that New Ulm is situated on a terrain which extends from the Minnesota River to the high bluff 6,000 feet distant and nearly parallel to the stream, the flow of which is about due south. Next to the river is a stretch of alluvium 2,100 feet in width and rising suddenly above this is a bench or terrace 1,300 feet wide, on which the business quarter of the town is built. This slopes gradually upward to a crest from which a second terrace 2,600 feet wide falls off gradually to a slough running the length of the town at the foot of the main bluff. Folwell Papers.

[33] See the Appendix, no. 3, for a symposium of varying accounts of this battle. The personnel of the party which made the sally to the outlying houses has remained a matter of dispute, but Daniel Shillock was probably the leader. See the map on page 140, *post.*

The news of the outbreak at the lower agency reached
St. Peter "about sundown" of the same day, August 18.
Why the tidings were not spread through the place and the
citizens roused that evening remains a matter for wonder.
They slept in peace until the arrival, between three and four
o'clock in the following morning, of the messenger sent from
New Ulm. It is not known to whom the message was addressed, but at four o'clock William B. Dodd, the first citizen
of St. Peter in point of time and influence, was dispatching
messengers to arouse the settlers of the surrounding neighborhoods. Having delivered his message, the same envoy
passed on through the town to the house of Charles E.
Flandrau, associate justice of the state supreme court, a
mile away at Traverse des Sioux.[34]

That a summons had been addressed to this personage
need not be wondered at. Some one has said that Judge
Flandrau was the best-known man in the state after Governor Ramsey. Certainly he was so known in the Minnesota
Valley. After leaving school at the age of thirteen he went
to sea for about two years and then gave three years to a
mechanical trade. Next he studied law and, after two
years' practice at the bar in New York, his native state, he
came to Minnesota in 1853 at the age of twenty-five. Not
long after he settled at "The Traverse," which was soon to
become a city of great expectations, but nothing more.
His enterprise, physical vigor, wit, and bonhomie soon
gained him friends, and his influence with juries rapidly
extended his reputation. In 1856 his neighbors sent him to
the territorial Council and in the same year President Pierce
appointed him agent for the Sioux Indians. While holding
that office he sat in the constitutional convention, where,
as we have seen, he was a conspicuous figure. Still in the
same year, 1857, President Buchanan permitted him to

[34] Galbraith, in Indian Office, *Reports*, 1863, p. 275; Asa W. Daniels, "Reminiscences
of the Little Crow Uprising," in *Minnesota Historical Collections*, 15: 323-336; Flandrau, in
*Minnesota in the Civil and Indian Wars*, 1: 731. For a biographical sketch of William B.
Dodd, accompanied by his portrait, see William G. Gresham, ed., *History of Nicollet and
LeSueur Counties*, 2: 128-131 (Indianapolis, 1916).

exchange his Indian agency for a seat on the supreme bench of the territory. At the first state election, which was held in that year, he was elected to the same position, from which he resigned in 1864, before the expiration of his term. The *Minnesota Reports* bear testimony to his industry, acumen, and sound judgment, but contemporaries were of the opinion that Flandrau was at his best at the bar. The arena and the forum were congenial to his nature. A colleague said of him: "He was not of the ordinary type of man. He was original, unique, picturesque, versatile, adventurous; and his career is illuminated by the light of an heroic spirit."[35]

It was to this "cavalier of the border" that the affrighted people of New Ulm naturally and confidently turned when refugees were streaming in with their dead and wounded and their tales of rapine and murder. They were not to be disappointed. Without delay Flandrau sent the message on down the valley and hastened to St. Peter, where he found "the situation . . . fully comprehended" and the people aroused and alert but without organization. More than a hundred volunteers were soon enrolled and they elected him their captain and William B. Dodd his lieutenant. Arms, ammunition, blankets, food, and transportation were assembled with all possible expedition. Before noon the party of sixteen mounted men, afterwards called "the Boardman Cavalry" from the name of their leader, took the road, as already stated, to reach New Ulm in the afternoon about the time the Indians disappeared. The main body of volunteers started in wagons at one o'clock and, swelled by accessions from Le Sueur until it numbered about 125, reached the Redstone Ferry about two miles below New Ulm at eight o'clock in the evening. It was probably about ten o'clock when the column, having crossed

[35] Greenleaf Clark, "The Life and Influence of Judge Flandrau," in *Minnesota Historical Collections*, 10: 771-782 (part 2); William H. Lightner, "Judge Flandrau as a Citizen and Jurist," in *Minnesota Historical Collections*, 10: 819-828 (part 2). A biographical sketch of Judge Flandrau by Isaac Atwater, an intimate friend, is in the *Magazine of Western History*, 7: 655-666 (April, 1888).

the river, entered the central part of the town. Guarded by
a line of sentinels, the townsmen and their guests passed
the night in security, if not in repose.[36]

Of all the frontier towns of the valley New Ulm was most
exposed to Indian attack. By native instinct the savages
had selected it and Fort Ridgely as their proximate objec-
tives. Could they capture either place, the other would be

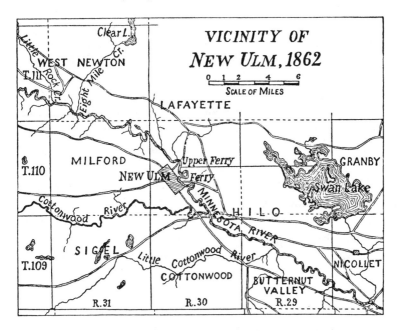

VICINITY OF
NEW ULM, 1862

SCALE OF MILES

likely to share its fortune. The whites also instinctively
divined the probability of an attack in force and resolved to
be prepared for it. The next two days were spent in waiting
and in preparation. The able-bodied men of the place were
now organized into several companies and were equipped
as well as the circumstances permitted. The need of a
superior authority was of course apparent and the officers

[36] Flandrau, in *Minnesota in the Civil and Indian Wars*, 1: 731; Thomas Hughes and
others, *History of the Welsh in Minnesota*, 77 ([Mankato], 1895); Salmon A. Buell, "Judge
Flandrau in the Defense of New Ulm during the Sioux Outbreak of 1862," in *Minnesota
Historical Collections*, 10: 784-789 (part 2).

of the companies elected Justice Flandrau to the command
and gave him the honorary title of colonel with permission
to appoint his assistants. He at once named William B.
Dodd his second in command. For the important duties of
"provost marshal, chief of staff and general manager,"
he chose Salmon A. Buell, a citizen of St. Peter who had
served in the navy and who had ideas about organization.
A provost guard was established for the maintenance of
order, the barricades were better connected and strengthened, and some elementary military exercises were practiced.
On the twentieth a hundred men came in from Mankato,
and on that day or the next a company from South Bend,
another of the ephemeral cities of the time, arrived. Two
companies from Le Sueur and three from Nicollet County,
of unequal numbers, materially increased the force of defenders. The men from South Bend left on hearing a report
that their homes were in danger from the Winnebago.[37]

On Saturday morning, the twenty-third, the smoke of
burning farmhouses and stacks of hay and grain was seen
arising off to the northeast beyond the Minnesota River.
Colonel Flandrau thought it possible that the Sioux had
captured Fort Ridgely and were coming down in triumph
on that side of the river to attack New Ulm. The ruse was
partially successful. To ascertain the design of his enemy
and, if necessary and possible, to give him a check, the commander sent Lieutenant William Huey of Traverse des Sioux
with a detachment of seventy-five men across the river.
The extent of the opposition which he met with is not known,
but it was sufficient to cause that leader to retire with his
party along the road to St. Peter. At Nicollet about fourteen miles away he met Captain E. St. Julien Cox coming
with his company of "Frontier Avengers." With some part

[37] Flandrau, in *Minnesota in the Civil and Indian Wars*, 1: 732; Buell, in *Minnesota Historical Collections*, 10: 789-791 (part 2). It is traditional that Dodd desired the chief command but that the majority voted against him because they feared that he would be too reckless of danger. See the map on page 140, *post*.

of his command he joined that body and marched back
to New Ulm the next day.[38]

After this unfortunate depletion about 250 guns were left
to defend the place against a foe of double that number at
least, already forming in battle array a mile to the west of
the town. The terrace slopes gently upward for about a
third of a mile to a crest, whence the higher bench or terrace
slopes also gently to the high bluff of the valley. The Indian
leaders leisurely deployed their warriors near the foot of the
bluff in a thin line which extended the whole length of the
town, with flanks curved forward, thus threatening a complete envelopment.

Under Colonel Flandrau's direction Captain Dodd put his
men in line just behind the crest separating the two slopes
and his skirmishers well out on the higher bench. The
advance of the Indians, as described by Colonel Flandrau,
"upon the sloping prairie in the bright sunlight was a very
fine spectacle." The movement, at first slow, increased in

[38] Flandrau's report of August 27, 1862, in *Minnesota in the Civil and Indian Wars*,
2: 203-207. Flandrau says: "I thought it best to send a detachment to ascertain the
design of the enemy, and if possible, give him a check. Lieutenant Huey . . . volunteering
to perform the service, I detailed 75 men with him, and they crossed at the ferry opposite
the town about 9 o'clock A.M." In his narrative in the same work, 1: 732, he says: "Lieutenant Wm. Huey having gone with about 75 men to guard the approach by the ferry, and
crossing to the other side of the river was cut off and forced to retreat toward St. Peter. It
was simply a mistake in judgment to put the river between himself and the main force."
So it was, but whose? In his *Minnesota*, 153, Judge Flandrau repeats the language of his
narrative. Bryant and Murch, in their *Great Massacre*, 166, say, "The commandant here
made the mistake of detailing seventy-five of his men, who were well armed . . . to go
across the river." Lieutenant Huey came upon a large body of Indians and retreated before
them to the ferry by which he had crossed. Here he was fired on from the New Ulm side.
Some thirty of his men broke and ran. The remainder retreated to Nicollet and joined Cox.
In regard to Huey's losses, see Bryant and Murch, *Great Massacre*, 167, and Buell, in
*Minnesota Historical Collections*, 10: 794 (part 2). The question naturally arises why Huey
did not retire downstream to the Redstone Ferry, effect a crossing there if possible, and
attack the Indians on their left rear, instead of chasing off across the prairie exposed to
ambush and flank attack for fifteen miles. See Jacob Nix, *Der Ausbruch der Sioux-Indianer
in Minnesota, im August, 1862*, 39 (New Ulm, 1887), for a statement about the Huey
detachment which differs from the other accounts. A party of over a hundred men, Nix
relates, was ordered across the Minnesota and was cut off completely by a superior force of
the enemy; and the captain and several men were lost. Buell, in *Minnesota Historical
Collections*, 10: 794 (part 2), states that "He [Colonel Flandrau] deemed it prudent to send a
detachment, large enough to reconnoiter in force on the other side of the river," and that
Lieutenant Huey "was sent . . . with additional instructions to reconnoiter well at and
about the ferry before crossing." Heard, in his *Sioux War*, 120, says that "The men under
Captain Cox, who reached New Ulm on Sunday morning, were dispatched by Colonel Sibley
[*from St. Peter*] on Saturday."

velocity and when they were "within about double rifle-shot" the savages raised "a terrific yell and came down . . . like the wind" on the waiting line of citizen soldiers. But the

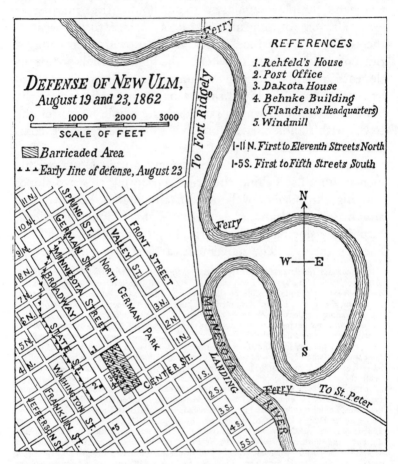

line did not wait long; the terrific yell followed by rifle shots unsettled the men and the whole army broke for the rear. The men stopped only when they were safe inside the barricades and the adjacent buildings. The Sioux swept on but, instead of rushing over the barricades pell-mell with the citizens, they halted, separated into groups, and took possession of abandoned outer buildings and other cover. Flandrau and his aids strove "with good effect" to rally and reform the line. The panic soon passed and courage came back, and the Indians found it beneficial to keep out of sight. A group of marksmen, of whom there were many, was established in the windmill and another group occupied the brick post office. A brisk fusillade from them kept the savages at bay about the upper part of town. "It got to be," says Colonel Flandrau, "a regular Indian skirmish, in which every man did his own work after his own fashion." It must indeed have been a very lively skirmish to have caused a loss of "60 men in about an hour and a half, 10 killed and 50 wounded." To prevent the occupation of nearer buildings by the Indians, adventurous individuals bravely crept out and set them on fire. The Indians also fired some buildings. An open space was thus formed, over which they did not care to advance.

A large body of the attacking force at length concentrated about the lower part of town, where they set fire to many buildings, hoping to have the flames carried into the barricaded area by the brisk south wind. At two o'clock Colonel Flandrau saw that a check must be given to the steady approach of the Indians upon his southern barricade. A concentration of Indians on the easterly side of the main street and behind buildings, apparently in preparation for an assault, gave Colonel Flandrau some concern when he remembered that his "boys had proved unequal" to resist the stampede of the morning. As he had anticipated, a party of some sixty Indians came charging furiously around a sheltering grove of oaks. To the commander's satisfaction and, perhaps, surprise, his boys "stood firmly, and advanced with a cheer, routing the rascals like sheep." Two of the brave defenders were killed and others were wounded. A volley from the barricade at short range now settled the fortunes of the day. The Indians continued to fire occasional shots from close cover until dark. When night fell the commander ordered all the remaining buildings outside the barricades—"some forty" in number—to be fired; 190 structures in all were thus destroyed by the Indians and the defenders. The following night passed in anxiety, but without attack or alarm. On Sunday morning a few Indians appeared and indulged in some harmless long-range shooting and drove off, or attempted to drive off, some wandering cattle.[39]

This was no sham battle, no trivial affair, but an heroic defense of a beleaguered town against a much superior force of infuriated savages alive to the strategic advantage of a capture and keen for scalps and plunder. It cost the lives of twenty-six citizen soldiers and wounds for many more. Seven of the total number killed were members of Captain John Belm's company of New Ulm—good proof that there were Germans in New Ulm who could fight. Six belonged to Captain Flandrau's St. Peter Frontier Guards.[40]   Among

[39] See *ante*, p. 134, n. 32; Buell, in *Minnesota Historical Collections*, 10: 794-803 (part 2); Flandrau, in *Minnesota in the Civil and Indian Wars*, 1: 732, and his report, in the same work, 2: 203-207.  In the Folwell Papers there is a copy of a statement made by Andrew Friend to Thomas Hughes, on August 23, 1913.  Friend took part in the affair on August 19 and in the battle of the twenty-third.  His recollections are coherent and they corroborate the best accounts, but it may be doubted that he made so many killings with his trusty double-barreled rifle as he remembers.  Flandrau, in his report, says that the fact that the wind was from the lower part of the town directed the larger part of the enemy to that point; in his narrative, he merely speaks of a "great conflagration . . . raging . . . in the lower part of the town"; while in his *Minnesota*, 151, he states that the main body took "possession of the lower end of the main [*Minnesota*] street below the barricades."  See also Buell, in *Minnesota Historical Collections*, 10: 795, 798 (part 2).  There is reason for believing that a considerable number of Indians had stealthily crept down opposite the lower part of the town over the low ground between the first terrace and the river.  In his report, Flandrau gives the number killed in the charge as two.  In his *Minnesota*, 155, he says, "I lost four men killed in this exploit."  In the latter he says that the Indians were chased for at least half a mile and then held at bay by the brave sallying party until six or seven o'clock.  From that position the commander sent back a party which burned every building outside the barricade in that quarter.  "We then abandoned our saw logs and returned to the town, and the day was won."  See the statement of Captain Nix, in his *Ausbruch der Sioux-Indianer*, 36.  Buell, in *Minnesota Historical Collections*, 10: 799 (part 2), says that there were two killed and several wounded.  The Reverend Robert J. Creswell, in his *Among the Sioux. A Story of the Twin Cities and the Two Dakotas*, 27 (Minneapolis, 1906), says: "Little Crow . . . was the acknowledged leader of the Indian forces. . . . He had under his control a large force of Indian warriors armed with Winchesters; and on the morning of the battle, he mustered on the hills around New Ulm, the largest body of Indian cavalry ever gathered together in America."  This is not an unusual exaggeration.

[40] Flandrau, in *Minnesota in the Civil and Indian Wars*, 1: 732; 2: 206.  See Sheriff Charles Roos to Ramsey, September 15, 1862, and Roos's sketch map of New Ulm showing the buildings left after the fire, in Governor's Archives, file 255.  The monument erected on the

those whose lives were sacrificed was Captain William B. Dodd, the second in command. Observing, as it is related, some men in white man's dress approaching from the south, he presumed that they were Huey's detachment or a part of it returning to the combat or, if not, some other reenforcement. He at once mounted and started out, followed by a party of volunteers on foot, to welcome the men or, perhaps, to give them warning of the danger of a flank attack. He had ridden but a short distance beyond the southern barricade when he and his horse received several shots apiece from Indians in hiding. He wheeled the animal around and rode back to or near to the barricade, where he was received by his friends. He was carried into a building outside the barricade and died soon afterwards. He was the founder of the village of St. Peter and was widely known and respected for his character and his services. His was a stalwart figure and, if likenesses may be trusted, he was endowed with unusual manly beauty.[41]

The numbers of the enemy have been variously estimated. In his report to Governor Ramsey, Colonel Flandrau suggests 350; but in his revised estimate in his narrative he places the number at 650, as advised by intelligent mixed-bloods, whom he had consulted in the meantime. The Indian losses

New Ulm battle ground gives the names of twenty-four killed in the battle of New Ulm. See "Notes to Judge Flandrau's Narrative," in *Minnesota in the Civil and Indian Wars*, 1:818f. Flandrau's first estimate, in his report, was ten killed. In his *Minnesota*, 156, he adds four to the number killed. Buell, in *Minnesota Historical Collections*, 10:800 (part 2), gives the number of killed as nine and that of the severely wounded as about fifty; but on page 814 he increases the number to "10 killed and 51 wounded." Satterlee, in his *Victims of the Indian Massacre*, gives the number of killed in this battle as twenty-six.

[41] Buell, in *Minnesota Historical Collections*, 10:798 (part 2). Flandrau, in his report, in *Minnesota in the Civil and Indian Wars*, 2:205, states that Captain Dodd "charged down the street" accompanied by "someone else"; in his *Minnesota*, 152, he says: "my first lieutenant, William B. Dodd, galloped down the main street," and gives the impression that he was alone and without aim; while in his narrative, in *Minnesota in the Civil and Indian Wars*, 1:732, no mention is made of the event. Sources agree for the most part in placing the fall of Captain Dodd at or about noon, certainly before Flandrau's final charge about three o'clock. But Dr. A. W. Daniels, one of the surgeons present who attended his brave townsman and friend in his last moments, places the event not earlier than five o'clock and Dodd's death as occurring about six o'clock. See Daniels, in *Minnesota Historical Collections*, 15:330; Daniels to the author, October 9, 23, 25, December 7, 1917, July 29, 1921, in the Folwell Papers; and Nix, *Ausbruch der Sioux-Indianer*, 35. Nix states that Dodd was accompanied by one Krieger of Milford.

remain a matter of conjecture.[42]  His own force Colonel
Flandrau at the time estimated at two hundred and fifty;
but in his narrative he places the number of effectives, after
the departure of the South Bend company, the Huey detachment, and some individuals, at not over two hundred.  The
total number of names on the rosters of the companies that
participated is between eight hundred and nine hundred.
As the lists were not made, or at least were not fully made,
at the time, it may be presumed that persons only construc-
tively present may have had their names inscribed on the
roll of fame.[43]

For five days some twelve hundred noncombatants had
been cooped up in the small area within the barricades.  The
women and children had been "huddled in cellars and close
rooms like sheep in a cattle car."  In a consultation of officers
on Sunday afternoon it was resolved to abandon further
defense and to evacuate the place.  At nine o'clock on the
following morning a column was formed of 153 wagons carrying the women, the young children, and the wounded, and
followed or flanked by others on foot.  A melancholy proces-
sion, it took the road to Mankato, about thirty miles away
to the southeast.  After the ford of the Cottonwood had been
crossed the road lay over open prairie.  The distance was
covered in a single march without molestation, but Colonel
Flandrau with 150 men halted at a point about halfway to
repel a possible night attack on his rear.  On the morning
of the twenty-sixth he moved on to Mankato, where his

[42] Flandrau, in *Minnesota in the Civil and Indian Wars*, 1:732; 2:204.  In his *Minnesota*,
151, Flandrau says that the Indian forces were "some six hundred strong."  Buell, in
*Minnesota Historical Collections*, 10:812 (part 2), estimates their number as "at least 650,
and probably 1,000 or more."  In *Sisseton and Wahpeton Claim Case Record, Evidence for
Defendant*, 295, 336, 352, 362, three Indian witnesses estimated the number to be about
seven hundred, and a fourth, about eight hundred.  Three of these witnesses gave the
number of killed as two and gave no testimony as to the number of wounded.  The notable
concurrence of these witnesses in this and in other points suggests previous conspiracy or
instruction.  Flandrau, in his *Minnesota*, 156, states that after the fight they "found
ten dead Indians in burned houses, and in chaparral."  No corroboration of this has been
discovered.
[43] Flandrau, in *Minnesota in the Civil and Indian Wars*, 1:733; 2:204.  For the rosters
see the same work, 1:754, 757, 758, 760, 764, 767, 770, 774, 776, 818a, 818b.

extemporized army, "being barefooted, overworked and required at their homes," disintegrated.[44]

Within two days after their disastrous assault on New Ulm the Indian warriors with their families, their captives, their camping outfits, and their plunder began a movement in retreat up the west side of the Minnesota. On the twenty-eighth they encamped near the Hazelwood mission five miles above the upper agency, where for the present we may leave them.[45]

It was but natural that the white people of Minnesota should suspect that the infection would spread to the other Indian nations residing within the borders of the state — the Winnebago on their small reservation in Blue Earth County and the Chippewa, who were still roaming over the immense ceded tracts in the northern wildernesses, although they were supposed to be residing on their reservations. Some testimony was later adduced that the Winnebago chief, Little Priest, and a dozen of his warriors took part in one of the battles of Fort Ridgely, but General Sibley's court-martial failed to convict them when they were arraigned for it in November. The Winnebago agent in his report for 1862 testified to the undoubted loyalty of his wards.[46] There

[44] Flandrau, in *Minnesota in the Civil and Indian Wars*, 1:733; 2:206. See also his *Minnesota*, 156-158. In his report Colonel Flandrau estimates "the inhabitants, women and children, sick and wounded, to the number of about 2,000"; in his narrative he suggests "about 1,200 to 1,500 non-combatants, consisting of women, children, refugees and unarmed citizens"; in his history, he gives the same numbers. A. W. Daniels, in *Minnesota Historical Collections*, 15:333, sharply criticizes the abandonment of the place, which was ordered without a consultation with the medical officers. Captain E. St. Julien Cox, in his formal report to Governor Ramsey, September 1, 1862, in Governor's Archives, file 255, says: "I will here state I differed with the others on this point and desired to remain with my Command but was overrulled. I think the town *should* have been held and the frontier thus protected." Colonel Flandrau states in his report that the evacuation was determined upon in "a council of the officers," but adds, "all the people decided that they would abandon the town the first opportunity." Such being the case, an orderly evacuation was better than disorderly flight. See also Flandrau to Ramsey, August 20, 1862, in *Minnesota in the Civil and Indian Wars*, 2:165. Nix, in his *Ausbruch der Sioux-Indianer*, 43, suggests that Colonel Flandrau was persuaded to undertake the exodus by persons expecting some personal advantage therefrom, but this is difficult to imagine.

[45] Brown, *In Captivity*, 14 (serial 4029).

[46] Proceedings of the Military Commission; *Sisseton and Wahpeton Claim Case Record, Evidence for Defendant*, 277, 288, 307, 347. The witnesses' estimates of the number of

was some ground for a rumor which spread far and wide that the Chippewa, or some of them, had made peace with the Sioux and were coming down in thousands to massacre the whites. There was in fact a small disturbance among two or three bands of the Chippewa of the Mississippi resulting in some trifling depredations, which alarmed many people and frightened one person to death. It was suppressed without bloodshed after the assemblage of troops and a tedious series of councils.[47]

Winnebago present at the battle of Fort Ridgely varied from none to thirty-five. See also Indian Office, *Reports*, 1862, pp. 22, 58, 93 (Agent Balcombe's report of September 15, 1862); *Official Records*, series 1, vol. 13, p. 694. See Bryant and Murch, *Great Massacre*, 460, for the discharge of Little Priest and eleven Winnebago by a military court. Nix, in his *Ausbruch der Sioux-Indianer*, 22, reports a statement of Little Priest that there was an agreement with Little Crow under which the Winnebago would have attacked Mankato as soon as the Sioux leader had captured New Ulm. The statement may be doubted.

[47] See the Appendix, no. 4, *post*, for an account of the Chippewa disturbance of 1862.

## VI. THE INDIAN CAMPAIGN OF 1862

IT WAS noon of Tuesday the nineteenth of August when the messenger sent by Agent Galbraith from St. Peter the previous evening reached Governor Ramsey in St. Paul with the tidings of the outbreak. The governor at once drove over to Fort Snelling to ascertain what troops could be got ready for movement. At three o'clock in the afternoon arrived Sergeant William J. Sturgis, who had been sent to that post the previous evening at eight forty-five o'clock by Lieutenant Thomas P. Gere, in command at Fort Ridgely. His dispatch brought the additional news of the slaughter of Captain Marsh's men.[1] On the instant Governor Ramsey perceived that he had to do with an Indian insurrection of magnitude and he lost not a minute in nice consideration of his constitutional war powers. Nor did he need to consume time in comparing the claims and qualifications of aspirants to command. There was one who was as eminently qualified for the position as he was incapable of seeking it, Ramsey's old political foe and personal friend, Henry H. Sibley; and it was to him that Governor Ramsey instantly turned. Sibley, still in middle life, was robust and athletic and accustomed to outdoor life; he was widely experienced in great affairs and greatly trusted and respected; he spoke the French and understood the Dakota language; he was familiar with the Sioux country and acquainted with many of the leading men of the four tribes; and, above all, he

[1] The *Saint Paul Press* of August 20, 1862, says: "Yesterday noon Mr. Wm. H. Shelley arrived in this city . . . with dispatches from Thos. J. Galbraith. . . . Before evening, other messengers arrived." Governor Ramsey in his message to the legislature, September 9, in *Executive Documents*, 1862, p. 5, says, "When the first vague news of the revolt at Red Wood was received on the evening of the 19th, I hastened immediately to Fort Snelling." The *Pioneer and Democrat* of August 20 says that Ramsey received Lieutenant Gere's dispatch "yesterday afternoon." See also Galbraith, in Indian Office, *Reports*, 1863, p. 275. For a description of Sturgis' ride, see Wall, *Sioux Massacre*, 110-117, and a copy of a letter from Sturgis to Wall, dated December 23, 1907, in the Folwell Papers. See also Gere, in *Minnesota in the Civil and Indian Wars*, 1:250.

possessed a profound knowledge of Indian character and habits. Ramsey at once drove over to Mendota, where Sibley was still living in his stone house, and laid the duty upon him. The same evening a commission of colonel and commander of the Indian expedition was placed in Sibley's hands.[2]

On the following morning Sibley was moving up the Minnesota by steamboat with four companies of the Sixth Minnesota Infantry not yet mustered into the United States service. That night he disembarked and bivouacked at Shakopee and the next day he marched to Belle Plaine, where he found the people "absolutely crazy with excitement." A further march of thirty miles brought him and his little command to St. Peter late on Friday the twenty-second. Here he learned from Jack Frazer, the half-breed, who had stolen out of Fort Ridgely, the nature and the magnitude of the task before him. It was not the mere pursuit and arrest of some crazy chief and a deluded band; the whole body of the annuity Sioux, it appeared, numbering over seven thousand, was in open war. Their fifteen hundred warriors, many mounted and, for Indians, well armed, were to be fought and subdued. The whole Sioux nation out to the Missouri, twenty-five thousand strong, might be rising. Four companies of raw infantry ill armed and equipped and utterly undisciplined were no adequate force for an offensive movement.[3]

[2] Nathaniel West, *The Ancestry, Life, and Times of Hon. Henry Hastings Sibley, LL.D.*, 254 (St. Paul, 1889); report of the adjutant general, in *Executive Documents*, 1862, p. 267; Governor Ramsey's message, in *Executive Documents*, 1862, p. 5. For a diary of the campaign, see the extracts from Sibley's letters to his wife, August 21 to November 4, 1862, in the Sibley Papers.

[3] Sibley to his wife, August 21, 24, 1862, Sibley Papers; *Minnesota in the Civil and Indian Wars*, 2: 165-198; West, *Sibley*, 255. See Edwin Bell, "Early Steamboating on the Minnesota and Red Rivers," in *Minnesota Historical Collections*, 10: 99 (part 1), for the commandeering of the steamboat on the Minnesota River. On Frazer, see *ante*, 1: 298 and note.

Four unpublished letters from Sibley to Ramsey in Governor's Archives, file 255, contain interesting details. From Shakopee on August 20 Sibley writes that he is sending Captain Grant to Fort Ridgely by way of Glencoe and that he himself will proceed to St. Peter and, if necessary, to Mankato, New Ulm, and Fort Ridgely. He has no advice to give about reënforcements. In a second letter of the same date he asks for a supply of Springfield rifles, stating that all the men needed can be got in the upper valley. On the twenty-first, writing from Belle Plaine, he reports that it is almost certain that Fort Ridgely

Colonel Sibley wisely, as he believed, halted at St. Peter and waited for more men, for arms, for ammunition, for subsistence, and for transportation. Governor Ramsey and his adjutant general, Oscar Malmros, responded to his requisition with great activity. Six companies of the Sixth Minnesota Infantry were filled up by transfer and consolidation, armed with Springfield rifles intended for another regiment, and dispatched to the front.[4] On the twenty-first Governor Ramsey issued his proclamation calling on the militia of the valley counties to report to the commander of the expedition with horses, arms, and a few days' subsistence. The response was gratifying. On the next day squads of mounted men armed in motley fashion were pouring "in a living stream up the Minnesota Valley." At the end of three days Sibley had a force of some fourteen hundred men, including three hundred very irregular cavalry. They were ill provided with supplies, and for transportation the teams and wagons of reluctant farmers had to be impressed.[5]

has been destroyed and that he has ordered Captain Grant to rejoin him at St. Peter. He repeats his requisition for Springfield rifles. "But for Heaven's sake, send me no more Austrian rifles, for they are in many cases utterly worthless & unserviceable." He says that he will leave "tomorrow morning in teams." At 10:00 P.M. of the same day in a second letter he calls for five hundred additional men officered by the best men and armed with Springfield rifles, and a goodly supply of fixed ammunition. "If they are not wanted, so much the better, the effect will be good, and reassuring to the people. In such an emergency, the expense cannot properly be considered."

[4] Report of the adjutant general, in *Executive Documents*, 1862, pp. 235-237, 243, 269, 418. The command of the suddenly gathered Sixth Minnesota was at first intrusted to Captain A. D. Nelson, U. S. A., who at the time was on duty at Fort Snelling as mustering officer. He accepted, joined the regiment, and made a day's march. It then occurred to him that as an officer of the regular army it was improper for him to serve as a subordinate to a colonel of state militia without leave from the war department. He therefore resigned his commission in the morning of the next day. William Crooks of St. Paul, who had been for two years a cadet at West Point and then engaged as engineer in constructing the first section of what is now the Great Northern Railroad, was appointed and at once took command. The resignation of Captain Nelson has been the occasion of sharp criticism. See Holcombe, in *Minnesota in Three Centuries*, 3:392. For Colonel Crooks's view, see Johnson, in *Minnesota in the Civil and Indian Wars*, 1:303.

[5] *Minnesota in the Civil and Indian Wars*, 2:193b; report of the adjutant general, in *Executive Documents*, 1862, pp. 418, 236. In a letter to Ramsey, dated August 21, Sibley says: "Alex. Faribault is said to be at St Peter with a company of men from Faribault waiting for me." See also two letters from Major William J. Cullen, former superintendent of Indian affairs of the northern superintendency, to Ramsey, dated August 22 and 23. In the latter, which was written at dark, Cullen says: "I have in all Two Hundred Men." They had organized as the "Cullen Frontier Guards." He was expecting the arrival at Henderson of the Minneapolis company in a few minutes. These letters are in Governor's Archives, file 255. The three companies mentioned aggregated four hundred men.

On the twenty-fifth Colonel Sibley in a general order gave his "army" a temporary organization. It consisted of the Sixth Minnesota, under Colonel William Crooks; a regimental organization of all mounted volunteers to be consolidated into full companies, under the command of Colonel Samuel McPhail, who had been a captain of volunteers in Mexico; and a regimental organization of all unattached unmounted men, under the command of Lieutenant Colonel Stephen H. Fowler. This last "organization" seems not to have been organized in fact. These regimental commanders were directed to complete their organizations and to furnish muster rolls. William H. Forbes, George A. Nourse, and Alexander Faribault were named as aids.[6]

On the following day a march of six miles was made toward Fort Ridgely. A "vanguard" of Colonel McPhail's mounted men, which continued the march through the night, arrived at the fort early in the morning of the twenty-seventh, to the great joy of the beleaguered garrison and refugees. In the afternoon of Thursday the twenty-eighth the whole "army" came up and was established in a well-disposed camp outside the fort. A large number of the refugees who had been shut up in the fort from the first day of the outbreak were sent to St. Paul the next day in the wagons which had brought up subsistence for the troops.[7]

For ten days the bodies of the murdered settlers of the vicinity had been lying unburied about their ruined homes or along the roadsides under the August sun. Their surviving relatives who had escaped to the fort now besought Sibley to give these bodies burial. After ascertaining through his scouts that the region was probably sufficiently

[6] Sibley's Order Book, 8, 9, in the possession of the Minnesota Historical Society. The appointment of McPhail could not have been pleasing to Major Cullen, who arrived before him with his two hundred Cullen Guards.

[7] McPhail to Ramsey, August 31, 1862, in Governor's Archives, file 255; Sibley to his wife, August 28, 29, 30, 1862, Sibley Papers; diary of Private, afterwards Captain, Le Vinne P. Plummer of the Sixth Minnesota. This diary was lent to the author by Captain Orlando C. Merriman of Minneapolis. See also West, *Sibley*, 258. "Vanguard" is the word there used. See the Appendix, no. 6, for divergent accounts. For a list of those who sought refuge at Fort Ridgely, 238 in number, see the report of the adjutant general, in *Executive Documents*, 1862, pp. 384-392.

clear of Indians to permit this pious duty, he decided to
send out a burial party under an escort large enough to protect it against any roving squads. The command of the
party was intrusted to no less a personage than Major
Joseph R. Brown, whose erratic career has been crossed at
so many points in this narrative. He had a perfect knowledge of the territory to be covered and was a master of
"Indian sign." He was instructed to examine the country
and to ascertain the movements and whereabouts of the
Sioux, so far as was consistent with his principal errand.
He was also warned by Sibley to use the greatest caution
against surprise and ambuscade, a caution, one would think,
superfluous for so experienced a man. Agent Galbraith, a
few refugees and other citizens, and some officers of the main
force attached themselves to the column. In the forenoon
of August 31 Brown moved out on the agency road and soon
found sad employment for his burial squad. Sixteen bodies
were given tardy burial on that road. After an easy march
the command bivouacked on the Minnesota bottom at the
mouth of Birch Coulee opposite the lower agency.[8]

On the following morning the command was divided.
The infantry, after burying some twenty bodies of Captain

[8] West, *Sibley*, 259; Brown's report to Sibley, September 4, 1862, in *Minnesota in the
Civil and Indian Wars*, 2: 212a. This report was not printed in the original edition of 1893.
See also Jared W. Daniels, "Indian Outbreak, 1862," p. 10. This narrative is probably the
best account of the expedition. It is one of a number of unpublished articles in the possession
of Dr. Daniels' daughter, Mrs. H. B. Hill of Faribault, to whom the author is under obligation. The Minnesota Historical Society has copies of the articles. Dr. Daniels was at
the time assistant surgeon of the Sixth Minnesota. From 1855 to 1862 he had been physician
at the upper agency. A biographical sketch of Daniels accompanies the narrative. There
is a concise account of the expedition, probably written by Return I. Holcombe, in the
*St. Paul Dispatch* of September 3, 1894. Numerous accounts of the affair give the number
of the party as 150, or about 150. Sibley, in his report to the adjutant general, September
4, 1862, says that there were seventy-five infantrymen, fifty-five cavalrymen, and an armed
burial squad of twenty, but he makes no mention of teamsters, of whom Major Brown says
there were seventeen. An effort to ascertain the number more precisely was without
results. For Sibley's report, see West, *Sibley*, 460, and Sibley's Order Book, 66-70. Major
Brown was most explicitly cautioned not to go into camp near a mound or near a ravine.
Captain Hiram P. Grant in his narrative, in *Minnesota in the Civil and Indian Wars*, 2: 215,
states that on August 31, while his men were engaged in burying the dead around the ferry
he sent a party across the Minnesota to reconnoiter and to bury the dead and that after he
left the ferry he moved five miles up the river and went into camp, where he was soon
joined by Captain Anderson. His memory is clearly at fault here and it may have failed
him in other particulars. Captain Grant's original report was destroyed by him for reasons
stated on page 219. The narrative here cited was furnished many years later.

Marsh's men, moved up the north side of the river to Beaver
Creek and then eastward across the prairie to the "upper
timber on the Birch Coolie" some three miles above its
mouth.   There Captain Grant selected a camp ground, a
spot ill chosen in the judgment of Captain Joseph Anderson.[9]
With the mounted force Major Brown crossed over the
Minnesota to the lower agency, rode through Little Crow's
abandoned village, and satisfied himself that the Sioux had
moved off toward the upper agency.   He recrossed by an
upper ford and at sunset gained the camp already selected
and did not order a new selection.   It was pitched on the
open prairie some two hundred yards west of the timbered
coulee.   Grant had parked his wagons in a partial circle in
open order and had joined them by ropes to which the team
horses were fastened.   A picket rope was stretched on the
south part of the circle for the cavalry horses.   Six Sibley
and other tents were raised in the central area, but most of
the men disposed themselves about the wagons.   Foragers
had brought in plenty of food for the men and the animals.
After a welcome supper the camp guard was posted and
sleep fell early on the tired soldiers.[10]

The night passed in unbroken quiet.   Just before dawn on
the second of September a single shot rang out, a bloodcurd-
ling yell issued from the throats of two hundred or more

[9] Daniels, "Indian Outbreak," 10; *Minnesota in the Civil and Indian Wars*, 2: 212a;
Holcombe, in *Minnesota in Three Centuries*, 3: 343; Captain Anderson to his wife, September
4, in the *Pioneer and Democrat*, September 7, 1862.   Dr. Daniels states that Major Brown
said that he had instructed the infantry captain to encamp at the head of Birch Coulee
near the old Abercrombie road and that Sibley intended, if he received expected reënforcements, to join him there with his whole force and to make the march to Yellow Medicine
on the east side of the Minnesota.   For a similar statement by Sibley, see his report, in
West, *Sibley*, 460.

[10] *Minnesota in the Civil and Indian Wars*, 2: 212a, 216.   Major Brown states that the
camp "was made in the usual way."   Holcombe, in *Minnesota in Three Centuries*, 3: 345,
remarks correctly that it was "virtually . . . a corral."   His account of the affair, derived
from interviews with participants, is full of incident.   He made a personal visit to the battle
field.   For a description of the camp, see J. W. Daniels, "Indian Outbreak," 13.   See also the
sketch of the battle field accompanying a letter from Levi Longfellow to the author, November 12, 1920, in the Folwell Papers.   In a letter to the author, November 15, 1917, in the
Folwell Papers, Dr. A. W. Daniels writes: "In talking with Gen. Sibley concerning that
battle, he told me that Maj. Brown was in command, and should have been court martialed
for camping in that exposed position, but he was so recently from civil life he was disposed
to be as lenient as possible."

THE BATTLE OF BIRCH COULEE, SEPTEMBER 2, 1862

*From the circular panorama by Gág, Heller, and Schwendinger*

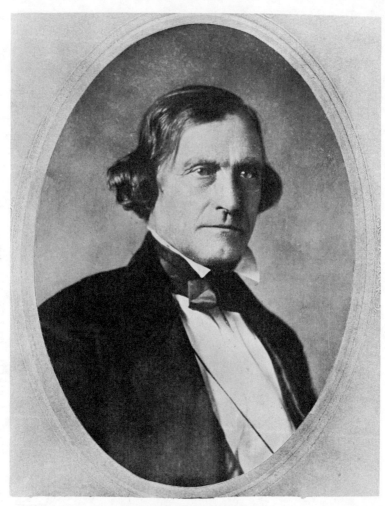

JOSEPH R. BROWN
*A daguerreotype taken in the 1850s*

Indians, who, bounding forward to within fifty or sixty yards of the camp, poured in a murderous volley, apparently from all quarters. Captain Anderson's men took cover behind the wagons and opened fire on the foe. The infantry started to fall in and form, but their captain ordered them to find cover behind the wagons and begin firing. These orders were so well obeyed that the Indians were soon driven to the shelter of the woods, which unfortunately were not distant. Many of the hundred horses or thereabouts were killed in the first half hour. The men immediately crawled behind the lifeless carcasses of the animals and found them a good protection. The fight proper was over in an hour and most of the casualties occurred during this time. The Indians, however, kept up a desultory fire throughout the day, and a few men were killed or wounded later. Major Brown having been wounded, Captain Grant at once set about arranging cover. The dead bodies of horses were strung along the front. Three spades and a shovel, all that could be obtained, were put into service. These, with sabers, bayonets, pocketknives, and tin plates, were used so industriously that by noon there was sufficient protection for all who kept to the ground. A few foolhardy men refused to do this and paid the penalty. At about two o'clock in the afternoon a loud report was heard, the repetition of which was assurance that it came from one of Sibley's cannon. Relief, however, was not to come for many hours.[11]

The sound of the battle was heard early in Sibley's camp at Fort Ridgely. He promptly dispatched a relieving party consisting of three companies of the Sixth Infantry, fifty mounted rangers, and a section of artillery — in all 240 men — under the command of Colonel McPhail. It was the sound of their guns shelling the timber and tall grass of the

---

[11] *Minnesota in the Civil and Indian Wars*, 2:212b, 212d, 216, 220; A. J. Ebell in the *Saint Paul Press*, September 6, 1862; Captain Grant in the *Press*, September 7; William R. Marshall in the *Pioneer and Democrat*, September 6, 1862; Captain Anderson to his wife, September 4, in the *Pioneer and Democrat*, September 7, 1862. The different accounts vary as to the number of horses, but Major Brown in his report states that all but six were killed, and that those were left behind wounded.

east branch of the coulee which cheered the hearts of the impounded men of Brown's command. As the party approached the main coulee a lively demonstration was made on its front by a detachment of Indians, which was soon dispersed by a few artillery shots. Two scouts came in unhurt but had their horses killed under them. McPhail, believing himself, for reasons unknown, to be "almost completely surrounded" by Indians, and ignorant of the location of Brown's camp, moved his command back of the east branch of the coulee, corralled it, and sent Lieutenant Sheehan and Interpreter William L. Quinn back to Ridgely for reënforcements.[12]

Upon the arrival of McPhail's message, Sibley at once put on the road his whole remaining force of six companies of the Sixth Regiment and two companies of the Seventh, which had reached his camp that day, and not long after midnight they came into McPhail's bivouac. At daylight the whole command was aroused and at length moved forward, the guns shelling the timber and grass of the coulee. The Sioux, perceiving themselves outnumbered, delivered some harmless parting shots into the camp and disappeared about eleven o'clock. No pursuit was attempted.[13] When Sibley rode into camp a pitiful spectacle was before him. Thirteen men lay stark in death and three more had received mortal wounds; forty-four were severely wounded and many more

[12] Report of the adjutant general, in *Executive Documents*, 1862, p. 419; *Minnesota in the Civil and Indian Wars*, 2:214, 217; Franklyn Curtiss-Wedge, *History of Renville County*, 1:167 (Chicago, 1916). In regard to the numbers of the detachment on record, see West, *Sibley*, 259, n.1, quoting a letter from Sibley to his wife. An extract from this letter, dated September 2, 1862, is also in the Sibley Papers. Captain Orlando C. Merriman, who commanded Company B of the Sixth Minnesota, told the author that he offered to take his company and one gun and march right into Brown's bivouac, but he was not given permission. He could have done it, but he probably would have lost some men. The author's interviews with participants are recorded in his notebooks as follows: Merriman, 2:63; Sheehan, 2:140; Longfellow, 8:50.

[13] Sibley's report, in West, *Sibley*, 460. Compare West's statement on page 260. Colonel McPhail's cavalry seems to have neglected its opportunity. See also Big Eagle's account, in *Minnesota Historical Collections*, 6:396, and Galbraith, in Indian Office, *Reports*, 1863, p. 278. Daniels, always friendly to Sibley, in his "Indian Outbreak," 17, is constrained to remark: "Maj. Brown's camp was fourteen miles from Ft. Ridgely, an easy march in five hours, yet it took twenty-eight [hours], after the firing was heard on the morning of the 2d, before Sibley's troops reached him and from three o'clock until 11 on the morning of the 3d, to make the three miles."

had received scratches and abrasions. The survivors, who had lain on the ground behind their slight defenses for more than thirty hours under a burning sun followed by a chilly night without water or food, were faint with hunger and fatigue. But five rounds of ammunition per man remained, the place was littered with the nameless débris of a disordered bivouac, and the air was full of the stench of decaying bodies.[14] One who was present says, "You never saw a skimmer so full of holes as those Sibley tents." On the afternoon of September 3 Sibley buried his dead, loaded his wounded into wagons, and led his troops back to Fort Ridgely where he arrived at midnight. The bodies of many of the dead were later removed to their homes.[15]

On the second day out Captain Grant had come upon a white woman, Justina Kreiger, who had been wandering up and down Beaver Creek for a fortnight with a wound in her shoulder. She was so much exhausted that she could not speak until after some hours' rest. She was placed upon a bed of grass in a wagon and taken into camp, where she was cared for by the surgeon, Dr. Jared W. Daniels, whose personal bravery and professional activity throughout the affair deserve the highest praise. Her wagon was the only one not turned on its side to make cover. In it she lay without food or water until the relieving party came. It was found that the wagon had been literally shot to pieces and that two hundred bullet holes had been made in the blankets and robes about her, but that the woman had received no wounds. The intensity of the Indian fire may be inferred.[16]

---

[14] West, *Sibley*, 261, and Sibley's report in the same, 461. Galbraith says: "We had killed and mortally wounded 24 men, and wounded, as near as I can ascertain, 67 men." See his report, in Indian Office, *Reports*, 1863, p. 278. Holcombe, in *Minnesota in Three Centuries*, 3: 349, follows Galbraith closely: "The loss of the whites was twenty men killed, four mortally wounded, perhaps sixty wounded more or less severely." See also Egan's statement in *Minnesota in the Civil and Indian Wars*, 2: 222; the *Saint Paul Pioneer Press* of May 7, 1894; and Satterlee, *Victims of the Indian Massacre*.

[15] Captain Merriman in an interview recorded in the author's notebooks, 2: 63-71; Sibley's report, in West, *Sibley*, 461; Captain Grant, in *Minnesota in the Civil and Indian Wars*, 2: 219; *Saint Paul Press*, October 25, 1862.

[16] Grant, in *Minnesota in the Civil and Indian Wars*, 2: 215; Daniels, "Indian Outbreak," 11, 16; narrative of Justina Kreiger, in Bryant and Murch, *Great Massacre*, 319-321.

In the foregoing account Major Joseph R. Brown has been recognized as the person in command of the Birch Coulee detachment, although that distinction has been claimed for another, Captain Hiram P. Grant of Company A, Sixth Minnesota Infantry, already mentioned. Even if documentary evidence were lacking, it might be presumed that Sibley would have selected for the duty his old and trusted client, who was particularly qualified by age, experience with the Sioux, and intimate knowledge of the local terrain. With such a person available it is not credible that he would have intrusted the control to a young man who had had no experience with frontier life or with Indians, who had no acquaintance with the geographical situation, and whose commission as an infantry captain was only a fortnight old. It is both affirmed and denied that Major Brown, being a civilian or merely an aide-de-camp on staff duty, could not really exercise command over the troops and that he did not in fact exercise command.[17]  The matter may be dismissed with the reflection that, when the unfortunate outcome of the expedition, resulting from gross lack of judgment and foresight, is considered, one may well wonder why either party to the controversy should desire to win its cause. Admirable as was the behavior of the men who made the gallant defense at Birch Coulee, nobody now considers it a victory in any sense. The innate cowardice of the Indians alone saved the whole personnel from massacre. The affair may have had the effect, however, of diverting the Indians from an enterprise which might have resulted in much mischief, as we are presently to see.

While Colonel Sibley is detained at Fort Ridgely waiting for men, for ammunition, for clothing, and for subsistence, it will be convenient for the reader to attend to some minor hostilities which followed closely on the affair at Birch Coulee. The hasty retirement of the Indians behind the Yellow Medicine River after their repulse at New Ulm on

---

[17] On this controversy and the Birch Coulee monuments, see the Appendix, no. 7, *post*.

August 23 was a strategic movement.  They had three objects in view: one was to place their families in a less exposed situation; another was to invite, if not to compel, the full coöperation of the upper tribes in the war; the third was to gain a more commodious base for further operations.  The Indian control had then no intention of suspending hostilities.  Suspension, indeed, would have bred dissension, and dissension would have soon led to abandonment.  The Dakota warriors had been repulsed but not subdued.  They were as keen as ever for plunder and for the coveted eagle feather.  It may be granted that in the pressing need for subsistence they were disposed to subordinate killing to robbery.

Within three days after the arrival of the Indians in the new camps on August 28 two grand forays were planned.  One was the dispatch of a force of several hundred men down the south side of the Minnesota to recover the large amount of supplies left at the lower Indian villages on their hasty retirement and then to move on down perhaps as far as New Ulm, cross the river, and make a demonstration in Sibley's rear.  The capture of his supply trains would be worth some adventure.  The suggestion made at the time and industriously repeated that the Indians intended with the small force to make descents upon Mankato and St. Peter and even on the river towns down to St. Paul cannot now be taken seriously.[18]  This expedition left the camps at the mouth of the Yellow Medicine on September 1, the day when Major Brown was reconnoitering about Little Crow's village and beyond.  That he did not encounter the advance of the party is remarkable.  On reaching that village about sunset the Indians saw across the Minnesota Valley Brown's troopers moving eastward across the prairie.  The Indian scouts soon ascertained that they had gone into camp at the

<hr />

[18] Flandrau, in *Minnesota in the Civil and Indian Wars*, 1: 737; West, *Sibley*, 216; Big Eagle's account, in *Minnesota Historical Collections*, 6: 393.  It may be doubted whether so ambitious a project as a campaign down the valley would have been undertaken in the absence of Little Crow with a strong body of warriors.

head of Birch Coulee. The infantry, which had passed at an earlier hour, they did not see and therefore presumed that the mounted squad was all that they had to deal with. To surround the small party under cover of darkness and butcher it at daylight was too promising an enterprise to be neglected. Two hundred men were selected for the attack, of which an account has already been given. The accidental division of their force and the loss of time seem to have diverted the Indians from prosecuting their original plan, whatever it may have been.[19]

The other expedition, which started on the same day, was led by Little Crow in person with a following of a few more than a hundred warriors. It may be reasonably conjectured that the original plan was to engage in plunder on the skirts of the Big Woods, to feel toward the larger party sent to creep around in Sibley's rear, and, should circumstances favor, to unite with it. The plan was much too like white men's war to please the majority of the tribesmen, who were ambitious to loot some of the towns toward the Mississippi. On the second day out, September 2, at noon two-thirds of the party seceded. The two factions, however, marched on parallel roads for the remainder of the day and at night went into separate bivouacs in Acton Township, Meeker County, where we may leave them for the moment.[20]

At an early hour on August 20 Judge Abner C. Smith of Forest City, Meeker County — one of the many cities of great expectations of the day — dispatched this message to Governor Ramsey: "The Indians have opened on us in Meeker. . . . Send us, forthwith, some good guns, and ammunition to match." Seventy-five Springfield rifles were all that could be spared. Forty-four were sent to Forest City and the remainder to Hutchinson, where they were delivered on the twenty-third. In both towns home guards were promptly organized, armed with the rifles, and sent out in detachments to relieve outlying settlements. One of

[19] Big Eagle, in *Minnesota Historical Collections*, 6: 393.
[20] Holcombe, in *Minnesota in Three Centuries*, 3: 357.

these from Forest City fell into an ambuscade of Indians, who killed four of the number. Another got warning of a like reception and beat a needlessly precipitate retreat without loss.[21]

In response to repeated calls for aid, Governor Ramsey on August 24 ordered Captain Richard Strout of the Tenth Minnesota Regiment — later of the Ninth — to proceed with his company to Meeker County to protect and to reassure the inhabitants. The command arrived at Forest City on the twenty-seventh. On the evening of September 2, as it was returning from a superfluous excursion to Glencoe, it chanced to make its bivouac at the Acton post office, as ignorant of the near presence of the two Indian crews as the latter were of the presence of each other.[22] A message of warning from Forest City that a further advance northward would bring him in contact with Indians known to have been lurking in the next township reached Captain Strout late in the night. At daylight he put his sixty-four men on the road by which they had arrived — the old Pembina and Henderson trail. When they were about two miles out the

[21] Abner C. Smith, *Random Historical Sketch of Meeker County*, 45–49, 51 (Litchfield, 1877). On page 56 the author gives a humorous account of a "wild flight" of forty men from twenty or more Indians. "In the flight our amiable Captain lost his hat and was unable to recover it, on account of two or three Indians that were within a half mile of them." Judge Smith's account of the activity of Captain George C. Whitcomb of Forest City is distorted by prejudice. See Smith to Ramsey, August 30, 1862, a copy of a captain's commission issued to Whitcomb, dated August 20, 1862, and John H. Stevens to Ramsey, August 18, 1862, in Governor's Archives, file 255. Stevens says: "Mr. Whitcomb is reliable in every particular. He will give you all the news." The recollections of Mrs. George C. Whitcomb, which include an account of the military activities of her husband at the time of the outbreak and with Hatch's Battalion, are in the *Pioneer Press* of January 17, 1909.

[22] Report of the adjutant general, in *Executive Documents*, 1862, p. 270; Smith, *Meeker County*, 64. John H. Stevens, the pioneer settler of Minneapolis — not St. Anthony — became in 1856 a pioneer of Glencoe. He had served in the Mexican War in the quartermaster's department and knew much about military affairs. When the news of the outbreak came he rallied his neighbors and, with their aid and that of refugees whose flight he halted, he prepared for defense. He was still a brigadier general in the state militia and in his letter to Governor Ramsey of August 18, 1862, he wrote, "I had a mind to call out the militia." In another, written on the twenty-first, he says, "I wish you could let my Brigade be armed." See Governor's Archives, file 255, and Bryant and Murch, *Great Massacre*, 211. For biographical sketches of Stevens, see John H. Stevens, *Personal Recollections of Minnesota and Its People and Early History of Minneapolis*, 401–404 (Minneapolis, 1890), and Holcombe, in *Minnesota in Three Centuries*, 3: 100. No attack was made on Glencoe. The statement regarding Captain Strout's march to Glencoe, in Smith, *Meeker County*, 64, is unjust. Strout's orders specifically directed him to that place. Report of the adjutant general, in *Executive Documents*, 1862, pp. 274, 468.

small advance guard sent back word that there were Indians on the road. The company was deployed as skirmishers, moved forward, and presently came against a line of Little Crow's warriors waiting to receive it. The Indians opened fire, which the soldiers promptly returned. At the third volley one of the soldiers fell mortally wounded. Not accustomed to that kind of fighting, the Indians began to give way. At this moment a party of Indians, mounted and possibly sixty strong, was seen coming up in the rear at full gallop. The captain instantly detached ten files under his second lieutenant to check this attack. The Indians did not care to make a direct onset and, leaving a small number behind, circled round by the right of the company to connect with Crow's line. As there was a lake on the left of the company, it was now surrounded. With admirable resolution Captain Strout decided to fight his way out. His first lieutenant, William A. Clark, gallantly led the main body of the force, probably in open order, in a charge with fixed bayonets against Little Crow's line, which gave way altogether and left the road to Hutchinson clear. An attempt of his teamsters to race away was stopped by the captain and his few mounted men. Unfortunately the commander, whose conduct so far had been brave and judicious, allowed his men — unwillingly, it may be granted — to betake themselves to a precipitate and disorderly flight to Hutchinson, where they arrived in the afternoon. The Indians hovered on the flank of the column for some miles, firing from a safe distance. Two more of Strout's men were killed, three were mortally wounded, and many more were wounded more or less severely. The dead were left where they fell. Nine horses were lost, as well as most of the ammunition, the rations, and the camp equipage. A Meeker County historian criticizes too severely the inexperienced commander in the so-called "Battle of Acton."[23]

[23] Smith, *Meeker County*, 69-78. Holcombe, in *Minnesota in Three Centuries*, 3: 359-362, follows closely Smith's account. The *Saint Paul Press* of September 5, 1862, gives Strout's meager report. He places the wounded at fifteen. Other accounts raise the number to as

Two incidents resulting from this raid deserve comment here. One was a second exodus of settlers from a range of counties including Stearns, Kandiyohi, Meeker, Wright, and McLeod. Many hundreds abandoned their homes and their harvest fields and fled with their wagons loaded with their families and such portable gear as could be hung on. On August 22, the day before the guns sent by Governor Ramsey were received at Forest City, seventy-two teams had passed that place headed for the east bank of the Mississippi River. In the previous week 170 such had passed through the place. Many of the fugitives did not return until long after and some never returned.[24] The other incident was the brave resolution of the people of the larger villages, who were mostly of American birth, to stay and defend themselves. They had begun the erection of so-called "forts" on receipt of the news of the original outbreak. These were generally stockades ten or twelve feet high and a hundred feet or more square, with simple flanking arrangements. But there were some interesting variations. At Maine Prairie a fort of two stories was built. At St. Joseph three pentagonal works were placed so as to command all approaches. At Sauk Centre a small inclosure was replaced with a larger one containing an acre of ground to accommodate the animals as well as the people. One of three fortifications at St. Cloud was circular, with concentric walls four feet apart filled in with earth. The whole space was floored over with heavy beams and planks covered with sod. On top was erected a bullet-proof tower, also circular, and loopholed for twelve sharpshooters. It was called "Fort Holes." These "forts" formed a chain from Little Falls to Glencoe. Two of them were attacked.[25]

high as twenty-three. See Marion P. Satterlee, "Narratives of the Sioux War," in *Minnesota Historical Collections*, 15:361-364. Satterlee's information was obtained from survivors named on page 363. The *Minneapolis Journal* of August 22, 1909, gives an account of the fight from the diary kept by William C. Allan of Minneapolis. In the issue of August 29 there is a description of the fight by J. C. Higgins, a participant, with a cut of a free-hand sketch of the field. See also the map on p. 416, *post*.

[24] Smith, *Meeker County*, 46; Ramsey's message, September 9, and report of the adjutant general, in *Executive Documents*, 1862, pp. 9, 462.

[25] Report of the adjutant general, in *Executive Documents*, 1862, pp. 464, 470, 478-482; S. V. Carr, "Letter from Fort Abercrombie," in *North Dakota Historical Collections*, 2:180.

In the afternoon of September 3, after their successful stampede of Captain Strout's men, the two factions of Little Crow's force reunited. After a brief rest at Cedar Mills about half of the warriors were detached for a night march and a daybreak attack on Forest City, some twenty miles to the north. At three o'clock of the following morning, September 4, twenty mounted Indians rode into the place and

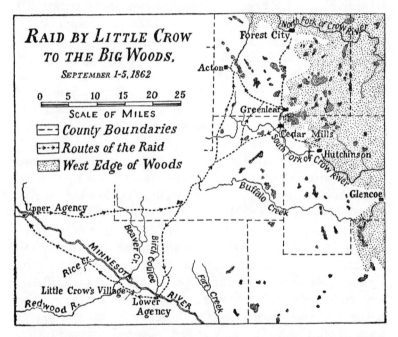

RAID BY LITTLE CROW
TO THE BIG WOODS,
SEPTEMBER 1-5, 1862

0    5    10    15    20    25
SCALE OF MILES
County Boundaries
Routes of the Raid
West Edge of Woods

fired a volley to create alarm. But there was no alarm. The two hundred refugees, mostly women and children, were protected by forty armed men and by the solid stockade which had been completed the day before. Foiled in their main purpose, the Indians turned to the plunder and burning of houses and the running off of sixty horses. By five o'clock they had departed on three different roads, along which they set fire to farmhouses.[26]

[26] Smith, *Meeker County*, 80, 86-90; Holcombe, in *Minnesota in Three Centuries*, 3: 362, 365-367.

Little Crow with the other moiety of his men remained in bivouac until morning and so timed his eight-mile march as to reach the neighborhood of Hutchinson at about eight or nine o'clock, when the men of the place might be scattered to the harvest fields. Whether they had received warning of a possible attack is not known, but the 125 armed men, including the remnant of Captain Strout's company, were held so closely that the Indian commander was able to distribute his force on three sides of the place, the fourth being left open in expectation of a flight of the people toward Glencoe, when they would be conveniently butchered from ambush. The Indians soon perceived that an assault would be useless and they retired out of ordinary rifle range. For some hours they leisurely devoted themselves to looting and burning. Many of the best residences were destroyed and along with them the pride of the village, the Hutchinson Academy. Soon after four o'clock the Indians took their departure with many wagonloads of plunder and many cattle and horses left by refugees on the neighboring prairie. On the following day all set out for Yellow Medicine, Little Crow with a few of his own band going by way of his old village.[27]

A third operation similar in nature to the two just described may here be related. In 1856 the war department sent an exploring expedition to Devil's Lake, Pembina, and the Red River Valley, with instructions to select a suitable site for a military post in that valley. It may be presumed that the motive for the establishment of such a post was the

[27] William W. Pendergast, "Sketches of the History of Hutchinson," in *Minnesota Historical Collections*, 10: 70, 80-84 (part 1); addresses given at the fiftieth anniversary celebration of Hutchinson by Dr. Leo M. Crafts, Dr. Kee Wakefield, and R. H. McClelland, in the *Hutchinson Leader*, October 6, 1905. Holcombe's account of the raid to the Big Woods, September 2-4, in *Minnesota in Three Centuries*, 3: 367-370, which was derived from the accounts of Smith and Pendergast and from interviews with Joe (Antoine J.) Campbell, the half-breed interpreter who accompanied Little Crow, is reliable. On page 371 Holcombe gives an account of Little Crow's behavior at the battle of Acton and an estimate of that leader's military qualities. For accounts of the preparations for defense at Hutchinson, see an article by Edward A. Bromley, with a cut showing the location of the buildings, in the *Hutchinson Leader*, October 6, 1905, and letters to Ramsey from Pendergast, August 24, and from Captain Lewis Harrington, August 27, 1862, in Governor's Archives, file 255. Hutchinson was founded by members of the widely known family of singers of that name from New Hampshire.

protection of the Red River trade, which was soon to assume a new importance. In the winter of the following year, in part through the instrumentality of Delegate Rice, a treasury permit was granted for the transportation in bond through St. Paul of the goods of the Hudson's Bay Company, which had previously found their outlet to market through Hudson Bay. In 1857 about five hundred Red River carts arrived in St. Paul. In the same winter Congress authorized the establishment of the proposed post.[28] The site chosen was that recommended by Lieutenant Colonel Charles F. Smith, commander of the exploring party, at the head of navigation of the Red River of the North on the west bank about forty miles north of Lake Traverse. A detachment of troops sent out in 1858 began the necessary constructions, but a report to the war department that the site was liable to flooding led to an abandonment the following year. The expansion of the Red River trade and its further development expected from the beginning of steamboat navigation on the river in 1859 were made grounds for a reëstablishment. There was also the added demand of a fringe of pioneer settlers for protection against possible raids by Sioux and Chippewa Indians. The place was reoccupied in the summer of 1860 and building was resumed on a better terrain. The completed fort was named "Fort Abercrombie." Small garrisons of regular troops were maintained until the outbreak of the Civil War, when details were made from Minnesota volunteer regiments. At the time of the Sioux Outbreak the garrison consisted of Company D of the Fifth Minnesota, eighty-four strong, under the command of Captain John Vander Horck.[29]

[28] Report of Lieutenant Colonel Charles F. Smith, December 30, 1856, in Secretary of War, *Reports*, 1858, vol. 1, pp. 426-454 (35 Congress, 2 session, *Senate Executive Documents*, vol. 2; *House Executive Documents*, vol. 2, part 2 — serials 975, 998); Russell Blakeley, "Opening of the Red River of the North to Commerce and Civilization," in *Minnesota Historical Collections*, 8: 46; Neill, *Minnesota*, 633 (fourth edition); Williams, *Saint Paul*, 303-306; *Statutes at Large*, 11: 204.

[29] Secretary of War, *Reports*, 1858, vol. 1, p. 432 (serials 975 or 998); 1859, vol. 1, p. 576 (36 Congress, 1 session, *Senate Executive Documents*, vol. 2 — serial 1024); Blakeley, in *Minnesota Historical Collections*, 8: 47-52; James H. Baker, "History of Transportation in Minnesota," in *Minnesota Historical Collections*, 9: 19; George E. Warner and Charles M.

In 1862 arrangements had been made for a treaty authorized by Congress with the Red Lake and Pembina bands of
Chippewa. A train of thirty or more wagons loaded with
Indian goods and a herd of some two hundred cattle, to be
used as such goods and animals were wont to be used at
Indian treaties, reached the vicinity of Fort Abercrombie
in the middle of August. On August 23, the commander of
the post received an order to detain the goods and the animals and with it came a newspaper clipping apprising him
of the outbreak of the Sioux at the Redwood agency on the
eighteenth. The wagons and the herd were at once brought
across the river and corralled near the post. On the same
day the commandant recalled a detachment which was about
fifty miles away down the Red. He sent out an order to all
citizens who could be reached to come into the fort immediately if they desired protection. Nearly eighty responded,
a small number bringing families. The commander at once
set his soldiers and citizen volunteers to piling up cordwood
and timber about the barracks and establishing emplace-
ments for his three twelve-pound howitzers. The company
was composed mostly of Germans and fortunately there were
a number who had been trained as artillerists.

The days passed in quiet until the thirtieth of August,
when a small band of Indians suddenly appeared in the distance and drove off the larger part of the stock, which had
been let out on the range to pasture. Forty of the cattle
were recovered the next day by a reconnoitering party.
Again all was peace until the early morning of September
3, when a body of Indians, in part mounted, attacked the
place, chiefly on the south front where the stables were
located outside the barricade. Armed citizens, whose
animals were in danger of capture, gallantly led by the post

Foote, eds., *History of Hennepin County and the City of Minneapolis*, 606 (Minneapolis,
1881); Linda W. Slaughter, "Fort Abercrombie," in *North Dakota Historical Collections*,
1: 412-415; Vander Horck, in *Minnesota in the Civil and Indian Wars*, 1: 255; report of the
adjutant general, in Minnesota, *Executive Documents*, 1862, p. 405. See also Major C.
Powell Adams to Lieutenant David L. Scott, December 4, 1865, which gives a brief
history of Fort Abercrombie, in the Adams Papers in the possession of the Minnesota
Historical Society.

quartermaster, Captain T. D. Smith, soon repulsed the attacking group. One civilian and two soldiers were wounded. Desultory firing continued for some hours without further casualties.[30]

Again on the sixth of the month there was another daybreak attack, also directed mainly on the stables, although demonstrations were made all around the post. The Sioux seem to have deemed it an easy task to hold off a surprised and terrified garrison while they escaped with the horses and mules. A ten minutes' encounter convinced them of their error and they retired from that quarter. Shots were exchanged elsewhere for some time and the howitzers broke up assemblages of warriors on the prairie as they appeared. One of the garrison was killed and two were wounded, one of them mortally. As usual, the Indian loss could not be ascertained and, as usual, in the reports it was declared to be much greater than that of the whites. A participant relates that the Indians "left two of their number dead in the stack yard, who were planted the same day."[31]

The small loss of the garrison was doubtless due to the foresight of the commandant in fortifying the place as soon as it was threatened and to his indisposition to expose the lives of his men to the fire of an enemy whom he believed outnumbered his garrison many times over. He estimated the Indian force in the first attack at four hundred and that in the second at not less than twice that number, though a later historian gives as the deliberate opinion of a participant known to him that in neither of the affairs did the Indians number over one hundred. This husbandry of his

---

[30] Indian Office, *Reports*, 1862, p. 14; Vander Horck, in *Minnesota in the Civil and Indian Wars*, 1:255; Bryant and Murch, *Great Massacre*, 232-241; report of the adjutant general, in Minnesota, *Executive Documents*, 1862, p. 489; Holcombe, in *Minnesota in Three Centuries*, 3:385-387. For resolutions praising Captain Smith for bravery in the defense of Fort Abercrombie and indirectly censuring the military commander, see the *St. Cloud Democrat* of October 16, 1862. The censure was probably unjust.

[31] Vander Horck, in *Minnesota in the Civil and Indian Wars*, 1:257; report of the adjutant general, in *Executive Documents*, 1862, pp. 490-493; *Saint Paul Pioneer*, September 28, 1862. See also a letter from P. Lamb to William B. Mitchell, September 22, and another of the same date to the editor, signed "W.," in the *St. Cloud Democrat* of October 2, 1862.

command gave occasion to charges of a lack of courage. In the night preceding the first attack, while the commandant was making the rounds of his guards, a disconcerted sentry, mistaking him for a prowling Indian, fired on him, fortunately with no greater harm than a wound in his right arm.[32]

The date upon which Governor Ramsey received the tidings of danger to Fort Abercrombie has not been found, but, relying on his unfailing activity, we may make a guess that it was on September 6 or the day before. On September 6 he gave orders for the dispatch of a relieving force. The nucleus was composed of sixty men of the Third Minnesota Regiment, to which were immediately attached two companies of recruits at Fort Snelling. On the eleventh the march was begun. Two days later the column was overtaken by a detail in charge of a fieldpiece. Companies or squads of mounted volunteer militia sufficient to raise the number of the party to something over four hundred were later absorbed. Captain Emil A. Buerger, who had been a lieutenant in the Second Company of Minnesota Sharpshooters and had been left wounded in the hands of the enemy at Fair Oaks, was in command. He had served many years in the Prussian army and therefore had qualities which fitted him for command. After a laborious march from Fort Snelling to St. Cloud and thence diagonally across the state, he arrived at Fort Abercrombie late in the afternoon of September 23. On the morning of the same day Captain Vander Horck, unaware of the approach of the relieving party, dispatched a courier to St. Paul with a message that assistance was still needed. When the escort of twenty men sent out with the messenger had come within a mile of the

[32] Vander Horck, in *Minnesota in the Civil and Indian Wars*, 1:256; Holcombe, in *Minnesota in Three Centuries*, 3:387. In his testimony in the *Sisseton and Wahpeton Claim Case Record, Evidence for Defendant*, 284, Vander Horck said that he was satisfied that about eight hundred Indians took part in the attack of September 6. See also the *St. Cloud Democrat*, October 2, 16; *State Atlas* (Minneapolis), October 15, 1862; C. P. V. Lull to Ramsey, Fort Abercrombie, September 22, 1862, in Governor's Archives, file 32. For documents relating to the attacks and sketches showing the plan of the fort, see Libby, in *North Dakota Historical Collections*, vol. 2, part 2, pp. 10-18, 96.

fort on its return, Indians in ambush fired and killed two of the party. A strong detachment sent out the day after, it is related, found the two bodies mutilated to such a degree that little resemblance to human bodies was left. After the arrival of Captain Buerger's force there were no more molestations of a serious character.[33]

While Colonel Sibley was detained inert at St. Peter and Fort Ridgely a most praiseworthy activity was displayed in providing protection for the southwestern frontier. Although Governor Ramsey in his proclamation of August 21 had called only for the militia of the Minnesota Valley and the counties adjoining the frontier, that of distant southeastern counties volunteered with alacrity. On the twenty-fifth Captain Alonzo J. Edgerton, afterwards a brevet brigadier general and a United States senator, appeared at the Winnebago agency with a company, which was soon after merged into the Tenth Minnesota, and sent a message to Sibley, telling him of the excitement and fear at the agency. The report had been widely spread that the Winnebago, who could muster six hundred warriors, were in alliance with the Sioux and that if they had not already joined in the outbreak they might at any moment do so.[34] On the day after his arrival at St. Peter, Sibley had sent Captain Cox to assist Flandrau at New Ulm and Captain Anderson

---

[33] Report of the adjutant general, in *Executive Documents*, 1862, pp. 287, 493-500. On page 499 Adjutant General Malmros gives an account of an attack at seven o'clock in the morning of September 26 by a party of Indians on a company of soldiers watering their horses. A teamster was mortally wounded. If any of the Indians were killed or wounded, their bodies were carried away. At a distance of two miles a camp was found by a pursuing detachment, but the Indians fled at their approach. In the abandoned camp a considerable quantity of plunder was found, including "a stock of liquors." Doane Robinson, in his *History of the Dakota or Sioux Indians*, 296 (*South Dakota Historical Collections*, vol. 2, part 2 — Aberdeen, 1904), attributes this attack to Little Crow and his small party of refugees who had fled on the twenty-fourth from the neighborhood of what was later called Camp Release. As the distance between the two points is more than a hundred miles, it is not credible that a march with considerable plunder could have been made in the interval. Malmros, in his report in *Executive Documents*, 1862, p. 500, speaks of another attempt of a small party of Sioux to gain cover in order to fire on troops watering horses on the twenty-ninth. One of the soldiers was wounded in the skirmish which followed.

[34] Ramsey's message, September 9, in *Executive Documents*, 1862, p. 5; *Minnesota in the Civil and Indian Wars*, 2: 193b, 209; report of the adjutant general, in *Executive Documents*, 1862, p. 501. See also p. 149, *ante*.

was sent two days later to the same place.[35]   On August
27 Judge Flandrau, in his letter of advice transmitting his
report of that date of the second battle at New Ulm, stated
that Sibley had put him in charge of affairs in that part of
the country, but that without men and arms he was powerless.   In a postscript he added: "I cannot hold any commission, and don't want any. . . . Give me some kind of
a roving, irregular commission."   On the next day Governor
Ramsey issued a proclamation authorizing the Honorable
Charles E. Flandrau to proceed to the Blue Earth country
and there to take measures to secure that frontier and restore
confidence to the people.   In particular he was to organize
military companies and to control them and any others
found in the locality or detailed by Colonel Sibley.[36]

If Judge Flandrau had scruples about accepting a military
office while a member of the supreme court of the state,
Governor Ramsey had none about his authority to appoint.
On September 3 his adjutant general sent a colonel's commission to Flandrau with a complimentary message and a
special order to assume command of all troops in the Blue
Earth country.   It appears from a postscript to a letter of
the same date that Colonel Flandrau's scruples had faded
away, as he speaks of a project to raise a regiment for a fall
and winter campaign.[37]   Volunteer militia companies from
southeastern counties were immediately ordered to report to
Flandrau and a few companies of men enlisted but not yet
mustered into the new Minnesota regiments were sent to
him.   He established his headquarters at South Bend, an
abortive village at the elbow of the Minnesota River, and
arranged a line of frontier posts from New Ulm down the
Minnesota and up the Blue Earth to the Iowa boundary, a

[35] *Minnesota in the Civil and Indian Wars,* 2: 196, 197; report of the adjutant general, in
*Executive Documents,* 1862, p. 423; Heard, *Sioux War,* 120.  For Captain Cox's report,
see his letter to Ramsey, September 1, 1862, in Governor's Archives, file 255.

[36] *Minnesota in the Civil and Indian Wars,* 2: 202, 208.

[37] Special Order no. 7, which accompanied Flandrau's commission, directed him to
report with his command to Colonel Sibley.  Flandrau soon became independent in the Blue
Earth Country.  Note his farewell order of October 5, 1862.  *Minnesota in the Civil and
Indian Wars,* 2: 210, 211, 266.

distance of eighty miles. Advanced posts were placed at
Madelia and the Chain of Lakes. Captain E. St. Julien
Cox, commanding at the former post, built a strong and
"artistic fortification." All the stations were fortified in
some manner — that at Garden City, with saw logs. No
attacks were made on the military posts and but few settlers
were disturbed, but on the tenth of September a party of
Sioux warriors, perhaps twenty in number, appeared in the
valley of Butternut Creek, a few miles from Colonel Flandrau's headquarters in the northwest part of Blue Earth
County. Twenty-two persons of the Welsh colony who had
been warned of Indians lurking in the neighborhood were
assembled in the house of one of their number. There was a
noise outside and the door was opened; shots through the
opening killed one man and wounded another. That the
whole unresisting assemblage was not massacred was due to
the fact that these Indians were just then more intent on
horse-stealing than on murder. On the same morning the
assassins came upon a threshing crew and killed one of them
and wounded another. They also killed another man in the
vicinity. They then made their escape so effectually that
the men sent out to find them had a fruitless excursion. On
the fifth of October Colonel Flandrau and all his companies
of militia were relieved by the Twenty-fifth Wisconsin Regiment, which had been sent on to Minnesota under the requisition of Major General John Pope, who had been placed in
command of the Military Department of the Northwest.
Flandrau returned to his judicial duties and was widely and
sincerely praised for the military services he had so efficiently
and gallantly rendered.[38]

On his arrival at St. Peter on August 22 with the nucleus
of his little army Sibley learned that the whole Indian force
was in arms and that the emergency was one not "to be

[38] Flandrau, in *Minnesota in the Civil and Indian Wars*, 1:739; 2:266; Flandrau, *Minne-sota*, 162-166; report of the adjutant general, in *Executive Documents*, 1862, pp. 501-509. Bryant and Murch, in their *Great Massacre*, 257-269, lift Adjutant General Malmros' account. See also Hughes, *Welsh in Minnesota*, 103-109, and Hughes, *History of Blue Earth County*, 113, 119-123 (Chicago, [1909]).

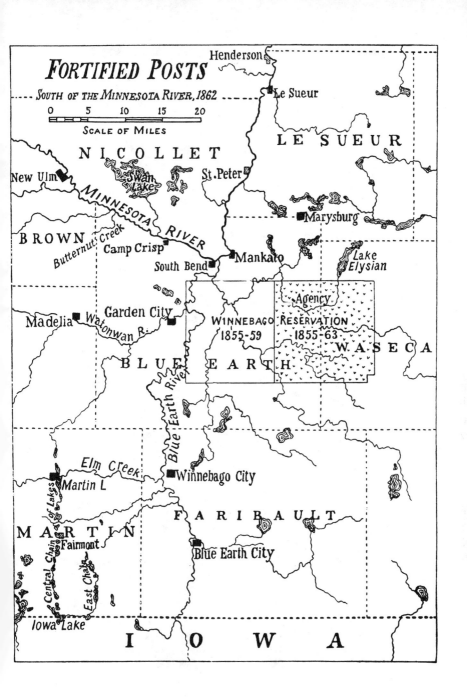

FORTIFIED POSTS

SOUTH OF THE MINNESOTA RIVER, 1862

0    5    10    15    20
SCALE OF MILES

NICOLLET

LE SUEUR

Henderson

Le Sueur

New Ulm

Swan Lake

St. Peter

Marysburg

MINNESOTA RIVER

BROWN

Butternut Creek

Camp Crisp

South Bend

Mankato

Lake Elysian

Garden City

Madelia

Watonwan R.

WINNEBAGO 1855-59

Agency

RESERVATION 1855-63

WASECA

BLUE    EARTH

Blue Earth River

Winnebago City

Elm Creek

Martin L

MARTIN

Fairmont

Central Chain of Lakes

East Chain

Iowa Lake

FARIBAULT

Blue Earth City

I    O    W    A

THE BATTLE OF WOOD LAKE, SEPTEMBER 23, 1862

*From A. P. Connolly, The Minnesota Massacre, 1896*

dallied with in the circumlocution office." Had he been furnished with a squadron or even a troop of cavalry and one or two fieldpieces he might have relieved Fort Ridgely the next day. With a mere collection of raw recruits and rawer militia — all utterly undisciplined and some of them provided with worthless muskets — with ammunition of the wrong caliber, and with no food nor transportation except such as was impressed from day to day, it was impracticable to take the field at once against a numerous foe, mounted in part and armed, who might be lurking in ambush behind the bluffs which bounded the town on the west.[39] None the less there was abundant complaint of Sibley's tardiness by persons sitting comfortably in armchairs at home. Lieutenant Governor Donnelly, however, who, it was said, had been sent up "to spy on Sibley," had no fault to find. Writing to Governor Ramsey on August 25 he said, "I found it not necessary to urge upon him [*Sibley*] a forward movement." That Sibley's mounted men reached Fort Ridgely on the twenty-seventh and were followed by the whole body of his force on the following day was all that could be reasonably expected. He had no intention to delay his march at this point and appointed a movement for the thirty-first. A rainstorm preventing this, he planned to march on the second of September, to absorb Brown's detachment, and to move up the east bank of the Minnesota. The disaster at Birch Coulee put a check on this scheme, strategically wise at the moment.[40]

An additional reason for postponement was now presented. It was a matter of general belief that Little Crow, although he was the brains of the Sioux insurgents, had, up to the moment of the outbreak, counseled against war on the whites. Assuming it to be in some degree probable that

[39] *Minnesota in the Civil and Indian Wars*, 2: 165, 196.
[40] Donnelly to Ramsey, August 25, in the *Saint Paul Press*, August 27, 1862. See also Donnelly's letters to Ramsey, August 25, 4 P.M., from Belle Plaine, August 25 from St. Peter, and August 26 from St. Peter, in Governor's Archives, file 255; Sibley to his wife, August 30, 31, in the Sibley Papers; and Sibley to Malmros, September 1, 1862, in West, *Sibley*, 458.

after the repulses he had suffered the chief might be coming to himself and might be glad to entertain some plan for ending the war, Sibley left on a split stake on the Birch Coulee field this message: "If Little Crow has any proposition to make to me, let him send a half-breed to me, and he shall be protected in and out of camp." To this Crow replied from Yellow Medicine on September 7. He gave as his reasons for the commencement of the war the misconduct of Agent Galbraith and the insolence and extortions of the traders and he casually remarked that he had a great many prisoners, intending Colonel Sibley to understand that a proposition from him might be entertained. Sibley's response on the following day must have satisfied the shrewd chief that his innocent allusion to prisoners was understood. "Return me the prisoners, under a flag of truce," wrote Sibley, "and I will talk with you then like a man." A communication from Little Crow a few days later renewed the covert suggestion that he was holding the prisoners as hostages and that the price of their delivery would be immunity for himself and all his warriors. Probably at Little Crow's instigation, rumors were spread that it was his intention, if he should be attacked, to place the prisoners between himself and the attacking party and, if he should be surprised, to put them all to instant death. To recover these unfortunates and to punish those who had taken them from their homes now became the double object of the campaign.[41]

A happy turn of affairs now took place which, it was hoped, would simplify a difficult problem. The half-breed, Thomas A. Robertson, who brought Crow's last communication, brought also, unknown to Crow, a letter signed by Chiefs Wabasha and Taopi, who had taken no hostile part except under compulsion. They expressed their desire to be

[41] Copies of Sibley's and Little Crow's letters are given verbatim in the report of the adjutant general, in *Executive Documents*, 1862, p. 444. Gabriel Renville, in "A Sioux Narrative of the Outbreak in 1862, and of Sibley's Expedition in 1863," in *Minnesota Historical Collections*, 10: 603 (part 2), states that Charles Crawford, whom he had sent down to Birch Coulee to look for dead, found and brought to him the paper left by Sibley on the battle ground, which Renville read in council.

taken under Sibley's protection and proposed that he name a place where they might meet him with their families and all the prisoners they could secure.[42]   The reply to this was that in two days Sibley's troops would all be mounted and in three days they would be on the march.   All Indians who desired protection had only to assemble on the prairie with their prisoners in full sight of the troops and hoist a white flag.   With a leaven of dissension working in the Indian camps, Sibley was less disquieted with the delays which prevented his advance.   Little Crow and his adherents, however, had sufficient influence to hold the support of the main body of warriors.   They could expect little mercy should they surrender and that, he assured them, they need not do.   They could whip the raw and inexperienced white volunteers in a fair fight in the field.   Little Crow therefore collected his warriors opposite the mouth of the Chippewa River to await Sibley's advance.[43]

Meanwhile the little army at Fort Ridgely was gaining coherence and learning its business.   The companies were drilled daily, chiefly in skirmishing.   One diarist makes record of "Dress parade, as usual."   On Sundays the men assembled in front of Colonel Sibley's tent to hear sermons from the Reverend Stephen R. Riggs, the veteran missionary whom the commandant had attached to his staff as chaplain, doubtless with the purpose of having his services as interpreter and interlocutor with the Sioux.   With only an extemporized transport, supplies indispensable for the campaign were delayed.   A consignment of fifty thousand cartridges arrived on September 11.   On the thirteenth and fourteenth a supply of provisions and a partial supply of

---

[42] Report of the adjutant general, in *Executive Documents*, 1862, p. 446; Heard, *Sioux War*, 149. Robertson, who in 1923 lived in Veblen, South Dakota, states in his reminiscences that the letter signed with the names of Wabasha and Taopi was written by him at the dictation of Good Thunder.   These interesting reminiscences, written in the winter of 1918–19, were lent by the author to the Minnesota Historical Society.   Good Thunder, who was a Christian Indian, lived and died at the little Sioux colony near Morton.

[43] Sibley Order Book, 22; report of the adjutant general, in *Executive Documents*, 1862, p. 447; *Minnesota in the Civil and Indian Wars*, 2: 228; Heard, *Sioux War*, 147.

clothing came up. The Seventh Regiment had received no overcoats.[44]

Finding all his "craft" to induce Little Crow to surrender his prisoners without avail, Sibley closed the correspondence with him on the twelfth. On the next day Sibley was gratified by the arrival of 270 enlisted men of the Third Minnesota Infantry, who had been paroled after the surrender of the regiment at Murfreesboro. He expected that these well-drilled soldiers, experienced in the campaign in the South, would inspire confidence in the other regiments and would render the whole command more effective. As the officers of the regiment had been retained as prisoners of war, Major Abraham E. Welch of the Fourth Regiment had been placed in command. He had been a first lieutenant in the First Minnesota and had been wounded and taken prisoner at Bull Run. After his release and recovery he was given the promotion indicated. He had but one commissioned officer of the Third, Lieutenant Rollin C. Olin, who had not been included in the surrender at Murfreesboro. The companies represented were commanded by experienced sergeants, some of whom were afterwards properly promoted. The battalion had made a circuitous march through Carver, Glencoe, Hutchinson, and Forest City. As it passed through the town of Acton, burial was given to the three men of Captain Strout's company who had been left where they fell in the precipitate flight of that command on the third of September.[45]

During these days the commander of the expedition, so lately impressed from private life, was subjected to a variety

[44] Plummer Diary; *Minnesota in the Civil and Indian Wars*, 2: 228, 235.

[45] Sibley to his wife, September 10, 13, 14, 1862, Sibley Papers; *Minnesota in the Civil and Indian Wars*, 2: 230; report of the adjutant general, in *Executive Documents*, 1862, p. 443, and the insert opposite page 308. A letter from Major Welch to Governor Ramsey, dated Fort Ridgely, September 13, 1862, in Governor's Archives, file 255, reports his arrival "this morning." He had found sufficient forces at Glencoe, Hutchinson, and Forest City and therefore thought his men "could not be better employed than by aiding an advance movement." In regard to the burial of the bodies in Acton, see Smith, *Meeker County*, 75, and Andrews, in *Minnesota in the Civil and Indian Wars*, 1: 158. Major Welch, in his letter cited above, merely says, "On our march . . . we . . . buried the body of a man who had been murdered by the Indians. No one could identify him."

of trials which one more experienced would have taken less seriously.  Lacking an experienced staff, he was obliged to attend to a multitude of administrative details, which wore him out.  His undisciplined soldiers caused him trouble. He had to stay up nights to watch his guards.  He found some of the men committing acts of wanton mischief and appropriating private property without authority and he was obliged to direct company officers to report such offenses for punishment.  He had to forbid shooting in camp or elsewhere without leave and selling liquor without his express permission.  He also found it necessary to order the arrest of civilians represented as making unauthorized impressments of horses and wagons with which to carry off stolen property.[46]

Another and a weightier cause of grief was the incontinent departure of nearly all Sibley's mounted men within three days after their arrival at Fort Ridgely.  Captain Anderson's company of fifty-five men remained to form a part of the Birch Coulee detachment.  Of the doughty cavaliers who left him for their homes, Sibley wrote that they "in most cases basely deserted this Corps."  Such disappointment was natural, but the commander might have remembered that these men, who were above military age, had left their work and had mounted their family horses and ridden away to help stop an imminent tide of insurrection.  They were not equipped for a campaign.  But Sibley's appreciation of the need, many times reported, of a mounted force was worthy of an experienced Indian fighter.  On September 11 he had but twenty or twenty-five horsemen left and they were occupied with herding cattle.[47]

[46] Sibley to his wife, August 25, 28, September 4, 5, 17, 1862, Sibley Papers; Sibley Order Book, 15, 27, 30.

[47] In a letter to his wife, dated September 17, 1862, Sibley writes: "The horsemen . . . have . . . skedaddled in view of dangerous service."  See also Sibley to Malmros, September 4, in Sibley Order Book, 66; the report of the adjutant general, in *Executive Documents*, 1862, p. 436; Heard, *Sioux War*, 130; and *Minnesota in the Civil and Indian Wars*, 2: 228. In a letter from Fort Ridgely, September 3, 1862, in Governor's Archives, file 255, John S. Prince writes: "Great complaint is made by Lieut Sheehan at what he calls the scum of creation that came up hear as mounted men or cavalry.  They would not submit to any

Colonel Sibley was unduly sensitive to the attacks which continued to be made upon him for his alleged inexcusable tardiness in reaching his base at St. Peter and in advancing from there to Fort Ridgely and for his parleying with Little Crow. One newspaper called him a "snail" who "falls back on his authority and assumed dignity, and refuses to march." Another stigmatized him as the "State undertaker, with his company of grave-diggers."[48]    It was charged that he intended to obtain the release of the captives by a treaty with Little Crow and to reëstablish the privileges of the Indian traders. The vile insinuation was made that he had many friends, not to say relatives, in the Indian camps whom he would not like to injure. Stung by such assaults, he offered his resignation to Adjutant General Malmros within a week after his arrival at Fort Ridgely. In letters to his wife he repeats his desire to return to his family and to private life. He found, however, some consolation in observing that the howlers in St. Paul had somewhat mitigated their onslaughts after the affair at Birch Coulee. They had concluded that the Indian expedition was something more than a picnic.[49]

disaplin, and when called upon to swear into the service for Thirty days and organize themselves so as to be effectiv, they suddenly learned that they had urgent business at home." For Riggs's reference to the "string-bean cavalry" called home to see sick wives by clairvoyant messages, the humor of which does not disguise a scintilla of contempt, see his *Forty Years with the Sioux*, 165. On September 7 the men in Captain Anderson's company were discharged, as their horses had been killed at Birch Coulee and remounts were not available. Sibley Order Book, 25.

[48] *Hastings Independent*, September 4, 1862; *St. Cloud Democrat*, September 11, 1862. In Governor's Archives, file 255, may be found complaints to Governor Ramsey of Sibley's alleged torpidity and inefficiency. Charles Roos, sheriff of Brown County, wrote on September 4: "Col. Sibly lying lassy in the Fort and the damnd dutsch in Brown County may go to hell. . . . Send a young ernest men to take Command instead of Col. Sibly, and he will do more with the present force than Col. Sibly ever will do with 10 or 15,000 men, he is in my mind a Coward and a Rascal." Jane G. Swisshelm wrote on September 5: "For God's sake put some *live* man in command of the force against the Sioux & let Sibley have 100 men or there about in his undertaker's corpse." Horace Austin wrote on September 9: "No State Administration can long possess the confidence of the people which shall appoint H. H. Sibley to command. . . . That a man who defrauded you out of the executive chair on the strength of Indian votes . . . should be appointed by *you* . . . and then *continued* in power while murder, rapine and plunder surround his imbecility [*sic*], staggers us all." This letter is indorsed, "an impudent letter." The event fully justified Sibley's Fabian policy.

[49] Sibley Order Book, 66, 70; West, *Sibley*, 459, 461; *Central Republican* (Faribault), September 10, 17, October 8, 1862; Sibley to his wife, September 4, 5, 7, 11, 17, 27, 1862, Sibley Papers.

When it was at length ready for the field, Sibley's command consisted of the Sixth Minnesota, with the exception of one company, commanded by Colonel William Crooks, whose West Point education rendered him exceedingly useful; five companies of the Seventh Minnesota under Lieutenant Colonel William R. Marshall, who was to command a brigade at Nashville and later to be twice elected governor of the state; fragments of all the companies of the Third Minnesota; one company of the Ninth Minnesota attached to the Sixth; thirty-eight Renville Rangers; twenty-eight mounted citizen guards; and sixteen citizen artillerists — in all, 1,619 men.[50]

With clearing weather Sibley issued on the eighteenth of September a formal order of march. As the whole command had to be ferried across the Minnesota in a single scow, but three or four miles were made on the nineteenth. Three days' leisurely marching along the government road brought the army at the close of the twenty-second to the neighborhood of the Yellow Medicine. A few mounted Indians had shown themselves on the flanks of the column and their scouts had fired several of the small bridges on the road, causing some delay.[51] The halt was made on the right of a small lake of good water from which issued a small rivulet which meandered through a swale a quarter of a mile in width.[52] This at first curved to the north and east and then took a southeastwardly direction down a ravine which deepened toward the Minnesota. In so favorable a camping place Sibley disposed his troops behind sufficient extempore

[50] Report of the adjutant general, in *Executive Documents*, 1862, insert opposite p. 308. William Crooks was a son of Ramsay Crooks, Sibley's old chief and patron in the fur trade.
[51] Sibley Order Book, 32; Plummer Diary; Sibley to his wife, September 19, 1862, Sibley Papers; *Minnesota in the Civil and Indian Wars*, 2: 234; Heard, *Sioux War*, 167-169, 173. Heard was with the expedition.
[52] Probably through some blunder of a guide, the lake was miscalled "Wood Lake." The name belongs to another lake in the next township on the west. The name which should have been used was "Lone Tree Lake." It lay in the northwestern quarter of section 9, township 114, range 38. See Heard, *Sioux War*, 173, and Andrews, in *Minnesota in the Civil and Indian Wars*, 1: 159. Maps of the battle ground and vicinity made by W. A. Truesdell, a government surveyor, in October, 1871, may be found in his "Field Notes of Wood Lake and Birch Coulie Battle Fields," a manuscript notebook in the possession of the Minnesota Historical Society. See also the map on page 184, *post*.

intrenchments. The Third Regiment lay along the crest of the southern slope of the swale, and on its left rear was placed the Sixth, fronting the lakelet. The Seventh held the ground on the right rear behind the ravine with its right somewhat refused. The wagons and the artillery were in the area thus partially inclosed.[53]

The half-breeds who brought Little Crow's message on the seventh of September assured Sibley that the Indians would give him battle at or near the Yellow Medicine. Later information that they had concentrated at Red Iron's village twelve miles above the Yellow Medicine led to the unfortunate inference that they would await his attack at that place. Had he appreciated as well as Little Crow the advantages of the deep timbered gorge of the Yellow Medicine with its precipitous banks as a line of defense; had he been able to keep out an advance guard of cavalry, no matter how small, if efficient; and had his scouts possessed the enterprise of those of the enemy, Sibley would not have been ignorant of the fact that the Sioux were marching down the Minnesota while he was marching up.[54] Nor would a war council have been held by the Indians while Sibley's soldiers were sleeping unapprehensive some three miles away. Why it was not there decided to fall on Sibley's column while it was threading its way down the long sloping road descending into the valley, up the corresponding one rising from it, or across the intervening swale with the considerable rivulet running through it, may remain for the present, at least, a matter of conjecture. The Indian council seems not to have entertained this idea and it positively rejected a proposal for a night attack. It finally agreed on a plan for a daylight attack, but one involving the favorite Indian tactics of an ambush. In pursuance of this Little Crow divided his warriors into three parties. One of them was placed across the

[53] As described to the author on the ground, October 18, 1910, by Judge Loren W. Collins of the Seventh Minnesota; recorded in the author's notebooks, 6: 82.

[54] Sibley to his wife, September 8, 1862, Sibley Papers; *Minnesota in the Civil and Indian Wars*, 2: 227, 228. Big Eagle, in *Minnesota Historical Collections*, 6: 397, says, "Our scouts were very active and vigilant, and we heard from him [*Sibley*] nearly every hour."

government road in the skirt of timber about the Yellow
Medicine gorge; another was placed in line along the east
side of the road and concealed in the tall grass and the swells
of the prairie; the third was hidden in the ravine opposite
Sibley's right.[55] The whole number of Sioux warriors who
marched down to the battle was, by actual count, 738, but
a portion not easy to estimate either kept out of the fight or
gave ineffective support.[56]

Crow had observed that Sibley, for lack of cavalry, had
few and sometimes no flankers to his column and no advanced picket guard for his camp. His scheme was to wait
until the white soldiers, careless of danger, were strung out
on the road in the morning, when his warriors at a signal
should spring from their ambushes and stampede the whole
body with their yells and their gunfire.[57] The Sioux warriors
evidently cherished the delusion that the white volunteers
would not fight in the open and that if there were no barricades for refuge they could be run down and slaughtered like
sheep. The ingenious and audacious scheme might have
been carried out but for an accident.

The men of the Third Minnesota, who, as Heard asserts,
"had acted in a very boisterous manner ever since it joined
us," were not unwilling to show the raw levies of the Sixth
and Seventh how the standard ration could be improved
upon if they were allowed to diverge from the line of march.
A number of them had learned that an abundance of potatoes had ripened in the Indian gardens about the mouth of
the Yellow Medicine and they arranged a foraging party.
It has been asserted that leave was not obtained, but the

[55] Renville, in *Minnesota Historical Collections*, 10: 607 (part 2); Mrs. Nancy Huggan to
Holcombe, May 27, June 14, 1894, Holcombe Papers; *Sisseton and Wahpeton Claim Case
Record, Evidence for Claimant*, 87, 117, 170. Witnesses for claimants in the Sisseton and
Wahpeton claim case testified that Little Crow proposed in council a night attack on Sibley's
camp but was dissuaded from it by friendly Indians. Big Eagle, in *Minnesota Historical
Collections*, 6: 397, says that "some . . . men" were placed "behind a hill to the west."
The old government road running northwesterly has been obliterated and replaced by new
roads on section lines.

[56] Brown, *In Captivity*, 21 (serial 4029). A notable dispute on this point is touched upon
in the Appendix, no. 12, *post*.

[57] Big Eagle, in *Minnesota Historical Collections*, 6: 397.

fact that wagons were allowed to go out indicates that at
least no objection was made. The men started about seven
o'clock in the morning, crossed the creek by the bridge, and
diverged from the road toward the east. They had gone not
more than half a mile from camp when they were fired on by
Indians lying in the grass. Several were wounded—one,
mortally. The men of the Third who had remained in camp,
seeing their comrades thus attacked, seized their arms and
rushed to the front without waiting for orders. Being well-
drilled troops, they assembled in companies as they ran and
formed a line on the crest of the swale. Major Welch deployed half the command as skirmishers and ordered, or at
least permitted, an advance. It was a gallant deed, but only
a successful event could have justified so rash a movement
by a single battalion without orders from the commander of
the field responsible for the disposition of his forces and
supposed to be capable of forming some plan of action under
any circumstances.

The Indians were at first not in force at the point and gave
way before the advance of the little battalion until it had
gained a distance of about a mile from camp. By this time
the enemy had gathered in force on its front and had deployed in their usual "fan-shaped" fashion threatening its
flanks. Sibley saw the danger and sent a staff officer with
an order for the Third to retire. Major Welch, however,
was so confident that he could hold his ground that he delayed compliance. Sibley, not so confident and probably
doubtful about the behavior of his untried regiments, instead
of ordering the latter up to support the Third, repeated his
order to the Third to retire. Through a misunderstanding
of a command the retreat became for a time disordered, but
the battalion was presently reëstablished somewhat to the
front of its camp, where it held its ground against the Indian
center. The Renville Rangers, who had bivouacked on the
immediate right of the Third, had a part in this movement
hard to comprehend from the slender information now

accessible; but the claim has been made that they played a part quite as heroic as that of the men of the Third. Observing a movement of Indians toward the ravine on the right, Colonel Sibley ordered Lieutenant Colonel Marshall to repulse them. With his five companies of the Seventh and one of the Sixth, aided by the six-pounder gun, Marshall not only drove back those Indians but cleared from the ravine the detachment which had been lying in ambush there, fortunately with small loss. Marshall's left was supported by an advance of the Renville Rangers and the Third Minnesota. On the extreme left a threatened attack in considerable force was repelled by one or two companies of the Sixth under Major Robert N. McLaren. Captain Horace B. Wilson, afterwards state superintendent of public instruction, received a painful, but not disabling, wound. After about two hours of desultory firing the Indians upon signal disappeared and Sibley deemed it inadvisable to order his handful of raw troopers in pursuit.[58]

So ended the "battle" of Wood Lake, so called for it seemed to be such to the inexperienced troops. Chaplain Riggs called it "quite a little fight" and General Pope mentioned it as a "skirmish." Sibley referred to it in his report as a "conflict of a serious nature." Still, it ended the campaign so far as fighting was concerned. The losses were seven killed or mortally wounded and thirty-four others

[58] Heard, *Sioux War*, 173-175; Andrews, in *Minnesota in the Civil and Indian Wars*, 1:159; recollections of Captain Ezra T. Champlin, in *Minnesota in the Civil and Indian Wars*, 2:244-247. There is much variation in regard to the size of the foraging party. General Andrews says that there were four or five teams with civilian teamsters and four soldiers to each wagon, which is probably correct. The teams, of course, were quickly turned and started for camp. Colonel Sibley, in his report in *Minnesota in the Civil and Indian Wars*, 2:240-242, states that when about three hundred Indians came dashing toward his bivouac, "whooping and yelling in their usual style and firing with great rapidity," the "Renville Guards, under Lieutenant Gorman, was sent by me to check them." Did the commander expect a successful check by forty men? See the last paragraph of the report. See also West, *Sibley*, 271, for a slightly variant account, and Colonel Marshall's report, in *Minnesota in the Civil and Indian Wars*, 2:242. General Andrews in his narrative represents the Third Regiment men and the Renville Rangers as making "a simultaneous and determined charge" along with the companies of the Seventh. Captain Champlin in his recollections states that Lieutenant Olin with fifty men of the Third "made a wild charge into the midst of the savages, completely routing them in our front." Interviews with participants are recorded in the author's notebooks as follows: Major James M. Bowler, 4: 49; 6: 21; Judge Collins, 4: 102; Reverend H. H. Wallace, 8: 98.

more or less severely wounded.⁵⁹   Fourteen bodies of Indians
were collected and buried in front of the position occupied
by the men of the Third.   Additional casualties—and it is
probable that there were such—have not been ascertained.⁶⁰
In an order published the day after the engagement Sibley
expressed his extreme pain and mortification over the
scalping of the Indians who were slain and threatened severe
punishment should such brutality be repeated.   "The bodies
of the dead," said he, "even of a savage enemy shall not be
subjected to indignities by civilized & christian men."⁶¹

After leaving the field the Indians returned at once to
their rendezvous at Red Iron's village, which they reached
at sunset.   They were fully aware of the completeness of
their defeat in a final stand taken on a chosen battle ground.

⁵⁹ *Minnesota in the Civil and Indian Wars*, 2: 240, 257; letter of Dr. Riggs, September 23,
in the *Saint Paul Press* of October 3, 1862.  "In my opinion," Riggs adds, "our men did
well."  Sibley, in his letter to his wife of September 23, in the Sibley Papers, called it "a
desperate fight of two hours."  In regard to the number of casualties, see Sibley's field
returns for September, in the report of the adjutant general, in *Executive Documents*, 1862,
pp. 307, 308; *Proceedings of the Dedication of the Monument Erected in Honor of the Volunteer
Soldiers at the Battle of Wood Lake*, 6 (Minneapolis, 1911); *Minnesota in the Civil and Indian
Wars*, 2: 243, 244; and Satterlee, *Victims of the Indian Massacre.*  Two of the killed and three
of the mortally wounded were from the Third Regiment, as were also twenty-seven of the
wounded.

⁶⁰ *Minnesota in the Civil and Indian Wars*, 2: 241; *Dedication of the Wood Lake Monument*,
11.  Two witnesses in the *Sisseton and Wahpeton Claim Case Record, Evidence for Defendant*, 290, 322, give the names of sixteen Indians killed at Wood Lake.  The reader may
observe that ten of the sixteen were Sisseton and Wahpeton, and the other six, lower
Sioux.

⁶¹ Sibley Order Book, 35.  On October 18, 1910, there was dedicated a monument of
marble and granite, of tasteful design and sufficiently imposing, which had been erected at a
central point of the Wood Lake battle field at the expense of the state by a board of commissioners.  The legislature of 1907 had appropriated the sum of five hundred dollars for the
purchase of a tract of not less than one acre of the Wood Lake battle ground, and an act of
1909 had authorized the erection of a suitable monument and appropriated two thousand
dollars for the purpose.  See *General Laws*, 1907, p. 459; 1909, p. 441.  The inscriptions are
as follows: On the north side, "To the memory of the men who here lost their lives in an
engagement between Minnesota volunteer soldiers and the Sioux Indians, Sept. 23, 1862";
on the east side, "Anthony C. Collins, Richard H. McElroy, Ernest Paul, Charles E. Frink,
Edwin E. Ross, De Grove Kimball and Matthew Cantwell were killed and thirty-four men
were wounded in the action"; on the south side, "The soldiers were commanded by Col.
Henry H. Sibley; the Indians by Chief Little Crow"; on the west side, "Erected by the state
in 1910 under the supervision of commissioners appointed by the governor, Loren W.
Collins, Ezra T. Champlin and Mathias Holl, participants in the battle."  The Honorable
Loren W. Collins, chairman of the board of commissioners and a former associate justice
of the state supreme court, presided at the dedication.  The principal addresses were made
by Governor Adolph O. Eberhart, Judge Collins, Captain Champlin, and the author of this
work.  The proceedings, including the addresses made, were published in an octavo pamphlet
of thirty-two pages, which contains a photograph of the monument and copies of the inscriptions on it.

The next day the hostiles of all bands represented took their families and departed to "scatter out over the plains" beyond immediate pursuit. Many who had been friendly also took to flight, fearing that the white soldiers would not discriminate but would regard all Indians as enemies.[62]

Had Sibley been governed by military considerations only, he would have left the battle field in the afternoon of the twenty-third, would have passed the gorge of the Yellow Medicine, and by a forced march would have reached the neighborhood of the Indian camp by nightfall. His chief concern now was the recovery of the captives, estimated to number about three hundred, in the hands of the disappointed savages, who might delight in giving a dramatic close to their campaign by an indiscriminate slaughter and a glorious harvest of scalps. There is testimony that Little Crow on the day after the battle declared to his assembled warriors that "the captives must all be killed." Fortunately his influence had already ended. Sibley knew of the dissidence in the Indian ranks and had learned that friendly half-breeds had formed a separate camp and soldiers' lodge. He therefore allowed his army to rest at Wood Lake that day and the next. On the twenty-fourth he wrote to three loyal chiefs that he was delaying his advance for fear that the war party would murder the prisoners before they, the friendlies, "could make . . . arrangements." He then added, "Now that I learn . . . that most of the captives are in safety in your camp I shall move on tomorrow."[63] It was but a leisurely march that he made on the morrow, September 25, to the Hazelwood mission, where he treated the command to a dress parade in the afternoon.[64] On the morning of the twenty-sixth he marched a few miles farther and halted near an Indian camp of 150 lodges. The occupants consisted of a nucleus of Mdewakanton, headed by Wabasha and Taopi, who had been well disposed from the

[62] Brown, *In Captivity*, 21 (serial 4029).
[63] Brown, *In Captivity*, 22; *Minnesota in the Civil and Indian Wars*, 2: 249.
[64] Plummer Diary.

beginning; a larger number of the same bands who within the last three days had become repentant and were willing to submit to the mercies of their conquerors; a considerable body of Wahpeton full-bloods and mixed-bloods; a small Sisseton element; and the captives.   Years after a contro-

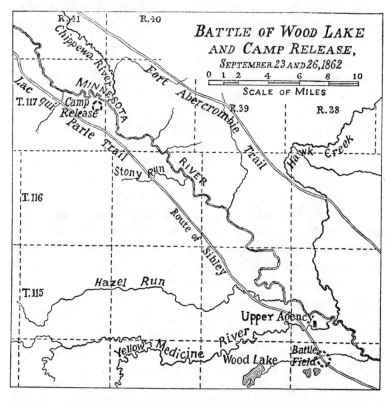

BATTLE OF WOOD LAKE
AND CAMP RELEASE,
SEPTEMBER 23 AND 26, 1862

versy arose over the question whether lower Sioux or upper dominated that camp and were entitled to credit for rescuing and releasing the captives.[65]

In the afternoon of September 26 Colonel Sibley, attended by his staff, his corps commandants, and an escort of troops,

[65] *Minnesota in the Civil and Indian Wars*, 2: 254; Brown, *In Captivity*, 22.  Brown gives the number of lodges as about 150.  In a letter to the author he says the number of souls to the lodge under the circumstances may have been ten.  Seven was the usual rule.  On the controversy mentioned, see the Appendix, no. 12, *post*.

proceeded unmounted but in stately fashion, with "drums beating and colors flying," to the Indian camp. With his officers, Sibley "entered . . . to the centre of the circle formed by the numerous lodges." He at once, through an interpreter, ordered all the captives to be brought before him. He expressed his "views of the late proceedings" to an assemblage of Indians and mixed-bloods and listened to extenuating oratory from the chiefs and headmen. Ninety-one white captives and about 150 mixed-bloods were turned over to him. These numbers were presently increased to 107 whites and 162 half-breeds — in all, 269. Most of the women, among whom were persons of education and refinement, hailed their deliverer with tears of joy and gratitude, but some had been so wrought upon by the scenes through which they had passed that they seemed dazed and stolid. In place of the Indian clothing that they had been forced to wear, the Indian women had supplied what they could from their stores of plundered wardrobes. Our prosaic diarist records, "They looked rather hard, but not so bad as we would expect." A few could bear testimony to kind treatment and many to the faithful efforts of Christian Indians to secure their safety and deliverance. They were, of course, cared for as well as the circumstances permitted. Some of the soldiers gave up their underclothing for the comfort of the captives. On the next day they were sent down to Fort Ridgely.[66]

<hr>

[66] Plummer Diary; Juni, in Fritsche, *Brown County*, 1:122; West, *Sibley*, 274-277. "He entered the camp," writes the biographer, "with an air of sovereignty and military supremacy, as if he owned the universe." West gives Sibley's own account from "Private Notes," which unfortunately have not been found. The biographer indulges in a lofty flight of rhetoric. See also *Minnesota in the Civil and Indian Wars*, 2:255. For the number of captives released, see the report of the adjutant general, in *Executive Documents*, 1862, p. 455. He speaks of some twelve or fifteen still remaining in the hands of the savages. Of these captives no further account has been found. Sibley in letters to his wife dated September 27, 28, October 10, 1862, in the Sibley Papers, mentions the case of a married woman who had become infatuated with the Indian who had captured her. For a list of the captives released, which may possibly be incomplete, see the *Mankato Semi-Weekly Record*, October 11, and the *Central Republican* (Faribault), October 8, 1862. In 1893 the legislature appropriated $2,500 for the erection of a monument on the site of Camp Release. See *General Laws*, 1893, p. 380. The half-breeds had not at any time been in danger of their lives.

The double object of the campaign — the defeat and dispersion of the Sioux and the release of the captives — had now been accomplished. Within a week after the affair at Wood Lake President Lincoln made Colonel Sibley a brigadier general of volunteers.[67] Up to this time he had occupied without protest from any quarter the anomalous position of a Minnesota militia colonel at large, exercising command over troops mostly enlisted for, but not mustered into, the service of the United States. Up to this time, moreover, it had been a Minnesota state war. Governor Ramsey had not failed to notify the secretary of war of the outbreak and of his dispositions for defense and he had appealed to the department to extend the dates set for the draft. Senator Wilkinson telegraphed the president of the existence of "a most terrible and exciting Indian war." His request for postponement of the draft being denied by the iron secretary, Ramsey appealed to the president. He received this characteristic reply by telegraph, dated August 27: "Yours received. Attend to the Indians. If the draft cannot proceed of course it will not proceed. Necessity knows no law. The Government cannot extend the time. A. LINCOLN."[68]

The reports and applications from Minnesota were at first not taken very seriously at Washington. On the sixth of September, at five o'clock in the morning, Ramsey

[67] On March 11, 1863, the Senate rejected this appointment by vote of 17 to 21. Three days later a reconsideration was voted, but the session ended without further action. Ramsey, writing to Donnelly from Washington on March 18, says, "I had Sibleys case, which had been disposed of by his rejection the day before I reached this reconsidered, but for lack of a quorum could not have him confirmed." The letter is in the Donnelly Papers. On March 20, 1863, the appointment was renewed by the president, and it was finally confirmed on April 7, 1864. Sibley was later appointed major general of volunteers by brevet. He did not retire from the service until late in 1866. See *Senate Executive Proceedings*, 13: 60, 128, 189, 231, 283, 298, 310, 349, 457, 458, 459, 461, 479; *Minnesota Historical Collections*, 3: 280-282; and West, *Sibley*, 278, 296-301, 335-340. Daniels, in his "Indian Outbreak," 19, expresses doubt as to whether the promotion was deserved for holding an intrenched camp with fifteen hundred men against an Indian force of one-third that number. But the promotion was for the conduct of the whole campaign and was deserved.

[68] *Minnesota in the Civil and Indian Wars*, 2: 194, 199, 200, 201. The dispatch from Wilkinson was signed also by William P. Dole, commissioner of Indian affairs, and John G. Nicolay, one of the private secretaries of the president, who was of the commissioner's party for the treaty with the Red Lake Chippewa.

telegraphed the president: "Those Indian outrages continue. . . . This is not our war; it is a national war.
. . . Answer me at once. More than 500 whites have been
murdered." Before the close of that day a war department
order named Major General John Pope, U. S. A., commander
of a newly created Military Department of the Northwest.
The letter of the secretary communicating this order was
couched in terms so complimentary that it must have been
truly consolatory to a general officer who had lately lost
command of a great army in the field after a series of defeats, provided that he had no sense of humor. Pope was
authorized in orders to employ whatever forces might be
necessary to suppress hostilities, but he seems to have been
left to pick up whatever scattered battalions he could.[69]

General Pope's first letter of advice and instructions,
dated St. Paul, September 17, did not reach Sibley until
he was one day out from Fort Ridgely in pursuit of Little
Crow. Pope made no change in Sibley's plans, but only
urged him to push on and exterminate or ruin all Indians
engaged in the outbreak. The new department commander was not without experience on the border and he
knew the Sioux. He understood the futility of chasing
mounted Indians with infantry. Without delay he formed a
large plan of operations, both defensive and offensive. He
proposed to station one thousand men, half of them mounted,
at Fort Abercrombie, five hundred mounted men at Otter
Tail, one thousand men at Fort Ripley, and five hundred
mounted men and five hundred infantry at Crystal Lake;
to furnish Sibley with one thousand cavalry; and to establish
at Fort Ridgely a base of supplies for them and for other
troops. General in Chief Halleck informed Pope, however,
that the organization of a large force for an Indian campaign
was not approved by the war department as it was deemed
unnecessary and that his extravagant requisitions for war
supplies could not possibly be filled. Pope in his reply

---

[69] *Minnesota in the Civil and Indian Wars*, 2: 225.

represented to Halleck, no doubt in good faith, that there were 2,600 Sioux warriors at the upper agency waiting to devour Sibley's little force of 1,600 men. The Chippewa and the Winnebago were on the verge of outbreak and all the tribes clear to the mountains were moving. Pope was finally permitted to borrow for a short time five companies of a Wisconsin regiment and five hundred cavalry from Iowa with which to relieve the militia companies and squads holding the line of posts along the Blue Earth.[70]

On the ninth of October Pope was able to inform Halleck that the Sioux war might be considered at an end. Not many days passed before he had occasion to expect that his connection with it might presently cease. On October 27, "because of a thousand rumors," he inquired of the general in chief whether he should remain in St. Paul the next winter. In response to this inquiry, Halleck on the twenty-eighth telegraphed: "It is proper . . . for me to say to you that there has been urged upon the President a proposi-tion to remove you and appoint a civilian (a member of Congress) in your place. I need not add that I have and will oppose it."[71] The civilian thus referred to was none other than Senator Henry M. Rice, whose term was soon to expire. Mention has already been made of the tardy acquiescence of that senator in the resolution of the government to go to war for its supremacy through the whole area of the country and of his complete and cheerful devotion to the Union cause after the war for the Union had begun.[72] The proposi-tion to give him military rank and command, especially in a quarter where his great experience in Indian affairs would come into service, was not devoid of reasonableness.. Heard, the leading chronicler of the Sioux war, expresses the opinion that had Rice been in superior control, Colonel Sibley would not have begged in vain for cavalry. Sibley in a letter to his wife, who had evidently expressed to him her disgust at

[70] *Minnesota in the Civil and Indian Wars*, 2: 233, 238, 266.
[71] *Minnesota in the Civil and Indian Wars*, 2: 270, 284.
[72] See *ante*, pp. 70, 73-76.

the prospect that Rice would be given command over her husband, lets her know that he would prefer to serve under his old political foe rather than under some stranger from without the state.    General Pope, as might have been expected, had his view of the proposition, to which he gave expression in a letter to Halleck, dated November 20. "Sibley," said he, "has lived here longer than Rice . . . and is, besides, a high-toned, honorable man, who has the respect of everybody, as he has conducted a successful campaign against the Indians, and endured all the hardships and exposures of such service.    The appointment of Rice, who has done nothing, will be a great and unmerited humiliation to him."    General Sibley was spared the humiliation and Rice did not score another triumph over his long-time political enemy.    Pope was presently authorized to move his headquarters to Madison, Wisconsin, leaving Sibley in command of the District of Minnesota carved out of the Department of the Northwest.[73]

[73] Heard, *Sioux War*, 181; Sibley to his wife, November 3, 1862, Sibley Papers; *Official Records*, series 1, vol. 12, part 3, p. 826.  See the *Saint Paul Press*, October 24, 25, November 8, 23, and the *Saint Paul Pioneer*, November 23, 1862, for spicy remarks.

# VII. THE PUNISHMENT OF THE SIOUX

THE military power of the Sioux had been shattered at Wood Lake on September 23 and three days later the white captives, (269) in number, preserved by the effective intervention of the friendly Indians, had been delivered to Colonel Sibley. Two further objects of his campaign now remained to be accomplished. One of them, the utter expulsion of the Sioux nation from Minnesota territory, which was universally demanded, was necessarily postponed. Without cavalry, without adequate commissariat, with transportation mostly impressed from farmers, a campaign out on the treeless prairies stretching to the Missouri River was impossible, especially as the early frosts would soon render the buffalo grass unfit for consumption by the animals. There was talk enough about an extreme and lively pursuit of the fiends and some active effort was made toward it; General Pope got some four hundred men of the Third Regiment mounted and Governor Ramsey endeavored to hasten the formation of a regiment of mounted rangers, as authorized by the war department; but the season and the elements decided adversely.[1]

There remained a second objective to be accomplished —the punishment of the Sioux. As the terrible news of the massacre of August 18 spread throughout the settled parts of the state, there rose everywhere the cry: "Death to the murderous Sioux. . . . Exterminate the fiends. . . . Let vengeance swift, complete and unsparing teach the red-skinned demons the power of the white man." That there was well-grounded palliation for such an outbreak of passion cannot be denied. In spite of his genuine respect for the good

---

[1] *Minnesota in the Civil and Indian Wars*, 2: 257, 259, 277, 282b; Sibley Order Book, 124; report of the adjutant general, in Minnesota, *Executive Documents*, 1862, pp. 241, 247, 249, 251; Plummer Diary.

traits in Indian character, his long friendship with many
of the leading men among the Sioux, and his own eloquent
appeal in Congress for justice to the Indian, Sibley was
not able to stem the current of popular demand for bloody
retribution.  On August 24 from St. Peter he wrote to Governor Ramsey of "these miserable wretches, who, among all
devils in human shape, are among the most cruel and
ferocious. . . . My heart is steeled against them, and if I
have the means, and can catch them, I will sweep them with
the besom of death."  It is worth while to note here that
at this very time Sibley was complained of for inaction and
for unwillingness to do harm to his old Indian friends.[2]

General Pope was at least equally affected by the common
sentiment.  In a dispatch of September 28 he instructed
Sibley to make no treaty with the Indians.  "The horrible
massacres of women and children . . . call for punishment
beyond human power to inflict. . . . It is my purpose
utterly to exterminate the Sioux if I have the power to do
so. . . . They are to be treated as maniacs or wild beasts."
Sibley, however, was too wise and too humane to take his
superior officer in earnest.  On the same date that these
instructions were sent he was organizing of his own motion
a military commission of five of his officers "to try sum-
marily" such Indian prisoners as he might bring before them
"and pass judgement upon them if found guilty of murder
or other outrages upon the whites during the . . . hostilities."  He had already in custody sixteen men whom a
sifting committee of officers had picked from the warriors
in the friendly camp who, when Little Crow's bands broke
up, had preferred surrender to flight.  On the same date
Sibley, in a letter notifying Pope of the appointment of the
commission and of the sixteen prisoners ready for trial, says
of the latter: "If found guilty they will be immediately
executed, although I am somewhat in doubt whether my
authority extends quite so far.  An example is, however,

[2] *Minnesota in the Civil and Indian Wars*, 2: 198.  For Sibley's speech in behalf of the
Indian, see *Congressional Globe*, 31 Congress, 1 session, 1506-1508.

imperatively necessary, and I trust you will approve the act."[3]

The commissioners set to work at once and presently found themselves confronted with a task bigger than they or their commander had expected. In the friendly camp there were at the time of surrender about 150 lodges sheltering some 1,200 souls. This number began immediately to swell. At first individual Indians and small parties came in and gave themselves up. Informed by these of larger bodies hovering in the neighborhood, General Sibley on October 3 sent runners to warn them to come in under a flag of truce and promised protection to all who were innocent. Already the question of feeding so many as had surrendered was pressing. To simplify this, on the fourth 1,250 Indians under a sufficient guard were sent down to the upper Sioux agency, to subsist on the remnants of the crops of the farmer Indians. In a week they had gathered several thousand bushels of corn and potatoes. After their departure a separate camp of Indians was formed adjacent to that occupied by the troops, which had been named "Camp Release." Within the guard line of this second camp were placed the newly arrived Indians as they came in, sometimes in parties of twenty lodges and more. In the course of a week they numbered probably five hundred. For those of them who had improvidently devoured all the subsistence they had gathered in their late forays there was no alternative to surrender. To remain on the open prairie meant death.[4]

[3] *Minnesota in the Civil and Indian Wars*, 2: 256, 257; Sibley Order Book, 36, 37, 46. The military commission appointed on September 28, 1862, consisted of the following officers: Colonel William Crooks of the Sixth Minnesota Infantry, Lieutenant Colonel William R. Marshall of the Seventh, Captain Hiram P. Grant of the Sixth, Captain Hiram S. Bailey of the Sixth, and First Lieutenant Rollin C. Olin of the Third. Lieutenant Olin was judge advocate, but the duties of that office were mainly performed by Isaac V. D. Heard, a lawyer of St. Paul who had enlisted as a private in Captain Anderson's company of mounted men called the "Cullen Guards." He has been erroneously mentioned as the recorder of the commission. After a few days' sessions Lieutenant Colonel Marshall was relieved and his place was filled by Major George Bradley of the Seventh.

[4] *Minnesota in the Civil and Indian Wars*, 2: 254, 261, 263-265, 267, 272, 276; Brown, *In Captivity*, 24 (serial 4029). Brown says that about six thousand bushels of potatoes and fifteen hundred bushels of corn were gathered at the upper agency. The name "Camp Release" is attached to the township embracing the site — township 116 north, range 41 west, in Lac qui Parle County. Rose, *Yellow Medicine County*, 71.

A few days later an expedition of 252 men was dispatched under the command of Lieutenant Colonel William R. Marshall of the Seventh Minnesota Infantry to scour the country westward toward the James River. But thirty-nine men and about one hundred women and children were brought in. A smaller expedition sent out under the command of Captain Orlando C. Merriman of the Sixth surprised and captured a camp of sixty-seven Indians on Lac qui Parle, whose wagons had still some goods plundered from the whites.[5]

General Sibley informed Pope on September 30 that the "work of the military commission still continues" and added that arrests were made daily. On October 4 he reported  that twenty-nine cases had been tried and that the majority had been convicted and sentenced to death. In order not to discourage wandering parties of Indians from coming in, arrests were now suspended for a week and more and Sibley notified Pope that he would send prisoners thereafter arrested to Fort Ridgely for trial by a military commission. This declaration points to the probable receipt of a notice from the superior officer that Sibley's trial commission would presently be superseded by one which Pope would himself appoint. The disposition of those already sentenced appears to have been left to the commander in the field, for on October 7 Sibley informed Pope that he had "20 prisoners under sentence of death by hanging. I have not yet examined the proceedings of the military commission, but although they may not be exactly in form in all the details I shall probably approve them, and hang the villains as soon as I get hold of the others." On the following day notice was given to Pope that the men of a party of twenty lodges then arriving would be sent to Fort Ridgely to be tried. After this no further allusion is found to a commission to sit at Ridgely.[6]

[5] *Minnesota in the Civil and Indian Wars*, 2: 275, 279, 282. Plummer in his diary says that they were a "hard looking lot."
[6] *Minnesota in the Civil and Indian Wars*, 2: 259, 264, 267, 269.

Three days later, on October 11, Sibley informed his department commander that in obedience to an imperative order he would suspend the execution of the twenty convicts and would send them along with other Indians to Fort Snelling to be subject to Pope's direction.  General Pope, who was at the time representing to the war department the necessity of numerous executions, apparently was not satisfied with the deliberate procedure of his subordinate, in spite of the assurance of the latter that the guilty Indians would receive small mercy at his hands.[7]  Accordingly General Sibley, as instructed, on the night of the eleventh reënforced the guards around the second camp and "purged" it of eighty-one warriors, whom, together with the twenty convicts, he chained by the ankles two and two.  Under his orders the officer commanding the guard at Yellow Medicine two days later put under arrest 236 others.  To effect this wholesale batch of arrests at Yellow Medicine an operation which has been called a "justifiable piece of strategy" was resorted to.  An interpreter was directed to notify all the Indians in the camp to appear on the following morning at the agency to be counted by Agent Galbraith preparatory to receiving their unpaid annuities for the year.  "This ruse worked like a charm."  The unsophisticated savages appeared at an early hour, to find the agent and the military commandant seated at a table outside the ruin of the stone agency building with clerks "hard at work on the rolls."  The families came up, were counted, and were motioned to pass on.  As they came to a doorway the men were told to step inside to be counted for extra pay.  As they entered they were asked to give up their arms upon a promise that they would receive them back "shortly."  Two hundred and thirty-six of Little Crow's warriors were thus safely

[7] *Minnesota in the Civil and Indian Wars*, 2: 267, 273.  Pope's imperative order seems to have been to send all Indians down to Fort Snelling to be subject to his direction.  In a letter to his wife, dated October 11, 1862, Sibley mentioned a dispatch from Pope, and added: "I shall, at any rate, be saved the task of hanging a large number of the scoundrels . . . by turning them over to General Pope, to be dealt with at Fort Snelling.  Say nothing about this however."  Sibley Papers.

placed in custody and were presently "fixed" in the same
way as their comrades at Camp Release. A military necessity may have justified this "strategy," but the reader may
judge whether it was calculated to increase the Indians'
respect for either the truthfulness or the bravery of the white
man.[8]

The fifteenth of October was an eventful day at headquarters in Camp Release. In a dispatch of that date
Sibley informed Pope that he was about to send all his
prisoners "below" for trial by the tribunal to be established
there. He would also forward the proceedings in the cases
of the twenty already convicted, after noting his action
thereon. No sooner had the dispatch been started on its
way than two communications dated October 10 came from
St. Paul countermanding in part previous orders relative to
the disposition of the convicted prisoners. Responding to
these communications on October 15, Sibley expressed his
approval of the plan of trying the Sioux prisoners in the field
rather than at Fort Snelling, where it might be difficult to
obtain evidence, and announced that he would set his trial
commission at work again as soon as possible. He also
stated that he would remove his camp to the lower agency
and, after executing those found guilty, would send all the
other Sioux under guard to Fort Snelling.[9]

In a dispatch of October 21 Sibley informed Pope that
his commission was proceeding as rapidly as possible, that
more than 120 cases had been disposed of, and that nearly
300 remained on the docket. He said also that in conformity
with a communication from Pope dated October 17 he would
change his plans. He would execute no Indians "until the
pleasure of the President is known."[10] By October 25,

[8] Sibley to his wife, October 13, 15, 1862, Sibley Papers; *Minnesota in the Civil and Indian Wars*, 2: 274, 276, 277; Brown, *In Captivity*, 24 (serial 4029). Two things may be wondered at: (1) Why had the Indians not been disarmed at the time of their surrender? (2) Why was a "ruse" needed under the circumstances?

[9] *Minnesota in the Civil and Indian Wars*, 2: 277, 278.

[10] *Minnesota in the Civil and Indian Wars*, 2: 256, 257, 281. Up to this time neither Pope nor Sibley seems to have learned that neither of them was authorized to execute death sentences. General Pope should not, however, have been ignorant of Article of War 65.

the little army and its two thousand Indian prisoners of war had been marched down and put into camp at the Redwood agency. Here Sibley found the "greatest difficulty" in preventing intercourse between his own camp and that of the Indians. Notwithstanding his strong line of guards, soldiers would "manage to get among the *gals*, — and the latter, I notice, take care not to give any alarm."[11]

The trial commission resumed its labors in La Bathe's log kitchen to dispose of some three hundred cases. From these labors it rested on the fifth of November, having tried 392 prisoners, of whom 307 were sentenced to death and 16 to imprisonment. Sibley promptly approved all the proceedings except in one case and transmitted them to the department commander.[12] He had instructed the commissioners not to concern themselves about the degree of guilt if they were satisfied that prisoners had been guilty

[11] Sibley to his wife, October 22, 25, 1862, Sibley Papers; Plummer Diary, October 25, 1862. Plummer says that the "men ran most of the way." Brown gives the number of Indians surrendered at Camp Release on September 26 and later, or captured, as 1,918. See his *In Captivity*, 23 (serial 4029). See Sibley Order Book, 42, 47, 55, for stringent orders prohibiting soldiers from passing through the line of sentinels.

[12] Heard, *Sioux War*, 239, and the woodcut opposite. The exception was Indian no. 381, a brother of Other Day, remitted at his solicitation and because the evidence was by no means conclusive. The indorsement, in the manuscript record of the trials, is in Sibley's hand. The record was carried to St. Paul by the Reverend Stephen R. Riggs. See his *Forty Years with the Sioux*, 182. In February, 1909, the record of the trials, long believed to be lost, was discovered by the author, with the aid of Senator Knute Nelson, in the files of the United States Senate. It appeared that President Lincoln had sent the whole record in response to Senator Wilkinson's resolution. See *post*, p. 209. The cases of the Indians condemned to death had been separated from the others. After a few instances, the specifications became stereotyped, as follows: "Charge: Participation in the murders, outrages and robberies committed by the Sioux tribe of Indians on the Minnesota frontier. Specification: In this, that the said . . . a Sioux Indian [*or* half breed] did join with and participate in the murders, and outrages committed by the Sioux tribe of Indians on the Minnesota frontier, between the 18th day of August, 1862, and the 28th day of September, 1862, and particularly in the battles at the Fort, New Ulm, Birch Coolie, and Wood Lake." In a large proportion of the cases the proceedings were very brief, consisting of an arraignment and a confession by the accused that he had been in one or more of the battles. Believing that they would be considered as prisoners of war, the Indians had no hesitation in confessing to presence in the battles. Some amusing pleas in abatement were offered. One Indian pleaded that he had fired, but that his gun was so short that he could not have harmed anybody. Another said that he had a bad gun; it did not go off; he did not fire at the white men, but at the houses. Paywashtay said that he belonged to the church and thought the Devil had been in him since the outbreak. Indian no. 331 fired at a mule but believed he did not hit it.

The result of the author's count from the record of the commission is as follows: whole number tried, 392; acquitted, 65; not proven, 5; sentenced to prison, 16; sentenced to death, 306; Other Day's brother remitted, 1. The reduction to 303 he cannot account for.

of voluntary participation in the murders and massacres. He believed that at least seven-eighths of the convicts had committed most flagrant outrages, many having violated women and murdered children.[13]   In a letter written on November 6 to Governor Ramsey, General Pope stated that the Sioux prisoners, meaning those convicted, would be executed "unless the President forbids it, which, from the tenor of his dispatches, I am sure he will not do."   Evidently he did not as yet realize the need of the affirmative action of the president.   He did, however, forward a telegram giving the names of the 303 Indians condemned to death.   To this the president replied personally on November 10: "Please forward as soon as possible the full and complete record of their convictions. . . . Send all by mail."   This command was, of course, obeyed, but in no haste.   On receiving the record on one of the last days of November, Lincoln placed it in the hands of two persons in whom he had confidence, with directions to sift the evidence carefully and in particular to select those who had been proved guilty of violating women and to distinguish between those who had committed wanton butcheries and those who had only participated in battles.[14]

The rapidity with which the military commission disposed of the cases brought before it is easily explained by remarking that by far the larger number were those of warriors charged with presence at and participation in the battles. Believing themselves to be simply prisoners of war, they severally pleaded guilty and were sentenced to be hanged. The cases of murder and outrage were conducted with more, and perhaps sufficient, deliberation; but the Reverend Stephen R. Riggs, who was constantly present, publicly stated at the time that, when forty cases were disposed of in six or

[13] *Sisseton and Wahpeton Claim Case Record, Evidence for Defendant*, 400.

[14] *Minnesota in the Civil and Indian Wars*, 2: 288, 289; message of President Lincoln on *Indian Barbarities in Minnesota* (37 Congress, 3 session, *Senate Executive Documents*, no. 7 — serial 1149); *Saint Paul Pioneer*, November 18, 23, 1862. The issue of the *Pioneer* for November 23 states that the *New York Times* "very properly" remarks that the cost of the telegram, four hundred dollars, should be deducted from Pope's salary.

seven hours, there was not full opportunity for elucidation of evidence. He had no particular liking for the manner of procedure generally followed and expected that the meager-ness of the record would lead to new trials. Still, he admitted that "a terrible necessity — the demand of public justice — requires that the great majority of those who are condemned should be executed."[15] Numerous suggestions were thrown out that Riggs was unduly lenient toward the unfortunate people among whom he had spent the prime of his life. There is evidence enough to acquit him of that. It was with his assistance that a large number of the accused were identi-fied and arraigned. The leading historian of the war, Isaac V. D. Heard, relates that Riggs assembled the half-breeds and others in a tent and interrogated them concerning suspected persons, and adds, "He was, in effect, the Grand Jury of the court." Riggs believed, as did many among the Sioux, that there were certain Indians who were guilty of crimes for which they deserved punishment and which could not be condoned as acts of war.[16]

[15] Letters of Riggs, November 27, December 3, in the *Saint Paul Press*, November 29, December 7, 1862; Riggs, *Tah-koo Wah-kan; or, the Gospel among the Dakotas*, 333 (Boston, [1869]). Dr. J. W. Daniels disapproved of the condemnations on the ground that "a large number were condemned on general principles, which was more in harmony with the predjudices of the whites, than justice." See his "Indian Outbreak," 20. John P. Williamson, in a letter dated November 5, 1862, in the *Missionary Herald*, 59:14-16 (January, 1863), says: "I have no doubt that very many of them are guilty, but I am not satisfied with the way the trials are conducted. Four hundred have been tried in less time than is generally taken in our courts with the case of a single murderer." Williamson did not understand that the tribunal was a military commission and not a court of law. "Again, in very many of the instances," he continues, "a man's own testimony is the only evidence against him." (None other was needed in cases of confession.) "If he denies, he is cross-examined with all the ingenuity of a modern lawyer. . . . They are not allowed counsel, and are scarcely allowed a word of explanation themselves. As they know nothing of the manner of conduct-ing trials, if a mistake occurs, they are unable to correct it; and often, not being acquainted with the English language, they very imperfectly understand the evidence upon which they are convicted. . . . The services of Mr. Riggs . . . have been invaluable." See page 16 of the same volume for the opinion of Thomas S. Williamson that the trials had "been con-ducted with too much haste and under the influence of undue excitement." West, in his *Sibley*, 280, asserts that Sibley gave strict instructions for fair trials, the best possible defense, and the concession of every reasonable doubt to the accused.

[16] Heard, *Sioux War*, 251; letter of Riggs, November 27, in the *Saint Paul Press*, Novem-ber 29, 1862. Riggs says that he took no pleasure in doing his duty at the trials. In the *Press* of December 17, 1863, Riggs reviews at length Heard's *Sioux War*. He praises the author's industry and his desire to ascertain and to relate the truth, but suggests that he is much too confident that he has in all cases been successful. After offering certain corrections, which need not be noted at this point, the reviewer proceeds to rebut Heard's statement that

The business of the commission was much expedited and
simplified by the instrumentality of one Otakle or Godfrey,
a mulatto son of a French Canadian by a negro mother.
He had married a Sioux woman and had lived at the lower
agency five years. He was the first to be put on trial,
charged, first, with the murder of seven whites, more or less,
and, second, with participation in the hostilities between
August 19 and September 28. His plea was "not guilty"
and he alleged that he had been forced to accompany the war
parties. The witnesses could only testify to his brags that
he had killed so many persons and to the apparent satisfaction with which he wore breechclout and paint, fighting and
acting like an Indian. The commission acquitted him of
participating in the massacres but found him guilty of the
second specification and sentenced him to death. Pending
the decision in his case Godfrey became, according to Heard,
"the greatest institution of the commission." His memory
of persons and transactions was remarkable and he charmed
all present with his melodious voice and fits of musical
laughter. "He seemed," it is related, "specially designed as
an instrument of justice."[17]

he, Riggs, had served as "a kind of a grand jury" to the military commission of 1862. On
account of his experience in spelling Indian names he had filled up papers at headquarters
with the names of prisoners and witnesses. In no sense had he acted as an accuser. He did
not know personally more than one-fourth of the prisoners, because they were mostly lower
Sioux, among whom he had never lived. He was present at the trials only on a few occasions,
but he read all the evidence and the findings. While he sympathized with the almost universal feeling in camp that all who had taken part in battles should be convicted, "over
some of their cases" he "felt very sorely." After the lapse of a year Riggs broke silence to
say that the trials were conducted in too much haste, that the records were generally too
meager, and that the pressure brought on prisoners to convict themselves was not in accordance with military regulations or with the spirit of Christianity. Many were guiltier than
they appeared to be and "many were condemned to death on insufficient evidence." He
charitably adds that the excitement and exasperation of the time unfitted them for doing
justice to Indians and says: "We all did as nearly right then as we knew how. But we will
not now . . . defend the wrong whatever it may be; but rather confess it and ask God's
forgiveness."
[17] Heard, *Sioux War*, 251-271. The charges and specifications in this typical case,
with a digest of the evidence, may be found on pages 252-254. See also Heard's letters in the
*Saint Paul Pioneer*, November 15, December 11, 1862. In his letter in the issue of November
15, Heard states that in some cases the prisoners were brought in eight at a time, chained in
pairs. The charges were read by Antoine Freniere. Each one was interrogated and witnesses
were called when necessary. The proceeding was summary but just. Some of the pleas
offered in extenuation were of the most ludicrous sort. About two-thirds of the culprits
admitted that they had fired two or three shots, but said that they had killed no one. If

The trials having been completed, there was no need of maintaining a large Indian camp so remote from the base of supplies. On November 7, Lieutenant Colonel Marshall, with a sufficient guard conducted the uncondemned men and the women and children of the camp to Fort Snelling. The column stretched out at times to four miles in length. After much hardship to the women and young children, for whom but few wagons were provided, the fort was reached on November 13 and a bivouac was made about a mile distant on the north bank of the Minnesota. As the wretched prisoners traveled through Henderson, the people — men, women, and children — with guns, knives, clubs, and stones, rushed upon them and, before the guard could drive them back, maltreated many. One infant, snatched from its mother, was so injured that it died a few hours later. "The body was quietly laid away," a witness relates, "in the crotch of a tree."[18]

Two days after the departure of the main body of the Sioux prisoners Sibley marched his troops and the convicted warriors to the Blue Earth River and placed them in camp at South Bend, a short distance to the west of Mankato. The column was passing through New Ulm on a day when the bodies of the victims of the battles and massacres thereabout were being removed for appropriate reburial in the cemetery. The sight of the condemned Indians so inflamed

one had taken a horse, it was a little one. If he had driven off a yoke of oxen, it was for his wife. Bellyache was a frequent basis of an alibi, as was hunger, which kept some behind the firing line cooking and eating. Several confessed "the whole thing" and wound up by saying that they were church members. Some said that they were cowards and had not joined in the battles. For Godfrey's own account of the outbreak, see Heard, *Sioux War*, 191-201. On page 255 Heard defends the attitude and the action of the commission. A reading by the author of the original record of the trials found in the Senate archives justifies Heard's humorous remarks.

[18] West, *Sibley*, 281; Brown, *In Captivity*, 25-27 (serial 4029). Brown says that the column departed on November 9 and arrived at Fort Snelling on the fourteenth. The *Saint Paul Press* of November 14, 1862, gives the date of arrival as November 13 and states that the company was made up of from forty to fifty male adults, one or two hundred half-breeds, and women and children enough to swell the total to over eighteen hundred. See also the letter of John P. Williamson, November 28, 1862, in the *Missionary Herald*, 59:43 (February, 1863). Williamson, who accompanied the column, erroneously gives the date of arrival as November 20. "Had they," he writes, "been in charge of a less efficient officer [*than Marshall*], I do not doubt they would have been mobbed, and many of them killed."

the people that they attacked them with such weapons as could be picked up. Sibley did not dare order his guard to fire upon the rabble, but he drove it back with a bayonet charge. Fifteen of the prisoners and some of the guards were seriously injured. Fifteen or twenty of the citizens were arrested and were marched twelve miles to the next camp. After a sharp reprimand they were released and allowed to return on foot to their town.[19]

From the beginning of his campaign Sibley had persistently urged that he be furnished with a cavalry force. With a few hundred troopers, or even one squadron, of trained cavalry he could disperse and disarm the hostile Sioux. Pope was not indifferent to these demands, but he could not prevail on the war department either to send him mounted troops ready for the field or to recruit new ones. All he could do was to get authority to buy a few hundred horses on which to mount infantrymen. But October was half gone before some five or six hundred men, mostly from the Third Infantry, received their mounts.[20]

There was no delay in giving the raw cavalry employment. Soon after the concentration of the troops and the Indians at the lower agency Lieutenant Joseph H. Swan was sent with four or five hundred men on an expedition to Lake Shetek in Murray County. The object was the arrest of the perpetrators of the murders at Lake Shetek, erroneously supposed at the time to have been Yankton Sioux instead of lower Sisseton. There was a circuitous march of five days to the lake, a rest of a few days, and a return march to Fort Ridgely. After a short rest the command was ordered to Fort Snelling, where it was dismounted and given a furlough. No Indians were seen in the desolated region traversed by

[19] Sibley to his wife, November 12, 1862, Sibley Papers. "The Dutch she devils! — They were as fierce as tigresses," Sibley writes. See also West, *Sibley*, 280; the *Mankato Semi-Weekly Record*, November 15, 1862; and a letter from Riggs, dated December 8, in the *Saint Paul Press*, December 11, 1862. Brown, in his *In Captivity*, 25, says that there were 392 convicts, 17 women, 4 children, and 4 friendlies, in all 417 under guard.
[20] *Minnesota in the Civil and Indian Wars*, 2: 228, 231-233, 236, 242, 254, 257-260, 264, 268.

the expedition.  Some bodies of murdered settlers were given
burial.[21]

By this time it was evident to all that no campaign of
any considerable range could be made in a prairie country
at this season of the year.  Soon after the establishment of
"Camp Lincoln" near Mankato, therefore, Sibley turned
over the command to Colonel Stephen Miller of the Seventh
Minnesota, lately promoted from the lieutenant-colonelcy of
the First, and assumed command of the Military District
of Minnesota, with headquarters at St. Paul.[22]

No sooner was it known that President Lincoln had taken
the disposition of the condemned Indians into his own
hands than he was inundated with "appeals": appeals for
mercy, on the one hand, from friends of the Indian who
never had seen one, from people opposed to the death penalty, and from those who regarded the convicts as prisoners
of war.  Among the last was the commissioner of Indian
affairs, who entered his formal protest against "an indiscriminate punishment of men who have laid down their
arms and surrendered themselves as prisoners."[23]  On the
other hand, there was no lack of "appeals" to the president
from the highest sources in Minnesota to hang the whole
batch without delay or discrimination.  On the very day
on which the record was called for by the president, Governor Ramsey telegraphed him expressing the hope that
every Sioux Indian condemned would be executed.  "Private
revenge," he said, would otherwise "take the place of official
judgment."  General Pope on the next day volunteered his
opinion that "the criminals condemned ought in every
view to be at once executed without exception."  Unless

[21] Sibley to his wife, October 20, 1862, Sibley Papers; Andrews, in *Minnesota in the Civil and Indian Wars*, 1: 161.  See also the same work, 2: 270, 278, 281, 282b-282e.  The "re-port" of Lieutenant Joseph H. Swan, dated July 27, 1894, is much expanded with unimportant details.

[22] West, *Sibley*, 284.  Sibley assumed command of the district on November 25, 1862.

[23] West, *Sibley*, 284; *Indian Barbarities in Minnesota*, 1 (serial 1149); William P. Dole to Caleb B. Smith, November 10, 1862, in Indian Office, *Reports*, 1862, p. 69.  This letter may be found also in the *Saint Paul Pioneer*, December 7, 1862.  Dole said that the act would be "a stain upon our national character and a source of future regret."

such execution should be done, and that speedily, nothing could save the fifteen hundred women and children and innocent old men prisoners at Fort Snelling from indiscriminate massacre. Evidently expecting his counsel to prevail, he asked the president to advise him by telegraph of his decision.[24] A memorial of the citizens of St. Paul demanded that the United States authorities, being the chosen instruments of divine vengeance, should perform their plain duty. If they did not, there would be no security for the future. The memorialists also hoped that the friends and relatives of those "foully murdered by those Indian devils, will not be compelled to take vengeance into their own hands, as they assuredly will if Government shall fail in its duty." Citizens of Blue Earth County demanded a "great *atonement*." Not less notable is an address to the president signed by one of the Minnesota senators — not Senator Rice — and by both representatives. These men alleged a number of horrible murders and outrages committed by individuals as a reason why three hundred men should be hung. They raised one point so clearly that the president should have been indebted to them, although he did not concur with them. "These Indians are called by some prisoners of war. There was no war about it. It was wholesale robbery, *rape, murder*." They urged the president to "*let the* Law *be executed*" for, if not, "the outraged people of Minnesota will dispose of these wretches without law." Riggs advised that the "*great majority*" of the condemned be executed.[25] The Minnesota newspapers did not neglect the occasion for the display of lurid rhetoric. In an editorial article headed "Boston Philanthropy," the *Saint Paul Press* of November 30 calls for "a lesson which shall ring in their [*the Indians'*]

[24] *Minnesota in the Civil and Indian Wars*, 2: 289.

[25] *Indian Barbarities in Minnesota*, 2-6 (serial 1149); *Saint Paul Pioneer*, November 27, December 9, 10, 1862. The original address of the Minnesota congressmen is in the possession of the Minnesota Historical Society. Wilkinson, Windom, and Aldrich were the signers. Senator Rice did not sign the address, but in a letter published in the *Pioneer* two days later he said: "Every guilty Indian should perish—not one should be spared that he might boast to the Indians of the Plains of his brutal feats." See also letters from Riggs in the *Saint Paul Press*, November 29, December 7, 11, 1862.

ears to the latest generation of them all, that death, swift, relentless and terrible, is the inevitable punishment of murder, and that they had better have not been born than lift a hostile hand against a citizen of Minnesota, in all time to come." General Sibley, having approved the sentences, seems not to have volunteered any advice. In a letter to his wife, he says: "I shall do full justice, but no more. I do not propose to murder any man, even a savage, who is shown to be innocent."[26]

There was much concern throughout Minnesota that a soft-hearted president would yield to the persuasions of Quakers and other philanthropists and fail to have justice done to the Sioux convicts. The editor of the *Saint Paul Press* proposed that the civil authorities of the state should have them indicted by the grand jury. Others were not so fastidious about conforming to regular procedure. There must have been widespread agitation which did not appear in print about securing the execution of all the Indians convicted and possibly about other irregular proceedings.  On November 24 Pope informed the president that he had official information of organizations being rapidly made for the massacring of those Indians and that he was concentrating a large body of troops to protect them. "Humanity," he wrote, "requires an immediate disposition of the case." Four days later Governor Ramsey telegraphed a second time to the president in characteristic style: "Nothing but the speedy execution of the tried and convicted Sioux Indians will save us, here, from scenes of outrage. If you prefer it, turn them over to me and I will order their execution."[27]

[26] October 20, 1862, Sibley Papers. This was written before the president had taken a hand in the matter and after General Pope, presuming that he had power to order the executions, had, as Sibley wrote, devolved the whole matter on him. "This power of life, and death, is an awful thing to exercise, and when I think of more than three hundred human beings are subject to that power, lodged in my hands, it makes me shudder." Sibley to his wife, October 17, 1862, Sibley Papers.
[27] *Saint Paul Press*, November 12, 1862; *Minnesota in the Civil and Indian Wars*, 2: 290; Windom to Donnelly, December 11, 1862, Donnelly Papers; message of Governor Ramsey, January 7, 1863, in *Executive Documents*, 1862, p. 28.

On the night of December 4 a loosely organized crowd estimated at from 150 to 200 persons collected at the old Mankato House, where an abundance of liquid refreshments was served free by some generous citizen, and started from Mankato for South Bend intent on making a demonstration, if not an attack, on the Indian prison. Colonel Stephen Miller, who had been apprised of the movement in time, ordered out a company of cavalry to intercept the mob. When those at the head of the straggling column reached West Mankato they halted to allow the rear to close up and a parley took place as to precisely what was to be done. While they were so detained, Captain Horace Austin arrived with his cavalry company, surrounded the crowd, and ordered them to move toward headquarters. At first they refused, but, when at the captain's command a hundred sabers flashed, obedience seemed to be judicious. In reply to his inquiry as to the occasion for their assemblage at an untimely hour, Colonel Miller was assured that their mission was wholly peaceful and that they had no intention of breaking the law. The colonel listened patiently and discreetly assumed that he had to deal only with a party of curiosity-seekers and not with a mob intending to break the peace. He therefore allowed them to depart with an appropriate warning.[28]

General Sibley seems not to have held the matter so lightly. On December 6, reporting the transaction to his immediate superior, he advised him that it would take a thousand "true men" to protect the prisoners and that it was doubtful whether those already present under Colonel Miller could be relied on. "Any hour," he said, "may witness a sad conflict." On the same date Governor Ramsey, believing there was great danger of a mob attempt to put the whole body of convicts to death, issued a proclamation

[28] *Saint Paul Press*, December 10, 1862. A half-breed squaw informed Colonel Miller about noon. See also the address of the Honorable Lorin Cray, in the *Mankato Free Press*, June 26, 1912. Judge Cray was a corporal in Company D of the Ninth Minnesota at the time and was one of a party which went from St. Peter to attend the affair.

entreating citizens not to disgrace the state with conduct worthy of savages. Either the danger was not so great as he feared or, if it was, his proclamation saved the state from disgrace.[29]

There was one man in Minnesota who was not swept off his feet by the tide of passion which raged throughout the state. This was Henry Benjamin Whipple, who in November, 1859, at the age of thirty-seven had come to Minnesota as the first bishop of the Protestant Episcopal Church. He was descended from distinguished Revolutionary stock and was richly endowed with bodily and mental gifts. Debarred by infirm health in youth from completing the traditional classical education, he was thrown into business and political relations, which perhaps gave him a better training for his future work than he might have got from the odes of Horace and Pindar. His theological education was obtained not in a divinity school, but from that great teacher, William Dexter Wilson, professor of philosophy in Hobart College for many years and later a professor in Cornell University, of which he may be called one of the founders.[30] If ever a man was fitted for the time and the place, Bishop Whipple was. Tall and strongly built, gracious but not patronizing in manner, he easily won the good will of men of every class and creed. His enthusiasm was tempered by a saving common sense and an abounding humor. He magnified his office, but only to do the greater service to those to whom he was called to minister. He loved all men; he feared no man. He had been in Minnesota but a fortnight when he made an excursion to Fort Ripley to ascertain the condition of the mission to the Chippewa at Gull Lake. This mission had been established

[29] *Minnesota in the Civil and Indian Wars*, 2: 290; Sibley to Ramsey, December 6, Colonel Benjamin F. Smith to Ramsey, December 9, 1862, in Governor's Archives, file 255; *Saint Paul Press*, December 11, 1862.

[30] George C. Tanner, *Fifty Years of Church Work in the Diocese of Minnesota, 1857–1907*, 286-293, 299 (St. Paul, 1909); Whipple, *Lights and Shadows*, 1, 4-6. For a time Professor Wilson maintained in his own house in Geneva, New York, a veritable school of the prophets.

some seven years before by the enthusiastic James Lloyd
Breck, but had been suspended in 1857 because of the
turbulence of the Indians due to the inundation of fire water
which followed the treaties of 1854 and 1855. This journey
and its experiences kindled in the heart of the young bishop
an interest in the red man which never abated to the end of
his life. Before a year had passed he had established the
Reverend Samuel D. Hinman in a mission at the lower
Sioux agency.[31]

Bishop Whipple informed himself of the condition and
prospects of both nations and soon became satisfied that
much of their wretchedness was chargeable to the indifference, not to say the rascality, of white men. On April 9,
1860, he addressed to President Buchanan a letter showing
the utter powerlessness of the laws and the administration
to stop the flow of fire water into the Indian country and
offering suggestions toward their betterment. The compre-
hensive remedy he found in the abolition of treaties with
Indians as equal powers and in the assumption by the
government of the character of guardian to Indian wards.
Ten years later this view prevailed. Again on the sixth of
March, 1862, Bishop Whipple addressed an open letter to
President Lincoln, in which he summarized the iniquities
of the Indian system and insisted on the supreme importance
of placing the Indians under a government of law, ad-
ministered by honest and capable men selected for their
merit and fitness and not as a reward for political services.

[31] Tanner, *Diocese of Minnesota*, 59-88, 300; Whipple, *Lights and Shadows*, 61. It is
notable that Dr. Williamson, who had labored among the lower Sioux since 1846, did not
follow them to their reservation but established himself in 1852 among the Wahpeton above
the Yellow Medicine. Riggs moved from Lac qui Parle to the same neighborhood two years
later. The Pond brothers found good reason in the degeneration of the Mdewakanton under
the operation of the treaty of 1837 to warrant giving up mission work among them when
they were removed to the new reservations in 1853. The annuities paid semiannually had
destroyed the influence of the old chiefs and had begot a horde of dissolute "sons of Belial"
impervious to civilization and Christianity. See *ante*, 1: 211; Riggs, *Forty Years with the
Sioux*, 130; and Samuel W. Pond, Jr., *Two Volunteer Missionaries among the Dakotas, or the
Story of the Labors of Samuel W. and Gideon H. Pond*, 211 (Boston, [1893]). Bishop Whipple
had a clear field for a mission at the lower agency, but John P. Williamson was about to
resume his work at the time of the outbreak.

Knowing as he did better than any other man in Minnesota, unless it was Sibley, the operation of the Indian policy and the machinations of selfish and dishonest officials, traders, employees, and half-breeds, he was not surprised at the outbreak in August, 1862.  In June he had been on the Sioux reservation and had seen unmistakable signs of danger, but he, no more than Agent Galbraith or any other, was able to guess when the smoldering volcano would burst into eruption.[32]

In the fall of 1862 Bishop Whipple was in Washington and, in company with his friend and relative, General Halleck, he called on President Lincoln.  In the course of their interview he gave an account of the outbreak, its causes, and the sufferings of the Sioux.  That he did this with the force and eloquence of which he was so capable may be inferred from a remark made by the president not long after: "He came here the other day and talked with me about the rascality of this Indian business until I felt it down to my boots."[33]  It is not likely that this impression had faded out when the president came to act upon the findings of the military commission.  In December Bishop Whipple published in the St. Paul newspapers a calm, clear statement of the train of events which had led to this terrible explosion.[34]

So far as is known, he was the only public man who had the courage to face the whirlwind of popular denunciation of all Indians and of the Dakota in particular.  To punish the guilty would avail little if the traditional Indian policy was to be left unreformed.  In some quarters the bishop

[32] Whipple, *Lights and Shadows*, 50-52, 106, 510-514; Greenleaf Clark, "Bishop Whipple as a citizen of Minnesota," in *Minnesota Historical Collections*, 10: 709 (part 2).  In a letter of January 9, 1869, in the *Pioneer Press*, January 12, 1869, Bishop Whipple arraigns the Indian system because of (1) the violation of treaties with the Indians; (2) the awarding of agencies for political services; (3) the formation of "Indian rings" to enrich themselves out of Indian contracts; (4) the lack of any system of government, civilization, or property rights; and (5) the widespread demoralization about the agencies.  See also Whipple to Sibley, December 8, 1862, in West, *Sibley*, 294.

[33] Whipple, *Lights and Shadows*, 136.

[34] *Saint Paul Pioneer*, December 3, 17, 1862; *Saint Paul Press*, December 4, 1862.

came in for denunciation almost as spiteful and unsparing as that directed against the Sioux themselves, but he never retracted a syllable nor budged an inch.

On December 5 Senator Wilkinson introduced into the United States Senate a resolution requesting the president to lay before that body the information in his possession relating to the late Indian barbarities in Minnesota and the evidence upon which some of the principal actors had been condemned to death. In a special message of December 11 the Senate was informed that the president had first caused a careful examination to be made of the records of the trials for the selection of such as had been proved guilty of violating women. "Contrary to my expectations," he wrote, "only two of this class were found." A further examination was then ordered to distinguish those who had committed  wanton murder on unarmed citizens from those who had participated in battles. Forty such, including the two mentioned, were found. An abstract of the evidence was prepared for the president, which he doubtless carefully scanned. Upon the recommendation of the military commission he commuted the sentence of Otakle, or Godfrey, to ten years' imprisonment. He then wrote out in his own hand on December 6 his order to General Sibley to cause thirty-nine of the condemned Indians and half-breeds designated by name and number to be executed on Friday, the nineteenth of December.[35]

This leniency was disappointing to the people of Minnesota, but there was less of outcry and denunciation than was expected. Because the necessary preparations could not be made after the receipt of the executive order, which had been delayed in transmission, a supplementary order

[35] 37 Congress, 3 session, *Senate Journal*, 30 (serial 1148); *Indian Barbarities in Minnesota* (serial 1149); Richardson, *Messages and Papers*, 6:144. Lincoln's original message to the Senate, his order for the execution of the Indians, and the report of George C. Whiting and Francis H. Ruggles, who selected the forty convicts for execution, are in the possession of the Minnesota Historical Society. For an account of their presentation, see the annual report of the society for 1868, p. 8. This is also in *Executive Documents*, 1868, p. 692.

was secured postponing the execution for one week. To guard against any possible outbreak of savagery a considerable force of troops was collected at Mankato, martial law was declared over a district of ten miles in radius, and a special patrol was established to visit all places where intoxicating liquor might be dispensed in disobedience of orders. On December 27 General Sibley telegraphed to the president "that the 38 Indians and half-breeds ordered by you for execution were hung yesterday at Mankato, at 10 A.M. Everything went off quietly." One of the condemned, Tatemima, or Round Wind, had been respited. The spectacle was witnessed by a great crowd and was described and illustrated in the newspapers with extreme detail.[36]

The old Sioux missionaries who were present had the satisfaction of seeing all the condemned but two accept Christian baptism. Doubtless through the influence of the half-breed fellow convicts, twenty-four of them received  the sacrament at the hands of the Catholic Father Ravoux, although he had not ministered among the Sioux for many years. The Protestant missionaries gladly witnessed the work of grace, although it was not in accordance with their own practice. It remains to add this melancholy finale: In a memorial sermon on Joseph R. Brown nine years later Riggs used the following remarkable language: "To him was given the duty of selecting the thirty-nine whose names were on that roll. It was a difficult duty, because in several

[36] *Official Records*, series 2, vol. 5, pp. 84, 86; *Minnesota in the Civil and Indian Wars*, 2: 292; Riggs, *Forty Years with the Sioux*, 185; Riggs, *Tah-koo Wah-kan*, 349; *Mankato Review*, December 27, *Saint Paul Pioneer*, December 28, *Saint Paul Press*, December 28, 1862. The confession and protests of the condemned taken down by Riggs are notable. West, in his *Sibley*, 289-291, revels in details of the executions. For Sibley's attitude in regard to the punishment of the convicted Sioux, see page 293 of the latter volume. "Even in the hour of execution," says West, "he felt that the Indian, though guilty, and righteously punished, yet died the victim of the white man's avarice, injustice, and wrong." The record of the suspension of Round Wind's sentence has not been found. The *Mankato Weekly Record* of December 26, 1862, states that the order was received by Colonel Miller on December 24. In a written statement, dated March 31, 1879, and subjoined to a facsimile of Lincoln's order for the execution of the Indians, in the possession of the Minnesota Historical Society, Colonel Miller gave as the reason for the postponement of the executions that he had no supply of the proper kind of rope.

Executive Mansion,

Washington, December 6ᵗʰ, 1862.

Brigadier General H. H. Sibley
St. Paul
Minnesota.

Ordered that of the Indians and Half-breeds sentenced to be hanged by the Military Commission, composed of Colonel Crooks, Lt. Colonel Marshale, Captain Grant, Captain Bailey, and Lieutenant Olin, and lately sitting in Minnesota, you cause to be executed on Friday the nineteenth day of December, instant, the following named, towit

"Te-he-hdo-ne-cha."          No. 2.   by the record.
"Tazoo" alias "Plan-doo-ta." No. 4.   by the record.
"Wy-a-tah-to-wah"           No. 5.   by the record.
"Hin-han-shoon-ko-yag."      No. 6.   by the record.
"Muz-za-bom-a-du."          No. 10.  by the record.
"Wah-pay-du-ta."            No. 11.  by the record.
"Wa-he-hud."                No. 12.  by the record.
"Sna-ma-ni."                No. 14.  by the record.
"Ta-te-mi-na,"              No. 15.  by the record.

"Hda-hin-hday."             No. 373. by the record.
"O-ya-tay-a-koo."           No. 377. by the record.
"May-hoo-way-wa."           No. 382. by the record.
"Wa-kin-yan-na."            No. 383. by the record

The other condemned prisoners you will hold subject to further orders, taking care that they neither escape, nor are subjected to any unlawful violence.

Abraham Lincoln, President of the United States,

LINCOLN'S ORDER FOR THE EXECUTION OF SIOUX PRISONERS
*The beginning and end of the manuscript are shown here*

THE EXECUTION OF THIRTY-EIGHT SIOUX AT MANKATO
*From a contemporary lithograph published by Wise and Clark, Mankato*

cases there were two or three of the same name in prison. It was a matter of regret that any mistakes were made, but I feel sure they were not made intentionally."[37]   A long and bitter course of punishment still awaited those whose lives were spared.   Thousands of Minnesota people long believed that there could be "no good Indian but a dead Indian."

[37] Augustin Ravoux, *Reminiscences, Memoirs and Lectures*, 72-81 (St. Paul, 1890); Riggs, *Forty Years with the Sioux*, 184; Pond, *Two Volunteer Missionaries*, 222-224; briefs of letters from Riggs and Williamson, in the *Missionary Herald*, 59:72 (March, 1863). A manuscript copy of Riggs's sermon was lent to the author by Mr. George G. Allanson of Wheaton.   The number of convicts baptized by Father Ravoux is given as twenty-four, of those by Williamson, fifteen.   These numbers, deliberately stated, may, if accepted as exact, indicate that all the convicts condemned to death, excluding Otakle, the one whose sentence had been commuted, and including Tatemima, the one reprieved, were baptized.

# VIII.  CAUSES OF THE SIOUX OUTBREAK

AFTER the lapse of a generation, during which the heat of passion has abated and a better understanding of the character of the Indian and of his relations to the white man has been reached, it is possible to sum up without prejudice the causes of one of the bloodiest of Indian outbreaks on the continent.  At this time no one will be found to attribute the Sioux Outbreak to machinations of secessionist emissaries, as did so high an authority as Senator Rice.  Nor will the short and economical explanation of the Reverend Stephen R. Riggs satisfy the more rational inquirer of today.  In a letter published on December 7, 1862, the worthy missionary says: "They [*the Sioux*] were undoubtedly instigated by the devil. . . . Such a demoniacal possession of a whole people it was exceedingly difficult to withstand."  Only the Christian Indians, it appears, were able to withstand it.  Agent Galbraith concurred in this statement.  It should be said, however, that in their depositions made before the claims commission a year later both Riggs and Galbraith elaborated a catena of human causes so cogent that the importation of diabolical initiative seems quite superfluous.[1]  And it is not necessary to import any extraneous fundamental origin of the outbreak and its atrocities.  That may be found in human nature itself. Whether as a result of "man's first disobedience" or as a survival of the primitive beast nature in man, from which he has tardily evolved, anger is a universal passion.  Perhaps no human being is able to restrain at times an excessive display of it.  It is contagious in family and tribal groups, and breaks out in riots and forays.  In civilized communities

[1] *Pioneer and Democrat*, September 16, 1862; *Saint Paul Press*, December 7, 1862; Galbraith, in Indian Office, *Reports*, 1863, p. 282; *Claims for Depredations by Sioux Indians*, 6-12 (serial 1189).  An interview with William L. Quinn, the Indian interpreter, on the causes of the outbreak, is recorded in the author's notebooks, 1: 88.

infuriated gangs wreak their wrath on obnoxious individuals or groups in contempt of the law of the land. Of this truth no better illustration could be found than that of the draft riots in July, 1863, in New York City, in which more than twice as many murders were committed and much more property was destroyed by white savages than by Indians during the outbreak of 1862.[2] Among our own people, moreover, lynchings are still too numerous. The Dakota Indians were human beings who had never been subjected to a government of law and who found their remedy for injuries in rapine and murder. It was Indian nature to torture and kill people who had wronged them. Under such an indisputable major premise we may marshal the principal causes of the outbreak of 1862.[3]

One of these underlying causes may be found in the traditional Indian policy of the United States government. The central vice of that system was the negotiation of treaties with Indian tribes as with equal contracting parties and the violation of such treaties without cause and without

[2] *American Annual Cyclopædia and Register of Important Events*, 1863, pp. 684-689, 811-816 (New York, 1871). The number of killed and wounded in the riots was estimated by the police at at least one thousand. Claims for damages were made to the amount of $2,500,000. Descriptive articles, editorials, and illustrations may be found in *Harper's Weekly*, 7: 466, 482, 493, 494, 498, 530, 546 (July 25, August 1, 8, 22, 29, 1863). The editor states that "These deeds were done . . . with the tacit approval of leading politicians and their newspaper organs," the pretext being "that negroes would supersede white men [Irish] as laborers." For graphic accounts, see Rhodes, *United States*, 4: 322-328; Rossiter Johnson, *The Story of a Great Conflict; a History of the War of Secession*, 290-306 (New York, 1894); an article by Anna E. Dickinson in the *Pioneer Press* (St. Paul and Minneapolis), August 2, 1877; and the *New York Tribune* and the *New York Times* for July 14, 1863. Johnson gives the number of rioters killed as more than twelve hundred. Numerous documents relating to the draft riots may be found in *Official Records*, series 1, vol. 27, part 2, pp. 875-939. Note also the massacre at Herrin, Illinois, in June, 1922. For a discussion of various estimates of the numbers killed and wounded in the Sioux Outbreak, see the Appendix, no. 8, *post*.

[3] Galbraith, in Indian Office, *Reports*, 1863, pp. 280-289, says, "The radical moving cause of the outbreak is, I am satisfied, the ingrained and fixed hostility of the savage barbarian to reform, change, and civilization." Samuel W. Pond, in *Minnesota Historical Collections*, 12: 379, says: "It was the work of a mob, begun by the few and carried on by the many, who were drawn into it by a great variety of motives. Some were influenced by that clannish feeling . . . to stand by their own people whether they were right or wrong. Some were intimidated by the insane violence of those who were drunk with blood. Many joined in the fight because they thought that, if the Dakotas were overcome, little discrimination would be made by the victors between the innocent and the guilty. . . . After all, a great many Indians on the Reserve held themselves aloof from deeds of violence, and did what they could for the preservation of the captives."

shame.  Indian treaties were necessarily farcical.  The
disparity of power and interests reduced them to a grant
to the weaker party of such conditions as it would stand
without too much resistance.  At the same time it must be
remembered that our democratic sentiments and traditions
made it impossible for us to establish over the American Indian a firm and beneficent guardianship for his good.  Some
one would have suggested "slavery" as the proper name for
this.  While keeping up the pretense that Indian tribes were
independent nations, by means of the agency and annuity
systems we reduced them in fact to the status of dependents,
not to say beggars.  The Indian agent in too many instances
was appointed solely for political services, and the trifling
salary — fifteen hundred dollars until of late years — was
too often construed as implying the expectation of Congress
that agents might increase their incomes from other sources.
Otherwise it is hard to account for the fact that applications
to fill vacancies were "innumerable."  The agency system
was complicated almost necessarily with that of licensed
trading.  As late as 1865 the commissioner of Indian affairs
was advising Congress to make it a penal offense for an agent
to be interested with any licensed trader.  When profit on
sales to Indians ranged from one hundred to four hundred
per cent it was comfortable for the agent to have a share in
the business.  It was due largely to this mixture of interests
that it was so easy for traders to have "claims" for money
due from individual Indians allowed and paid out of tribal
funds.  The payment of annuities in money was notoriously
demoralizing but the influence of politician traders had long
prevailed to prevent a change.  Substantially all the money
paid out for annuities went immediately into the pockets of
the traders in payment for past "credits"; whereupon the
Indian at once began to buy against his next accruing annuity.  It was not to be expected that politician agents at
fifteen hundred dollars a year should be men of high character devoted to the welfare of the Indian.  Still less could that

be looked for in the swarm of interpreters and employees about him. The salary of an interpreter was four hundred dollars a year. It might be expected that the traders would make it an object to him to look after their interests on the treaty ground. The missionaries had constantly to labor against the profanity, drunkenness, and debauchery of the people about the agencies. A Sioux Indian once asked Bishop Whipple if the Jesus of whom he preached to them was the same talked to by the white men at the agency when they were drunk.[4]

The seduction of Indian women and the multiplication of half-breeds contributed to the general demoralization. The half-breed was a misfit. Generally he despised his Indian relatives, but his affection expanded the moment some land or some annuity or other money was to be distributed to Indians; then he was Indian to the manner born. A "rake-off" for the half-breeds was for generations an element in every Indian treaty for cession of lands. The half-breed should have been denied this double nationality and considered as a white man unless he chose to identify himself with the savages.[5]

The effect of the white man's treaties and administration had been to break up the ancient totemic system of the Indians and to weaken the power and influence of the chiefs. The rule of a wise and experienced chieftain may be as good as such a people can enjoy, and that of the worst chieftain is better than no government. The United States took from the Indian his ancient and traditional customary law and

[4] The evils of the old Indian system are matters of common knowledge, but the reader may see Bishop Whipple's preface to Helen Hunt Jackson's *A Century of Dishonor; a Sketch of the United States Government's Dealings with Some of the North American Tribes*, v (London, 1881); Whipple, *Lights and Shadows*, 124-126, 517, 523-525; a footnote from the unpublished private notes of Sibley in West, *Sibley*, 294; Indian Office, *Reports*, 1865, p. 2 (reprinted in 39.Congress, 1 session, *House Executive Documents*, vol. 1 — serial 1248); and the report of the secretary of the interior for 1861, in 37 Congress, 2 session, *Senate Executive Documents*, 1:448 (serial 1117). See also *ante*, p. 207.

[5] Galbraith, in his report dated October 1, 1861, says, "Mixed bloods ought in no case to be recognized in any other light than as citizens of the United States — 'white men.' " Indian Office, *Reports*, 1861, p. 93 (reprinted in 37 Congress, 2 session, *Senate Executive Documents*, vol. 1 — serial 1117).

left him in a state of anarchy. If all the forms, safeguards, and sanctions of law in a civilized community should be abolished at a stroke, would it be long before it would sink into a state below that of the savage? In the Indian country there was no jurisdiction, no tribunal, no punishment for crime, and the Indian had no idea of obtaining redress for the white man's crimes against him other than by the torch, the rifle, and the scalping knife. If we consider human nature and Indian nature, the traditional Indian policy of the United States was calculated to invite outbreaks of passion and revenge.[6]

There were also more direct causes of the Sioux Outbreak. It was more than two hundred years after the white man began to encroach upon Indian country before the pressure of his advance was felt on the upper Mississippi. When the Sioux in 1837 ceded a little area in the crotch of the Mississippi and the St. Croix, they were giving up lands held by a slender title. Only a few of them had to leave their homes, which were already mostly west of the Mississippi. By the treaties of 1851 the Sioux were induced to alienate their right of occupancy of a magnificent empire over which their ancestors had ranged and hunted and to consent to be concentrated on an insignificant shoe-string tract drained by the upper Minnesota. The story of how those treaties were made in 1851 and were amended and finally ratified in 1853 has been told.[7] The Sioux, rightly or wrongly, believed at the time that they had been overreached in the transaction. In particular they resented the distribution of some four hundred thousand dollars in "hand money" among traders and half-breeds without any scrutiny of their claims. This transaction ever after rankled in the breasts of even their best chiefs. Further, it was commonly asserted among the tribes that at the time of the treaties they were assured that,

[6] For a vigorous arraignment of our Indian policy and the responsibility of white men for Indian crimes and outrages, see the report of the Brunot commission of 1869, in Indian Office, *Reports*, 1869, p. 47 (reprinted in 41 Congress, 2 session, *House Executive Documents*, vol. 3 — serial 1414).

[7] See *ante*, 1: 160, 266-304.

besides the money they would receive, the Sioux people were to have all the good things "they wanted": one blanket a year to every soul; a gun and ammunition to every hunter; coffee, tea, tobacco, pork, flour, and sugar "ota" — that is, in plenty; and white men to do all their work. That the treaty commissioners made or authorized any such promises is not believed; that persons who expected to get, and did get, a large part of the treaty money did so delude these Indians, as yet inexperienced in treaty-making, is quite credible. At any rate, the Sioux never ceased to reiterate these extraneous promises. Agent Galbraith says that they formed the text and the conclusion of nearly every Indian orator's speech he had heard, and he had heard not a few. In his opinion there was some ground for the claims. They were discussed in the councils and formed "a perpetual source of complaint, discontent, and annoyance."[8]

As already related, the four tribes were not removed to the reservations on the Minnesota River until late in 1853. They soon learned that the land was not to be their own. One of the amendments made by the Senate in 1852 and consented to by the new-made chiefs was that the government should pay the Indians ten cents per acre for the proposed reserve and that the president should at his discretion remove them to some region outside the ceded territory. It might have been well had this provision been carried out. The executive, however, permitted them to remain and Congress tardily sanctioned his action and, further, authorized him to confirm to the Sioux forever the reserved lands. This he never formally did and it remained an open question whether they had anything better than a tenancy at will.[9] It was not strange, therefore, that the

[8] Galbraith, in Indian Office, *Reports*, 1863, p. 285.
[9] *Senate Executive Proceedings*, 8:126, 368. For the amounts, see pages 398, 401. See also *Statutes at Large*, 10:326, and *ante*, 1:291. For an unseemly political squabble in which an attempt was made to throw the entire blame for the massacre on Governor Ramsey because of his action as treaty commissioner in 1851 and his alleged failure to obtain from the government proper military protection for the whites and farmer Indians on the reservation, see the issues of the *Pioneer and Democrat* for September 10, 13, 14, 17, 24, and those of the *Saint Paul Press* for September 12, 13, 14, 16, 23, 1862.

Sioux harbored a lurking suspicion that a tenure thus conceded might at any time be revoked by the insidious white man.

The Sioux had not been fairly settled on their reservations when it began to be whispered to them that they had more land than they needed and that it would be better for them to swell their annuities by a sale to the government. In the spring of 1858 delegations of chiefs and braves, appropriately selected from all the bands, were taken to Washington by Agent Joseph R. Brown and amid the allurements of the capital city they were induced to agree to a pair of treaties for the cession of their lands, nearly a million acres, as then estimated, on the north bank of the Minnesota, at a price to be fixed by the Senate. It is highly probable and there is some evidence that the Indians were again allowed to think that they would be placed beyond want. They were so confident of generous treatment that their delegations consented to treaties which completely transferred their rights to the lands but which left the purchase price to be fixed by the Great Council of the Great Father, the United States Senate. The two treaties, framed in exactly the same language except as to the descriptions of the lands, provided, according to bad usage, for the payment of debts due to the licensed traders from individual Indians, fixing a maximum sum which might be allowed by the chiefs in open council. The treaties were signed on July 19, 1858, but two years ran by before the Senate by resolution awarded the Indians the sum of thirty cents per acre for land worth five dollars per acre. On March 2, 1861, Congress appropriated in payment for the ceded lands, to the lower Sioux, $96,000 for 320,000 acres, and to the upper Sioux, $170,880 for 569,600 acres. When the traders' claims allowed by the secretary of the interior had been paid, the lower Sioux had virtually nothing coming to them and the upper Sioux, perhaps one-half of the amount voted.[10] When the Indians after three

---

[10] *Statutes at Large*, 12: 237. For further discussion of the treaties of 1858, see the Appendix, no. 9, *post.*

SIOUX DELEGATION TO WASHINGTON, 1858

*Upper photo, standing left to right: Big Eagle, Traveling Hail, and Red Legs; seated: Medicine Light, The Thief, and Taconlipeiyo (?). Below, standing: Joseph R. Brown, Antoine J. Campbell, Has a War Club, Andrew Robertson, Red Owl, Thomas A. Robertson, and Nathaniel R. Brown; seated: Mankato, Wabasha, and Henry Belland (?).*

LITTLE CROW, SIOUX LEADER IN THE OUTBREAK OF 1862
*Photograph by Joel E. Whitney of St. Paul*

years of waiting found their lands gone and the beggarly proceeds largely absorbed by traders, there was a degree of exasperation among them which white men under similar circumstances might righteously have exhibited. "From the first day of my arrival upon the reservation, up to the outbreak," wrote Galbraith, "this matter was a perpetual source of wrangling, dissatisfaction, and bitter, ever-threatening complaints on the part of both the upper and lower bands."[11]

It must not be inferred that the treaties of 1858 had no other ostensible object than that of reducing the size of the reservations. They involved a noble scheme of Indian civilization. In October, 1857, Joseph R. Brown assumed the duties of Sioux agent in place of Charles E. Flandrau, who had been elected one of the judges of the state supreme court. Related by marriage to the Sioux and in earlier years long engaged in the Indian trade, this much-experienced man possessed a knowledge of the Dakota tribes not surpassed by that of any other man of the time. Without indulging in extravagant expectations of rapid advances in letters, arts, and religion, he did believe that the Indian could be guided into paths which would lead to the abandonment of savage life, to the adoption of fixed abodes, and to the cultivation of the soil. It was doubtless at his instance that the civilization clauses were written into the treaties. The leading provision was for the allotment of eighty acres of land to heads of families and to single persons above the age of twenty-one years — the land to be inalienable for a period to be determined later and, in the discretion of the president, to be patented to the allottee.[12]

---

[11] Galbraith, in Indian Office, *Reports*, 1863, p. 286.

[12] Brown's report dated September 30, 1858, in Indian Office, *Reports*, 1858, pp. 49-57 (reprinted in 35 Congress, 2 session, *Senate Executive Documents*, vol. 1, *House Executive Documents*, vol. 2, part 1 — serials 974, 997); *Statutes at Large*, 12:1031, 1037. For a compliment to Brown by Flandrau, see his report dated September 24, 1857, in Indian Office, *Reports*, 1857, p. 60 (reprinted in 35 Congress, 1 session, *Senate Executive Documents*, vol. 2, *House Executive Documents*, vol. 2, part 1 — serials 919, 942). Agent Brown's was an interim appointment made in September, 1857. It was not confirmed by the Senate until April 14, 1858. See *Senate Executive Proceedings*, 10:361. For a sketch of Brown, see *ante*, 1:231-234.

No sooner had the treaties been ratified than Agent
✱ Brown began to put his favorite policy into operation. In
his annual report for 1859 he noted an "extensive . . .
sudden, and . . . complete" change at his agencies. Over
two hundred men, mostly heads of families, had discarded
the blanket, had had their hair cut, had donned white man's
clothes, and were locating on the lands allotted to them by
the treaty of 1858. With their families, seven hundred were
thus counted as "Farmer Indians," according to Commissioner Greenwood. These and others to follow their example, said Brown, would presently become "respectable
farmers and useful citizens." If the necessary oxen, plows,
wagons, cows, swine, and chickens were supplied, in another
season he would have five hundred farmers. Major Cullen,
northern superintendent, reported with enthusiasm on the
experiment as "an assured success" and Commissioner
Greenwood prophesied that in three years the "blanket
Indians" would be fewer than those who two years before
had put on white man's dress.[13] At the mission stations of
Williamson and Riggs near the upper agency, where an
association of Indians called the Hazelwood Republic had
been formed under a constitution and a simple code of by-
laws, the teachers at length expressed encouragement. Jane
Williamson, teacher of the mission school near Yellow Medicine, testified to the industry of the men and to the better
housekeeping of the women. "In many instances a decent
bed is substituted for the dirty buffalo skin in former use.
Instead of a group with wooden bowls, horn spoons, and
perhaps a butcher knife, seated on the floor near a kettle of
ducks, fish, or hominy, the family may be seen surrounding
a table decently furnished, on which, with other articles of
well-cooked food, is often well baked bread, and sometimes
butter."

Agent Brown, however, in his next report, for 1860,
says that he had established a probation system to check

[13] Indian Office, *Reports*, 1859, pp. 5, 59, 79-82 (reprinted in 36 Congress, 1 session, *Senate
Executive Documents*, vol. 1 — serial 1023).

the accession of "bad men" intent on getting gratuitous clothing, food, and tools. He refers also to mischievous teasing and petty larceny by the "blanket Indians." In 1860 one hundred and eighteen families were living in houses. In his report for that year the farm superintendent at Redwood says that the Indians had done all their plowing without the assistance of white laborers. The farmers had given up their heathen feasts and dances and were "a law-abiding, quiet, and *sober* people," comparing "favorably" with the white settlers surrounding them. Agent Brown repeats this, and says also that the Indians would have a surplus crop of corn, for which they would have trouble to find a market.[14]

The exigencies of party politics caused the retirement of Major Brown from the Sioux agency early in 1861; a calamity, this, for the Sioux nation and for the United States. He made a good beginning on a good plan. Had he been left in office there would have been trouble enough awaiting him, but he might have succeeded. He might have induced many thousands, as he had many hundreds, of the Sioux to live in houses, to till the soil, to use domestic animals, and slowly to assume the ways of civilized men. Had he not succeeded it would have been for lack of intelligent and consistent support and because of diabolical interference by white men without bowels and conscience. What Joseph R. Brown could not do with and for the Sioux Indians could not be done.

Into his place came Thomas J. Galbraith, a man of character and ability, who obtained the appointment not on account of actual qualifications for the position but because he had been a stanch Republican wheel horse in late political campaigns. He had presided temporarily over the Republican end of the constitutional convention of Minnesota four years before. Major Galbraith believed in and proposed to

[14] Indian Office, *Reports*, 1858, pp. 49-52; 1859, pp. 92-96; 1860, pp. 54-70. For an interesting sketch of "Aunt Jane" Williamson, see Robert J. Creswell, *Among the Sioux; a Story of the Twin Cities and the Two Dakotas*, 72-78 (Minneapolis, 1906).

carry out the policy of 1858, but he was soon to encounter
difficulties.  From the beginning of the experiment the
"blanket Indians" had ridiculed and tormented those who
were adopting the life of the white men, whom they stigmatized as "white men" and "dutchmen," thus likening them
to the unwarlike German settlers in the valley.  These
blanket Indians stole pigs, drove the cattle off, and raided
the cornfields.  The importation of whisky with which to
ply the farmer Indians was much resorted to as a means of
recalling them to their old life.  There were a few cases of
relapse, but Galbraith reported that not one of the farmer
Indians had used a drop of intoxicating liquor in several
months.  The one hundred and twenty-five families settled
on farms in 1861 were very lonesome, however, among some
seven thousand wild Sioux, and their numbers were not
increasing greatly after Major Brown's retirement.  That
agent had felt the need of military protection for his farmers
and had obtained it for a short period.  His successor notified
the Indian department that such support was indispensable.
The Hazelwood Republic, under the adverse influences
surrounding it, had disbanded before the end of Brown's
administration.[15]

It is now easy to see that Fort Ridgely should have been
moved to the Yellow Medicine and that a strong force of
cavalry should have been placed at Big Stone Lake to protect
the annuity Indians from the wild Sioux of the plains.  The
farmer Indians were, of course, in large proportion those
who had been impressed if not converted by the missionaries.
Against them the hostility of the medicine men, who were
still numerous and influential, was intense and bitter.  The
latter were renegades and miscreants unfit to live.  It must

---

[15] Indian Office, *Reports*, 1860, p. 58; 1861, pp. 88-94; 1863, p. 283.  In an interview
with Mr. Thomas Hughes on November 27, 1903, Judge Martin J. Severance said that Galbraith "was a red-haired man and was a hard drinker.  His excessive use of liquor had
brought about a serious impairment of his mental faculties and he was really unfit to hold
any official position.  Half the time he was out of his head.  He had no diplomacy and
treated the Indians arrogantly.  He was wholly unfit to manage a turbulent lot of savages,
who had long standing grievances and were disposed to be ugly."  A typewritten copy of
the report of this interview is in the Folwell Papers.

be remarked that as a general fact, with notable exceptions, the Indian traders were opposed to the civilization experiment and that the half-breeds did not render such aid as might have been expected. The experiment, which had promised so much, became a source of suspicion and dissension and instead of mitigating the Indian's natural hatred of the paleface only inflamed it the more.

The residence of the Dakota tribes on the extreme frontier had given them, with the exception of a few chiefs, slight opportunity for learning the white man's numbers and power. It was a stupid policy which, adhered to against the counsel of those most able to advise, failed to give them frequent and adequate demonstrations of the government's might. Five years before the Sioux Outbreak of 1862 occurred a preliminary massacre, on no great scale but sufficiently atrocious to cause great alarm, of which notice was purposely omitted in a foregoing chapter. In the early spring of 1857 a small renegade band of lower Sioux led by an outlawed chief named Inkpaduta—in English, "Scarlet Point"—fell upon a white settlement on Lake Okoboji in Dickinson County, Iowa, just across the Minnesota line, murdered over thirty persons, and departed with four women captives and the plunder of their stables and cabins, to encamp on Heron Lake in Jackson County, Minnesota. From this place they moved on to the small settlement then called Springfield, which later became Jackson. Here they brutally murdered several persons, after which they departed for their usual abode in the Big Sioux Valley in South Dakota.

In expectation of the latter attack messengers had been sent to the lower agency. Agent Flandrau at once made a requisition on the post commander at Fort Ridgely for a military force to pursue the scoundrels. An infantry detail of two company officers and forty-eight enlisted men was sent to the scenes of the murders. After an absence of three weeks, during which no little hardship was undergone, the

detachment returned, as might have been expected, without
having effected its object.  Reports of the outrages were soon
spread throughout the settlements of southwestern Minnesota and panic ensued.  Hundreds of families living south of
the Minnesota abandoned their claims and fled to New Ulm,
Mankato, St. Peter, Traverse des Sioux, Henderson, and
other towns, and some fled southward into Iowa.  In these
towns companies of volunteers were raised which stood
guard at home and patrolled their respective neighborhoods.
They encountered no Indians except some small parties
peaceably engaged in hunting muskrats and making maple
sugar, which they incontinently drove off to the reservations.

The panic became so intense and widespread that a
detachment of three infantry companies of regulars was sent
from Fort Snelling to the seat of war.  After long marches
continued for many days the troops returned without having
seen any Indians, but the settlers were so heartened that
many soon returned to their homes.  Agent Flandrau continued his requisitions for a mounted force sufficient to
follow Inkpaduta to his retreat, but it did not please the
authorities at Washington to grant it.  Instead, the Indian
office adopted a scheme of requiring the loyal Indians to capture the outlaw and, to stimulate their activity, announced
that no annuities would be paid until he should be brought
in a prisoner.  To relieve his people of the hardship thus
imposed upon them, Little Crow volunteered to lead a party
of Indians in a man hunt.  It was a futile chase of a hundred
miles and more into South Dakota and back.  The Indian
office was now obliged to recede from its perfectly absurd
scheme and used the convenient pretext that as the loyal
Indians had done what they could they need not suffer.[16]

The unfortunate result was not merely that the murderers
remained at large but also that the Great Father had shown
himself incapable of apprehending them.  Either he had not
warriors enough, or those that he had were too cowardly to

[16] For a more detailed account of the Inkpaduta or Spirit Lake massacres, see the Appendix, no. 10, *post.*

fight the unconquerable Sioux. It was the deliberate judgment of Dr. Thomas S. Williamson, the experienced Sioux missionary, that the "utter neglect" of the government to punish the Spirit Lake murderers was the "primary cause" of the Sioux massacre.[17]

All the foregoing remote causes but augmented and sharpened the loathing and lodged hatred of the red man toward the white. It must also be remembered that the Minnesota Sioux were the smaller fraction of the great nation whose hunting grounds reached from the Iowa line and below to the Canadian boundary and west to the Rocky Mountains. With the nearer tribes of the Sioux of the plains the Minnesota tribes were in close association. The Yankton, indeed, asserted an important interest in the lands ceded in 1851 and extorted in some years from the upper Sioux a portion of their annuities. The Sioux felt themselves to be a powerful people. This consciousness was often stimulated by martial demonstrations calculated to arouse pride and *esprit de corps*. An officer of the Second Minnesota, Captain Jeremiah C. Donahower, who was present with a detachment of that command at the upper agency at the time of the payment of 1861, describes the parade of the upper bands on the day of the "counting." This writer in the course of the Civil War "witnessed many reviews and impressive martial pageants . . . where the arena glittered with bristling bayonets, and where flags . . . floated proudly and defiantly in the breeze; where staff officers rode swiftly, and where batteries of light Artillery drawn by horses under whip and spur rushed madly into the fray, but never witnessed any military display that so

[17] Letter from Williamson, August 29, in the *Saint Paul Press*, September 3, 1862. For concurring opinions of Brown and Galbraith see Indian Office, *Reports*, 1858, p. 54; 1863, p. 298; a letter from Riggs, dated August 27, in the *Saint Paul Press*, August 29, 1862; Riggs's deposition before the Sioux commission, in *Claims for Depredations by Sioux Indians*, 11 (serial 1189), and his *Forty Years with the Sioux*, 144; Thomas Hughes, "Causes and Results of the Inkpaduta Massacre," in *Minnesota Historical Collections*, 12: 278-280, 282; Horace Austin, "The Frontier of Southwestern Minnesota in 1857," in *Glimpses of the Nation's Struggle*, fourth series, 140; and Asa W. Daniels, "Reminiscences of Little Crow," in *Minnesota Historical Collections*, 12: 520. Dr. Daniels was physician to the lower Sioux from 1854 to 1861.

deeply impressed his youthful, imaginative heart, as did that
Grandly Spectacular scene presented by the more than four
thousand Indians on foot, preceded by the three hundred
and twenty mounted Indians richly adorned with feathered

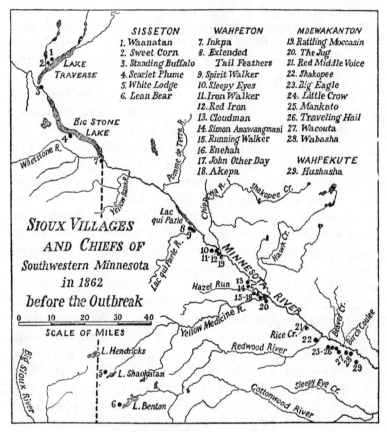

*SISSETON*
1. Waanatan
2. Sweet Corn
3. Standing Buffalo
4. Scarlet Plume
5. White Lodge
6. Lean Bear

*WAHPETON*
7. Inkpa
8. Extended
   Tail Feathers
9. Spirit Walker
10. Sleepy Eyes
11. Iron Walker
12. Red Iron
13. Cloudman
14. Simon Anawangmani
15. Running Walker
16. Enehah
17. John Other Day
18. Akepa

*MDEWAKANTON*
19. Rattling Moccasin
20. The Jug
21. Red Middle Voice
22. Shakopee
23. Big Eagle
24. Little Crow
25. Mankato
26. Traveling Hail
27. Wacouta
28. Wabasha

*WAHPEKUTE*
29. Hushasha

SIOUX VILLAGES
AND CHIEFS OF
Southwestern Minnesota
in 1862
before the Outbreak

head gear of varied colors, with their guns held aloft, swaying
their bodies and singing, as in two extended lines they came in
sight and rode swiftly toward us."[18]

For half a century Indian commissioners and friends of the
Indians had harped upon the importance of "concentrating"

[18] Indian Office, *Reports*, 1858, p. 54.   Captain Donahower's account, written in 1906,
is in the Folwell Papers.

them on reservations of moderate extent. There was sense in the proposition when understood to involve the civilization of the red man, his abandonment of war and the chase, and his subsistence from the fruits of the soil. The concentration of wild Indians could work nothing but mischief and ruin. One object of the removal of the Minnesota Sioux to the reserves on the Minnesota River was to concentrate them. Later, in 1858, the same policy by treaty cut down the area of the Minnesota Sioux lands by one-half. Some hundreds of farmer Indians were nominally "concentrated." The great majority, however, were not, because free hunting grounds, upon which the buffalo still ranged in countless numbers, extended indefinitely to the west. Every season strong hunting parties left the reservations to return laden with robes and pemmican. Still there was enough of concentration to work mischief. The close neighborhood of the villages and camps made it easy for malcontents to assemble frequently to growl and fret together over grievances — the bad faith of the Great Father in making and keeping treaties, the shortcomings of the agent, the sharp practices of the traders, the abuse of women by white men generally; all these were constant themes for oratory in the councils. The Pond brothers foresaw this in 1852 and decided not to follow the lower Sioux, among whom they had labored for eighteen years, to the reservations.[19]

Another desideratum much discussed from year to year by those who in good faith wished to protect the Indian from his friend the white man was his isolation as complete as possible. Reservations, therefore, were to be remote and to consist of solid areas of land, with natural boundaries if possible. All these conditions were ignored in laying out the Sioux reserves. Together they were originally one hundred and fifty miles long and twenty miles wide, and later they were half that width. They nearly solved the problem of

[19] S. W. Pond, Jr., *Two Volunteer Missionaries*, 211; S. W. Pond, in *Minnesota Historical Collections*, 12: 379.

embracing the smallest area within the longest boundaries. An hour's walk brought the Indian to the edge of his country, to meet his deadliest foe, the white man with his whisky jug. The Great Father was powerless to protect his Indian children from this vilest of all unconvicted criminals. Plenty of good law there was of nation and of state; but the frontier had too many engaged in its violation. Few witnesses to lawbreaking could be found willing to testify; no jury on the border of an Indian reservation could be got to find against a whisky-seller.

We have now discussed the predisposing causes which coöperated to maintain and aggravate the ancient native hostility of the Dakota tribes in Minnesota to the whites. There were additional immediate causes of exasperation which might have affected the conduct of civilized men. In the season of 1861 the corn crops of the Sisseton were totally destroyed and great damage was done to those of the three other tribes by cutworms. The agent was obliged to buy on credit flour and pork to eke out the living of all. He fed a thousand and more women and children and old and infirm men of the Sisseton from the middle of December, 1861, until nearly the following April. But for this assistance they would have perished. With the opening of the new season all the bands, in particular the farmers, planted extensively. This done, all awaited the payment, which custom gave them the right to expect so soon as the prairie grass was high enough for pasture. This time was commonly toward the end of June for the lower bands and a fortnight later for the upper. About the twenty-fifth of June of this year, 1862, Agent Galbraith assured a delegation of the upper Indians that they need fear no default, but that the payment could not be made before July 20. What was his surprise on the fourteenth of July, when returning from a visit to the lower agency, to find that four thousand upper annuity Indians and a thousand Yanktonai from the plains had assembled at Yellow Medicine "with nothing to eat." The provisions and goods for the payment had been received and were stored in the large brick warehouse at the agency. The money had not come and there were no advices in regard to it. It was the established custom to make the payments of provisions, goods, and money at the same time, probably because of the saving of time in making a single count and in filling up and signing a single set of rolls. The agent thought he could not depart from the custom, but he did so, as will be seen. For three weeks he doled out provisions enough to keep the hungry crowd alive, along with their fishing and root-digging.[20]

With a fine disregard of red tape the Indians could not understand why they should go hungry when the flour, pork, lard, sugar, and other provisions which belonged to them were locked up in the warehouse. On the morning of August 4 four hundred mounted men and one hundred and fifty more on foot suddenly appeared and surrounded the camp of the infantry guard which had been sent up from Fort Ridgely a month before. It had become customary for a guard of soldiers to be present at the annual payments. On this occasion the guard consisted of parts of two companies of the Fifth Minnesota Volunteers, about one hundred strong, commanded by Lieutenant Timothy J. Sheehan, with whose gallant behavior at Fort Ridgely the reader is already acquainted. While this demonstration was going on a party of braves broke open the door of the warehouse and began carrying out sacks of flour. Sheehan's men loaded a mountain howitzer and trained it on that door. With a sergeant and sixteen men Sheehan boldly marched down a lane formed by the Indians to the government building. Leaving his sergeant and his squad to hold off the exasperated Indians, the lieutenant went into the agent's office in the warehouse and, after a long parley, induced Galbraith to make an issue of pork and flour, if the Indian leaders would promise to take their people away and come to a council the

[20] Galbraith, in Indian Office, *Reports*, 1863, pp. 267-274, 287.

next day. The promise was given and some food was issued, but the still exasperated Indians lingered about clamoring for all their goods and provisions in store, and they did not leave the neighborhood until after the whole detachment of troops, with the two howitzers, was formed in battle order in front of the warehouse. The situation was critical. The removal of the Indian camp some miles away on the same day indicated active hostilities.

Lieutenant Sheehan had sent immediately for Captain Marsh, his superior officer at Fort Ridgely, who arrived soon after noon on August 6. Galbraith had sent to the Hazelwood mission for Dr. Riggs, who came probably on the next day. The agent's state of mind may be inferred from his appeal to the missionary. "If there is anything," said he, "between the lids of the Bible that will meet this case, I wish you would use it." The good minister thought there was; he advised a council with the principal men and himself arranged with Standing Buffalo, head chief of the Sisseton, for an assemblage that afternoon, August 7. The Indians admitted that the attempt to get possession of the provisions belonging to them in advance of a regular issue was unlawful and agreed that the warehouse door should be repaired out of their money. Thereupon Agent Galbraith, working out either his own "plan" or one urged upon him by his councilors, proposed that the Indians take their annuity goods and some provisions and go back to their villages, where they should await his summons to the agency to receive their cash annuities. In the course of three days the goods were distributed and the Indian camp was empty. "Peace and quiet," says Dr. Riggs, "now reigned at the Yellow Medicine." In the belief that payment trouble for the year was over, Captain Marsh started Sheehan and his detachment of Company C back to Fort Ripley, to be recalled to Fort Ridgely on August 18, as already related. Agent Galbraith regretted that this event passed without the punishment of a single Indian and that, without power to punish, he had been constrained to adopt the same "sugar plum" policy which had been resorted to in the case of the Spirit Lake massacre by Inkpaduta's band five years before.[21]

The upper Sioux had an additional ground for dissatisfaction, which seems to have caused them intense exasperation. It was the established custom for deductions to be made from cash annuities to reimburse white people who had suffered losses of property by depredations of individual Indians. As the amounts were usually small, little objection was made. In 1860 claims for such depredations were lodged in the Indian office in Washington and were allowed to the amount of nine thousand dollars. Of this sum fifty-five hundred dollars were awarded to a partnership at Big Stone Lake for loss by robbery of its store. At the payment of 1861 the amount was deducted from the annuities, which were forty-five thousand dollars, against the protest of the Indians, who alleged that the loss was not over three hundred dollars, the mischief having been done by two men who entered the store once and carried off some groceries, for which they were willing to pay. Riggs, who was familiar with the affairs of the upper Sioux, lays stress on this transaction and remarks upon their exasperation.[22]

At and about the Redwood agency there were no riotous assemblages, no open demonstrations of hostility. The lower Sioux waited sulkily in their villages for the hoped-for payment. They had passed the winter and spring without assistance, but the summer found them in need. Early in July the

[21] Galbraith, in Indian Office, *Reports*, 1863, pp. 274, 298; Gere, in *Minnesota in the Civil and Indian Wars*, 1: 245-248; Riggs, *Forty Years with the Sioux*, 151; Riggs, *Tah-koo Wah-kan*, 324-326. Riggs gives no account of any hostile demonstration of the Indians, but he was not present on August 4. See also the testimony of Sheehan, somewhat vitiated by a willingness to emphasize his personal influence and courage, in *Sisseton and Wahpeton Claim Case Record, Evidence for Defendant*, 271-273, 278, 281. Colonel Sheehan's recollections of the affair of August 4, 1862, are in the *Pioneer Press* of September 1, 1902; an interview with him on the subject is recorded in the author's notebooks, 2: 140. See also a communication dated August 23 from P. M. Clark, chief of the finance division of the office of Indian affairs, in the *Pioneer Press* of August 24, 1902. Clark gives Gabriel Renville's opinion on the cause of the outbreak, which is noteworthy.

[22] Riggs, in *Claims for Depredations by Sioux Indians*, 10 (serial 1189); letter of Riggs, August 27, in the *Saint Paul Press* of August 29, 1862; report of Superintendent Thompson dated October 30, 1861, in Indian Office, *Reports*, 1861, p. 69.

agent, as he says, issued to them "a good supply of pork, flour, powder, shot, and tobacco, and . . . left them apparently satisfied." When Agent Galbraith was engaged in issuing provisions to the upper Sioux as related, Little Crow was present and, willing to extort a further distribution to his people, obtained, under circumstances which made refusal undesirable, a promise of a further issue to them from the storehouse at Redwood. This promise the agent did not keep, probably for reasons similar to those which caused him to refuse to supply the upper Indians until he was virtually forced to do so.[23] The Indians then demanded that their traders should furnish them food on credits to be liquidated at the expected payment. The traders had already extended credits to amounts possibly equaling the cash to be paid out. They were also angered because the soldiers' lodge had proposed that traders should not be allowed to approach the pay table and get their money without consent in open council. They therefore refused to enlarge existing credits. A last appeal was made to them about August 15 in a parley with the agent and representatives of the traders. After futile attempts to get definite information as to the time of payment, Little Crow, speaking for some hundreds of Indians present, said: "We have waited a long time. The money is ours, but we cannot get it. We have no food, but here are these stores, filled with food. We ask that you, the agent, make some arrangement by which we can get food from the stores, or else we may take our own way to keep ourselves from starving. When men are hungry they help themselves."

The interpreter was so much disconcerted and alarmed by the threat that he refused to interpret it. The Reverend

---

[23] Galbraith, in Indian Office, *Reports*, 1863, p. 273. In his testimony in *Sisseton and Wahpeton Claim Case Record, Evidence for Defendant*, 274, Sheehan said, "I was present when the agent consented to the issuing of the rations to the Upper Indians, and told Little Crow and his men that they would immediately issue rations to the Lower Indians." When he was asked if he knew whether those rations were issued, he replied, "I know that they were not." In answer to a following question, Sheehan said, "I think that probably the immediate cause and the real cause of the grievance of Little Crow and his men and the Soldiers' Lodge were not issuing those rations as agreed to." See also page 359.

John P. Williamson, who had very lately resumed work on a mission he had begun in the preceding spring, was present. He was the son of Dr. Thomas S. Williamson and had learned Dakota in childhood. Little Crow and he had played together as boys at Kaposia. Turning to him, Agent Galbraith said, "Williamson, you tell us what Little Crow says." Williamson immediately complied. The agent then turned to the storekeepers and asked them what they would do. After a brief consultation apart, one of them said, "Whatever Myrick does, we will do." Andrew J. Myrick was the only one of the four present who had a proprietary interest in the stores. He started to leave without response, but was called back by the agent, who insisted upon a statement. He deliberately said, "So far as I am concerned, if they are hungry, let them eat grass." The interpreter again refused to translate and the agent called on the missionary. In a clear voice he gave the Dakota version. There was a moment of silence, followed by savage whoops and wild gestures, with which the Indians disappeared. The heartless and insolent statement of the trader must have deeply incensed the Indians. In his reply to Colonel Sibley's split-stick message left on the Birch Coulee battle field, Little Crow gave it as one of the reasons for beginning the war, naming the trader who made it and quoting his words with an addition variously rendered. Myrick was one of the first to be shot to death on the morning of the outbreak and when his body was found by a burial party from Sibley's column the mouth was stuffed with the grass commended to the Indians for food.[24] All the bands were agreed

[24] Holcombe, in *Minnesota in Three Centuries*, 3: 285; Winifred W. Barton, *John P. Williamson, a Brother to the Sioux*, 18, 46, 48-52 (New York, [1919]). The author of the latter work is the daughter of the Reverend John P. Williamson and had the account from her father, who doubtless repeated it many times. See also in the Folwell Papers letters to the author from Winifred W. Barton, February 6, April 21, 1919, October 4, 1920, September 25, 1922; from John P. Williamson, September 28, 1922; from Jesse P. Williamson, September 2, 1922; from Thomas C. Williamson, September 23, 1922; and from Mrs. Susan Williamson, November 17, 1922, all concurring in the statements of Mrs. Barton in her book. A paragraph on page 49 of Heard, *Sioux War*, may refer to this council. The allusion to grass-eating in Little Crow's first letter to Colonel Sibley adds a degree of credibility. See West, *Sibley*, 263. It is difficult to assign a date for the "council" other than August 14 or 15. Galbraith did not come down from the upper agency until August 13. He mentions

in the belief that their traders had been guilty of frauds under treaties and of extortions for goods sold to the Indians.

June had ended, July had passed, August days were multiplying — and no payment. The agent had no advices and could only temporize with vague excuses. The natural anxiety and suspicions of the Indians were heightened and inflamed by the behavior and language of whites and half-breeds among them. The traders generally had belonged to the "old moccasin Democracy" of the territory and state and had no expectation of better times under "black Republican" rule. Altogether there was a considerable "copperhead" element on the reserve. Half-breeds who could read kept the leading Indians informed of the progress of the Civil War and doubtless the defeat of McClellan's right wing at Gaines's Mill and the flight of his whole army to the James were pictured in strong relief. The Great Father, they were told, was whipped — "cleaned out" — and "niggers" would get the money due the Indians. He had taken five thousand men out of Minnesota already and was calling for as many more. The Indians compared the volunteer soldiers sent to Fort Ridgely unfavorably with the regulars who had previously formed the garrison there. The absurd story, which later gained circulation, that secessionist emissaries penetrated the villages and poisoned the minds of the warriors was wholly devoid of truth. There was no need of importing rebel emissaries, since, as Galbraith said, "rebel sympathizers did all in their power to create disaffection among the Indians." Riggs rather gingerly suggests that "men of the opposite political faith were not careful in their conversation" and that they kept the Indians informed of disasters to the Union Army "with some exaggerations," which "was a political sin."[25]

an interview with Little Crow on the fifteenth, but makes no mention of any council. See Indian Office, *Reports*, 1863, p. 275. John P. Williamson, it is related by Mrs. Barton, left Redwood the morning after the alleged council and saw the newspaper announcements of the outbreak on reaching some point in Ohio.

[25] Galbraith, in Indian Office, *Reports*, 1863, p. 286; Riggs, *Forty Years with the Sioux*, 148, 152; Riggs, *Tah-koo Wah-kan*, 329-331; Galbraith and Riggs, in *Claims for Depredations*

There was a custom among the Sioux when on their great seasonal hunts to organize a kind of provost guard to enforce a necessary discipline over the party. In particular it had to see to it that no individual hunter passed beyond the bounds set in council for the day's hunt, to disturb the game. Sibley, who on one occasion joined one of the hunts, inadvertently transgressed the rule. By making a timely present he saved his tent from destruction, but he was obliged to consent to a commutation of his costly fur cap. The members of this guard camped together and were called collectively the "soldiers' lodge." During the season under consideration many of the braves conceived the idea that their chiefs were not efficient in securing subsistence and the payment of the annuities. It should be kept in mind that, since the custom of paying directly to heads of families and single individuals had been adopted by the government, the disciplinary power of the chiefs had been greatly weakened. Early in the summer 150 warriors of the lower bands formed themselves into a quasi soldiers' lodge. The leading question for consideration was whether or not they should forcibly protest against the attendance of troops to help the traders collect their credits at the coming payment. The statement of Galbraith that "the real object of this lodge was to adopt measures to 'clean out' all the white people at the time of payment" has no warrant of record or of circumstance. That the outbreak was deliberately planned in a subsequent meeting of the lodge is equally inadmissible. It may perhaps be reasonably conjectured that in one or another of the convocations

by Sioux Indians, 8, 10, 11 (serial 1189). Examples of the rebel emissary theory are numerous. An editorial in the Saint Paul Press of September 21, 1862, says, "That the secession sympathizers and agents have been instrumental in causing the difficulty with the Indians is evident." In a letter dated September 9, 1862, in the Saint Paul Pioneer of September 16, 1862, Henry M. Rice says, "The Sioux Indians were induced by rebels and traitors to make war upon our people." Caleb B. Smith, secretary of the interior, in his report for 1862, in 37 Congress, 3 session, House Executive Documents, vol. 2, p. 8 (serial 1157), says, "I am satisfied that the chief cause is to be found in the insurrection of the southern States." He also quotes from a letter, dated September 5, 1862, from the Reverend P. J. De Smet to the commissioner of Indian affairs. See also Pope to Halleck, October 2, 1862, in Official Records, series 1, vol. 13, p. 705. A. W. Daniels, in Minnesota Historical Collections, 12:524, says that "Little Crow watched the war . . . with the deepest solicitude."

there was some display of patriotism in the glowing imagery of Indian eloquence. The great Dakota nation, it may have been pictured, could "clean out" the little guard of volunteers at the fort, swarm down the Minnesota, and wipe out all the settlements in the valley. The Great Father would have to buy their lands over again and pay for them.[26]

The August days were passing and still, in spite of suspicions and anxieties, all was outwardly quiet at the agencies and throughout the reservations. Agent Galbraith perambulated the farms and villages and found all at peace and the fields full of promise. On the fifteenth he had a friendly interview with Little Crow, for whom he was building a brick house, and he believed that he had completely secured that chief's good will and coöperation in the work of civilization. He "understood" that the chief was ready to abandon the blanket Indians and to "become a white man." So confident was the agent of continued peace that he decided to take a short leave from his post. Some forty young men, mostly employees on the reservation who were soon to be discharged, had signified their willingness to enlist in the Union army under a new call for volunteers issued in August. Because they could not agree upon a leader, Agent Galbraith undertook to enlist them and take them down to Fort Snelling and even farther, if permitted. On the afternoon of the fifteenth he left the agencies in charge of his assistants and took his recruits to Fort Ridgely. The party traveled by way of New Ulm, where a day was spent, and was in St. Peter about sundown of August 18, where we have already found

[26] Henry H. Sibley, "Reminiscences of the Early Days of Minnesota," in *Minnesota Historical Collections*, 3: 259; Pond, in *Minnesota Historical Collections*, 12: 362; Galbraith, in Indian Office, *Reports*, 1863, p. 287; Riggs, *Tah-koo Wah-kan*, 326; Riggs, in *Claims for Depredations by Sioux Indians*, 12 (serial 1189); Holcombe, in *Minnesota in Three Centuries* 3: 281, 285. Holcombe calls the soldiers' lodge "a-ke-che-ta tepee," but Riggs calls it "*Tee-yo-tee-pe.*" Riggs, *Forty Years with the Sioux*, 153.

It was Joseph R. Brown's judgment that the commanding officers at Fort Ridgely for some years previous to the outbreak sympathized with the lower Sioux and even promised to protect them if they should refuse the allowance of traders' debts at payments. See Samuel J. Brown to the author, October 26, 1921, in the Folwell Papers.

them. Of the part taken by Captain James Gorman's Renville Rangers in Colonel Sibley's campaign of 1862 an account has already been given.[27]

Teased by the traders, who themselves were exasperated by the delay of the payment, misinformed by half-breeds, and deluded by "copperheads," the lower Indians became more and more anxious and suspicious. There were two causes of delay. The first was the tardy action of Congress. The reader will properly wonder why congressional action was necessary, since the appropriations for 1862 had been made in the previous year. The goods and provisions for 1862 had been purchased and were in the storehouses of the two agencies. There were no separate items of money appropriations, but lump sums were named to include all dues for a year under the treaties. The reports of agent, superintendent, commissioner, and secretary throw no light upon the subject. The uncontradicted explanation of Riggs must therefore be relied upon. He relates that the "government" — the new Republican administration — decided in 1861 to change the money annuities into goods and began in the fall of that year by sending on goods to the value of twenty thousand dollars to be divided equally between the upper and the lower Sioux and to be accepted by them in lieu of so much cash at the next payment, that of 1862. The goods were accepted but the proposition to reduce the cash payment was repugnant. The exasperation of the Indians was so intense that the "government," advised through the Indian officials, did not dare to depart from the treaties and custom, but was constrained to make the usual money payment to the truculent savages. The twenty thousand dollars expended for the extra issue of goods had to be replaced from the appropriations for the next year, 1863. The bill for those appropriations, which was passed by the House on February 24, 1862, was not passed by the Senate until May 16 and then with many amendments. Some of these were not agreed

[27] Galbraith, in Indian Office, *Reports*, 1863, pp. 272, 275.

to by the House and the bill went to conference.  The report
of the conferees was not agreed to by the Senate and a second
conference took place.  The act was at length passed and
approved on July 5, 1862.  The amendments and the discussions had no relation to the appropriations for the
Sioux.[28]  In as much as Congress was occupied with Civil
War finance measures of high importance and had no advice
that any portion of the Indian appropriations for 1863 was
to be diverted to making up an extraordinary deficiency in
those of 1862, no blame attaches for the congressional
tardiness.

The other cause of delay arose in the treasury, when the
question was asked why these Indians might not be paid with
the United States notes later known popularly as "green-
backs."  More than a month passed before a decision was
reached.  Advised by the Indian officials concerning the risks
attending a departure from custom if not from faith and
honor, Secretary Chase on August 8 ordered the deputy
treasurer at New York to deliver seventy-one thousand
dollars in gold to the order of the commissioner of Indian
affairs.  A keg said to contain gold coin of that value
reached St. Paul on August 16, whence it was dispatched on
the next day to Fort Ridgely.  It reached there at midday
on the eighteenth, by which hour some hundred white
people lay in or about their homes dead or bleeding from
wounds.  Had the arrival taken place a few hours earlier
and been made known to the Indians, the Sioux Outbreak
would have had no place in Minnesota history.[29]  There was

[28] *Statutes at Large*, 12: 231; Riggs, *Forty Years with the Sioux*, 147-149; Riggs, *Tah-koo Wah-kan*, 328; *Congressional Globe*, 37 Congress, 2 session, 938, 2162, 2215, 2494, 2588, 2595, 2659, 2675, 2840-2842, 2906, 3050, 3062, 3120.  J. W. Daniels, in his "Indian Outbreak," 23, says this handling of the annuity greatly exasperated the Sioux.  See also Riggs's review of Heard, *Sioux War*, in the *Saint Paul Press* of December 17, 1863.

[29] Holcombe, in *Minnesota in Three Centuries*, 3: 284; *Saint Paul Press*, August 24, 1862; Charles E. Mix, acting commissioner of Indian affairs, to Commissioner Dole, August 13, 1862, in Indian Office, *Reports*, 1862, p. 68.  Mix states that "Secretary Chase had agreed to order Mr. Cisco [*deputy treasurer of the United States*] to pay the $71,000 in coin."  He says also that efforts to get gold "appear, from present appearances, to have been success-ful."  Some Chippewa payments were afterwards made in greenbacks.

absolutely no truth in the slanderous rumor of the time, later revived, that Indian officials had held back the gold while they used it in speculations. The reader has, of course, divined that there was no payment in 1862. The keg of gold was taken back to St. Paul by the guards who had brought it up to Fort Ridgely. They had remained in the fort during the battles and until after the arrival of Sibley's troops.[30]

On Sunday, August 17, Little Crow attended the morning service in the Episcopal chapel at the lower agency and, according to Big Eagle, shook hands with everybody. When the sun set that day over that consummately beautiful and peaceful valley, no one doubted that it would rise on a happy day of industry and pleasure. But beneath the surface lay an explosive magazine ready for some casual detonating spark. On that same Sunday, about noon, at a settler's house in Acton Township, Meeker County, three white men, one woman, and a girl were treacherously murdered by a party of four Indians. They were a detachment of a hunting party belonging to a small body of blanket Indians who had seceded from Shakopee's band and had established themselves in a new village on Rice Creek, a diminutive tributary of the Minnesota some miles above the mouth of the Redwood. The exciting cause of the separation is not well known, but they were a band of malcontents, all heathen and opposed to civilization. There had been accessions from other bands, both upper and lower. They frequently extended their hunts to the Big Woods of Kandiyohi and adjacent counties.[31] For some days this hunting party had been looking for deer in the Big Woods and possibly for

---

[30] Galbraith, in Indian Office, *Reports*, 1863, p. 287.

[31] *Sisseton and Wahpeton Claim Case Record, Evidence for Defendant*, 291, 302, 309, 319, 367, 388; Holcombe, in *Minnesota in Three Centuries*, 3: 274, 302. An error locating Rice Creek on the left bank of the Minnesota is notable because Holcombe had been on the ground more than once. It has been suspected that he mistook Middle Creek in Renville County for Rice Creek. Pond, in *Minnesota Historical Collections*, 12: 329, says that the party at Rice Creek was led by Shakopee's brother, "a bold bad man," though not a chief, and an abler man than Little Crow. Pond seems to have had a low opinion of Little Crow.

Chippewa scalps. It is both affirmed and denied that the Indians were drunk. Their behavior before the shooting lends countenance to the hypothesis of intoxication, but the fact that the assassins departed leaving the settler's liquor untouched discredits that hypothesis. The deed done, the miscreants seized four horses belonging to neighboring farmers and rode at top speed to Rice Creek, where they may have arrived before dark.[32]

The statement has been made that a council — it could not have been a general council — had that day been held at Rice Creek, in which it had been agreed that all the able-bodied men should go in a party to the lower agency, thence to Fort Ridgely, and even on to St. Paul to demand an early pay day. Nothing was said about war.[33] Galbraith states that a council of relatives was held immediately upon the return of the murderers. Doubtless there was some consultation, of which the result was that the leader of the local band, who was not a recognized chief, took the young men to Chief Shakopee at his village near the mouth of the Redwood. That chief was willing enough to spill white man's blood, but he was not ready to take the warpath on his own responsibility. He preferred concerted action and therefore took the young men, and doubtless some attendants from Rice Creek and his own village, to Little Crow's village, situated about two miles above the lower agency. It may be presumed that Shakopee sent runners to the heads of all the lower bands summoning them to a rendezvous. If an orderly council took place, it must have been brief. "Blood had been shed, the payment would be stopped, and the whites would take a dreadful vengeance because women had been killed." The resolution was for immediate war on

---

[32] Big Eagle, in *Minnesota Historical Collections*, 6: 388-390. For details of the Acton murders, see the Appendix, no. 11, *post.*

[33] Holcombe, in *Minnesota in Three Centuries*, 3: 302; Bryant and Murch, *Great Massacre*, 60; Hughes, *Welsh in Minnesota*, 65. The last two accounts lack confirmation, and are improbable.

all whites and all "cut-hairs" who would not fight with their people. Little Crow, at first scornful or indifferent, accepted the chief command, probably because it would restore his lost distinction as speaker of the lower Sioux and would give him opportunity to display his military talent, of which, not without reason, he was vain. He at once ordered the attack on the agency in the morning, the killing of the traders, and the looting of the stores.[34]

[34] Galbraith, in Indian Office, *Reports*, 1863, p. 288; Big Eagle, in *Minnesota Historical Collections*, 6: 384-389. Big Eagle's statement that Wabasha and Wacouta were present at a council at Little Crow's house is improbable, as their villages lay some miles below the agency. His résumé of the causes of the outbreak is reasonable and in excellent temper. Note his account of the Acton murders on pages 388-390. Concerning Little Crow's loss of his position as speaker for the lower Sioux, see the Appendix, no. 9, *post*.

## IX. SEQUEL TO THE SIOUX WAR OF 1862

THE effects of the battle of Wood Lake in the capture of nearly two thousand Indians and the dispersion of perhaps twice as many more were no sooner clearly apparent than Pope in a series of letters to Halleck informed him that the Indian war was over and that he could spare some of the troops of his department. Governor Ramsey in a letter of October 22 to the president said that the war was "virtually closed" and that he was sending his acting chief quartermaster, Colonel Richard Chute, to present the bill of the state for its outlays in the campaign.[1] The Democratic press of the state charged that both Pope and Ramsey had made haste to announce the end of the war for the purpose of discouraging the administration from appointing Senator Henry M. Rice a major general of volunteers to supersede Pope in his command in the Northwest. Whether any such "low juggling" took place or not, Minnesota was not deprived of her patriotic and efficient senator and Sibley received no affront.[2] Ramsey and Pope were soon apprised from many quarters that the Indian war was not over in any sense to justify the removal of the troops from the theater of that war. Ramsey was informed by a leading journal that if he should suffer "a soldier of this State to be withdrawn until this matter is satisfactorily settled, the blood of his thousand murdered constituents" would "cry out against him, and the arms of their living kin be raised for his destruction." In a letter of November 6 to Ramsey, Pope expressed his intention of holding troops enough, although they were much needed in the South, to give the people of Minnesota ample security for returning to their farms and villages.

[1] *Minnesota in the Civil and Indian Wars*, 2:264, 270, 272, 274, 282e.
[2] *Saint Paul Pioneer*, October 23, November 7, 9, 1862.

He had never thought of abandoning any of the frontier posts occupied. He would therefore send only the Third Regiment south and would retain the Sixth, Seventh, Eighth, Ninth, and Tenth. His change of station late in November devolved the distribution of these five infantry regiments and a battalion of the First Mounted Rangers upon Sibley, who had been placed in command of the Military District of Minnesota.[3]

The Sixth Regiment was given headquarters at Fort Snelling with five companies. Three other companies were placed at Glencoe and the remaining two, at points in the Big Woods. The Seventh, with headquarters at Mankato, extended a line of posts westward and southward through Madelia and Fairmont to the Iowa border. The Eighth was disposed along an east-and-west line with headquarters at Fort Ripley. There was a company at Princeton and another at Anoka to cover the "Twin Cities" from assault by the Chippewa of Mille Lacs; posts at Sauk Centre, Alexandria, Fort Abercrombie, and intermediate places were intended to protect the white settlements on the north from attacks of the Pillagers and other bands of the Chippewa of the Mississippi. The Ninth Regiment had a central position at Fort Ridgely with four companies and headquarters and single companies were sent to South Bend, St. Peter, Glencoe, Judson, Hutchinson, and Fort Abercrombie. The principal duty assigned to the Tenth Regiment was the intimidation of the Winnebago Indians, still suspected of hostility on their reservation in Blue Earth County. Two companies were posted at the Winnebago agency; two others were placed at Le Sueur with headquarters; two companies were sent to Henderson; one company was added to the garrison of Fort Ridgely; and the remaining three were posted at as many less important places. It is not difficult to observe that economic considerations had their part in the location of the troops.

[3] *Saint Paul Pioneer*, October 23, 1862; *Minnesota in the Civil and Indian Wars*, 2:284, 287, 293.

What with the building of stockades, outpost duty, and military drills the winter passed quickly, without alarms, and the spring of 1863 found the regiments in excellent condition for further service.[4]

The military operations for the protection of the frontiers were not allowed long to delay exertions for the relief of the families mourning for their dead and wounded and their abandoned homes. The legislature which met in extra session on September 9, 1862, at once authorized a loan of a hundred thousand dollars, which was taken by Thompson Brothers, bankers, of St. Paul, at seven per cent and a small premium. Twenty-five thousand dollars were devoted to the immediate relief of refugees and to this sum were added private contributions of over five thousand dollars. These funds were expended by Commissioner Peter Berkey of St. Paul, mostly on the people who had swarmed into St. Paul after the outbreak. The legislature of 1863 also made an appropriation of three thousand dollars to be drawn on by county commissioners and paid out for the support of widows and young children.[5]

The remaining seventy-five thousand dollars of the state loan were expected to be sufficient to pay the costs incurred by the state in the Indian war and "would have been sufficient," said Governor Ramsey, "had the State been called upon to discharge only the expenses of the Militia" while it was under her control. But the state was obliged to continue her disbursements after the government took control and to furnish much of the transportation and subsistence needed in the Indian war. At the beginning of operations against the Indians Governor Ramsey had expressly authorized commanders to impress horses, oxen, wagons, and needed supplies. The militia called out by his proclamation of August 21 was directed to take its

[4] *Minnesota in the Civil and Indian Wars*, 1:314, 353, 386, 416-418, 456.

[5] *General Laws*, 1862, extra session, 50, 52-54, 65, 66; 1863, pp. 99-103; reports of the state treasurer, in *Executive Documents*, 1862, p. 605; 1863, p. 365; Governor Ramsey's message, January 7, 1863, in *Executive Documents*, 1862, pp. 4, 7, 9.

own horses and a few days' subsistence and the commanders were authorized to provide for all exigencies. This liberal authority was soon so much abused that it was revoked before the assemblage of the legislature. To ascertain the amounts due private individuals for such impressments of their services and the use of their animals the legislature elected a board of three auditors of war claims. Subsequent acts perpetuated this board.

Governor Ramsey's appeal to the secretary of war for reimbursements drew out the information that the advances made by the state could be met only by a future appropriation by Congress. In the following session of Congress an appropriation of $250,000 was made for the purpose, which was received and credited on account. A large additional amount was held charged against the United States and many years passed before that account was closed. The whole amount obtained by the state was about $365,000. The multiplication of claims by individual citizens appears to have been stimulated by the industry of attorneys.[6]

Compensation for property damages wrought by the Indians was not undertaken by the state. The legislature of 1862 in the extra session, voicing a general sentiment, adopted a memorial to the president praying that citizens of Minnesota be reimbursed for their property losses out of annuities to be regarded as forfeited by the Indians by their insurrection.[7] There were patriots enough in Minnesota to conceive the idea that the United States might properly be called upon to reimburse her citizens whose relatives had been butchered, whose homes had been destroyed, and who themselves had been driven far by

[6] Governor Ramsey's message, January 7, 1863, in *Executive Documents*, 1862, pp. 10, 11; *Minnesota in the Civil and Indian Wars*, 2:194, 285; *Statutes at Large*, 12:754. The details of this long-drawn-out account would not greatly, if at all, interest the general reader. The following citations will assist those who may desire to follow them up: *Statutes at Large*, 13:350; 16:40; Minnesota, *General Laws*, 1862, extra session, 19;1863, pp. 17-21, 124; 1864, p. 69; and the annual reports of the state auditor and treasurer, in *Executive Documents*, 1862-70.
[7] *General Laws*, 1862, extra session, 87.

the terror of the Indian wards of the nation. But the suggestion of a scheme whereby a generous nation might dispense a great charity apparently without cost must have been the conception of some individual wise and expert in things political. The writer regrets that he has not learned his name for record here.

On December 2, 1862, Cyrus Aldrich, representative from the second Minnesota district, introduced into the third session of the Thirty-seventh Congress a bill which finally got the title, "An Act for the Relief of Persons for Damages Sustained by Reason of Depredations and Injuries by Certain Bands of Sioux Indians." This bill, in the form in which it passed the House, proposed to divert for the relief of sufferers the sum of $1,500,000 from Sioux annuities due and to accumulate. Aldrich informed the House that, as the payment would come from Indian trust funds, it would not increase the indebtedness of the United States. It was "not in the true sense of the term an appropriation." The money was needed to relieve ten thousand people living on charity. Windom urged the passage of the bill in a brief but impassioned address. The Indian outrages had been committed chiefly in his own district. Over a thousand persons had been butchered with brutalities beyond description. Thousands had been driven from their homes without a moment's warning, taking nothing with them, and were living on charity. "They look imploringly to you, gentlemen," said he. "Do not refuse them justice and disappoint their hopes by unnecessary delays." There was but slight opposition to the bill in the House, but rather indifference, as indicated by the lack of a quorum on three attempts at passage.

The Senate committee on Indian affairs was unwilling to recommend the disbursement of $1,500,000 or of any sum for damages in advance of an enrollment of beneficiaries and an inventory of their several losses. The substitute it reported abrogated all existing treaties with the Minnesota

Sioux and declared "all lands, rights of occupancy, annuities, and claims, heretofore accorded to said Indians . . . to be forfeited to the United States." Provision was made for an appropriation of a hundred thousand dollars for immediate relief of personal sufferers, being two-thirds of the amount of annuities due the Sioux for the present year, already appropriated but not expended; and a commission was to be appointed to entertain claims for damage to property, take testimony, ascertain the loss of each deserving claimant, and report to the secretary of the interior, who in turn should report to Congress. Senator Rice, supported by Wilkinson, made a brave but vain effort to secure the passage of the House bill with its ready-made appropriation of a million and a half. After a tedious debate in which the Minnesota senators assured the Senate that a hundred thousand dollars would be a ridiculously trifling gratuity, they persuaded the Senate to double that sum and to take the additional amount out of Sioux annuities of the next year, thus recognizing the "principle." The bill passed without division and was approved on February 16, 1863. It was to have a long history. The reader will have observed that if the House bill had been enacted into law there would have been good times in Minnesota and he need not doubt that the whole bounty would have been promptly absorbed.[8]

The report of the Sioux commission of 1863 is an important document. The testimony upon which it is based covered nearly twenty thousand pages of legal cap paper and embodied a number of narratives of survivors of the Sioux Outbreak and depositions of Agent Galbraith and Dr. Riggs.

[8] 37 Congress, 3 session, *House Journal*, 30, 102, 128-132 (serial 1155); *Senate Journal*, 83, 136, 151, 294 (serial 1148); *Congressional Globe*, 4, 144, 179-181, 192, 440-442, 509-518; *Statutes at Large*, 12:652-654. The debate in the Senate fills twenty-seven columns of the *Globe*. The incongruity of abrogating all pecuniary obligation to the Sioux and still relieving sufferers out of their annuities as if still due and payable seems not to have occurred. It is notable that the leading St. Paul newspapers are silent on the measure for the abrogation of the treaties and the relief of sufferers. People in Minnesota seem to have been more concerned about the removal of the Indians. Jane G. Swisshelm made an address "of uncommon power" in Washington in favor of expulsion. *Saint Paul Pioneer*, March 1, 1863.

The commission allowed a total of $1,370,374 to 2,635 claimants. Of the $200,000 already appropriated $184,392 were apportioned for immediate relief of heads of families or their survivors and the remainder was applied in satisfaction of the total damages awarded them and others. The balance of $1,170,374 was appropriated by Congress in an act approved on May 28, 1864. A tradition has survived that the commission in distributing this Indian money was becomingly generous and that attorneys for claimants on shares were well compensated.[9]

It would not have been strange if, while the laws were in fact suspended throughout several counties and parts of counties, persons usually obedient to them felt themselves at liberty to carry off and appropriate the movable effects left by the affrighted refugees in and about their homes. To a considerable number of such Agent Galbraith gave the name "Algerines." "The teamsters and transient visitors," said he, "literally *pitched into* this business." Dr. Riggs left the following emphatic declaration: "It appeared, too, that not only had the devil taken possession of the Indians, but of almost everybody else. Multitudes of white men and women turned plunderers. . . . As the people fled from one town, the inhabitants of town or country beyond, fleeing also, came in and plundered the houses; and when the panic had somewhat subsided, there were harpies who passed around through the depopulated districts and gathered up wagon loads of property, such as the Indians had left untouched. Many tools and implements of husbandry disappeared in this way." The commission itself recorded its conviction that "the freebooter and the army completed what the impotence of the savage had spared." To what extent the

[9] *Claims for Depredations by Sioux Indians* (serial 1189); *Statutes at Large*, 13: 92. A mass of papers of the commission, including part of the testimony, has recently been located in the Indian office in Washington, and a calendar of this material, with copies of a few of the documents, is now in the possession of the Minnesota Historical Society. See the *State Atlas* (Minneapolis), November 4, 1863, for criticisms of extravagant claims. Thousands of dollars were claimed for damages to rutabagas. If all the rutabagas claimed to have been destroyed by the Sioux "were evenly spread over the entire State, the whole surface would be covered to the depth of one foot." The claims presented amounted to about $2,500,000.

aggregate awards of the Sioux commission were swelled by the losses so incurred will never be known.[10]

In his order for the execution of the murderers at Mankato, President Lincoln directed General Sibley to hold the other condemned prisoners subject to further orders, "taking care that they neither escape nor are subjected to any unlawful violence." The reasons for not making such further orders until after the whole ensuing winter had passed have not been revealed. In the meantime a most remarkable revolution was taking place in the prison at Mankato. In the first place, as Riggs wrote, the prison was "one great school." Groups of ten or more were gathered as pupils about fellow convicts who had attended the mission schools. Riggs extemporized a spelling book and had four hundred copies printed in St. Paul. A hundred copies of Bunyan in Dakota, which John B. Renville and others had cached, were found and put in use. All over the prison groups were practicing writing with pens and paper or slates and pencils. Before spring four hundred letters were taken down to the camp at Fort Snelling to members of convicts' families. Fortunately a Dakota Indian was not condemned to learn the vagaries of English orthography. His own spelling, thanks to the Pond brothers, was strictly orthographic. "These Sioux," wrote Riggs, "have made as much progress in education as in twenty-six or twenty-seven years."

But the revival of learning in the Mankato prison was far less wonderful than that of religion. Williamson, their faithful missionary, spent much of his time with the prisoners

---

[10] *Claims for Depredations by Sioux Indians*, 6, 12, 16 (serial 1189); *Mankato Semi-Weekly Record*, August 30, September 6, 27, 1862. In a letter to Captain Skaro, September 16, 1862, in *Minnesota in the Civil and Indian Wars*, 2:233, Sibley says, "This system of plunder must be suppressed and the criminals punished." Sheriff Roos of Brown County, writing to Governor Ramsey on September 4, 1862, says, "Our Town is plundered out entirely every thing we left here [has been] . . . taken away . . . *by white thiefes*." The letter is in the Governor's Archives, file 255. In his testimony in *Sisseton and Wahpeton Claim Case Record, Evidence for Claimant*, 132, John B. Renville says, "There were many white people . . . that represented themselves as Indians and were marauding through the country."

and preached to them every Sunday. His influence, however, was more effective through the aid of his former ruling
elder in the Yellow Medicine church, Robert Hopkins
Chaskay. Hopkins had been convicted on his own confession of presence in battles and on the testimony of
David Faribault, Sr., that he had heard him say that he
had shot a white man. Riggs deposed that it was Hopkins
who had saved the Williamson family and had rescued the
widow of Amos W. Huggins. Although he was "strongly
recommended to mercy," the sentence of death by hanging
stood of record. Robert Hopkins became the ruling spirit
in the Mankato prison. He spent his days and some whole
nights conversing and praying with the anxious. The
commander of the prison guard ordered his chains taken
off. A fortnight had barely passed after the execution when
convicts began to speak and pray in the evening meetings.
A few extemporized copiously, as if aided by the Holy
Spirit. There was abundance of singing. Many asked to
be baptized. Williamson sent for Gideon Pond, with whom
and a local Presbyterian minister he took counsel. It
was agreed that under like circumstances the apostles
would have baptized generally.

The Dakota medicine men, who had egged on their
people to wage the war against the whites, had fled to the
plains after the collapse at Wood Lake. The white man's
"medicine" had triumphed. Inveterately religious, these
Indians were now ready to accept the white man's cult
and kneel at the altar of his religion. Williamson prepared
a confession of faith and a covenant such as he thought
proper for the occasion. On February 3, 1863, he and Pond
poured the water of baptism on the heads of 274 willing
candidates. As each knelt the missionary said, in substance: "My brother, this is a mark of God which is placed
upon you. You will carry it while you live. . . . This
ends your superstition and from this time you are to call
God your father. Remember to honor him. Be resolved

to do his will." Each responded, "Yes, I will." Other baptisms of convicts, mostly in the same month, raised the number to 305 or 306, including "all the Indians at Mankato except one woman." Study and prayer continued to fill the hours of dull imprisonment. There were three seasons of prayer a day. The officers and soldiers of the guard were duly remembered and the divine blessing was besought on the prisoners' families in the camp at Fort Snelling. Robert Hopkins handed to the missionaries a written resolution that all would continue constant in praying for three things — a country, a sanctuary, and teachers. The hearts even of Mankato people were softened by these blessed fruits of religion.[11]

The further disposition of the convicts at Mankato seems to have been the subject of much consideration at Washington. The Indian office naturally refused to take any charge of them while they were military prisoners. On the last day of February Halleck informed Pope that his letter requesting orders had been submitted to the cabinet. On April 14 he further informed the department commander that the matter would be considered at an early meeting of the cabinet.[12] Meantime the disposition of the convicts was not forgotten in Minnesota. In his message of January 7, 1863, Governor Ramsey proposed to the legislature a careful consideration of the question whether these criminals were not still amenable to Minnesota justice. The state had been invaded and the state under constitutional privilege had waged a war of defense. The commander of her troops appointed under state authority had instituted a tribunal which had tried and convicted these murderers. "May she," he said, "raise armies and take prisoners, and shall she not dispose of those prisoners when taken?" The state of Virginia had tried and punished John Brown for

[11] *Indian Barbarities in Minnesota*, 7 (serial 1149); *Missionary Herald*, 59:72, 149, 201-205 (March, May, July, 1863); Pond, *Two Volunteer Missionaries*, 223; Riggs, *Tahkoo Wah-kan*, 343, 347, 352, 360; Proceedings of the Military Commission (Indian no. 163). The missionaries believed that Faribault's testimony was false.
[12] *Official Records*, series 1, vol. 22, part 2, pp. 117, 127, 217.

invading her soil. In as much as the convicts were at
this time in the hands of United States troops the legislature
made no response to the proposition, which may have been
a pardonable play to the gallery. So, rejoicing in their
new-found faith, these convicts in the Mankato prison
passed the winter of 1863 in a riot of religious exercises.
That the good missionaries saw in answer to their prayers
a special visitation of the Third Person of the Trinity need
not be wondered at.[13]

The melancholy horde which Lieutenant Colonel Marshall
escorted from Redwood to Fort Snelling in November was
put into a camp on the bottom land of the Minnesota near
the fort, surrounded by a high board fence within which the
Indians pitched their tepees. Fed from the government
stores, they passed the winter of 1863 more comfortably
than they might have done in their own villages before
their desolation. A census dated December 2, 1862, showed
a total population of 1,601. It included 112 loyal half-
breeds belonging mostly to families who had located their
half-breed scrip on the upper Minnesota and had established
homes on their lands. The Freniere, Faribault, Laframboise,
Robertson, and Renville families were represented. Their
homes desolated, they could do nothing but follow their
Indian relatives and share their rations as they were allowed
to do. There were a few other half-breeds, among them
Jean Jacques Frazer and Charles Crawford, who were
reserved for scout service in a future expected campaign.
Of the nearly fifteen hundred Indians not more than ten
per cent were male adults, as shown by the lists.

In this camp there took place a revival of learning and
religion like that at Mankato, which involved nearly all
the adults. Hundreds became interested in learning to read
and all except the young children and a few very old men
became deeply religious. There was no such native leader
as Robert Hopkins, but there was a young missionary to

[13] *Executive Documents*, 1862, p. 29.

SAUK CENTRE STOCKADE, 1864

*Oil by an unknown artist owned by the Sauk Centre Public Library*

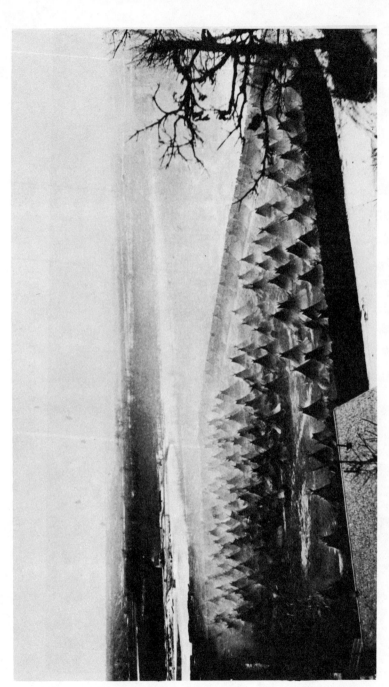

SIOUX PRISONERS ENCAMPED NEAR FORT SNELLING, 1862–63
*Photograph by B. F. Upton of St. Anthony*

be their beloved leader and guide.[14] John Poage Williamson, the eldest son of Dr. Thomas Smith Williamson, after finishing his theological education at the Lane Theological Seminary was informed from home of the unhappy condition of the lower Sioux and offered himself to the American Board as a missionary to them. It was in the late fall of 1860 that he came to Redwood. From childhood he had spoken Dakota and he knew what Gideon Pond strained himself to learn, the "inside of an Indian." At first Williamson took his lodging and held his religious meetings in the tent of an Indian who had been his playfellow at Lac qui Parle. In the spring of 1862 he began the building of a church from lumber which cost the mission nothing, doing most of the work with his own hands. He had also the material ready for a dwelling when the outbreak occurred and the Indians and the army did away with his lumber. He rejoined the scattered flock as soon as Sibley's army had collected the remnants of the tribes at Redwood and accompanied the Indians to Fort Snelling. He never left the Sioux but spent the remainder of his life in their service. From day to day through that long winter he labored with and for those who had become in an eminent sense his people. There was a scarcity of books and writing materials but many learned to read. The religious interest soon became powerful. After holding meetings in tepees Williamson got the use of the garret of an old government warehouse in which as many as five hundred could be seated Indian fashion. Here nightly meetings for prayer and praise were held. Hopeful conversions and requests for baptism were soon abundant. In regard to these the younger Williamson was not so liberal as his more experienced father, who suited the covenants to the circumstances. The converts at Fort Snelling were put before the session of the church

[14] Riggs, *Forty Years with the Sioux*, 191; Renville, in *Minnesota Historical Collections*, 10: 610 (part 2), speaks of much sickness. For the census of the Indian camp, see Indian Office, *Reports*, 1863, pp. 313-316. Antoine Freniere's explanation of the reason the half-breeds stuck to the Indians in captivity is given in the *Saint Paul Press* of February 22, 1863. A sufficient reason was to support their families on army rations.

and subjected to an examination as to piety and knowledge
as thorough as the young pastor had "been accustomed
to see in any of our churches." He records but 140 admissions and three of these were of backsliders. Had he been
pleased to use the generous standard adopted at Mankato
the flock might have been increased by many hundreds.
As it was the missionary feared that there might be some
tares in the wheat.[15]

Little is known of the ministrations of Father Augustin
Ravoux in the Indian camp at Fort Snelling. His own brief
statement is that he visited it often and baptized 184 persons,
almost all young children. The labors of the Reverend
Samuel D. Hinman, missionary of the Protestant Episcopal
Church, seem to have been blessed. As first fruit he baptized fifty-two adults and ninety-two children in the presence
of four hundred Indians. Wabasha and most of the head
men came under his instruction. His congregations increased from thirty to three hundred and he had three
hundred children under his care. On March 18, 1863,
forty-seven of his converts were confirmed by Bishop
Whipple.[16]

Still that camp was not wholly a scene of happiness.
There was some sickness and there were not a few deaths.
It is traditional that the corpses were not allowed an indefinite repose. It was a hard place for children. There were
temptations for men and women, even for virtuous women.
"The devil . . . is ever on the alert to bring our religion
into disgrace by the fall of such," wrote John Williamson.
The idle creatures were tantalized with rumors, probably
brought in by half-breeds who could read English, that
the thirty-eight men hanged at Mankato were but the
first installment of wholesale executions and those not

[15] Barton, *John P. Williamson*, 45-47, 50; *Missionary Herald*, 59: 133, 205 (May, July, 1863).
[16] Ravoux, *Reminiscences*, 81; Tanner, *Diocese of Minnesota*, 397; Bishop Whipple, in his *Lights and Shadows*, 133, states that Hinman spent the winter in the camp at Fort Snelling and that one night a gang of white roughs broke into the stockade and beat him nearly insensible.

so put to death or made slaves would be banished either
to some island where they would have to live on fish alone
or to some hot country where they would die of fevers.
Their guards and keepers, who were equally ignorant of
the undeclared policy of the government, could give them
no intimation of their probable fate.[17]

There was no doubt as to what the voice of the people
of Minnesota was with regard to disposing of the Sioux
prisoners both at Mankato and in the Fort Snelling camp;
loud demands for extermination at length gave place to
clamor for exile. Governor Ramsey in his message of
September 9, 1862, had voiced a unanimous sentiment.
"The Sioux Indians of Minnesota," he said, "must be
exterminated or driven forever beyond the borders of the
State. The public safety imperatively requires it. Justice
calls for it. . . . The blood of the murdered cries to
heaven for vengeance on these assassins of women and
children . . . amenable to no law; bound by no moral
or social restraints — they have already destroyed . . .
every pledge on which it was possible to found a hope of
ultimate reconciliation. They must be regarded and treated
as outlaws." The newspapers, without exception so far as
has been found, echoed this voice but enlarged its volume
to include every Indian of every tribe in the state. The
legislature addressed by Governor Ramsey seems not to
have been greatly excited by his sanguinary counsel. It
remains a question why it merely agreed to a memorial
to the president asking for the removal of the harmless
and besotted Winnebago but made no immediate appeal
for the exile of the Sioux. Instead of that it agreed to a

---

[17] Barton, *John P. Williamson*, 64; Riggs, *Forty Years with the Sioux*, 190; *Missionary
Herald*, 59: 43 (February, 1863). An interesting document is the petition accompanied by
a letter of Agent Galbraith dated December 17, 1862, and signed by thirty-eight chiefs
and headmen, all friendlies, to be allowed to go back to their farms and live like white men.
See the *Congressional Globe*, 37 Congress, 3 session, 514. In the *Saint Paul Press*, December
14, 1862, is a letter of Antoine Freniere, in which he says the signers of the petition had their
share of plunder on the first day of the outbreak and had any quantity buried at both
agencies. See *Sisseton and Wahpeton Claim Case Record, Evidence for Defendant*, 359, for
Hakewaste's account of the signing.

memorial requesting the president of the United States to
appoint an impartial commission to investigate the management of Indian affairs in Minnesota "and all other matters
pertaining to the Indian outbreak," suggesting that there
may have been causes tending to inflame the Indians and
expressing fear that the just and humane policy of the
government had not been faithfully carried out. It is
noteworthy that the same legislature industriously locked
the door after the horse had been stolen, by passing a very
drastic act forbidding the sale of intoxicating liquors to
Indians. Immediately after the organization of the legislature of 1863 memorials were offered in the lower house for
the removal of all Indian tribes from the state. They
were adopted by the House but were rejected by the Senate.[18]

Under the presumption that banishment would be meted
out to the Dakota, if not to all other Indians in the state, a
variety of projects were broached. General Sibley's plan
was to locate all the Sioux on a reservation about Devil's
Lake in North Dakota and surround them with a strong
cordon of United States troops which would shut them off
from all but licensed intercourse with whites. This plan
implied turning these Indians over to the care of the war
department. Agent Galbraith proposed the establishment
of a reservation on the north end of the Coteau des Prairies
in North Dakota, also to be surrounded by a military
reservation to keep the whites from penetrating the inclosed
Indian area. He would have a code of laws for the Indians
abolishing all the "accursed paraphernalia of Indian war"
and enforcing the adoption of the habits and customs of
enlightened Christian civilization. He would furnish the
Indians with means for tilling the soil and would compel

[18] *Executive Documents*, 1862, p. 12. The *Saint Paul Press* of October 10, 1862, says,
"The wilderness and starvation should be their doom." See also the *Press* of January 1,
1863; *General Laws*, 1862, extra session, 55, 92, 94; *House Journal*, 1863, pp. 23, 42, 79, 108;
and *Senate Journal*, 42, 97, 102. About January 1, 1863, a secret society of "Knights of the
Forest" was organized at Mankato for the purpose of having both the Sioux and the Winnebago removed from the state. Sublodges were soon organized in neighboring places. It is
supposed that the society exercised some influence on the legislature. Hughes, *Blue Earth
County*, 138.

them to use them. No traders were to be tolerated but the government would supply needs in return for labor performed. The Indians would need no money. This scheme for a beneficial slavery could not be entertained by a nation just then at war for the liberation of slaves and its operation presumed a degree of virtue and honesty not yet possessed by any large body of citizens and an exalted purity of character in public officials not to be safely attributed. No notice was taken of the plan.[19] General Pope communicated to Governor Ramsey in a letter of November 6, 1862, the policy which he had already proposed to the government. He would remove all Indians from Minnesota and would place them where they could not endanger settlers; he did not designate the place. He would treat all Indians as irresponsible persons, as the states do lunatics. He would feed and clothe them cheaply out of forfeited annuities and would allow them no dangerous weapons. Deprived of arms, forbidden to wander, and removed from evil influences of gamblers, whisky-sellers, unprincipled white men, and half-breeds, the Indian might be influenced by Christianity and education and the labors of missionaries might at length bear fruit.[20] Of all the propositions none had more dramatic features than that of James W. Taylor of St. Paul, then a well-known public character. As a suitable home for outlawed Indians he chose Isle Royale near the north shore of Lake Superior. In a long series of newspaper articles he advocated the selection of that

[19] Message of Governor Stephen Miller, in *Executive Documents*, 1864, p. 31; Galbraith, in Indian Office, *Reports*, 1863, pp. 295-298.

[20] *Minnesota in the Civil and Indian Wars*, 2:288. Pope elaborates this scheme in his report to the secretary of war, February 11, 1864. Commissioner Dole denounced the plan as a "mammoth scheme of colonization" which seemed to be "fraught with insuperable difficulties." St. A. D. Balcombe, who was the agent for the Winnebago and had temporary care of the Santee, made a proposition similar to Pope's. Colonel Clark W. Thompson recommended that the Indians be distributed among the white population, not more than two families in any county, on eighty-acre farms, and that their children be sent to the district schools. See Indian Office, *Reports*, 1864, pp. 398-402, 413, 424-429 (reprinted in 38 Congress, 2 session, *House Executive Documents*, no. 1 — serial 1220). Pope's report may be found also in *Official Records*, series 1, vol. 34, part 2, pp. 259-264. In a letter to General Grant, June 14, 1865, Pope said that the question before the government was "either the extermination of the Indian tribes, or a humane policy." Indian Office, *Reports*, 1865, p. 198.

island, from which escape could easily be made impossible, as a secure place of exile for 46,880 Sioux, Chippewa, Winnebago, and Menominee. He had no lofty humanitarian scheme for the civilization of these Indians but would leave them to live and die together as best they might. *"Let not the work of the Lord be done negligently!"* was his pious exhortation.[21] In December, 1862, Caleb B. Smith, secretary of the interior, recommended to the House committee on Indian affairs the removal of the Sioux to some point in the Missouri Valley and furnished a draft of an act for the purpose.[22]

The act of Congress of February 16, 1863, which abrogated all treaties with the Sioux, left them homeless. A subsequent act of March 3, 1863, following the recommendation of Secretary Smith, provided for the removal of all then in the custody of the government to some place outside of any state. The president decided to locate them on the Missouri River somewhere within a hundred miles of Fort Randall, where they would be secure from intrusion by whites. The removal was intrusted to Clark W. Thompson, the superintendent of Indian affairs for the northern superintendency, which included Minnesota. His instructions were given to him in person at Washington in April and ample funds were placed at his disposal. On the twenty-eighth he reported from St. Louis to the commissioner that he had made large purchases of implements, machinery, and provisions, and had employed engineers, sawyers, blacksmiths, and laborers. On June 1 the superintendent further announced that after examining the Missouri Valley for some distance he had selected a reservation with "good soil, good timber, and plenty of water," on the northeast bank of the river about eighty miles above

---

[21] *Saint Paul Press*, October 21–25, 1862. These articles were reprinted in pamphlet form under the title, *The Sioux War: What Shall We Do with It? The Sioux Indians: What Shall We Do with Them?* (St. Paul, 1862).

[22] 37 Congress, 3 session, *House Reports*, no. 13 (serial 1173).

Fort Randall. The place was some six hundred miles above St. Louis.[23]

The Indian office did not wait for the selection of the particular tract to be assigned to the exiled Sioux but prepared to ship them off like so many cattle. On May 4 the steamer "Davenport" took on 770 head. At the St. Paul levee there was hooting and stone-throwing but no serious damage was done to the defenseless cargo. The Reverend Samuel D. Hinman accompanied this party. On the following day 540 persons were put on board the steamboat "Northerner." John P. Williamson gives the following account of the departure of these friendless pilgrims: "The last one was counted on just at dusk, after which, an escort of soldiers being brought aboard, we shoved off. . . . We are, however, hardly under way when from all the different parts of the boat where they are collected, we hear hymns of praise ascending to Jehovah — not loud, but soft and sweet, like the murmur of many waters. Then one of them leads in prayer, after which another hymn is sung; and so they continue till all are composed; and drawing their blankets over them, each falls asleep." The smaller of the two parties was transferred to railroad cars at Hannibal, Missouri, and carried to St. Joseph. There it waited some days for the arrival of the "Davenport" with the larger detachment. On to this steamer was crowded the whole body of exiles. There was not room enough for all to lie down at night and they were forced to sleep by relays. The weather was already hot and the rations of pork and hardtack were musty. The steamer laboring against the powerful current of the Missouri did not reach its destination until May 30. As a result of that "middle passage" the hills about Crow Creek were soon covered with graves.[24]

[23] *Statutes at Large*, 12:652, 819; Indian Office, *Reports*, 1863, pp. 303-305, 308-311.
[24] *Minnesota History Bulletin*, 2:422 (May, 1918); Barton, *John P. Williamson*, 72-74; *Missionary Herald*, 59:205 (July, 1863); George W. Manypenny, *Our Indian Wards*, 135 (Cincinnati, 1880); Indian Office, *Reports*, 1863, p. 311. West, in his *Sibley*, 292, erroneously states that the number was reduced to one thousand before the destination was reached. See Riggs, *Tah-koo Wah-kan*, 366, and his *Forty Years with the Sioux*, 196.

It was too late when the Santee — as the amalgamated lower Sioux have since been called — arrived at Crow Creek to plant potatoes and too dry for corn to make good growth. Still quasi prisoners of war, the Indians were not allowed to range the country for the berries and roots which would have added to their rations. It early became evident that the government would have to furnish food during the coming winter of 1864 not only to the Santee but also to some two thousand Winnebago who had been moved to Crow Creek and placed on a reservation separated from that of the Santee by an air line only. A large amount of provisions was sent from St. Paul and Mankato by wagon train which reached its destination after twenty days of actual travel. The food thus shipped proved to be of inferior quality as well as insufficient in quantity. About two hundred of the Santee and as many Winnebago were allowed to go down to the Yankton agency near Fort Randall to beg for food and fuel. There was hunger in the bark tepees and starvation threatened many already enfeebled. But there came an unexpected and happy deliverance to the Santee from that danger. In midwinter a Santee hunter escaped from the guard with a gun he had kept concealed. He returned to tell John Williamson that there were buffalo on the plains and that he could kill enough with his own gun to keep the people alive. Williamson extorted a reluctant permission from the agent for a buffalo hunt on condition that he would go along. All the men, some fifty in number, with their families made up a party of perhaps five hundred. They had half a dozen guns with ammunition, some rations of pork and flour, and two horses, one of them Williamson's. The route lay northward up the valley of the James River, a hundred miles or more. A permanent hunting camp was made north of Redfield, South Dakota. Vast herds of buffalo were met with, many as fat as stall-fed beeves, and a large and welcome addition to the food supply was secured. Throughout the excursion, morning and evening, those Christian Santee, standing in the snow, sang their hymns and listened to prayer and reading of the Scriptures. The Santee have never forgotten this service of their "Saint John." Reader, join your tribute with theirs to heroic John Poage Williamson, "Brother of the Sioux."[25]

The story of the removal of the Santee from the impossible Crow Creek reservation after three years of distress to a more suitable one near the mouth of the Niobrara cannot here be told. The adoption of white man's clothing and dwellings, the abandonment of the chase for agriculture, and the multiplication of schools and churches have resulted in the transformation of the savage tribes into civilized, law-abiding, self-supporting Christian communities. Especially notable is the progress made by the sixty families who in 1869 and 1870 broke away from the agency, gave up all government aid, and took their way on foot, carrying their goods and papooses on their backs, to the valley of the Big Sioux south of Flandreau, South Dakota, where they took up homesteads. In 1878 Williamson wrote of them, "The Flandreau Indians are citizens and without doubt are the most advanced in civilization of any of the Sioux nation." It was his judgment that independence outside of the reservation nest was what the Indian most needed.[26]

[25] *Missionary Herald*, 60: 102, 203, 261 (April, July, September, 1864); Barton, *John P. Williamson*, 78-86; Manypenny, *Our Indian Wards*, 136-138. A letter from Thomas S. Williamson, H. D. Cunningham, John P. Williamson, and Edward R. Pond to the secretary of the interior, September 8, 1864, gives a connected account of the fortunes of the exiled Santee to that date. See Indian Office, *Reports*, 1864, pp. 420-422. "Santee" is a shortened form of "Isanati," a name given by the Sioux of the Missouri to those of the Mississippi. The explanations in Stephen R. Riggs, *Grammar and Dictionary of the Dakota Language*, 92 (Washington, 1852), and in Warren Upham, *Minnesota Geographic Names*, 249 (*Minnesota Historical Collections*, vol. 17 — St. Paul, 1920), are doubtful. For the circumstances attending the removal and the reluctant departure of the Winnebago, see Thomas Hughes to the author, April 22, 1922, with the accompanying statement of Judge A. J. Edgerton, in the Folwell Papers; Hughes, *Blue Earth County*, 138; and the same author's "History of Steamboating on the Minnesota River," in *Minnesota Historical Collections*, 10: 151 (part 1). Some two thousand were taken away by steamboat between May 9 and 17. Concerning the expedition — known as the "Moscow Expedition" — which brought the provisions from Mankato to Crow Creek, see the Appendix, no. 14, *post*.

[26] Indian Office, *Reports*, 1866, pp. 35, 47; Riggs, *Forty Years with the Sioux*, 238-240; Barton, *John P. Williamson*, 106, 108, 138-143.

The exile of the Sioux of the Mississippi, as decreed, left the convicts in the Mankato prison in the hands of the military to undergo such punishment as might be meted out to them.  No formal commutation of their death sentences has been found.  On April 22, 1863, a steamboat quietly received them on board and, after dropping at Fort Snelling some fifty who had not been condemned, delivered them at Davenport, Iowa, near which place the government had some military barracks.  After a short time their chains were removed and, as none attempted to escape, wide liberty was allowed them.  Many were permitted to go to the town to sell the bows and arrows, mussel shell rings, and trinkets of their manufacture.  With the money received they bought books and writing materials as well as pipes and tobacco.  A few worked on farms in the neighborhood.  Most of them asked to be allowed to enlist in the volunteer army but the secretary of war decided that it would be inexpedient to grant the request.  For two years and more their devoted teacher and pastor, Dr. Williamson, clung to them.  Wisely discerning their needs, he divided them into classes according to their former villages and gave each a leader who presided at the daily morning and evening gatherings for singing and prayer.  It was something like a Methodist organization, according to Riggs.  With the addition of about a hundred military prisoners and with deaths amounting in three years to about a hundred and twenty, the number of those in the prison was variable.  In 1864, at the urgence of Williamson, some forty were pardoned and in April, 1866, the then remaining number of two hundred and forty-seven were pardoned by the president and turned over to a special agent, who on June 12 delivered them at the Niobrara agency in Nebraska to rejoin their families.[27]

[27] *Missionary Herald*, 60:13,137 (January, 1864); Riggs, *Forty Years with the Sioux*, 193-196; Barton, *John P. Williamson*, 104; Indian Office, *Reports*, 1866, p. 46 (reprinted in 39 Congress, 2 session, *House Executive Documents*, vol. 2 — serial 1284); Riggs, *Tah-koo Wah-kan*, 369-374, 418. The Minnesota Historical Society has a manuscript copy of the special order of the war department for the release of Big Eagle.

The shipment of thirteen hundred lower Sioux to Crow Creek in the early summer of 1863 left some two hundred out of the fifteen hundred counted by the census of December, 1862, at Fort Snelling unaccounted for. About that number who had been steadfastly friendly to the whites had been allowed to depart for their old homes on the reservations. No formal authorization for their departure has been found. The act of March 3, 1863, which provided for the exile of the Sioux tribes, authorized the secretary of the interior to locate meritorious individual Indians on tracts of eighty acres on their old reservations, selecting those on which improvements had been made.[28] This benevolence was utterly futile. The settlers swarming in in advance of survey and sale and after would not tolerate Indian neighbors. As outcasts these Indians wandered about. A small group settled at Mendota on land belonging to Sibley. A larger number pitched their tents near Faribault on property of Alexander Faribault, in whose woods they hunted and dug ginseng. He supplied them with food and gave them work when he could and credit when he had no work. In the course of three years he had laid out nearly four thousand dollars. In a special report dated April 20, 1866, the commissioner of Indian affairs stated that his effort of the previous year to locate Mendota Indians on eighty-acre farms had failed because of "feeling among whites." He therefore approved a recommendation of the missionary, Hinman, indorsed by Bishop Whipple, that these homeless Indians be moved to the Santee reservation on the Missouri, with the exception of some who would not, as suggested by Sibley, be welcomed there. In his annual report for 1866 the commissioner stated that Alexander Faribault had been appointed to collect the scattered remnants of these Indians and take them to the Santee agency. No record of any such removal has been found and it may be assumed that none took place. For many years the groups at Men-

---

[28] *Statutes at Large*, 12:819.

dota and Faribault lived in peace, though gradually dying off. A larger body, of which the Faribault Indians formed the nucleus, collected at Morton, Minnesota, across the Minnesota from the Redwood agency; and a number of survivors — peaceable Christian Indians engaged in small farming and other industries — still dwell there.[29]

Before dismissing these meritorious Indians from our view mention must be made of an effort to reward a few of their number for exceptional proofs of loyalty. By an act passed on February 9, 1865, Congress made an appropriation of $7,500, one-third of which was specifically awarded to John Other Day; the remainder was left for distribution to individuals to be selected. The commissioner of Indian affairs imposed upon Bishop Whipple the duty of making the selection. In consultation with Sibley, Williamson, Riggs, and others, he made up a list of thirty-six persons, which the special agent of the Indian office accepted without change. In his report Bishop Whipple declared the amount a "miserable . . . pittance" and expressed the opinion that John Other Day, who had made his escape with his white wife along with the missionaries from Yellow Medicine, was far less deserving than other men who had stayed with their people, sheltered the white captives, and saved their lives. The appropriation had been reduced from $10,000, as at first proposed, to $7,500, probably because the number of beneficiaries was supposed not to exceed fifteen, as Representative Windom informed the House. The original bill did not contain the assignment of $2,500 to John Other Day, which was made by a Senate amendment. A letter from ex-Agent Galbraith gratefully attributing the rescue of his wife and children to that Indian, read to the Senate, seems to have had its effect.[30]

[29] Indian Office, *Reports*, 1866, pp. 47, 225-227; Tanner, *Diocese of Minnesota*, 401.

[30] *Statutes at Large*, 13:427; Indian Office, *Reports*, 1866, pp. 235-239; *Congressional Globe*, 38 Congress, 1 session, 2014, 2222, 3516.

# X.  INDIAN WARS OF 1863–65

A T THE CLOSE of the Indian war of 1862, about 1,500 of the 2,312 (627 adult males) lower Sioux who were numbered on the pay rolls of 1861 were in the prisons at Mankato and Fort Snelling.  The remainder, about 800 persons, at first scattered over the prairies between the Red River and the Missouri, concentrated for the winter on the Missouri River near Fort Rice.[1]  The upper Sioux, who in 1861 numbered 4,026 (909 adult males), lingered in or near their villages on Lake Traverse for a little time after the battle of Wood Lake.[2]  General Sibley deemed it wise to give them an opportunity to surrender and perhaps expected them to do so.  On the day after the battle he sent a letter to Standing Buffalo, head chief of the Sisseton, promising safety to him and to those of his people who wished to be friends of the Great Father.  In a later letter he advised them to remain in their own villages and await his coming for a council.  But the chief and his people were in no mood to trust themselves to the white chief with an army full of zeal to kill Indians.  The many individual warriors who had tasted blood in the outbreak or had carried away loot could not believe that their behavior would be condoned.  The upper Sioux, therefore, did not wait for Sibley to come with his soldiers but departed for the north and at length made a winter camp about Devil's Lake.  It was now believed that the renegade Sioux of both divisions, reënforced by a horde of Yankton and Yanktonai, would descend upon the Minnesota settlements in the coming season.  General

[1] *Sisseton and Wahpeton Claim Case Record, Defendants' Brief and Argument*, 12; record of an interview of the author with Dr. Charles A. Eastman, May 24, 1919, in the Folwell Papers; *Official Records*, series 1, vol. 22, part 2, p. 123. See the *Saint Paul Press*, September 20, 1863, for the story of a white boy, John Schurch, who was captured by the Sioux and spent the winter on the Missouri with them.

[2] *Sisseton and Wahpeton Claim Case Record, Evidence for Claimant*, 94; *Defendants' Brief and Argument*, 10. See the map on page 226, *ante*.

Sibley in October, 1862, estimated that twenty-two hundred warriors would take the warpath. General Pope, believing that another great Indian war was imminent, in the following February stated that concurring reports indicated that Little Crow had united several bands of the upper Sioux and would bring as many as seven thousand warriors into the field, a "number . . . perhaps overestimated."[3]

Still commanding the Department of the Northwest with headquarters at Milwaukee, General Pope early laid plans for a punitive expedition against the Sioux, which were approved by the war department. The scheme provided for two advancing columns: one, largely of infantry, to move from the neighborhood of Fort Ridgely northward to Devil's Lake; the other, mostly of cavalry, to ascend the Missouri Valley from Fort Randall, to cut off a retreat beyond that river, and at length to diverge northeastward toward Devil's Lake. The converging columns, it was expected, would destroy or capture the whole Indian fighting force. That the possibility of a pursuit across the Canadian border was entertained is proved by a dispatch from Halleck to Pope stating that the president "directs that under no circumstances will our troops cross the boundary line into British territory without his authority." To Brigadier General Sibley was intrusted the organization and the command of the infantry column, with authority to use all the troops in his district, except enough to hold the line of posts and patrols already established in the frontier counties.[4]

Early in June, 1863, the district commander concentrated at Camp Pope, in the angle formed by the Redwood and Minnesota rivers, 2,200 infantry, 800 cavalry, 150 artillery, 70 scouts, and 100 pioneers — in round numbers, 3,300 men. A train of 225 wagons, each drawn by six mules,

[3] *Minnesota in the Civil and Indian Wars*, 2: 250, 262, 280; *Sisseton and Wahpeton Claim Case Record, Evidence for Claimant*, 32, 81, 93, 141; *Official Records*, series 1, vol. 22, part 2, p. 116. West, in his *Sibley*, 303, estimates the number of warriors at nearly four thousand.

[4] *Official Records*, series 1, vol. 22, part 2, pp. 123, 186, 198, 211, 289, 304, 381, 385, 403-406. In a letter to Sibley, February 25, 1863, Pope suggested that the original plan of having a third column move north from the Big Sioux be eliminated. See also West, *Sibley*, 319, n.

carried subsistence for ninety days.  About a hundred others
followed for the transportation of ammunition, bridge
material, camp equipage, and quartermaster and medical
supplies.  A herd of many hundred cattle was driven along
to furnish beef on the hoof.[5]  In reply to Sibley's early
request for a larger body of troops, Pope had reminded him
that two thousand men had always been considered a
large force for Indian operations and begged him to say no
more about it.  Political enemies and some critical friends
had prophesied that the movement would be a failure.  Such
a lumbering outfit led by a torpid commander would never
catch or kill a single Indian.  The savages would steal his
horses, stampede his mules, and pick off his men from
ambush.  All these were things to be guarded against
but none of them came to pass.[6]

The column, five miles in length, left Camp Pope near
present-day Redwood Falls on June 16 and in the course
of ten days reached the point between Lakes Big Stone and
Traverse where the village of Brown's Valley now lies.
There a stop of three or four days was made to repair wagons
built of green lumber and to cooper many shaky barrels.
Already 17,500 rations of hard bread had been lost.  A four
or five days' march over prairies as dry as in November,
under a sky clouded by swarms of grasshoppers (locusts),

[5] The round numbers given are from the *Saint Paul Press* of June 20, 1863.  West, in
his *Sibley*, 304, seems to assume that the infantry regiments were full, which was probably
not the fact.  West's statements of fact may generally be relied upon, however much the
reader may feel obliged to discount his excess of eulogy.  In a note West cites Sibley's
diary of the campaign.  The writer has had this diary in hand but unfortunately it has
since been lost or mislaid, so that citations cannot be revised.  The troops selected for the
expedition were the following: the Third Battery of Light Artillery, under Captain John
Jones, artillerist at Fort Ridgely; one hundred pioneers from the Ninth Minnesota Infantry,
under Captain Jonathan Chase; seventy Indian and half-breed scouts, under Majors
Joseph R. Brown, George A. McLeod, and William J. Dooley; nine companies of the Minnesota Mounted Rangers, under Colonel Samuel McPhail; the Sixth Minnesota Infantry,
under Colonel William Crooks; nine companies of the Seventh Minnesota Infantry, under
Lieutenant Colonel William R. Marshall; and eight companies of the Tenth Minnesota
Infantry, under Colonel James H. Baker.

[6] *Official Records*, series 1, vol. 22, part 2, pp. 119, 380, 381; *Saint Paul Press*, July 7, 10,
1863; *Central Republican* (Faribault), June 10, 17, July 8, 15, 1863.  As late as July 18
General Pope understood that Sibley had taken but 2,800 men.  Halleck wrote to Pope that
Senator Wilkinson and others of high standing had reported in Washington that Sibley's
command was much too large and he suggested that part of it be recalled.

brought the command to the Big Bend of the Sheyenne
River.   Here it made a halt of a week, from the fourth to the
eleventh of July, awaiting the return of a detachment sent
to Fort Abercrombie for supplies.   The march was resumed in a northwesterly direction and a point some
forty miles to the southeast of Devil's Lake was reached
on July 18.   On the day previous two Red River buffalo
hunters joined the column and gave to Sibley the information
that a large body of Sioux — "600 lodges" — had lately

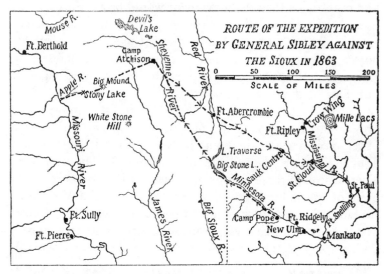

ROUTE OF THE EXPEDITION
BY GENERAL SIBLEY AGAINST
THE SIOUX IN 1863
SCALE OF MILES

left Devil's Lake and were now encamped about seventy-
five miles distant toward the Missouri.   The commander
immediately decided to follow those Indians and, should
they prove to be hostile, to attack them.   He therefore
devoted one day, July 19, to rest and preparation.   An
intrenched camp called "Camp Atchison" was formed to
be occupied by two companies from each of the three infantry
regiments, a company of cavalry, a section of artillery, all
disabled men and animals, and superfluous transportation.
    Early on the morning of July 20 the reorganized expedi-
tion of 1,400 infantry, 500 cavalry, three sections of artillery,

and all the pioneers and scouts, with rations for 2,300 men for twenty-five days, in wagons with loads reduced to 1,500 pounds, set out in a southwesterly direction. At the close of the day's march a visit was received from two hundred Red River buffalo hunters whose camp of from five hundred to six hundred carts was some three miles westward. They were all mounted and rode "like arabs of the desert." Prominent among them were two former members of the Minnesota legislature, Charles Grant and John B. Wilkie, the latter captain of the hunt. Father André, their priest, was spokesman and in fluent French he assured Sibley that as American citizens who had suffered at the hands of the Sioux they would not be sorry to have those Indians punished. The information concerning the whereabouts of the Indians was confirmed.[7]

On July 24 at about one o'clock scouts reported to the general, who had ridden ahead of the column to select a camping place, that many Indians could be seen on the prairie two or three miles away and that a large camp was not far distant to the southward. The column having already marched fifteen miles, the general decided to halt and encamp. On the eastern shore of a small salt or alkali lake he corralled his transportation and disposed his troops about it. The Sixth Regiment held the northern front, the Tenth and Seventh the eastern, and the cavalry the southern. The usual sod intrenchments were begun. This deliberation was probably used to give opportunity for Standing Buffalo and any other chiefs disposed to be friendly to appear in person or by delegate. Meantime Indians in large numbers showed themselves on a range of hills a mile or more to the east of the camp. A numerous group occupied the summit and western slope of a surmounting peak which had or took the name "Big Mound." From this height Indians rode toward the camp and were met by some of Sibley's scouts

[7] West, *Sibley*, 304-307, 325; *Minnesota in the Civil and Indian Wars*, 1:353; Jared W. Daniels, "General Sibley's Campaign, 1863," pp. 1-4, Daniels Papers; William R. Marshall's manuscript journal of the expedition, 10-13, Marshall Papers.

on a hillock about a fourth of a mile from the camp. The general's hope or expectation of a show of friendship was disappointed. A son of Little Paul came in to see his father but brought no message from Standing Buffalo and he said that the young men would certainly fight. Gabriel Renville, one of the trustiest scouts, fell in with his father-in-law, Scarlet Plume, a principal Sisseton chief, and got from him a warning of a plot to entice Sibley and his chief officers into a council and there to assassinate them.

No other dispositions were made for battle but about three o'clock a fight was suddenly precipitated. Dr. Josiah S. Weiser, surgeon of the cavalry regiment, who had some acquaintance among the Indians, rode out and joined the group on the hillock. While he was talking with one of them, a young Indian, either a fiend or an idiot, came up behind him and shot him through the heart. The group instantly dispersed and the report of the gun was understood to be the signal for battle. General Sibley ordered a company of the Seventh Regiment armed with Colt six-shooters to deploy on the left front of the camp and a squadron of cavalry with two companies of the Seventh on the right front. He led in person a half section of artillery out to an elevation halfway to the Big Mound. A few spherical case shot cleared its summit of Indians. Captain Eugene M. Wilson's troop of rangers, dismounted, was at once sent forward to occupy it. Lieutenant Colonel Marshall got leave to advance five of his companies of the Seventh Regiment. Halfway to the Big Mound he deployed them as skirmishers, pushed the line over the crest of the range south of the Big Mound, wheeled it to the right, and drove the Indians off the eastern slopes a long distance southward. The squadron of cavalry first sent out now dismounted and, with the two companies of the Seventh Infantry, cleared the western slopes of the range. Near the southern end of the range Marshall recrossed the crest, followed by a part of the cavalry, which had been unable to charge on account of the numerous ravines and intervening ridges running down from the crests of the hills. The rangers now passed to the front and Captain Horace Austin led his troop in a charge against a belated group of Indians. A bolt of lightning from a passing thundercloud, from which only a few drops of rain fell, killed one of the men and his horse. It was late in the afternoon when Sibley from a commanding elevation saw the whole body of warriors, from a thousand to fifteen hundred in number, as he estimated, in full retreat westward. The unequal battle was over. Marshall states in his narrative that "probably not one half [*of the thousand and more Indians*] had fire arms" and that they were careful of their ammunition. Still they made some use of what they had, for in his report Marshall states that one of his soldiers had his hat damaged, another had the stock of his gun hit, while balls occasionally kicked up the dust and, more rarely, whistled past.

While the battle was thus raging the Indian women in their camp south of the Big Mound range loaded up what stuff they could in their wagons, on travois, and on backs of ponies and dogs and took their flight with their children toward the Missouri. The warriors gallantly covered the rear as best they could. Sibley ordered the rangers, all somewhat tardily rallied and remounted, to pursue the fugitives until nightfall and sent the Seventh Regiment, one company of the Tenth, and a piece of artillery in support. The ardent rangers pressed on until nearly dark, repeatedly gaining contact with the retreating Sioux and laying many of them low, as they believed, with their "deadly carbines." They reached a point fifteen miles distant from the first point of attack. The infantry support was left five miles behind, although it was put on the double-quick. At about nine o'clock Marshall halted, posted his guards, and, after they had eaten of the dried meat abandoned by the Indians, put his men into bivouac on beds of buffalo robes which the Indians had thrown away. The tired soldiers had had but an hour's repose when Colonel McPhail came back with his cavalry, which had just been reënforced by three of his troops. Sibley's order to bivouac on the prairie, so understood by Marshall, was misunderstood by the cavalry officer. It was daybreak of the following morning when the jaded men and horses of the cavalry and the infantry support straggled back to the brigade camp. The Sixth and Tenth regiments had but a small part in the battle of Big Mound. The former command was promptly deployed by its colonel to cover the left of the advancing troops, but it met with no resistance and was ordered back to camp. The Tenth also was not engaged, but one company participated with the Seventh in the pursuit and four other companies which started in pursuit were recalled.[8]

The day following the battle was lost while the men and animals engaged in the pursuit were taking a needed rest in a new camp situated near good water and grass. On the morning of the twenty-sixth the march was resumed at an early hour. For miles the line of advance southwestwardly was strewn with immense quantities of buffalo robes, dried meat, tallow, kettles, and all the gear of an Indian hunting camp abandoned in precipitate flight. After a march of fourteen miles, as the head of the column approached a site selected for encampment near a lake on the shore of which lay the head of a dead buffalo, Indians

[8] The account in the text was digested from the following sources: Sibley Diary; West, *Sibley*, 308-310; reports of Sibley, McPhail, Crooks, Marshall, and Baker, in *Official Records*, series 1, vol. 22, part 1, pp. 352-354, 359, 361, 364-370, 907-909; Daniels, "Sibley's Campaign"; Marshall Journal; *Minnesota in the Civil and Indian Wars*, 1:316,354,457, 521,670; narrative of Marshall and letters of Riggs, July 30, 31, August 5, 6, in the *Saint Paul Press*, August 15, 1863; A. L. Van Osdel, "The Sibley Expedition," in the *Monthly South Dakotan*, 2:97-100 (October, 1899); Robinson, *Sioux Indians*, 318-322; testimony of Little Fish, Iron Hoop, Daniel Paul, and Antoine J. Campbell, in *Sisseton and Wahpeton Claim Case Record, Evidence for Claimant*, 194, 210, 236, 263; critical editorials and letters, in the *Central Republican* (Faribault), September 23, 1863; and an interview with Henry Belland, January 31, 1907, recorded in the author's notebooks, 4:27. Marshall's reports, his narrative, and his journal are in close resemblance, with occasional discrepancies. Daniels writes that Surgeon Weiser had said to him: "Let us go and shake hands with our friends; I know them." Daniels doubted that all the Indians were friendly and did not go. He thought the surgeon's mind was not in a normal state at the time. In *Harper's Weekly*, 7:580 (September 12, 1863), there are pictures of Sibley crossing the James River and of his pursuit of the Indians after Big Mound from sketches by George H. Elsbury of the Seventh Minnesota. Descriptions are given on page 587.

appeared in front as if threatening an attack. The men of the Sixth Infantry, who had the advance, were at once deployed as skirmishers and, aided by a section of battery and a troop of cavalry, soon drove the savages a distance of one and a half miles. Four companies of the Seventh were sent forward to strengthen the right of the Sixth but returned to camp without having been annoyed. A squadron of cavalry gallantly repulsed "the audacious devils, that were very nearly successful in gobbling up the teams and loose animals." The battle of Dead Buffalo Lake was over and the troops, with the exception of the one cavalryman who had been mortally wounded, passed a quiet night in camp.[9]

On the twenty-eighth of July took place the "greatest conflict" of the series in point of number of Indians participating — the battle of Stony Lake. As the brigade was taking the road at five o'clock in the morning Indians appeared in great numbers on front and flanks, forming an enveloping curve of two-thirds of a circle. If their plan had been to make a concentrated rush on the white man's camp "ere the morning star," they arrived too late. The artillery and musketry of the skirmish lines, promptly thrown out, kept them at a safe distance. Sibley coolly resolved to waste no time in formally disposing his troops for battle, as doubtless the Indians hoped he would do. Instead of that, after a brief delay, he put them on the march in what had become the usual order: a regiment of infantry — on this occasion the Tenth — in front with two others on the flanks, and the wagon train between, with the cavalry and artillery available for emergencies. The enemy soon disappeared and the column made an unmolested march of eighteen miles to encamp on Apple River, a small tributary of the Missouri emptying some ten miles south of Bismarck. An undisturbed march of fifteen miles

[9] Reports of Sibley, Crooks, and Marshall, in *Official Records*, series 1, vol. 22, part 1, pp. 354, 362, 366; West, *Sibley*, 310; Marshall Journal, 20-23; Van Osdel, in the *Monthly South Dakotan*, 2: 115-119 (November, 1899).

on the following morning brought the brigade to the dense timber and thickets along the Missouri River. After the woods had been shelled by artillery the Sixth Infantry made its way through the tangle of prickly ash and thorn to the river bank and, looking across, saw the hills swarming with the savages, inviting the white soldiers by derisive gestures to come over.[10]

The reader has probably already divined the nature of the battles just described. The Indians whom Sibley's column had taken by surprise were no war party with out-lying scouts and flankers, but a body of hunters — probably a combined body — engaged in getting their meat for the coming winter in a region in which buffalo abounded because its numerous lakes and springs kept the buffalo grass fresh. Whether the parley which was begun at the Big Mound on July 24 might have been followed by a grand council and a capitulation need not be considered. The Indians knew well that the whites would take immediate revenge for the atrocious murder of Dr. Weiser at the Big Mound. The tactics instantly adopted by them were both wise and heroic. The mounted warriors, displayed in a long line, by ferocious demonstrations delayed the advance of the white troops while the old men and the women and children broke their camp in the rear and fled toward the Missouri. Doubtless the savages would willingly have embraced any opportunity

---

[10] West, *Sibley*, 311-314; Loren W. Collins, "The Expedition against the Sioux Indians in 1863, under General Henry H. Sibley," in *Glimpses of the Nation's Struggle*, second series, 194; reports of Sibley, Crooks, and Baker, in *Official Records*, series 1, vol. 22, part 1, pp. 355, 363, 370. Sibley in his report expresses the opinion that no cool and dispassionate observer could have placed the number of warriors present at the battle of Stony Lake at less than from 2,200 to 2,500 and that the number of souls in their enormous camp was nearly, if not quite, 10,000. In his dispatch to Pope of August 7, 1863, in West, *Sibley*, 316, he states that he had "three desperate engagements" with 2,300 Sioux warriors. The numbers and names of the various tribes represented in the battles must remain a matter of conjecture in the absence of an actual enumeration. In a letter to Pope of September 16, in *Official Records*, series 1, vol. 22, p. 912, Sibley made a careful estimate of the combined Indian tribes defeated by his column as follows: Minnesota River bands, remnants, 250 warriors; Sisseton Sioux, 450 warriors; east Yanktonai, 1,200 warriors; and other bands, including Teton Sioux, 400 warriors — making an aggregate of 2,300. Dr. J. W. Daniels' eyesight at the time or his memory later could not have been good, as he speaks of "may be three hundred" Indians at Stony Lake. See his "Sibley's Campaign," 7. Collins mentions the battle of Stony Lake as a "little episode" which "detained us some two hours."

for stampeding animals, cutting off exposed detachments, and breaking through weak points in their enemy's line. But they got no beef, nor plunder, nor scalps and were content to be on the safe side of the Missouri, with a loss of lives small in comparison with the numbers of their people rescued from death and capture. There was grievous loss of property. They abandoned more than a hundred wagons and carts and their loads at the crossing. Because of the weak resistance of the Indians, with inferior arms and no artillery, the casualties of the whites were few.[11] Sibley's

[11] Reports of Sibley, McPhail, and Crooks, in *Official Records*, series 1, vol. 22, part 1, pp. 357, 360, 363. On page 357 of his report and in his dispatch to Pope of August 7, in West, *Sibley*, 316, Sibley gives the Indian losses as at least 150. In his general order of congratulation, on page 317 of the latter work, he places the number at from 120 to 150, and adds that 44 bodies had been found. In a letter of September 2 to Meline, in *Official Records*, series 1, vol. 22, part 1, p. 910, Sibley gives the number of dead bodies found as 46 and reports an admission by Standing Buffalo that the Indians lost many lives at the crossing of the Missouri, but that not more than 13 were killed in the battles. West, in his *Sibley*, 316, says that nearly 150 Indians were killed or wounded; on page 309 he gives the number of killed and wounded in the battle of Big Mound as 80, "twenty-one being scalped in the last charge." On page 311 he mentions the killing of 9 Indians by one man. Sibley had recorded in his diary, which West used, that "nine were killed by *our* men, and I am ashamed to say all were scalped. . . . God's image should not be thus mutilated or disfigured." McPhail in his report, in *Official Records*, series 1, vol. 22, part 1, p. 360, gives the number of Indians known to have been killed at Big Mound by the mounted rangers as 31, "all found with the peculiar mark of cavalry upon them." Dr. J. W. Daniels, who accompanied the cavalry in its pursuit of the Indians after the battle of Big Mound, saw but 4 dead Indians — a lame man whom he knew, an old woman, and two old men, one of whom had the United States flag wrapped around him. In another paragraph he says that he was informed that there were 21 found dead on the trail after the battle. See his "Sibley's Campaign," 7. Marshall, in his narrative in the *Saint Paul Press*, August 15, 1863, says that the cavalry colonel told his men that it was bad to take scalps, but that he would not believe that any of them had killed an Indian unless he showed a full-sized scalp.

But one enlisted man of Sibley's army was killed in all these battles and he was killed by lightning. Another was mortally wounded. Two or three were slightly wounded. The only officer killed in battle was Dr. Weiser, but there were three other burials. Lieutenant Frederick J. Holt Beaver, an English gentleman thirty-three years of age who was traveling for his health and for information, was attached by General Sibley to his staff as an aid. He seems to have been zealous and efficient in duty and to have won general respect. When the Sixth Regiment was pushing its way on July 29 through the forest and tangle to the brink of the Missouri, Lieutenant Beaver undertook to carry a message to its commander, Colonel Crooks. He delivered the message but did not return with the answer given him. At night there was much concern about his absence from quarters. On the day following Colonel Crooks was sent with a strong detachment to scour the woods, dislodge any savages, and destroy their abandoned wagons. The body of Lieutenant Beaver was found pierced by three arrows and a bullet. Near it lay the body of a soldier of the Sixth Regiment. Of Beaver, Dr. J. W. Daniels, his messmate, wrote: "He was a genial, well educated English gentleman, who won the love and respect of all those having the pleasure of his acquaintance. To meet and not have him with us was a bereavement that filled our hearts with sorrow." See his "Sibley's Campaign," 9. In *Harper's Weekly*, 7:577 (September 12, 1863), there is a picture of the murder of Lieutenant Beaver. See also Riggs's letters and Marshall's narrative in the *Saint Paul Press*, August 15, 1863. The third burial was that of

energy, poise, and judgment, the readiness of his regimental commanders to take initiative, and the gallant behavior of officers and men generally are worthy of commendation. They were facing an enemy believed greatly to outnumber them, and that enemy was fighting for all that was held dear.

Of General Alfred Sully's column moving up the Missouri Valley, which was to meet him near Devil's Lake, Sibley had no tidings. Without Sully's support, with but a few days' subsistence in his wagons, and with his animals much exhausted, he made no attempt to cross the Missouri and fight more battles. Indeed, he was gratified with an already "complete success," which would forever prevent raids on the frontier of Minnesota. Still, he expressed his regret that the "remorseless savages" had not been extirpated root and branch. The brigadier general commanding therefore gave his men but two days' rest and issued a general order for a return march of the expedition. In this order he warmly complimented all the units of the command and commended his officers and soldiers for having destroyed great numbers of the savages and for having so dispersed and despoiled the survivors that they could scarcely escape starvation in the coming winter. He asked his men to unite in returning thanks to a merciful God for his manifest intervention.[12]

The column set out on August 1 and reached Camp Atchison on the tenth. On the eighth Lieutenant Colonel

Lieutenant Ambrose Freeman of the Mounted Rangers. This officer had left the column at an early hour on July 24 to hunt for game. At a distance of probably five miles from camp he was waylaid and shot by a party of Indians. McPhail in his report gives the impression that Lieutenant Freeman was killed in the battle of Big Mound. Dr. J. W. Daniels writes that the head men of the Indians at Big Mound had no intention of fighting, but that when the news of the killing of Lieutenant Freeman was brought in the young men became excited and wanted to try their hands. A companion of the murdered officer, George A. Brackett of the quartermaster's corps, escaped and made his way on foot back to Camp Atchison. For his account see the *Saint Paul Press*, August 13, 1863, the *Minneapolis Tribune*, May 29, 1921, and his little volume entitled *A Winter Evening's Tale* (New York, 1880). Brackett, who died in 1921, furnished the writer with a sketch of his route. See the *Minneapolis Journal*, April 3, 1914, for an article by A. P. Connolly, a companion of Freeman and Brackett. The murderous attack on the hunting party indicates that some of the Indians at least were hostile. Daniels says that Brackett, "by his social nature, and untiring energy, had won the good wishes of all." "Sibley's Campaign," 10.

[12] West, *Sibley*, 315, 317.

Marshall was ordered to St. Paul as bearer of dispatches. He took with him the headquarters and regimental reports which have been cited. A violent Republican enemy declared that the real errand of that experienced journalist was to advertise the results of the "Great Imposition" in a way calculated to disarm criticism. Marshall reached St. Paul on August 14 and on the following morning in the *Saint Paul Press* there appeared his story of the expedition "hastily prepared." The narrative of five columns follows closely the line of his formal reports, with additions here and there of some piquant personal details. Along with the reports mentioned went also a dispatch to be telegraphed to General Pope announcing "three desperate engagements" with from 2,200 to 2,500 Sioux warriors.[13]

On the homeward march large detachments were made from the main column. From Camp Atchison Colonel McPhail was sent with four troops of his cavalry regiment and a section of mountain howitzers to search the region from the James River to Fort Ridgely and capture or destroy a small but mischievous band of Yanktonai. At Fort Abercrombie a battalion of three troops of cavalry was detached to proceed to Fort Ripley by way of Otter Tail Lake to produce a moral effect upon the Pillagers and other Chippewa bands. At Sauk Centre the Tenth Infantry, accompanied by the cavalry troops which had been sent through the Chippewa country, was detached to follow the chain of frontier posts to Fort Ridgely. The main column, reduced to the Sixth and Seventh infantry regiments and two gun sections, reached Fort Snelling on September 13. The distance covered by it from Camp Pope to the Missouri and back to Fort Snelling was 1,039½ miles. On ten of the thirteen Sundays the command remained in camp and religious services were conducted by the regimental chaplains or by the Reverend Stephen R. Riggs, chief interpreter. Sibley's diary shows that he

---

[13] West, *Sibley*, 326; *Central Republican* (Faribault), September 9, 23, 1863.

was strenuously conscientious about the observance of the
Sabbath. The diary also shows how deeply he felt the loss
of a young son and a daughter by death, the tidings of
which reached him on the march.[14]

The results of the campaign gave Pope the greatest
satisfaction. The cheerfulness, endurance, and gallantry
with which the troops had surmounted hardships and
privations reflected, he wrote to Sibley, "the highest credit
upon them and upon you." As a reward for the whole
performance of duty he promised that they should be soon
transported to the South, where their soldierly qualities
and the military experience acquired in the campaign
against the Indians would secure for them a national reputation.[15]

The failure of Sully to keep his appointment with Sibley,
though disappointing, became the occasion for an Indian
victory all his own. The complicated causes of his detention
are not here important, but they prevented his departure
from his advanced base above Fort Pierre until August 21.
At the end of a week he reached the neighborhood of Sibley's
last camp on the Missouri. He learned from a "good
Indian" that the Indians Sibley had driven across the
Missouri had soon recrossed and that the larger portion
had gone to their old hunting grounds on the headwaters
of the James River. A rapid march of three days in a
southeastern direction brought him to a point in Dickey
County, North Dakota. At about three o'clock in the
afternoon of September 3 one of his battalions, on advanced

[14] *Official Records*, series 1, vol. 22, part 1, pp. 907-911; West, *Sibley*, 322-326; Sibley
Diary. See *Official Records*, atlas, vol. 1, plate 33, for a map by Private John H. Wagner
of the Sixth Minnesota showing the route of the Sibley expedition. On the same plate are
sketches by Joseph McCloud of the battle fields of Big Mound and Dead Buffalo Lake.

[15] *Official Records*, series 1, vol. 22, part 2, p. 497. On page 495 in a letter to Pope,
August 24, 1863, is an "appreciation" of Sibley by Colonel Stephen Miller, whom Sibley had
left in command of his district and of the troops retained for the defense of the Minnesota
frontier. Miller expressed his joy that his commander was so highly appreciated at headquarters and added: "Poor General Sibley! I know him well. He is gallant and glorious
in conflict, but in executive and administrative capacity he is but the wreck of his former
self." General Sibley survived his generous subordinate many years to fill a variety of
administrative positions with great acceptance. For hostile partisan criticism of the campaign see the *State Atlas* (Minneapolis), July 22, August 19, September 9, 16, 23, 30, 1863.

scouting duty, came suddenly upon a large camp of unsuspecting Indians and formed a line of battle within
fifty rods of it. A messenger sent back to Sully reached him
in camp ten miles in the rear at four o'clock. He instantly
remounted his men and led them on the gallop to the front.
Meantime the battalion commander occupied himself with
reconnaissances to right and left and with a palaver with
chiefs who had come in under a flag of truce. They were willing to give up some chiefs, but they refused to make the unconditional surrender demanded, preferring to repeat the
tactics successfully used at Big Mound. When Sully
arrived at five o'clock with his main force, he found the
Indians leaving and carrying off everything they could.
After sending his Nebraska regiment to the right and an
Iowa battalion to the left, the general himself with the
battery and three companies charged through the center
of the encampment. As the warriors rallied from point to
point to cover the flight of their families, they made, Sully
reported, "a very desperate resistance" and the battle
became quite a "respectable engagement." Had not darkness, much to his regret, put an end to it, he believed that he
would have annihilated the enemy. Such was the "battle
of White Stone Hill."

After two days spent in scouring the country, in dispersing
small bodies of Indians, and in destroying immense quantities of abandoned provisions, baggage, and other
"plunder," the expedition returned to its base on the
Missouri. That the battle of White Stone Hill was indeed
a serious affair is shown by the losses. Sully reported that
the ascertained loss of his own force was twenty killed
and thirty-eight wounded and that the estimated loss of
Indians was more than one hundred and fifty killed and
wounded. Thirty-two men and one hundred and twenty-
four women and children were taken prisoners. This
victory was entirely satisfactory to Pope and his approval
took the edge off his frank criticism of Sully's failure to

coöperate with Sibley in a campaign intended to crush the power of the Sioux forever.[16]

The story of Sully's campaign of 1863 would not be complete without the addition of a version written in that year by one in a situation favorable for hearing the Indian side of it. It is in a letter written on November 13, 1863, to Joseph R. Brown by his son, Samuel J. Brown, then nineteen years of age and interpreter at the Santee agency at Crow Creek on the Missouri. "I hope you will not believe all that is said of 'Sullys' successfull expidition,' against the Sioux I don't think he ought to brag of it at all, because it was, what no decent man would have done, he pitched into their camp and just slaughtered them, worse a great deal than what the Indians did in 1862, he killed *very few* men and took *no* hostile ones prisoners, he *took* some but they were friendly Yanktons, and he let them go again. . . . it is lamentable to hear how those women and children were slaughtered it was a perfect massacre, and now he returns saying that we need fear no more, for he has 'wiped out all hostile Indians from Dakota,' if he had killed men instead of women & children, then it would have been a success, and the worse of it, they had no hostile intention whatever, the Nebraska 2nd pitched into them without orders, while the Iowa 6th were shaking hands with them."[17]

While Sibley was making his laborious march and counter-march across the plains of Dakota, the settlers on the Minnesota frontier, supposed to be thus protected from Indian raids, were in no happy frame of mind. Pope, in a letter of instruction written to Sibley while the expedition was being organized, advised him that he need not keep up the small posts established for the winter but that he should

[16] Reports of Sully and his regimental and battalion commanders, in *Official Records*, series 1, vol. 22, part 1, pp. 555-568; letters from Pope to Sully, in the same work, series 1, vol. 22, part 2, pp. 434, 496, 502, 608. The reports, with the exception of that of Major House, may also be found in Secretary of War, *Reports*, 1863, pp. 495-507 (reprinted in 38 Congress, 1 session, *House Executive Documents*, vol. 5 — serial 1184). Sully's report is accompanied by a revised list of casualties. Seventeen enlisted men were killed and two officers and thirty-four men were wounded.

[17] Brown Papers.

break them up as he passed and take the troops along with his column.  As if anticipating such a plan, Governor Ramsey several days earlier assured Sibley that there was great anxiety throughout the frontier settlements, and fear that the troops would be unable to protect them from "stealthy encroachments" in the coming spring.  A sudden, unexpected attack would, he declared, create a panic as widespread and as frenzied as that of the preceding summer and would probably drive the white population of the western counties back to the Mississippi towns.  Sibley replied that he intended to protect the settlers and appease their fears but that he did not believe the hostile Indians would descend upon the border as long as they feared attack in their prairie haunts.  This confidence was not fully justified.[18]

About the middle of April, 1863, a party of Indians made an attack on settlers in the valley of the Watonwan.  Three persons — one a soldier — were killed and others were wounded and left for dead.  Household goods and provisions were seized and cattle, sheep, and horses were stolen.  Lieutenant Colonel Marshall, with a detachment of the Seventh Regiment and the Mounted Rangers, pursued the miscreants to Lake Shetek but failed to overtake them.  In May a citizen was killed within two miles of New Ulm, where a company of the Mounted Rangers was stationed.[19]

On May 23 Ramsey advised Sibley that something must be done openly to quiet the alarm raised by these murders and suggested that with five thousand troops in the state it ought to be unnecessary to call out the state militia.  To this the general replied that it was impossible to station a guard at every farmhouse on the border and that citizens must arm themselves for defense against small parties of lurking savages.  He also repeated his opinion that such

[18] *Official Records*, series 1, vol. 22, part 2, p. 123; *Minnesota in the Civil and Indian Wars*, 2:292-294.

[19] *Minnesota in the Civil and Indian Wars*, 1:353; 2:296; *Saint Paul Press*, April 19, 21, 25, May 6, 1863; Hughes, *Blue Earth County*, 140.  See the map facing p. 170, *ante*.

raids would cease as soon as his expedition should depart. Ramsey had already dispatched Emil Munch, a general officer of the state militia, to visit eight of the more populous counties most exposed to attack, and to urge the people to organize and arm for the protection of the whole western border. That officer reported a plan for advancing the established chain of posts to the border of settlement and for patrolling more efficiently between them.[20]

Sibley was probably influenced not only by Ramsey's urgency but also by abundant demands through newspapers and correspondents to make more extensive arrangements for the local defense of the frontier than he had believed necessary. On June 4 he issued an order rearranging the garrisons and placing a belt of company districts behind them as recommended by the militia brigadier general and detailing some two thousand of his troops to hold the long line of defense. The detail consisted of the whole Eighth Regiment, nine companies of the Ninth, one company of the Tenth, and three companies of the Mounted Rangers. Three companies of the Eighth were stationed at Fort Abercrombie to protect the Red River trains of the Hudson's Bay Company. The larger part of the cavalry detachment occupied Fort Ridgely.[21]

If the settlers on the border were comforted by these ample provisions for their protection, their confidence in them was soon to be dissipated. While the regiments were collecting at Camp Pope and the details for home-guard duty were moving to their several posts, a citizen of Brown County was murdered almost within sight of Fort Ridgely. On the night of June 7 a party of Indians penetrated to the heart of Wright County a hundred miles from the Minnesota River and not more than fifty miles from St. Paul

---

[20] *Minnesota in the Civil and Indian Wars*, 2:296; report of the adjutant general, in *Executive Documents*, 1863, pp. 339-341.

[21] West, *Sibley*, 305, n.; *Minnesota in the Civil and Indian Wars*, 1:387, 417, 457, 520; *Saint Paul Press*, June 5, 1863; report of the adjutant general, in *Executive Documents*, 1863, p. 341.

and stole some horses. On the day following Captain John S. Cady of the Eighth Regiment, with a squad of soldiers and one or more civilians, pursued the thieves through Wright and Meeker counties past the scene of the Acton murders of August 17, 1862, overtook them on the verge of the Kandiyohi lakes, and opened fire upon them. A return shot killed Captain Cady almost instantly. There was naturally great excitement in the region over the murder of so highly respected a citizen. Many persons imagined that they had seen "Indian sign" and stray animals were believed to have been stolen by Indians. There was, however, ground for anxiety and fear of lurking savages. On June 29 Amos Dustin, a citizen of Wright County, was traveling with his family in an open wagon near the site of the village of Howard Lake, within forty-five miles of St. Paul. A party of Indian fiends fell upon them from an ambush, shot three of them to death with arrows, and mortally wounded a fourth. It was a piece of sheer, unmitigated assassination. The bodies of the dead lay in the wagon for two days awaiting discovery. On July 1, two days after the Dustin murders, James McGannon was murdered while traveling on a road near Fairhaven in Wright County.[22]

A notable event took place on July 3, 1863, when a citizen of McLeod County, Nathan Lamson, and a son, Chauncey, both armed, were hunting for deer some six miles north of Hutchinson. In the evening of July 3 they came suddenly upon two Indians in a thicket engaged in picking berries and approached them within a few rods. Taking careful aim, Lamson fired and wounded, but did not disable, one of them. Both Indians instantly fired at him and wounded him slightly in the shoulder. The younger Lamson, who probably had not been seen, fired and killed the wounded Indian. The survivor mounted

[22] Report of the adjutant general, in *Executive Documents*, 1863, pp. 342-345; *Saint Paul Press*, June 13, July 3; *State Atlas* (Minneapolis), June 17, 1863. For an account of the Dustin murders, see the Appendix, no. 15, *post*.

a pony and fled. Late in the night the father and son made their way to Hutchinson. The next morning a party of soldiers went out and found the body of the dead Indian neatly laid out with a pair of new moccasins and a citizen's coat on or near it. They took the scalp and left the body. In the afternoon some boys brought the corpse into town in a wagon. Many persons recognized it as that of an Indian well known in the place. Some persons noticed a resemblance to Little Crow, but the complexion seemed too light for his. The mortifying carcass was thrown into the offal pit of a slaughterhouse.[23] Positive identification was furnished by an unexpected revelation.

Some of the Red River half-breed hunters whom General Sibley came upon soon after leaving Camp Atchison told him that a small camp of Sioux had not left Devil's Lake with the hunting party he was chasing. He therefore sent back by courier an order to the officer left in command of that camp to send out a detachment to discover and capture those savages. The search, which lasted a week, resulted in the arrest of one Indian, a young man half-starved and nearly naked. On the return of the expedition from the Missouri to Camp Atchison General Sibley obtained from him the substance of the following statement, which had already been given to the post commander and forwarded to the Minnesota press: "I am the son of Little Crow; my name is Wo-wi-nap-a; I am 16 years old. . . . Father went to St. Joseph last spring. When we were coming back he said he could not fight the white men, but would go below and steal horses from them . . . and then he would go away off. Father . . . wanted me to go with him to

[23] Testimony of Nathan Lamson in the case of Wowinapa, in "Proceedings of Military Commission Held at Fort Abercrombie D. T., & Fort Snelling, Minn., for the Trial of Certain Dakota Prisoners," an official manuscript copy of which is in the possession of the Minnesota Historical Society; *Saint Paul Press*, July 10, 1863; *Saint Paul Pioneer*, July 14, 1863; *Hutchinson Leader*, June 6, 1863; Satterlee, quoting J. B. Lamson in *Minnesota Historical Collections*, 15:367-370; Pendergast, in *Minnesota Historical Collections*, 10: 88 (part 1). For accounts of the treatment of Little Crow's body, see a letter from Captain John W. Bond, August 16, 1863, in the *Saint Paul Pioneer*, August 20, 1863, and Dr. John Benjamin's story in the *Hutchinson Leader*, October 6, 1905.

carry his bundles. . . . There were sixteen men and one squaw in the party that went below with us. We had no horses. . . . Father and I were picking red berries near Scattered Lake. . . . It was near night. He was hit the first time in the side, just above the hip. . . . He was shot the second time. . . . The ball . . . hit him in the side, near the shoulders. This was the shot that killed him. He told me that he was killed, and asked me for water. . . . He died immediately after. . . . A short time before . . . an Indian named Hi-u-ka, who married the daughter of my father's second wife, came to him. He had . . . a gray colored coat that he had taken from a man that he had killed to the north of where father was killed. He gave the coat to father . . . as he had no coat with him. . . . The Indians that went down with us separated, eight of them, and the squaw went north, the other eight went farther down. I have not seen any of them since after father was killed. I took both guns and the ammunition, and started to go to Devil's Lake."[24]

[24] *Saint Paul Pioneer*, August 13, 1863. See also the *Saint Paul Press*, August 13, 1863; *Official Records*, series 1, vol. 22, part 1, p. 908, and "Proceedings of Military Commission Held at Fort Abercrombie and Fort Snelling." Wowinapa was tried on two charges: (1) participation in the massacre of 1862, and (2) an attempt at murder and horse-stealing in 1863. Lamson testified to the shooting of Little Crow. William L. Quinn, a witness, gave the substance of Wowinapa's statement to him and Joseph Demarais, another witness, reported what Wowinapa had said to him. David Faribault, Sr., said that he drove Little Crow to the second attack on Fort Ridgely under compulsion and that five hundred warriors crossed the Minnesota on a bridge. Antoine J. Campbell swore that he had been forced to accompany Little Crow on his expedition to the Big Woods in 1862 with 150 men. Wowinapa was convicted and sentenced to be hanged. Sibley approved the proceedings and findings. Pope took no action but forwarded the record through the general in chief to the president. When it reached the secretary of war, he referred it to the judge-advocate-general. This authority returned it to Pope with the remark that he had not complied with the law requiring commanding officers to give a decision in such cases. Pope then wrote the judge-advocate-general that he had not confirmed the proceedings because of a doubt in his mind about the bearing of Article of War 65, forbidding a commanding officer to appoint a court-martial and then to prosecute officers of his command before it, and that he therefore solicited the opinion of the judge-advocate-general. The brief reply was that there seemed to be sufficient ground for disapproving the proceedings. This left the unconscious subject of the correspondence at the disposition of Pope, who on November 13 ordered him to be sent under guard to Camp McClellan, there to be confined until the president should act in the case. On December 7 General Sibley, in a letter to the judge-advocate-general, respectfully represented to that official that his military commission of 1862 had tried nearly four hundred Indians on charges preferred by himself, that thirty-eight of them had been hanged, and that the remaining convicts were then in prison at Davenport. He suggested that Article 65 related only to courts-martial and not to military

Sibley, who had heard of the killing of the Indian near Hutchinson, at once decided that it could have been no other than Little Crow. This conclusion had already been reached at Hutchinson. A deformity of one or both wrists caused by a gunshot wound received in a family feud was the most conclusive evidence of identity. The legislature of 1864 appropriated five hundred dollars as a reward to Nathan Lamson for the killing of Little Crow. The coat lying on or over the body was found to have belonged to James McGannon, who, as related above, had been murdered near Fairhaven two days before Little Crow was killed. Wowinapa's story cleared his father of that murder. There is no evidence that Little Crow was present at the killing of Captain Cady or at the butchering of the Dustin family, but there is little doubt that these murders were committed by members of his immediate group, for whose acts he may be held responsible. His ignoble end was not unfit. Persons who knew Little Crow have told the author that his manners were those of a gentleman, that his diplomatic talent and oratorical ability gave him an influence over the lower Sioux greater than that of abler and more honorable men. His military talent, in which he took pride, was but mediocre; but had his plan for the battle of Wood Lake been followed, the result might have been less fortunate for Sibley's sleeping soldiers.[25]

commissions and that its purpose was to protect officers from prejudiced commanders; it could not apply to enlisted men or to prisoners of war. The tardy protest had, of course, no influence on the administration, which was content to let the Indian boy live. Wowinapa grew to manhood, took the name "Thomas Wakeman," and became a Christian and a church deacon. See the record of an interview of the author with Dr. Charles A. Eastman, May 24, 1919, in the Folwell Papers. Mrs. Barton, in her *John P. Williamson*, 163, says that Thomas Wakeman was the founder of the Y.M.C.A. among the Dakota and that his son, the Reverend John W. Wakeman, was the pastor of the Yellow Medicine Church near Granite Falls. Another son was a Y.M.C.A. secretary among the Sioux.

[25] *Saint Paul Press*, August 21, 1863; *Official Records*, series 1, vol. 22, part 1, p. 909; Riggs's testimony in "Proceedings of Military Commission Held at Fort Abercrombie and Fort Snelling ; report of the state treasurer, in *Executive Documents, 1864*, p. 98. For estimates of Little Crow, see A. W. Daniels, in *Minnesota Historical Collections*, 12:513-530, and Pond, in the same volume, 325. Daniels' statements are, for the most part, eulogistic. In interviews with the author Dr. A. W. Daniels, Auguste L. Larpenteur, Samuel J. Brown, Henry Belland, and Return I. Holcombe all spoke some good words for Little Crow. These interviews are recorded in the author's notebooks, 2:130, 133; 3:137; 4:89, 116; 5:70. In the Minnesota Historical Society Scrapbooks, 2:91, is a clipping of a letter of John Wakeman,

After the murders above described the belief spread far and wide that the Big Woods were full of Indians. Baseless fears that the Chippewa and the Winnebago were also moving were indulged. In Wright and adjoining counties a panic like that of the previous year set in. The whole population took the roads to St. Paul with their live stock and household stuff. But as there were no further murders the "crazy fugitives" soon began to return to their farms. A considerable number, however, abandoned their claims. To abate this panic, prevent its recurrence, and afford protection to the region most infested — which the soldiers

half brother of Little Crow, in which he pictures Little Crow as doing his best to protect the captive women and children at his house at the time of the outbreak of 1862, providing food for them at the risk of trouble with his men. The letter closes with the declaration that Little Crow was not responsible for the massacres. The Minnesota Historical Society, in its *Annual Report*, 1868, p. 12, acknowledged the gift by William Grube of the scalp of Little Crow, with the remark, "It is *tanned*, and thus in a measure imperishable." For many years it was displayed, with Little Crow's skull and wrist bones, among the exhibits of the society. Dr. J. W. Daniels, in his "Indian Outbreak," 23, speaks of Little Crow's "suavity of manners in which he was gifted beyond any other Indian I ever met"; and Daniels had lived among the Sioux for seven years. Frederick W. Hodge, in *Handbook of American Indians*, part 1, p. 769 (Bureau of American Ethnology, *Bulletins*, no. 30 — Washington, 1910), gives Little Crow's real name as *Chetan wakan mani*, "the sacred pigeon-hawk that comes walking." Little Crow signed the treaty of Mendota, August 5, 1851, under the name *Taoyateduta*, "his people are red." Cyrus Thomas, in *The Indians of North America in Historic Times*, under the picture of Little Crow opposite page 353 (*The History of North America*, vol. 2 — Philadelphia, [1903]), gives Little Crow's name as *Taoyatechata*.
   The whereabouts of Little Crow during the winter of 1862-63 cannot be confidently stated. Pope placed him on the Missouri River 150 miles above Fort Pierre. The more common opinion was that, with a following of about 150 persons, he was at or about Devil's Lake. Samuel J. Brown, in a written memorandum for the author's use, in the Folwell Papers, states that Little Crow and part of the lower Sioux spent the winter "in Turtle Mts (neighborhood of St. Joseph, D. T.)." The question where and how he hibernated is not important, since we know of his first move at the opening of the season of 1863. About May 29 he appeared at Fort Garry, now Winnipeg, with sixty followers to beg for food and ammunition. Some provisions were granted to prevent them from helping themselves, but ammunition was refused. With so small a retinue it may be presumed that the chief was sincere in his profession that he wanted ammunition only for hunting. Little Crow's principal request was that the governor of Rupert's Land intercede with the United States authorities for the return of the prisoners in their hands. He complained bitterly that the Indians had been induced unfairly to surrender the prisoners they had taken while the whites had kept all that they had captured and had hanged some of them. He gave as the reasons for beginning the war bad treatment for many years, bad faith, and delay of payments. Holcombe's statement that Little Crow appealed to the Canadian authorities to furnish him a cannon and men to fight the Americans has not been verified. It may be assumed that on his return from Fort Garry in June Little Crow gave up all thought of continuing the war and, disappointed in the hope of military glory, came down to the ignoble occupation of horse-stealing, with a possible murder or two for variety. *Official Records*, series 1, vol. 22, part 2, p. 123; Holcombe, in *Minnesota in Three Centuries*, 3:407-409; Heard, *Sioux War*, 296.

on patrol seemed unable to do — Adjutant General Oscar Malmros conceived the plan of collecting a special mounted force of professional hunters and trappers and, in the absence of Governor Henry A. Swift, issued on July 4 a general order for the enlistment of a corps of experienced hunters and marksmen as "volunteer scouts" to scour the Big Woods from Sauk Centre to the north end of Sibley County. Each volunteer was required to arm, equip, and subsist himself at his own expense. For his service he was to receive two dollars per day. It was not until July 20 that the corps was wholly mustered in, but squads had already been doing duty as authorized.[26]

In the meantime it was reported that Indians had been seen in the western part of Dakota County and it became known that horses had been stolen in Rice County. On July 15 two men cutting hay near Waterville in Le Sueur County saw three Indians riding westward and carried the news to that village. An armed party started in pursuit and in the night discovered the camp fire of the unsuspecting Indians. The next morning they overtook the Indians on the bank of Scotch Lake in the town of Cleveland. They fired on the savages and fell back to reload. The Indians fired and killed a horse and then disappeared. After a search a wounded Indian was discovered lying behind a log. Six bullets relieved him of his pain. On the shore of the lake was found a complete outfit of clothing, ornaments, and arms for one Indian and it was presumed that the owner had taken to the water; but neither he nor the third of the party was found. Three stolen horses, however, were recaptured. This event aroused an unjust suspicion of the Winnebago, for they had just started on their journey to Crow Creek, but a squad of the volunteer scouts was ordered to operate south of the Minnesota River.[27]

[26] *Official Records*, series 1, vol. 22, part 2, p. 494; message of Governor Swift, in *Executive Documents*, 1863, p. 20; report of the adjutant general, in the same volume, 192, 195, 196, 345.
[27] *Saint Paul Press*, July 22, 1863; report of the adjutant general, in *Executive Documents*, 1863, pp. 347-349.

To stimulate the activities of the volunteer scouts the order of July 4 promised a compensation of twenty-five dollars for each scalp of a male Sioux Indian delivered by any of them at the office of the adjutant general. A second order of July 20 promised a reward of twenty-five dollars to any scout who should kill a hostile Sioux Indian and furnish satisfactory proof of the act. This order contained a new provision offering a reward of seventy-five dollars to any person not in military service for every hostile Sioux warrior killed by him in the state on the production of satisfactory proof. To increase the number of such "Independent Scouts" and to multiply that of dead Indians shot on sight, the governor on September 22 raised the bounty to two hundred dollars per head. The business seems not to have prospered, for the only payments found of record are the following: July 6, bounty for scalp, $25.00; August 7, bounty for killing one Sioux warrior, $75.00; August 31, tanning an Indian scalp, $5.00; October 9, bounty for killing one Sioux warrior, $25.00. These were paid out of the adjutant general's contingent fund. The state treasurer paid $25.00 for one Sioux scalp. The activity of the volunteer and independent scouts soon made horse-stealing and murder unsafe for marauding Sioux, if any of them were lurking in the timber, and settlers returned to their farms. At the close of their term of enlistment on September 20 the volunteer scouts were paid and mustered out of service. The pay of the company amounted to $11,375.24.[28]

As already stated, there were persons of influence who predicted the failure of Sibley's expedition of 1863. By some of them it was represented to the war department that to check the incursion of numerous raiding parties of the Sioux bent upon pillage and murder — which Sibley's expedition could not intercept and destroy — there should be organized a regiment of troops especially equipped for service against Indians and commanded by a man of

[28] Message of Governor Swift, in *Executive Documents*, 1863, p. 21; report of the adjutant general, in the same volume, 192-198, 217, 223-226, 349, 403.

practical qualifications. Such a force, it was represented, would dispose of the Sioux in a brief and decisive campaign. Ex-Senator Rice and Senator Wilkinson, politically opposed to each other, coöperated in obtaining the attention of the secretary of war and his approval of the plan. On June 12 he issued an order through the provost marshal general authorizing Major Edwin A. C. Hatch to raise in Minnesota and adjacent Indian territories, not a regiment, but an independent battalion of two companies of cavalry and two of infantry for three years or the war and to appoint the officers, subject to the approval of the war department. "Indians," read the order, "may be enlisted." Subsequent orders eliminated the infantry and authorized five companies of cavalry, but only four were organized in 1863. The command was called "Hatch's Independent Battalion of Cavalry" — for short, "Hatch's Battalion."[29]

The citizen thus suddenly advanced to a field officer's rank, given an independent command, and authorized to appoint his officers, had been a resident of St. Paul since 1848 and of the territory and state since 1843. Still he was not widely known in the state because of his continuous and extensive travel in Indian country for trade and exploration. In 1856 he was appointed agent to the Blackfeet. A Republican newspaper denounced him in offensive language as a "relic of the Buchanan dynasty." His knowledge of Indians was believed by his friends to qualify him for service against Indians without military experience; and a great many gentlemen had been appointed officers with more slender equipment. His year of service furnished no opportunity for the display of military talent in general or of eminent ability in Indian warfare.[30]

The recruiting of a command in his military department without his recommendation was by no means agreeable

---

[29] *State Atlas* (Minneapolis), July 22, August 19, 1863; *Saint Paul Press*, June 23, 25, July 12, 1863; *Official Records*, series 1, vol. 22, part 2, pp. 493-495. An official copy of the order of the war department, dated June 12, 1863, and signed by J. W. Fry, provost marshal general, is in Governor's Archives, file 222.

[30] Newson, *Pen Pictures*, 82; *Central Republican* (Faribault), July 1, 1863.

to Major General Pope. In a letter of July 13, 1863, to the war department he asked to be favored with a copy of the order under which Hatch was acting and suggested that "of course" Hatch had no authority to announce that he was to command troops and to make campaigns at his pleasure in the Department of the Northwest. He further objected, with much emphasis, against employing Chippewa Indians in the war against other Indians. Pope did not hesitate to express his judgment that the proposed battalion would be simply a source of great and unnecessary expense and he recommended that the order, if not revoked, should be modified to exclude Indians and to confine the battalion to one arm of the service. Brigadier General Sibley was no better pleased with the implied condemnation of his conduct and ability by the raising of an independent command in his military district to perform the service with which his troops in the field were charged. The following extract from his diary in the entry under Wednesday, July 8, may illustrate his attitude: "Learned of the order granting authority to Major Hatch to raise two companies of infantry and two of cavalry to serve against the Indians during the existence of this war. The whole thing I regard as a miserable scheme got up by Rice and others, who hate General Pope and do not love me and who wish to annoy and humiliate us both. I have a contempt for the whole humbug inventor and all."[31]

Under amending orders conforming partly to the counsel of Pope, three companies of cavalry were recruited and mustered in in August and September, 1863. The fourth company, partly recruited at the same time, was not mustered in until some time in November. Upon a suggestion of Sibley the battalion was at once ordered to Pembina, apparently to defend against a possible incursion

[31] *Official Records*, series 1, vol. 22, part 2, pp. 371, 384, 494, 498. Halleck wrote to Pope on July 20, 1863, that he knew nothing of the authority granted to Hatch. In a letter to Stanton, August 29, 1863, Pope wrote, "Hatch is but an instrument of Rice." Pope informed Sibley that the battalion was under his, Sibley's, command.

of the Sioux who had taken refuge in Canada after the outbreak, as well as to be conveniently out of the way. The command did not receive its equipment of arms and horses at Fort Snelling until the last days of September, so that it was not able to depart until October 5. The march of four hundred miles by way of St. Cloud and Georgetown was not completed until November 13, when winter with high winds, heavy snows, and low temperature had set in. Many of the oxen and mules of the long wagon trains perished. Upon the arrival of the command the erection of a cantonment was begun on the later site of Pembina, to be finished late in December. In the last days of that month the mercury fell to forty degrees below zero and on January 1, 1864, it stood at sixty degrees below.[32]

The industrious commander did not wait until his troops and animals were housed before beginning war on the Indians. Soon after his arrival at Pembina information came in that a party of Sioux was encamped in the neighborhood of St. Joseph, a British, later an American, trading post some forty miles to the west. On or about December 15 a dismounted party of twenty or less was sent out to dispose of those Indians. A rapid march brought the detachment unseen to the Indian camp about three o'clock in the morning. "A short though decisive engagement ensued, and all was over," says the historian of the battalion. "Several Indians were killed — passed to their 'happy hunting grounds.'" Had a party of Indians surrounded a camp of sleeping white men and shot them one by one as they looked out from their tents it would have been called an atrocious massacre. This was the only battle fought by Hatch's Battalion.[33]

---

[32] Charles W. Nash, "Narrative of Hatch's Independent Battalion of Cavalry," in *Minnesota in the Civil and Indian Wars*, 1: 595-598; diary of Sergeant Calvin Mooers of Hatch's Battalion, lent to the author; *Official Records*, series 1, vol. 22, part 2, p. 569. Major Nash's statement that the battalion was raised originally for duty at Pembina is erroneous.

[33] Nash, in *Minnesota in the Civil and Indian Wars*, 1: 598, 601. Nash exaggerates the numbers of killed and captured. In a letter to Hatch, January 5, 1864, in *Official Records*, series 1, vol. 34, part 2, p. 29, Sibley speaks of the killing of six Sioux as "very satisfactory." See also the same volume, 249, and Mooers Diary.

Soon after this battle a message was received from the governor of the province of Rupert's Land stating that some Sioux were willing to give themselves up to the United States authorities under merciful conditions. Hatch offered by letter to receive and feed them all on condition that they give up their weapons and surrender Little Six and seven or eight of the principal murderers. There was no general acceptance of the offer, but on January 4 forty-two Indians arrived at Pembina and were confined as prisoners of war. Before the end of the month forty-nine more arrived. The united parties were sent below and arrived at Fort Snelling in April, 1864. Among the murderers whom Hatch desired to secure were the notorious Shakopee or Little Six and the less-known, but equally criminal, Medicine Bottle. So desirous was he to arrest them that he resorted successfully to a novel proceeding involving a violation of Canadian soil, with the connivance, however, of British subjects. In the spring of 1864 the two were taken to Fort Snelling. In November and December of that year they were tried for murder and convicted, but the sentence of death was not executed until November 11, 1865.[34]

After a winter of idleness and hardship, in which three-fourths of the animals died of starvation and cold, the battalion was ordered to Fort Abercrombie and until its muster out in 1866 it garrisoned that post and others on the frontier and patrolled the Red River Valley. On August 31 and September 1, 1864, two additional companies were added and on the fifth of the latter month Major Hatch, who had resigned in June, was succeeded by Lieutenant Colonel — afterwards Brevet Brigadier General — C. Powell Adams, who had been mustered out in the same rank with the First Minnesota Infantry on May 4, 1864. The

[34] Mooers Diary; John H. McKenzie and Onisime Giguere, *Capture of Little Six and Grey Iron in 1864*, 2. This statement, "ordered printed by the legislature, February 1, 1867," is in the form of an eleven-page pamphlet, a copy of which is in the library of the Minnesota Historical Society. The story of the capture of Little Six and Medicine Bottle is told in the Appendix, no. 16, *post*. The other prisoners were sent to Camp Kearny, Davenport, on June 6, 1864. See *Official Records*, series 1, vol. 34, part 4, pp. 209, 210, 289.

prolonged service of the battalion until June, 1866, was honorable and saved the trouble and expense of detaching troops from the seat of war in the South.[35]

The operations of Sibley and Sully against the Indians in 1863 were by no means conclusive. The great hunting parties overtaken by them had been dispersed with much loss of the slender store of property precious in their sight, but with small loss of fighting men. The savages had not been crushed by the armies of the Great Father. The new year, 1864, had hardly opened before Sibley began to lay plans for the defense of his district. Reports from his agents on the frontier, the principal one of whom was Joseph R. Brown at Fort Abercrombie, convinced him that active operations against the Sioux should be resumed. The upper Sioux were reported as wintering between the Red River of the North and the Missouri near the Canadian border. A remnant of the murderous lower Sioux, estimated at from eight hundred to one thousand, was in British settlements along the Red River of the North and the Assiniboine, rationed by the British authorities. All of them were supplied with ammunition by Canadian traders and it was the general's opinion that they would be pleased to have the Indians remain hostile to the Americans. The war must therefore be carried once more into the enemy's country. Sibley laid out a plan of operations for the ensuing season. As this plan was merged into a greater one, it is sufficient to observe that it involved the reënforcement of Forts Ripley, Abercrombie, and Ridgely and the dispatch from the last named of an armed expedition to "beat up the camps of the prairie Indians," whether they should be found on the upper Sheyenne, at Devil's Lake, or on the Missouri Coteau.[36]

Pope had not waited for advice from his subordinate commander but had developed a plan of his own on a greater scale, which provided not merely for the defense of the

[35] Nash, in *Minnesota in the Civil and Indian Wars*, 1: 600, and the roster, 602-611.
[36] *Official Records*, series 1, vol. 34, part 2, pp. 69, 152.

Minnesota frontier but also for the protection of settlements on the Missouri and for operations far beyond that
river. Gold had been discovered some years before in
northern Idaho and in 1860 five thousand gold-seekers had
penetrated to the region of the Salmon River. In the
next two years the rush increased. The invasion of these
lands was displeasing to the seven tribes of the Teton Sioux,
who not only protested but in 1862 attacked one party of
emigrants and killed a number of them.[37] Pope was advised
by the war department to have the protection of these gold-
seekers in view, but he had anticipated the general in
chief in this respect. After receiving an approval of his
general plan and after a consultation with Sibley and
Sully, Pope issued to them on March 15, 1864, his instructions for their operations. The plan was a double one. The
first part provided for the construction of four posts to be
garrisoned by strong details of infantry and cavalry. These
were to be located at Devil's Lake, on the James River
at a point as nearly as practicable due west of the head of
the Coteau des Prairies, on the Missouri near the point
reached by Sibley's expedition the year before, and on the
Yellowstone. The last three posts would be nearly on the
emigrant route from the upper Mississippi to the gold mines
of Idaho. Well-marked trails were to be opened between
them. The other and greater part of the plan was a military
expedition against the whole Sioux nation, which was spread
over a great area extending from the Platte River to the
British possessions and from the Red River to the Rocky
Mountains. Pope expected that it would encounter some
six thousand warriors furnished with ammunition and other
supplies by the British half-breeds and traders of the Red
River. Sully was to command this "Northwestern Indian
Expedition," which was to include his own troops and a
large detachment from the District of Minnesota.[38]

[37] *American Annual Cyclopaedia*, 1862, p. 770, article on Idaho.
[38] *Official Records*, series 1, vol. 34, part 2, pp. 607, 622-625; series 1, vol. 41, part 1,
p. 134. The total strength of the expedition was about 2,200.

By well-timed marches the two brigades commanded by Sully met on the Missouri at a point but a few miles below that where Sibley had reached it in 1863. The Minnesota brigade — the Second — was composed of the Eighth Minnesota Infantry mounted on Canadian ponies, six companies of the Second Minnesota Cavalry, and two sections of Captain John Jones's Third Minnesota Battery.

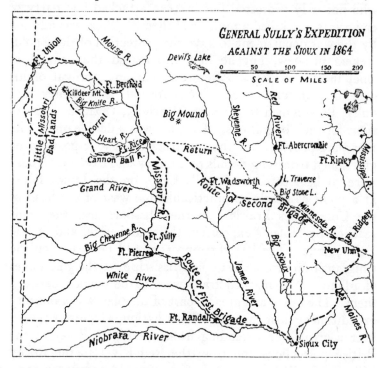

The First Brigade was made up of cavalry troops from Iowa and Dakota Territory, a battery of artillery, a battalion of the Thirtieth Wisconsin Infantry, and about seventy scouts. Attached to the First Brigade was Brackett's Minnesota Battalion of Cavalry, which had been relieved from service in the South as part of an Iowa regiment and had been given an independent position after reënlistment. Sully here learned that the Indians he had expected to

oppose him on the east side of the Missouri had crossed
that river and had moved westward into a hilly region in
the bend of the Little Missouri. He understood that the
Indian force consisted principally of Teton tribes, Yanktonai, and some Santee Sioux. He therefore put his command across the Missouri by steamboats and on July 19
moved westward up the valley of the Cannon Ball River
for five days. Another day's march in a northerly direction
brought him to the Heart River. Here he left in a guarded
corral all his baggage except food and ammunition and
at three o'clock on July 26 he set out for the Indian camp,
which was reported to be near the Knife River. At ten
o'clock on July 28 that camp was seen at a distance of ten
miles, situated on the side of a high hill forming one of a range
known as the Killdeer Mountains, broken by ravines and
heavily timbered. The number of lodges was estimated
by Sully at over sixteen hundred and that of warriors at
from five thousand to six thousand. In front of the camp
was a very rolling prairie. On its swells and on hills to right
and left the Indians had taken strong but isolated positions.
They were aware of the approach of the white man's soldiers
and were prepared to entertain them. Their women had
come out to witness the spectacle. These remote and
inexperienced savages still cherished the foolish idea that
their warriors, armed with shotguns and bows and arrows,
could defeat the white man in battles.

The command was at once formed in battle order, with
two strong battalions in front, a battalion in support of
each wing, and the two batteries with support in rear.
After an advance of two or three miles with slight opposition,
the front line was dismounted and the men were deployed
as skirmishers at close intervals. The Indians made vigorous
but desultory opposition to their advance. "The ground
over which we advanced," says one battalion commander,
"was very uneven, and the Indians would gather behind
knolls and in ravines on our front and fire upon us and

scatter away on their swift-footed ponies." The batteries pushed forward to points of vantage and scattered groups of Indians to whom artillery fire was a novelty. Attacks on the flanks were repulsed by the cavalry reserves. Brackett's Battalion made a gallant charge on a force assailing the right flank, in which two of his men were killed and eight wounded. Before sunset the Indians gave up the unequal contest. Their women and children had fled to the mountains, leaving behind their lodges, tons of pemmican, great quantities of dried berries, buffalo robes, tanned buffalo, elk and antelope skins, brass and copper kettles, and mess pans. They even left their dogs and their ponies tied to pickets. The total white loss was five killed and ten wounded; the Indian loss was uncertainly estimated at from one hundred to one hundred and fifty.[39]

After a day spent by part of the command in destroying the property abandoned by the Indians, Sully returned to his corral on the Heart River on July 31. After a rest of two days the expedition moved westward and ten days later, on August 12, it reached the Yellowstone River. On August 8 and 9, while passing through the notorious Bad Lands of the Little Missouri, the command experienced much annoyance, without casualty, from Indians firing from the safe cover of buttes and ravines. The colonel of the Eighth Minnesota, in his report wrote of the affair on the eighth: "The Indian shotguns and bows and arrows were no match for the accurate aim and long range of our rifles and carbines, and when the artillery sent shell into their assemblies on the hills and into their retreats in ravines, the cowardly rascals soon learned that they were no match for soldiers that had come 1,000 miles to fight

[39] *Minnesota in the Civil and Indian Wars*, 1:387-390, 544-546, 672; David L. Kingsbury, "Sully's Expedition against the Sioux in 1864," in *Minnesota Historical Collections*, 8:449-456; W. E. Seelye, "Early Military Experiences in Dakota," in *North Dakota Historical Collections*, 3:243; John Pattee, "Dakota Campaigns," in *South Dakota Historical Collections*, 5:305-310; reports of Pope, Sully, and Sully's regimental and battalion commanders, in *Official Records*, series 1, vol. 41, part 1, pp. 135, 141-143, 157, 160, 165, 168, 170-172.

them." Sully described the Bad Lands as "hell with the fires put out." Some of his men had literally to dig roadways through narrow ravines while the main command, disposed in a judicious manner, kept the Indians at a distance. The return march of the column from this extreme distance was made without notable event. The route was down the left bank of the Yellowstone to its mouth, where the Missouri was crossed, and then along the left bank of that river to Fort Rice, which was reached on September 9. The Minnesota brigade, relieved at that point, returned to Fort Ridgely, where it arrived on October 8, after having marched 1,625 miles in four months and three days. An officer of the Eighth Minnesota in a spirited narrative states that on the march down the Missouri buffalo herds were so great in number that the command was frequently corralled for protection.[40]

But two of the forts included in Pope's plan were built. On reaching the limit of his march up the Missouri, Sully selected a position for a military post and left his detachment of Wisconsin infantry to build the work named "Fort Rice." Sibley, using the discretion allowed him to locate the post west of the head of the Coteau des Prairies, sent out a detachment, also of Wisconsin infantry, which built Fort Wadsworth on a site better situated for wood and defense than that originally designated by Pope.[41]

The account of the Indian wars in which Minnesota was concerned may be closed with the campaign of 1864. Her infantry regiments were soon sent to the South. The Second Cavalry Regiment was retained for patrol duty on the northern and western borders until the close of the Civil War and some portions were retained a year longer. Brackett's Battalion was again sent to Sully's district in

---

[40] Reports of Sully and Thomas, in *Official Records*, series 1, vol. 41, part 1, pp. 143-153, 167-170; Kingsbury, in *Minnesota Historical Collections*, 8: 457-462. The diary of Lewis C. Paxson, in *North Dakota Historical Collections*, vol. 2, part 2, pp. 141-147, gives an itinerary of the expedition.

[41] Reports of Sibley, Pope, and Sully, in *Official Records*, series 1, vol. 41, part 1, pp. 39, 135, 153.

the spring of 1865 and for a year it patrolled the country
east of the Missouri, extending its marches to Devil's
Lake and the Missouri River. The Third Battery of
Light Artillery was divided among the three Minnesota
forts for the winter of 1864–65. In the summer of 1865
three sections, commanded by Captain Jones, marched to
Devil's Lake, to no purpose, as it turned out. The muster
out of the battery did not take place until February, 1866.
No Indians were encountered in any of the excursions
named.[42]

The opinion has been expressed that the money expended
upon the Indian campaigns might better have been given
to the Indians in annual installments. But nothing would
suit the people of the Northwest but Indian blood. "The
only good Indians are dead Indians," was ever the word.
Politicians and army contractors knew how to turn this
sentiment to their advantage, and the Minnesota troops
were not averse to campaigns much less bloody than those
south of the Potomac and the Ohio. Still, it must not be
forgotten that the soldiers were patient in their laborious
marches and exposures, and gallant in action whenever
the enemy could be overtaken.

The costly campaigns against the Sioux had not long
passed before it became apparent that nothing had been
gained financially by the confiscation of their annuities
in the winter of 1863. The policy of the act was also called in
question as being too sweeping and indiscriminate in its
operation on innocent and guilty alike. This was not
merely a sentimental view of philanthropist friends of the
Indians. The commissioner of Indian affairs, the Honorable D. N. Cooley, in his report for 1866 gave expression to
a "deliberate conviction" after "thorough examination"
that the Sioux generally had not been treated fairly by the
government and that the forfeiture of all their annuities
by the act of Congress of February 16, 1863, was unjust

[42] *Minnesota in the Civil and Indian Wars*, 1:394, 550, 583, 675. For Sully's operations
in 1865, see his reports, in Indian Office, *Reports*, 1865, pp. 204-211.

to a large number who had taken no part in the outbreak of 1862 and to many more who had only an unwilling part in it. In a special report to the secretary of the interior, dated April 20, 1866, he furnished a recital of the existing locations, numbers, and conditions of the separated fragments of the Sioux tribes and recommended that Congress at once restore to them the gross sums forfeited in 1863, less the amount paid by the government for the damages of the outbreak of 1862. This action was urged on three grounds: (1) justice, to the large number, especially of upper Sioux, who had not participated, particularly to those who had done faithful military service; (2) mercy, to the sufferers at Crow Creek and Davenport, already sufficiently punished, to the small remnant of outcasts on or near their old reservations in Minnesota, and to the homeless wanderers on the prairies of Dakota; (3) economy, because the government had been paying out more for their subsistence than the interest on the sums forfeited. The commissioner estimated the amount of the annuities at $5,161,800 and the appropriations for damages during the outbreak at $1,380,374. The remainder, $3,781,426, at five per cent, would yield annually $189,071, a sum not much below the annual appropriations for support.[43] He furnished a draft of a bill to effect the proposed restoration. The secretary of the interior did not notice the commissioner's advice in his annual report and Congress gave it no attention. A proposition for a blanket immunity for all the Sioux of the Mississippi could not then, nor at any time since, be entertained. The upper Sioux, however, were so situated as to oblige the government soon to entertain their claim for restoration, to secure an admission of injury done them, and, later, to collect large sums of money.[44]

---

[43] Indian Office, *Reports*, 1865, p. 195; 1866, pp. 46, 225-229.
[44] The story of the "Sisseton and Wahpeton claim," which extended over a period of more than forty years, is treated in the Appendix, no. 12, *post*. A long-pressed and finally successful claim by the Santee for indemnity for their confiscated annuities is discussed in the Appendix, no. 13, *post*.

# XI. MINNESOTA TROOPS IN THE CIVIL WAR

IN A PREVIOUS chapter an account of the enlistment and organization of the Minnesota regiments and battalions raised for the Civil War was given and sketches of some notable experiences of the older commands in their earlier years were attempted. We may return now from the long digression devoted to the Indian war and may properly resume our story of the Minnesota troops in the later years of their service. The scope of this work cannot include elaborated histories of the several commands, but it would be unjust to omit particular accounts of the performances of some regiments favored above others in opportunity for displaying the fighting qualities possessed by all. In patriotism, courage, pride, and grit they were equal; in opportunity alone were they unequal.

Most of the Minnesota troops served in the western armies, but the Second and Fourth regiments and the First Battery of Light Artillery made the march with Sherman from Atlanta to Savannah and thence to the national capital. The Eighth Regiment was detained in the North until late in October, 1864, passed two months in Tennessee, and was sent east with the Twenty-third Army Corps in January, 1865, to participate with credit in Sherman's Carolina campaign.[1] The First Regiment alone completed its full term of service in the Army of the Potomac. Upon its muster out on May 5, 1864, enough officers and men re-enlisted or held over to form a nucleus of two companies of the First Battalion of Minnesota Infantry Volunteers. This organization was ordered to the Army of the Potomac just after the slaughter at Cold Harbor and was placed in

---

[1] Narratives of these units may be found in *Minnesota in the Civil and Indian Wars*, 1: 79-122, 198-220, 386-400, 640-649. See especially page 395 for William H. Houlton's account of the Eighth in the affair at Murfreesboro, Tennessee, December 7, 1864, in which ninety of its members were killed or wounded in thirty minutes.

the same brigade to which the "Old First" had belonged. It shared all the subsequent fortunes of the Second Army Corps, suffering heavy losses. By December there were but "little more than thirty men present for duty." A recruiting detail was sent to Minnesota and the ranks of the two companies were soon filled and a third company was added. Thus strengthened, the battalion had its honorable part in the Appomattox campaign. Five additional companies were added only in time to be sent home for discharge.[2]

As fast as the Minnesota infantry regiments employed in the Indian wars were relieved they were ordered south. All were merged into the Union armies for service in the field except two, the Third and the Sixth. The Third, after performing indispensable service in connection with the siege of Vicksburg, was sent to Arkansas for the remainder of the war period. From September, 1863, to the end of April, 1864, it occupied Little Rock, the capital of the state, and conducted itself in a manner to encourage loyal sentiment and conciliate rebels. In January, 1864, a state convention framed a free-state constitution under which a loyal government was established which continued until the final reconstruction. While thus stationed in Little Rock twenty-three officers and enlisted men were promoted to offices in United States colored infantry regiments and nearly enough able-bodied freedmen to fill a regiment were recruited in the neighborhood. The command suffered greatly with malarial fevers, especially while stationed at Pine Bluff, some eighty miles below Little Rock on the Arkansas River, in the summer of 1864. Thirty of the original members of the regiment died and the regimental surgeon reported eighty-nine deaths among recruits and thirty among drafted men. The regiment was engaged in a number of minor affairs. In one of these, called the "battle of Fitzhugh's Woods," Colonel, afterwards

[2] Report of the adjutant general, in *Executive Documents*, 1865, insert opposite p. 40, pp. 94-111, 169; Lochren, in *Minnesota in the Civil and Indian Wars*, 1: 44-47.

Brigadier General, Christopher C. Andrews displayed tactical ability worthy of a much greater arena. On April 1 Andrews marched from Augusta, on the White River, with a detachment of 231 men to break up a camp of rebel conscripts some miles from that place. He found the camp deserted and learned that the able Confederate commander had disposed his brigade of some six hundred conscripts in a manner to cut off the returning Union column. While Andrews' detachment was halting for a brief rest a sharp attack was made upon it by a mounted force. The men of the Third, with a volley fire, soon dismounted some of the enemy and drove the remainder into the woods. After the Union column had marched two miles farther a fierce onset was made on the rear guard, but it was repulsed. Almost at the same moment the left flank of the column was assailed. The Third faced into line and drove the enemy out of range. Immediately after this the right flank was attacked in force. The gallant colonel faced his men about and led them in an effective and decisive countercharge with the bayonet. Andrews' horse was killed by a shot which narrowly missed shattering the rider's knee. The command then made its way without molestation to the transport, which carried it back to its station at Little Rock. The loss was eight killed and twenty-one wounded out of one hundred and eighty actually engaged.[3]

The Sixth Infantry, long detained in the state, reached Helena, Arkansas, on June 23, 1864, 940 strong. Malarial fevers at once attacked the men with such virulence that on August 15 there were fit for duty but 7 officers and 178 men. In September that number was reduced to 140. Six hundred had been sent to northern hospitals. On October 8, 1864, Dr. Levi Butler, a state commissioner, wrote confidentially: "I do not feel that it is expedient to report

[3] Andrews, in *Minnesota in the Civil and Indian Wars*, 1:164-174; reports of Colonel Andrews and Major Everett W. Foster, in *Official Records*, series 1, vol. 34, part 1, pp. 863-868, reprinted in *Minnesota in the Civil and Indian Wars*, 2:432-437; Holcombe to the adjutant general of Minnesota, January 28, 1896, and the statement of Brigadier General Dandridge McRae, Confederate commander, in the latter work, 2:437-437f.

the true condition of the Sixth Regiment to the public.
. . . on Monday last only two hundred and twenty,
all told, were able for duty." He feared that the command
would be destroyed if kept at Helena sixty days longer.
Late in that month the command was ordered to St. Louis,
where it arrived on November 11 to be assigned to provost
guard duty. Convalescents in considerable numbers here
rejoined it. On January 29, 1865, the regiment embarked
for New Orleans, whence it was ordered a little more than
a month later to join the force collected for the siege of
Mobile. In the attack on Fort Blakely on April 9 the
regiment performed very creditable service without material
loss. The country should ever remember that the fourscore
men who died of fever at Helena were as deserving of its
gratitude as if they had fallen in battle.[4]

The Seventh, Ninth, and Tenth regiments had a somewhat common experience after the close of their activity
in the Indian campaigns of 1862–63. The Seventh left the
state early in October, 1863, under the command of Lieutenant Colonel William R. Marshall, in place of Colonel
Stephen Miller, who was about to resign in expectation of
election to the governorship of Minnesota. The Ninth
and Tenth regiments followed in the same month. All
were held in Missouri through the succeeding winter,
employed in provost duty or in guarding railroads. Colonel
James H. Baker of the Tenth was soon appointed commander
of the post at St. Louis and never rejoined his regiment.
The command fell to Lieutenant Colonel Samuel P. Jennison.
In the early summer of 1864 the Seventh and Tenth regiments were merged into the Sixteenth Army Corps, which
also absorbed the Ninth after that regiment returned from
the disastrous expedition under Sturgis into northern
Mississippi in June of that year for the destruction of a
railroad. The Ninth took part in the battle of Guntown,
or Brice's Cross Roads, on the tenth of June and by its

stout rear-guard fighting in the three days following probably
saved the whole force, eight thousand strong, from dispersion
or capture. Its losses on the field were not large — nine
killed and thirty-three wounded, twenty of whom were
left where they fell. A sacrifice, however, of six officers
and two hundred and thirty-three men as prisoners of war
had to be suffered on the retreat. Most of the enlisted
men taken prisoners were sent to the notorious rebel prison
at Andersonville, Georgia. One hundred and nineteen died
in prison, an additional number died within a year after
their release, and many of the survivors were permanently
broken in health. Had these men fallen on the battle
field, a monument, or at least a tablet in the rotunda of the
Capitol, would commemorate their gallantry. The writer
of these lines offers his humble tribute of gratitude to these
men of Minnesota who gave up their lives and strength in
the cause of their country as surely as if they had fallen
charging a rebel division in battle. The conduct of Colonel
Alexander Wilkin in remaining with his command when the
commanding general, most of the mounted officers, and
the cavalry had fled ingloriously to the rear, leaving him
to handle the rear-guard fragments, deserves a worthier
recognition than has yet been accorded.

In June, 1864, an expedition of some ten thousand men
was sent into northern Mississippi to cut a railroad, likely
to be used to embarrass Sherman, and to amuse Forrest's
forces and others hanging on Forrest's rear. The three
Minnesota regiments mentioned were included in the
detachment. At Tupelo on July 14 a Confederate force
under Forrest was encountered and a sharp fight ensued
which resulted in a victory for the Union force, but it does
not appear that a railroad was cut. The Minnesota losses
were not heavy, but they included the death of Colonel
Wilkin, who was hit by a rebel bullet while he was sitting
on his horse directing the movements of his brigade. Again
in the autumn months of 1864 the three regiments were

engaged in the pursuit of Price in Arkansas and Missouri. There was suffering from long marches in vile weather, but the losses in action were nominal. The splendid performances of four Minnesota regiments at Nashville in December, 1864, will be sketched on a later page.[5] The limits of this work do not permit accounts of the services of the First and Second batteries of Minnesota Light Artillery in sufficient detail to be satisfactory. Both were recruited in the winter of 1861–62 and both served through the war. The First Battery got its baptism of fire at Shiloh in the famous "hornet's nest." Its captain, Emil Munch, was severely wounded early in the day and had his horse shot under him. The command was engaged at Vicksburg and Atlanta and made the march to the sea with Sherman. The Second Battery, commanded throughout the war by Captain William A. Hotchkiss, when he was not serving as a chief of artillery, played a distinguished part at Perryville and Chickamauga and was engaged at Stone River and Chattanooga.[6]

We now turn to some brief account of exploits of regiments whose fortunes led them onto great battle fields. The First Minnesota, which had been engaged at Fair Oaks, Savage's Station, and Fredericksburg and had been so severely punished at Antietam, had awaiting it a

[5] *Minnesota in the Civil and Indian Wars*, 1:355-358, 418-428, 461-466; 2:469-474. The administration of Colonel Baker was so efficient and the behavior of the Seventh and Tenth Minnesota regiments was so satisfactory that a committee of the city council of St. Louis waited upon Secretary Stanton in Washington to request that Baker might remain in command and that the troops be a permanent garrison for the city. The secretary declined to leave the troops in St. Louis, but consented to the continuance of Baker's detail. He was later put in command of a large subdistrict including St. Louis and was made provost marshal general of Missouri. At the close of the war he was complimented in orders and brevetted brigadier general.

For an account of an attempt of forty-one men of Companies C and K of the Ninth Regiment to anticipate the Emancipation Proclamation in November, 1863, by liberating a negro family from slavery — an adventure which cost them two months' detention in the guardhouse in Jefferson City, Missouri — see Colin F. Macdonald, "Narrative of the Ninth Regiment," in *Minnesota in the Civil and Indian Wars*, 1: 419. On January 11, 1864, Senator Wilkinson introduced into the United States Senate a resolution asking the secretary of war for information as to the cause of the imprisonment. The next day the secretary telegraphed an order for the release of the men. See 38 Congress, 1 session, *Senate Journal*, 67 (serial 1175), and *Congressional Globe*, 145. For the part of the Minnesota regiments at Nashville, see *post*, pp. 322-327.

[6] *Minnesota in the Civil and Indian Wars*, 1: 640-648, 655-663.

decimation hardly equaled in modern warfare. General Herman Haupt, chief of the bureau of United States military railroads in the Civil War, who had been selected for that position by Stanton because of his West Point education, his high standing as a civil engineer, and his large experience in railroad management, was in Harrisburg, Pennsylvania, on the thirtieth of June, 1863. Having been in former years a professor in the little college at Gettysburg, he knew the topography of the region. The Confederate troops, who had reached the opposite bank of the Susquehanna, had suddenly broken away to the south by certain roads. The practiced eye of the military engineer instantly divined the situation. A telegram to Meade gave him the certain information that Lee was rapidly concentrating on Gettysburg, intending to attack the leading Union corps and destroy them before support could arrive.

On June 30 the First Minnesota rested near the Pennsylvania line after a march of thirty-three miles on the previous day. The company officers worked on their pay rolls, from which many brave men were soon to be dropped. In the forenoon of July 1 the march was continued to a point some three miles from the battle field, where, at about nine o'clock, the division bivouacked. On the second it was "roused up . . . ere the morning star" and, after moving to the field, was halted near general headquarters, where it was placed in reserve. Late in the afternoon the First Minnesota, detached from its division and its brigade, was sent off to the south, following the well-known Cemetery Ridge, along which the Union line had been drawn out, to a point about half a mile away, where on a salient of the ridge a battery was in position. The regiment was stationed in support on the left of the battery. Three companies, C, F, and L, were absent; one was supporting a battery near the cemetery, a second was on provost guard duty, and the third was skirmishing toward Sickles' left. For two hours and more, resting at ease, the eight companies in line watched from their elevated position the ebb and flow of Sickles' disastrous struggle against the rebel divisions enfilading both legs of the right angle formed by his lines at the Peach Orchard. The unequal fight was continued until near sunset, when the shattered battalions of the Third Corps came pouring to the rear, some in tolerable

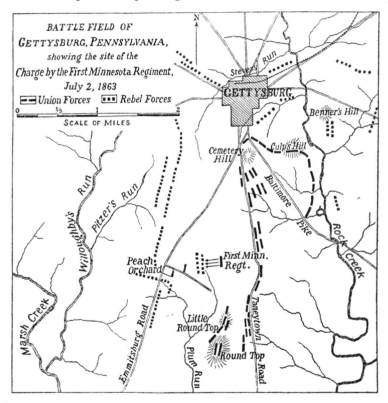

*BATTLE FIELD OF GETTYSBURG, PENNSYLVANIA,* showing the site of the *Charge by the First Minnesota Regiment,* July 2, 1863
Union Forces ▪▪▪ Rebel Forces
0   ½   1   2
SCALE OF MILES

order, many straggling singly or in squads. They passed by or through the line of the First and hurried on to rally on the lower ground in the rear. Sickles had been wounded and Hancock had been ordered to command Sickles' corps along with his own, the Second. The advance of the Third Corps to the unfortunate positon on the Emmitsburg road early in the day had left a long stretch of the ridge,

north of Little Round Top, bare of troops. Hancock
observed the repulse of Sickles' brigades and instantly
devoted all his energies to filling this open space with
troops from the reserves.

Meantime Anderson's division of A. P. Hill's corps was
advancing north of the Peach Orchard in lines parallel to
the ridge, with great rapidity and confidence. It was but
a short half mile that they had to come. A few minutes
more and they would be on the crest, unless arrested.
Hancock, with a single aid or orderly, rode furiously up
and down to meet the reënforcements he had ordered; they
were coming on the run, but they did not arrive, and the
precious minutes were passing. From the salient where the
battery stood he overlooked the ground for a moment and
then galloped to the center of the supporting regiment on
its left. "What regiment is this?" he asked of Colonel
Colvill. "First Minnesota," was the reply. "Charge
those lines!" said Hancock firmly, pointing to the front of
Wilcox's brigade not more than four hundred yards away.
Colvill and his men knew what that meant — a sacrifice to
save five minutes' time. The usual orders put the little
battalion in movement at right shoulder shift on double
time. The line was less than one hundred yards long. The
ground to be traversed was an old pasture field. At the
foot of the considerable slope of three hundred yards there
was a dried-up ditch or "run." From the start the enemy's
fire began to thin the ranks, but not a man flinched. When
near the foot of the slope Colvill ordered "Charge!" and, on
full run with bayonets fixed, the Minnesotans rushed upon
the Confederate line, which was momentarily disordered
while climbing up the hither bank of the run. The mass was
small but velocity gave momentum to the onset. The men
of the South scrambled back across the run and gathered
into little groups. The fire poured in convinced them that
further progress to the front would be dangerous and they
gave up the attempt. The moral effect of this charge may be

inferred from the report of Wilcox, the commander of the Confederate brigade thus put out of the fight: "Still another line of infantry descended the slope in our front at a double-quick. . . . Without support . . . my men were withdrawn, to prevent their entire destruction or capture."

Many brave officers and men had fallen by the way on the slope; some of them were smitten by fire from the right of their little front, thrown in by one of Wilcox's regiments which had not been so suddenly halted in its advance. At dusk the battle ceased, the enemy drew back to the pike, and there was leisure to reckon the living and the dead. Of the 262 officers and men of the First Minnesota who began that fatal charge, 47 answered to roll call and 215 lay dead, dying, or wounded in the pasture, on the slope, or in the swale below, *according to Judge Lochren's statement.* Colvill was crippled for life. Lieutenant Colonel Adams, Major Downie, and Adjutant Peller were severely wounded. A high authority announces this to be the heaviest loss known in the records of modern warfare. Hancock said later: "There is no more gallant deed recorded in history. I ordered these men in there because I saw I must gain five minutes' time. . . . I would have ordered that regiment in if I had known that every man would be killed. It had to be done." No one blundered as at Balaklava. The sacrifice was necessary; those Minnesota troops knew it, and marched proudly into the jaws of death. "When shall their glory fade?"[7]

[7] Herman Haupt, *Reminiscences*, 208-222 (Milwaukee, 1901); Frank A. Flower, "General Herman Haupt," in the same volume, xxix-xxxii; personal interview of the author with General Haupt, August 26, 1905; dispatches in *Official Records*, series 1, vol. 27, part 1, pp. 69-72; report of Wilcox, Confederate brigade commander, in the same work, part 2, p. 618; Lochren, in *Minnesota in the Civil and Indian Wars*, 1:32; the same author's account of "The First Minnesota at Gettysburg," in *Glimpses of the Nation's Struggle*, third series, 42-56; Holcombe, *First Regiment*, 327-348; dispatch of Captain H. C. Coates to Governor Ramsey, July 5, 1863, with an official list of killed and wounded, and Coates's report of August 3, in nearly the same terms as his dispatch, in *Minnesota in the Civil and Indian Wars*, 2: 372-377; William F. Fox, *Regimental Losses in the American Civil War, 1861-1865*, 28 (Albany, 1889). A vivid description of the battle is to be found in a letter signed "Sergeant" and dated July 28, 1863, in the *Saint Paul Pioneer*, August 9, 1863. Colonel Colvill's account is contained in a letter to Hanford L. Gordon published in the *Minneapolis Tribune*, July 28, 1884. In the Folwell Papers is a statement dictated to

But another decimation awaited the little band of surviving heroes. They slept that night under the stars, near the line they defended, and early in the morning of July 3, Company F having returned, they rejoined their brigade, which was already posted in the front line next but one on the left of that brigade of the Second Corps which became the objective of Pickett's charge. The impetus of that charge was sufficient to push back the first line upon its support. The First Minnesota moved on a full run by its flank to the right, mingled with the supporting regiments, and helped to beat back the wave of rebellion which there reached "high tide at Gettysburg." At the very moment of its arrival at the apex of the Confederate onset came Captain Farrell with his Company C — which until then had been absent on provost guard duty — to share in the final repulse. A minute later Farrell found himself in

the author by Colonel Colvill on December 24, 1904. The author has also in his notebooks, 1: 11, 35, records of interviews with Colvill on September 7, 1902, and December 16, 1904. An account of the charge of the First Minnesota as reported by a veteran field officer of the Civil War, dated Gettysburg, June 28, 1897, is reprinted from the *New York Sun* in the *Pioneer Press*, July 3, 1897. See also an article entitled "Colonel of the 'Old First' Dead," in the *Minneapolis Journal*, June 13, 1905, and John Talman, *Minnesota in Panorama: An Historical Poem*, 22-27 (Mapleton, 1923). For complimentary references to the behavior of the regiment at Gettysburg, see John Day Smith, *History of the Nineteenth Regiment of Maine Volunteer Infantry, 1862-1865*, 69, 71, 75, 83, 84 (Minneapolis, 1909). This regiment was brigaded with the First Minnesota. Judge Smith's history is more than a record of the activities of his regiment and is a valuable contribution to the general history of the Civil War. An excellent map of the Gettysburg field, simplified from that in *Official Records*, atlas, vol. 1, plate 43, is in Josephus N. Larned, *History for Ready Reference*, 5: 3500 (Springfield, Massachusetts, 1895).

The author is so well satisfied that his account of the charge on the evening of July 2, 1863, derived from the narrative of Judge Lochren and the signed statement of General Colvill and corroborated by members of the "Old First," is true, that he does not deem it worth while to do more than refer to a claim that Lieutenant Colonel C. Powell Adams was in command throughout the day and until after the charge began, when Colvill rode up. See the *Minneapolis Journal*, December 2, 1903. See also the signed statement of William Lochren, March 11, 1906, and letters to the author from Major J. N. Searles, June 23, 1920, March 8, October 4, 1921, and from George H. Hazzard, September 19, 1921, with accompanying statements of Chester S. Durkee and John O. French, members of the First Regiment, in the Folwell Papers. A reference to the matter is in a letter in the Adams Papers from Adams to Major General John M. Corse, from Fort Abercrombie, November 23, 1865, describing Adams' military career. "After 2nd Fredericksburg, I was promoted to the Lieutenant Colonelcy of my [*First Minnesota*] Regt and was with it in the fight at Haymarket, Va, and subsequently commanded it in the Battle of Gettysburg, Pa." The statement, if true — and it may be — is not an adequate assertion of command at the time of the charge on the evening of July 2. Adams was an officer of undoubted bravery and capacity. The losses of the First Minnesota at Gettysburg are discussed in the Appendix, no. 17, *post*.

command of the regiment, Captain Messick having fallen dead. In another minute he himself lay on the field mortally wounded. All the color guard being disabled, Corporal Henry D. O'Brien seized the flag, its staff already shot in two, and rushed forward "keeping it noticeably in advance of every other color." As he fell stricken with two wounds he passed it to Corporal W. N. Irvine, who carried it on. The Minnesota men sprang forward to protect it and were in at the death. Fifty-five names were added to the list of casualties.[8]

On July 2, 1897, there was unveiled a monument of granite and bronze on that part of the Cemetery Ridge from which the First Minnesota launched its charge on the same day of the month thirty-four years before. All the survivors who were able to leave their homes and travel were

---

[8] The head of Pickett's charge struck the left of the Second Brigade, under Webb, as the men in gray were "pouring over the stone fence." Hall, the commander of the Third Brigade, next on the left, perceiving the imminent danger, retired his line slightly and moved it on a run to the right behind Webb's men. The First Brigade (Harrow's), including the First Minnesota, immediately followed the movement. The three brigades were thus massed and organization was temporarily lost. Man-to-man fighting became general. The loss of twenty-three killed or mortally wounded and possibly of thirty-two officers and men more or less severely wounded in the *mêlée* is good proof that the Minnesota remnant of some hundred and fifty men did its full share of the fighting. See the reports of commanders in *Official Records*, series 1, vol. 27, part 1, pp. 416, 420, 423, 424, 426, 428, 437-441. For graphic accounts of the participation of the First Regiment in the battle of July 3, see Holcombe, *First Regiment*, 369, and Lochren, in *Minnesota in the Civil and Indian Wars*, 1: 36-38. Judge Lochren, for many years the author's nearest neighbor, gave him the same account in frequent interviews. According to Lochren, the men even picked up stones and threw them. An article describing the activities of "Co. C. at Gettysburg" on the same day is in the *Minneapolis Journal* for June 30, 1897. See also Wright, "Company F., First Regiment," 603-618. The concluding paragraph of the description of this day's events may be quoted as an example of the latter author's literary style. "After the care of the wounded . . . our next care was something to eat . . . we built little fires and made coffee. . . . and as we drank our coffee we decided to bury Hamline that night. Search was made for a spade and after some time a shovel was found. With this a shallow trench was dug beside a walnut tree, near which he had been killed, struck by four bullets. His blanket and tent-cloth were spread in it, he was then laid upon them and covered with the remaining portions. Then those present knelt in silence about him, with uncovered, bowed heads. I do not now recall that a word was spoken. . . . Then we covered him over with the dirt and stones we had thrown out of the trench and placed at his head a board, on which his name, company and regiment, had been marked. Then we went back to where *three* stacks of guns marked the position of Co. F. in the line — one of the largest companies in the regiment. . . . we laid down to sleep and in a few minutes were oblivious to all of the suffering and sorrow about us." See pages 594-596 for the engagement of Company F as skirmishers on July 2. Wright's account of the long march from the Rappahannock to the Gettysburg field, beginning on page 534, is good reading. For an account of Wright's narrative see *ante*, p. 86, n. 4.

transported to Gettysburg and back at the expense of the state. Addresses were delivered by the governor of Minnesota, David M. Clough, Judge William Lochren, General Colvill, Senator Cushman K. Davis, and others, including Major Martin Maginnis, whose description of the charge is the most graphic that has been found. The monument consists of a base and die of granite, surmounted by the figure of a private soldier running with his gun at a charge bayonet.[9]

A bronze statue of General William Colvill, designed and modeled by Mrs. George J. Backus of Minneapolis and erected by the Colvill Monument Association under the dome of the State Capitol, was unveiled on March 31, 1909, with addresses by Captain Jasper N. Searles, by Governor John A. Johnson, read by Lieutenant Governor Eberhart, and by James J. Hill, read by Judge John Day Smith, and with singing by Mrs. Alma Johnson Porteous. A reporter

[9] *Minneapolis Tribune*, July 3, 1897; *Pioneer Press*, July 3, 1897. For Senator Cushman K. Davis' speech at the dedication of the monument see Holcombe, *First Regiment*, 432-438. A picture of the monument is opposite page 350. The figure of the soldier was designed and modeled by Jacob H. G. Fjelde of Minneapolis, a Norwegian by birth and training who had made his home in America. He died on May 5, 1896, a year and two months before the unveiling. In conversation with the author, Fjelde said that he had given up his preference for a design less bold and spectacular. Among the works left by this gifted artist may be mentioned the statue of Ole Bull in Loring Park, Minneapolis, the figure of "History" on the facade of the Minneapolis Public Library, the exquisite allegorical figures which adorn the atrium of the library of the University of Minnesota, and portrait busts of President Cyrus Northrop and the author. The appropriation of twenty thousand dollars for the monument was made by the legislature of 1891, which provided that the sum be expended by a commission of three men appointed by the governor to serve without compensation. A preamble to the act states that the regiment charged a Confederate force more than twenty times its size and suffered a loss of more than four-fifths of its numbers. See *General Laws*, 1891, p. 292. An additional appropriation of five thousand dollars was made on April 3, 1897, for the dedication of the monument by the governor of Minnesota and his staff in the presence of veterans of the regiment who participated in the charge of July 2 or who would have taken part but for wounds or sickness on the march to the battle ground and any who had previously been discharged from service for wounds. There were 165 veterans present. See *General Laws*, 1897, p. 112, and the *Pioneer Press*, July 8, 1897. It should be mentioned here that the memorial of 1897 replaced a simpler one erected by members of the regiment in 1867. To pay for the erection of this monument, the regimental band instruments were sold for $350 and that sum was raised to $1,000 by subscriptions. Governor Stephen Miller attended to the expenditure of the money. The structure then erected was of white marble surmounted by an urn, the whole about six feet high. On the face of the die was a dedication by survivors and on the reverse was the name of the regiment; on one side was inscribed the motto, "The dead shall not have died in vain," on the other, "All time is the millennium of their glory." The monument erected in 1867 was "the first special decoration permitted or erected in the Soldiers' National Cemetery" and permission to erect it was given reluctantly. *Saint Paul Press*, November 10, 1867; Miller to Adams, January 16, 23, March 28, 1865, Adams Papers.

says that there was "scarcely a dry eye" at the close of Hill's address. A replica of the statue was unveiled on May 29, 1909, at Cannon Falls, Minnesota, where Colvill's body had been buried in 1905. Addresses by Governor Johnson, Frank M. Wilson, and Major Martin Maginnis and some stanzas of a poem by Hanford L. Gordon, who had served in the regiment, were read. A bronze tablet commemorative of the First Regiment, with emphasis on the charge at Gettysburg, was installed in the rotunda of the State Capitol.[10]

Criticism of Meade's leisurely movements after his repulse of Lee at Gettysburg may be left to the military historian. Moving on parallel lines separated by the Blue Ridge, the two armies marched southward, to confront each other on the line of the Rappahannock in the last days of July. In the middle of August the First Minnesota was placed in a provisional brigade which was sent to New York to assure the authorities of that city of the preservation of order after the suppression of the draft riots of July 11 to 16. The detachment spent a fortnight in comfortable camps on Governor's Island and in a Brooklyn park, without being called upon to use its arms. It returned to the Army of the Potomac on September 16, after an absence of a month and a day. The remnant of the First, equal to about two full companies fit for the field, saw no more rough service. By midwinter it was ascertained that there would be no

[10] *Pioneer Press*, April 1, 1909; *Minneapolis Journal*, May 30, 1909; Holcombe, *First Regiment*, 392, 443, 446. The cost of the bronze statue in the Capitol was paid out of an appropriation of ten thousand dollars by the legislature of 1907. See *General Laws*, 1907, p. 81. The address of Major Maginnis at the unveiling of the replica of the statue at Cannon Falls was read by Major William D. Hale. Gordon's poem, written in 1884 under the title "Gettysburg: Charge of the First Minnesota," was printed as a four-page pamphlet and placed in Holcombe, *First Minnesota*, as a loose insert. The poet's pictures of Hancock "spurring his panting charger till his foaming flanks dripped blood" and of the First Minnesota springing "like a fierce pack of hunger-mad wolves that pant for the blood of the prey" is in sharp contrast to Judge Lochren's prose. In another version of the poem, printed as a four-page folder, Gordon represents Hancock shouting, "Here — by the God of our fathers! — here shall the battle be won." A picture of the bronze tablet in the Capitol is in Holcombe, *First Regiment*, opposite page 418. A separate monument at Gettysburg consisting of a base and die surmounted by an obelisk of granite commemorates the participation of the fragment of the regiment in the repulse of Pickett's charge on July 3, 1863. A picture of the latter monument may be found in Holcombe, *First Regiment*, opposite page 378.

general reënlistment. As its three-year term of enlistment would expire before the opening of a new campaign, the command was ordered to Fort Snelling, where it was mustered out of the service on May 5, 1864.[11]

On the crest of the "Snodgrass Ridge" in the national park at Chickamauga, Tennessee, stands a tasteful monument of bronze and granite, on which is inscribed "The Second Regiment, Minnesota Veteran Volunteer Infantry, occupied this position Sunday, September 20th, 1863, from 2:30 P.M. to 7:30 P.M." It is not necessary for the present purpose to relate the maneuvers which brought the Union Army under Rosecrans face to face with the Confederate force under Bragg in the valley of Chickamauga Creek on September 20, 1863. With numbers swelled somewhat above those of his enemy by the arrival on the day before of two divisions of Longstreet's corps detached from Lee's army in Virginia, Bragg planned to turn the Union left, disperse the troops intrenched there, seize on the two gaps through Missionary Ridge, and destroy or capture the whole Union Army. The plan failed because of the stout resistance encountered but an unexpected opportunity for a change of the rebel tactics was soon presented. The issue of an order by Rosecrans through a misunderstanding of the situation and its stupid interpretation by a division commander resulted in the retirement of a whole division from the general line of battle. Through the gaps thus opened the Confederate troops plunged with tremendous ferocity and put the whole Union right and part of its center into headlong flight on the roads leading back to Chattanooga.

Rosecrans and some of his general officers, swept along with the tide, hastened to Chattanooga to rally and reform the fugitives. But he left behind an abler general — Thomas, ever after known as the "Rock of Chickamauga" — with orders to take command of the field and hold the enemy

[11] Lochren, in *Minnesota in the Civil and Indian Wars*, 1:38; Wright, "Company F, First Regiment," 676-727, 844-875.

in check as long as possible. It was Thomas' corps, the
Fourteenth, which in the morning had frustrated the
movement to turn the Union left. In rear of his left ran
nearly east and west an elongated hillock known as the
"Snodgrass" or "Horseshoe" Ridge. It extended about
a mile, to abut on the eastern slope of Missionary Ridge,

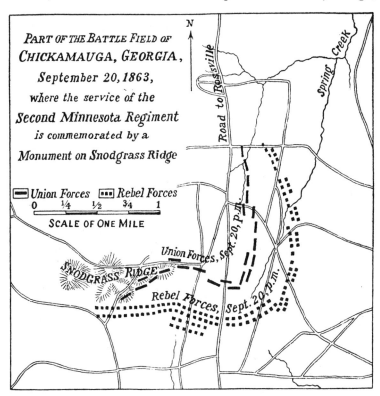

leaving a narrow space for the Dry Valley road to MacFar-
land's Gap. Its elevation was almost a hundred feet
above the plain of the valley and it had several terraces.
On the crest of the Snodgrass Ridge Thomas, still holding
in check the Confederate right, posted in single line one
of his still unbroken divisions and to it he rallied such
fractional commands as his aids and orderlies could summon.

Longstreet, who had been in command of the left wing of
the Confederate Army, had now a battle of his own before
him.  With a change of front forward of four divisions he
launched brigade after brigade on Thomas' thin line lying
along the crest of the Snodgrass Ridge.  He would doubtless
have carried the ridge but for the arrival in mid-afternoon
of General Granger with two divisions of his reserve corps,
which he had marched four miles *au canon*, bringing some
wagonloads of ammunition.  Late in the afternoon Longstreet flung forward Preston's division, which had not yet
been engaged.  The fresh battalions in successive charges
swept up the southern slope of the hill, denuded of brush-
wood by the hail of bullets, but were repulsed within a
few paces of the crest.  But Thomas' thin line of heroes
held the crest until sunset and then, its sacrifice accomplished, it marched away for the Rossville Gap, leaving
behind all the dead and most of the wounded of the day's
battle.  The Confederate troops slept on the field after their
great victory, but they had neither legs nor stomachs for
pursuit.  The Second Minnesota, commanded by Colonel
James George, had a part in the defense of the Snodgrass
Ridge.  It nobly performed that part and richly earned
the monument erected by a grateful commonwealth.
Including some small casualties of the day before and those
of the morning, its losses were 45 killed, 103 wounded, and
14 captured while caring for wounded — 162 casualties
out of a total of 384 engaged.  Not a single man was missing.[12]

[12] See Judson W. Bishop, *The Story of a Regiment: Being a Narrative of the Service
of the Second Regiment, Minnesota Veteran Volunteer Infantry, in the Civil War*, 113-142
(St. Paul, 1890); the account by the same author in *Minnesota in the Civil and Indian Wars*,
1:95-101; and his *Van Derveer's Brigade at Chickamauga*, a paper read before the Minnesota
Commandery of the Loyal Legion, on May 12, 1903, and published with a map of the
battle field as a twenty-four-page pamphlet (n.p., n.d.).  Chaplain Levi Gleason, in "The
Experiences and Observations of a Drafted Man in the Civil War," in *Glimpses of the
Nation's Struggle*, sixth series, 554, gives an appreciation of Bishop.  See also James K.
Hosmer, *Outcome of the Civil War, 1863-1865*, 23-40 (*The American Nation: A History*,
vol. 21 — New York, 1907); reports of Rosecrans and his corps, division, brigade, and
regimental commanders in *Official Records*, series 1, vol. 30, part 1, all easily found by means
of the roster, on pages 40-47, and the index.  On pages 182-221 may be found the dispatches
— for several weeks before and after the battle — from Charles A. Dana, assistant secretary of war, to Stanton.  In his *Recollections of the Civil War; with the Leaders at Wash-*

THE SECOND MINNESOTA AT THE BATTLE OF MISSIONARY RIDGE

*Oil by Douglas Volk in the Minnesota Capitol*

THE THIRD MINNESOTA ENTERING LITTLE ROCK, ARKANSAS

*Oil by Stanley M. Arthurs in the Minnesota Capitol*

The Second Minnesota and the army to which it belonged were soon to recover their prestige, however. Soon after the rout at Chickamauga Bragg seized on Missionary Ridge, overlooking Chattanooga from the east, and Lookout Mountain, dominating the place from the south, and stretched a long line of intrenchments between them. Confederate batteries shut off steamboat navigation on the Tennessee. The railroad to Nashville was useless and there remained but a single wagon road connecting the Union Army with the base of supplies. Chattanooga was besieged. The army was put on half rations and thousands of animals died of starvation. The necessary transfer of Rosecrans to other service was ordered on October 19 and four days later Grant, who had been put in command of the Military Department of the Mississippi, arrived at Chattanooga. Under his orders the blockade of the Tennessee was raised in the course of five days and subsistence and forage arrived in abundance. Reënforced by a part of Sherman's army and two corps brought by Hooker from the Army of the Potomac, he was ready within a month to try to dislodge Bragg, who had been weakened by the departure of Longstreet's divisions to attack Burnside at Knoxville. Heavy rains caused a few days' delay, but on November 24 a carefully studied movement began. Sherman's army was established on the northern end of Missionary Ridge, which flattened out as it neared the river. Hooker on the same

ington and in the Field in the Sixties, 104-131 (New York, 1908), Dana greatly moderated the tone of the dispatches. See Official Records, series 1, vol. 30, part 1, pp. 58, 101-105, 645-647, for correspondence of Rosecrans and Wood regarding the responsibility for the break in the line. In the same work, series 1, vol. 30, part 2, by using the roster on pages 7-11 and the index, may be found the reports of Bragg and his subordinate commanders. Longstreet and his general officers claim that Thomas' line was dislodged from the Snodgrass Ridge, but the regimental and battalion commanders agree that they were unable to reach the crest and were obliged to cease their charges. Daniel H. Hill, a Confederate officer, in an article entitled "Chickamauga — The Great Battle of the West," in Battles and Leaders of the Civil War, 3: 661 (New York, [1884]), admits that Thomas held on until nightfall. See also Joseph S. Fullerton, "Reënforcing Thomas at Chickamauga," in the same work, 3: 665-667, in which the author, a Union officer, gives high praise to General Granger. For maps of the battle field, see Official Records, atlas, vol. 1, plates 46, 47, 48. Fifteen thousand dollars were appropriated by the Minnesota legislature for monuments at Chickamauga and Chattanooga. General Laws, 1893, p. 378.

day drove the enemy from Lookout Mountain and connected with the right of the Army of the Cumberland, now commanded by Thomas. The sun of November 25 rose upon the final act. Sherman, in the saddle before daybreak, roused his sleeping corps to their task of doubling back the Confederate right and seizing Bragg's communications. Hooker's activity on the Union right was giving the enemy plenty of occupation. The Army of the Cumberland, arranged in double lines, lay in front of the fortified center

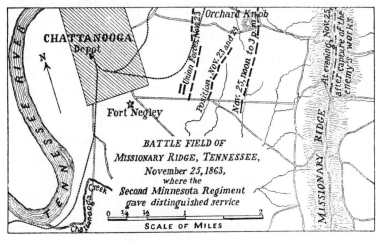

BATTLE FIELD OF
MISSIONARY RIDGE, TENNESSEE,
November 25, 1863,
where the
Second Minnesota Regiment
gave distinguished service

SCALE OF MILES

of the enemy. The rumor had run down the line that this army was to take an object lesson from Sherman and Hooker and was to be allowed to participate in the pursuit of the routed enemy. The hours wore on. Noon came and passed. Sherman's army was fighting its best, but it could not gain ground much beyond "the tunnel," two miles away from Thomas' left. Bragg had sent every man he dared to take from other portions of his line. Grant became anxious about Sherman's condition, the more so because Hooker's expected attack on the Confederate left had been delayed four hours by the crossing of Chattanooga Creek. It was late in the afternoon when he gave Thomas the order to advance on the enemy's first line at the foot of Missionary

Ridge, a mile away. Under a heavy fire of artillery and musketry the corps moved forward with lines dressed as if on parade. When it arrived at the foot of the ridge a brief halt was made and then the whole body, without orders, it is alleged, sprang forward and swarmed tumultuously up the rugged hillside and over the Confederate breastworks, capturing guns, colors, and prisoners. It was a soldiers' battle.

The part of the Second Minnesota was conspicuous and honorable. To it was assigned the duty of leading its brigade. Lieutenant Colonel — afterwards Brigadier General — Judson W. Bishop led forward the command deployed as skirmishers and drove back with loss a strong line of the enemy posted in rifle pits on a ridge a little in advance of the foot of the main hill. Here he held his ground under artillery fire for twenty minutes while the brigade was coming up. From this point his men joined in the scramble for the ridge and in the crowning jubilee. The Army of the Cumberland had won the battle. The Second Minnesota lost eight killed and thirty-one wounded. Six out of seven members of the color guard fell. The Second Minnesota at Missionary Ridge is the subject of one of the paintings which decorate the State Capitol. The subject is worthy of such distinction and of the artist, Douglas Volk, long resident in Minnesota.[13]

[13] Dispatch of Dana to Stanton and reports of Grant, Thomas, Baird, Van Derveer, and Bishop in *Official Records*, series 1, vol. 31, part 2, pp. 27-35, 69, 92-97, 507-510, 527-529, 533-536. Van Derveer says, "Especial credit is due Lieutenant-Colonel Bishop for the management of his regiment when skirmishing in front of the brigade, and in the gallant manner in which his command carried the rifle-pits at the foot of the ridge." In the same volume, pp. 664-683, are the reports of Bragg and of his subordinate commanders. Bragg could find no possible excuse for the conduct of his troops, but he offered as an explanation the effect produced upon them by beholding the immense forces of the enemy in plain sight for two days. According to all accounts, the battle of Chattanooga on Thomas' front was nothing but a stampede from start to finish. See also Ulysses S. Grant, *Personal Memoirs*, 2:77-82 (New York, 1886); Adam Badeau, *Military History of Ulysses S. Grant, from April, 1861, to April, 1865*, 1:503-513 (New York, 1881); and Ulysses S. Grant, "Chattanooga," in *Battles and Leaders of the Civil War*, 3:704-708. Grant writes of the final charge: "Without awaiting further orders or stopping to re-form, on our troops went to the second line of works; over that and on for the crest." The Minnesota reader will be interested in the article on pages 676-678 of the last work, "The Little Steamboat that Opened the 'Cracker Line,'" by William G. Le Duc, a pioneer Minnesotan. See also the maps in *Official Records*, atlas, vol. 1, plates 49 and 50, and a simplification of these in Larned, *History for Ready Reference*, 5:3510.

It was the fortune of the Fourth Minnesota to partake in numerous movements and actions without heavy losses. In the siege of Vicksburg its behavior was so efficient and gallant as to secure, along with its brigade, the honor of leading the victorious column into the surrendered fortress. It was a further compliment that the regiment was detailed as provost guard of the city for the remaining summer months. Here sickness and death wrought greater havoc than the weapons of the enemy. In August there were 631 officers and men absent, "nearly all sick in hospitals." The promotion of Colonel John B. Sanborn to the rank of brigadier general left the command of the regiment to Colonel John E. Tourtellotte, an excellent officer. The Fourth had a full share in the glory won by the little garrison of 1,944 men, which, under the command of General Corse, "held the fort" at Allatoona on October 5, 1864, against a Confederate division 7,000 strong. The historian of the regiment records that "Several of our men fought in this battle after the period of their enlistments had expired, and some of these were killed in the action."[14]

Sherman occupied Atlanta on September 2, 1864, but the Confederate garrison of forty thousand veterans had escaped and presently, under the leadership of the bold and enterprising Hood, it threw itself by a rapid march upon Sherman's communications north of the captured city. Sherman followed with a superior force and chased Hood nearly to Chattanooga, when the Confederate general, unwilling to risk a battle, withdrew into eastern Alabama and occupied a position from which he could fall upon Sherman's communications at will. Sherman now decided, with Grant's approval, to abandon those communications and Atlanta itself and make the famous march to the sea. It was his belief, as well as Grant's, that Hood would strike

[14] Brown, in *Minnesota in the Civil and Indian Wars*, 1:198-219; Brown, *Fourth Regiment*, 106, 131, 213, 305-329; report of Lieutenant Colonel John E. Tourtellotte, May 24, 1863, in *Executive Documents*, 1863, pp. 245-250. A large mural painting in the governor's office in the Minnesota Capitol portrays General J. B. Sanborn leading his brigade, including the Fourth Regiment, into the fortress of Vicksburg.

for the north to sweep up the separated detachments of Union troops in Tennessee and Kentucky. As it appears from Hood's own later statements, it was his expectation to occupy Nashville and from there to dominate Tennessee. With his battalions well recruited and abundantly supplied he intended then to move on to a point of vantage in Kentucky, such as Richmond in Madison County, prepared to fight Sherman, should he return, or to march through Cumberland Gap and attack Grant in rear. Sherman provided for this emergency by sending Thomas to Nashville to assemble an army sufficient to defeat Hood or at least to hold him in check. To gain time for concentration and equipment, Thomas was obliged to order Schofield to fight the bloody battle of Franklin with less than twenty-five thousand men. Here on November 30, only twenty miles south of Nashville, Hood gained a technical victory indeed, but one which cost him nearly seven thousand men and impaired the morale of his army for the battle which he hoped might restore the prestige of the Confederacy in the West. He immediately followed up his apparent advantage and on December 3 besieged Nashville.[15] He probably believed that he had Thomas there bottled up, as Bragg had fancied with regard to Rosecrans' army at Chattanooga.

The whole North was alarmed and the war department was in a panic. Stanton authorized Thomas to impress horses and property of every kind needed for military purposes wherever he could find them, and to call upon governors of all western states for militia. Every available man in western departments was ordered to Thomas. On December 2 Grant urged Thomas to attack before Hood had time to intrench and four days later Grant

---

[15] William T. Sherman, "The Grand Strategy of the Last Year of the War," in *Battles and Leaders of the Civil War*, 4: 254-257; John B. Hood, "The Invasion of Tennessee," in the same work, 4: 426; reports of Thomas, Wood, Schofield, and Hood, in *Official Records*, series I, vol. 45, part I, pp. 45, 124, 341-344, 654; pertinent correspondence in the same volume, pp. 1085, 1106, 1108, 1169-1171. For a map of the Franklin battle field, see *Official Records*, atlas, vol. I, plate 72.

peremptorily ordered a movement. On the ninth an order relieving Thomas and placing Schofield in command at Nashville was made out. Before it could be dispatched a telegram came from Thomas saying that a "terrible storm of freezing rain" made it impossible for him to fight to advantage but that should it be thought best to relieve him he would "submit without a murmur." Grant thereupon suspended the order "until it is seen whether he will do anything." On December 11 Grant telegraphed, "Delay no longer for weather or reënforcements" and reminded Thomas that a rebel army moving for the Ohio would force him to fight whatever the weather might be. His patience exhausted, on December 13 Grant ordered Logan to Nashville and started there himself. By that time Thomas was "ready" and on the evening of the fourteenth he issued his order of battle.[16]

The main operation of the battle of December 15 was a general left wheel which drove the Confederates from their intrenchments but did not prevent them from occupying new positions in the rear which they held until nightfall. Because of this retirement the losses were not heavy. The night following was passed by both armies in preparation for the great battle which they knew awaited them. Hood withdrew to a range of hillocks running nearly east and west and formed a new line some two and a half miles long with both flanks sharply refused. In portions stone fences were used as revetments and elsewhere such defenses as time and means allowed were established. Thomas' men slept where the day's fighting had brought them.

After sending his cavalry and Schofield's corps on a detour around the left flank of the enemy, Thomas on the sixteenth leisurely gave his main force a right wheel which brought

[16] *Official Records*, series 1, vol. 45, part 2, pp. 17, 28, 29, 36, 39, 70, 75, 96, 114, 115, 143, 155, 171, 180, 183, 195. For correspondence of Grant and Sherman touching Thomas' delays, see the same work, series 1, vol. 44, pp. 612, 636, 726, 740, 788, 841. Thomas' order of battle is in series 1, vol. 45, part 1, p. 37.

it roughly parallel to the Confederate position at distances
varying from three hundred to six hundred yards. At
three o'clock in the afternoon a gallant charge was made
by a brigade of Wood's corps on Overton's Hill held by
Hood's right, and held so firmly that the attempt was
a failure and was attended by a loss of five hundred brave

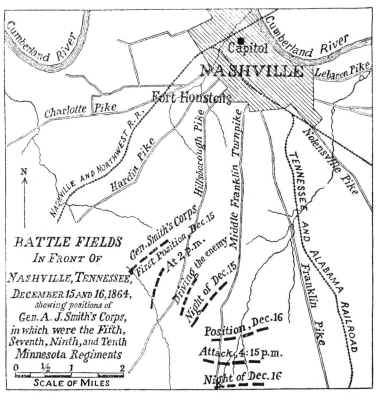

men. Thomas, believing that Hood had weakened his
left to resist that charge, resolved to attack it and selected
McArthur's division of A. J. Smith's corps to make the
initial assault. McArthur's First Brigade was to lead off
and when it should be halfway up the hill the two other
brigades on his left should advance. After some delay,
McArthur sent word to his superior that, unless forbidden,

he would advance. Having received no reply, about four
o'clock he ordered his first brigade — McMillen's — with
the Tenth Minnesota on the left of his first line to begin
the assault up the considerable hill in his front. "At the
appointed time" Hubbard, commanding the Second Brigade,
with the Fifth and Ninth Minnesota forming his first line,
received his order and led his eager men forward. Marshall,
commanding the Third Brigade with the Seventh Minnesota
on the left of his first line, received no order but, seeing
Hubbard on his right moving and in need of support, he
took up the charge. These brigades, which advanced over
nearly level ground, probably arrived at the enemy's
works at about the same time as the First. It was now late
in the day and the sky was cloudy and showers of cold
rain were falling. The intervening ground was partly a
muddy cornfield and generally was strewn with boulders
and obstructed by stone walls, ditches, and rail fences.
The enemy had a cross fire of artillery and musketry over
nearly its whole extent. Led by their gallant commanders,
mounted, the three brigades went for the rebel line, with
bayonets fixed, as rapidly as it was possible to march over
such ground, with never a halt nor a break. With men falling
fast and thick, they swept over the enemy's parapets, without stopping to fire, and seized guns and battle flags and
took hundreds of prisoners. Some regiments claimed to
have taken more prisoners than they had men in line. A
general charge along the whole front now easily broke
up and captured or put to rout the whole Confederate
Army and virtually ended the war in the West.

This glorious charge was not made without serious
losses. The Minnesota regiments left 302 of their numbers
on the field. Jennison, lieutenant colonel commanding the
Tenth, was struck down with a disabling wound as he was
leading his battalion over the works and Hubbard was
wounded and had his horse shot under him. The colors of
all the regiments were repeatedly shot down. Three color

bearers of the Fifth were killed and four of the color guard were wounded. The question has never been settled as to which one of the North Star regiments was first to plant its colors on the enemy's parapet or which took the greatest number of guns, battle flags, and prisoners. The contention will go on as long as any of the veterans are living. When they have passed away, all will share equally in the gratitude of their country. Marshall and Hubbard both became governors of Minnesota. The latter won his star at Nashville and the former was especially complimented in the report of the division commander as "an officer of rare merit."[17]

[17] Reports of Thomas, Smith, McArthur, McMillen, Sanders, Hubbard, Gere, Marsh, Marshall, and Bradley, in *Official Records*, series 1, vol. 45, part 1, pp. 38-40, 434-436, 437-440, 441-443, 444-448, 449-452, 452-454, 460-462, 466-468. All these reports except that of Thomas are printed in part or in full in *Minnesota in the Civil and Indian Wars*, 2: 580-606b, and with the further exceptions of those of McArthur, McMillen, Smith, and Marshall, in Minnesota, *Executive Documents*, 1865, pp. 145-165. A critical reader may observe a departure in Marshall's report as printed in *Minnesota in the Civil and Indian Wars*, 2: 601, from that given in *Official Records*, 461. In the former version the general distinctly asserts that he moved his brigade without orders, that the brigades advanced "*en échelon*," and, therefore, arrived successively at the enemy's works. McArthur's compliment to Marshall, "His admirable management and example stamp him as an officer of rare merit," was, it may be presumed, called out by Marshall's leading his brigade in the charge without orders. See also Lucius F. Hubbard, *Minnesota in the Battles of Nashville, December 15th and 16th, 1864*, an address delivered before the Minnesota Commandery of the Loyal Legion (St. Paul, [1905]). This paper, first published in pamphlet form, is reprinted in *Glimpses of the Nation's Struggle*, sixth series, 259-284, and in *Minnesota Historical Collections*, 12: 597-614. In this account Hubbard uses language calculated to convey the impression that all the brigades of McArthur's division began the charge simultaneously and reached the enemy's works at the same moment, thus making a slight departure from his original report. Hubbard is in error in stating that the four Minnesota regiments formed a continuous line. The Twelfth Iowa on the right of the Third Brigade line separated the Seventh Minnesota from the Fifth, which formed the extreme left of the adjoining Second Brigade. See *Official Records*, series 1, vol. 45, part 1, p. 463. General A. J. Smith, corps commander, states in his report in the same volume, p. 436, that Hubbard had three horses shot under him, but the latter makes no allusion to this. The battles of Nashville are described by the historians of the regiments concerned, in *Minnesota in the Civil and Indian Wars*, 1: 274-277, 358-361, 430-433, 466-469. A striking oil painting of the battle of Nashville by Howard Pyle hangs in the governor's room at the Capitol; along with it are paintings of the First Minnesota at Gettysburg, the Second at Missionary Ridge, the Third at Little Rock, and the Fifth at Corinth. The author takes the occasion to express the opinion that such memorials of a war between sister states in the American Union are not in good taste. The Roman custom of preserving no memorials of a civil war is one that America, now united forever, may properly follow.

# XII. GLEANINGS

IN A CLOSING chapter we may gather up some matters occurring in the Civil War period which are worthy of record and which have been passed over for the sake of preserving an unbroken narrative.

The legislature of 1860, the same which proposed the amendment to the state constitution expunging from that document the Five Million Loan article of 1858, by an act approved on March 6 directed the governor to foreclose on behalf of the state all the mortgages covering the properties of the four land grant railroad companies and in his discretion to bid them in for the state at the sale. The proceedings of foreclosure by action were conducted with unimpeachable accuracy and, with one exception, were brought to completion on June 23 and October 16. Temporary injunctions sued out by two of the companies were ignored by the executive as trenching on his constitutional prerogative. In each case Governor Ramsey bid for the state the sum of one thousand dollars and bought all the right of way, lands, property, franchises, privileges, and immunities of the corporation. When the transactions were consummated the state was again in full control in trust of all lands granted for railroads in 1857 and had to the good 240 miles of graded roadbed, somewhat the worse for flood and frost.[1]

---

[1] *General Laws*, 1860, p. 269; message of Governor Ramsey in *Executive Documents*, 1860, no. 1, p. 10. In Governor's Archives, Records, A, 206-208, 254, are copies of the certificates of sale of the Minnesota and Pacific, the Transit, and the Southern Minnesota railroad companies, the two former dated June 23 and the latter, October 16. See the *Pioneer and Democrat*, June 24, 1860, for "Bluff Aleck's" direction to Auctioneer Benjamin W. Brunson to "go on" and pay no attention to the protest of James M. Winslow, presented by Attorney George A. Nourse, that the sale was illegal in view of the injunction issued a few days before by the Ramsey County district court. The mortgage on the Minneapolis and Cedar Valley road was foreclosed later by the trustees. For Engineer J. S. Sewall's report on the amount and cost of construction by the companies, see *Proceedings of the Board of Commissioners under the Provisions of an Act Approved February 28, 1866*, 47-52 (Five Million Loan Pamphlets, no. 13). The bibliography of railroads by J. Fletcher Williams, in *Minnesota Historical Collections*, 3: 44-50, gives the titles of many early publications. See *ante*, p. 56.

The need and desire of the people for railroad communication with the outside eastern world was now even more pressing. If there was any expectation that lively competition would set in for the new franchises and grants held in trust, it was disappointed. The credit of the state had suffered in the course of its railroad operations during the last three years. Money was still scarce and interest ranged from two per cent a month upward. There were plenty of opportunities for railroad investments in other and older states. When the legislature of 1861 convened no throng of promoters and contractors distracted the members. The whole winter passed in reflection and planning for the revival of building. The four companies, although stripped of all their belongings, had maintained their organizations. Among their stockholders were men of some means, of high character, and with great faith in the future of the state. If liberal conditions could be granted they were willing to resume the construction of the roads. The legislature was, or became, willing to be liberal. On March 8, 1861, it sanctioned four separate acts releasing and restoring to the companies all property and assets covered by the several foreclosures, free from all claims and liens. Construction was to begin immediately and three of the companies were to have ten miles of road ready for operation before the close of the calendar year; the fourth company was to construct twenty miles in the same length of time; certain mileages were to be completed in several periods of years following; the sum of ten thousand dollars in cash or in public stocks was to be deposited with the governor, to be forfeited upon failure of compliance with conditions; and, in case of default by any company, any other persons or company might take over the property and franchises under like conditions. In the cases of two companies annual payments of a percentage of their gross earnings were to be in lieu of all taxation and assessment.[2]

---

[2] *Special Laws*, 1861, pp. 213-238.

The year 1861 was not a favorable period for opening new enterprises and raising money. The ear-piercing fife and the spirit-stirring drum rudely drowned the negotiations of market and exchange. One only of the four companies, the Minnesota and Pacific, succeeded in making a beginning of construction that year—on its main line out of St. Paul northward—and that was disappointingly meager. At the close of the season its contractors had laid ties and rails on fourteen hundred feet of track on the roadbed of 1858, starting from the St. Paul levee, over which they had moved the single locomotive purchased to a place of storage for the winter. The company had done what it could and had forfeited its rights under the acts of 1861.[3]

Another winter passed in consultations and negotiations. The outcome was four separate statutes—all approved on March 10, 1862—to "facilitate" the construction of the several roads by amending previous legislation. These acts technically created four new corporations, which represented substantially the same interests with changes of personnel. The Saint Paul and Pacific Company, successor to the Minnesota and Pacific, was the only one which promptly began construction. It was required by law to build to St. Anthony by September 1. The track laying reached that place on July 2, but regular operation was of course delayed. The newspapers of October 14 printed "Time-Table No. 1," announcing four trains each way daily. The fare was sixty cents, including the omnibus fare at both ends. Late in the fall of 1863 two companies had completed forty-six and one-half miles of road; in the next year three companies built forty-three and one-half miles. The year 1865 was more fruitful: all four of the companies built unequal stretches aggregating 110 miles. The total mileage at the close of the year was 210.[4]

[3] Annual message of Governor Ramsey, in *Executive Documents*, 1861, p. 21.

[4] *Special Laws*, 1862, pp. 226-255; annual message of Governor Ramsey, in *Executive Documents*, 1862, p. 22. In Neill, *Minnesota*, opposite page 786, is a table giving the mileage constructed by each railroad annually from 1862 to 1881. See the map opposite page 38, *ante*.

THE "WILLIAM CROOKS," MINNESOTA'S FIRST LOCOMOTIVE

EARLY PASSENGER TRAINS ON THE NORTHERN PACIFIC LINE

LAYING TRACK NEAR NEW ULM
*Photograph by Sattler and Meyer, New Ulm*

How the admission of Minnesota was obstructed by the proslavery propaganda has been told.[5] Another interesting example of obstruction to her progress is found in the long delay of the Homestead Law. Already mooted in occasional utterances, the proposition to give free lands to settlers on the public domain became a public question in 1852, when the Free-soil–Democratic convention held at Pittsburgh on August 11 made it a plank in its platform. Seven years later — 1859 — a homestead bill was passed by the House of Representatives by a vote of 120 to 76. There were but two southern votes in favor of the bill and but seven northern votes against it. The Senate rejected the bill. At the next session, in 1860, the House passed the same bill, in substance, by a vote of 115 to 65. Not a single southern vote was given for it and but one from the North was cast against it. The Senate amended the bill; the House refused concurrence. Both agreed to the report of the conference committee and passed the bill. President Buchanan vetoed it in an elaborate message, giving his objections in nine numbered paragraphs, all of which but the first were superfluous, if it was valid. Congress, argued the president, has no power under the Constitution to give away the public lands of which it is a trustee; and perhaps this was good law. In 1861, with a western man in the White House, the western members of Congress were hopeful of a better issue. On July 8 Cyrus Aldrich of Minnesota introduced the homestead bill into the House in the first session of the Thirty-seventh Congress. It was not taken up until the second session, when it passed easily through the usual stages. It was approved on May 20, 1862. In the three-year period from 1863 to 1865 inclusive, 9,529 homestead entries for 1,237,722.13 acres were made in Minnesota.[6]

[5] See *ante*, pp. 9-21; 1: 390-392.
[6] *Statutes at Large*, 12: 392-394; Donaldson, in his *Public Domain*, 332-356 (serial 2158), gives the history of the bill, the text of the act, statistics of homesteading, and President Buchanan's veto message. Buchanan's objections were: (1) Congress had no power to make such donations; (2) the act would prove unjust and unequal in its operation among the settlers themselves; (3) it would work an injustice to old soldiers by reducing the value of

That the Homestead Act was beneficent at first and in great part cannot be questioned. It operated to spread over great areas of arable land a population whose industry enriched the country and the government far more than the sale of the land could have done. Whether the active promoters of the measure had any expectation that its provisions might be twisted out of their obvious line of operation is not known. It is the fact, however, that not long after the passage of the act individuals, firms, and corporations found out how to use the law to gain possession of great areas of Minnesota pine lands at moderate cost. The procedure was simple. Individual persons were hired to "enter" quarter sections, to make a show of settlement, and to maintain each a constructive residence for the full five-year period or, more commonly, for six months, when the entry could be legally commuted for by the payment of $1.25 per acre. At length the title would mature and a patent would issue to the pretended settler, who conveyed to his employer for an agreed compensation. The transaction involved, of course, perjury on the part of the ostensible settler and subornation of perjury on that of the principal. It was a bold and impudent fraud practiced upon a generous nation. By means of this process many thousands of square miles of pine lands have been acquired by persons who would much dislike to have their transactions disclosed and called by their true names. It may be said, however, that in the rough ethics of the pineries a process so extensively operated, so rarely denounced, and tolerated by the government and by government officials seemed not to be so very wrong. There was little sense of guilt. Indeed, so numerous and influential were those engaged in the operations that

land warrants held by them in reward for their services; (4) it was unjust because it was confined to a class of people—the farmer class; (5) it was unjust to the old states; (6) it would open a vast field for speculation; (7) it favored declarants of foreign birth; (8) it was unjust to future preëmptors, who were required to pay twice as much per acre as existing preëmptors; (9) it would prove to be a great loss to the treasury by destroying a source of revenue. He added that such "charity" would "go far to demoralize the people, and repress this noble spirit of independence." Between May 20, 1862, and June 30, 1880, there were made in Minnesota 62,379 entries of 7,346,038.96 acres.

they seemed not merely innocent but positively meritorious. It was "business." It may be remembered that in the minds of the American people almost up to the present time a forest has been something to be cut down and burned up or otherwise to be got out of the way of cultivation. Hence, there were no effective protests against these operations.[7]

The annual election of 1862 was a warmly contested one, but the Republican party generally elected its candidates by sufficient majorities. This party, however, would have been less successful but for a bit of legislation enacted at the special session of September, 1862, enabling Minnesota soldiers to have their votes received and counted at their several places of residence. The act provided also for the appointment of commissioners to visit the camps both within and without the state, to receive the ballots of soldiers, securely sealed, and to send them by mail or deliver them to the judges of election of the proper precincts. The act was effectively carried out and it assured, as was expected, comfortable majorities for the Republicans. William Windom was reëlected to Congress from the first district and Ignatius Donnelly was chosen from the second, each by a majority of slightly over two thousand. Both of these men were retained in their positions by reëlections until March 4, 1869, and both were conspicuous figures in state and national politics for a long time after that.[8]

The chief interest of the election of 1862, however, lay in the circumstance that the legislature then elected would choose a United States senator to succeed Henry M. Rice, then in the last year of his term. It was, of course, impossible that the Democrats, divided in their sentiments and discredited for holding alleged "copperhead" sentiments, could

[7] There are, of course, no records of the transactions, but the notorious facts cannot be questioned.

[8] General Laws, 1862, extra session, 13-18; Saint Paul Press, November 4, 15, 25, 1862; Legislative Manual, 1870, p. 91.

expect to name his successor. As already noted, the Republicans were far from unanimity in their preferences. A powerful faction hoped to secure the election of Cyrus Aldrich, then a member of the House from Hennepin County. Among his supporters were many Republicans of the sort who later might have been called "stalwarts," who were dissatisfied with the national administration for its alleged lack of energy and thoroughness in the prosecution of the war. One of their journals said of Lincoln that his speeches showed "about as much eloquence and enthusiasm as would be found in a basswood log." Ramsey was believed to sympathize with the conservative position of the administration. No such fault, however, could be found with Donnelly, who was aspiring to succeed Aldrich and did succeed him in Congress. In his speech to the Republican convention which gave him the nomination Donnelly said: "Where the wrath of the nation falls it must fall as of old fell the wrath of God, in fire and in ashes. We must make rebellion synonymous with desolation; and the track of our armies must be as a shining track of ruin." It is highly probable that the speaker had in mind the possibility of an occasion for the appearance of a dark horse in the coming senatorial contest.[9]

The legislature of 1863 had no sooner met and organized than it grappled with the problem awaiting it. The contest would be decided in the Republican caucus, numbering forty-six. On the first ballot Ramsey's supporters were nineteen. On the second they gained one adherent. Then for nine successive ballotings the number stood at twenty. On the twenty-fourth balloting it ran to twenty-three, with no prospect of the accession of the one other necessary vote. The caucus adjourned. On the next evening twenty-six votes were cast for Governor Ramsey at the first trial and his election awaited only the formal action of the two

[9] *State Atlas* (Minneapolis), August 13, 1862; *Saint Paul Press*, July 31, 1862. See *ante*, pp. 106-108.

houses in joint convention on January 14, 1863.[10] The injurious insinuations by friends of the defeated aspirants as to the influences which won the odd votes have not been sufficiently corroborated.

Governor Ramsey did not relinquish office until July following, when he retired to take his place in the Senate at the extra session of Congress. Donnelly, who had been lieutenant governor, had resigned on March 6, 1863, and the Minnesota Senate had on the day before elected as its president *pro tempore* the Honorable Henry A. Swift of St. Peter, who thereupon became lieutenant governor and, upon Ramsey's resignation, governor, under section 6 of article 5 of the state constitution. He held office but six months, which passed without important political event. Governor Swift had come from Ohio, where he had held public office, and had settled in St. Paul in 1853. Three years later he had forsaken that village for the future great city of St. Peter. He bore the reputation of a singularly pure and amiable character. Upon his death, five years after his retirement from office, a successor in his inaugural address eulogized Swift as "noble, generous, and self-sacrificing" and well worthy of a place in the list of "war governors."[11]

Governor Swift was succeeded by the Honorable Stephen Miller, a native of Pennsylvania, who came to the state in 1858 and entered upon a business venture in St. Cloud. He was a good stump speaker and at once entered ardently into Republican campaigns. His support of Ramsey and of the administration in the fall of 1859 gave him a claim to a share in the political appointments of 1860, which he did not fail to press. The anti-Ramsey faction, however, was able to defeat his expectations; but it was not able, and probably did not attempt, to hinder his appointment to the lieutenant-colonelcy of the First Minnesota Infantry in the spring of 1861. At the first battle of Bull Run, at

[10] *Saint Paul Pioneer*, January 13, 14, 1863; *House Journal*, 1863, p. 29.
[11] *Senate Journal*, 1863, pp. 326, 337. For a biography of Swift, see James H. Baker, *Lives of the Governors of Minnesota*, 111-127 (*Minnesota Historical Collections*, vol. 13—St. Paul, 1908).

Fair Oaks, and in many affairs he showed military ability and gave undisputed proof of bravery. The colonelcy of the First became vacant twice. To this he did not aspire to succeed, but he did desire to command every one of the later formed regiments in succession and left Governor Ramsey in no doubt as to his wishes. In September, 1862, the governor gladly promoted Miller to the head of the Seventh Minnesota, of which he took command soon after the battle of Wood Lake. When General Sibley was promoted to the command of the newly created Military District of Minnesota on November 25, 1862, he placed Colonel Miller in command of the troops guarding the Indian prisoners at Mankato and left to him the details of the execution of the thirty-eight Sioux convicts selected by President Lincoln out of the three hundred and more sentenced to death by the military commission. While Sibley was absent on his expedition to the Missouri in the summer of 1863, Colonel Miller, because he was physically unfit for field service at the time, remained in command of the troops left behind to defend the Minnesota frontier. His physical disability was only a part of the consideration which decided him to retire from military service, in which he had made a very creditable record, and try his fortune in the field of politics. In 1862 he had seriously contemplated an endeavor to secure the nomination for representative in Congress which went to Donnelly. Believing that "the masses" were now for him, as the event proved them to be, and assured of the support of Governor Ramsey, he accepted the nomination for the governorship of Minnesota, tendered by acclamation by the Republican state convention on August 19, 1863. He therefore did not accompany the Seventh Regiment when it departed for St. Louis on October 7, 1863. On the twenty-sixth of that month he was appointed brigadier general of volunteers and within a few days he resigned his colonelcy.[12]

[12] West, *Sibley*, 284, 288-291; Baker, *Governors of Minnesota*, 134-136; Miller to Ramsey, June 13, 17, July 8, 30, 31, August 13, September 16, 1861, February 5, April 5, 17, 25,

No Republican had contributed so much to the elections of Ramsey, both to the governorship and to the Senate, as had William R. Marshall through his newspaper, the *Saint Paul Press*, and otherwise. He had been in Minnesota almost ten years before Stephen Miller arrived and was one of the organizers of the Republican party. Had he demanded the governorship it could not have been denied him, at least by Governor Ramsey's following. With fighting blood in his veins, he was content to postpone political preferment and succeed to the command of the Seventh Minnesota Regiment. The Democrats nominated Henry T. Welles of Minneapolis, an educated man much respected for business ability and probity of character. He was no match for General Miller on the stump and made no great efforts to gain votes. The official canvass gave Miller 19,628 votes and Welles 12,739 — a result indicating that even after Gettysburg and Vicksburg there were many citizens in Minnesota who were not confident about the triumph of the Union arms or the justice of its cause.[13]

In the first year of his term Governor Miller was much occupied in securing additional recruits to meet the calls of the war department. The opportunities for enlistment for the Indian service, for which recruits had been obtained with little difficulty, had mostly passed; but there still remained abundant opportunity for joining the old fighting regiments, which promised no holiday campaigns. Under rulings of the war department promotions in those regiments were suspended until their numbers should be

May 4, 8, 20, 25, 27, 30, July 23, 31, August 8, 11, 1862, Ramsey Papers; *Saint Paul Pioneer*, August 20, 1863; *Senate Executive Proceedings*, 13:350. When Senator Rice's death was falsely predicted, Colonel Miller wrote to Governor Ramsey on May 20, 1862, and asked to be appointed to serve the remainder of the term. Upon Rice's recovery, Miller proposed in a letter to Ramsey on September 29, 1862, that the Minnesota regiments which had been engaged in the Indian war be sent south as a brigade with himself in command. These letters are in the Ramsey Papers. See *Minnesota in the Civil and Indian Wars*, 1:26, for Judge William Lochren's testimony to the bravery and modesty of Miller. A eulogy of Miller by Hanford L. Gordon is in the *Anoka County Union*, June 1, 1887.

[13] For brief biographies of Marshall and Welles, see Upham and Dunlap, *Minnesota Biographies*, 490, 836. The report of the secretary of state, in *Executive Documents*, 1863, appendix C, gives the total vote for governor; on page 49 of the same report the total soldier vote is estimated at 4,750.

increased. Hence there were loud calls upon the governor
from their officers for recruits. There were some reënlistments and some new recruits for the old regiments and
battalions, but they were not enough. The draft which
had been appointed for January 5, 1864, but postponed
was enforced in May and again in September. From the
records of the adjutant general's office it appears that
14,274 names were listed for draft in the two Minnesota
districts; 6,517 were exempted before the draft and 4,989
afterwards; 2,497 failed to report for duty and 2 deserted;
269 were held for service and among those exempted were
272 who procured substitutes; so that the actual number
of men added to the muster rolls was 541.[14] The draft
was a melancholy farce, but Governor Miller took it most
seriously, lamenting in his first annual message "this base
and cowardly conduct on the part of a small portion of our
people" as "deeply humiliating." He suggested an amendment to the constitution "attaching the high penalties of
disfranchisement and confiscation to the crime of desertion."[15]
The legislature to which this advice was given did not
please to act upon it. Three years later a delayed and
pent-up indignation broke out in the lower house, which
on March 2, 1867, passed a bill by a party vote of 25 to 11
providing for such an amendment, subject to ratification
by the people. Three days later the Senate adopted a
report from its committee on federal relations declaring
that the very small body of persons who would be affected
were less blamable than that larger number of citizens "who
remained at home during the war and spoke, and wrote
and used their influence against its vigorous prosecution
and counseled and encouraged their friends to evade the
military service."[16]

[14] Report of the adjutant general, in *Executive Documents*, 1864, pp. 238, 334. The
number of reënlistments in 1864 was 1,445; the number of recruits sent to old regiments
was 2,663.
[15] *Executive Documents*, 1864, p. 33.
[16] *House Journal*, 1867, p. 267; *Senate Journal*, 243, 247, 261.

To fill up her quota Minnesota was forced to the same action taken by other states, that of raising new organizations and granting commissions to aspiring gentlemen who could gather recruits. Had it been possible from the beginning to limit the number of regiments or battalions to be furnished by each state and to require the states to keep their ranks filled up the cost of the war might have been materially lessened and its length curtailed. In 1864 there were 2,972 men raised for new organizations. Among these, already mentioned, were the Second Regiment of Cavalry formed upon the expiration of the term of the First Mounted Rangers; the Eleventh Regiment of Infantry, over a thousand strong; and the First Regiment of Heavy Artillery, about seventeen hundred officers and men. The Eleventh Infantry was commanded by Colonel James Gilfillan, afterwards chief justice of the state supreme court, and the "First Heavy" was commanded by Colonel and Brevet Brigadier General William Colvill, who led the First Minnesota Infantry in its forlorn charge at Gettysburg. Both regiments were sent late in 1864 to Tennessee, where they performed the useful duty of garrisoning posts and guarding railroads, thus relieving veteran troops for operations in the front.[17]

A table compiled by the late Lieutenant Colonel Charles J. Humason, for many years record clerk in the office of the adjutant general of Minnesota, gives the following figures for Minnesota troops in the Civil and Indian wars: First Infantry Regiment, 1,285; First Infantry Battalion, 709; Second Infantry Regiment, 1,782; Third, 1,402; Fourth, 1,601; Fifth, 1,158; Sixth, 1,253; Seventh, 1,127; Eighth, 1,041; Ninth 1,086; Tenth, 1,090; Eleventh, 1,005; Mounted Rangers, 1,284; Second Cavalry, 1,347; Hatch's Battalion, 720; Brackett's Battalion, 613; First Heavy Artillery, 1,750; First, Second, and Third batteries of light artillery, 694; First and Second companies of sharpshooters, 208;

[17] Report of the adjutant general, in *Executive Documents*, 1864, p. 238. Narratives of these organizations may be found in *Minnesota in the Civil and Indian Wars*, 1: 488-491, 543-551, 612.

unassigned substitutes and drafted men, 441; three-months men, 220; detachments of United States engineers, 94; colored troops, 72; total, 21,982.[18]

The year 1865 was marked by the return of the Minnesota troops and their dispersion to their homes to resume the pursuits of industry. There was never so happy a year in all the land. Governor Miller in his last message congratulated the people on the return of peace with honor and with the country again united. He regretted, however, their failure at the last election to adopt the proposed amendment to the constitution extending the suffrage to negroes. He thought it worth while to advise the legislature to appropriate money to light the Capitol with gas, to introduce "heaters" in place of stoves, and to repair the fences inclosing the Capitol grounds.[19]

Two legislative events of the year 1865 deserve attention. One was the election of Daniel S. Norton of Winona as United States senator to succeed Morton S. Wilkinson. Wilkinson's oratorical power and his ardent support of administration measures had given him importance in Washington, at both ends of the Avenue. President Lincoln so much desired Wilkinson's reëlection that he wrote an open letter urging the Minnesota Republicans to return him. The senator, however, had not been successful in retaining support at home. It was charged that he was not diligent in attending to the requests of constituents and that when they visited the Capitol he was not as hospitable as Rice, who was eminently so. It was believed that he had not been so influential in securing appointments as was naturally to

---

[18] These figures were corrected to January 30, 1912, from all sources then available. The compiler was unable to obtain permission to examine the files in the war department at Washington for corrections of a great many possible errors. An earlier version of the table is in Holcombe, *Minnesota in Three Centuries*, 3: 214. A table of casualties of Minnesota troops in Fox, *Regimental Losses in the Civil War*, 514, reprinted in Holcombe, *Minnesota in Three Centuries*, 3: 215, shows 34 officers and 601 men killed or mortally wounded and 32 officers and 1,872 men who died from disease, from accident, in prison, and from other causes—a total of 2,539. The figures in this table do not check with lists in the office of the adjutant general of Minnesota but may be taken as approximately correct. The whole number of desertions was 540, about three men to a company.

[19] *Executive Documents*, 1865, pp. 3, 20, 21.

be expected and the charge was made that he had formed an alliance with Rice, which compromised his standing in the party. The latter complaint was voiced perhaps most bluntly by Major General John Pope in a letter to Secretary Stanton, written on August 29, 1863: "The alliance between Wilkinson and Rice is well enough understood in Minnesota. Wilkinson has been discarded by his party. . . . In his desperation at the certainty of falling into total obscurity after his term expires, he has joined Rice, who is about as desperately broken down as himself. Whilst the one has political purposes, the other has financial." Wilkinson afterwards affiliated with the Democratic party. He served a term in Congress from 1869 to 1871 and two terms in the state Senate in the seventies. A contemporary characterized him as "stately, gifted, eloquent."

The Republican caucus had thirty-two ballotings. In none of them did Wilkinson receive over twenty-three votes and twenty-five were necessary for a choice. In "the field" were Windom, Swift, and Norton, agreed in nothing but the defeat of "Wilk." For many successive trials there were no material changes in the voting. It has been believed by the friends of Governor Swift that nothing but his indifference and inaction prevented his nomination. At a moment when a deadlock seemed inevitable, two Republican delegates hurried to the residence of Henry M. Rice and besought him to allow them to announce him as a candidate. As he had approved the Emancipation Proclamation, had stood for a vigorous prosecution of the war, and had supported Lincoln in 1864, he might consistently have accepted unsought favors from the Republicans of Minnesota. But Rice, who had been too long a standard-bearer of Democracy to desert its colors and who was possibly looking forward to new honors not far away, declined. Nevertheless, he was voted for on the nineteenth to the twenty-seventh ballotings and received a maximum of thirteen votes. After the usual dickering and after great effort on the part of his friends, Norton had two

votes to the good on the last ballot. His election in joint
convention of the legislature followed, of course. The
opposition against him in caucus was grounded upon the
facts that he had bolted his party in his district and had
refused as a state senator to favor soldier absentee voting
and upon allegations of a coalition with "copperheads" to
secure the pending election.[20]

The other matter of moment which came before the
legislature of 1865 was the ratification of the thirteenth
amendment to the national Constitution for the abolition of
slavery. The joint resolution for the amendment had
originated in the first session of the Thirty-eighth Congress.
It passed the Senate on April 8, 1864, but failed in the House
for lack of a two-thirds vote. Due notice was immediately
given for reconsideration, but the friends of the measure preferred to let action go over to the second session. It was
there promptly brought forward and was debated from time
to time until January 31, 1865, when the reconsideration
was ordered by a decisive vote. The main question on
adoption was at once carried by a vote of 119 to 56, eight not
voting. Senator Ramsey wrote to Governor Miller expressing the hope that Minnesota might be the first state to ratify.
On February 8 the Minnesota House adopted a joint resolution to ratify by a vote of 33 to 5. The vote in the Senate on
February 15 was unanimous. The Senate amended the bill
on a point of "style" and the House concurred.[21]

[20] Harlan P. Hall, *Observations: Being More or Less a History of Political Contests in Minnesota*, 61-68 (St. Paul, 1904); *Official Records*, series 1, vol. 22, part 2, p. 494; William B. Dean to the author, May 27, 1907, Folwell Papers; proceedings of the Republican convention, in the *Saint Paul Press*, January 10, 1865; *House Journal*, 1865, p. 27. Baker, in *Governors of Minnesota*, 123, quotes from a letter from Swift to his wife, "For a few minutes I was afraid I might be elected." Governor John S. Pillsbury told the author that he and John Nicols paid that visit to Rice. The *Press* of January 10, 1865, said, "Mr. Rice came in late as a compromise candidate" but "locality" was against him. For Rice's support of Lincoln and his policy, see *ante*, pp. 74-76, and the letter from Rice to Blakely in the *Press* of September 29, 1865. "Vindications" of Norton appear in the same paper for January 10, 12, 13, 17, 1865. The attitudes of the St. Paul papers of the time are notable. The *Press* of January 10 coolly hopes that Norton will justify the expectations of his friends; the *Saint Paul Pioneer* of January 11 praises Norton for political sagacity and rejoices at his triumph over a clique of "venal demagogues"; the *Press* of the following day regrets the excessive laudation of the Republican nominee by the "copperhead" organ.
[21] 38 Congress, 1 session, *Senate Journal*, 311-313 (serial 1175); *House Journal*, 812, 818

Upon the muster-out of his regiment, the Seventh, Colonel and Brevet Brigadier General William R. Marshall was ready for political employment. The Republican convention of 1865 gave him its nomination for governor over two other aspirants whose following was so strong and so evenly balanced as to delay the necessary plurality vote.[22] In opposition to Marshall the Democrats put up their best vote-getter, Henry M. Rice. The leading organs of the parties waged a bitter warfare of words, as may be seen by an examination of their files from the time of the convention in September to the election in November. The *Press* had easily the advantage in outpourings of venom. It assailed Rice on account of his activity in the Minnesota and Northwestern Railroad juggle of 1854, his tardy conversion to the Union cause in 1862, and his opposition to conscription in 1863. The violence of these attacks probably recalled to the support of their object many war Democrats who remembered Rice's loyalty to Minnesota and her interests. It was impossible to smirch Marshall after his gallant career in the Indian and Civil wars. The principals in the contest maintained a becoming dignity. There is a tradition that in the joint discussions held by them in many of the principal towns they spent so much time in paying amiable compliments to one another that little was left for discussion of the issues. Rice vigorously advocated the support of President Johnson, the taxation of government bonds, and the refusal of suffrage to the negro — all of which points Marshall traversed. The Republicans had good reason for anxiety as to the outcome of the campaign. The canvass of the votes showed that a shift of 1,739 would have defeated their candidate.

(serial 1179); *Congressional Globe*, 1479-1490, 2977-2995, and the index under "Constitution of the United States"; 38 Congress, 2 session, *House Journal*, 168, 170 (serial 1215); *Congressional Globe*, 530; Minnesota, *House Journal*, 1865, pp. 125, 163; *Senate Journal*, 130, 133, 135, 176.

[22] *Saint Paul Press*, September 7, 1865. The two other aspirants were Colonel John T. Averill and Charles D. Gilfillan, whose supporters finally gave their votes to Marshall. Twenty-five ballots were taken.

Rice survived the contest by nearly thirty years, in modest retirement, occasionally accepting a local office or service on an Indian commission.[23]

The footings of an intermediate state census taken in 1865 showed a population of 250,099, an increase of forty-five per cent over the total of 1860. As eighteen counties had not been included, the secretary of state, who had charge of the census, estimated the probable true number at 264,600. Governor Miller was confident that it ought to be placed at 275,099. There was no enumeration according to nationalities, but it may safely be assumed that the immigration into the rural communities was largely American. The new settlements were confined mostly to the hardwood areas and did not extend on to the prairie for such reasons as the following: (1) scarcity of wood for fuel, fencing, and building; (2) lack of forest protection for man and beast; (3) remoteness from markets; (4) a belief that the prairie was deficient in fertility because it was bare of trees.[24]

Notwithstanding the reduction of the labor force by the absence of so many thousands of able-bodied men serving in the Civil and Indian wars, the period was one of no little prosperity. Under the operation of the Homestead Act an increasing immigration of farmers more than filled the places of the absent soldiery and extended the area of settlement and cultivation. The mowing and reaping machines, the high-powered threshing machine, and many improved implements and vehicles made it possible to plant and harvest crops from an expanding acreage. In that period of inflation of paper money, prices rose and mortgages and old debts were cleared off with comparatively small sacrifices of labor and produce. The price of wheat

[23] *Saint Paul Press*, September 8, 16, 24, 26, 28, October 3, 5, 12, 1865; *Saint Paul Pioneer*, October 6, 7, 1865. The vote stood as follows: Marshall, 17,318; Rice, 13,842. Minnesota, *Legislative Manual*, 1870, p. 130.

[24] Message of Governor Miller and report of the secretary of state, in *Executive Documents*, 1865, pp. 17, 417-445.

in Minneapolis rose from about fifty cents a bushel in 1861 to three times that sum in 1866, and this may be taken as an index of the general rise of prices.[25] Large expenditures of government money in the state for soldiers' pay and subsistence and for forage for animals stimulated production and exchanges. This was so notable that Major General Pope charged in an official paper that influential citizens were conspiring to prolong the Indian war for the sake of maintaining this profitable market.[26] City and village life was cheerful, notwithstanding the absence of pavements, water and lighting works, and furnace heating for dwellings. In the larger places there was much social and literary activity and probably more than ordinary religious endeavor. The abundance of literary, historical, and scientific articles in the columns of the leading newspapers of the time indicates a higher standard of taste than has prevailed since the newspaper has become so greatly commercialized.

Sully's expedition of 1864 was expected to hold all bodies of hostile Sioux far from the Minnesota frontier and it did so. The line of military posts maintained under Sibley's orders from Fort Ridgely to the Iowa line, with intervals patrolled by mounted men, was relied upon to arrest incursions in that quarter of Indian horse-thieves ready to commit incidental murders. Relying on such protection, settlers resumed work on their farms. Early in the spring the lines were broken and on August 11 two Indians came upon Noble G. Root and two sons engaged in stacking oats in Shelby Township, Blue Earth County. They fired, wounded Root mortally and one of the sons slightly, and fled upon Root's horses. On the same afternoon Jesse Mack and two others loading grain espied two Indians in time to make their escape by running their team. Still in the same township the same or two other savages shot

[25] Robinson, *Agriculture in Minnesota*, 59.
[26] *Official Records*, series 1, vol. 34, part 2, p. 792.

Charles C. Mack, who was cutting hay, killing him instantly. A settler's home was ransacked and everything of value was destroyed or carried off. The news of the outrages spread rapidly and by nightfall all the settlers in three townships had fled to the stockade at Vernon Center. The next morning a party of Shelby militia started in pursuit, but it soon lost the trail in Watonwan County. A captain with eight men started from Fort Ridgely and came in sight of eight Indians, who saw them and hid in the grass. It was thought imprudent to undertake dislodging them. A company of mounted militia dispatched from Mankato made a march of more than a hundred miles, but overtook no Indians. A company of the Second Minnesota Cavalry and twenty men of Brackett's Battalion were ordered out from Fort Snelling. All these expeditions were, of course, fruitless, as the scoundrels had the start and could easily outmarch them. But no more raids were made that season.[27]

Sully's expedition of 1865 far beyond the Missouri occupied all the hostile Sioux then held together in federated bands, but it did not and could not arrest marauding gangs of Indians separated from their people. It was believed, probably with good reason, that vagabonds from the camps of those lower Indians who had fled to Canada in 1862 after the battle of Wood Lake might again resume depredations in Minnesota. That Sibley's line of military posts for the protection of the exposed southwestern counties could not completely stop all gaps against Indian bandits was demonstrated by atrocious murders committed some five miles west of Garden City, Blue Earth County, in the season of 1865. Andrew J. Jewett, who had been a resident and postmaster of Garden City, had moved on to his farm in the northwest quarter of section 33 of Rapidan Township. On May 2, 1865, he and his family were taking their breakfast when a number of Indians burst into the house.

[27] Hughes, *Blue Earth County*, 143-145; *Mankato Weekly Union*, May 20, 1864.

It is not known what demonstrations they made, but the members of the family felt that their lives were in danger. The wife snatched her two-year-old boy and ran out. Eight rods away she was shot dead and the child was severely wounded. Jewett followed and was killed when about four rods from the house. His aged father was shot and tomahawked as he was rising from the table. He lived until the next day but was too weak to give an account of the murder. He could say only that there were five or six Indians. The grandmother was killed in her bed by blows of a tomahawk. Charles Tyler, a hired man at work in a neighboring ravine, was discovered and killed.

A neighbor who had occasion to come to the Jewett house about eight o'clock saw the bodies and noted that the house had been ransacked. The alarm spread from farm to farm and neighbors gathered in. About midday two citizens carrying the news to Mankato came upon a stranger, evidently a half-breed, whose account of himself was not satisfactory. They arrested him and took him to Mankato, where he was lodged in the county jail. In the following night a small party of citizens, apparently with the connivance of the jailer, took him out of the jail and examined him with a rope about his neck, uncomfortably tightened. He persisted in denying all knowledge of the murder and said that he was a Winnebago half-breed named Pelky. His clothing was taken off and two pairs of women's stockings were found on his feet under ill-fitting shoes.

On the following morning the half-breed was identified by two or more citizens so clearly that he was obliged to abandon his first account of himself. He said that his name was John L. Campbell and admitted that he was a deserter from Brackett's Battalion. He said that there were nine bands of Indians in the woods of Blue Earth County, intent upon theft and murder. He gave the numbers and named the leaders of each band. He had been brought down from the north by one of these bands against his will. The Indians had forced him to carry baggage and to perform other menial services. He had been unable to escape from them until the previous day and at the time of his arrest he was on his way to Traverse des Sioux, evidently to see his mother.

Early in the day there was a large assemblage of people from the town and adjoining settlements and there was talk of summary punishment without further inquiries. Against this a body of citizens protested and they succeeded in gaining consent to an orderly, if not a regular, examination. Early in the afternoon an organization was formed which proceeded to elect a judge, a panel of jurymen, a prosecuting attorney, and an attorney for the accused. The principal witness was a young woman who had been working in the Jewett family. On the day before she had identified the clothing worn by Campbell as that of Jewett. In his statement the prisoner admitted that the suit was not his own but said that some Indians whom he had met with in the timber had given it to him after taking his own from him. He repeated the story about the nine bands of Indians lurking about. At the close of the trial, which lasted four hours, the jury gave a verdict of "guilty" and recommended that the prisoner be kept in jail to be arraigned before the district court, which was soon to convene. By this time the assemblage, or a large part of it, had become a mob and loud protest was voiced against delay of punishment. It was cried out that if the prisoner was not punished immediately the military authorities would take him down to Fort Snelling, hold him in confinement for a short time, and let him go. The mob prevailed and the wretch was soon dangling at the end of a rope thrown over a convenient limb. The executioners had not thought to tie his hands. He clutched the rope, drew himself up, and begged to see a priest. He was thereupon lowered into the wagon and was allowed five minutes for a conference with a Catholic priest who was present. The interview was in the French language; what manner of confession was made is not known. The execution then proceeded and John L. Campbell ended, if accounts are to be trusted, a long career of crime.

The motive for the crime, as discovered later, was the desire of the man to get five hundred dollars believed by him to be in the possession of Jewett. Campbell had learned that an officer of Brackett's Battalion had sent that sum of money to Jewett to make a payment on a piece of land. He therefore deserted, gathered to him four or five half-breed confederates, and with them committed the murders. It is said that he told the priest that he had hidden the money in the jail and that $470 were found in the bunk that he had occupied.

This painful story of a local crime need not have been related but for more than local effects. The panic in the vicinity was extreme. It was believed that there might be truth in Campbell's statement that the Sioux were about to descend in force upon the Minnesota frontier. The minute men of Mankato were ordered out and in Garden City and other outlying villages squads of volunteer scouts were organized, who ranged the country from Lake Shetek to the Yellow Medicine. It occurred to some ingenious citizen that a pack of bloodhounds would be more efficacious in capturing Indian bandits than General Sibley's soldiers and the local militia. The commissioners of Blue Earth County appropriated five hundred dollars and that sum was raised to thirteen hundred dollars by private contributions and appropriations from three other counties. An agent was sent to the South, where it was supposed the breed of hounds formerly kept for the pursuit of runaway negroes might still survive. He found none, but he bought thirteen foxhounds, some of which were said to have a strain of bloodhound, and brought them home. The expenses of the trip and the cost of the hounds amounted to $1,226. There was no use for them and the pack soon disintegrated. The state authorities effected an enlistment of a battalion of six hundred men at Mankato and another at St. Cloud. Some ammunition was shipped up the Minnesota. General Curtis, commanding the District of Minnesota, sent up from Fort Snelling a company of the Second Minnesota Cavalry not yet mustered out and himself appeared on the scene. Governor Miller, who was in Washington, laid the matter before President Johnson, who assured Miller that he would use his best endeavors to satisfy the people.

The *Mankato Union* in its first account laid the blame for the Jewett murders upon Sibley. His expedition of 1863, and impliedly that of Sully in 1864, had been farcical. The Sioux war was not yet over. Sibley replied in a letter of May 5 that if his influence and appeals had been of any avail all the fiends concerned in the outbreak of 1862 and in later ones would long since have been dangling in the air at the end of stout ropes; that it was only at his urgent request that troops had been kept in the state; that he was maintaining a strong line of posts and patrols from Alexandria to the Iowa line; that it was impossible to station a guard at every settler's house and that settlers ought to be organized for defense against petty raids penetrating the cordon of troops. The *Saint Paul Pioneer* thought that the public ought to be satisfied with General Sibley's apology, but the *Press*, while it did not specifically blame him, insisted that a sufficient military force be sent at once into the Indian country to exterminate completely all hostile Sioux. To the ferocious proposition of the *Press* "*to hunt the Indians to their holes* and kill them" the Reverend Dr. Riggs offered the pertinent suggestion that the camps of the hostile Sioux were all north of the Canadian line and that the British government ought either to surrender them to the United States or effectually to restrain them from guerrilla warfare across the border. John Campbell, who had got his deserts, evidently expected to return with his booty and be protected by the Canadian authorities.

The panic soon subsided when scouting parties caught
no Indians, although they reported seeing Indian sign.
The battalions of militia were disbanded.  If a correspondent
of the *Pioneer* from Fort Wadsworth may be trusted, the
only party of hostile Sioux which had come down from the
north was John Campbell and five others, four of whom
had been killed.  But the people of the Minnesota Valley
may easily be excused for giving away to panic after murders
so sudden and atrocious, committed in a well-settled community.  An incident shows the state of mind in Mankato.
On the evening of the day on which the Jewett murders
were committed the missionary, Dr. Thomas S. Williamson,
preached in Mankato before the Minnesota Presbytery
and counseled moderation in this particular case and
sympathy in general for Indians, who were much sinned
against.  The next morning a committee of citizens waited
upon him and advised his immediate departure, which
counsel he thought it prudent to take.[28]  The Sioux war
was ended except for lawsuits and raids upon the United
States treasury, and they continued for many years.[29]

---

[28] *Mankato Union*, May 5, 12, 1865; *Saint Paul Press, Saint Paul Pioneer*, May 6-27;
report of the adjutant general, in *Executive Documents*, 1865, pp. 173-175.  A well-studied
account of the murders is in Thomas Hughes, *Blue Earth County*, 149-158.  The reader's
attention is called to accounts by Mr. Hughes of pursuits of Indians by a detachment of the
Second Cavalry in which one of the cavalrymen was shot; of the picketing of the agency
road by volunteers from Mankato and Winnebago City and the killing of a boy of ten by
the Indians; and particularly his account of a battle between some Indians and a party of
half-breed scouts led by "One-armed Jim" which resulted in the killing of four Indians
and the wounding of another.  The sixth and last of the gang would have been accounted
for had not One-armed Jim's gun exploded.  With due respect to Mr. Hughes, it must be
stated that all these incidents seem to need corroboration.  For slight variations from the
author's account, see the letter of J. Bookwalter, in the *Minneapolis Journal*, October 6,
1920.  The issue of the *Pioneer* for May 7, 1865, contains a sketch of Campbell by Heard, the
historian of the Sioux massacre.  The man was a half-breed son of Scott Campbell, the
favorite interpreter of Major Taliaferro.  His brother, Baptiste, was one of the convicts
executed at Mankato.

[29] See Sisseton and Wahpeton Bands of Sioux Indians *v*. United States, *Amended Petition of Plaintiffs*, 44 (Court of Claims, no. 33,731).  The petition is dated March 23, 1920.
Under ten counts the attorneys for the Indians pray for judgment against the United States
for $20,394,951.48, with uncomputed interest at five per cent for different terms, amounting
to a sum nearly equal to the principal.  See also the *Minneapolis Sunday Tribune*, August 22,
1920, section 4, p. 6.  This case is not to be confounded with the previous cases in the court
of claims, nos. 22,524 and 33,728, which are discussed in the Appendix, nos. 12 and 13, *post*.

# APPENDIX

# 1. THE STATE CONSTITUTION[1]

THE constitution adopted by vote of the people on October 13, 1857, and approved by Congress on May 11, 1858, follows in point of order a fashion of American constitutions long established. A preamble expressing gratitude to God for civil and religious liberty precedes three preliminary articles.

Article 1 is the "Bill of Rights," a title dating far back in Anglo-American history. By silent implication it recognizes the contract theory of the state and forbids the invasion of rights believed to belong to civilized men anterior to their political organization — among them the rights of freedom of speech, of the security of the home, of private property, and of every man to worship God according to the dictates of his own conscience. The article further includes restrictions on the government to be established by the constitution: the legislature is forbidden to maintain a standing army in time of peace, to pass bills of attainder and *ex post facto* laws, to imprison for debt, to deny the right of trial by jury and the speedy and public trials of persons accused of crimes; and the courts are forbidden to require excessive bail, to impose excessive fines, and to inflict cruel or unusual punishments. A provision of far-reaching import is that declaring all lands in the state to be alodial — in other words, that private proprietors own in their own right and are not tenants of the state.

Article 2, on "Name and Boundaries," is merely a repetition of provisions in two acts of Congress, the enabling act of February 26, 1857, and the act of admission to the Union of May 11, 1858. It serves only as a memorandum.

Article 3, entitled "Distribution of the Powers of Government," with the exception of the clause forbidding the overlapping of powers, has no significance.

The constituting articles establishing the frame of government begin with article 4, entitled "Legislative Department." This article vests all lawmaking power in a legislature consisting of a senate and a house of representatives, but requires that all its acts, before becoming law, be presented to the governor for his approval or disapproval. In case of the governor's disapproval of an act, passage may be effected by a two-thirds vote of both houses. The legislature is authorized to divide the state into legislative districts, to determine the number of senators and

[1] See *ante*, p. 1.

355

representatives, and to fix their compensation. The separate powers of the houses are defined and the privileges of members are stated. Regulations in regard to the process of lawmaking abound.

Article 5 creates the executive department, to consist of a governor, a lieutenant governor, a secretary of state, an auditor, a treasurer, and an attorney-general—all to be chosen by the electors. In general the powers and duties of these officers are left to be implied by their titles or to be determined by law. Certain exceptional powers, however, are conferred upon the governor. He is made commander of the armed forces of the state on land and water; he holds the pardoning power, the power to appoint such officers as may be provided for by law, and the suspensive veto power over all laws passed by the legislature. The article might have been abridged by the omission of such details as the fixing of salaries.

Article 6 vests the judicial power of the state in a supreme court, district courts, probate courts, justices of the peace, and in any other courts, inferior to the supreme court, which the legislature by a two-thirds vote may please to establish. All the judicial offices are made elective and the jurisdictions of the several courts are defined. The article requires that judges of the supreme and district courts must be "men learned in the law"—that is, they must be lawyers—and that their compensation must not be diminished during their continuance in office, thus forbidding the legislature to embarrass or suppress the judiciary.

Article 7 is on the "Elective Franchise." The right to vote, which has since been greatly extended, is reposed in white citizens of the United States, foreign declarants for citizenship, Indian half-breeds, and civilized Indians. All elections are required to be by ballot, but the further regulation of the franchise is left to the legislature.

Articles 4, 5, 6, and 7, which establish the frame of government, still are not fundamental. There is a power back of all the powers reposed in these articles, the power of a majority of electors to amend or revise the constitution. This ultimate power is reserved in Article 14, "Amendments to the Constitution." Particular amendments are made by a majority of electors voting on propositions submitted by majorities of both houses of the legislature. A revision of the whole constitution must be made by a convention voted for by a majority of electors upon a proposition submitted by two-thirds of all members elected to both houses of the legislature. No revision has yet been made. The fourteenth article is in fact a superconstitution. A majority of electors have it in their power to make any changes they please except as they are limited by the national Constitution. They might lodge the legislative power in a grand committee of thirty or any other number of men, the executive power in a triumvirate appointed by the legislature, the judicial power in judges appointed for life. They might limit the elective franchise to persons forty years old and upwards, to high school graduates, or to owners of property worth three thousand dollars.

The remaining articles — 8 on education, 9 on finance, 10 on corporations, 11 on counties and townships, 12 on militia, 13 on impeachments, and 15 on miscellaneous subjects — are all of a legislative character, but were added, according to prevailing custom, principally to place restrictions upon lawmaking and administration.

The remaining provisions, of a temporary nature, are grouped at the end under the barren title "Schedule." The most important provides for an election at which the draft constitution shall be voted upon and for the canvass of the vote. Less important, because they may be taken for granted, are provisions that territorial laws shall remain in effect until altered or repealed by the state legislature, that all territorial officers shall retain their offices until superseded by state authority, and that all judicial proceedings shall go on as if no change had been made.

## 2. THE STATE SEAL[2]

The question of a state seal and coat of arms was brought up in both bodies of the constitutional convention of 1857. In the Republican section on August 6 a special committee, which had been appointed a week before, submitted a report accompanied by a design. The central feature was a waterfall — supposed to be that of Minnehaha — within a shield, symbolical of the abounding lakes and rivers of Minnesota. Above the shield were three pine trees, typical of the three great pine regions — those of the St. Croix, the Mississippi, and Lake Superior. On the right of the pines was a distant view of Lake Superior, with a ship in sail; on the left was a view of the Minnesota River with a steamboat ascending it. On the right of the shield was the figure of a white man with a sheaf of wheat and implements of agriculture at his feet; on the left was the figure of an Indian asking the white man by an imploring gesture where he shall go; at the feet of the Indian were a bow, a quiver, and a tomahawk. The committee said that the central waterfall was proposed by a number of delegates, but that accessory features were suggested by R. Ormsby Sweeny, an artist and designer of St. Paul. It rejected the motto *Fulget intaminatis honoribus*, and recommended Webster's "Liberty and union, now and forever." On August 8 in committee of the whole the motto was amended by striking out the words "now and forever." A delegate suggested that "we can tell about the future when that becomes the present." On August 18 the committee on state seal submitted a report giving, as it said, "a brief and more correct description of the Seal and Coat of Arms." The only notable change was the addition, "Above

<hr>

[2] See *ante*, p. 26.

these [*the three pine trees*] appears the North Star." On August 20 in committee of the whole it was agreed to add the words "and canoe" after the word "steamboat." The convention concurred and ordered the substitute report as amended to be engrossed for its third reading. No further action was taken in the Republican body, as the joint compromise committee of the two bodies was already at work compiling the one constitution.[3]

The Democratic wing of the convention had among its standing committees one on the "Seal of the State, Coat of Arms and design of the same." Joseph R. Brown was a member. The brief report of this committee, submitted on August 15, expressed the opinion that it was the appropriate work of the legislature to prepare a seal and proposed a draft section reading: "There shall be a Seal of the State, which shall be kept by the Governor, and used by him officially, and shall be called the 'Great Seal of the State of Minnesota.'" The compromise committee ignored the proceedings of the Republican committee in the matter of the seal and acceded to the principle announced by the Democratic committee, whose draft it modified, however, so as to make the secretary of state the custodian of the seal. The constitution as adopted charged the legislature with the duty of providing for an appropriate device and motto.[4]

On January 6, 1858, State Senator William H. C. Folsom gave notice of a bill to provide for a state seal and on January 30 he submitted a design identical in its main features with that laid before the Republican convention. The only noteworthy departure was that the three trees above the waterfall were no longer all pines, but were of three different species. A pine in the center typified the great pine region; an oak on the left, the south and southwest parts of the state; and a maple on the right, the north and northwest parts of the state. The North Star did not appear. On March 18 the committee to which the matter had been referred reported the design and description presented by Senator Folsom and recommended the adoption of a joint resolution to legalize it. [5] The matter received no further attention until after the opening of the adjourned session on June 2, 1858. On the twenty-fourth of that month the Senate adopted, by a vote of 19 to 3, the resolution declaring the seal recommended by its committee to be the great seal of the state. The House was notified of this action on the same day and it gave the resolution

[3] *Debates and Proceedings* (Republican), 182, 336, 411, 520, 557.
[4] *Debates and Proceedings* (Democratic), 519; Constitution, article 15, section 4.
[5] *Senate Journal*, 1858, pp. 86, 181, 332. The original resolution is in Secretary of State's Archives, Legislative Papers, 1857–58, Senate Files, miscellaneous, in the custody of the Minnesota State Archives. In William H. C. Folsom, *Fifty Years in the Northwest*, 658 ([St. Paul], 1888), is a woodcut which the author states represents the design presented by him to the Senate.

a precipitate and indefinite postponement. On the day following the House reconsidered the postponement and as precipitately adopted the resolution without roll call. On the twenty-sixth the Senate received notice of the House concurrence.[6]

The bill thus recorded as passed by both houses did not become a law. The *Senate Journal* contains no report of the enrollment of the bill or of its transmittal to the governor. It has not been found in any message announcing the governor's action on bills. The only further reference to it that has been discovered—and it is a doubtful one—is a "Joint Resolution" offered in the Senate on July 16 requesting the governor "to return to the Senate the Joint Resolution No. 2, adopting the Great Seal of Minnesota." The motion was "laid over under the rules."[7] The mover, Senator Isaac Van Etten, may have learned that the resolution to adopt the seal was in the hands of the governor and may have proposed his "Joint Resolution" to arrest its progress. If the bill was in the hands of the governor and was not recalled nor disapproved by him within three days, it would have automatically become a law. But it was not printed in the laws of 1858. If the Van Etten resolution was intended to recall the resolution adopting the seal, there was an error in the number given to it. Joint resolution no. 2 was an ancillary one authorizing the governor to cause the seal to be engraved. That was duly passed and approved and was printed in the laws of 1858.[8]

Governor Sibley seems to have acted promptly upon his authority to cause the seal of the state to be engraved. The *Pioneer and Democrat* of August 25, 1858, contained an advertisement of an engraver and an editorial reference stating that he had been employed by the state officers to get up the official seals of the state. It may be presumed that the great seal was the principal one. In the absence of directive legislation, Sibley appears to have exercised a liberal discretion in determining what was the seal of the state that he was authorized to have engraved. He apparently assumed that the territorial seal already in use might with some modifications be considered to be the seal of the state. The notable changes

[6] *Senate Journal*, 1858, pp. 460, 466; *House Journal*, pp. 737, 742. On June 14 a bill for an act to provide for a state seal was introduced in the House by a select committee on state seal. This bill, which proposed to authorize the governor to procure a seal "with an appropriate device and motto," was passed the following day and sent to the Senate, where, on June 18, it was referred to the committee on state seal. *House Journal*, 599, 663; *Senate Journal*, 416, 437, 442; Secretary of State's Archives, House file 284.

[7] *Senate Journal*, 1858, p. 533. The *Pioneer and Democrat* of July 17, 1858, in a report of the legislative proceedings of the previous day, said: "Mr. Van Etten offered the following resolution. *Resolved*, That the Governor be respectfully requested to return to the Senate the resolution adopting the Great Seal of the State of Minnesota. During the discussion . . . the Private Secretary of the Governor appeared and informed the Senate that the resolution had been signed and approved, and the resolution was laid over for one day under the rules."

[8] Constitution, article 4, section 11; *Senate Journal*, 1858, pp. 340, 471, 533; *House Journal*, p. 795; *General Laws*, 1858, p. 338.

made were: (1) the title, "The Great Seal of Minnesota, 1849," was
replaced by "The Great Seal of the State of Minnesota, 1858"; (2) the
outside diameter was reduced from three to two inches; (3) the drawing
was reversed so as to show the Indian riding westward toward the setting
sun and the farmer—in boots—plowing eastward; (4) the absurd Latin
motto was erased and the French words for the North Star, "L'Etoile du
Nord," were inserted.[9]

Knowledge of the new seal must presently have got abroad, for on
September 11 the *Minnesotian* poured out vials of sarcasm upon "Mister"
Sibley for selecting a motto from the Canadian French patois, the only
French known to him, and one conveying no appropriate sentiment. The
*Pioneer and Democrat* responded in a vein much too serious. The wordy
battle continued for some days. The *Minnesotian* suggested that "Mister"
Sibley should have designed an entire new seal—"with a *Huge Moccasin*,
rampant; on a *Prairie*, vert; *with an Indian Trader*, prominent; and the
motto issuing from his mouth of '*Big Indian me*—Ho!'" Without
serious protest the modified seal doubtless came into early use.[10]

In 1860 the Reverend Edward D. Neill became superintendent of
schools. Desirous to conform to the law requiring all state officers to
use the seal of the state, he inquired of Acting Governor Donnelly what
constituted the seal of the state, since the legislature had not acted under
its constitutional mandate. The inquiry was referred to Attorney-
General Gordon E. Cole, who replied that the modified territorial seal
which Sibley had provided might properly be used. Its employment had
been sufficiently sanctioned by usage. The opinion contains a suggestion
that the governor had acted without authority.[11] In the following year,
to remove doubts and to heal all defects and errors, the legislature pro-

[9] For information concerning the compensation of the seal engraver, see *House Journal*,
1860, pp. 85, 237, and *General Laws*, 1860, p. 236. See any recent *Legislative Manual* for
the two seals; the territorial seal is reproduced *ante*, 1: 461. There is a tradition that Sibley
desired to have the North Star appear in the original territorial seal, but when reminded by
Governor Ramsey that Pennsylvania farmers did not plow by starlight he did not insist.

[10] *Minnesotian*, September 10, 11, 14, 18, 1858; *Pioneer and Democrat*, September 12, 15,
17, 1858. The *Minnesotian* still refused to consider "Mister" Sibley's election as legitimate.

[11] Neill to Donnelly, May 16, Cole to Donnelly, May 17, 1860, in Governor's Archives,
Records, A: 194. The original of Cole's letter is in Governor's Archives, file 567; it is printed
in *Opinions of the Attorneys General of the State of Minnesota*, 116 (St. Paul, 1865). The
attorney-general informed Donnelly that the seal at the head of a circular which Neill had
inclosed in his letter was not the great seal of the state; that Neill was in error in saying that
the legislature had taken no action in regard to the seal, for chapter 5, section 13, of the
*Public Statutes of the State of Minnesota, 1849-1858*, 126 (St. Paul, 1859), provided that the
governor should renew the seal when it was worn out or defaced; that it was doubtful whether
the governor had power to change the seal; that, whether the governor's action in providing
a seal differing from the territorial seal was authorized by law or not, the seal thus adopted
had been used and treated as the great seal of the state. See Milliken's report to Governor
McGill on the seals of Minnesota (see *ante*, 26, n. 49). The report conveys much information mingled with errors.

vided by law that the seal which had been in use should be the great seal of the State.[12]  The conjecture may be hazarded that Sibley much preferred the perpetuation of the simple territorial seal which he had assisted in selecting to the elaborate pictorial devices favored by the legislative bodies and that some friend who knew his views arranged, without suggestion, to have the bill mislaid and not presented for approval. As a matter of taste the result is commendable.

## 3. THE FIRST BATTLE OF NEW ULM[13]

The question, "Who saved New Ulm on August 19, 1862?" has been mooted ever since that date.  Citizens of New Ulm have been industrious in supporting the claim that to the German townsmen alone should the credit wholly or in chief be given.  A narrative attributed to Charles Roos, sheriff of Brown County at the time of the battle, is probably the most emphatic in the assertion of this claim.  According to this narrative, at noon on Monday, August 18, a man rode through the town shouting, "The Indians are coming. . . . They have murdered the recruiting party."  Sheriff Roos believed that only some drunken Indians needed to be arrested and called out a posse.  Thirty men armed with rifles, shotguns, and other weapons responded.  During the half hour consumed in preparations the sheriff ordered the New Ulm militia to be in readiness for service and to barricade a part of the town.  The eventful excursion of the sheriff and his posse to the town of Milford is not of present concern.  On his return, about ten o'clock in the evening, he found that picket guards had been stationed, some houses had been fortified, and signal fires had been lighted.  He at once summoned the Brown County militia and placed in command Jacob Nix, who had returned from a reconnoissance toward the agency with tidings that the Indians were "murdering everything."[14]

On Tuesday morning Sheriff Roos sent a message to Governor Ramsey asking for men and ammunition.  The forenoon was spent in organizing and equipping the company and in lodging refugees.  Farm wagons were added to the barricade as fast as they were driven in.  At noon a few

[12] *General Laws*, 1861, p. 165.  In his report of January 1, 1861, the secretary of state notified the legislature that the state had "no legally authorized Seal." *Executive Documents*, 1860, no. 4, p. 7.

[13] See *ante*, p. 133.

[14] The manuscript of Roos's narrative, the date of which is unknown, is in the possession of the family.  A copy of it, made for the author, is in the Folwell Papers.  The *New Ulm Post*, August 30, 1912, contains a statement by Sheriff Roos in the form of an affidavit in which he represents that before his departure for Milford he organized the militia of Brown County, appointed Jacob Nix *Platzkommandant* with the rank of major, and gave him authority to organize the citizens into companies.  On his return at about eleven o'clock at night he found the companies and several squads organized.

farmers came in on foot and reported that they had been chased by Indians as far as the Cottonwood River. Fifteen riflemen were immediately sent to reconnoiter the region. This little band had gone only a short distance when thirty more men with double-barreled shotguns were sent to their support. This left in the town but two or three rifles and about forty other guns. It was during the absence of these forty-five men with all the better arms that the Indians, advancing as far as the post office, began firing on the people behind the barricades. The forty guns left in town were loaded and fired as rapidly as possible. At an hour not noted the two bands which had been sent out on reconnoissance returned and took up the best available positions within the "fortifications." The Indians, seeing their approach, seemed to lose courage. Meanwhile it had begun to rain. Between four and five o'clock a band of seven men, armed with rifles, came from Nicollet County to aid in defending the besieged town. Some of these thought it advisable to make a sally to prevent the burning of more houses. Twenty men volunteered but only ten of them reached Fred Rehfeld's house, from which they observed the movements of the Indians and checked their further advance. "With the approach of night every Indian had disappeared."[15]

The account of Captain Nix agrees in general with the foregoing but is much more circumstantial. He places Roos's return from Milford, his own immediate appointment as *Platzkommandant*, and his muster in of the militia late in the afternoon of Monday, the eighteenth. Messengers were then dispatched to Mankato and St. Peter for aid in a danger common to all and an armed force was organized. When mustered the force consisted of a squad of fourteen men armed with rifles, another of eighteen men equipped with double-barreled shotguns, and a third, numbering twelve, provided with common shotguns. There were also from fifteen to eighteen men, with firearms of various sorts, who would not enroll in any of the squads. To all these was added a reserve, not enumerated, furnished with stable forks and hayforks, axes of all sorts, and a few revolvers. The building of barricades was begun and prosecuted through the night by torchlight. The sheriff and the commandant spent an anxious night in conference upon and oversight of the means of defense in progress. Mention is made of the dispatch of the two parties to rescue farmers on the Cottonwood reported to be in danger, but the fact and time of their

[15] Roos's narrative; Roos to Ramsey, August 19, 1862, in Governor's Archives, file 255. Roos's letter to Ramsey is also printed in the *Saint Paul Press* and in the *Pioneer and Democrat* of August 22, 1862. The sheriff asked for a thousand men and expressed a desire to have every Sioux Indian, with the exception of those who were civilized, killed. In his affidavit, in the *New Ulm Post*, August 30, 1912, Roos states that a number of the militia were killed and wounded in the affair of August 19. He adds that a few militiamen from Nicollet made their appearance during the fight. See the map on page 140, *ante.*

return are left to be guessed at. Nix remarks that the false report which led to this weakening of the garrison cost the lives of many brave men.

In the forenoon of Tuesday, Nix continues, the barricades were manned, the inner and outer guards were doubled, and all preparations were made for a warm reception of the redskins. It was nearly three o'clock when the Indians were seen through a telescope to be approaching. They came from the direction of Milford, separated into two divisions near the cemetery, and, in curving lines, advanced upon the town. "Auf Eure Posten! Fertig zum Gefecht!" shouted the commandant. Foaming with rage, the savages approached the barricades. In a moment the desperate battle began. Soon there were dead and wounded on both sides. A girl of thirteen, who in defiance of orders had stepped out of a door on Minnesota Street, was killed. At the same moment and by the same bullet the commandant lost his ring finger. More and more Indians appeared on the field, all well armed, and more furious were their attacks. As they stormed forward, Theobald, Spenner, Hauenstein, Brandt, Pfau, and other riflemen gave them such a fusillade as to discourage further advance. But still more Indians confronted the barricades and the battle went on. Charge after charge was made, accompanied by barbaric yells horrifying enough to appall brave men who had never heard such. The most impetuous charges of all were those repeatedly made for the capture of the barricades on the south end of the town, from which the Indians retired with "bloody heads." They were no more successful on the northwestern defenses, but they succeeded in firing three outlying houses. From a charge on the northeast they were sent back carrying a number of dead and wounded. Foiled in all these local onsets, the Indians, now probably further reënforced, attacked from all quarters and a fearful struggle ensued. The murderous conflict was going on when, about half past four o'clock, a dark cloud arose out of the southwest, accompanied by fearful thunder and a deluge of rain. The elements commanded peace and soon after five o'clock the battle was over. "The German city," writes Captain Nix, "was defended and saved . . . by Germans." An exception may be noted later. The captain found the local surgeon so prostrated with fatigue from caring for the wounded that he would not allow him to dress his injured member. Emphatic protest is made against the claim that the "Boardman Cavalry" had anything to do with insuring the victory. It did not arrive until the battle was in fact over, when it was comfortably housed in the two principal hotels of the town.[16]

[16] Nix, *Ausbruch der Sioux-Indianer*, 16-18, 20-24, 27-29. See *General Laws*, 1881, p. 240, for a joint resolution requesting the Minnesota delegation to obtain from Congress a captain's pension for Captain Jacob Nix for valiant and heroic conduct in defending New Ulm both before and after he had been wounded so severely in the hand that he later lost the use of it.

Rudolph Leonhart, the German schoolmaster of the time, includes in his recollections a graphic account of the occurrences of August 18 and 19, 1862. About noon Sheriff Charles Roos came to Leonhart's schoolhouse and advised him to send his children to their homes to warn their parents of a possible attack by the Indians. The sheriff at once organized a company to go to the relief of the recruiting party which in the morning had gone out in the country to the westward. It returned late in the day bringing the bodies of three persons whom the Indians had killed. During the absence of the relieving party citizens fell to work building barricades of wagons, boxes, and other materials and arranged for a night watch. The forenoon of Tuesday, the nineteenth, was spent in busy preparation for a probable attack. Many farmers came in from the surrounding country, some of them armed, and joined the defenders. After the noon meal a great cloud of smoke arose in the southwest from fields of grain which had been fired by the Indians. About three o'clock mounted Indians were seen on the prairie near the town. At the same time a dense storm cloud, accompanied by thunder and lightning such as could be heard and seen only on a western prairie, spread over the scene. A downpour of rain followed during which the thunder continued to roll overhead, while the shrieks of frightened women and children and the crack of rifles below added to the din. The shower was soon over but the gunfire kept on livelier than ever. The citizens had by this time recovered from their first panic and thronged toward the southwest quarter of the town, where the Indians had attempted to fire some out-lying houses. The rain, however, had thwarted their attempt and, seeing "our men" advancing in a solid body—"entschlossen phalanx"—they disappeared on their fleet ponies as quickly as they had come. The writer makes no reference to Captain Nix or his exploits as *Platzkom-mandant*. Nor does he mention the Swan Lake party or the "Boardman Cavalry." "Our men"—"die Unserigen"—alone had saved New Ulm. Leonhart is careful, however, to say that he writes only what he saw or experienced. He saw the dead body of a girl in the main street and learned afterwards that it was that of Emilie Pauli, who a year before had been the ornament of his school. Leonhart was one of those who left the state for the east after the evacuation of New Ulm, never to return.[17]

In an illustrated pamphlet on New Ulm, Fred W. Johnson follows the Roos narrative closely, but divides the honor of the victory between the brave citizens of New Ulm and "the little band of seven from Nicol-let," of which mention will be made later.[18]

The Reverend Alexander Berghold gives an account which varies somewhat from the foregoing accounts. When Captain Nix returned

[17] Leonhart, *Erinnerungen an New Ulm*, 19-22.
[18] *A Glimpse of New Ulm* (New Ulm, 1894).

from his reconnoissance in the afternoon of the eighteenth he found that fifty men had been lined up in front of the Dakota House by a former Austrian soldier. They at once unanimously elected Nix as their captain because of his reputed experience in arms. Not more than fifty guns—and those mostly "old, rusty and useless"—could be found; only twelve of them were rifles. The building of fortifications was at once begun and was continued through the following night. The Indian attack on the nineteenth caused great "excitement and terrible fear." The Indians were several hundred in number and they seemed to have been but an advance guard boldly attempting to capture and loot the place before the main body should arrive. When Captain Nix ordered his command to the barricades twenty responded but only six were willing to fall into line. Their inferior arms "were a mere nothing" against the "magnificent rifles" of the Sioux. Earlier in the day Henry A. Swift and five others, well armed with rifles, had come from St. Paul on business. "No sooner had they learned the state of affairs than they wanted to turn back; but they were finally persuaded by Captain Nix to remain." A heavy rain had a great deal to do with the saving of the town. After the fight was over twenty-five horsemen under Captain Boardman arrived from St. Peter. "The proposal of Captain Nix that these twenty-five men should pursue the Indians was not accepted."[19]

The denials of credit to the "Boardman Cavalry" for saving New Ulm have naturally raised the question: Who else claimed such credit? Perhaps the most emphatic ascription of the credit to these horsemen is that of the historian Heard, writing not many months after the event. Early in the morning of August 19 a general alarm was spread through St. Peter. The people assembled and resolved on the collection of arms and ammunition. At a reassemblage an hour later an organization was made and the Honorable Charles E. Flandrau, associate justice of the state supreme court, was elected captain. At eleven o'clock Flandrau dispatched sixteen mounted men, "tolerably well armed," in charge of Sheriff L. M. Boardman with orders "to scout toward New Ulm." The party reached that place while the Indian attack, which had begun at four o'clock, was in progress, to find the people in "a state of utter frenzy" and without any kind of organization. The people were huddled like a flock of sheep within barricades of "wagons, barrels, and all kinds of trumpery." The St. Peter men at once rode out beyond the barricades, opened a vigorous fire on the Indians, and drove them away about dark. "It is conceded," says Heard, "that these men saved the town."[20]

[19] Berghold, *The Indians' Revenge*, 112-119. The Sioux had few rifles. Their guns were shotguns with reënforced breech to allow the use of so-called "traders' balls."
[20] Heard, *Sioux War*, 78-80.

In his narrative of the Indian wars of 1862-64, Flandrau gives an account similar in tenor to that of Heard. At about four o'clock in the morning of August 19 a messenger from New Ulm came to Flandrau's house in Traverse des Sioux, about one mile north of St. Peter, with the news of the outbreak. After making provision for his family, he repaired to St. Peter, where he found the situation already comprehended. Volunteers were called for and 116 promptly enlisted and elected Flandrau their captain. Before noon two men, Henry A. Swift, afterwards governor of Minnesota, and William G. Hayden, had started to the front. By noon sixteen mounted men commanded by Sheriff L. M. Boardman followed. Flandrau remarks that at an earlier hour a "squad from Swan Lake, some fifteen miles nearer to New Ulm than St. Peter, under Samuel Coffin, had gone to New Ulm to find out what was the matter." The advance guard—the "Boardman Cavalry"—reached New Ulm about four or five o'clock, "just in time to aid the inhabitants in repelling an attack of about one hundred Indians upon the town. They succeeded in driving the enemy off."[21] The Sioux commission of 1863 in its report says, "By sundown the next day [*August 19*] a detachment of Captain Flandrau's company reached and saved New Ulm from capture."

Lieutenant Governor Donnelly, in a report to Governor Ramsey written from Fort Ridgely on August 29, 1862, states that the attack on New Ulm on Tuesday by from two to three hundred Indians began about three o'clock and continued all the afternoon. The company under Captain Flandrau reached the town at six o'clock. The cavalry charged upon the Indians and drove them back, killing at least twelve or fifteen of them.[22]

Oscar Malmros, adjutant general of Minnesota in 1862, writes that a detachment of some fifteen members of the St. Peter relieving party sent forward in advance "arrived at a time when the battle was raging in its greatest fury." The Indians, surprised by the sudden appearance of reënforcements and presuming that a much larger force would follow, immediately fell back and retired from the conflict.[23]

[21] *Minnesota in the Civil and Indian Wars*, 1: 731; Flandrau's report of August 20 to Governor Ramsey in the same work, 2: 165. Flandrau's party of ninety reached New Ulm between nine and ten o'clock on the evening of the nineteenth to find the citizens, along with his advance guard, "engaged in a brisk battle with the Indians, which lasted about two hours and resulted in the repulse of the Indians." Judge Isaac Atwater, an intimate friend and at one time a law partner of Judge Flandrau, states that the St. Peter party of about 115 men reached New Ulm in the evening and none too early, since a hundred Indians were already attacking the place, a considerable portion of which was in flames. "The command," he continues, "advanced upon the town, drove out the Indians, extinguished the fires and calmed the excitement of the people. The timely arrival of these citizen troops undoubtedly saved New Ulm from destruction and the people from massacre." *Magazine of Western History*, 7: 660 (April, 1888).

[22] *Pioneer and Democrat*, September 2, 1862; Indian Office, *Reports*, 1862, p. 62.

[23] *Executive Documents*, 1862, p. 422.

The account given by Mrs. Harriet E. Bishop McConkey varies some-what from the foregoing. Judge Flandrau was roused before daylight and had 150 men "true as steel" ready to march by noon. At four o'clock three hundred Indians besieged New Ulm. The whole population was huddled in two squares, utterly powerless from fright. Fortunately a party of eighteen men had preceded the main body from St. Peter; but their efforts to rally the panic-stricken citizens were vain. "This brave little body," therefore, "hastily organized and advanced to meet the skulking foe," and "several red skins 'bit the dust' in mortal agony." At six o'clock Judge Flandrau arrived. His cavalry charged on the Indians and drove them back, killing twelve or fifteen.[24]

Mr. Thomas Hughes relates that at four o'clock in the morning word was sent to Flandrau from St. Peter to come and help form a company. He found the people busy organizing a company to go to the relief of New Ulm. By noon Boardman had set out with sixteen men. Judge Flandrau followed with over a hundred men and was joined by a squad of men from Le Sueur County. Boardman with his sixteen men arrived at New Ulm "just in time to help save it at the first battle."[25]

The account of Major Salmon A. Buell, a member of the Boardman relief party, gives Flandrau a prominence which the latter modestly tried to avoid. Upon his early arrival from his home, Flandrau informed the citizens of St. Peter that he had forwarded the message from New Ulm into Le Sueur County and down the valley and that he now desired to raise an armed force for the protection of the frontier. Over a hundred volunteers from Nicollet and Le Sueur counties at once rushed to his standard and made him their captain. The captain's first order was that eighteen men should raise arms and horses and hasten to New Ulm. Henry A. Swift and William G. Hayden were first to obey the order and they were soon followed by sixteen others, one of whom was Boardman, in command. When within ten miles of New Ulm, the party rested in an unoccupied farmhouse during "a most terrific rain storm." Between four and five o'clock it dashed into the town. The inhabitants were principally engaged in defending the place against an attack upon the upper end of the town, where a barricade had been erected across Minnesota Street. Some men, under the superintendence of Samuel Coffin of Swan Lake, were observed building another barricade across the same street lower down. In a consultation of Henry A. Swift and some leading citizens of New Ulm with the Boardman party, it was deemed advisable

[24] *Dakota War Whoop: or, Indian Massacres and War in Minnesota, of 1862–3*, 82–84 (St. Paul, 1864). It may be surmised that the writer had the Swan Lake party in mind but that she erroneously gave St. Peter as its starting place. The party was not Judge Flandrau's cavalry, which she mentions later.

[25] *Welsh in Minnesota*, 77.

to send another messenger back to Flandrau. Boardman had the best horse and gallantly volunteered for the duty. About sunset the Indians discontinued the attack and retired. In an interview with the author Major Buell stated that it was while the party was resting during the rainstorm that Boardman was elected captain. Immediately upon reaching the upper barricade Boardman gave the order to move out and Buell at once jumped his horse over the barricade. The citizens present begged so earnestly that the men should not expose themselves to the Indians' fire that the captain yielded and revoked the order. Thereupon took place the consultation which resulted in Boardman's departure homeward. Buell made no claim of a deployment or a charge upon the Indians.[26]

Another member of the Boardman party, Postmaster J. K. Moore, writes that the citizens of the beleaguered town were found gathered in the main street, doing their best in the apparently hopeless task of saving themselves. As Moore was hitching his horse in a vacant lot Indian bullets whizzed past him thick and fast, but the firing soon ceased and no Indians were heard from thereafter.[27]

An inscription on the state monument at New Ulm, dedicated on August 22, 1891, contains the following statement: "On the afternoon of the 19th of August a force of about one hundred warriors attacked the town of New Ulm. . . . While the battle was in progress, the advance of Captain Charles E. Flandrau's company from Nicollet county, about fifteen strong, under the command of L. M. Boardman, entered the town and the savages withdrew. The defense up to this time was in charge of Captain Jacob Nix." [28]

An interesting variant on the story of the "Boardman Cavalry" should find place here. In an interview with the author, Horace Austin, a member of the Boardman party and governor of Minnesota from 1870 to 1874, gave his recollections. At an early hour on Tuesday the people of St. Peter were astir and in great excitement. Mounted messengers had arrived with the news that the Sioux Indians had arisen and had murdered

[26] Buell, in *Minnesota Historical Collections*, 10: 784-798 (part 2). Notes on the interview with Buell, December 21, 1905, are recorded in the author's notebooks, 2: 125.

[27] Moore to the author, October 19, 1905, Folwell Papers.

[28] *Minnesota in the Civil and Indian Wars*, 1: 818e. See the *New Ulm Review*, August 26, 1891, for an account of the dedication of the monument. The orator of the day stated that a small body of men led by Captain Boardman put in an appearance, joined with the New Ulm company commanded by Captain Nix, and put the Indians to flight. The German orator expressed his disappointment in the monument, which was less imposing than had been expected, and his regret because of errors in the inscription. He said that the New Ulm men fought gallantly and drove the Indians away before the arrival of outside assistance. The editor of the *Review*, Fred W. Johnson, appealed to the press of the state to give currency to the corrections. He did, however, acknowledge the assistance of the Nicollet company, which, he says "has never been given the credit that it deserved."

many settlers west and north of New Ulm and that an attack on that place was expected. There was no formal assemblage or organization that he remembered. A number of men, most of them young, who had gathered at the Ewing House agreed to get guns and horses and to start for New Ulm as soon as possible. They started about eleven o'clock. Sheriff Boardman, the most popular man in the company, was recognized as the leader, but he was not formally elected. After some delay at the Redstone Ferry, the party dashed into New Ulm about four o'clock. As they approached the place mounted Indians were seen dashing hither and thither on the high bench of land overlooking the town. The people were in the business center, huddled together as closely as they could be packed. Fear and panic had apparently seized them all. A few men, including some from Swan Lake, were constructing barricades across the main street three or four blocks apart. Jacob Nix and Daniel Shillock in a very excited manner were vainly calling for order. Shillock at once made the suggestion that the horsemen should ride out and drive the Indians away while he and others should strive to calm the excited crowd. With Boardman in the lead the men put spurs to their horses and rode out the street leading to the open country, where the Indians, who were about to begin a deployment, appeared to be most in evidence. At this moment Boardman halted his men and, after informing them that he did not feel competent to lead them in battle, resigned the command. After it had been refused by others it fell upon Horace Austin. He at once deployed the squad and ordered a charge. "On we dashed," said Austin, "regardless of consequences." While the lines were too far apart for any danger, the Indians fired off their guns and disappeared behind the second bench of land. "Some historians," he added, "attach more importance to the services of these mounted men than I do, one historian saying that the little company 'undoubtedly saved the town.' It is my judgment that there was at no time on that somewhat eventful day a greater number of Indians in the immediate vicinity of New Ulm than there were white men in this relieving party."[29]

The glory of saving New Ulm on August 19, 1862, cannot be accorded either to the burghers of that town or to the gallant cavalry from St. Peter until after a third claim has been considered. The editor of the *Minnesota Statesman* gave, in substance, the following account. On Tuesday Indians appeared and dismounted in the rear of the first table-land and from its crest they opened a long-range fire on the place. About

[29] Governor Austin later recorded the substance of this interview for the author's use. The typewritten manuscript is in the Folwell Papers. There is also recorded in the author's notebooks, 2:76, an interview with Governor Austin on the subject. In the *Pioneer and Democrat* of August 26, 1862, is a letter from Senator Guy K. Cleveland in which he estimates the number of Indians at twenty-five. A similar estimate of numbers is in the *Saint Paul Press*, August 27, 1862.

one o'clock a party of eighteen men arrived from Swan Lake and the town of Nicollet to find the people huddled in two squares of the main street. They were in utter confusion and the men could not be rallied for defense. The Swan Lake men organized by electing A. M. Bean captain and Samuel Coffin lieutenant. Thereupon they moved out and gained the shelter of a house from which they could deliver an effective fire. Four or five of the number pushed out to another house but could not hold the position. Six good rifles in the company did such execution that the Indians at length gave up and fell back, after several of their number had been felled. "Just at this time" Boardman and eleven other men, all mounted, arrived from St. Peter. On seeing them enter the town, the Indians disappeared. Praise is given to the "eighteen noble heroes" and their brave and competent leaders. "Had they [the Germans of New Ulm] been Americans, familiar with the Indian nature, they could have rallied and held the enemy at bay."[30]

The account given by Bryant and Murch follows so closely the article in the Minnesota Statesman as to warrant the surmise that the writer had it before him. On Tuesday afternoon at four o'clock mounted Indians appeared in rear of the first table-land, dismounted, and advanced on the town. The people were gathered in the buildings in the center of the village, "perfectly panic-stricken and nearly helpless." Most of their arms were unfit for use in a fight and they were seemingly in a hopeless condition. Fortunately a party of eighteen men, well armed, from Nicollet and St. Peter reached the town about one o'clock. They organized by electing A. M. Bean captain and Samuel Coffin lieutenant and immediately advanced upon the enemy. They reached a house on the edge of the table-land, from which they effectually returned the Indians' fire. A few of their number gained a more advanced position but were unable to hold it. "At this time" L. M. Boardman and eleven others from St. Peter, all mounted, entered the town. On seeing this reënforcement the savages retreated.[31]

[30] Saint Paul Press, August 27, 1862, which quotes the article from the Minnesota Statesman (St. Peter), August 22, 1862. See also in the Folwell Papers a letter from Gideon S. Ives to the author, October 9, 1917, accompanied by a copy of part of an article in the Saint Peter Tribune and a clipping of the article in the Minnesota Statesman.
[31] Great Massacre, 164-166. On pages 425-427 the reader may find an alternate account written by Bryant. On the morning of August 19 there was a state of unwonted confusion in St. Peter. Couriers had arrived before daybreak with the alarming news that New Ulm was on fire and that the inhabitants were being massacred. By nine o'clock horsemen from Nicollet and Le Sueur counties began to arrive. The men collected horses, teams, and provisions. Busiest of all in the work of organization were Charles E. Flandrau and Captain William B. Dodd. About ten o'clock Flandrau, with 135 men armed as well as they could be, took the road to New Ulm. Since they expected to meet savages on the way, a few men were kept in advance as skirmishers. Before dark the entire force reached the Redstone Ferry and crossed to enter New Ulm, which was soon "frantic with the mingled shouts of the delivered and their deliverers."

APPENDIX (3)                              371

A remarkable reassertion of this account may be found in a letter written by Henry A. Swift to Lieutenant Governor Donnelly on September 3, 1862, criticizing Donnelly's report of August 29, mentioned above, and in particular the statement that Flandrau had arrived at six o'clock and had thereafter driven the Indians away. The Indians attacking New Ulm on Tuesday, not more than fifty in number, were only a marauding band and were driven off five hours before Flandrau arrived. "The cavalry *did not* charge upon the Indians, nor did *they come in time to see an indian*. The Indians were driven from the town by a party of about a dozen men . . . named in the report of the affair in the 'Minnesota Statesman' of the 22nd ult. It was all done *before* the *Cavalry*, or Flandrau's infantry reached the town. I happened to be one of the party who did it, and *saw* it all, whether 'magna pars fui' or not." [32]

An account furnished by the Honorable Gideon S. Ives, lieutenant governor of Minnesota from 1891 to 1893 and a son-in-law of Governor Swift, carries such a degree of probability that it should not be omitted from this catena. "The news of the outbreak reached St. Peter in the early morning of August 19, 1862. The messenger came to the House of Governor Swift very early and within a short time thereafter he started for New Ulm driving his own horse and taking with him Mr. Hayden who at that time was the County Auditor of Nicollet county. On this trip to New Ulm they drove through Nicollet and the Swan Lake region and aroused these other men whose names appear in the statement [*of the Minnesota Statesman*] and who lived in the vicinity of this road and they evidently joined Swift at the time. When they arrived at the town, everything was in a disorganized state. . . . There was certainly no organization. . . . As soon as these men got there they organized and pushed on to the table land above the town and after considerable fighting drove the Indians off before any reinforcements came. The Boardman party did not reach the town until late in the afternoon and had no part in this fight." Mr. Ives states that his information came from many talks with William G. Hayden and other members of the party of eighteen.[33]

In 1897, thirty-five years after the Sioux Outbreak, William G. Hayden wrote his recollections of the affair at New Ulm on August 19, which may be given in substance as follows: Early in the morning messengers brought to St. Peter tidings that the Sioux were on the warpath, which were soon confirmed by the arrival of refugees. By nine o'clock a company of about a hundred men had been organized, with Flandrau as its commander, to go to the relief of Fort Ridgely. For some reason Swift deemed it desirable to ascertain the condition of things at New Ulm and invited

[32] Donnelly Papers. See *ante*, p. 366.
[33] Letter to the author, October 9, 1917, Folwell Papers. The names of the Swan Lake party are given in Bryant and Murch, *Great Massacre*, 165.

Hayden to accompany him thither in his own conveyance. Flandrau approved of the suggestion and "detailed" the two volunteers to proceed at once to New Ulm and upon their arrival to report the situation there. They left St. Peter about eleven o'clock. Among the numerous refugees they met hurrying eastward was a German minister, whose name unfortunately is not known. He decided that if those two men could go to New Ulm so could he, and turned the head of his "fine pony" in that direction. When the three arrived at the town about three o'clock no Indians had been seen. As the talk was in German, it was difficult to obtain definite information, but enough was learned to warrant sending a message to Flandrau advising him that his company should be brought to New Ulm. Among the crowd of distracted people were a few who were trying to establish order and to organize a defense. The few citizens who had arms had only hunting pieces. Some who had no firearms had provided themselves with pitchforks.

"Leaving our guns at the Dacota House," writes Hayden, "we [apparently the three persons mentioned] walked to the top of the hill or bluff just back of the hotel. . . . Standing on this ridge or hill we could see the whole space from the river to the second bluff. We soon noticed a number of persons coming over the farthest bluff and also a small body of horsemen riding down the prairie toward the west end of the town, but supposing them to be settlers coming in, or scouts who had been looking for Indians, we paid but little heed to them." A discharge of guns toward the west, however, soon attracted their attention and started them back to the hotel to get their guns. When near the hotel they looked back and saw "several Indians" standing where they had been two minutes before and firing over their heads into the crowded street. One woman, standing in the doorway of a store, was killed.

After securing their guns they went out into the street, where they learned that the Indians had possession of a house at the west end of the village. "A dozen or more men armed with guns and revolvers decided to attempt driving them out, and by keeping behind buildings as much as possible until near the house they made a rush for the front door. The Indians, after firing once, fled through the back door." About this time it began to rain and thereafter the fighting was confined to an exchange of shots with Indians lying just over the crest of the hill. Most of their shots went over the heads of the people. The cross streets leading to the ridge were now hastily barricaded. Several citizens of Nicollet arrived during the afternoon, making up a company of sixteen acquaintances. At about ten o'clock the St. Peter company arrived. The number of Indians was estimated to be from thirty to forty.[34]

[34] The manuscript of Hayden's recollections is in the possession of the Minnesota Historical Society.

General James H. Baker, writing in 1908, furnishes a version which involves some notable complications. He relates that when the news of the Indian outbreak reached St. Peter on Monday, August 18, Swift asked Hayden to go with him to New Ulm the next day. According to agreement the two left at noon on the nineteenth. Meantime A. M. Bean, with sixteen men, had started from Nicollet and reached New Ulm about one o'clock. About a hundred Indians began an attack about four o'clock. Very soon after the battle began Swift and Boardman, with sixteen well-armed men, arrived on the scene and, "taking an active part, turned the tide of battle. . . . Senator Swift's prompt action in aiding in rallying men and going to that place with the others . . . was probably the salvation of the town." On the same page Baker adds, "In the St. Peter Tribune . . . we find Swift's name with that of his companion Hayden as two of the company of eighteen men who arrived in New Ulm on the 19th and took an active and gallant part in the first defense of the town."[35]

The reader may remember that Captain Nix made an exception to his broad statement that his brave fellow townsmen saved the town. That was "Herr Swift," who, with his long Kentucky rifle, rendered efficient service in the action. There might have been one or two others present from St. Peter but he could not avouch it. The name of Henry A. Swift is to be found in the lists of both the "Boardman Cavalry" and the Swan Lake party. It appears that, having a fast-traveling horse, he either overtook the Swan Lake people or reached New Ulm soon after them. The messenger he sent back met Boardman at Courtland, ten miles away.[36]

An edifying contribution to the story of the salvation of New Ulm is that of Captain Theodore E. Potter. The news of the outbreak reached Garden City in the morning of August 20. In four hours a company of sixty mounted men was enlisted and, after partaking of a good dinner supplied by the ladies, started on its march. At sunset it arrived on the high bluff overlooking New Ulm. Formed in four ranks the men galloped into the eastern part of the city while Indians were scalping men, women, and children in the western part. It is further related that, as the Garden City company was nearing the place, it met with two other companies— one, from St. Peter, under command of Captain Dodd and the other, from Le Sueur, under command of Captain Sanders. A moment later a third company from Mankato, under Captain Bierbauer, came at full speed. There were now present full two hundred men, all mounted. With

[35] *Governors of Minnesota*, 118-120.
[36] Nix, *Ausbruch der Sioux-Indianer*, 28. The suggestion of Mr. Ives in his letter to the author, October 9, 1917, that Swift and Hayden raised the Swan Lake party and led it to New Ulm may be true, but it has not been sufficiently corroborated.

Captain Sanders in the lead they swept four abreast through the main business street as fast as their horses could carry them.  They took the Indians
by surprise and caused "every one of them instantly to drop his torch and
scalping knife and to mount his pony in the utmost haste and scatter."
If these military companies had not arrived in time the Indians would
have burned the whole town and massacred the people that night.  Later
on the same page the writer adds that Colonel Charles E. Flandrau, a
former Indian agent, had arrived from St. Peter during the afternoon
and had been placed in command of the city.[37]

This appendix illustrates the difficulty often presented to historians of
extracting truth from discordant statements of worthy persons ill informed or infirm of memory, or possibly biased by pride or some personal
interest.

## 4. THE CHIPPEWA DISTURBANCE OF 1862[38]

The agency for the Chippewa of the Mississippi in 1862 was located
on the Gull Lake reservation, comprising some 450 square miles west of
the Mississippi River and north of the Crow Wing in what is now Cass
County.  The site of the agency was on the north side of the Crow Wing
some three miles from its mouth.  Opposite the junction of the two rivers
stood the small village of Crow Wing, clustered about the ancient trading
post.  Seven miles below the junction, on the west bank of the Mississippi,
stood Fort Ripley, consisting of some small one-story buildings arranged
on three sides of a square open to the river.  There was a garrison of about
thirty men of Company C of the Fifth Minnesota Infantry.[39]

On the very day of the Sioux Outbreak, August 18, Lucius C. Walker,
the Chippewa agent, learned that a number of warriors were collecting
on Gull Lake in the northern part of the reservation and were threatening
to attack the agency.  He at once dispatched a messenger to Fort Ripley
asking for military protection.  On the following morning the agent was
so much impressed with what he believed to be immediate impending
danger that he abandoned the agency and started for the fort.  At Crow
Wing he met a detachment of twenty soldiers from the fort on their way

---

[37] "Captain Potter's Recollections of Minnesota Experiences," in *Minnesota History
Bulletin*, 1:439-443 (November, 1916); Potter, *Autobiography*, 161-165 (Concord, New
Hampshire, [1913].

[38] See *ante*, p. 146.

[39] Indian Office, *Reports*, 1862, p. 72; Mrs. Abbey Fuller Abbe, "Remarks and Reminiscences on Hole-in-the-Day and the Sioux Outbreak, 1862," p. 2, an unpublished manuscript
in the possession of the Minnesota Historical Society; Fobes, in *Minnesota in the Civil and
Indian Wars*, 1:257; record of an interview with Major Edwin Clark, Chippewa agent from
1865 to 1867, in the author's notebooks, 8:62; manuscript history of Fort Ripley, presum-
ably by Jasper W. Johnson.  Concerning this history, see *ante*, p. 127, n. 24.  For maps of
the Fort Ripley Reservation, consult the files of the Minnesota Historical Society.

to the agency. Walker, believing that the notorious Hole-in-the-Day, head chief of the Chippewa of the Mississippi, was responsible for the disturbances, gave the commander of the detachment a written order for his arrest. A squad chased the chieftain to his frame house not far distant, from which he escaped to the opposite bank of the river. After an exchange of shots with the soldiers, he fled to join the gathering on Gull Lake.

It was now learned that a large number of Pillagers from Leech Lake, who had robbed the private and government buildings there and were holding seven persons in temporary captivity, were coming down. A few cattle had been killed and some horses had been stolen on both reservations. Bad Boy, a Pillager chief or headman unfriendly to Hole-in-the-Day, had come down to the fort with his family and a few others and had given the alarm of a possible attack, not only on the agency but also on the fort. The commander at the fort at once proclaimed martial law over the surrounding region and called upon the settlers to come into the post for the protection he could not give them at their homes and for the common defense, if need be. The garrison and the refugees who came in at once began preparations for defense. Sergeant Frantzkey of the ordnance corps of the regular army, who was on duty at the post, found some ammunition for the four six-pound howitzers but no cartridges for the rifles. Bullets were molded and cartridges were made by candlelight. But no attack was made upon the agency or upon the fort and no further depredations were committed. Still the alarm spread rapidly along the northern frontier, causing a stampede to the fort or to the less exposed settlements. From these settlements frantic appeals were made to Governor Ramsey for troops or arms. Volunteer companies were raised at Marine, Taylor's Falls, Stillwater, Sunrise, and other points and the Ramsey County Picket Guard marched off northward. Colonel Francis R. Delano was placed in command of all the volunteer militia of the St. Croix Valley. A large number of refugees collected at Fort Ripley and fifty men volunteered to aid in defense.[40]

[40] Indian Office, *Reports*, 1862, pp. 14, 16, 73, 76; Fobes, in *Minnesota in the Civil and Indian Wars*, 1: 257-259; report of the adjutant general, in *Executive Documents*, 1862, p. 515. For the possibility of a raid on the whites by the Chippewa, see Whipple, *Lights and Shadows*, 107; John Johnson Enmegahbowh, "Extracts from Letters Written to Hon. Nathan Richardson," 8-12, a manuscript narrative in the possession of the Minnesota Historical Society; Abbe, "Remarks and Reminiscences"; the *Pioneer and Democrat*, August 22, 1862; and the *St. Cloud Democrat*, August 21, 1862. For numerous appeals for protection see letters to Ramsey from H. Z. Mitchell, St. Cloud, August 25; from twelve citizens of Chisago County, August 25; from J. H. Allen, Princeton, August 28; from Hermann Trott, Chengwatana, August 28, September 1; from L. O. Tombler, Wyoming, August 28; from John S. Cady, Anoka, September 1; from James Starkey, Sunrise City, September 1, 3; and the report of F. R. Delano, Sunrise, September 2, 1862 — all in Governor's Archives, file 255. Exact dates of important arrivals and events at Fort Ripley are given in the entries from August 18 to September 26, 1862, in a daybook kept by the Reverend E. Steele Peake, in the possession of the Minnesota Historical Society.

Agent Walker did not tarry at Fort Ripley, but started with his family for St. Paul. On reaching St. Cloud, fifty miles below the fort, on August 20 he found his superior officer, William P. Dole, United States commissioner of Indian affairs, with a considerable party about to leave for the long journey to the Red River country, where a treaty was to be negotiated with the Red Lake and Pembina Chippewa. The unfortunate agent was by this time in a state of such distraction that he could give the commissioner no coherent account of the nature and the causes of the Chippewa disorder. Pursuing his way toward St. Paul, he warned all persons whom he encountered to fly from the Indians who were on his track. At Monticello he was seen to be mentally much disturbed and three miles below that place, on August 22, he ended his life with a pistol.[41]

The commissioner very soon learned that his Red River journey must be given up, for a time at least, because of the forays of the Sioux in the region he must traverse to reach Fort Abercrombie. He deemed it imprudent, and it probably was, to proceed into the Indian country without greater military protection than that afforded by the little garrison at Fort Ripley. He therefore returned to St. Paul to confer with Governor Ramsey, who at once dispatched two companies of infantry in addition to the one already sent forward at the request of the post commander. It was not until the twenty-ninth that the commissioner arrived at Fort Ripley under the escort of the troops. He at once dispatched a runner to Hole-in-the-Day, who was still at Gull Lake, to summon him to council. He did not come. The message was repeated day by day, but it was not until the tenth of September that, after having moved his camp to a point between the agency and Crow Wing, he condescended to appear, not at the fort, but at that village. He came in great state, attended by a large body of followers in war paint and dress. A detachment, numbering "some two hundred" according to the commissioner's estimate, was sent "around through the brush" to surround the council ground and to take possession of the road to the fort. Upon the commissioner's demand the chief consented that civilians, but civilians only, might use the road. In council he was insolent and even defiant. He made no charges against the government or its agents and gave no explanation of his conduct other than that he had been fired upon by the military. The council was without result and the chief broke his engagement for another the next day.[42]

[41] Indian Office, *Reports*, 1862, pp. 14, 15, 73, 77; *Pioneer and Democrat*, August 26, 1862. Thomas B. Walker, in his "Memories of the Early Life and Development of Minnesota," in *Minnesota Historical Collections*, 15: 462, gives his reason for believing that Walker was murdered.

[42] Dole to Ramsey, August 20, 25, 30, September 2, 11, 1862, in Governor's Archives, file 255; Indian Office, *Reports*, 1862, pp. 17-19, 73, 77-82; Abbe, "Remarks and Reminiscences," 4. In *Harper's New Monthly Magazine*, 26: 186-191 (January, 1863), is an article on Hole-in-the-Day by John G. Nicolay, who was a secretary to President Lincoln and who

Deeming further parley with the truculent chieftain useless, the commissioner on September 12 took his leave for St. Paul, leaving instructions with Special Agent Ashley C. Morrill for proceedings which, perhaps, he did not care personally to execute. The agent was to avoid a collision with the Indians, but was to advise them to move their camp off the road between the fort and the agency and, whenever the commander should decide to withdraw the troops from the agency, Morrill was to abandon the agency and remove the property to the fort. In a final sentence the commissioner made an order calculated, if not intended, to bring matters to a crisis. "You will," it read, "issue no further provisions or goods of any kind to the Indians until directed so to do by the superintendent." The Indians had been furnished with food to keep them from raiding the agency and the settlements.

The order had its effect upon a stormy council of chiefs the same night. In vain did Hole-in-the-Day plead for an attack upon the agency for the provisions in store there. The chiefs did not care to face three companies of infantry. In the night a delegation came to the agent to ask for a council the next day. The request was granted and the council was attended by the large majority of the insurgent Indians. The chiefs denounced Hole-in-the-Day as the fomenter of the trouble and expressed sorrow for their bad acts, but urged the failure of the Great Father to keep promises as some extenuation. He had not furnished enough iron for the blacksmith; the carpenters he had promised to build houses for the old men and chiefs had not been seen; their wives and children were not warmly clothed; though their children went to school, they were not made wise; ten boxes of money and goods of equal value which had been promised eight years ago had not come; in all, sixty boxes of money (sixty thousand dollars) were due them. They would not, however, blame the Great Father himself. He doubtless sent them all their dues, but, "as the road from Washington is long and crooked, and the fore car moves so very fast, perhaps they drop off and are lost over the road." They were willing to pay their share of the damage which had been done. On the day following, September 14, they moved their camp to the agency and delivered up some horses and other property. Supplied with rations for the journey, 364 Pillagers took their departure on the same day for their homes on Leech Lake. A small number only remained attached to Hole-in-the-Day, but they also turned in the plunder which they had taken.[43]

accompanied Commissioner Dole. A well-known woodcut of Hole-in-the-Day is at the head of the article. On page 190 is a pen picture of the chief. For sketches of Hole-in-the-Day, see Julius T. Clark, "Reminiscences of Hole-in-the-Day"; Alfred Brunson, "Sketch of Hole-in-the-Day"; "Death of Hole-in-the-Day," reprinted from the *Saint Paul Press* of June 30, 1868; and "Murder of Hole-in-the-Day," reprinted from the *St. Cloud Journal*, July 9, 1868—all in *Wisconsin Historical Collections*, 5: 378-409.

[43] Indian Office, *Reports*, 1862, pp. 19, 73, 75, 83.

In a last interview Hole-in-the-Day had suggested to the agent a means of settling the difficulties, the only one in his judgment which could be conclusive. Let the government turn over to him and his people ten thousand dollars worth of goods and they would give no further trouble. He had in mind, doubtless, the goods brought by the commissioner for use in making the proposed treaty with the Red Lake Chippewa. The proposition was, of course, immediately and decisively rejected. The special agent now considered the outbreak at an end and reported, "All danger is passed."[44]

The play, however, was not to end without the traditional afterpiece. The reports from the Chippewa country did not at first create great alarm in St. Paul. The Chippewa had always been friendly and amenable to white man's guidance. The troops sent up would be able to hold Fort Ripley and to overawe Hole-in-the-Day and any faction he might gather about him. But the long delay in settling the disturbance became a cause of anxiety, all the greater because the head of the Indian department seemed to exercise little influence or effective authority. The legislature of Minnesota met in extra session on the ninth of September. Soon after its organization Governor Ramsey communicated a letter from the commissioner of Indian affairs—then still awaiting the pleasure of His Mightiness, Hole-in-the-Day—asking for additional military force. Feeling that the public, already excited to a high pitch of anxiety by the Sioux Outbreak, would expect some action, the houses lost no time in considering questions of jurisdiction, quietly ignored that clause of the Constitution of the United States which reposes in the president and the Senate the power of making treaties with Indians, and straightway appointed a commission to act in conjunction with the commissioner of Indian affairs and requested the governor to repair with it to the scene of trouble. The membership of the commission was judiciously made up. It embraced Senator Henry M. Rice, whose long and intimate relations with the Chippewa qualified him in an eminent degree for the duty; David Cooper, one of the first territorial judges, who possessed the confidence of Hole-in-the-Day, having served as his counsel; the Reverend Frederick Ayer, the pioneer missionary to the Chippewa; and Edwin A. C. Hatch.[45]

The commissioners and Governor Ramsey left St. Paul in the evening of September 13. At two o'clock in the morning at Anoka they met the Indian commissioner on his return from Crow Wing and learned of his failure to effect an adjustment with the disgruntled Chippewa. The commissioner, however, according to his statement, advised them of the

[44] Indian Office, *Reports*, 1862, pp. 19, 86.
[45] *Senate Journal*, 1862, extra session, 22, 25; *House Journal*, 28, 139.

probable submission of the Indians and of the consequent futility of reopening negotiations. He declined to give them passports to the Indian country but, seeing that they were resolved to execute their mission, furnished a letter to the governor in which he gave his assent to a council and promised his coöperation in measures for peace. In a second letter he requested the governor to act through Special Agent Morrill. The commissioner pursued his journey to the seat of government and the Minnesota delegation proceeded to Crow Wing. The tidings that the Indians had submitted and had departed for their homes, communicated to the commissioners by a messenger encountered between St. Cloud and Fort Ripley and again by the commandant at Fort Ripley, did not discourage them. The Gull River chiefs were recalled by runners without the knowledge or consent of Agent Morrill and a council was held at Crow Wing on the fifteenth, which he would certainly have prevented if he could. The result of an all-day palaver, with an intermission for consultation, was a formal treaty duly signed in triplicate by the plenipotentiaries. The name of the special agent was written in the list of witnesses. The first article bound the high contracting parties to continued peace and friendship; the second provided for a joint board of arbitrators to investigate and adjust the claims of the Indians and the equities of the government; the third and last article guaranteed the full payment of the annuities, about due, without deductions, that is, without reparation for the late depredations. Major Morrill sharply criticized the commission because, as the Indians had departed for their homes without having exacted any concessions, its action was superfluous; because it diminished the authority of the officers charged with the care of the Indians; and because it virtually rewarded the Indians for the outrages which they had committed.[46]

The high commission returned and reported its action to the legislature, which presently memorialized the president to carry out the stipulations of the agreement. It is hardly needful to say that, advised by the incensed Chippewa agent and his superior, the commissioner, President Lincoln did not trouble himself about the extraordinary, not to say superfluous, negotiation. It may have had a temporary soothing effect upon the

[46] Indian Office, *Reports*, 1862, pp. 20, 74, 83-86. One of Dole's criticisms of the "treaty" was that it called for an investigation by a commission entirely independent of the department of the interior. He was unprepared to believe that "the government" would thus "surrender its legitimate and constitutional control of Indian affairs." It was, of course, impossible that either Governor Ramsey or Senator Rice believed that their commission had power to make a binding treaty with the Indians. It may be surmised that they expected that an uninformed public would easily believe they had such power and that their action would be approved for the assurance of peace which it seemed to guarantee. In his report for the following year, in Indian Office, *Reports*, 1863, p. 30, Dole makes the statement that the Chippewa treaty of 1863 was made "in lieu" of the unratified treaty of 1862, negotiated under the authority of the legislature of Minnesota.

disappointed Chippewa and upon the distracted settlers along the upper
Mississippi. A week after the treaty some fifty chiefs and braves of the
Chippewa appeared at St. Paul, in gorgeous costume, to offer their services
in the war against the Sioux. The offer was, of course, tactfully declined
by both Governor Ramsey and Major General Pope. After a council of
farcical solemnity, the savages were duly feasted and started for their
homes, enjoying the treat of a ride in the "fire-wagon" all the way to St.
Anthony Falls.[47]

Because the Chippewa trouble broke out on the same day on which
the massacres by the Sioux began, it was natural that it should occur
to many that there must have been some agreement or understanding
between the two Indian controls for a simultaneous attack upon their
common enemy, the hated white man. That rumor spread far and wide
and carried alarm over many counties unaffected by the carnage and
plunder going on in the Minnesota Valley. The direct evidence of an
understanding between the head chiefs of the nations is meager. The
Indian preacher, Enmegahbowh, who was continuing the mission at Gull
Lake established and abandoned by Breck, told the post commander at
Fort Ripley that he heard Hole-in-the-Day say in council that an outbreak had been arranged with the Dakota and that the whites could not
resist their united forces. The Chippewa were to kill their agent, seize
the agency and the fort, and sweep down the Mississippi. In his printed
narrative Enmegahbowh states that he had heard that Hole-in-the-Day
had received a message from Little Crow.[48]

Bishop Whipple in his autobiography relates that at Crow Wing not
many days before the outbreak he saw a letter from Little Crow to Hole-
in-the-Day which made it evident to him that "some treaty of peace"
had been made between them. The letter purported to notify the Chippewa chief that Little Crow could not restrain his soldiers from taking

---

[47] *House Journal*, 1862, extra session, 90, 93, 124, 130, 133-139; *Pioneer and Democrat*,
September 19, 24, 1862; *Saint Paul Press*, September 23, 24, 1862. The "embassy" departed on September 13, arrived at Fort Ripley the following day, and held councils with the
Chippewa chiefs and headmen on September 15, after which they returned. In the *Press*
of October 2, 1862, is a six-column "History" of the Chippewa trouble by Superintendent
Clark W. Thompson. By implication the action of the government agents is approved and
that of the Minnesota legislature and its commission is condemned. A number of important
documents are included in this article.

[48] Captain Francis Hall to Ramsey, August 23, 1862, in Governor's Archives, file 255;
John Johnson Enmegahbowh, *Enmegahbowh's Story: An Account of the Disturbances of the
Chippewa Indians at Gull Lake in 1857 and 1862 and Their Removal in 1868*, 18 (Minneapolis, 1904). For a sketch of Enmegahbowh's part in the disturbance of 1862, see Leroy
Jackson, "Enmegahbowh—A Chippewa Missionary," in *North Dakota Historical Collections*,
2: 483-488, and Whipple, *Lights and Shadows*, 110. Bishop Whipple probably exaggerates
the part of Enmegahbowh. On pages 497-510 of the latter work is Enmegahbowh's story
of his life. He is mentioned frequently throughout the book. Enmegahbowh was an
Ottawa Indian born in Canada. On the mission at Gull Lake, see *ante*, p. 206; 1: 181.

vengeance upon some Chippewa who had killed one of his people. "Look out," it ended. This letter, if authentic, certainly imported a friendly relation between the two men. While it may be doubtfully granted that the two had had a personal understanding, that Hole-in-the-Day should brag about it in a council of Chippewa chiefs and braves is improbable. Such an alliance would have surpassed belief and would not have been tolerated for a moment.[49]

Whatever may have been the motive and the object of the insurrection, it did not involve the whole body of the Chippewa of the Mississippi, much less any of the Lake Superior bands. But two of the eight bands of the former group of Indians, Hole-in-the-Day's own band at Gull Lake and that of the Pillagers at Leech Lake, took part. That this coalition, mustering not more than five hundred warriors, without transportation or commissariat, should seriously contemplate war on the United States may be doubted.[50] A probable explanation of the affair may be found in a concurrence of minor exasperations with Hole-in-the-Day's vanity and greed. There was the matter of promised goods and money long withheld, as claimed. Agent Walker had incurred the dislike of influential Indians, which had been fanned into enmity by traders with whose unlawful traffic in whisky he had interfered. Hole-in-the-Day had been in Washington not long before and had learned of the magnitude of the Civil War and of the defeats suffered by the Union armies, and he inferred from the presence of recruiting agents in his country enlisting half-breeds that the government must be in great need of soldiers.[51] He had learned also of the intended expedition to the Red Lake country, with the usual great train of cattle, provisions, and presents. He came home exasperated because his complaint of Agent Walker had not been entertained. He therefore conceived the plan of a hostile demonstration

---

[49] Whipple, *Lights and Shadows*, 107. Jacob V. Brower, in his *Kathio*, 86 (*Memoirs of Explorations in the Basin of the Mississippi*, vol. 4—St. Paul, 1901), says that Chief Bad Boy notified the commandant at Fort Ripley of a conspiracy between Little Crow and Hole-in-the-Day. In the Fuller Papers is a letter to Miss Elizabeth Fuller written at Fort Ripley by Mrs. Samuel B. Abbe on August 25, 1862. Mrs. Abbe, who with her family had gone to the fort at the time of the Chippewa disturbance, says that Johnson (Enmegahbowh) told her family that Hole-in-the-Day in council said that he and Little Crow had met in St. Paul the previous spring and "had agreed upon this thing and the time was to be indicated by letter," which Hole-in-the-Day had received, for "we saw it." The plan was to burn the agency, kill everyone there and at Crow Wing, and sweep the country to St. Paul. The Chippewa killed Johnson's team to keep him from the whites, but he slipped off to Crow Wing. In the *Minneapolis Journal* of December 4, 1916, is a letter of Major Edwin Clark, in which he states that "the bead belt and pipe sent by Little Crow . . . to the head chief of the Chippewas of Red Lake, requesting the Chippewas to join in the massacre, was presented to me by the chief and is now deposited in the pioneers' museum at the Godfrey house."

[50] Indian Office, *Reports*, 1862, p. 16. For the size of the two bands as given by Agent Morrill, see pages 70 and 72.

[51] Fobes, in *Minnesota in the Civil and Indian Wars*, 1: 260; *Enmegahbowh's Story*, 11-17.

which, under the circumstances, might extort from a government not desiring another Indian war the payment of long-standing claims and perhaps a new and more liberal treaty, with the usual accompaniments of gifts and bonuses, of which he would receive a generous share. He would pose before his people as the powerful chief who had brought the Great Father to terms. As the reader already will have observed, this grand scheme degenerated into one of blackmail.

## 5. MONUMENT TO MOUZOOMAUNNEE[52]

The considerations which moved the legislature of Minnesota in 1913 to appropriate eight hundred dollars for the erection of a monument on the site of Fort Ridgely in honor of the Mille Lacs Chippewa Indians and in particular of Chief Mouzoomaunnee have not been revealed and are not easy to imagine.[53] It is notorious that the Mille Lacs bands were devotedly loyal in 1862. They sent a large delegation to Fort Ripley to assure the United States commissioner of Indian affairs of their friendliness. There was no occasion for exertion by their chiefs to dissuade them from accepting the invitation of Hole-in-the-Day, the Gull Lake chief, to join in an outbreak. There is no record that any Mille Lacs chief was conspicuous in such superfluous service. That Mouzoomaunnee was a chief at all may be doubted. The name "Mosomonnee" appears on a pay roll of 1866 as that of a member of a Mille Lacs band, not that of a chief. In that year the agent distributed monetary rewards for loyalty to Chippewa chiefs and headmen whose names were included in a list prepared for his use by three men well qualified to make the selection. Mouzoomaunnee's name does not appear, but there need be no doubt of the man's existence. A reputed son of his was present at the dedication of the monument on August 20, 1914, but made no recital of the valorous deeds of his father. One of the speakers made the statement that the Indian died on September 3, 1896, but added that he signed the treaty of 1863, which was utterly erroneous. The reasonable suggestion has been made that if there were good reasons for raising a monument to a distinguished loyal Chippewa, a site other than that of Fort Ridgely should have been chosen.[54]

[52] See *ante*, p. 133, n. 31.

[53] *General Laws*, 1913, p. 582. The name is inscribed on the monument as "Mon-zoo-man-nee."

[54] Letter of the Mille Lacs chiefs, in Indian Office, *Reports*, 1862, p. 79; letter of Major Edwin Clark, in the *Minneapolis Journal*, August 19, 1914. The signatures to the treaty of 1863 are in *Statutes at Large*, 13: 45. Mrs. Abbe, in her "Remarks and Reminiscences," 1, speaks of Mouzoomaunnee as a reputed Chippewa chief and ridicules statements made during the controversy. In the entry for June 22, 1821, in his journal, Major Lawrence Taliaferro mentions a visit from "Mossomoni," a Chippewa chief, at the St. Peter agency. For a description and a picture of the monument and an account of the dedication ceremonies and addresses, see the *Fairfax Standard*, August 27, 1914. For other contributions to the controversy, see the *Minneapolis Journal*, August 16, 19, and the *St. Paul Dispatch*, August 20, 27, 1914. See also the *Minnesota History Bulletin*, 3: 306 (February, 1920).

## 6. RELIEF OF FORT RIDGELY[55]

The question,"Who relieved Fort Ridgely?" has been the subject of controversy. The relief of the fort has been commonly attributed to Colonel Samuel McPhail, commander of Sibley's mounted men. In his report of August 31, 1862, to Ramsey, McPhail related his all-night march with part of a company from Fort Snelling, his arrival at St. Peter on the twenty-fourth, and the organization on that day of a mounted force of 450 men. He received no orders until the twenty-sixth, when he was directed to prepare for a march. At four o'clock in the afternoon he called for 150 men to make a forced march by night to the fort. "Having obtained the number," he writes, "at Sunset we mounted Six miles west of St Peter and at Sun Rise next morning Dismounted at the fort." The statement presumes McPhail's personal command of an undivided detachment.[56]

The unknown author of a biographical sketch of Anson Northup claims for him the honor of being first to bring joy to the beleaguered garrison. In this account Captain Northup is represented as marching from Minneapolis direct to Fort Ridgely with a company which he had hastily recruited in that town. "It is but simple justice," the author writes, "to state here that Captain Northrup was the first to relieve the distressed inmates of the fortress. Others, with less modesty, and as surely with less honesty, have claimed the laurels due only to this old patriot."[57]

A surviving member of the Northup company has furnished in manuscript the following account, in substance: It was the purpose of the company before reporting to Sibley at St. Peter to go direct to Fort Ridgely. When Sibley ordered it to halt in St. Peter the men felt mutinous. Under the pretense of watering their horses outside the guard lines, they held a consultation and decided to make the march without orders from Sibley. Under the guidance of Major Brown they started about three o'clock and arrived at the fort "at the earliest crack of dawn."[58]

Colonel Timothy J. Sheehan in the Sisseton and Wahpeton claim case testified that "Anson Northrop, with 175 mounted men, arrived on the morning of the 27th at daylight. Those men were mostly raised at Minneapolis and gathered up on the line as they went."[59]

---

[55] See *ante*, p. 150.

[56] Governor's Archives, file 255.

[57] George E. Warner and Charles M. Foote, eds., *History of Hennepin County and the City of Minneapolis*, 607 (Minneapolis, 1881); *Central Republican* (Faribault), September, 17, 1862.

[58] This account, written by John F. Barnard, accompanies a letter from him to the author, dated January 16, 1918, in the Folwell Papers.

[59] *Sisseton and Wahpeton Claim Case Record, Evidence for Defendant*, 282.

Judge William Lochren in an article on Minneapolis in the Civil War says of Captain Northup that he brought the first relief to the garrison at Fort Ridgely.[60]

Captain Simon P. Snyder, a lieutenant of Northup's company, writing in 1880, states that "we went through to the Fort . . . and were the first body of men, by at least twenty-four hours to reach and relieve Fort Ridgley."[61] This statement called out from Colonel McPhail a rejoinder, in which he gave his recollections of the march as follows: He set out late in the afternoon, accompanied by William R. Marshall as a volunteer. At Cullen's farm, seven miles from St. Peter, he rested and fed his horses. Just before sunset the march was resumed, with Northup's company in front. After marching a mile, that company broke into first a trot and then a gallop. McPhail remonstrated with the captain for increasing the gait without orders. Northup petulantly told him that, as he was not subject to McPhail's orders, he would not obey them and thereupon took his men out of the column and turned to the rear. Marshall remonstrated with Northup to no purpose and then called out, "All that are for the relief of Fort Ridgely forward, and let cowards turn back." After the march had been continued for several miles, Northup sent a lieutenant forward with the message that he was rejoining the column. McPhail sent back an order for Northup to leave his men in the rear and report in person at the head of the column. From that time McPhail, Northup, Marshall, and another led the march and rode into the fort just after sunrise. Colonel McPhail's statement is immediately followed by a letter from Colonel Sheehan certifying that he was relieved by Colonel McPhail on August 27, 1862.[62]

A published account prepared by Dr. Alonzo Barnard, a member of the Minneapolis company, is in substance as follows: Mounted men were called to volunteer for a night march from St. Peter to the fort. Northup's company of about one hundred men responded and other volunteers raised the number to 175, all under the nominal command of Colonel McPhail. The cavalcade started about five o'clock, headed by Northup and Antoine Freniere. When it was a few miles out the horses, which had been all the way without water, on seeing a lake started off at a lively gait, which the men did not take pains to check. McPhail came to the front and there was a brief altercation between him and Northup, who suddenly took his men out of the column and led them to the rear. "As we were passing the St. Paul squad," Barnard writes, "William R. Mar-

[60] Isaac Atwater and John H. Stevens, eds., *History of Minneapolis and Hennepin County, Minnesota*, 2: 819 (New York, 1895).

[61] *Pioneer Press* (St. Paul and Minneapolis), March 4, 1880, p. 6.

[62] *Pioneer Press* March 16, 1880, p. 8. See the issue of February 27, 1880, p. 5, for a slightly variant account drawn from the *Saint Peter Tribune* of February 25.

shall . . . with mingled emotions of indignant surprise, contempt and disgust . . . could not repress the exclamation: 'You d——d Hennepin county cowards!' . . . Instantly a dozen guns were raised and a dozen furious voices broke upon the air with a profanity too profuse for full expression here: 'Take that back, d——n you; take that back quick; repeat that if you dare!'" The column moved on and the members of Northup's company gathered in a circle for consultation. It was decided that McPhail's indiscreet attempt to subject them to the discipline of veteran soldiers should not swerve them from their duty. They reformed, spurred their horses into a gallop, and were soon at the head of the column. Upon arriving in sight of the fort early in the morning, they saw the flag flying over it. Freniere, the guide, suggested that it might be a lure into an ambush. While others hesitated, Northup, Freniere, and three or four others dashed into and through the intervening gorge and in a few minutes emerged safe near the fort. Barnard gives from memory the names of ninety-two members of the company; no proper roster has been found. Members of the company obtained pensions for the service.[63]

Another story, carefully written by Richard H. Chittenden, who subscribes himself as "Late Capt. 1st Wisconsin Cavalry, and of 'Northrup Guard,'" deserves attention. According to Chittenden, 130 of the most prominent business men of Minneapolis and St. Anthony, forming "the most thoroughly organized and effective mounted corps connected with the Expedition," set out soon after notice of the Indian outbreak had been received. They reached St. Peter on Sunday, the twenty-fourth, at five o'clock in the afternoon and their leader asked leave to proceed immediately to the relief of New Ulm. The request was denied. On the next day Captain Northup again asked permission to advance at once to New Ulm or Fort Ridgely. This request also was denied. On Tuesday, the twenty-sixth, the "Northrup Guard" was kept in the saddle all day and was not allowed to refresh either men or animals. At five o'clock it was placed under the command of Colonel McPhail. The men were exasperated by the delay and by being put under the command of a man whom they did not know nor trust. Six miles out of St. Peter they refused to go farther under his command. Captain Chittenden, however, prevailed upon them to proceed upon the understanding that McPhail would not interfere with them. After an all-night ride, they reached the fort at daylight on the twenty-seventh. On the twenty-eighth they made a reconnoissance in the vicinity. On the twenty-ninth a detail of fifty men made a reconnoissance to Little Crow's village and the vicinity of Birch

---

[63] Atwater and Stevens, *Minneapolis and Hennepin County*, 2: 838. A footnote indicates a previous publication of the account. The author can vouch for Dr. Barnard's honesty from a long acquaintance.

Coulee and ascertained that there was no enemy near. They believed that Sibley's enlisted troops could take care of any Indians who might appear. Because of their refusal to serve under McPhail they were now refused rations and a threat was made to commandeer their horses. The "Guard" therefore marched for home.[64] It may be added that Captain Northup was wagon master of the First Minnesota, on furlough at the time.

## 7. THE BIRCH COULEE MONUMENT CONTROVERSY[65]

The Minnesota legislature of 1893 provided by law for the erection of an appropriate monument on "the land on which was fought the battle of Birch Coulie," made an appropriation of $2,500 for the purpose, and committed the execution of the work to seven commissioners named in the act. In the spring of 1894 it became known that the commissioners had not been pleased to give to the phrase quoted above its literal and obvious meaning but had selected a site for the monument a mile and three-quarters south of the battle ground and three-fourths of a mile east of the village of Morton on the fair grounds of the Renville County Agricultural Society. Morton lies on the left bank of the Minnesota two miles above the mouth of Birch Coulee. A branch of the Minneapolis and St. Louis Railroad crosses the river near the town. Protests were soon heard. To these no formal replies were made, but the public became informed that among the considerations which had governed the board were such as these: (1) that the site of the "corral" was remote and lonely; (2) that the owner of that site had undertaken to exact an exorbitant price for it; (3) that the preferred site was beautiful because of its situation on a high bluff overlooking the Minnesota River for long distances up and down; (4) that the monument would overlook the battle ground and would be visible to railroad travelers; (5) that a sufficient area had been donated and would be graded, inclosed, and beautified without cost to the state; (6) and that, after all, as the Indians had passed over the place on their retreat, it might be considered a part of the battle ground. The attorney-general, it is said, had advised the commissioners that the change of site was within their discretion. As no injunction was sued for, the monument, which was of Rockville granite forty-six feet high and of a conventional design, was erected in the summer of 1894 and the third day of September was appointed for the dedication.[66]

[64] *State Atlas* (Minneapolis), July 1, 1863, p. 2. Sibley's biographer, writing doubtless under inspiration, makes the ambiguous statement that "McPhail's vanguard" reached the fort on the day preceding the arrival of the main expedition. Holcombe attributes the relief of the fort to McPhail and Northrup. West, *Sibley*, 258; Holcombe, in *Minnesota in Three Centuries*, 3: 394.
[65] See *ante*, p. 156.
[66] *General Laws*, 1893, p. 381; *Pioneer Press*, May 7, 11, 24, 25, September 4, 5, 1894. There is a tradition that the change of location implied a land speculation and a desire to

One of the published letters to the press supporting the commissioners in their location of the monument was that of Captain Hiram P. Grant, who signed it as "Commanding the forces at Birch Coulee." He had already published a statement in the form of a report in which he claimed to have had "full charge" in the affair.[67] These called out from Mr. Samuel J. Brown, a son of Major Brown, an elaborate response, in which he marshaled the documentary evidence of his father's right to be recognized as the commander of the expedition. The principal citations were: (1) Colonel Sibley's report of September 4, 1862; (2) Major Brown's report of the same date; (3) Captain Anderson's report to Major Brown, also of the same date; (4) Sibley's letter to his wife, also of the same date; (5) Colonel Flandrau's narrative; (6) Judge Egan's statement; and (7) the accounts of the historians, Mrs. McConkey, Heard, and Neill. All these, if examined, will be found to concur in representing Major Joseph R. Brown as the commander of the expedition. Mr. Brown further asserted that his father was a duly commissioned major in the state troops and that he did in fact command as such, while Captain Grant, not having been mustered in, was technically a civilian. Captain Joseph Anderson declared in a letter to the *Pioneer Press* that during the whole time that the detachment was out he recognized and obeyed Major Brown as "the rightful and only commander" and that he received no orders from Grant.[68]

To these allegations Captain Grant replied that he had been mustered in as a captain on August 16, while Brown held no commission entitling him to command and that Brown's Third Regiment of Minnesota Militia had never existed. Major Brown, he said, obeyed his orders just as other civilians did. He remarked that Colonel William R. Marshall in his account of the battle made no mention of Major Brown but spoke of the expedition as being under Grant's command. Grant embodied in his reply three letters in support of his contention. One of them, dated May 25, 1894, was from Colonel William Crooks, who commanded the Sixth Minnesota. Crooks stated that he made the detail of Captain Grant's

secure an object of interest on the Renville County fair grounds. For a map showing the locations of the monument and the battle field, see Ray P. Chase, *Statement to the Nineteen Hundred Twenty-three Legislature*, 29. This is a report by the state auditor of Minnesota on state parks and playgrounds.

[67] *Pioneer Press*, May 25, 1894; *Minnesota in the Civil and Indian Wars*, 2: 215-219.

[68] *Pioneer Press*, June 4, August 6, 16, September 2, 1894; Sibley's report, in West, *Sibley*, 460, and in his Order Book, 67; Flandrau, in *Minnesota in the Civil and Indian Wars*, 1: 736; reports of Brown and Anderson and statement of Egan, in the latter work, 2: 212d, 219; Sibley to his wife, September 4, 1862, Sibley Papers; McConkey, *Dakota War Whoop*, 171; Heard, *Sioux War*, 131; Neill, *Minnesota*, 730 (fourth edition). See Curtiss-Wedge, *Renville County*, 2: 1344, for the statement of Dr. J. W. Daniels, one of the monument commissioners: "I know that Major Brown was the commander of all of us." Dr. Daniels withdrew from the commission after it was voted to recognize Captain Grant as commander. In his "Indian Outbreak," 9, Dr. Daniels recognizes Major Brown as commanding at the time. See also Daniels to Holcombe, October 15, 1894, in the Holcombe Papers.

company by direction of Colonel Sibley and that "Capt. Hiram P. Grant, of Company 'A,' being the ranking officer, was placed in command of the whole detachment. He received his instructions and orders from me." The second letter, dated June 15, 1894, was from Major Timothy J. Sheehan and was based on his minutes made at the time. He related that on the evening of August 31 he was at the headquarters of Colonel Sibley when a detachment was ordered to be detailed by Colonel Crooks and placed under the orders of Captain Grant. Major Brown, who was present, requested permission to accompany the force to look after his family, still in the hands of the Indians. In the third letter, which was written to Grant by a company clerk, the statement was made that Major Brown gave no commands during the battle. Captain Grant in his letter further said that by his personal knowledge there was a secret meeting of "the Indian Ring" at half past nine o'clock on the morning of September 4, 1862, at which it was agreed and arranged to make it appear that Major Brown was in command at Birch Coulee. He noted that General Sibley had made no denial to his claim published in the St. Paul newspapers years before.[69]

The day appointed for the dedication of the monument came and a great concourse of citizens assembled. After the formalities had been disposed of Captain Grant made an address describing the Indian outbreak of 1862 and the events following it, without referring to disputed matters. Governor Ramsey followed with interesting reminiscences. William R. Marshall then broke out in a fervid address in which he denounced the location of the monument and its inscriptions as falsifying history. Judge Flandrau, according to the *Pioneer Press*, "straddled the commander question by referring to the camp as 'Maj. Brown and Capt. Anderson's camp.'" Captain Anderson asserted in the most positive terms that Major Brown was in command at Birch Coulee. Captain Grant declared his willingness that the legislature should make an investigation of his claim and closed by saying: "So help me God, Maj. Brown did not give me an order." The *Pioneer Press* in an editorial article expressed regret that the dedication had been made an occasion for "acrimonious controversy . . . barely preserved . . . from the indignity of a heated quarrel."[70]

The matter rested until the following winter (1895), when it was brought before the legislature by a memorial from the Sixth Minnesota Infantry Association, which doubtless desired and expected the vindication of a comrade. To the disappointment of the association, a joint committee of the two houses in a unanimous report declared that the

[69] *Pioneer Press*, July 16, 1894.
[70] *Pioneer Press*, September 4, 5, 1894.

commissioners had erred in their choice of a site and in inscribing on the monument the name of Captain Grant as commander of the forces. The committee therefore recommended the relocation of the monument and the correction of the inscriptions. By a unanimous vote in the Senate and by seventy-two ayes in a total vote of seventy-five in the House a bill was passed providing that the adjutant general should have the monument moved onto the land on which the battle of Birch Coulee was "actually fought" and the inscriptions corrected to conform with the truths of history. "In particular," reads the text of the act, "said inscriptions shall show . . . that Major Joseph R. Brown, of the state militia, was in general command of the state's forces and that Captain H. P. Grant, of Company A, Sixth regiment of Minnesota infantry, and Captain Joseph Anderson, of the 'Cullen Frontier Guards,' (cavalry) were in subordinate commands at and in the battle of Birch Coulie."[71]

Nearly thirty years have passed and the monument still looks out over the Minnesota Valley from its sightly bluff near Morton and the inscriptions remain unchanged. The suggestion that political motives had something to do with the failure of the governor in 1896 to require the adjutant general to obey the mandate of the legislature without delay has not been verified. The appropriation of twelve hundred dollars long ago lapsed under the rule relating to unused appropriations.[72]

The subject might here be dismissed to debating clubs looking out for questions which have two sides, were it not for some points which later studies have brought to light. Sibley's intention to place Major Brown in charge of the expedition seems beyond question; so also does his official assertion that Major Brown did have charge. Still, his order for the dispatch of the detachment does not mention Major Brown. It directs Colonel Crooks to detail one of his companies and Colonel McPhail to send Captain Anderson's mounted men. Colonel Crooks, who had a military education, may naturally have inferred that, since no commander had been designated, the ranking officer named would have charge and may have so informed Captain Grant. At the same time, it may be presumed that Colonel Sibley, not yet versed in the customs of the service, thought that, as he was sending out merely a burial squad, as Neill suggests, he deemed it unnecessary to name Major Brown in an order for the detail of the military escort.[73] There was no expectation of a battle.

[71] *Senate Journal*, 1895, pp. 180, 611, 688; *House Journal*, 675, 833; *General Laws*, 1895, pp. 776-778.
[72] Curtiss-Wedge, *Renville County*, 2: 1345.
[73] Sibley's Order Book, 14; *Pioneer Press*, May 27, 1894; Neill, *Minnesota*, 730 (fourth edition); Dr. J. W. Daniels to Holcombe, October 15, 1894, in the Holcombe Papers, with accompanying reminiscences of the battle of Birch Coulee drawn from Daniels' diary; Daniels, "Indian Outbreak," 9.

In his manuscript report of the battle Major Brown signed himself as "Maj᷷ Gen¹ 3ʳᵈ Division Min. Vol. Militia." It is not known that Colonel Sibley seriously resented this assumption of a rank somewhat superior to that held by himself. It is more probable that he was amused by the ingenuous simplicity of his old client. As if to remove doubts as to Brown's military status, Colonel Sibley on September 20, 1862, by authority conferred by the governor of Minnesota, appointed Joseph R. Brown "to be Major to rank as such from the 25ᵗʰ day of August," without assigning him at the time to any particular arm or command of the service. Brown's report as printed in *Minnesota in the Civil and Indian Wars* is signed "Joseph R. Brown, Major Third Minnesota Volunteer Militia."[74] Between October 29 and November 5 he signed five of Sibley's general orders as "Major Indian Expedition, A A A Gl [*Acting Assistant Adjutant General*]." On the field return for the month of September he is carried as "Major, August 25, A. D. C."[75] The reader should note that, according to custom, he had held the courtesy title of Major ever since he became agent to the Sioux in 1857.

On a site adjacent to that of the Birch Coulee monument stands another to "The Faithful Indians." The Minnesota Valley Historical Society was organized at Morton, Minnesota, on February 2, 1895. The president was the Honorable Charles D. Gilfillan, who modestly kept himself behind the screen of an organization while he furnished substantially all its funds. Return I. Holcombe, already more learned in Minnesota Indian lore than any other living person, was historiographer. Beginning in 1898 the society erected substantial granite tablets, suitably inscribed, at the lower agency and on the Birch Coulee battle field. It erected also granite monuments to Captain Marsh and his men at the Redwood Ferry and to James W. Lynd at the lower agency. In 1899 it raised the monument to the friendly Indians. The idea of it was to celebrate and perpetuate the memory of certain Sioux Indians who had preserved an exceptional loyalty. It was decided to put on the monument the names only of those full-bloods who had remained unbrokenly loyal and who had saved the life of at least one white person. After a careful investigation of many names, but five were found which stood the test. When the monument, fifty-two feet high and made of granite from a local

---

[74] The original report as signed by Major Brown is in Governor's Archives, file 255. See also the *Saint Paul Press*, September 14, 1862; *Minnesota in the Civil and Indian Wars*, 2: 212d; and Sibley's Order Book, 119.

[75] Sibley's Order Book, 51-55; *Executive Documents*, 1862, p. 311. See the *Saint Paul Pioneer*, January 28, 1863, for an editorial in which it is charged that Adjutant General Malmros, to gratify Governor Ramsey, in his annual report for 1862 had maliciously ignored Major Brown as commander at Birch Coulee. Governor Ramsey, said the writer, had not forgotten that Joseph R. Brown was a member of the board of canvassers of the vote for governor after the election of 1857. See also the *Saint Paul Press*, January 30, 1863.

quarry, was completed in December, 1899, the names of Other Day, Little
Paul, Lorenzo Lawrence, Simon Anawangmani, and Mary Crooks were
shown on the die. Another name, that of Snana, then living, was added
after her death in a place reserved for it.[76]

## 8. THE NUMBER OF KILLED AND WOUNDED IN THE SIOUX OUTBREAK[77]

It is a matter of regret that no census was taken of the killed and
wounded in the Sioux massacre of 1862 and in military operations which
followed in that year.  The legislature of 1862 in extra session provided
by law in September for the appointment by the governor of a commission of three citizens to ascertain the names, relationship, and number
of the persons killed and the kind, amount, value, and ownership of
property destroyed or injured.  The commission was given three months for
the performance of the duty and was granted a compensation of three
dollars a day and ten cents per mile for traveling.  In his message to the
legislature of 1863 Governor Ramsey was obliged to inform that body that
he had been unable to employ any competent persons to perform the service
in the time limited for three dollars a day in state scrip.  His recommendation for the appointment of a new commission to be allowed plenty of
time and to be headed by a lawyer who should be well paid was not acted
upon.[78]  Again in 1881 an act was passed enjoining town assessors to
obtain and report all possible attainable information in regard to the
killed and wounded, both whites and Indians.  County auditors were
directed to furnish blanks for the purpose.  As the law provided no compensation for the service and attached no penalty to nonperformance, it
seems to have been wholly neglected.[79]

The social and newspaper gossips of the time, having no reliable
statistics to restrain their imaginations, allowed them to range at great
liberty.  Many hundreds, then a thousand, then more hundreds up to two
thousand killed were current estimates.  Governor Ramsey's conservative
estimate in his message of September 9, 1862, was about five hundred.
President Lincoln, in his message of December 1, 1862, placed the number
at not less than eight hundred.[80]  Agent Galbraith, as favorably situated

[76] Minnesota Valley Historical Society, *Monuments and Tablets Erected in Renville and Redwood Counties*, 3, 6, 10, 46-63; Curtiss-Wedge, *Renville County*, 2: 1342-1345.  No lower Sioux, not even Wabasha or Good Thunder, were found capable. In an interview recorded in the author's notebooks, 8: 42, Mrs. Mary Schwandt-Schmidt said that Snana had saved and protected her.
[77] See *ante*, p. 213.
[78] *General Laws*, 1862, extra session, 52-55; Ramsey's message of January 7, 1863, in *Executive Documents*, 1862, pp. 12-14.
[79] *General Laws*, 1881, p. 153.
[80] *Executive Documents*, 1862, p. 9; Richardson, *Messages and Papers*, 6: 132 (serial 3265).

as anyone at the time for collecting the information, recorded his estimate of the killed, which he thought "very nearly correct," as follows:

CITIZENS MASSACRED

| | |
|---|---|
| In Renville county, including reservations | 221 |
| In Dakota Territory, including Big Stone Lake | 32 |
| In Brown county, including Lake Shetek. | 204 |
| In the other frontier counties. | 187 |
| | 644 |

SOLDIERS KILLED IN BATTLE

| | |
|---|---|
| Lower Sioux ferry, Captain Marsh's command | 24 |
| Fort Ridgely and New Ulm | 29 |
| Birch Coolie | 23 |
| Fort Abercrombie, Acton, Forest City, Hutchinson, and other places, including Wood Lake (4). | 17 |
| | 93 |
| Aggregate | 737 |

The agent estimated the wounded at one half the number killed and the property damage at over two millions of dollars.[81]

Mr. Marion P. Satterlee of Minneapolis, while editing the *Annandale Advocate* about 1897, became interested in the story of the massacre and began collecting the names of the white people who lost their lives in it and in the subsequent battles. After devoting his leisure for many years, exhausting the published accounts, visiting most of the places of slaughter, and interviewing survivors and relatives, he has made up lists of the victims so nearly complete that few if any additions are likely to be made. From these lists the following summary has been made: 91 were massacred in Brown County, 13 in Jackson, 24 in Kandiyohi, 11 in McLeod, 11 in Meeker, 17 in Murray, 12 in Nicollet, 14 in Redwood, 126 in Renville, 15 in the vicinity of Fort Abercrombie, and 23 in other parts of the state— making a total of 357 killed in massacre. The total number of those killed in military operations was 90; of these 25 were killed at Redwood Ferry, 26 at New Ulm, 19 at Birch Coulee, 7 at Wood Lake, and 6 each at Acton and Fort Ridgely. This would make a total of 447 killed in the Sioux massacre and war of 1862.[82] When reminded that the total number of Minnesota officers and men killed in the course of both the Civil and Indian wars was but 635, one may excuse exaggerations of statement when over two-thirds as many were done to death in about forty days.[83]

[81] Indian Office, *Reports*, 1863, pp. 291, 294; *Claims for Depredations by Sioux Indians*, 9 (serial 1189).

[82] Satterlee, *Victims of the Indian Massacre*. This list, which is dated 1919, is a revision of lists compiled earlier by Mr. Satterlee. The first list, which is in the form of a printed pamphlet, is dated August, 1914. The Minnesota Historical Society has two other lists compiled by Mr. Satterlee, one in manuscript dated May, 1916, and a photographic copy of another presented by the compiler in October, 1917. In a recast of Mr. Satterlee's lists dated September 7, 1923, in the Folwell Papers, Dr. Warren Upham names three additional persons massacred—one each in Brown, Nicollet, and Watonwan counties.

[83] See *ante*, p. 340, n. 18, and Holcombe, in *Minnesota in Three Centuries*, 3: 215.

Contemporaries in their excited imaginations not only exaggerated the numbers of the killed and wounded, but also circulated stories of atrocities of the most fiendish and horrible character. Governor Ramsey in a deliberate public statement gave voice to a general belief: "But massacre itself," said he, "had been mercy if it could have purchased exemption from the revolting circumstances with which it was accompanied. . . . Infants hewn into bloody chips of flesh, or nailed alive to door posts to linger out their little life in mortal agony, or torn untimely from the womb of the murdered mother and in cruel mockery cast in fragments on her pulseless and bleeding breast; rape joined to murder in one awful tragedy . . . women held in captivity to undergo the horrors of a living death; whole families burned alive; and as if their devilish fury could not glut itself with outrages on the living, its last efforts exhausted in mutilating the bodies of the dead." The moderated judgment of Dr. Williamson was that most of the killing was done by shooting, and that mutilations of either the living or the dead were rare, and later investigation has confirmed that conclusion.[84]

The Indian losses have never been ascertained. It is of record that sixteen were killed at Wood Lake; the losses in other affairs remain matters of conjecture. It was a maxim of Indian warfare for warriors to expose themselves as little as possible; and if any were slain their bodies were carried off or concealed from the enemy.[85]

## 9.  THE TREATIES OF 1858[86]

For a complete understanding of the treaties of 1858 a knowledge of some details of the negotiations, of the ratification, and of subsequent proceedings is requisite. The reader needs to remember that the Senate amended the treaties of 1851 by striking out the provisions for reservations in Minnesota and authorizing the president to select new homes for the Sioux outside the limits of the state. The Indians were to be credited with ten cents per acre for the reservation lands, which were to be added to the main cession. The Sioux consented to the amendment, under protest, late in 1852. So great was their reluctance to another and distant removal

[84] Message of Governor Ramsey, September 9, in *Executive Documents*, 1862, p. 8; *Saint Paul Press*, September 21, 1862. See *Congressional Globe*, 37 Congress, 3 session, 13, for an impassioned statement of Senator Morton S. Wilkinson.

[85] Holcombe, in *Minnesota in Three Centuries*, 3: 406. According to the concurrent testimony of Indian witnesses for the government in *Sisseton and Wahpeton Claim Case Record*, *Evidence for Defendant*, 288-290, 306, 308, 321, 336, 363, the number of hostile Indians killed in battle was as follows: New Ulm, 2; Fort Ridgely, 2; Birch Coulee, 2; and Wood Lake, 16. The names are given of those killed. Heard's estimate in his *Sioux War*, 248, of a total of forty-two Indians killed in battle is excessive. For the Sioux customs of war, see S. W. Pond, in *Minnesota Historical Collections*, 12: 450-453.

[86] See *ante*, p. 218.

that the president, as advised by the Indian officials concerned, delayed
their ejectment and selected no new homes. At length, in July, 1854, he
was authorized by law to allow the Indians to reside indefinitely on the
Minnesota reservations and to confirm their titles. He took no formal
action. Meantime the Indians had received credit for the proceeds of the
lands at ten cents per acre and had been paid installments of interest thereon. The uncertainty of tenure and residence delayed the concentration
of the Indians on the reservations. In 1856 the agent reported that the
upper Sioux still refused to settle on theirs.[87]

Why both agencies had been located on the south side of the Minnesota
is not known, but the effect was to attract the Indian settlements about
them and thus leave the ten-mile strip on the north side of the river a
no-man's land. That the strip was not much needed by the Indians would
naturally occur to some one. William J. Cullen, the northern superintendent, in his report for 1857 suggested that reservations bounded on
the east by the Minnesota would be quite sufficient. In his report for the
same year, Agent Flandrau suggested that a treaty should be negotiated
• with delegations of chiefs and braves at Washington where they would be
free from the domination of their young men.[88]

With the consent of the Indian office a delegation of eighteen chiefs
and headmen of the lower Sioux, headed nominally by Wabasha but in fact
by Little Crow, and another of nine chiefs and headmen of the upper Sioux,
headed by Red Iron, appeared in the capital city in the spring of 1858.[89]
Agent Joseph R. Brown was in charge of the united party. It was at a
late hour on the nineteenth of June that the lower Sioux delegation, in
full costume, met with the commissioner of Indian affairs to close the
negotiation of their treaty and add their signatures. The commissioner
recited the contents of the several articles and suggested as the first subject
for consideration the filling of the blank left for the insertion of the amount
of money to be allowed for the payment of the debts due the licensed traders
from members of the tribe. He remarked that he had found Little Crow
well informed on the subject and a pretty fair accountant, although somewhat influenced by speculators. He had, however, obtained the reluctant
consent of the Great Father to allow the sum of $40,000, as recommended
by the chief. Agent Brown remarked that the amount should be raised to
$45,000, to cover some items which had been overlooked. Little Crow
• made this the occasion for a long and impassioned harangue on the wrongs

---

[87] See *ante*, p. 217; 1:291-294, 354, n. 8; *Statutes at Large*, 10: 52, 235, 326; Indian
Office, *Reports*, 1856, p. 54 (reprinted in 34 Congress, 3 session, *Senate Executive Documents*,
vol. 2, *House Executive Documents*, vol. 1, part 1 — serials 875, 893).

[88] Indian Office, *Reports*, 1857, pp. 51, 60. It is easy to surmise that there were "interests"
desirous of a "reduction" of the Sioux reservation.

[89] *Statutes at Large*, 12: 1035, 1040.

suffered by his people through broken treaties and unfulfilled promises. At its close the commissioner said to the orator: "You are talking like a child now. You have been here three months, and the very matter put into the treaty at your own instance, you find fault with, and pretend not to understand. If you talk in this way, you can go home as soon as you please, and I won't see you any more." Little Crow said he was only pleading for justice. The commissioner continued: "You have had the paper in your possession and slept eight nights upon it, after a full interpretation and explanation. You still want the paper explained. I repeat that you are like a child. . . . Your delegation asked permission to come here and promised to pay all the expenses of the trip out of your annuities. I have, however, paid those expenses out of the National treasury."

The matter of the debts was then temporarily laid aside to give place to the consideration of an article in the draft authorizing individual Indians to reside outside their reservation and become citizens without forfeiting annuities and tribal privileges. Upon this Little Crow made a spirited attack. He did not want Indians to become citizens. "If they go among the whites they become corrupted, drink liquor and act badly. . . . If you let the Indians run about the country, they will . . . hunt deer for traders and take whiskey for pay." Because he wished them to act rightly, he would keep his people together under the control of the agent and the chiefs. And then he launched into another discourse on the bad faith of the white man. The commissioner, after calling upon Little Crow to stop and attend to the business of the meeting, erased the offensive paragraph. It was now near midnight. A long debate then took place among the members of the delegation, Little Crow appearing to desire agreement to some proposition. The commissioner, observing this, inquired of them who was their chief and asked whether they had a dictator. He added that if the delegates were influenced by bad men present or absent not to sign the treaty, it would bring suffering on their women and children. "I will not remain here all night," he added. Little Crow hoped the Father would be patient and again referred to the broken treaties. As to the traders' debts, he said, "We want to pay them ourselves, and we know then they are paid." The commissioner reminded him that none could be paid without the consent of the Indians and told the chief that his head must be very thick not to understand that. At the close of the dialogue Little Crow told the commissioner that the delegation wished the blank filled with $45,000 for the debts and $25,000 as presents for themselves and expressed the hope that his Father would not call him a child again. The commissioner hoped that he would never have occasion to. The article so long debated was now modified so as to authorize the chiefs and headmen in their discretion in open council to allow a sum not exceeding $70,000 for the debts *and* the goods which the delegation would take with them for their bands. All accounts were to be scrutinized by the secretary of the interior. It was long after daylight when, the signatures having been made, the council was dismissed.[90]

Such observations as the following may here find place: (1) the extraordinary zeal of the commissioner may have been justified by considerations not of record; (2) much of the irrelevant oratory of Little Crow was addressed to his colleagues and not to the Indian commissioner; (3) the matter was so handled that the principal sum to be paid for the ceded lands was kept out of controversy. Because the president had never formally exercised the power conferred upon him to confirm the Indians' title to the reservations and because the Indians had received credit and money on account for the lands at ten cents per acre, the question was brought up whether they had ever owned the land and had any legal title and right to convey. The Indians, believing their right indisputable, easily consented to submit the question to the arbitrament of the Senate; and, expecting a favorable decision, they left also to the Senate the question of the compensation they should receive. It will be seen that they had reason to look for a generous valuation. It was further provided in the same article of the treaty that, in case the Indian title should be sustained and compensation should be accorded, the Senate should decide the further question whether a specific sum of money should be paid or whether the lands should be sold and the proceeds, less the costs of survey and sale and the amount credited under the ten-cents-per-acre provision of the amended treaty of 1851, should be distributed. It may be surmised that in the prefatory consultations the price spoken of was so satisfactory that there was no need of discussion at the definitive council.

The treaty with the upper Sioux was in exactly the same language, even as to the amount of money to be allowed for debts and presents. No account has been found of the final council and signature, but it is safe to assume that no difficulties were encountered. The upper Sioux had always been the more tractable. Both treaties were reported by Senator Rice on March 9, 1859, and received the ratification of the Senate without amendment. The legal effect was that the Indians made complete cessions of their lands north of the Minnesota, nearly a million acres as estimated, trusting to the magnanimity of the white man's government to accord them fair compensation.[91]

The Senate was not in haste to take up the duty of arbitration imposed upon it. Nearly a year lapsed before that duty received attention of any

[90] *Pioneer and Democrat*, July 8, 1858, quoting from the *St. Louis Republican; Statutes at Large*, 12: 1033, 1038. The report prepared for the *Pioneer and Democrat* had been destroyed in the fire which consumed the steamboat "Galena" at the Red Wing landing on July 1, 1858.

[91] *Senate Executive Proceedings*, 11:95. For the text of the treaties, see *Statutes at Large*, 12: 1031-1042.

kind. Meantime there were those not so indifferent to action. The Sioux agent, Joseph R. Brown, in his report for 1859 asked for fair treatment of "a deeply wronged portion of the human family." He argued that the Sioux, the Indian office, and Congress had treated the Indian title as perfect since the act of July, 1854. The president had virtually conceded it. As for the manner of payment, he favored neither a specific award of money nor a sale and distribution of proceeds. The lands, he said, were some of the best in Minnesota, had twice as much timber as those of the retained reservations, and were well worth five dollars an acre even in the existing hard times. It would, however, be useless to put them up for sale in the market because the settlers, who were already numerous, would combine and hold the price down to the minimum. He preferred the plan of opening the lands to preëmption at the established price of a dollar and a quarter an acre. After the proper deductions mentioned above were made, there would remain a price of about one dollar per acre and, he wrote, "the Indians should receive that sum for it." The fund thus arising would place every Sioux family, with the exception, perhaps, of a few upper Sisseton, in a comfortable house within two years and would put them beyond future want. The northern superintendent and the commissioner of Indian affairs both approved the recommendations of the agent and urged early action by the Senate.[92]

On February 16, 1860, Senator Rice obtained a reference of all matters in the treaties requiring further action to the committee on Indian affairs, with instructions to report. The committee took time for deliberation and did not submit its unsigned conclusions until the nineteenth of June. It found that the Indians had held a "just and valid" title to the retroceded lands and were entitled to compensation. Under ordinary circumstances the committee would have recommended a sale and award of the proceeds, but because the Sioux were in immediate need of means to establish themselves comfortably on the retained reserves and to further their progress in the arts of civilization, it was constrained to advise a fair equivalent in money. After long consideration the committee had concluded that a price of a dollar and a quarter an acre would be fair and just.[93] To believe that these experienced statesmen did not suspect what might become of the money requires a degree of charity.

On June 27, the last day but one of the session of Congress, the chairman of the Senate committee obtained unanimous consent for consideration of the matter and offered a resolution declaring the Indian title just and valid but departed from the proposal of the committee by fixing the purchase price at thirty cents per acre, without deductions. It appears that the

[92] Indian Office, *Reports*, 1859, pp. 82–85.
[93] *Senate Executive Proceedings*, 11:144; 36 Congress, 1 session, *Senate Reports*, no. 284 (serial 1040).

departure was not detected. The chairman, upon request, explained the resolution, stating the facts already known to the reader and the deliberate judgment of the committee. He reminded the Senate that, as the government had already taken possession of the land—"It is our's now," he said —the Indians ought to be paid the fair price recommended. One senator said that it was no proper time to bring up the proposition at the close of an eight months' session and within ten minutes of adjournment. Another moved a postponement, which was not ordered. Senator Wilkinson of Minnesota spoke at length in explanation of the measure and declared its passage to be "absolutely necessary" for the preservation of peace on the Minnesota border. He showed a letter—it was not read—from the department of the interior advising immediate action to preserve peace on that border. Senator Fessenden objected to the passage at that time of a resolution calling for an appropriation. "We have hardly a quorum," he said, "and there is a great confusion, nobody listening, and nobody understanding it, and it is impossible for anybody to understand what it is." Senator Rice addressed the chair, but Chairman Sebastian took the word from him and told the Senate that the committee had given the subject most just consideration, that the senators from Minnesota had a just and lively interest in the passage of the resolution, and that it was a small matter involving only some $192,000. Still, small as it was, its passage was necessary to put a stop to murders and depredations. The senators who raised the alarm of murders and depredations did not offer any evidence of their allegations. As a fact, such crimes were then no more frequent in and about the Sioux reservations than in other parts of Minnesota and the Minnesota senators knew it. The Senate had evidently been prepared for decision. On the first vote the yeas were 19 and the nays 8 but there was not a quorum voting. The roll call was ordered and the result was: yeas, 31; nays, 6. So the resolution was agreed to.[94] Patient reader, do you wonder that Indian blood boiled?

It was, of course, too late for the appropriation of the money thus pledged to the Indians. The Indian appropriation bill of March 2, 1861, carried the following items: for payment to the Mdewakanton and Wahpekute Sioux Indians, $96,000 for 320,000 acres of land; to the Sisseton and Wahpeton Sioux, $170,880 for 569,600 acres of land. The total of $266,880 looks small beside the sum of $889,600 which would have resulted from the price of one dollar per acre as recommended by Agent Brown and still more insignificant when compared with the sum of $4,448,000, the fair value of the land at five dollars per acre, in Brown's opinion.[95]

[94] *Congressional Globe*, 36 Congress, 1 session, 3305.
[95] *Statutes at Large*, 12:237; Indian Office, *Reports*, 1859, p. 85. For disbursements under this act see Santee v. United States, *Evidence for Defendants*, 89 (Court of Claims, no.

The exasperation of the Sioux over the price of thirty cents per acre for the halves of their reservations ceded by the treaties of 1858 was sharpened by the disposition of the proceeds. In the case of the lower Sioux, who may be considered first, the amount was $96,000. It was stipulated in the treaty that a sum not to exceed $70,000, less the cost of the goods to be taken home by the delegation, might be devoted to the payment of such debts as the Indians in open council should acknowledge, as the northern superintendent should approve, and as the secretary of the interior should authorize. No proper open council was held, but Little Crow and a few chiefs or headmen were dealt with in an assemblage in the Episcopal mission schoolhouse at the lower agency on December 3, 1860. Bishop Whipple says of it, "What took place I do not know, but the following day Little Crow had a new wagon."[96]

On February 13, 1861, the northern superintendent, William J. Cullen, reported to the Indian office his approval of traders' claims against the lower bands to the amount of $102,290.92 for necessaries supplied prior to the ratification of the treaty on March 9, 1859. These were thoroughly investigated in the Indian office and on May 30, 1864, were submitted to the secretary of the interior, Caleb B. Smith, who ordered the distribution of $70,000 allowed in the treaty pro rata to the claimants, in full satisfaction. They accepted their several allotments, but under protest. At the council, so called, of December 3, 1860, the obliging chiefs were induced to "request" that if the sum of $70,000 should not be sufficient to pay all their just obligations, an additional amount should be paid from the remaining $26,000. It was not difficult to accommodate them. Traders' claims to the amount of $34,150.47 for supplies furnished *after* the ratification of the treaty, a period of twenty months, were found just by the superintendent and the Indian office. On August 27, 1861, the secretary of the interior authorized a ratable distribution of $25,954.35 to the creditors. An easy subtraction shows the lower Indians to have been still in debt to their traders to the amount of $8,196.12 on account of obligations incurred after the ratification of the treaty. It was the surrender of Little Crow to the traders which brought him into such disrepute that he lost his position as principal speaker of his people, who elected Traveling Hail to his place. Still he seems not wholly to have lost prestige for, when the outbreak came, none other was thought of as leader.[97]

33, 728). To thirty-five certified claimants $167,400.08 were paid; $123,657.70 were paid to six claimants, individuals or partners, as follows: to the Myricks, $36,550.63; to Robert, $23,923.22; to the Browns, $21,597.57; to Sweetzer, $16,747.35; to Fuller, $12,428.93; to Sibley, $12,410.00.

[96] *Statutes at Large*, 12: 237; Whipple, *Lights and Shadows*, 138.

[97] 43 Congress, 1 session, *Senate Reports*, no. 225, p. 3 (serial 1586); *House Reports*, no. 75, p. 3 (serial 1623); Big Eagle, in *Minnesota Historical Collections*, 6: 386. See *ante*, p. 240. In the Brown Papers there is an unsigned, undated memorandum, in the hand-

The upper Sioux, with $170,880 coming to them under their treaty, had over $100,000 left for distribution among their bands after the payment of $70,000 to traders on account of debts claimed to be due them at the time of the ratification, which amounted to $93,737.68. There remained due on traders' claims $24,371.80. An article in the treaty of 1867 awarding this amount was struck out by the Senate. As these claims both before and after the ratification of the treaties had been approved by the northern superintendent and the Indian office, it was not to be expected that the traders would be content with partial payments. In 1870 the secretary of the interior, Jacob D. Cox, was persuaded that the claims for the out-standing remainders were "probably just" and he recommended them to the attention of Congress.[98] It was not until May 16, 1874, however, that an act was passed by that body appropriating a sum not to exceed $70,000 to be paid out of the treasury for the discharge of all obligations of the United States to creditors of the upper and lower Sioux bands under the treaties of July 19, 1858. Upon favorable reports of committees of the two houses the bill passed without opposition.[99]

## 10. THE SPIRIT LAKE MASSACRE, 1857[1]

The Wahpekute tribe of the Dakota was never a numerous one. At the time of the outbreak of 1862 it had dwindled to two small bands, which after the removal westward in 1863 lost their identity altogether. Their hunting grounds had been in Nicollet's Undine Region, with their principal rallying place where the city of Faribault now stands.[2] About the year 1840 there was a rebellion in the tribe, led by a subchief named Black Eagle, which resulted in the murder of the well-known old head chief

writing of Joseph R. Brown, of traders' claims for debts against both upper and lower Sioux. All the old traders are represented. Dr. J. W. Daniels, in his "Indian Outbreak," 21, correctly gives "violated treaty obligations on the part of our government" as the great cause of Indian troubles; but he is wrong in stating that Joseph R. Brown secured for the Sioux all that was their own under the treaties of 1858.

[98] *Senate Executive Proceedings*, 15: 736 (part 2); 43 Congress, 1 session, *Senate Reports*, no. 225, p. 3 (serial 1586). On the treaty of 1867 see *post*, pp. 418–420.

[99] *Statutes at Large*, 18: 47. The amount paid under this act appears to have been $67,559.23. See Santee v. United States, *Evidence for Defendants*, 78. The bill, H. R. 420, was ingeniously merged into a large body of private claims and passed without notice. 43 Congress, 1 session, *Senate Journal*, 999; *House Journal*, 605; *Congressional Record*, 2783, 2792.

[1] See *ante*, pp. 223-225. The title "Spirit Lake Massacre" long ago became unalterably established, although but one of the murders was committed on the shore of that lake. With this exception the murders in Iowa were committed on the southern shores of East and West Okoboji lakes in Dickinson County, in the townships next south of Spirit Lake; those in Minnesota were committed in Jackson County about nine miles north of Spirit Lake. See Alfred T. Andreas, *Historical Atlas of the State of Iowa*, 49 (Chicago, 1875).

[2] Hodge, *Handbook of American Indians*, 2: 890. Riggs, in his *Grammar and Dictionary of the Dakota Language*, vii, gives the number of Wahpekute in 1852 as five or six hundred. Holcombe, in *Minnesota in Three Centuries*, 3: 273, says that but one band remained in

Tasagi and the flight of Black Eagle with a small band of partisans to the south and west of the old Sioux country. They roved about in the valleys of the Vermilion, the Little Sioux, and the Des Moines and became so separate from the old tribe that they were regarded as outlaws. They had no part in the treaty of 1851, but by threats of violence exacted participation in one or more payments under it.[3]

Little is known of the activities and changes in leadership of these outlaws for many years, but it is well known that in 1857, with numbers reduced to some ten or fifteen warriors, they recognized one Inkpaduta (Scarlet Point) as their chief. The motives which impelled this miscreant to make a descent upon the settlements of northwestern Iowa and southwestern Minnesota in the winter and spring of 1857 cannot be definitely stated. Some accounts give as a motive a desire for revenge for the murder of a tribesman by a white man; another states that the raid resulted from the scarcity of game in an unusually inclement season; and others give as a cause the improbable one of a quarrel with a white man whose dog had been shot by an Indian.[4] After committing depredations in Clay County, Iowa,

1862, not counting the group residing about Faribault, which never moved to the reservation. Doane Robinson, in his article on "Sioux Indian Courts," in *South Dakota Historical Collections*, 5: 405, expresses the opinion that Inkpaduta's gang was originally made up of outlawed men. The Sioux appear to have had a customary proceeding to sentence a person to outlawry.

[3] Holcombe, in *Minnesota in Three Centuries*, 3: 220, 253; Charles E. Flandrau, "The Ink-pa-du-ta Massacre of 1857," in *Minnesota Historical Collections*, 3: 387. Tasagi is frequently mentioned as a visitor at the St. Peter's agency by Taliaferro in his journals. See especially the entries under June 17, August 13, 1829, August 19, 21, 1830. The evidence regarding participation in the payments is conflicting. Flandrau, in his "Official Account of the Late Indian Difficulties," dated April 11, 1857, in Indian Office, *Reports*, 1857, p. 71, states that in 1854 and 1856 payments were refused to Inkpaduta's band. In *Minnesota Historical Collections*, 3: 388, he repeats the statement. Major Kintzing Pritchette, in his report of October 15, 1857, in Indian Office, *Reports*, 1857, p. 101, states that Inkpaduta received annuities for eleven persons in 1855 and 1856. His accompanying statement that the Inkpaduta band was resident on the reservation near the Sioux agency in the fall of 1856 has no ascertained support, but Bryant and Murch, in their *Great Massacre*, 38, repeat it. Robinson, in his *Sioux Indians*, 343, says that Inkpaduta appeared at each annual payment up to 1856 and bulldozed the Indians into sharing with him. See also Thomas Teakle, *The Spirit Lake Massacre*, ch. 8 (Iowa City, 1918). This useful study was published too late to be of use to the author in the preparation of this account.

[4] Holcombe, in *Minnesota in Three Centuries*, 3: 222, 224; Hughes, in *Minnesota Historical Collections*, 12: 265-269; Indian Office, *Reports*, 1857, pp. 69, 101; Flandrau, in *Minnesota Historical Collections*, 3: 387, 388; Robinson, *Sioux Indians*, 233; Abbie Gardner Sharp, *History of the Spirit Lake Massacre*, 59 (Des Moines, 1885); Teakle, *Spirit Lake Massacre*, ch. 9. Dr. J. W. Daniels' reasonable account, in the Daniels Papers, may be briefed: Inkpaduta's band had been kindly treated by the settlers about the Okoboji lakes and continued to hunt thereabouts. The winter of 1857 was a very severe one, so severe that the settlers could not spare food for the Indians, who were begging for it. One of the Indians was bitten by a settler's dog and in anger killed the dog. The settler assaulted the Indian and beat him so that he was hardly able to get back to his camp. Fearing trouble, the settlers went to the Indians' camp, took their guns away, and told them to leave the country. One of the chief's grandchildren died of starvation. Infuriated by impending starvation, the Indians recovered their guns and began the killing. Dr. Daniels

in the valley of the Little Sioux, the Indians went northward to the Okoboji lakes in northern Iowa.  There, on March 8 and 9, they fell upon six
settlers' cabins, murdered some thirty of the unsuspecting inmates, and
took captive three women.  After spending four days in the neighborhood
in looting, feasting, and dancing, they departed for Heron Lake in Jackson County, Minnesota, to encamp for some time.  On the way they
murdered a settler named Marble on Spirit Lake and took his wife captive.[5]

Some twelve miles southeast of Heron Lake was a small settlement on
the Des Moines River on a site where later grew up the village of Jackson,
which was to become a well-known county seat.  It was then called
Springfield or Des Moines City and was on the extreme frontier of settlement.  Late on March 9 one of the members of the Okoboji settlement
returned from an expedition in search of strayed oxen to discover the
lifeless bodies of members of the Gardner family.  He fled at once northward, passing the houses where the other murders had been done, and
found shelter for the night with a settler on Spirit Lake, whose cabin was
almost exactly on the state boundary.  The next day these two men and
another carried the news of the tragedy to Springfield and on the eleventh
two members of that community were dispatched to the lower Sioux
agency to ask for protection.  The distance in an air line was about sixty
miles, but it took the men a week to make the necessarily roundabout
journey.

The settlers at Springfield, perhaps thirty-five in number, were alarmed
but not stampeded.  With the exception of a man named Shiegley and
two brothers named Wood who had a store on the west side of the Des
Moines and had no fears of Indians, they at once arranged to gather, if
danger threatened, in two of the log houses best adapted for defense.  Two
of Inkpaduta's men came to the store and made some purchases, paying
in gold.  The days passed in quiet and in hope of the arrival of the pro-
tecting force asked for, until the twenty-sixth of March, when Inkpaduta
with most of his men surrounded the Thomas house where many of the
settlers were lodged.  One of the settlers, seeing a man approaching in
white man's dress and supposing him to be one of the messengers returning
from the agency, called the people out to welcome him.  From their
hiding places the Indians fired, killing one boy and wounding two men and

adds the story of the wife of the Indian who killed the settler's dog, which agrees with his
own.  She says that her husband was not the same man after the white man had beaten him.
In a council he became excited when he heard the starving children crying and his sister
moaning over her dead baby and called upon the Great Spirit to help him destroy those
bad people.

[5] Arthur P. Rose, *History of Jackson County, Minnesota*, 54-56 (Jackson, 1910); Sharp,
*Spirit Lake Massacre*, 61-84; Teakle, *Spirit Lake Massacre*, chs. 10-14; L. P. Lee, *History
of the Spirit Lake Massacre! and of Miss Abigail Gardiner's Three Months' Captivity among
the Indians, According to Her Own Account*, 15-19 (New Britain, Connecticut, 1857).

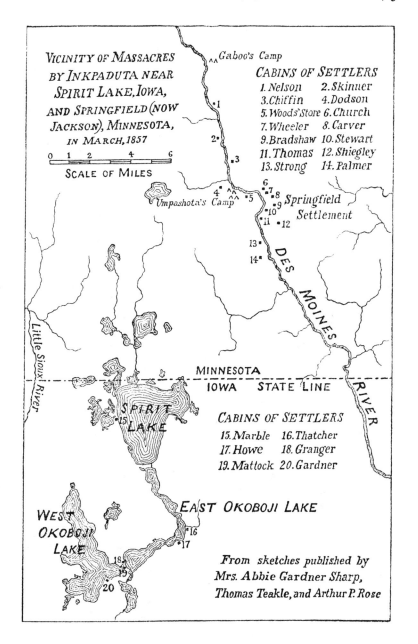

VICINITY OF MASSACRES
BY INKPADUTA NEAR
SPIRIT LAKE, IOWA,
AND SPRINGFIELD (NOW
JACKSON), MINNESOTA,
IN MARCH, 1857

0   1   2   4   6
SCALE OF MILES

Gaboo's Camp

CABINS OF SETTLERS
1. Nelson        2. Skinner
3. Chiffin       4. Dodson
5. Woods'Store   6. Church
7. Wheeler       8. Carver
9. Bradshaw     10. Stewart
11. Thomas      12. Shiegley
13. Strong      14. Palmer

Umpashota's Camp

Springfield
Settlement

DES MOINES RIVER

Little Sioux River

MINNESOTA
IOWA    STATE LINE

SPIRIT LAKE

CABINS OF SETTLERS
15. Marble    16. Thatcher
17. Howe      18. Granger
19. Mattock   20. Gardner

EAST OKOBOJI LAKE

WEST OKOBOJI LAKE

From sketches published by
Mrs. Abbie Gardner Sharp,
Thomas Teakle, and Arthur P. Rose

404 A HISTORY OF MINNESOTA

a woman. All but the murdered boy ran into the house, closed the door, tore up the puncheons, and barricaded the door and the windows. Firing through holes in the chinking, they kept the Indians at bay for the remainder of the day. The women loaded guns for the men and one of them is said to have disabled, if not killed, the only Indian hurt. The Wood brothers were brutally murdered. A man named Stewart was decoyed from his house and shot down. His wife ran out with two small children to share his fate. A third child, a boy of eight, hid himself and was not discovered. Toward night the fiends departed, driving off all the horses they had found. Seven persons had been murdered and three had been wounded.[6]

On the morning after the murders the gang departed for the northwest and after leisurely marches lasting many weeks reached the James River near the latitude of forty-five degrees north, where they may be left for the present. It should be noted, however, that as they crossed the Big Sioux River one of the woman captives, Mrs. Elizabeth Thatcher, was wantonly thrown into the stream and beaten and shot to death as she struggled to gain the shore. Some days later another, Mrs. Lydia Noble, was clubbed to death for resistance to one of the brutes said to have been a son of Inkpaduta. The fortunes of the two remaining captives may be reserved for later mention.[7]

The incredible atrocities of Inkpaduta and his crew, abundantly described in many works, need not be dwelt upon at length because they do not relate to the subject now in hand so much as do certain resulting transactions. The two messengers from Springfield delivered their tidings to the Sioux agent, Major Charles E. Flandrau, at the lower Sioux agency on March 18. He repaired at once to Fort Ridgely, consulted with the commandant, and made requisition for troops for the relief of the affrighted settlers. On the next day, March 19, Captain Bernard E. Bee of the Tenth Infantry, with a lieutenant and forty-eight enlisted men, began his march. At the same time Agent Flandrau, accompanied by Philander Prescott and a French Canadian *voyageur*, provided with a fine team and a light sleigh, and well outfitted, started in advance. He chose the road down the Minnesota to Mankato, where he turned southwestward and pushed on to the cabin of a settler named Slocum on the Watonwan, some twenty-five miles distant. Here he could obtain no definite information about the danger at Springfield and there was no "beaten track" beyond. He therefore returned to meet Captain Bee and at once advised that officer

[6] Rose, *Jackson County*, 38, 42, 58-67; Sharp, *Spirit Lake Massacre*, 85-90; Hughes, *Blue Earth County*, 82; Teakle, *Spirit Lake Massacre*, chs. 15, 17, 18.

[7] Sharp, *Spirit Lake Massacre*, 150, 175, 216-219, 230. Mrs. Sharp says that they reached a large Yankton camp on the site of Old Ashton, in Spink County, South Dakota. See also Teakle, *Spirit Lake Massacre*, 215-224, 234.

to abandon his expedition on account of the almost impassable condition of the roads for such an outfit as his. The gallant captain declined to accept the advice and resolved to go forward until he should be stopped by some impassable obstacle. He accordingly proceeded to South Bend, obtained some supplies, and moved on to Slocum's cabin. The journey from the fort and a day's rest at this point had consumed a whole week, although the distance is not more than seventy miles measured on an air line.[8]

It was therefore not until March 26, the day of the massacre at Springfield, that the march was resumed. Before the detachment broke camp two settlers from the Des Moines came in with a report that the Indians were in camp in a grove near the cabin of one Coursalle, an Indian trader living eight miles north of Springfield. Captain Bee at once directed his march across the trackless prairie to that point. In his report he gives the narrative of a single day as a history of the whole march. "Wading through deep drifts; cutting through them with the spade and shovel; extricating mules and sleighs from sloughs, or dragging the latter up steep hills or over bare spaces of prairie; the men wet from morning till night, and sleeping on the snow." After three days of such laborious marching they reached Coursalle's grove, only to find that Inkpaduta had gone on westward to Heron Lake. On the night of the twenty-eighth Captain Bee asked for volunteers to continue the pursuit the next day. The whole company stepped to the front. A march of fifteen miles, as estimated, with Coursalle for guide, brought the command to Heron Lake. "The camp was there, with all its traces of plunder and rapine; books, scissors, articles of female apparel, furs and traps." A detail mounted on the thirteen led mules was pushed out on the Indians' trail to another grove some four miles beyond. A halt had been made here by the Indians, but the signs, as read by the guide, were two days old. Further pursuit in a region destitute of provisions was, of course, useless. The next day Captain Bee sent a detachment to Spirit Lake to inter any unburied dead and himself moved to Springfield, where he found the bodies of the victims of the massacre awaiting burial. Several settlers had followed the expedition back and word was sent out to others that they would be protected. Leaving his lieutenant with twenty-two men as a guard, Captain Bee, led by the "invaluable guide, La Framboisé," returned to Fort Ridgely, mostly across country, in four marching days. It may be believed that, in his own words, he had used "the best energies" of his "nature" to accomplish the purposes of his expedition, but it must remain a matter of regret that the messengers from Springfield to the agency consumed so

[8] Flandrau, in *Minnesota Historical Collections*, 3: 390; Rose, *Jackson County*, 75; Teakle, *Spirit Lake Massacre*, chs. 15, 16; reports of Bee and Flandrau, in Indian Office, *Reports*, 1857, pp. 62, 70.

much time on the way and that so many marching days were occupied by
the military in their outward journey. Could the men have been equipped
with snowshoes and a few *trains de glace* to carry provisions and blankets,
the massacre at Springfield need not have taken place. It was Flandrau's
opinion that the "poor troops . . . were about as fit for such a march as
an elephant is for a ball room." The Sioux were doubtless amused that
the Great Father should try to catch Indians with foot soldiers wearing
leather boots and a mule train hauling provisions and full camp equipage.[9]

That Inkpaduta should be allowed to continue his wanderings and probable massacres, holding the captive women as hostages, was, of course,
not to be tolerated in any quarter. The territorial legislature met in extra
session on April 27, 1857. The roll of the house had hardly been called
when Joseph R. Brown offered a resolution, which was at once passed under
a suspension of the rules, declaring the imperative need of protection for
the southern frontier. The same member also gave notice of a bill to
authorize the governor to raise a force of volunteers, in case the United
States government should fail to furnish troops for the emergency. On
the twenty-ninth Governor Medary, who had been in the territory hardly
a full week, in his message to the legislature recommended a memorial
to the president praying him to send a body of mounted men to scour the
region in which Inkpaduta might be lurking and also to appoint an efficient superintendent of Indian affairs for the territory. The outcome of
the Brown resolutions and the governor's counsel was the passage of an
act, approved on May 15, appropriating ten thousand dollars to effect,
not the capture of Inkpaduta, but the release of the female captives, "by
purchase, stratagem or otherwise"! The legislative action probably took
this direction by a suggestion from Governor Medary, who had meantime
attended a conference at Fort Snelling on May 6, at which the Indian
superintendent was also present. It was agreed in this conference that an
effort should be made to rescue the women before any troops should be
employed in pursuit of Inkpaduta because the fiend would undoubtedly
put the unfortunates to death on the approach of soldiers. It was also
agreed that it would be best that a party of loyal Sioux under the lead of a
discreet half-breed should be sent to bring them in. What progress may
have been made in working out the plan is not known and the inquiry is
superfluous because a fortunate incident made the execution of the plan
unnecessary.[10]

[9] Indian Office, *Reports*, 1857, pp. 63-67; *Henderson Democrat*, May 7, 1857; Teakle,
*Spirit Lake Massacre*, ch. 20; Flandrau, *Minnesota*, 106; the same author, in *Minnesota
Historical Collections*, 3:390. In both works Flandrau inadvertently wrote as if he had
accompanied Captain Bee's expedition the whole distance. In his report in Indian Office,
*Reports*, 1857, p. 57, he is careful to say that he accompanied it only part of the way.
Had he gone on from Slocum's cabin instead of turning back to meet Captain Bee,
results might have been different.

[10] *House Journal*, 1857, extra session, 4, 8; *Laws*, 317; Indian Office, *Reports*, 1857, p. 73.

About May 20 one of the captives, Mrs. Margaret Ann Marble, was brought to Yellow Medicine by two Wahpeton hunters, doubtless presuming that they would be well rewarded, and was delivered to the missionaries in exchange for shot, powder, blankets, and other gear. Through Dr. Riggs they made a formal claim in writing on the Sioux agent for five hundred dollars apiece, in money and not in goods. Agent Flandrau thought it wise to pay the sum without question but he had only half the needed amount in hand. To make up the other moiety he and Dr. Riggs united in a bond pledging the territory or its citizens to pay the two Indians five hundred dollars within three months. The traders cashed the obligation without hesitation.[11]

Aware now of the whereabouts of the other women, Major Flandrau lost no time in arranging for their rescue. With such generous recompense in sight there was no lack of volunteers for the enterprise. He selected three Wahpeton, one of them being our well-known John Other Day. The agent bought on credit from the traders four horses for $600, a wagon and harness for $110, and other outfit to the amount of $179.12; and on the twenty-third of May he saw his emissaries on their way to the Big Sioux country. On the twenty-ninth they discovered the lifeless body of Mrs. Lydia Noble and on the day following they found Miss Abbie Gardner alive in a camp of Yankton. After about three days of bargaining the envoys bought her for two horses, two kegs of powder, twenty-two yards of blue cloth, seven and a half yards of calico, and some other small articles which had cost the agent about four hundred dollars. It was precisely one month after their departure, June 23, when the three Indians delivered Miss Gardner with much ceremony to Governor Medary in St. Paul. Agent Flandrau paid each one four hundred dollars and made presents to other Indians who had shown kindnesses to the rescued women. The ten-thousand-dollar appropriation bill contained no provision for borrowing on a bond issue, there was no money in the territorial treasury, and the act would have been altogether inoperative had not

[11] Riggs, *Forty Years with the Sioux*, 139-141; *Pioneer and Democrat*, June 9, 1857; Teakle, *Spirit Lake Massacre*, ch. 27. See also Flandrau in *Minnesota Historical Collections*, 3:393-396; the same author's "State-Building in the West," in *Minnesota Historical Collections*, 8: 485; and his *Minnesota*, 106. Flandrau remarks that when the missionaries stripped Mrs. Marble of the jaunty squaw costume in which she had been dressed by the mother of her two Dakota rescuers and rehabilitated her in an ill-fitting calico dress which they were pleased to call more Christian raiment, they committed a deadly assault upon beauty, either in nature or art. Robinson, in his *Sioux Indians*, 239, states that the missionaries found Mrs. Marble content to remain with her new friends, but persuaded her to return to her white relatives. In a letter of February 25, 1885, to Mrs. Sharp, Mrs. Marble gives no warrant for this statement. She says that the missionaries bought her a suit of clothing, soap, and other articles, and took her to visit in their families. She speaks of great kindness shown her by her rescuers, who wanted to adopt her. At parting the Indian father kissed her and shed tears. Sharp, *Spirit Lake Massacre*, 183-189.

Governor Medary used his personal credit for enough to cover the expenses of the rescues.[12]

The way was now clear for the employment of troops in the pursuit of Inkpaduta. About May 25 the commandant at Fort Ridgely was engaged in preparations for an expedition to start as soon as the grass should be grown enough to feed his animals. For reasons which will presently appear neither this expedition nor any other was sent out from the fort. The Indians naturally assumed that either the Great Father had no soldiers to spare or, if he had, they would not dare to fight the unconquerable Dakota.

The progress of events was now varied by an episode which, although it was of no great magnitude, had notable effects. Two days after Agent Flandrau had paid his Indians for the rescue of Miss Gardner, he received a note from a trader at the upper agency advising him that Inkpaduta with some or all of his following had come to the neighborhood, probably for the purpose of extorting shares in the coming payment. With characteristic energy he at once drove over to the fort and easily obtained a detail of a lieutenant and fifteen men, who marched the same day to the agency. In the meantime a party of a dozen mounted civilians, including two guests and his interpreter, Antoine J. ("Joe") Campbell, had been made up. The expedition, with the soldiers in wagons, set out from the lower agency at dark on June 30 for a night's march of thirty miles. At a point about midway between the Redwood and the Yellow Medicine, where the trail led over a hill, was found John Other Day seated and smoking his pipe. In response to Flandrau's request to the missionary at Yellow Medicine for a guide, this Indian had been sent to meet him. Other Day informed the leader that Inkpaduta himself was not in the neighborhood, but that a small number of his people were in an outlying camp of Sisseton some distance up the Yellow Medicine, to which he was ready to guide the party.

In the gray of the morning the camp was reached, and the soldiers were sent in file along the edge of the river bank, while the horsemen charged down from the prairie. From one of six tepees emerged a man and a woman, who ran at utmost speed toward the ravine. The Indian was shot and later bayoneted and the woman was taken prisoner. The man proved to be Roaring Cloud, the oldest son of Inkpaduta, who had murdered Mrs. Noble. The woman was put in one of the wagons and the party started for the upper agency five miles below. On the way it was necessary to pass through the camps of some thousands of upper Sioux who had as-

---

[12] Flandrau, in *Minnesota Historical Collections*, 3: 396-400; *Pioneer and Democrat*, June 9, 24, 1857; *Laws*, 1857, extra session, 317; Teakle, *Spirit Lake Massacre*, ch. 28. Three thousand dollars were expended on the rescue of Mrs. Marble and Miss Gardner. The latter died at Colfax, Iowa, about January 26, 1921. *Minneapolis Journal*, January 27, 1921.

sembled for the payment, among whom were some of her relatives.  Her outcries called them from their tepees and the agent's party was soon surrounded by hundreds of armed warriors.  Their appearance was so threatening that Flandrau thought it prudent to let the captive go. Upon arriving at the agency the party took refuge in a log house, where it remained until Major Sherman's battery, which had been sent up from Fort Ridgely to be present at the payment, arrived on July 5.  The imprisonment of the agent and his guards for two or three days did not increase the respect of the Sioux for the Great Father.  Within a few days Major Flandrau took his departure to sit in the constitutional convention, which was to open on July 13.  He had already been appointed by President Buchanan an associate justice of the territorial supreme court, but he did not relinquish his office of Sioux agent for some time.[13]

We now reach a period in which was illustrated one of the most objectionable elements of the traditional Indian policy, that of refilling the offices of the service at the opening of every new administration with party politicians, either in reward for party labors or as consolation for elective offices lost.  Soon after his accession to the presidency, Buchanan bestowed the position of commissioner of Indian affairs upon James W. Denver of California.  Denver had been a state senator, a secretary of state, and a member of the house of representatives from his state.  He was doubtless a man of ability, but his notable successes in political stations permitted him to believe that he would be equally successful in managing Indian affairs, a task calling for experience as well as mere ability.[14]  This confidence was a source of a capital error.  The policy also placed in the office of northern superintendent of Indian affairs William J. Cullen of Indiana, who had served a term in the legislature and had aided in the election of Jesse D. Bright to the United States Senate.  The appointment was his reward. In the expressive language of Joseph R. Brown, Cullen did not know "the difference between . . . a Sioux Indian and a snapping turtle."[15]  It is just to state that the superintendent's lack of experience was later

---

[13] Flandrau, in *Minnesota Historical Collections*, 3: 402-407; *Pioneer and Democrat*, July 7, 8, 1857.  Dr. Thomas S. Williamson contributed to the *Missionary Herald*, 54: 54 (February, 1858), some interesting particulars.  It was he and Dr. Riggs who, upon Major Flandrau's request for a trusty guide, sent John Other Day.  The killing of the murderer and the capture of the woman, who was his wife, were "entirely owing" to the part admirably performed by Indians.  The Indians who surrounded the agency and clamored for the release of the woman were Wahpeton, some of whom were her relatives.  Flandrau was under the humiliating necessity of letting her go and of "telling them a falsehood."  Dr. Daniels on page 4 of his narrative of the Spirit Lake massacre states that Major Flandrau was taking breakfast at his quarters at the agency when the Indians demanded the release of the captive woman.  On their demand he also gave them two beeves for a feast for the braves.

[14] *Appletons' Cyclopædia of American Biography*, 2: 144.

[15] *Henderson Democrat*, July 16, 1857.

compensated for by a study of Indian character and needs and an honest effort to do the Indian service.

Upon early and imperfect information about the Spirit Lake massacre, Commissioner Denver assumed that it was a matter of trifling importance which he could dispose of from his desk with little or no aid from the war department—a conceit from which he was soon obliged to recede. It was the established usage in Indian management to hold whole tribes accountable for individual crimes and depredations and in some treaties there were stipulations that the tribes should arrest and deliver perpetrators for trial and punishment. The commissioner presumed that this was an ordinary case to be dealt with in an ordinary way. He did not understand that Inkpaduta led a band of outlaws, cordially hated by all the tribes, who had a good right to demand that the Great Father himself with his mounted soldiers should pursue them to their distant haunts and destroy them. He assumed that they were ordinary annuity Indians, temporarily absent from their bands, which could, if so disposed, easily run them down and capture them. As early as May 9 the commissioner issued instructions, which were repeated on May 30, to the effect that the whole body of the Sioux of the Mississippi, about seventy-five hundred in number, should receive no part of their annuities until all the participants in the Spirit Lake massacre should have been captured and delivered to the proper authorities. The annual payments were set for an early day in July and Superintendent Cullen, who had arrived at the reservation on July 3, at once made known to the assembled bands that there would be no payments until the Sioux had caught and brought in Inkpaduta's whole band. On the ninth he held a council with the upper Indians, and on the twelfth one with the lower bands. They were willing to unite in an expedition provided white soldiers were added to it. To this proposition the superintendent could not agree, for more reasons than one: Major Sherman's artillerymen were not fitted for such service and the infantry force was too small to spare a detachment; if soldiers were sent along they would be exposed to treachery on the part of the Indians and, at any rate, they would have to do all the killing and capturing; finally, it was the duty of the Indians to control their bad men. "Something had to be done soon," wrote the superintendent. In his perplexity he dispatched a messenger to Dunleith, Illinois, with a message to be telegraphed from that place to the commissioner at Washington, briefly stating the situation and asking, "What shall I do?" He got a brief reply from the commissioner, "Adhere to your instructions; there must be no yielding."[16]

[16] Indian Office, *Reports*, 1857, pp. 48-50, 74, 77-80, 103. Dr. J. W. Daniels, in his narrative of the Spirit Lake massacre, p. 5, says that Cullen arrived at the reservation on July 5. On page 6 Daniels gives an account of a council of upper chiefs and warriors in which they were persuaded by White Lodge and Standing Buffalo to unite in sending the

The state of mind into which the Indians were thrown by the postponement of the payments can here be illustrated by another episode. Major Sherman had remained at the upper agency after the release of Agent Flandrau from imprisonment and a reënforcement of twenty-five infantrymen had been sent to him. On July 15 an insolent Sisseton without provocation stabbed a soldier and was harbored in one of the lodges. An officer who was sent to demand his surrender was met by two hundred Indians with guns leveled toward him, but their spokesman promised that they would bring him the next day. Shortly after sunrise next morning an Indian brought word to Major Sherman that the criminal would be delivered to him; but it was near noon before a large body of Sisseton and Wahpeton, with mounted parties of Yankton on their flanks, arrived at his camp. The interval was one of suspense and anxiety. Guns had been loaded and arrangements had been made for resisting attack. Three braves came forward for a conference with Superintendent Cullen and told him that the man would not be delivered until they had received their annuities. They were informed that no communication would be had with them until they had turned over the man who had stabbed the soldier. Major Sherman then went forward, thinking that the Indians would deliver the man to him. He met with the same demand and returned a similar answer. The Indians then returned to their camp. But few of them had guns or bows and arrows and they were not disorderly. At nightfall they moved their camp well out of cannon range. In the afternoon the military moved their camp to a point overlooking the neighborhood and called all the employees and traders of the agency to come into it. The missionaries were content to remain in their homes under the protection of their Indian friends. Major Sherman's moderation in not insisting upon instant compliance with his demand and his "consummate prudence and coolness" in giving the savages time to sleep on the matter were effusively praised as preventing an immediate slaughter and averting a protracted Indian war.[17]

On the morning of the seventeenth Captain Alfred Sully arrived from Fort Ridgely with a full company of infantry and not much later a large

war party after Inkpaduta. Standing Buffalo said: "Our Great Father has asked us to do a very hard thing . . . to go and kill men and women that do not belong to any of our bands . . . His Agent . . . says we shall not have our annuities until the murderers are given up to him or killed. The leaves will fall and come again before we shall see what he has for us unless we listen to his words. Our children will suffer with the cold if the goods he has is not given us."

[17] This account follows Dr. J. W. Daniels' narrative on the Spirit Lake massacre, 7-14. Dr. Daniels was resident physician at the upper agency at the time. Special Agent Pritchette concurs, but he acknowledges indebtedness to a diary kept by Dr. Daniels. The dramatic story of Superintendent Cullen of "about twenty-five hundred warriors, all armed and painted, evidently prepared for fight," is perhaps excusably imaginative. Neither he nor Agent Pritchette makes any allusion to the demand of the Indians for their annuities before giving up the stabber. Indian Office, *Reports*, 1857, pp. 80, 103.

body of Indians appeared near the camp.  A detachment came on and
delivered up the Indian criminal with protestations of friendship, appearing to be glad to be rid of him.  The superintendent did not carry out his
resolution to hang the scoundrel, because the wounded soldier was re-
covering.  Five days later the prisoner eluded his guards and escaped in
the "turmoil and confusion" with several wounds; he was carried off in a
blanket by his friends.  It was not considered advisable to demand his
redelivery.  The reader may judge how much this affair added to the
Dakota's veneration for the Great Father and his soldiers.[18]

On July 18 another general council of chiefs was held.  Although the
superintendent had not yet received the order to adhere to instructions,
he was firm in warning the Indians that failure to deliver Inkpaduta and
his men meant war with the United States.  Little Crow, who, on hearing
that the upper Indians were meditating an attack, had shown his friendliness by hastening to the upper agency and offering his services to the
superintendent, now induced some of his tribesmen to consent to go after
Inkpaduta without white soldiers.  After some hours of deliberation,
expedited by a liberal distribution of blankets and beef, the upper Sioux
delegation also consented.  The party, led by Little Crow, was made up of
four warriors from each of the twenty-five upper and lower bands, six half-
breeds, and "Joe" Campbell, the interpreter.  It was supplied with provisions and transportation and departed from the Yellow Medicine on the
twenty-second of July.  The superintendent now issued provisions to the
Sisseton to "keep them from starving" and sent them home.  For some
days quiet reigned at the Sioux agencies.[19]

If the commissioner of Indian affairs was confident of his own ability
to manage Indian affairs in Minnesota fifteen hundred miles away, he was
not so sure of the competency of his northern superintendent.  He therefore appointed a special agent, by letter of July 22, to proceed with the

[18] Indian Office, *Reports*, 1857, p. 81; narrative of J. W. Daniels. Williamson, in a letter
to the *Missionary Herald*, 54: 56 (February, 1858), states that the Sisseton who stabbed the
soldier was allowed to escape by the advice of Riggs.  Williamson relates that, as he was
making his way through an excited crowd of Indians to render medical assistance to the
wounded culprit, the latter's sister would have plunged a large butcher knife into him had
not a bystander seized her in time to prevent the stroke.  In the afternoon the father of
the man was discovered about Williamson's house watching to kill him.  The Indian had
heard that his son was dead and, according to his savage creed, some white man should die.
Williamson's sister, "Aunt Jane," had the address to divert the man's passion by some
tempting food.  When he learned that his son was not dead he expressed thanks for his
entertainment.  The whole letter is interesting.  Dr. Daniels had a similar experience.
He followed the party carrying the wounded man a mile and more.  As he approached the
man the latter's mother made a lunge at him with a scalping knife, but a friendly hand
averted the blow.  The man had received seven slight wounds below the hips.  His friends
were grateful for the doctor's ministry.
[19] Indian Office, *Reports*, 1857, p. 81-83, 85, 87, 96.  Superintendent Cullen goes so far
as to say that he cannot speak too highly of Little Crow, whose services had "saved the
government from a long and tedious war."

greatest possible dispatch to the Sioux country to second the efforts of the superintendent. In particular the special agent was instructed to inform the superintendent that he must impress upon the minds of the Indians that no part of their annuities would be paid until they had delivered up all the participants in the Spirit Lake massacre, or — a notable clause — until they had used "their utmost exertions to do so"; and, further, that the government would punish in the most summary manner those who should stubbornly refuse to deliver the murderers. As the secretary of war had disapproved of Governor Medary's application for equipment for volunteers, the superintendent was to be directed to warn citizens not to interfere in any way with the operations of the regular troops. The special agent was enjoined to submit a final report, doubtless to enable the commissioner to dispose of the "apparent difficulties" in person. By a rapid journey the special agent reached the lower agency on August 2, two days before the return of Little Crow's expedition.[20]

Interpreter Campbell kept an itinerary of the marches and bivouacs of the journey out and back. He stated that on July 28 on the shore of Skunk Lake — now Lake Madison in Lake County, South Dakota — were found two deserted encampments of three lodges each. Little Crow, with a selected detail, followed the trail of the fugitives and came upon them at another lake some miles northwestward, probably that now known as Lake Herman. There was a fight of half an hour, which was stopped by night and a heavy rain. "Two women and a little boy," wrote the diarist, "fell into our hands; and on the morning of the 29th we ascertained that three men were killed . . . and one badly wounded." The superintendent and the special agent evidently felt the need of something more convincing than the hearsay evidence of Campbell and therefore interrogated three Indians of the party and had their statements recorded in English. One witness, Good Hail, was confident that two men whom he fired on had dropped dead in the reeds of the lake and he thought that a third also fell. A second witness, The Cloud, said that he went around the lake the next morning and saw three dead Indians, whose names he gave. He then followed the trail of another who was apparently badly wounded, but, becoming "lonesome and unhappy" because the rest of the party were all gone, he abandoned the pursuit. The other witness was our well-known John Other Day, who, being on foot, arrived too late to see much of the fight. On the next morning, however, he saw The Cloud raise three bodies from the reeds of the lake. Little Crow's evidence was not taken, although he was present when Good Hail fired on the men who had run into the lake. It is notable that Interpreter Campbell did not personally see and identify the dead Indians and that the examination did not reveal the

[20] Indian Office, *Reports*, 1857, pp. 75-78, 85, 96.

reason for the negligence. The scalps of the Indians killed would have been the customary and the best evidence. That none was produced has been attributed to a tradition that Dakota never scalped Dakota. Inkpaduta had not been captured nor had any of his warriors. The only fruit of the costly expedition was the capture of the two women and the little boy, who were presently released. One of the women, Shifting Wind, gave the names of all the men of Inkpaduta's band.[21]

The two local Indian authorities were quite content to accept the statements before them, but they were by no means content with the results of Little Crow's expedition and in a council with the lower chiefs on August 5 urged them to join in another effort to capture the vagabond Inkpaduta, repeating to them that they need expect no annuities until the remainder of the band of outlaws had surrendered or perished. On the tenth the same proposition was submitted to the upper chiefs separately at Yellow Medicine. The attempts were vain. The Sioux had done all they could do or would do and they further insisted that what they had already done ought to satisfy the Great Father of their loyalty and entitle them to their annuities. A suggestion from the special agent that if they, the Indians, would do nothing further they would still have to wait for their annuities until the warriors of the Great Father had followed and captured the murderers, did not move them. Upon "mature deliberation," the two officials came to the same conclusion: the Indians, having "used their utmost exertions to deliver up the murderers," ought not to be further punished. On the same day, August 10, the special agent started for Dunleith, where he arrived on the eighteenth and at once dispatched a message from the superintendent to the commissioner, asking authority to pay the Indians. He added a postscript for himself: "I concur in the above for reasons in letter mailed to-day." The immediate answer of the commissioner was "Before giving the order I shall wait for the reasons." On August 25 the Indian office telegraphed: "Reasons received this morning; annuities may be now paid."[22]

The troops returned to the fort on August 27, but various delays kept the lower Indians waiting for their money until September 11 and the upper Indians, until September 20. The superintendent in his annual report of September 28, 1857, declared the payment to have been highly satisfactory and that not a single Indian was drunk. The commissioner in his annual report announced that the outlawed and reckless band which had committed the Spirit Lake murders had been severely punished by their brethren, a better course than chastisement by troops. In a letter from the upper agency, written July 7, Joseph R. Brown had prophesied that

---

[21] Indian Office, *Reports*, 1857, pp. 86-90, 97.
[22] Indian Office, *Reports*, 1857, pp. 92, 95, 99, 108-112.

there would be crawfishing on one side or the other. It was not on that of Little Crow.[23] It is now evident that Dr. Williamson had reason to say that the failure to capture and punish Inkpaduta was a fundamental cause of the Sioux Outbreak.

## 11. THE ACTON MURDERS[24]

The township of Acton lies in the middle of the five townships which form the western tier of Meeker County in the edge of the Big Woods. In the early summer of 1857 two American born citizens, Howard Baker and Robinson Jones, took up preëmption claims on the north half of section 21, Baker on the northeast corner and Jones on the northwest. They built log houses and began farming. Jones opened a small store of general merchandise to which was added a barrel of whisky. He also gave lodgings to travelers, chiefly fellow immigrants. He obtained an appointment as postmaster and, being a man of much energy, acquired no little influence in the community. That he sold liquor to Indians is probable, but no evidence has been found of such misdemeanor. In 1861 Jones married the mother of Baker and the couple adopted two children of a deceased relative, Clara D. Wilson, a girl of fifteen, and her half brother, eighteen months old.[25]

Hunting parties of Indians from the reservation came and went from year to year without causing trouble or alarm. When the party from Rice Creek mentioned in the text arrived in the neighborhood on the morning of August 17 it divided into two or more fractions. We are concerned with one only, composed of four young Indians, two of whom had on white men's coats. It has been asserted that the group set out with the definite purpose of killing Jones, with whom one or more had contracted debts which the settler expected to have paid to him out of the annuities of the year. No proof has been adduced of this theory and the transaction shows that the scoundrels had not come to kill any particular person. Of all the explanations, that furnished by Big Eagle to Holcombe, although apparently trivial in character, seems most probable. "They came," he says, "to a settler's fence, and here they found

[23] Indian Office, *Reports*, 1857, pp. 2, 50, 93. In a letter of August 16, 1857, Special Agent Pritchette, writing while en route to Dunleith, ventured the opinion that it was impossible to force the surrender of Inkpaduta and the remainder of his band without chastising the whole Sioux nation, which would be unjust. Since the adoption of the per capita plan of paying annuities, the chiefs had lost their authority over their bands and "no common nationality" existed. Mounted troops alone could effect the extirpation of Inkpaduta's murderous outlaws.
[24] See *ante*, p. 239.
[25] Holcombe, in *Minnesota in Three Centuries*, 3: 304; memorandum of Nathan Butler, July 11, 1917, Folwell Papers. Mr. Butler owned a claim adjacent to those of Jones and Baker. The township of Acton is 119, range 32 west.

a hen's nest with some eggs in it. One of them took the eggs, when another said: 'Don't take them, for they belong to a white man and we may get into trouble.' The other was angry . . . dashed them to the ground and replied: 'You are a coward. You are afraid of the white man. You are afraid to take even an egg from him, though you are half-starved. Yes, you are a coward, and I will tell everybody so.' The other replied: 'I am not a coward. I am not afraid of the white man, and to show you that I am not I will go to the house and shoot him. Are you brave enough to go with me?' The one who had called him a

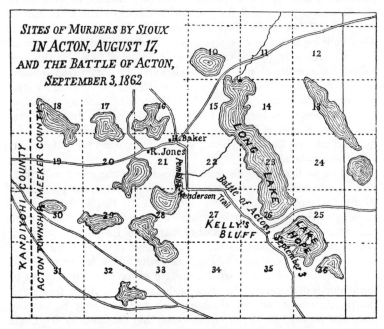

coward said: 'Yes, I will go with you, and we will see who is the braver of us two.' Their two companions then said: 'We will go with you, and we will be brave, too.' They all went to the house of the white man.'' It was reported that the Indians asked for liquor, were refused, and were so "cross" that Jones was alarmed and fled over to Baker's, whither his wife had already gone on a Sunday call. Because he left behind him the two children and because of the friendly interview which followed, it may be doubted whether he went to Baker's on account of fright.

At Baker's were two other persons, Viranus Webster and his wife, who had lately come into the neighborhood to select a homestead in that favored region. Their covered wagon stood near the house. The four Indians followed Jones somewhat leisurely and upon their arrival at Baker's appeared friendly. Jones, who could speak a little Sioux, traded Baker's gun with one of the Indians, who paid a small sum to boot. The Indians persuaded the white men to shoot at a mark, after which the Indians loaded their guns; the white men did not think to reload. Without warning the four Indians fired and killed or mortally wounded the three men and Mrs. Jones. Mrs. Baker with a child fell through a trapdoor to the cellar and Mrs. Webster was in the covered wagon. The miscreants did not search for them, but departed immediately without mutilating the bodies or disturbing the furniture or other property. It is remarkable that they did not seize the horses of Baker and Webster. As they passed to the westward one of them shot at the Wilson girl, probably through a door or window, and killed her. Here again they committed no depredation and they left Jones's whisky untouched. The murderers, conscious of the gravity of their crime and its possible consequences, thought of nothing but a headlong return to their village. They stole one pair of horses not far from the scene of the murder and probably others on their way.[26]

The surviving women, Mrs. Webster and Mrs. Baker, with the latter's two children, when all the victims were dead, made their way without visiting the Jones place to the house of a settler living near the north line of the township. From there a messenger took the terrible news to Forest City, distant not much less than twenty miles from the Acton post office. An armed party of villagers started in the evening and, with the exception of a large number who fell out by the way, reached the Jones house late in the night, where they found the body of the murdered girl and the little boy, who was unhurt. On the following day, August 18, a coroner's inquest was held, and the bodies of the five victims were buried in the cemetery of the Norwegian church a few miles away.[27]

[26] Smith, *Meeker County*, 43; Big Eagle, in *Minnesota Historical Collections*, 6: 388; Holcombe, in *Minnesota in Three Centuries*, 3: 303-306; *Pioneer Press*, July 1, 1894; Bryant and Murch, *Great Massacre*, 83-86; *Sisseton and Wahpeton Claim Case Record, Evidence for Defendant*, 291, 302, 309, 319, 367, 388; Indian Office, *Reports*, 1863, p. 288. A letter from Nathan Butler giving Mrs. Baker's story as told by a neighbor is in the *Litchfield Independent*, September 25, 1912. For a letter of M. S. Croswell stating the corroborating story of Mrs. Webster, see the *Saint Paul Press*, September 4, 1862. Mrs. Rosa Ann Webster in her testimony before the Sioux claims commission, stated that "soon 2 other Indians came, called or asked for a drink of water, which was given to them, three of them [the six Indians] then sat down & confered or conversed together a few minutes, one of the other 3 was sitting on the ground with his back to the three [in conference]." She then describes the four murders and adds that "the Indians all immediately left." Were the murders concocted in that conference? A typewritten copy of Mrs. Webster's testimony is in the possession of the Minnesota Historical Society. Heard, in his *Sioux War*, 55, states that the four conferred together before the murders.
[27] Holcombe, in *Minnesota in Three Centuries*, 3: 307-309; Heard, *Sioux War*, 56; Smith to Ramsey, August 19, 1862, in Governor's Archives, file 255; Smith, *Meeker County*, 17, 40-42. Judge Smith held the coroner's inquest over the bodies of the victims.

## 12. SISSETON AND WAHPETON CLAIMS[28]

The act of Congress of March 3, 1863, providing for the exile of all Sioux Indians from Minnesota, was superfluous as to the upper Sioux, the Sisseton and Wahpeton bands; they had removed themselves after the battle of Wood Lake. For five years they wandered over the prairies of Dakota, those who had been notoriously hostile occasionally concentrating at Devil's Lake and those who at length were disposed to be friendly, if they had not been so before, occasionally gathering about Fort Wadsworth. In 1866 a delegation of the latter Indians, who had made known to the government their desire to be at peace with the Great Father, met with three United States commissioners at Fort Rice. No treaty was made for the reason, as reported by the commission, that the Indians were dissuaded by Joseph R. Brown, who advised them to make an ill-timed demand for restoration of annuities and also sought to secure certain advantages for himself and his Indian relatives.[29]

Better success attended a council held at Washington on February 19, 1867, by the commissioner of Indian affairs and a colleague, with Gabriel Renville, the head chiefs of the Sisseton and Wahpeton bands, other headmen, and sixteen soldiers, twelve of them Sisseton. The treaty there made was afterwards spoken of as the "Great Treaty of 1867." If it had been concluded as originally negotiated it might have deserved that ascription. The preamble set forth that from twelve hundred to fifteen hundred members of the tribes had not only preserved their obligations to the government during and after the outbreak of 1862, but also had at that time risked their lives to rescue the residents on the reservations and to recover the captives from the hostile bands; and that another portion of the bands, from one thousand to twelve hundred in number, who had had no part in the massacres, had fled to the great prairies for fear of indiscriminate vengeance of the whites. By confiscating their annuities and reservations Congress had left these friendly and innocent people homeless, to wander and suffer for lack of food and clothing in a high latitude. The purposes of the treaty were to secure a recognition of their friendship to the government and the people of the United States, relief from their precarious life by the chase, and their settlement on the soil.

---

[28] See *ante*, p. 301.

[29] See *ante*, p. 258, and a letter to the commissioner of Indian affairs from the Edmunds-Guernsey-Reed commission, September 4, 1866, in Indian Office, *Reports*, 1866, p. 240. The commissioners bitterly arraigned Brown. In the Brown Papers is a draft of a "petition" of 188 lodges of Sisseton and Wahpeton to these commissioners in the handwriting of Joseph R. Brown, dated June, 1866. It contains the remarkable admission that from 175 to 200 lodges of those bands were engaged in the outbreak of 1862. The petitioners proposed to ingraft these hostiles into their bands and civilize them. The statement is made that had the Great Father protected the Sioux under the treaty of 1858 there would have been no outbreak.

The Indians had something to offer for the benefits they sought. They claimed to be owners of an area of land lying between the Red River of the North and the James and extending from Goose River to the treaty line of 1851. The Indian delegation agreed, not to cede to the United States any of this area, but to grant the right to construct wagon roads, railroads, telegraph lines, and other improvements over and across the lands. In consideration of this cession, of the faithful services claimed to have been rendered by the friendly bands represented, and of the confiscation of their annuities, reservations, and improvements, the United States was pledged to establish two reservations, which were afterwards known as the Sisseton and Devil's Lake reservations. In anticipation of the Dawes Act, passed twenty years later, allotments of 160 acres were to be made to heads of families and to single persons over twenty-one desirous to cultivate the soil. An allotment could be patented after the allottee had occupied it for five consecutive years and had fenced, plowed, and put in crop fifty acres. To enable the Indians to establish themselves on the land, $750,000 were to be expended upon the Sisseton reservation in four years, $450,000 on that of Devil's Lake, and $30,000 annually thereafter on both. It was provided that no goods of any kind should be furnished to the Indians except for labor or produce, but agents might relieve the aged, sick, or deformed. No trader was to be allowed on the reservations, but the agent would supply needed goods and provisions in payment for labor. Then followed four articles of a novel character. In the first of these the Indians guaranteed the safety of travel and of the mails in the territory which they claimed and the safety of the frontier settlers of Minnesota and eastern Dakota. To enable them to make good this guaranty, the president was to select a suitable person acceptable to the Indians and authorize him to organize a company of scouts not less than 250 in number and to exercise command over them under prescribed regulations. Each of the scouts so employed was to receive sixty dollars and rations per month for himself and his family and grain for his horse, but he was to provide his own horse, arms, ammunition, transportation, and equipment of all sorts. It was further provided that when the services of the scouts so employed were dispensed with the Indians themselves, under direction of the agent, might organize scouts to enforce laws and regulations prescribed by the government, or adopted in council, for securing life and property and advancing agriculture and civilization.[30]

As drawn and agreed to in council, the treaty was one of civilization and the reader does not need to be informed by what experienced and skillful person it was framed. With Joseph R. Brown, acting on his

[30] *Statutes at Large*, 15: 505-508. For the Sisseton and Devil's Lake reservations, see Charles C. Royce, *Indian Land Sessions in the United States*, map no. 11 (Bureau of American Ethnology, *Eighteenth Annual Report*, part 2—Washington, 1899).

experience in civilizing Indians from 1858 to 1860, as their agent and with
Gabriel Renville as chief of scouts, the end of the proposed four-year
term might have seen the upper Sioux living in houses, subsisting upon
the fruits of the soil, their children in schools, and a large proportion of
them embracing the Christian religion.[31]   The Senate, however, was not
ready for that kind of treaty with Sioux Indians.   The committee on
Indian affairs reported the treaty with a recommendation to amend by
striking out the last nine articles and replacing them with five others.
The most important change had to do with the provisions to expend
$1,200,000 in four years.   Instead of that it was proposed that Congress
should, "in its own discretion, from time to time, make such appropriations
. . . as Congress in its wisdom shall deem necessary to promote the
agricultural improvement and civilization of said Indians."   The articles
providing for scouts to guarantee protection to frontier settlers and safety
of travel and of the mails were cut out entirely.[32]   The contemplated
scheme to put the whole population into houses, to fence and plow fields,
and to have all hands at work on farms and gardens, with a new Hazelwood Republic in operation, did not commend itself to the wisdom of
the Senate.   That body preferred the policy of doling out annual driblets
of money, which were soon spent for petty objects.   Between 1867 and
1873 somewhat over $300,000 were appropriated for support.   Under an
agreement which became effective in 1873 the Sisseton and Wahpeton
sold all their lands outside of the two reservations, for which they were
paid $800,000 in ten annual installments terminating in 1882.   The per
capita distribution of sixteen dollars a year could do little or nothing toward civilization.   The old and vicious system was continued.[33]

The grants by the treaty of 1867 of new reservations on land which
already belonged to the Indians and the proposed large donation for
civilization were made in part in consideration of the confiscated an-

[31] Jared W. Daniels, "Sisseton Agency," 5, in the Daniels Papers. In the Brown Papers
there is a letter of twenty-three hundred words from Joseph R. Brown to the chairman of
the Senate committee on Indian affairs, dated March 11, 1867, in which Brown makes an
earnest and powerful appeal for the ratification of the treaty, which was then pending. An
article in the *Saint Paul Press*, March 19, 1867, criticizes the treaty adversely and condemns
Brown. For Brown's opinion of Indian treaties and his conviction, derived from experiment,
that the Sioux could be rapidly civilized, see his letter to William Welsh, April 13, 1869, in
Welsh, *Taopi and His Friends, or the Indians' Wrongs and Rights*, pp. 64-72 (Philadelphia,
1869).
[32] *Senate Executive Proceedings*, 736; *Statutes at Large*, 15: 505, 509. The Senate amendments were ratified by an Indian delegation in Washington on April 22, 1867.
[33] *Sisseton and Wahpeton Bands of Dakota or Sioux Indians*, 17, 18, 48-56 (55 Congress,
2 session, *Senate Documents*, no. 68 — serial 3593); *Statutes at Large*, 17: 456; 18: 167.
Credit must be given for commendable progress in the work of civilization during the
agency of Dr. J. W. Daniels, from 1869 to 1871. See his "Sisseton Agency" and his reports
for 1869 and 1870, in Indian Office, *Reports*, 1869, pp. 320-322; 1870, pp. 225-227 (reprinted
in 41 Congress, 3 session, *House Executive Documents*, vol. 4, part 1 — serial 1449). In his
"Sisseton Agency," 17, Daniels gives the reason for his transfer to another position.

nuities, reservations, and improvements. When Congress cut out the civilization fund and vaguely promised appropriations from time to time according to its wisdom and when the Indians perceived that they had received nothing substantial for their confiscated annuities, agitation for an ampler and more definite remuneration for those annuities was soon resumed. In 1869 a scheme was developed by which Joseph R. Brown was to undertake to secure the repeal of the act of confiscation as far as Indians who did not participate in the outbreak were concerned. He was aware that it would "cost a great deal of money . . . besides a long time and hard work." He was to hold a power of attorney for the purpose and, if successful, he was to receive one-third of all sums appropriated and one thousand dollars were to be paid annually to his family until 1880. It was proposed that he and his family should receive their compensations direct from the United States treasury and take no chances of having them handled by any intermediate custodian.[34]

Joseph R. Brown closed his notable career on November 9, 1870,[35] and the plan which might have reached success in his hands died with him, to be revived only after many years. There took place, however, after more than a decade, a partial restoration of forfeited annuities, which should not be passed without mention. The reader will have noted the presence of Indian scouts in the camps and on the marches of the white soldiers in the Indian wars. The rosters of Minnesota regiments show some names of Indian soldiers who fought in the Civil War. The number so employed or enlisted was variously and liberally estimated at from 200 to 270. Although the injustice of withholding annuities from these really loyal individual Indians, many of whom were mixed-bloods, was or ought to have been apparent, many years passed before an effort was made for their relief. In 1888 a bill for this purpose was reported to Congress from the House committee on Indian affairs with its favorable recommendation. The commissioner of Indian affairs in a long communication to the committee pleaded with fervor for justice to a deserving and long-neglected body of persons who had fought against disloyal tribesmen and secessionists. He estimated the number so engaged, together with their families, to be about one-fourth of all the upper Sioux and he therefore recommended that one-fourth of the whole annuities confiscated by the act of February 16, 1863, be restored to them. The secretary of the interior, less sympathetic, merely recommended consideration of the committee's proposition. The bill received no attention at that session and met with no better hospitality the following year.[36]

[34] Joseph R. Brown to Samuel J. Brown, February 16, 1869, Brown Papers. Forms for a petition to be signed by the Indians and the agent's certificate accompany Brown's letter.
[35] Upham and Dunlap, *Minnesota Biographies*, 84.
[36] *Indians Who Served in the Army of the United States* (50 Congress, 1 session, *House Reports*, no. 1953 — serial 2603); *Congressional Record*, 50 Congress, 2 session, 890, 3290.

A way was soon found by which an indifferent Congress could be induced to entertain the claim. The Dawes allotment act, passed in 1887, provided for the establishment of individual Indians on parcels of 160 acres of land within reservations, the subsequent sale of the surplus areas, the deposit of the proceeds in the treasury, and the payment of interest on the fund in perpetuity for the civilization of the tribes. In 1889 the allotment of the Sisseton reservation was practically complete and that of the Devil's Lake reservation was under way. On March 2, 1889, Congress specifically authorized negotiation for the purchase of the unallotted lands on both reservations.[37]  On December 12 of that year an "agreement" was made with the chiefs, headmen, and adult males of the Sisseton and Wahpeton tribes under which they sold to the United States all the unallotted lands of their reservations, more than a million acres, for the sum of two dollars and fifty cents per acre. With the main transaction we have no present concern. An ingeniously ambiguous article provided for the payment "to the Sisseton and Wahpeton bands of Dakota or Sioux Indians . . . the amount found to be due certain members of said bands of Indians who served in the armies of the United States against their own people . . . and their families and descendants." The amount so due was estimated at the rate of $18,400 per annum, one-fourth of each year's annuity from 1862 to 1901, the end of the fifty-year period of the treaty of Traverse des Sioux, in all some $700,000.

The agreement of December 12, 1889, did not come up for consideration in Congress until February 16, 1891, and then as section 26 of the Indian appropriation bill for the year. The following section making an appropriation of $376,578.37 toward carrying it out provided for payments per capita and declared that the sum so paid should be in full settlement of "all claims they [the scouts and soldiers] may have for unpaid annuities" up to June 30, 1890. As if to forestall any undesirable diversion of the money, the bill limited the amount payable to any agent or attorney to ten per cent of the appropriation. The bill became a law on March 3, 1891, without modification.[38]

The long delay of justice to the scouts and soldiers of the Sioux did not much encourage their friends, interested and disinterested, to urge Congress to restore to the Sioux generally the value of their forfeited lands and annuities. Still the fact that one-fourth of the annuities had been restored to the Sisseton and Wahpeton kept alive the hope that some day, either out of justice or mercy, a generous Congress might give back the whole

[37] *Statutes at Large*, 24: 388-391; 25: 892; Indian Office, *Reports*, 1889, pp. 15, 16 (reprinted in 51 Congress, 1 session, *House Executive Documents*, vol. 12 — serial 2725).
[38] *Statutes at Large*, 26: 1035-1039; *Congressional Record*, 51 Congress, 2 session, pp. 2764, 2809, 3879-3881. For payments under this agreement see *Sisseton and Wahpeton Bands of Dakota or Sioux Indians*, 18 (serial 3593).

of them. It was not until the winter of 1897, however, that a campaign was seriously opened. On February 2 the Senate committee on Indian affairs, of which Senator Richard F. Pettigrew of South Dakota was chairman, submitted a report recommending such restoration. The report was in substance a version of a statement prepared by an attorney for the Sisseton and Wahpeton Sioux.[39] No progress was made at that short session of Congress, but at the special session of a new Congress there came from the committee on Indian affairs, on March 23, 1897, a second report of the same tenor, with some enlargements. The bill introduced received no attention, but Congress was enough interested to insert in the Indian appropriation bill a paragraph directing the secretary of the interior to report to Congress as soon as practicable copies of all treaties or agreements made with the Sisseton and Wahpeton bands, and statements of all moneys paid under the treaties, of the extent of all reservations granted the two bands, and of amounts arising from the sale of their reservations or portions thereof. The secretary's report, submitted on January 15, 1898, and accompanied by a map, admirably fulfilled the requirements of Congress. A month later the Senate committee presented a new version of its report with a bill, which came up for consideration on June 16. Senator Allison of Iowa was its principal opponent. The end of the short session left the bill with unfinished business, although repeated efforts were made to obtain consideration.[40]

Upon the reassemblage of Congress for the winter of 1899, the industrious Senate committee on Indian affairs had ready another report, which was submitted on January 5. It was a rehash with some additional argument. At this session no separate bill was introduced, but when the Indian appropriation bill, which had come from the House, was under consideration on February 8, 1899, Senator Pettigrew proposed a new section to restore to the upper Sioux their forfeited annuities. Senator Allison objected under the rule that no amendment proposing general legislation should be received to any general appropriation bill and his objection was sustained; but the vice president generously allowed some speeches before announcing his ruling. On March 2, 1900, Senator Pettigrew presented a brief résumé of his previous reports.[41] Three bills were introduced into the Senate and two into the House relating to annuity restorations, all of which were referred to the committees on

---

[39] *Sisseton and Wahpeton Bands of Sioux or Dakota Indians* (54 Congress, 2 session, *Senate Reports*, no. 1384 — serial 3475).
[40] *Sisseton and Wahpeton Bands of Sioux Indians* (55 Congress, 1 session, *Senate Reports*, no. 9 — serial 3569); *Statutes at Large*, 30: 89; *Sisseton and Wahpeton Bands of Dakota or Sioux Indians* (serial 3593); *Congressional Record*, 55 Congress, 2 session, 6024, 6066.
[41] *Annuities of Certain Sioux Indians* (55 Congress, 3 session, *Senate Reports*, no. 1441 — serial 3739); *Congressional Record*, 55 Congress, 3 session, 1600-1606; *Sisseton and Wahpeton Indians* (56 Congress, 1 session, *Senate Documents*, no. 205 — serial 3854).

Indian affairs. No reports were made on the bills. It was apparent to claimants that Congress would give them no relief by direct appropriations. In the year following, 1901, a new strategy was adopted, which resulted in the insertion of a paragraph in the Indian appropriation bill conferring full jurisdiction upon the court of claims to ascertain and report to Congress what members of Sioux tribes had remained loyal to the United States and had not been concerned in the outbreak of 1862 and also what annuities under the treaty of 1851 would now be due those loyal Indians if the act of forfeiture of February 16, 1863, had not been passed. This was enacted into law.[42]

Some observations may properly be made at this point. The first is that, throughout all the reports mentioned and in the debates in Congress on the various bills for restoring annuities to the upper Sioux, it was repeatedly stated that the outbreak of 1862 was inaugurated by the lower Sioux and that no overt act of hostility had been committed by the Sisseton and Wahpeton bands. They had remained steadfastly loyal and patriotic. They had rescued many white captives from the hostile Indians and more than two hundred of their warriors had been employed or had enlisted in the military service of the United States. Senator Cushman K. Davis of Minnesota said in the Senate on February 8, 1899: "Congress, without any process of law whatever, arbitrarily confiscated" the annuities of all the bands. "Nothing is better known in the history of my own State where the tragedy occurred, [than] that three of those bands took no part in the massacre. It was perpetrated entirely by the Santees. . . . there is not a shadow of a doubt as to the fact or the merits. . . . it is going to pass some time. Why not do it now?" The great lawyer had not yet carefully studied all the chapters of Minnesota history.[43]

The Senate committee on Indian affairs, of which Senator Pettigrew was chairman, in two reports had estimated that the government had made a gain of $55,531,250 from the lands ceded by the upper Sioux in 1851, but in a third report it had reduced that "profit" to the more modest sum of $19,699,500. It was stated in one of the reports that in the treaty of Traverse des Sioux the Indians were promised $1,777,000, of which $1,472,000 were to remain in trust with the United States, but that "a subsequent article" provided that the fifty annual installments of interest on the principal sum should be in full payment of both the principal and the interest. The Indians had not so understood the bargain. Considering that the United States had never recognized in aborigines a possessory title to lands, the presentation of such an argument to the Senate suggests a degree of desperation. It is true that such provision

[42] 56 Congress, 1 session, *Senate Journal*, 19, 52, 61; *House Journal*, 35, 459; *Statutes at Large*, 31: 1078.
[43] *Congressional Record*, 55 Congress, 3 session, 1605.

was contained in a subsequent paragraph of the treaty of 1851, but in all the literature of the Sioux Outbreak the author has found no previous complaint by or for the Indians that such a fraud had been practiced. The Senate committee found still other grounds for repealing the confiscation act of 1863. It was, the committee said, clearly unconstitutional. Congress had not the right to take property away from those holding under the treaties, which were a part of the supreme law of the land and were also contracts not to be canceled, unless by the consent of all parties. Forfeiture of lands as a penalty for treason, for lifetime only, could be lawfully effected only by judicial process. Further, Indians, not being citizens, could not commit treason against the United States. A suggestion that the act of confiscation had an *ex post facto* operation was added. It was therefore represented to the Senate that the confiscation was "a most outrageous and unconscionable transaction" and "a great and monstrous wrong without parallel in the history of any civilized government."[44]

Another point of importance was the simultaneous claim of the lower Sioux for the restoration of their annuities. Indeed, their claim technically antedated that of the Sisseton and Wahpeton. Separate bills for their relief were before Congress in 1897 and again in 1898. After the reception, on January 15, 1898, of the report of the secretary of the interior mentioned above, the Senate committee added to the bill to restore annuities to the Sisseton and Wahpeton an amendment to exercise the same generosity toward the lower Sioux. The claim of the lower Sioux was merely an appeal to the nation to be generous to an unhappy people grievously punished for the fault of a few wrongdoers of a bygone generation. This contention was in itself fatal to the claims of both. An independent resort to the court of claims by the Sisseton and Wahpeton attorneys was the only course open. There was another feature in this bill and the amendment which excited opposition, namely, provisions for the payment of the fees of the Indians' attorneys directly from the treasury from sums to be immediately available to the Indians. In the case of the upper Sioux the amount to be immediately available was four hundred thousand dollars; in that of the lower Sioux, three hundred thousand dollars. The hope of enjoying such comfortable fees no doubt stimulated the industry of these friends of their poor and deeply wronged clients.[45]

[44] *Sisseton and Wahpeton Bands of Sioux Indians*, 1, 5 (serial 3569); *Annuities of Certain Sioux Indians*, 5, 17-21 (serial 3739); *Sisseton and Wahpeton Bands of Sioux or Dakota Indians* (serial 3475).
[45] *Amendment to Indian Appropriation Bill* (54 Congress, 2 session, *Senate Reports*, no. 1362 — serial 3475); *Affidavits and Petitions of Members of the Santee Sioux Tribe of Indians* (54 Congress, 1 session, *Senate Documents*, no. 85 — serial 3349); *Congressional Record*, 55 Congress, 2 session, 4423, 6024, 6026.

In March, 1901, the attorney for the Sisseton and Wahpeton Sioux filed in the United States court of claims his original petition. After reciting the various treaties and the acts relating to them, he asked the court to find as fact that the Sisseton and Wahpeton bands of Sioux had preserved their loyalty to the United States during the hostilities of 1862, that they had not been concerned directly or indirectly in the depredations on the lives and property of the whites, and that the total sum due those Indians on account of forfeited annuities was $2,969,204.46, less the amount of $615,778.37 already paid to scouts and some other small deductions to be ascertained. The presentation of evidence in the case took place in August and September, 1901, under the direction of a commissioner appointed by the court.[46]

The first witness, who was introduced by the claimants' attorney on August 5 at his home in Brown's Valley, Minnesota, was Samuel J. Brown, a son of Joseph R. Brown. The testimony of this witness as to facts within his knowledge was clear and consistent, but as he was a prisoner in Little Crow's camp from August 19 to September 23 his opportunities for observation were limited. In the record of the testimony there follows the remarkable narrative of Samuel J. Brown's experiences as a prisoner of the Sioux. Its introduction was mildly objected to because it was not "the best evidence of what it contains."[47]

At the Sisseton agency, beginning on August 10, 1901, seven Indians were interrogated, of whom the most prominent was Solomon Two Stars, recognized as the headman of the two tribes. All were representative members. Five mixed-bloods, including Charles Crawford, Joseph Laframboise, and Thomas Robertson, testified at that place. The three

---

[46] *Sisseton and Wahpeton Claim Case, Original Petition.* As the principal allegation of the claimants was innocency in the outbreak of 1862 and as the witnesses were interrogated in regard to their several experiences and observations, the record has become one of the best sources of information on that tragedy. The documents relating to this case in the library of the Minnesota Historical Society consist of the following: *Original Petition; Evidence for Claimant,* parts 1 and 2; *Evidence for Defendant; Brief for Claimants; Defendants' Brief and Argument; Claimants' Reply Brief; Defendants' Supplemental Brief; Defendants' Argument; Proposed Restoration of Annuities to the Medawakanton and Wahpakoota Sioux Indians* (report of the Senate committee on Indian affairs, March 28, 1906); *Supplemental Petition; Claimants' Supplemental Request for Findings of Fact and Conclusions of Law, and Brief; Defendants' Brief on the Last Jurisdictional Act of Congress and Request for Findings of Fact; Claimants' Reply Brief; Defendants' Supplemental Brief;* "Memorandum of Defendants' Supplemental Brief Filed Since the Oral Argument" (typewritten); *Defendants' Substitute Brief on the Last Jurisdictional Act of Congress and Request for Findings of Fact; Findings of Fact,* April 22, 1907; *Findings of Fact,* May 13, 1907; *Appeals from the Court of Claims* (in the Supreme Court, October term, 1907). The first three items are paged consecutively and the remaining, separately. Other documents, which the author has seen, are *Amended Supplementary Petition,* January, 1907; *Claimants' Supplemental Brief;* "Motion of Claimants to Amend the Findings of April 22, 1907"; and "Defendant's Objections to Amendment of Findings." The last two documents, relating to details apparently of minor importance, have not been printed.

[47] *Evidence for Claimant,* 25-74. On Brown's narrative see *ante,* p. 122, n. 18.

named were examined at great length. As all these witnesses would share in the hoped-for award of over two million dollars, they betrayed the bias natural to human nature. They had, no doubt, often conversed upon the subject and there is reason to believe that they had been prepared for the examination. There is evidence that they had been selected in council. There was a general denial of participation by the upper bands in the outbreak and in the four battles. The questioning of their attorney brought out repeated assertions of the absence of Standing Buffalo, Scarlet Plume, and Waanatan. These chiefs had gone down to Little Crow's camp at Hazelwood, had refused in council to join his force, and had returned to their homes on Lakes Big Stone and Traverse. Standing Buffalo had had two letters written to General Sibley. Cross-examination extorted some important concessions. Although innocent of participation in the war, the upper bands, including the innocent bands of the Sisseton chiefs mentioned, generally took flight after Sibley's victory at Wood Lake. They were so fearful of the white man's indiscriminate vengeance that even Sibley's promise of immunity to all good Indians did not call them back. It was admitted by different witnesses that, while the bands had not gone down to the massacre and the battles, some young men, having escaped from control, had gone down and had taken part. Seven of these witnesses were at the battle of Wood Lake, four of them in Indian dress and three of them armed, but they were there, as they claimed—perhaps truly—to communicate with Sibley or to rescue friends.[48]

The testimony of the mixed-bloods taken at the Sisseton agency was not strongly affirmative. Thomas Robertson, one of the "two Toms" who carried Little Crow's and, later, Taopi's letters to Sibley, was at the second battle of Fort Ridgely and at New Ulm. To the former he went to please the lower Indians and thus to secure protection for his mother and sisters, who were among them; "he had to go" to New Ulm. He saw no upper Indians at either battle. He did not know of any of them going down to Wood Lake, but heard some say that they had been there.[49] Laframboise, a mixed-blood Sisseton, went to Birch Coulee to see whether the hostiles would kill the white men with their clubs instead of having to shoot them, as they had boasted. Another reason was his fear that his sister Julia would be injured if he did not yield to threats. For appearance's sake he got into the fighting. His memory was infirm on many points, particularly in regard to the number of Sisseton who went to the battle of Wood Lake. Charles Crawford, a mixed-blood Wahpeton, brother-in-law of Joseph R. Brown, and later a Presbyterian minister, was at the

<hr>

[48] *Evidence for Claimant,* 75-188, *passim,* especially 93, 100, 103, 109, 125.
[49] *Evidence for Claimant,* 136, 141; Robertson's statement, in Proceedings of the Military Commission. See *ante,* p. 172.

last battle of Fort Ridgely by order of the soldiers' lodge, but he stayed
under the hill.  He also went to New Ulm from Fort Ridgely along with
two of the Renvilles, but his party stopped in a cornfield a mile from the
firing and cooked corn.  He was not asked about seeing the upper Indians.
At Wood Lake he was one of a party of friendlies who went down to see
what could be done to assist the troops or to notify them of attack.  He
and Gabriel Renville endeavored to send Angus Brown inside Sibley's
lines but failed.  The two spent the night in the edge of the timber,
watched the battle from a safe distance, and after it was over went into
Sibley's camp.  He did not remember seeing any members of certain
Sisseton bands named to him.  The Reverend John B. Renville testified
that he had stayed at his home at Hazelwood with his white wife until the
Indians had moved from there to Red Iron's village.  On the march he
was so closely guarded that he saw and heard little.  He had heard merely
that upper Sioux had taken part in the war.  Isaac Renville said that he
went with two other Wahpeton down to the second attack on Fort Ridgely
"to see what was going on," but he did not notice whether any upper
Sioux were there.  He did not know that any of them had participated in
the war against the whites.  He went to Wood Lake to keep Simon
Anawangmani from being hurt and to aid the whites, but he kept out of
the fight.  He was not asked whether upper Indians were engaged or
not.[50]

At the Devil's Lake agency, between August 28 and September 3,
1901, six Indian witnesses deposed.  Most of them agreed that at the
time of the outbreak of 1862 the bands of Standing Buffalo, Scarlet
Plume, and Waanatan were hunting buffalo near the Sheyenne River,
that two Wahpeton runners brought the news of the massacre, that a
council was held in which the chiefs warned the young men to keep away
from the scene, and that the bands kept together as they went back to
their villages.  Little Fish said, "We kept together, and none [of the
young men] went down there."  Some questions were then asked about
the attack on Fort Abercrombie and what Indians made it.  Two of the
Indians knew nothing about it and one of them, Little Fish, asserted
that it could not have been made by any of the bands of Standing Buffalo,
Scarlet Plume, or Waanatan.  Confident that the evidence recorded would
abundantly support the contention of the claimants that the upper
Sioux had not as bands participated in the outbreak and battles of 1862,
their attorney now tardily opened a new line of interrogation intended to
prove that they, at least the three prominent bands mentioned, were
equally guiltless in 1863.  Aside from some minor variations, five of
these Indian witnesses testified that in midsummer of 1863 the Sisseton

[50] *Evidence for Claimant*, 112, 129, 144, 167.

and Wahpeton tribes, with a few Mdewakanton in a separate body, were traveling after buffalo between the James and Missouri rivers; that the day before the battle of Big Mound they met the band of Inkpaduta, including perhaps some Yanktonai and a body of Teton who had come from their homes west of the Missouri; that the four parties had made separate camps south and west of Big Mound; that on the day of the battle Standing Buffalo, with his men, was going, or was getting ready to go, to meet General Sibley, who had demanded a conference with him; that, upon the sudden assassination of Surgeon Weiser by one of Inkpaduta's men who thought Sibley "had come to kill or to fight such as he," Standing Buffalo, finding it impossible to communicate with Sibley, hurried his people back to their camp and took little or no part in the big fight; and that all the Sisseton and Wahpeton after dark separated from the other Indians and "went up North." They could only state from hearsay that General Sibley followed Inkpaduta's men and the Teton to the Missouri. One of the Indian witnesses who deposed at Devil's Lake was Paul Mazakutemani's son, Daniel Paul, a Wahpeton, who, as related, left the Indian line and went over to Sibley's camp before the battle began. He could say that the Indians with whom Sibley was engaged after the battle of Big Mound were Inkpaduta's band, the Teton, and probably some Mdewakanton. He believed the Sisseton and Wahpeton had gone off "in another direction." In regard to the number of Indians killed at Big Mound, he testified that there were but five, all of whom he saw. Four were old men and one was a very old woman. The statement may be as far from fact as Colonel McPhail's estimate of eighty. According to Paul's judgment there were from 350 to 450 lodges of Indians present at the battle of Big Mound, which corresponds roughly to General Sibley's estimate of from a thousand to fifteen hundred Indians.[51]

The willingness of these witnesses to make Inkpaduta a scapegoat is clearly apparent. It is notable that no similar testimony was drawn from the Sisseton agency Indians. It may be admitted that the roving Inkpaduta had led his hunting party to this distant region and, if so, was only too happy to have a shot at the hated white man. The story that Inkpaduta was given or took the leadership of the warriors of the combined hunting parties and conducted their retreat with consummate skill, defeating Sibley's hope of capturing or destroying the whole Sioux force, is a romantic conceit not warranted, at least by the testimony in the claim case.[52] It may be true that the Sisseton and Wahpeton bands, considering themselves as friendlies, separated from the other Indians

[51] *Evidence for Claimant*, 192-195, 197, 202, 211, 214, 224-229, 231-233, 236-239, 241, 244; *Official Records*, series 1, vol. 22, part 1, p. 354.
[52] Robinson, *Sioux Indians*, 345.

regarded as hostiles and "turned north in the night," but testimony in addition to that given by the interested Indian witnesses at Devil's Lake in terms suspiciously uniform, would be desirable. If the upper Sioux had thus escaped and gone off north three days before, it is difficult to account for the presence of the large amount of transportation abandoned by the Indians who had fled across the Missouri and reported to have been destroyed by Colonel Crooks.[53]

An important contention of the claimants was that their tribesmen had rescued the white captives from the hostile Indians under Little Crow and had delivered them to Colonel Sibley at Camp Release. It was stated in evidence that when the lower Indians retreated to Yellow Medicine on August 28, their soldiers' lodge ordered a small group, mostly of Wahpeton half-breeds, which had the Brown family in its keeping to move into the general camp. This they refused to do and summoned the neighboring Wahpeton by runners to their defense. Several hundred responded, assembled at Hazelwood, pitched a large tepee in the center of the camp, and organized a soldiers' lodge. A delegation to the hostile camp secured the release of some property belonging to Mrs. Brown and others. A number of these friendlies maintained a separate camp on and after the march to Camp Release and, it was claimed, upon the dispersion of the hostiles after their defeat at Wood Lake, the friendly Mdewakanton who did not flee came over to that camp and brought their captives with them. The friendly upper Indians then turned the captives over to Sibley. As claimant witnesses admitted that there were, besides old men, women, and children, only some twenty warriors left in the friendly camp the day before the battle of Wood Lake, the hundreds of Wahpeton who had rallied at Hazelwood must have been in the hostile camp.[54]

The one mixed-blood examined at Devil's Lake, one of the Renville Rangers, threw no light on points in dispute, but volunteered his opinion that the Mdewakanton "made that massacre" and that the upper Indians were "very innocent about this Indian massacre." A former private soldier of Company D, Fifth Minnesota Infantry, sworn at St. Paul on September 14, 1901, was at Fort Abercrombie at the time of the main attack. He saw only four Indians and "did not believe there was 500 Indians in the outfit." He could not say what Indians were there. Another member of the same command was examined on the fourteenth at Minneapolis. He placed the number of Indians in the attack on Fort Abercrombie "at between 300 and 500." He could only say that Sweet Corn, a Sisseton Indian, had been about the fort before the attack.[55]

[53] *Evidence for Claimant*, 229. See ante, p. 275.
[54] *Evidence for Claimant*, 31, 52-54, 148, 155, 175; Renville, in *Minnesota Historical Collections*, 10: 605 (part 2); "Narrative of Paul Mazakootemane," translated by Stephen R. Riggs, in *Minnesota Historical Collections*, 3: 84-87.
[55] *Evidence for Claimant*, 217, 222, 247, 252.

The deposition of witnesses called by the defense—that is, the government—began at Minneapolis on September 11, 1901, with the exception of that of the well-known interpreter, William L. Quinn, which had been taken at an earlier date. Nothing had been elicited from Quinn but the fact that when Walking Spirit's band of Wahpeton was captured at Goose Nest Lake by Lieutenant Colonel Marshall in October, 1862, its wagons were loaded with plunder, but he would not say that it was white man's property. At Minneapolis, Captain John Vander Horck, who was in command of Fort Abercrombie in August and September, 1862, testified that the attack on that post was made by Sisseton and Wahpeton. He was absolutely certain of that because members of the garrison had buried some of those Indians and because he had recognized Chief Waanatan, with whom he had been personally acquainted. At the same place, Colonel Timothy J. Sheehan was examined at great length. His account of the affair at the upper agency on August 4, 1862, when the upper Sioux broke open the agency warehouse and were prevented from completely looting it only by the resolute action of Sheehan and his soldiers, was utilized later to show that the upper Sioux were then hostile and mutinous. The government counsel spoke of "this outbreak of August 4." On direct examination Colonel Sheehan testified that the attack on August 22, 1862, on Fort Ridgely, where he was in command, was begun by from 950 to 1,000 Indian warriors and that they were reënforced in the afternoon by at least 200 more. He estimated the number of lower Sioux warriors at from 475 to 500, thus leaving it to be inferred that there must have been a very large proportion of upper Sioux in action. Upon cross-examination, through a lapse in memory or confusion of thought, the witness raised the number of the reënforcement to from 300 to 400 and said that he had surmised at the time that they were Standing Buffalo's and Red Iron's Indians. It was evident that Colonel Sheehan was not desirous of underestimating the force which attacked the fort he so gallantly defended.[56] The young lieutenant, fighting his first battle, might easily err in guessing at the number of the savages who fought from cover or in detached bodies from different quarters.

Fourteen witnesses were produced by the government at Flandreau, South Dakota, and at the Santee agency in Nebraska in September. Ten of them were Mdewakanton, eight full-bloods and two mixed-bloods; three were Wahpeton, two full-bloods and one mixed-blood; and two were Yanktonai full-bloods. One of the last mentioned was called for the purpose of proving that no Yanktonai could have been in the region during the summer of 1862. If such were the fact it was to be inferred that Sisseton made the attack on Fort Abercrombie. One of the Wahpeton

⁵⁶ *Evidence for Defendant*, 268, 270-288; *Brief for Claimants*, 26.

witnesses swore that Amos W. Huggins was killed by one of his tribesmen, thus relieving the lower Sioux of the odium of that atrocious deed. Another Wahpeton witness testified that the four Acton murderers were his nephews and that they were all Wahpeton; but on cross-examination he admitted that they had all married Mdewakanton women, had lived on the lower reservation, and had drawn their annuities with the Santee.[57] Mrs. Maggie Brass, whose Dakota name was Snana, testified that "after they went up river" she saw in the Sisseton camp a scalp dance around a white man's scalp and also that at the time the captives were released there was but one camp.[58] The remainder, and the larger number, of the witnesses, Mdewakanton, were introduced chiefly for the purpose of showing that there were, and must have been, a great number of upper Indians present at the four battles. Six of them testified that one thousand Indians were engaged in the second attack on Fort Ridgely; one of them was careful to say that the number lacked seventy of being one thousand; and one put it at over nine hundred. Two deponents said that the number attacking New Ulm was seven hundred; others put it at eight hundred. The lowest estimate of the number of Indians at Birch Coulee by five witnesses who were there was seven hundred, the highest was one thousand, and the intermediate numbers were eight hundred and nine hundred. Five of eight witnesses who were questioned in regard to the Indian force at Wood Lake said that it was one thousand or more, one fixed it at eleven hundred, and the remaining two, at twelve hundred. All these witnesses averred that in the four battles large numbers of Sisseton and Wahpeton were fighting in their distinctive tribal dress. As it was well known that the number of lower Sioux warriors could not have much exceeded five hundred, there must have been that number or more of upper Indians in the battles, if these witnesses were telling the truth. That the tribes were "all mixed up" in the battles was a stereotyped phrase. Such conspicuous uniformity of statement excited the suspicion of the claimants' counsel, who in his brief sarcastically insinuated that the testimony had been prearranged by John Eastman, "the ever-present representative of the Lower Indians." A similar conformity occurred in regard to the number and even the names of Indians killed in the several battles and the number of upper Sioux who surrendered and were tried and convicted by the military commission.[59]

No little pains were taken to establish a contention that it was not any group of friendlies among the upper Indians who fed and protected the

[57] *Evidence for Defendant*, 319, 344, 388, 302, 390-392; *Evidence for Claimant*, 90, 126, 132, 143.
[58] *Evidence for Defendant*, 380-383. See *ante*, p. 391.
[59] *Evidence for Defendant*, 288-290, 307, 322, 336, 340, 345, 351, 362-364; *Brief for Claimants*, 50.

white captives and finally delivered them to Sibley but a body of loyal and faithful Mdewakanton, who risked their lives in so acting. Claimant witnesses had testified to the dispatch, under the utmost secrecy, of the letter of Taopi and Wabasha on behalf of friendly Mdewakanton. When asked why these lower friendlies had not opposed the hostiles of their own camp, the defendant witnesses said that they dared not for fear of their lives; and two of them added that they were also terrorized by Sisseton and Wahpeton in their camp. There could be no dispute that the captives had been closely guarded in Little Crow's camp up to the day of the Wood Lake battle. The only question left was whether the friendlies of the lower bands had held them until Sibley came up or had gone over with their prisoners to the camp of the friendly Wahpeton and allowed them the glory of releasing the captives. Against this claim the lower Sioux protested. The question is not of high importance and perhaps the best solution may be found in the simple words of Snana: "Just about the time that Sibley came they all pulled down their tents and put them near together."[60]

At the Santee agency on September 28 a last witness was produced for the claimants, the widely known Antoine J. Campbell, and he gave them little comfort. He testified that he was in the lower camp from August 18 to September 23 and that there was organized a big soldiers' lodge of about 150 warriors, composed of different bands "all mixed up." His estimate of the number of Indians who actually fought at Wood Lake was "maybe 300." He remarked that Standing Buffalo and the two other Sisseton chiefs had come down to Little Crow's camp and had said in council, "You people have cut our people's throat," that Traveling Hail, speaking for the lower Sioux, had replied that he had tried to make peace all the time, and that Standing Buffalo had then said, "We will go back from here, so they won't fight." He also remembered that Little Paul, a Wahpeton speaker, had told the lower Indians, in a gathering at Little Crow's place on the lower reservation, that he could not help them unless he got guns, powder, and balls from them. Campbell's recollection was that all the Indians were in one camp before the battle of Wood Lake. He said that he would have taken the prisoners out of camp and given them to Sibley, but he did not because he was warned that they would be attacked and killed. In answer to the question, "Then who had the prisoners when Sibley came?" he replied, "Well, it was mixed up, but

[60] *Evidence for Defendant*, 292, 307, 311, 320, 327, 330, 334, 356, 360, 374, 380. In a letter to Return I. Holcombe, May 1, 1894, in the Holcombe Papers, Nancy Huggan says: "I was taken prisoner with my husband [*David Faribault*] a[nd] kept for six weeks and had a very hard time. . . . When we knew that Gen. Sibley was close the half Breeds took all the white prisoners most of the Indians had gone to meet Gen Sibley and fight while they were gone the woman all dug holes to get into expecting when the Indians returned they would kill all of us."

there were more Lower Sioux than the Upper ones—a few of the Upper ones were there." When interrogated as to the battle of Big Mound in 1863, the scout related that when he was sent out by Sibley with a message to Standing Buffalo he told the crowd that he met that the general had not come out to fight them; he had come to make peace. "Well, they didn't want no peace at all, and they told me that it was best for me to leave them." He went back and told the general "that he had to look out, them Indians say they are going to fight." The general, he intimated, acted on that information and advice.[61]

The government produced certified copies of certain papers from the files of the Indian office: (1) an affidavit of Anton Manderfield, who deposed that the four haymakers, his companions, who were killed on Big Stone Lake on August 22, 1862, were murdered by the Sisseton band of Sioux; (2) affidavits of two of the Reverend Stephen R. Riggs's daughters, both of whom said that their father's house was pillaged by Wahpeton and Sisseton annuity Indians; (3) Dr. Riggs's deposition before the Sioux claims commission of 1863, in which he stated that the depredations at Hazelwood were committed by lower Sioux, aided by upper Sioux, the latter having plundered the mission houses at Hazelwood and Pajutazee. A letter from Sibley to the Honorable John P. Usher, dated December 19, 1862, was produced, in which, in answer to an inquiry, the statement was made that "the Wahpetons and Sissetons . . . were to a great extent equally guilty with the lower bands," and that the Sisseton were engaged in the attack on Fort Abercrombie.[62]

A large amount of printer's ink was expended on the record, briefs, and arguments, and counsel were heard by the court of claims. It was not until January 18, 1904, that the decision was rendered. The court found it impossible from the evidence to ascertain and identify the members of the two bands who had preserved their loyalty and, as there was then no occasion for any finding as to moneys which might have become due, it dismissed the petition. "A careful analysis of the whole evidence of the case, however," reads the opinion, "compels us to say that all of the responsible members of the bands in question at some time during the perpetration of the outrages in one way or another aided, abetted, assisted,

---

[61] *Evidence for Claimant*, 255-265. In his letter from Wood Lake, September 24, 1862, to Mazakutemani and others, Sibley wrote: "Now that I learn from Joseph Campbell that most of the captives are in safety in your camp I shall move on to-morrow." The passage seems to indicate the existence of a joint camp of lower and upper friendlies at that date. *Minnesota in the Civil and Indian Wars*, 2: 249.

[62] *Evidence for Defendant*, 399-409. The correspondence between Sibley and Usher is given in *Defendants' Substitute Brief on the Last Jurisdictional Act of Congress and Request for Findings of Fact*, 29-34. A letter from Sibley to Sanborn, January 13, 1878, in *Annuities of Certain Sioux Indians*, 3 (46 Congress, 3 session, *House Reports*, no. 95 — serial 1982), indicates that it was the opinion of the writer at that date that some of the upper chiefs did all in their power to restrain their men from taking part in the massacre and the battles.

or encouraged therein . . . if they did not actually participate therein."
Sibley's letter to Usher was cited.[63]

The now celebrated case did not end here. Bills were introduced into
the Senate in the years 1904 and 1905 for the relief of the Sisseton and
Wahpeton Indians, but they got no further than reference to the committee on Indian affairs.[64] The indefatigable friends of the Indians now
resorted to a stratagem which has had too many examples in Congress.
On April 13, 1906, the Senate committee on Indian affairs, the chairman
of which was the Honorable Moses W. Clapp, reported out the Indian
appropriation bill of the year, which had been sent from the House, with
numerous committee amendments. Among them was one for the relief
of the Sisseton and Wahpeton bands of the Sioux Indians. The two
senators from North Dakota, making no reference to previous action in the
matter, spoke briefly in explanation of the amendment as if it were an
entirely new matter. There had been an outbreak of Sioux Indians in
which these bands as a whole had had no part. Only a few young men who
had got beyond control of their loyal chiefs were guilty of depredations.
Nevertheless, Congress had arbitrarily confiscated the whole unpaid annuities of the bands. Commissioner Cooley's report of 1866 and Senator
Davis' speech on February 8, 1899, were cited as showing the grave injustice done the unfortunate Indians. The Senate was told that this was
the only case in which Indians who had been hostile had been finally deprived of annuities. After a trifling modification was made the rider was
agreed to. The House disagreed to the Senate amendments to the appropriation bill, which then went into conference. The conference report,
which retained the Senate amendment for the relief of the Sisseton and
Wahpeton with a slight modification, was agreed to and the bill was passed.
On its face the enactment was charmingly simple. The court of claims was
empowered to ascertain and determine the amount of money which would
be due if the confiscation act of 1863 had not been passed and the aggregate
of payments made the bands properly chargeable to the annuities and to
render judgment for the balance. The secretary of the interior was directed thereupon to make a roll of the Indians of the bands in question who
were living at the time of the passage of the act, excluding the names of
any whom he should determine to have been engaged in the outbreak,
probably not over half a dozen, the Senate was told; and, that done, he
was to distribute per capita the proceeds of the judgment. The faithful
attorneys were not forgotten. The secretary of the treasury was directed
to pay them out of the proceeds of the judgment such sum as the court of

[63] United States Court of Claims, *Cases Decided*, 39: 172-178.
[64] 59 Congress, 1 session, *Senate Journal*, 41, 138, 338, 384, 470 (serial 4902); 58 Congress,
3 session, *Senate Journal*, 174 (serial 4753).

claims, after hearing and considering any contracts they might have made with the Indians, should decide to be just and reasonable.[65]

No time was lost by the claimants' attorneys—now reenforced by two learned counselors, one of whom was ex-Senator Marion Butler of North Carolina—in filing their petition. They joyously interpreted the act of Congress as an unconditional restoration of the annuities and furnished this brief account:

Total annuities unpaid at the time of the forfeiture act of 1863 . . . . . . $2,919,309.12
Amount received by claimants since the date of said act . . . . . . . . . .   616,370.59

Balance due from the United States to claimants . . . . . . . . . . . . . $2,302,938.53

The attorneys claimed that there were and could be no other sums properly chargeable against annuities and suggested, with an unconscious sarcasm, that Congress itself might as well have struck the balance and have voted the appropriation. The government attorney, now aided by an assistant attorney-general, did not consider the matter "so simple and easy." Congress must at least have suspected that there were items of payment so chargeable or it would not have carefully instructed the court of claims to discover and determine them. Accepting an accounting furnished by the Indian office on a previous occasion, the government replied that after deducting payments found to be properly chargeable against the annuities, there remained due the bands the sum of $578,792.05. Upon this issue the case was argued and on May 13, 1907, it was decided. The court rejected the accounting of both parties and made one of its own, making use evidently of statistics given in a Senate document of the Fifty-fifth Congress. It refused credit to the government for $800,000 paid the bands for their North Dakota lands, to which their right was doubtful, but charged them an equal amount for damages and support, made chargeable in some cases in terms against annuities and in others, by implication. The court ordered a judgment of $788,971.53 for the claimants.[66]

The attorneys for the Indians, whose fees would obviously be greatly reduced by the decree, at once resolved to appeal to the United States Supreme Court, which they had a right to do under the jurisdictional act of 1906. The appeal was argued in January, 1908, and was decided on February 24 of the same year. The opinion, written by Judge Holmes,

[65] *Congressional Record*, 59 Congress, 1 session, 5181, 5794, 8352; *Statutes at Large*, 34: 372.
[66] *Claimants' Supplemental Request for Findings of Fact and Conclusions of Law, and Brief*, 6, 15; *Defendants' Brief on the Last Jurisdictional Act of Congress and Request for Findings of Fact*, 10; Court of Claims, *Cases Decided*, 42: 420–432; *Sisseton and Wahpeton Bands of Dakota or Sioux Indians*, 17–21 (serial 3593). In an interview recorded in the author's notebooks, 5:87, Samuel J. Brown said that Butler received fifty-three thousand dollars.

examined the items of accounts made by the court of claims and found all correct and just, with the exception of a trifling error of $104.66 which had been twice deducted.[67]

## 13. THE SANTEE CLAIM[68]

The claim of the Santee for the restoration of their forfeited annuities was kept before Congress from session to session. Petitioners on their behalf could not urge, as could those for the Sisseton and Wahpeton, that the lower Sioux took no principal part in the outbreak of 1862; but they could truthfully represent that those sent to Nebraska in 1863 and thereafter called Santee were a remnant including not more than one hundred able-bodied men, "wholly indigent, broken-hearted and without hope in the world." Of the lower Sioux who had been the active participants in the outbreak, thirty-eight had been hanged at Mankato, some three hundred had been imprisoned at Davenport, and a large number had fled to Canada in and after the fall of 1862. The poor remnant in Nebraska had suffered enough. The expectation that Congress would at length become weary of the continual petitioning of industrious counsel was fulfilled. On the last day of the existence of the Sixty-fourth Congress, March 4, 1917, an act was passed conferring jurisdiction on the court of claims "to hear, determine, and render final judgment" for any balance that might be found due the Mdewakanton and Wahpekute (Santee) Sioux Indians, giving them full credit for all the sums allowed them, without interest, by the treaties of 1837 and 1851, as if the act of February 16, 1863, had never been passed, and charging them with all sums paid them thereunder and all other moneys paid them since that date.[69]

[67] United States v. Sisseton and Wahpeton Bands of Sioux Indians, 208; *United States Reports*, 561.

[68] See *ante*, p. 301.

[69] *Statutes at Large*, 39: 1195. A detailed account of the progress of this measure, which was kept before six successive Congresses, would be wearisome and of trifling value to the ordinary reader. Anyone desirous from curiosity or interest to follow it up will find the following citations helpful: 59 Congress, 2 session, *Senate Reports*, nos. 2178, 2561, 5689 (serials 4905, 5060); 60 Congress, 1 session, *Senate Reports*, no. 486 (serial 5219); 60 Congress, 2 session, *House Reports*, no. 2153 (serial 5384); 62 Congress, 2 session, *Senate Reports*, no. 818 (serial 6122); *House Reports*, no. 444 (serial 6131); 63 Congress, 1 session, *Senate Reports*, no. 70 (serial 6510); 63 Congress, 2 session, *Senate Reports*, 759 (serial 6553); 64 Congress, 1 session, *House Reports*, no. 444 (serial 6131); 64 Congress, 2 session, *House Reports*, no. 1225 (serial 7110).

It appears that the claim had found ready hospitality in the Senate, but not in the House. The bill was passed by the Senate on August 5, 1916, without debate or division. It was immediately transmitted to the House, but it was not until after the opening of the second session of the same Congress, the Sixty-fourth, on December 16, 1916, that a substitute bill was reported from the committee on Indian affairs. It came up for consideration on February 5, 1917, and was that day debated and passed. The Senate refused concurrence and the matter went to conference. On March 2 the conference report was agreed to and the bill as amended was passed.

There were two points of disagreement between the houses, closely contested. The bill passed by the Senate on August 5, 1916, provided that the proceedings should be commenced

The attorneys for the Santee accordingly brought suit on March 6, 1917, but it was not until the filing of their amended petition of November 6 of the same year that their claim was definitely stated. They asked the court to find that the total amount due under the treaties of 1837 and 1851, without interest, was $3,380,000 in round numbers, and that offsets amounted to $900,000; and accordingly they asked judgment for the balance of $2,470,000. The government lawyer took a very different view of the account. He asked the court to allow the Santee $4,325,000 and to charge them with $4,445,000, leaving the poor Indians in debt to the United States to the amount of $120,000. Thereupon the industrious attorneys for the Santee made a new study of the records and produced a new balance sheet. They found credits amounting to $4,625,500 and debits to the amount of $2,904,000 and asked for the more moderate residue of $1,721,000.[70]

The case dragged along slowly until June 5, 1922, on which day the court, after hearings and a careful study of the records, rendered its decision. It awarded the Santee a larger minuend than had been claimed for them, placing it at $4,642,750, and made vast additions to the subtrahends proposed by their counsel, naming the sum of $4,256,152.11; and accordingly it determined that the Santee had the right to recover of the United States a balance of $386,597.89.[71]

The great difference between this pitiful allowance and the original claim for the Santee is accounted for by the resolution of the court to allow a set-off of nearly two million dollars for benefactions to these Indians under a treaty of April 29, 1868. This treaty, a memorable one, was negotiated by

" by petition, verified by the attorney or firm of attorneys so authorized by John Eastman, assignee of Charles A. Eastman or Charles Hill, the attorneys in fact employed by said Indians under a contract bearing date November 27 [1896], and by the Secretary of Interior July 1, 1897." The court of claims was authorized to award compensation to such attorneys upon a *quantum meruit* according to agreements to be filed with the court and the secretary of the treasury was authorized to pay them accordingly. The House substitute as passed on February 5, 1917, provided that the petition must be verified by one of the attorneys under the contract, but that fees should not exceed five per cent of the award nor more than twenty-five thousand dollars. When the House substitute came up for consideration on February 5, 1917, a brief debate ensued. Stephens of Nebraska, in charge of the bill, explained it and gave it as his opinion that the Santee ought to recover about a million dollars. They had been robbed of their just dues for twenty-five years by the wrangling of parties and attorneys. Clarence B. Miller, representative from the eighth Minnesota district, closed the debate. The bill, in substance, was identical with one he had drafted six years before and guaranteed to the Santee what was justly due them. Not one penny, however, should go to a certain attorney, at one time a senator in Congress, whose name he could give upon a proper occasion. The substitute bill would "cut out attorney fees and attorneys' rapacity." The bill which came out of conference and was passed provided for verification by the attorneys under the contract, but fixed their fees at not more than ten percent of the final award and not to exceed fifty thousand dollars. *Congressional Record*, 64 Congress, 1 session, 12167; 2 session, 462, 2648, 2655-2659, 2752, 4484, 4506, 4845.

[70] *Santee Claim Case, Plaintiff's Request for Findings*, 506 (Court of Claims, no. 33,728); *Defendant's Objections to Plaintiff's Request*, 5; *Plaintiff's Amended Request*, 16.

[71] Court of Claims, *Cases Decided*, 57: 357-379; *Minneapolis Journal*, June 22, 1922, p. 9.

a commission, of which General William T. Sherman was a member, in pursuance of an act of Congress passed on July 20, 1867, entitled "An Act to Establish Peace with Certain Hostile Indian Tribes." On April 29, 1868, at Laramie, Wyoming Territory, this treaty was signed by representatives of nine hostile Sioux bands and by seven delegates from the Santee. It has been said, probably with truth, that the latter, subdued and inoffensive Santee, were invited to send delegates to the conference that they might use their influence upon their wild brethren of the plains and induce them to make a great peace. The principal obligations on the part of the tribes were, first of all, to keep the peace; next, to stay quietly on a great reservation covering all the present state of South Dakota west of the Missouri; and, finally, to stop all opposition to the building of railroads on the plains. It was a civilization treaty as well as a peace treaty. The United States did not buy any land nor propose to pay any annuities, but agreed to supply provisions, clothing, cattle, farming implements, seeds, and some money; to employ an agent, a physician, blacksmiths, a carpenter, an engineer, a miller, and a farmer; and, most important, to furnish schoolhouses and teachers—most of them for a limited number of years.[72]

By the year 1917 the government had disbursed under the treaty of 1868 some sixty million dollars in all and some two million dollars to the Santee. Now the attorneys for the Santee before the court of claims contended that this money or money's worth was due the Santee under the treaty in consideration of their observation of its obligations; that in signing the treaty they had no thought of giving up their right for restoration of their confiscated annuities.[73] The government resisted this claim with vigor and successfully. The court of claims considered that, while the jurisdictional act provided that the treaty of 1868 should not be a bar to the recovery of annuities, it also provided that the "equities and benefits" of the treaty should be taken into account. The sum of $1,903,023.22, therefore, was charged the Santee for benefactions under that treaty.[74]

## 14. THE MOSCOW EXPEDITION[75]

It was near the first of June, 1863, when the thirteen hundred debilitated Santee and as many or more Winnebago were landed at Crow Creek. It was late for extensive planting and the succeeding drought so parched the ground and wilted the belated corn and vegetables that it became apparent that it would be necessary for the government to feed these

[72] *Statutes at Large*, 15: 17, 635-647; Charles J. Kappler, ed., *Indian Affairs, Laws, and Treaties*, 2:998-1007 (Washington, 1904).
[73] *Evidence for Defendant*, 152, 154; *Plaintiff's Amended Complaint*, 22, 36.
[74] *Defendant's Reply to Plaintiff's Amended Request*, 449; Court of Claims, *Cases Decided*, 57: 371, 379.
[75] See *ante*, p. 261, n. 25.

miserable exiles until the next year. The order to buy the provisions reached Colonel Clark W. Thompson, northern superintendent, on September 28, 1863. The normal procedure would have been to make the purchases at either St. Louis or Sioux City, or at both, and to ship the food up the Missouri River. Instead of that it was planned to buy the provisions in Minnesota and haul them overland under military escort to Crow Creek. Major General Pope, when asked to furnish the escort, expressed his doubt as to whether the journey could be made at that season of the year without great suffering to the men and loss of most of the animals; but, rather than have the military authorities blamed for withholding food from the Indians, he directed General Sibley to furnish the escort if he thought it would be possible for it to make the journey.[76]

The departure from the normal procedure of sending supplies up the Missouri at a cheaper freight rate is accounted for by the circumstance that certain persons, whose identity is obscure, had bought at nominal prices large quantities of condemned pork and flour, not fit for soldiers' consumption but good enough for hungry Indians.[77] The superintendent appears to have been brought to that mind. It was given out, however, that the overland haul was decided upon because the Winnebago, who had left their reservation in the early summer, had left behind them several hundred barrels of pork and flour. It was also given out that the proposed expedition would immediately open a "cartway" from that place to the Indian agencies on the Missouri. The project had the support of United States Senator Wilkinson. One of the Mankato newspapers spoke scornfully of the undertaking; another, supposed to be the senator's organ, was favorable to it. The St. Paul dailies in general spoke approvingly, but the *Press* gave an editorial the heading, "A Moscow Campaign." From this suggestion the phrase "Moscow Campaign" or "Moscow Expedition" came into common use. In the course of October 150 wagons were brought up, 300 yoke of oxen were collected to haul them, and the loading was concluded. The escort consisted of three companies of the Sixth Minnesota Infantry commanded by Captain Joseph C. Whitney of Minneapolis, a much respected Presbyterian minister who had volunteered for the war.[78]

[76] Indian Office, *Reports*, 1863, pp. 32, 310-312, 316, 321; 1864, pp. 394-396; Barton, *John P. Williamson*, 74, 78; *Official Records*, series 1, vol. 22, part 2, p. 671. James B. Hubbell of Mankato was the contractor. Hughes, *Blue Earth County*, 142.

[77] Interview with Charles W. Johnson, a member of the escort, recorded in the author's notebooks, 2: 73; manuscript narrative of Captain George E. Case, another member of the escort, accompanying a letter from his daughter, Miss Maud Case, to the author, March 1, 1919, in the Folwell Papers.

[78] *Mankato Record*, October 3, 10, 17, 24; *Mankato Union*, October 2, 30, November 6; *Saint Paul Pioneer*, November 22, December 30; *Saint Paul Press*, October 18, 28, 1863; Johnson, in *Minnesota in the Civil and Indian Wars*, 1: 317; Holcombe, in *Minnesota in Three Centuries*, 3: 437.

The head of the train left Mankato, which had been chosen as a convenient point of concentration and departure, about November 1, but a fortnight was consumed in getting the train together as a whole at the village of Leavenworth in Brown County, forty miles away. The contractors found it impossible to hire civilian teamsters even at three dollars and a half a day. They then offered to pay soldiers twenty-five cents a day, but none would engage. At a dollar and a quarter some men who had families to support accepted, but finally two dollars a day had to be paid to man all the teams. A variety of pranks were resorted to by the soldiers to compel the abandonment of the expedition, one of them being the removal of axletree nuts. The mischief was not ended until Colonel Crooks came up on the thirteenth and "set matters to rights" by giving them "to understand that it was a Government train and any efforts to hinder its progress would be treated with the utmost severity." Thereafter the expedition moved steadily toward its destination, which was reached on December 2 without material loss. One severe snowstorm with extreme temperature was encountered. The distance covered in the nineteen days of travel was 292 miles. The return journey of the escort was without important incident and terminated at Mankato on January 1, 1864.[79]

More important than the journey were the results upon the Indians at Crow Creek. The arrival of the provisions made "their hearts . . . glad," but there was disappointment when they sampled the pork and flour, which were not up to their expectations. The three hundred yoke of oxen were presently slaughtered and their carcasses were stacked up for beef. As the animals had endured the journey of nearly three hundred miles on dry prairie grass and a feed of corn meal a day, they had not become too fat. To economize the ration and to make it more agreeable to Indian taste, it was decided to install a cooking apparatus. A large wooden tank was built, into which a steam pipe was introduced. At night measured portions of flour, pork, and beef were thrown in and the tank was filled up with water. The steam was then turned on until the mixture was sufficiently cooked. In the morning the "rotten stuff was ladled out to the squaws."[80]

[79] Johnson, in *Minnesota in the Civil and Indian Wars*, 1 : 318-320; *Mankato Union*, November 6, 20, 1863; Indian Office, *Reports*, 1864, pp. 396, 405-407.
[80] Indian Office, *Reports*, 1864, p. 396; Samuel J. Brown to the author, May 13, 1919, Folwell Papers; Barton, *John P. Williamson*, 79. Mrs. Barton is in error in regard to the kind of teams employed and the extent of the losses incurred on the journey, and also in neglecting to mention that beef was added to the "cottonwood soup" — a name given by the Indians to the cooked rations because the tank was built of green cottonwood lumber. In an interview with the author, Samuel J. Brown, who as a young interpreter was at Crow Creek at the time, stated that he and a son of Lame Jim ladled out the rotten stuff. The Sioux, fearing that they might be poisoned, would not consume it until Brother John had tasted it. The Winnebago would not take it. This interview is recorded in the author's notebooks, 5 : 88.

## 15. THE DUSTIN MURDERS, 1863[81]

On June 29, 1863, Amos Dustin, who had resided in Wright County for some years, was moving his family to a new claim in the southwestern part of the same county. There were six in the party: Dustin and his wife, their three children—a girl of six and two sons, one four and the other two years old—and Dustin's widowed mother. The wagon in which they traveled, drawn by an ox team, was also loaded with their household goods. About noon they rested at the house of Aaron E. Cochran, a little over a mile east of Howard Lake, after which they continued their journey. Late in the afternoon Dustin's oxen came back, but Cochran, supposing they had been turned out to graze and had strayed away, thought nothing of it and put them into his yard until Dustin should return for them. The next day he mentioned the matter casually to two men, one of whom was a brother-in-law of Dustin. At first they thought it trivial, but after hearing that Indians were in the timber the three agreed to investigate. They started out from the Cochran farm at two o'clock and traveled warily in fear of encountering Indians. About a mile west of Howard Lake village, while looking in silence at some moccasin tracks in the road, they heard a moan. Was it a lure of Indians to entrap them? The moan was repeated and the men, preceded by Cochran, with cocked rifles, moved in the direction from which the moaning seemed to come, passed around the margin of a meadow to a point about fifty rods from the road, and there found Mrs. Dustin lying helpless and almost unconscious. She could only say, "They are all killed in the wagon by the Indians."

With wounds from two arrows, one of which had passed through her body from behind and protruded below the breastbone, Mrs. Dustin had started back on the road with the two surviving children, the little girl walking by her side. At the beginning of the attack the girl had dropped to the bottom of the wagon and her father's body, falling backward, had so covered her that she was not noticed by the assassins. The younger boy had been left unharmed by the roadside. Weakened and bewildered, Mrs. Dustin had lost the road and had lain down, as she thought, to die. The two children were found wandering in the tall grass of the meadow. As soon as Cochran's ox team could be obtained, the three were taken back to his house. Messengers were sent in different directions to give notice of the presence of Indians in the neighborhood and of the murders. Early on the following day relief parties from Rockford, Watertown, and other quarters convened at Waverly and went on westward to the scene of the murders, a place on the road, which ran through the timber, about two and a half miles beyond the site of Howard Lake. They found three lifeless bodies—those of Dustin, the older boy, and the grandmother. Dustin's

[81] See *ante*, p. 283.

left hand and both of his mother's hands had been cut off. Her mouth and nose had been slashed with a knife. No scalps had been taken. Some bedclothing and provisions had been carried off. Rude coffins were put together out of materials brought along and late at night the three bodies were buried at Old Waverly. Medical assistance was obtained for Mrs. Dustin, but her wounds were mortal and she died on July 3, to be buried beside her husband. Exaggerations concerning the mutilation of the victims are still current; for instance, it was reported that the Indians had cut out the heart of Dustin's mother and had put it on the end of a stick. It was also related that the arrows which had penetrated the body of Mrs. Dustin were pulled out by the Rockford blacksmith, who had brought along his horseshoer's pincers.

The personnel of the half dozen savages who assassinated the Dustins has never been ascertained. The conjecture that they were members of Little Crow's party is supported by the fact that it was in the neighborhood at the time. The two surviving children were soon adopted into reputable families, grew up and married, and are still living—Mrs. Alma Perkins in Minneapolis and Mr. Albert Dustin near Madison, Wisconsin.[82]

## 16. LITTLE SIX AND MEDICINE BOTTLE[83]

The grounds of Major Edwin A. C. Hatch's desire to secure possession of the persons of Little Six, or Shakopee, and Medicine Bottle, otherwise erroneously called "Grey Iron," are not known. No order nor official request for him to make the arrests has been found. He may have presumed that the capture of the greatest of the lower Sioux chiefs for condemnation and capital punishment would be a service acceptable to many citizens of Minnesota. It is difficult to place the exploit in any category of the duties of an officer in the service of the United States. Whatever may have been his motive or authority, he seems to have felt himself warranted in resorting to an extraordinary process.

On Christmas Day, 1863, a lieutenant of the battalion, equipped with a letter of introduction, called upon John H. McKenzie of Fort Garry and opened to him the subject of capturing the chiefs, assuring him "that it would be hundreds of dollars in his pocket if he would enter into this business with a whole soul" and would trust to the honor of Major Hatch.

[82] Report of the adjutant general, in *Executive Documents*, 1863, p. 343; narrative of John B. Walker in Curtiss-Wedge, *Wright County*, 1: 150-153; *Hutchinson Leader*, October 6, 1905; Farnham, in the *Wright County Eagle* (Delano), March 3, 1881; statement of Calvin Mooers, May 20, 1919, Folwell Papers; Mooers' recollections, in the *Northsider* (Minneapolis), June 30, July 7, 1921. Mooers, a boy of seventeen at the time of the murders, was a member of the burial party. The account of Mrs. Alma Dustin Perkins is given in the *Minneapolis Journal*, October 21, 1906, and a letter from her to the author, June 17, 1919, is in the Folwell Papers. The letter confirms an interview of June 12, 1919, recorded in the author's notebooks, 8: 102.

[83] See *ante*, p. 293.

Later a captain of the battalion informed McKenzie and a colleague, one Onisime Giguere, that if they could secure the surrender of the murderers, Andrew G. B. Bannatyne, who was furnishing the battalion with horse feed and other supplies, would provide teams and provisions needed to transport the whole band to Pembina. Upon inquiry they found Bannatyne willing and anxious to assist. On January 15 the two adventurers traveled to the Sioux encampment, some twenty-five miles up the Assiniboine River, and on the following day they met the chiefs and braves concerned. The suggestion of a willing surrender to the Yankees was rejected with scorn. A man named Lane, who was charged by the Canadian authorities with supplying the Indians with food, was then asked to tell them that he was going to stop their rations. Although anxious to assist, he could only say to them, "I do not know how soon your rations will be stopped." Giguere, however, "interpreted it a little different to suit the times" and stated definitely that the rations would soon be stopped. Little Six was greatly excited and declared that he would go down to see the governor of the province and the bishop.

Later in the day it was arranged that the two chiefs should have a free ride to Fort Garry, if they would start at once, and a glass of toddy upon their arrival at McKenzie's house. A jug of toddy and a good supper were enjoyed about midnight; all drank freely. The next day was Sunday and the Indian guests were persuaded to respect the white man's Sabbath and remain quiet at McKenzie's house. The generous host, "having plenty of alcohol, resumed the toddy work . . . Mr. Bannatine furnishing him with some laudanum to put in their drink." In the course of the day the chiefs went over to Bannatyne's house, where he "seized the opportunity of treating the two to a glass of wine and laudanum." In the afternoon they "went into the spree in good earnest, on raw whiskey made of alcohol," McKenzie pretending to be afraid of giving them too much and filling Giguere's tumbler mostly with water so as not to make him drunk. About nine o'clock Little Six became unconscious. A group of white men and half-breeds had the pleasure of seeing the terrible savage lying helpless on the floor. For fear that he might inopportunely wake up, Bannatyne applied a handkerchief saturated with chloroform to his nose. With hands and feet tied, the Indian was strapped on "a flat dog sled" spread with buffalo robes and "off Mr. McKenzie started with his prey for Fort Pembina." The intoxication of Medicine Bottle was not so complete and a lively struggle was necessary to tie and strap him on to a similar conveyance; then "off Mr. Giguere started in triumph." Bannatyne had furnished a relief of horses and about noon of the following day the two chiefs were delivered at Pembina to Major Hatch.[84]

[84] McKenzie and Giguere, *Capture of Little Six and Grey Iron.* In his report of December 21, 1863, to Sibley, Hatch inclosed a letter from Bannatyne, dated December 19, which

Here ends the exploit of John H. McKenzie and his companion in the irregular arrest of the two Indians and they should disappear from our horizon but for the fact that the Minnesota legislature of 1867 appropriated the sum of one thousand dollars for the services and expenses of John H. McKenzie and Onisime Giguere in the capture of Little Six and Medicine Bottle.[85]  At one time in our history such a violation of her sovereignty would have called forth from Great Britain a sharp demand for apology and reparation.  Little Six and Medicine Bottle, after being arrested in this infamous manner, were taken along with Major Hatch's returning battalion to Fort Abercrombie and from there were sent to Fort Snelling, where they arrived on May 27, 1864.[86]

The reason for a delay of ten months in bringing the two Indians to trial was doubtless the fact that Sibley's troops were so disposed at the frontier posts or detached for Sully's expedition of 1864 that he had not sufficient numbers of commissioned officers near his headquarters from which to select members of a military commission.  When at length he issued his order of November 18, 1864, for the commission, he was obliged to confine his selection to the officers of a single regiment, the Second Regiment of Minnesota Cavalry, which had not yet seen a year's service.  The commission consisted of two captains, a lieutenant, and the adjutant as judge advocate; it sat at Fort Snelling.

Medicine Bottle was arraigned on November 25 on two charges, murder and participation in the outbreak of 1862.  The specifications to the first charge were: (1) the killing of Philander Prescott by shooting; (2) the same with slight variation; (3) the shooting of sundry white people in wagons and other vehicles near New Ulm; (4) the killing of white persons in Brown, Renville, and other counties; and (5) the shooting and killing of sundry soldiers.  To the second charge there were three specifications: (1) a mere repetition of the charge; (2) the discharging of a gun into an inhabited house in Brown County with intent to kill; and (3) the killing of sundry white persons in wagons or other vehicles near New Ulm.  The prisoner was allowed two days to employ counsel, but on the reassemblage of the commission on November 28 he had none to introduce.

Five witnesses were sworn for the prosecution, two of them women. In regard to the murder of Philander Prescott, four of them said either that they knew nothing or that they knew only what they had heard.  The fifth

indicated that the settlers at Fort Garry were desirous of having these Indians captured. The letter is in *Minnesota in the Civil and Indian Wars*, 2 : 546.  In a letter to his son written at Pembina, February 15, 1864, Joseph R. Brown made the following statement: "Little Six and Black Dogs Brother are prisoners here.  They were taken in the English settlement and brought up here by some of the settlers."  Brown Papers.

[85] *Special Laws*, 1867, p. 390.

[86] *Minnesota in the Civil and Indian Wars*, 1: 601; 2: 551; *Saint Paul Pioneer*, May 27, 1864.

witness testified that he had heard the prisoner say at Little Crow's house that "on the day [*August 19*] they went down to the settlements, they, (the Indians) overtook Mr Prescott below and near the agency and killed him . . . he (the prisoner) and one other Indian shot at him." In regard to the killing of white people in wagons near New Ulm, one witness knew nothing and another had heard about it. Three witnesses testified in nearly identical language that they had heard Medicine Bottle boast that he had taken part in it. He, with the other Indians, saw teams coming into New Ulm loaded with white people, upon whom they had fired, killing and wounding men, women, and children, and the horses had run into New Ulm with the dead bodies in the wagons. As to firing into an inhabited house, four witnesses knew nothing about it; the fifth testified that he had heard the prisoner say that he and other Indians had ridden into a part of New Ulm, had discharged their guns into the houses, in which he had heard the men, women, and children scream and cry. No testimony was elicited in regard to the killing of soldiers. Upon the second charge, that of participation in the outbreak of 1862, there was a general agreement. All knew Medicine Bottle to have been so engaged. One witness testified that he had gone on war parties and had returned with white men's horses; that he had prevented friendly Indians from going to the whites; that before Wood Lake he went to all the tepees and told the men to come along to the battle and that those who did not go would be killed. One of the witnesses testified that she had seen Medicine Bottle in a party of Indians led by Little Crow coming very early to Forbes's store at the lower agency. This was the most damaging testimony.

The Indian had no witnesses and he did not cross-examine any. At the close of the testimony he was allowed twenty-four hours to prepare his defense. In his written statement he objected to the jurisdiction of the commission to try a person kidnapped from a foreign state, where the United States had no right to seize him. He denied that he had ever killed any white persons or that he had gone on any war parties. In regard to the killing of Prescott, he had only remarked, in reply to a question, that on their way to New Ulm some Indians had killed him. He was not at Myrick's store on the morning of the outbreak. He had gone off to the British possessions as soon as possible to be away from the warlike portion of his tribe. To this statement was appended a paragraph signed "Gorman & Davis, Attorneys," who begged leave to suggest to the court that the prisoner's plea to its jurisdiction was sound. " 'No government can,' " they said, " 'acquire right by its own wrong or by the wrong of any of its citizens.' No state can reach over into the domain of a foreign and neutral power and drag from its protection any criminal by force. The flagrancy of the original crime does not abridge his rights." Reference was made to

James Kent's *Commentaries on American Law*, volume 1, lecture 6, page 117, and to Secretary Seward's recent decision in the case of Mason and Slidell, taken by force from a British vessel. The counsel described the regular lawful procedure for obtaining by executive requisition the arrest and delivery of persons accused of crime who had taken refuge in a foreign country. On December 2 the commission found the Indian guilty of both charges and of all the specifications except that of willfully killing soldiers and sentenced him to death.

The trial of Little Six began on December 2 with his arraignment on the same two charges. His request for delay to allow him to introduce counsel was refused, probably for the reason that he had had ample notice of the time of trial. The first charge, that of murder, had five specifications, which in brief were: (1) the killing of sundry white men, women, and children in Brown, Renville, and other counties, on or about the eighteenth and nineteenth of August, 1862; (2) the killing of a white man and family of three or more in Renville County; (3) the killing of seven white persons in Brown or Renville County; (4) the killing of thirteen persons in Brown or Renville County; and (5) the killing of one or more soldiers between August 18 and September 23, 1862. The first specification to the second charge, that of participation in the outrages of 1862, alleged that Little Six did actively participate in the murders, massacres, and outrages; the second, that he fought in battles in which many soldiers were killed.

Six Indian witnesses were called, one of whom was the friendly Taopi, and two of whom were women. All were friendly Indians, none of whom had seen the accused kill anybody. Three of them, on the evening of the first day of the outbreak, had heard Little Six boast of having killed white people, but one gave the number as seven, another as thirteen, and the third as six. Taopi testified that eight days after the outbreak he heard Little Six brag of having killed a "bad talker" (a German) and his women and children. In reply to the question whether the prisoner was engaged in the murders and outrages, two said they knew nothing except what they had heard him say; another said he knew only what he had been told; three others, who answered, "he was," also based their testimony on remarks which they had heard Little Six make. The prisoner produced no witnesses but asked to be allowed to submit a statement in writing. The statement was brief. His father had been a good chief and always friendly to the whites. Little Six had tried to be like him and was friendly to the whites, but his people had made war on them without his knowledge and threatened to kill him if he opposed them. He recalled telling Little Crow that whites were killed, but he was never in any fight because he knew it was not right. While his people were fighting at Wood Lake he was moving up to the British territory. He would have remained there forever but was taken away. He never intended to see another American because he was ashamed for what his people had done. At its session on December 7 the commission found Little Six guilty of both charges and of all specifications except the fifth under the first charge, that of willfully killing soldiers, and the second specification under the second charge, that of participating in armed opposition to United States forces, whereby soldiers were killed or wounded. He was sentenced to death by hanging at a time to be fixed by the brigadier general commanding.

The proceedings, findings, and sentences of the commission were approved by Sibley on December 14 and the twentieth day of January, 1865, was named for the execution, "subject to the revision of the President of the United States." For a reason not understood it was not until the day set for the execution that Major General Pope confirmed the proceedings of the commission and forwarded them to Major General Joseph Holt, judge-advocate-general of the newly created bureau of military justice, for such action as the war department might deem expedient. In his letter of advice of December 14 Sibley informed Holt that it was a matter of notoriety that the two Indians were among the foremost in engaging in the indiscriminate butcheries of 1862 and in exciting their people to engage in them. As for their being kidnapped from British territory, he had no information other than that British subjects, anxious to be rid of their presence, had brought the two men into United States territory. They had not been seized nor abducted by any of our soldiers or citizens. He considered the testimony of the loyal Indian witnesses procured on the spot so conclusive that it was not necessary to summon others from a distance. From a knowledge of all the facts he was convinced of the deep criminality of the convicts and urged the approval of their sentences. Finally, he suggested that "their escape from punishment would have a very bad effect upon the Indians generally."[87]

On March 25, 1865, Major General Holt submitted to the president two opinions in nearly identical terms, quoted in large part from Sibley's letter of December 14, 1864. He added the suggestion that, as the British authorities had made no claim for their restoration, it did not rest with the prisoners to plead to the jurisdiction of the commission. He thought the proof of guilt amply sufficient and recommended the execution of the sentences. On August 29, 1865, President Andrew Johnson confirmed the sentences and on September 25 the decision was made known to the two

---

[87] An official manuscript copy, in two parts, of the proceedings of the military commission held at Fort Snelling, November 23–December 8, 1864, for the trial of Little Six and Medicine Bottle and a typewritten copy of Sibley's letter of December 14 to Judge-Advocate-General Joseph Holt are in the possession of the Minnesota Historical Society. The attorneys who contended that the commission was without jurisdiction were ex-Governor Willis A. Gorman and Cushman K. Davis, governor from 1874 to 1876.

men. They received the fatal news with the stolid calmness of their race. Shakopee said merely, "I am no squaw—I can die whenever the white man wishes"; and Medicine Bottle repeated the sentiment. On September 30 Major General John M. Corse, who had succeeded Sibley as commander of the District of Minnesota, fixed October 11 following as the date of execution. As that day drew near it is safe to assume that Father Augustin Ravoux, who had become the spiritual adviser of the condemned men, was exerting himself to secure a commutation. On October 2 the Right Reverend Thomas L. Grace of St. Paul, doubtless upon the suggestion of Father Ravoux, addressed the president in a remonstrance against the execution of the Indians, "in consideration of the treacherous manner in which they were brought within the jurisdiction" of the United States, which he described. "However guilty they may be," he wrote, "it is the instinct of every generous mind that the Government cannot execute punishment upon them under the circumstances, without dishonor to itself."

The tenth of October was a busy one for those concerned in the cases. The president had sent Bishop Grace's letter to the secretary of the interior, who, on that day, having failed to get information about the case from the war department, sent the letter back to the president with a recommendation that the sentences be suspended. The president instantly so ordered. On the next day, October 11, the governor of Minnesota, Brigadier General Stephen Miller, in the name of seven hundred victims of 1862, wrote to the president and appealed to him to give the cases careful personal consideration. In a later letter, written on October 31, he advised the secretary of the interior that the evidence was sufficient for execution in spite of Bishop Grace's objections. The judge-advocate-general now took up the cases again and on November 7 furnished the president with a final opinion and recommendation. In answer to Bishop Grace's remonstrance he cited Sibley's statement that the men had been brought across the British line before delivery to an American officer and maintained that therefore the prisoners had no ground for pleading to the jurisdiction. It was his judgment that Shakopee's boast of having killed white people and of having mutilated their bodies, as sworn to, as well as the plunder seen in his possession by the witnesses were sufficient proof of murder. Still convinced that a remission of the sentence "would have a very bad effect upon the Indians generally," he repeated his recommendation that both sentences be executed. A telegram of the same date ordered the execution of the two sentences within three days after its receipt.

When Colonel Robert N. McLaren, commandant at Fort Snelling, announced to the Indians through Father Ravoux that they would be hanged on Saturday at noon, they nodded and smiled. On the day appointed in orders, November 11, Father Ravoux came early and remained with the condemned unto the last. Medicine Bottle repeated the prayers and versicles the priest had taught them and Shakopee grunted in assent. The older man, Shakopee, gave his pipe to Colonel McLaren and handed him a letter and a small valise for his wife. The younger man had a letter and a small valise for his sister. The execution, carried out with proper military ceremonial, may be found described in full detail in the daily newspapers of St. Paul of November 12, 1865.

The reader must already have found himself questioning the justice meted out in these cases. The remarks of the editor of the *Saint Paul Pioneer*, printed the day before the execution, may perhaps voice his judgment: "We do not believe that serious injustice will be done by the execution to-morrow, but it would have been more creditable if some tangible evidence of their guilt had been obtained. . . . The evidence consists almost wholly of their own vapid boastings among their bands . . . and no white man, tried before a jury of his peers, would be executed upon the testimony thus produced. The general supposition that they are guilty, is very likely correct, but their execution will, nevertheless, establish the precedent of hanging without proving. . . . A government which is daily pardoning educated murderers should not deny a fair trial, even to guilty Indians." All this is no compliment to the trial commission, the general officers who approved the findings, the learned judge-advocate-general, or the governor of Minnesota. All of them seem to have had in view the predominating importance of giving a moral lesson to "Indians generally." A sentence of imprisonment along with their fellow miscreants at Camp McClellan would have been appropriate if not adequate; such punishment they well deserved for the lies, equally silly and shameless, told by them in their defenses at the close of the testimony. Had their lives been lengthened it may be doubted whether they would ever have been so well prepared for another judgment as they were under the devoted ministrations of Father Ravoux. About the only admirable element in the whole course of the cases was the serene and dignified behavior of the chiefs in their last hour.[88]

## 17. LOSSES OF THE FIRST MINNESOTA AT GETTYSBURG[89]

The charge of the First Minnesota on the afternoon of July 2, 1863, irrespective of the enormous resulting casualties, was a splendid, an heroic performance. A small battalion of eight companies of the regiment was

[88] *Saint Paul Pioneer*, September 26, October 8, 11, November 2, 9, 10, 12, 1865; *Saint Paul Press*, September 26, October 1, 8, 11, November 1, 9, 10, 12, 1865. Typewritten copies of the opinions submitted by Holt on March 25, the letters of the secretary of the interior, October 10, to the secretary of war and the president, respectively, President Johnson's suspension of the execution, October 10, and Holt's final opinion and summary of the case, incorrectly dated November 17, 1865, which includes a statement of Bishop Grace's contentions, are in the possession of the Minnesota Historical Society.

[89] See *ante*, p. 311.

ordered to assault without support two Confederate brigades advancing in regular lines, not to repulse them, but merely to check their onset, if possible, while troops were hurrying to fill a gap in the main line of defense on Cemetery Ridge. Hancock's terse order, "Charge those lines," meant sacrifice and every man of the forlorn hope knew it. To their everlasting glory not one flinched. The correction of a statistical error cannot diminish in the slightest degree the honor Minnesota and the country will forever accord those heroic officers and men.

The discrepancies in the statements regarding the whole number of casualties in the regiment during the two days' battle at Gettysburg are too slight to need further inquiry. In a dispatch dated July 5, 1863, mailed to Governor Ramsey by Captain Henry C. Coates, the total number of killed, wounded, and missing is stated as 232. The nominal list which accompanied the dispatch gives the total as 222. The table in the *Official Records of the Union and Confederate Armies* giving casualties in the Union forces at Gettysburg indicates the loss of the First Minnesota as 224. The official report of Captain Coates, dated August 3, 1863, was accompanied by a revised nominal list which aggregates 226; the report itself mentions two casualties omitted, probably inadvertently, from the list. The addition of these and the deduction of one for a duplication in the list results in a total of 227, which may be accepted as correct.[90]

A study of the revised nominal list and the report which it accompanied shows that 6 officers and 64 enlisted men were killed or mortally wounded in the two days' battle and 11 other officers and 163 other men were wounded. The indisputable number of casualties on July 2 in the eight companies that participated in the charge is 160. If there be added to this number 6 casualties sustained by the other companies while on detached duty and 43 which can be definitely assigned to July 3, a total of 209 is

[90] *Saint Paul Press*, July 25, 1863; *Minnesota in the Civil and Indian Wars*, 2: 374-377; *Official Records*, series 1, vol. 27, part 1: 176, 424. The dispatch of July 5, written on the battle field by acting adjutant William Lochren and signed by Captain Coates, appears also in the report of the adjutant general of Minnesota in *Executive Documents*, 1863, pp. 231-234, and, in part, in Neill, *Minnesota*, 741-745 (fourth edition). The original list, signed by Lochren, which accompanied this dispatch and an unsigned manuscript list which is doubtless a copy of the original list of August 3 are on file in the office of the adjutant general of Minnesota. The latter omits the names of commissioned officers wounded. The two names mentioned in the official report but omitted from the accompanying list as printed in *Minnesota in the Civil and Indian Wars*, 2: 375, are also those of commissioned officers wounded, Lieutenants George Boyd, Company I, and William M. May, Company B. Both are included in the list of July 5. The name which is duplicated is that of Edwin Paul of Company I. In his narrative of the First Regiment, Lochren, after a careful examination of the documents, adheres to the figure given in the dispatch. Fox's total agrees with that given in the *Official Records*. Holcombe gives a total of 245 casualties, which he bases on a nominal list made out on August 31 to accompany the regimental report for that month. This list, which cannot now be found, probably included casualties occurring after July 3. Lochren, in *Minnesota in the Civil and Indian Wars*, 1: 36, 38, 47; Fox, *Regimental Losses in the Civil War*, 26, 36; Holcombe, *First Regiment*, 378.

obtained. That leaves 18 unaccounted for: 3 of them died on July 3 but may have been mortally wounded on the second, 13 are recorded as having died from wounds after July 3 with no indication of the dates on which the casualties occurred, 1 is listed as killed or mortally wounded with no date given, and for 1 wounded man there is no date. If the whole number of the unascertained casualties be added to 160, the result is 178 in place of the 215 of Judge Lochren's narrative. If the 18 unaccounted for be added to the certain casualties of July 3, the aggregate is 61 in place of Holcombe's 58.[91] If somewhat proportionate assignments be ventured, the losses of the eight companies on July 2 would stand at 174 and those of the regiment on July 3 at 47. Percentages computed on these numerators could not be far from correct.

About the number who participated in the charge of July 2 there has also been much disagreement. Judge Lochren gives it as 262. His 215 casualties gives a percentage of 82, a figure which has been widely and currently reported. Unfortunately no authentic separate record of the numbers engaged in the charge of July 2 has been found. The regimental officers of the time preferred to merge the losses of the two days and made no separate careful statements of the numbers engaged on either day. The consolidated morning report of the regiment is blank from June 29 to July 15 inclusive. On June 28 the whole number of officers and enlisted men present for duty was 386. This number did not include the sharp-shooter company, which was not engaged with the regiment on either day and can be neglected. Company C, comprising three officers and fifty-nine men, which had been for some weeks on duty as provost guard at division headquarters, was treated as on detached service and was also not included in the footing given.[92] Nine companies therefore reached the battle field. Soon after noon on July 2 Company F was ordered on skirmish duty off toward Little Round Top. Without its personnel of 33 there were 353 officers and men. If but 262 joined in the charge of July 2, there would remain 91, a number much too large to be accounted for as noncombatants, detailed men, and possible stragglers.

[91] Holcombe says that one man was killed and one was wounded on July 2 before the regiment was moved to support the battery. He distributes the casualties of July 3 as follows: 3 officers and 23 men killed or mortally wounded; 3 officers and 29 men wounded not mortally. The total of these figures is given incorrectly as 55 instead of 58. Holcombe cites "the nominal list . . . as it is still preserved and of record" as his authority. No separate list of casualties on July 3 is now available, and it is probable that his figures are an inexact computation from one of the general lists. First Minnesota, 340, 369.

[92] As Lochren was not appointed acting adjutant until July 4, he probably had not examined this entry. This morning report was preserved in the office of the adjutant general of Minnesota and was there consulted by the author several years ago, but it cannot now be located. The entry for June 28 showed but twelve noncombatants present, two surgeons and ten musicians.

# INDEX

# INDEX

Abolitionists, attitude of Democrats and Republicans toward, 69

Acker, William H., 28n; adjutant general, issues orders relating to mobilization of militia, 78

Acton Township, Meeker County, warfare with Sioux, 158-160, 174; murders in, 239, 283, 392, 415-417, 432

Adams, General C. Powell, commands Hatch's Battalion, 293; wounded at Gettysburg, 311

Adams, Samuel E., 28n

Agriculture, *1860–66*, 64, 65n, 344. *See also* Homestead Act

Aiton, Mrs. Mary Briggs, 64n

Akepa, Sioux chief, 122

Aldrich, Cyrus, congressman, 28n; aspires to senatorship, 107; approves execution of condemned Sioux, 203n; introduces bill for relief of victims of Sioux Outbreak, 246; introduces homestead bill, 331; succeeded by Donnelly, 107, 334

Alexandria, 243

Allan, William C., 161n

Allanson, George G., 122n

Allanson, Mrs. George G., 122n

Allatoona, battle of, 322

Allison, Senator William B., 423

American House, St. Paul hotel, 4n

Ames, Alfred E., 28n

Anawangmani, *see* Simon Anawangmani

Anderson, Captain Joseph, 192n; at battle of Birch Coulee, 152, 153, 175, 387, 389; sent to New Ulm, 168

Anderson, Thomas L., congressman, 15

Andersonville, Georgia, 306

André, Father —, 269

Andrews, General Christopher C., 94, 304

Anoka, 378; designated railway station, 42; garrisoned, 243

Antietam, battle of, 86

Apple River, 273

Army of the Cumberland, 320, 321

Army of the Potomac, 9, 101, 102

Artillery, troops organized, 98; number engaged in Civil and Indian wars, 339. *See also* individual artillery units

Assiniboine River, 294, 444

Atwater, Judge Isaac, 366n

Austin, Captain Horace, 105; criticizes Sibley, 176n; deals with mob at Mankato,

205; on Sibley expedition of *1863*, 271; account of first battle of New Ulm, 368

Averill, Colonel John T., 343n

Ayer, Reverend Frederick, 378

Baasen, Francis, 4n, 25, 28n

Babcock, Lorenzo A., 17

Backus, Mrs. George J., artist, 314

Bad Boy, Chippewa chief, warns whites of attack, 375, 381n

Bailly, Alexis, 28n

Bailey, Captain Hiram S., 192n

Baker, Howard, 415, 416; killed, 417

Baker, Mrs. Howard, 417

Baker, General James F., 70n; on Sibley expedition of *1863*, 267n; commands post at St. Louis, 305, 307n; brevetted brigadier general, 307n; account of first battle of New Ulm, 373

Balcombe, St. A. D., Indian agent, 257n

Ball's Bluff, battle of, 86, 87

Banks, laws relating to, referred to by Sibley, 23, passed, 57, revision of, recommended, 62; failure of, 57; national, established, 58

Bannatyne, Andrew G. B., 444

Barnard, Dr. Alonzo, account of relief of Fort Ridgely, 384

Barton, Ara, 28n

Bean, A. M., 370, 373

Beaulieu, Clement, 28n

Beauregard, General Pierre G. T., 85

Beaver, Lieutenant Frederick J., killed, 275n

Beaver Creek, 152, 155

Becker, George L., 18, 28n, 53

Bee, Captain Bernard E., 404, 406n

Belland, Henry, Sr., 109

Belle Plaine, 148, 148n

Belm, Captain John, 142

Belmont, attacked by Sioux, 123

Berdan, Colonel Hiram, 99

Berghold, Reverend Alexander, account of first battle of New Ulm, 365

Berkey, Peter, 244

Berry, Charles H., 28n, 31

Bierbauer, Captain William, 373

Big Eagle, Sioux subchief, cited, 131n, 133, 178n, 179n, 239, 241n; pardoned, 262; explains Acton murders, 415

455

Camp Release, 168n, 192, 430; monument on site of, 185n; location, 192n; arrest of Indians at, 194, 195, 196n

Campbell, Antoine J. (Joe), interpreter, 163n; testifies before military commission, 285n; on expeditions in pursuit of Inkpaduta, 408, 412, 413; testifies in Sisseton and Wahpeton claim case, 433

Campbell, Baptiste, executed, 351n

Campbell, John L., Winnebago half-breed, 351, 351n; executed for Jewett murders, 347-349, 350

Campbell, Scott, 351n

Cannon Ball River, 297

Cannon Falls, statue of Colvill at, 315

Cantwell, Matthew, killed, 182n

Capitol, state, memorials to Minnesota troops in, 87n, 314, 315, 321, 322n, 327n

Carver, 174

Cass County, 374

Cavalry, organized, 99. *See also* Brackett's Battalion of Minnesota Cavalry; Second Regiment of Cavalry

Cavanaugh, James M., congressman, 18, 19

Cedar Mills, 162

Cemetery Ridge, 308, 313

Census, *see* Population

Centreville, 85

Chain of Lakes, fortified against Sioux, 170

Champlin, Captain Ezra T., 181n, 182n

Chase, Charles L., territorial secretary, 21

Chase, Captain Jonathan, 267n

Chase, Salmon P., secretary of the treasury, 238

Chaskay, Robert Hopkins, Sioux Indian, 250, 251, 252

Chattanooga, 316, 322; monument to Minnesota troops, 319; battle at, *see* Missionary Ridge

Chetan wakan mani, *see* Little Crow

Chicago Land Verein, 133n

Chickahominy, 101

Chickamauga, battle of, 91, 307, 316-318; monument commemorating Minnesota troops, 316, 319n

Chippewa (Ojibway) Indians, 277, 291; alliance with Sioux rumored, 124, 188, 380; loyalty to whites commemorated, 133n, 382; disturbance of *1862*: 146, 374-378; causes, 377, 381, negotiations following, 378-380, tribes participating, 381; attack by, feared, 243, 287; plan for exiling, 258; agency, 374; reservation, 374; treaty with Red Lake and Pembina bands postponed, 376; attitude toward whites, 378; offer services against Sioux, 380. *See also* Indian treaties; Indians; Missions

Chippewa River, 173

Chittenden, Richard H., narrative of relief of Fort Ridgely, 385

Churches, established, 64n. *See also* individual denominations; Missionaries; Missions; Y. M. C. A.

Chute, Colonel Richard, 28n, 38n, 242

Cities, incorporated, 21

Civil War, 234; public opinion prior to, 68-74; southern confederacy established, 76; Fort Sumter occupied by Confederates, 76; first tender of troops, 77; recruiting and organization of troops, 77-81, 88, 89-92, 95, 96, 98-101, 102-106, 234, 236, 337-339; military operations: first battle of Bull Run, 80, 82, 85, 87, 102, 335, Ball's Bluff, 86, 87, Peninsular campaign, 86, Antietam, 86, Fredericksburg, 86, Fair Oaks, 86, 336, Mill Springs, 91, 91n, 102, Perryville, 91, 99, 307, Chickamauga, 91, 307, 316-318, 319n, Missionary Ridge (Chattanooga), 91, 319-321, 327n, Murfreesboro, 92-95, 302n, Corinth, 95, 95n, 96, 98, 102, 327n, Iuka, 95n, 102, Farmington, 96, Shiloh, 98, 307, Fort Donelson, 99, second battle of Bull Run, 100, Savage's Station, 101, 102, Glendale, 102, Malvern Hill, 102, Cold Harbor, 302, Fitzhugh's Woods, 303, Vicksburg, 303, 307, 322, Little Rock, 303, 304, 327n, Fort Blakely, 305, Guntown (Brice's Cross Roads), 305, siege of Mobile, 305, Tupelo, 306, Gettysburg, 308-315, 327n, 339, 451, Allatoona, 322, Franklin, 323, Nashville, 323-327; departure of First Minnesota, 84; Minnesota troops in: number, 101, 103, 339, losses, 340n, 392, 451-453, Indians and half-breeds, 421; draft planned, 102, 103; return of troops, 340. *See also* individual batteries, companies, and regiments; Slavery

Clapp, Senator Moses W., 435

Clark, Major Edwin, Indian agent, 374n

Clark, Lieutenant William A., 160

Clearwater, refuge from Indians, 124

Cloud, The, Sioux Indian, 413

Clough, Governor David M., 314

Coates, Captain Henry C., 451

Cochran, Aaron E., 442

Coffin, Samuel, at first battle of New Ulm, 366, 367, 370

Coggswell, Amos, 70n

Cold Harbor, battle of, 302

Cole, Attorney-General Gordon E., 360

Colfax, Schuyler, 60

Collins, Anthony C., killed, 182n

Collins, Judge Loren W., 178n, 181n, 182n

Faribault, Alexander, 149n, 150; assists
Sioux settlers, 263
Faribault, David, Sr., testifies before
military commission, 250, 251n, 285n
Faribault family, 252
Faribault, designated railway station, 38,
42; Sioux settlement near, 263, 264; site
of Sioux habitat, 400, 401n
Farming, see Agriculture
Farmington, battle of, 96
Farrell, Captain Wilson B., at battle of
Gettysburg, 312
Fessenden, Senator William P., 398
Fifth Iowa Cavalry, Minnesota troops
in, 99
Fifth Regiment Minnesota Volunteer Infan-
try, organized, 95; in Civil War battles:
Farmington, 96, Corinth, 96, 98, 102,
Nashville, 326, 327; chaplaincy, 97; goes
to aid of settlers at Sioux agency, 112; in
battle of Redwood Ferry, 113, 392; aids
in quieting Indians at Yellow Medicine,
229, 230, 231n; memorial of, 327n;
number engaged in Civil and Indian wars,
339. See also Companies B, C, and D
Financial conditions, see Economic con-
ditions
First Battalion Minnesota Infantry Volunteers, Civil War service, 302; number in
Civil and Indian wars, 339
First Battery Minnesota Light Artillery,
mustered, 98; Civil War service, 98, 302,
307. See also Artillery
First Company Minnesota Sharpshooters,
Civil War service, 99; becomes Company
A, Second Regiment United States
Sharpshooters, 99
First Regiment Heavy Artillery, Minnesota
Volunteers, formed, 339; number engaged
in Civil War, 339
First Regiment Minnesota Mounted Rangers, 243, 339; organized, 105; on Sibley
expedition of 1863, 267n, 276n; detachment stationed at New Ulm, 281;
pursues Indian marauders, 281; detachments garrison frontier, 282; number
engaged in Indian wars, 399
First Regiment Minnesota Volunteer Infantry, 293, 303, 335, 336, 386; mobilization, 78-81, 88; service on Minnesota
frontier, 81, 88; mustered, 82; chaplaincy,
84, 84n; Civil War service: 84, 86, 87, 89,
302, 307, 315, at battle of Bull Run, 80,
82, 85, 102, 335, Second Company of
Minnesota Sharpshooters attached to, 86,
100, artillery attachment, 87, at battle of
Gettysburg, 308-313, 451; casualties, 85,
86, 311, 451; history published by state,

85; memorials to, 87, 313-315, 327n;
mustered out, 302, 316; number engaged
in Civil War, 339. See also Companies
C, F, and L
Fishing, 1860, 64n
Fisk, Robert M., 78n
Fitzhugh's Woods, battle of, 303
Five Million Loan, 22; bill providing for:
passed, 45, provisions, 46, 50, arguments
for and against, 47, submitted to electors,
47-49; failure to secure priority of lien for
bonds, 49-51; depreciation of bonds, 52;
repudiation of bonds opposed by Sibley,
52; Ramsey's plan for cancellation of
bonds, 53; attitude of public, 55; bonds
discussed by legislature, 56; bank failures,
57; foreclosures, 328. See also Railroads
Fjelde, Jacob H. G., artist, 314n
Flandrau, Judge Charles E., 28n, 50, 50n,
223, 224, 387, 394, 406, 407, 411; sketch,
135; notified of Sioux Outbreak, 135, 366,
367; organizes volunteers against Sioux,
136, 371; elected captain of volunteer
forces, 136, 138, 365, 371; at battle of
New Ulm, 139, 141, 142, 143, 366, 367,
370n, 371, 372, 374; services in Indian
campaign of 1862, 168-170; commissioned
colonel, 169; supreme court judge,
219, 409; account of first battle of New
Ulm, 366; address at dedication of Birch
Coulee monument, 388; Sioux agent:
pursuit of Inkpaduta, 404, 408, arranges
for rescue of captives held by Inkpaduta,
407, 408; in constitutional convention,
409
Flandreau, South Dakota, 261, 431
Folsom, William H. C., legislator, 31, 358
Forbes, William H., 28n, 150, 446
Foreigners, 1860, 64n
Forest City, 174; preparations against Sioux
attacks, 158, 159, 161, 174n; plundered by
Sioux, 162; number killed during Sioux
Outbreak, 392; sends party to scene of
Acton murders, 417
Forrest, General Nathan B., 92, 93, 306
Fort Abercrombie, 268, 376, 445; regular
troops relieved by detachment of First
Minnesota, 81; garrisoned by volunteers,
81, 164, 243, 282, 293; established, 164;
attacked by Sioux, 165-168, 428, 430,
431, 434; defense planned by Pope, 187;
detachment from, sent to Fort Ripley,
277; reënforcements planned by Sibley,
1864, 294; number killed during Sioux
Outbreak, 392
Fort Blakely, attack on, 305
Fort Donelson, battle of, 99
Fort Garry, 287n, 443, 444

Johnson, President Andrew, confirms sentences of Little Six and Medicine Bottle, 350, 448

Johnson, Fred W., account of first battle of New Ulm, 364, 368n

Johnson, John, see Enmegahbowh, John Johnson

Johnson, Governor John A., address by, 314, 315

Johnston, General Albert S., 85

Jones, Captain John, 130, 132; on Sibley expedition of *1863*, 267n; on Sully expedition of *1864*, 296; commands detachment sent to Devil's Lake, 300

Jones, Robinson, 415, 416; killed by Indians, 417

Jones, Mrs. Robinson, killed by Indians, 417

Jones, William A., 28n

Judiciary, see Courts

Judson, garrisoned, 243

Kandiyohi County, Sioux attacks in, 123; exodus of settlers during outbreak, 161; number massacred, 392

Kandiyohi lakes, 283

Kansas, admitted to Union, 10-12, 15

Kaposia, 233

Kimball, De Grove, killed, 182n

King, William S., denounces Rice, 71n

Kingsbury, William W., delegate to Congress, 28n; unseated after admission of Minnesota, 19-21

Kittson, Norman W., 28n

Kitzman, Paul, 120, 121

Knights of the Forest, society for the removal of Indians, 256

Knox, John J., 28n

Kreiger, Justina, 121n, 155

Krieger, ——, 143n

La Bathe, François, 196; murdered by Sioux, 109

Lac qui Parle, Indian murder, 121; capture of Indians, 193; mission at, see Missions

La Crescent, designated railroad terminus, 38, 42

Laframboise, Joseph, French half-breed, 117, 405; testifies in Sisseton and Wahpeton claim case, 426, 427

Laframboise, Julia, 427

Laframboise family, 252

Lame Jim, 441

Lamson, Chauncey, kills Little Crow, 283, 285n

Lamson, Nathan, wounds Little Crow, 283, 284n; rewarded, 286

Lawrence, Lorenzo, Sioux Indian, loyalty commemorated, 391

Laws, territorial, codified by first state legislature, 25. See also Banks; Corporation laws; Interest laws; Legislature; Military laws

Lean Bear, Sioux chief, 123n

Lecompton constitution, 10

Le Duc, William G., 321n

Lee, General Robert E., 308, 315, 316

Leech Lake, Pillagers at, join in insurrection, 375-382

Legislative districts, 1, 355

Legislature, territorial session of *1857*: railroad legislation, 40-43, appropriates funds for rescue of Inkpaduta's victims, 406; session of *1857-58*: organized, 4-6, status questioned, 5, 6, 13, 21, governors' messages, 5, 23, election of senators, 6, 17n, 21, legislation, 21, 25, 30-33, 57, 59, 63, 105, constitutional amendments, 22, Five Million Loan bill, 22, 45-47, 50, 50n; session of *1859-60*: governors' messages, 43n, 52, 53, 62, discusses railroad bonds, 55, constitutional amendments, 56, 242, election of senator, 62, legislation, 63, orders foreclosure of railroad mortgages, 328; session of *1861*: governor's message, 68, legislation dealing with school lands, 68, resolution on secession, 72, railroad legislation, 329, legalizes use of territorial seal, 360; sessions of *1862*: revision of militia law, 106, legislation resulting from Sioux depredations, 244, 245, 391, governor's message, 255, railroad legislation, 330, provides for soldiers' vote, 333, appoints commission to negotiate with Chippewa, 378; session of *1863*: election of senator, 108, 334, governor's message, 251; session of *1864*: rewards Lamson for killing Little Crow, 286; session of *1865*: governor's message, 340, election of senator, 340-342, ratification of thirteenth amendment, 342; session of *1867*: bill penalizing desertion, 338, rewards captors of Little Six and Medicine Bottle, 445; session of *1881*: orders compilation of data relating to Sioux Outbreak, 391; later legislation dealing with erection of monuments, 182n, 185n, 314n, 342n, 382, 386, 388

Leonhart, Rudolph, account of first battle of New Ulm, 364

Lester, Colonel Henry C., service in First Minnesota, 94; surrenders Third Minnesota, 94

Le Sueur, 136; headquarters Tenth Regiment, 243; sends reënforcements to New Ulm, 373

Le Sueur County, Indian depredations, 288

Renville, Reverend John B., testifies in
Sisseton and Wahpeton claim case, 249,
428
Renville County, Sioux attacks in, 110,
120; number killed during Sioux Outbreak, 392. *See also* Birch Coulee
Renville family, 252
Renville Rangers, 430; reenforce garrison
at Fort Ridgely, 129; casualties, 133n;
on Sibley expedition of *1862*, 177, 180,
181
Representatives, state: apportioned, 1, election of, in *1857*, 1, 2, in *1858*, 59, 62, in
*1860*, 68, in *1862*, 333; United States:
election of, in *1857*, 1, 2, 12, 18, in *1862*,
333, 334, 336; number: provided by
constitution, 12, debated in Congress, 13.
*See also* Cavanaugh, James M.; Donnelly,
Ignatius; Phelps, William W.; Windom,
William
Republicans, in elections: of *1857*, 2-4,
of *1858*, 59, of *1859*, 59, 61, 62, of *1860*,
66-68, of *1862*, 333, 334, of *1863*, 108,
336, 337, of *1865*, 340-342, 343; attitude
toward Five Million Loan, 48; control
legislature of *1859*, 62; of *1861*, 68;
attitude toward Abolitionists, 69; criti-
cize Sibley expedition of *1863*, 277;
denounce Major Hatch, 290; supported
by Miller, 335; by Marshall, 337
Reservations, *see* Blue Earth Reservation;
Gull Lake; Sioux reservations
Rice, Edmund, 39
Rice, Senator Henry M., 9, 89, 333, 397,
398; elected, 6, 8; seated, 17; credited
with securing passage of land grant bill
of *1857*, 38n; advocates passage of Five
Million Loan amendment, 48; attitude
on mandamus issued to Sibley, 51; in
political campaign of *1860*, 66; opposes
Civil War, 70, 71, 73; supports administration during Civil War, 74-76; accused
of political machinations, 108, 341;
instrumental in securing opening of Red
River trade, 164; suggested as successor
to General Pope, 188, 242; approves
execution of condemned Sioux, 203n;
explanation of Sioux Outbreak, 212;
supports bill for relief of victims
of Sioux Outbreak, 247; urges formation
of regiment for campaign against Sioux,
290; criticized by Sibley, 291; hospitality,
340; declines Republican senatorial
nomination, 341; candidate for governor,
343; member of commission negotiating
with Chippewa, 378; reports Indian
treaties, 396
Rice County, Indian depredations in, 288

Rice Creek, 239, 239n, 240, 415
Riggs, Reverend Stephen R., missionary,
196n, 248, 262, 350, 407, 409n, 412n;
mission stations, 118, 207n, 220; learns
of Sioux Outbreak, 118, 119; on Sibley
expedition of *1862*, 173, 181, 182n;
at trial of Sioux, 198; attitude toward
execution of condemned Sioux, 203;
preaches memorial sermon on Joseph R.
Brown, 210; explanation of Sioux
Outbreak, 212, 231; called to Yellow Medicine agency to quiet Indians, 230; testifies before Sioux claims commission,
247, 250, 434; ministration to Sioux convicts, 249; aids in listing loyal Sioux,
264; on Sibley expedition of *1863*, 277
River transportation, 65
Roads, provided for, 21; revision of laws
relating to, 63; Congress appropriates
funds for, 64
Roaring Cloud, Sioux Indian, 408
Robert, Louis, trader, 129n, 399n
Robertson, Colonel Daniel A., commands
Twenty-third Regiment of Militia, 28n;
criticizes Five Million Loan, 48; offers
regiment for Civil War service, 88;
rejection of regiment, 89-91
Robertson, Thomas A., Sioux half-breed,
172, 173n; testifies in Sisseton and
Wahpeton claim case, 426, 427
Robertson family, 252
Rochester, designated railroad junction, 42
Rockford, 442
Rolette, Joseph, legislator, 41
Roman Catholic Church, *see* Grace, Right
Reverend Thomas L.; Ireland, Arch-
bishop John; Ravoux, Father Augustin
Roos, Charles, Brown County sheriff, 362,
364; criticizes Sibley, 176n; account of
battle of New Ulm, 361
Root, Noble G., killed by Indians, 345
Root River Valley, provisions for railroad
along, 38
Root River Valley and Southern Minnesota
Railroad Company, chartered, 42. *See
also* Railroads
Rose, Edwin E., killed, 182n
Rosecrans, General William S., 96, 316, 319,
323
Rossville Gap, 318
Round Wind, *see* Tatemima

Sacred Heart, Sioux attack settlers of, 120
St. Anthony, 4, 82; designated railway
station, 38, 330; population, *1860*, 64;
opens telegraph office, 66; liberation of
slave, 69, 70n; refuge from Indians, 124;
sends reënforcements against Sioux, 385

St. Cloud, 292, 376, 379; activities of Mrs. Swisshelm, 33-36; designated railway station, 42; refuge from Sioux, 124; fortifies against Sioux, 161; sends force against Indians, *1864*, 350

St. Joseph, fortifies against Sioux, 161; battle with Sioux near, 292

St. Paul, 4, 83, 203, 260, 277, 282, 283, 376, 380, 381n; designated railway station, 38, 42, 330; Republican convention, *1859*, 59; population, *1860*, 64; opens telegraph office, 65; departure of First Minnesota, 84; refuge from Indians, 124; objective of Sioux, 133; Red River trade, 164; headquarters Military District of Minnesota, 202; relief of refugees, 244; embarkation of exiled Sioux, 259

St. Paul and Milwaukee Railroad Company, 38. *See also* Railroads

Saint Paul and Pacific Railroad Company, succeeds Minnesota and Pacific Railroad Company, 330. *See also* Railroads

St. Peter, 128, 138, 148, 148n, 149n, 205n, 236, 383, 384, 385; designated railway station, 38, 42; objective of Sioux, sends reënforcements to New Ulm, 134, 362, 365, 367, 368, 370, 371, 372, 373; learns of Sioux Outbreak, 135; founding, 143; Indian attack rumored, 157; arrival of Sibley's troops, 168, 176; refuge from Sioux, 224; garrisoned, 243

St. Peter Frontier Guards, 142

St. Vincent, designated railway terminal, 42

Sanborn, General John B., 28n; eulogizes Rice, 75; adjutant general, 90, 95; commands Fourth Minnesota, 95; promoted brigadier general, 322; painting of, 322n

Sanders, Captain Edwin C., 373, 374

Sanford, Henry S., 87

Santee (Mdewakanton, Wahpekute) Indians, 257n, 297, 432; removed to Crow Creek reservation, 259-261, 263, 439; significance of name, 260, 261n; removed to Niobrara reservation, 261, 262, 437; civilization of, 261; agencies, 262, 280, 431, 433; claim for restoration of annuities, 437-439. *See also* Indian treaties; Mdewakanton Indians; Moscow Expedition; Sioux Indians; Sioux Outbreak; Wahpekute Indians

Satterlee, Marion P., compiles lists of victims of Sioux Outbreak, 392

Sauk Centre, 277; fortified against Indians, 161, 243

Savage's Station, battle of, 101, 102

Scarlet Plume, Sioux chief, loyalty to whites, 122, 270, 427, 428

Scarlet Point, *see* Inkpaduta

Scattered Lake, 285

Schofield, General John M., 323, 324

School lands, schools, *see* Education

Schurz, Carl, 60

Scotch Lake, 288

Seal: of Minnesota Territory, modified and adopted as state seal, 26, 359-361; recommendation of Republican constitutional convention, 357; constitutional provision for, 358; legislative bill for, 358

Searles, Captain Jasper N., 314

Sebastian, Senator William K., 398

Second Battery of Minnesota Light Artillery, Civil War service of, 99, 307. *See also* Artillery

Second Company of Minnesota Sharpshooters, attached to First Minnesota Infantry, 86, 100; at battle of Antietam, 86

Second Regiment Minnesota Veteran Volunteer Infantry, 225; organized, 89-91; frontier service, 91; Civil War service: summarized, 91, at Missionary Ridge, 91, 319, 321, on Sherman's march, 91, 302, defense of Snodgrass Ridge, 318; memorials to, 316, 319n, 321, 327n; casualties, 318, 321; number engaged in Civil and Indian wars, 339

Second Regiment of Cavalry, Minnesota Volunteers, service against Indians, 296, 299, 346, 350, 351n; organized, 339; number engaged in Indian wars, 339; officers of, form military commission, 445

Second Regiment of United States Sharpshooters, 99, 100

Senators, state: apportioned, 1; United States: manner of election prescribed, 6, election of, *see* Legislature

Seventh Regiment Minnesota Volunteer Infantry, 192n, 193, 202, 336, 343; organized, 103, 104; commanders, 106, 305, 336, 337; on Sibley expedition of *1862*, 154, 174, 177, 178, 181; retained for protection against Sioux, 243; on Sibley expedition of *1863*, 267n, 269, 270, 271, 272, 273; pursues Indian marauders, 281; Civil War service: summarized, 305, 306, in battle of Nashville, 307, 326; number engaged in Civil and Indian wars, 339

Severance, Judge Martin J., estimate of Galbraith, 222

Seward, William, 13; delivers political address in St. Paul, 66; supported for presidency by Minnesota Republicans, 67